THE PEOPLE'S
TEAM

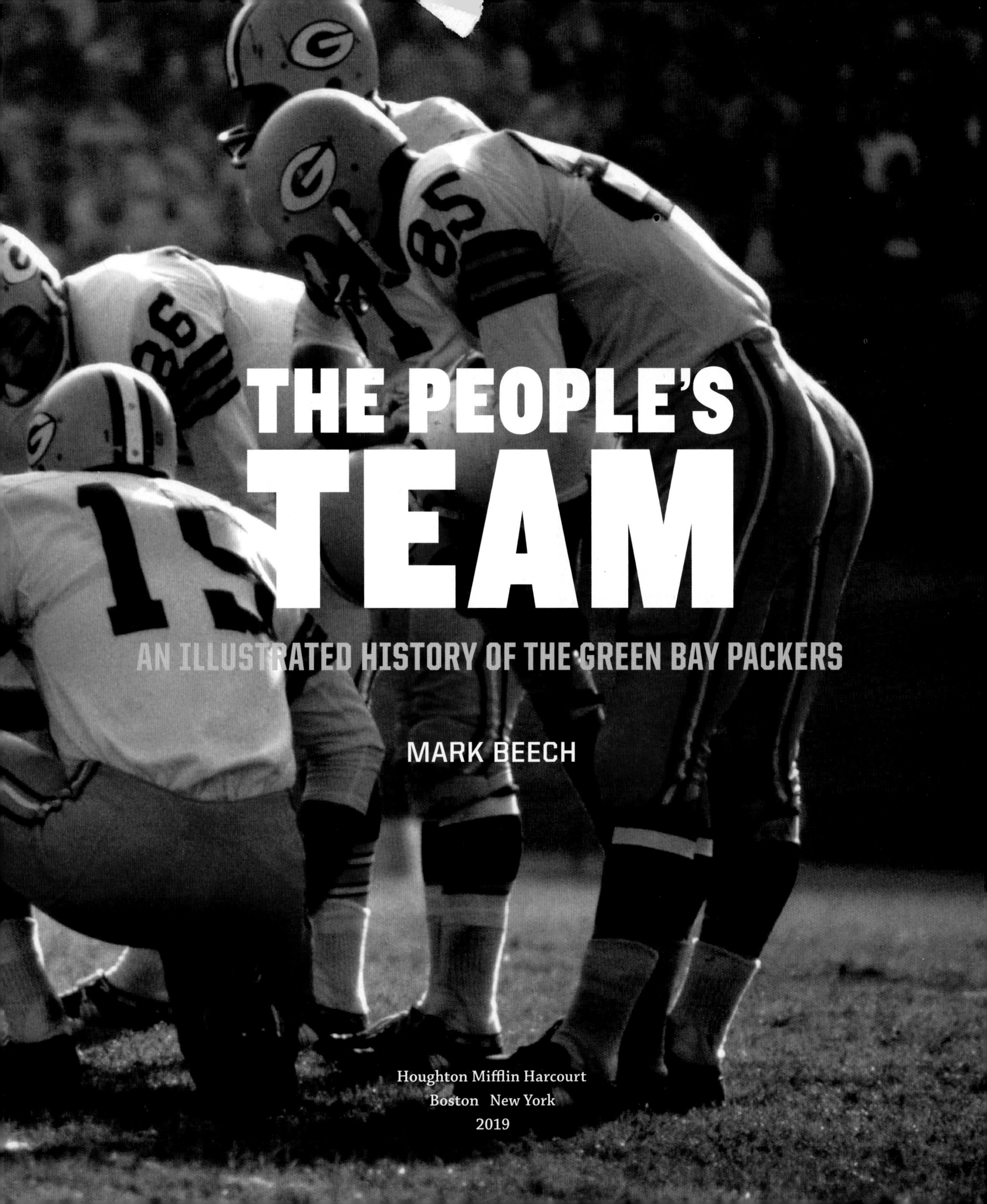

THE PEOPLE'S TEAM

AN ILLUSTRATED HISTORY OF THE GREEN BAY PACKERS

MARK BEECH

Houghton Mifflin Harcourt
Boston   New York
2019

For information about permission to reproduce selections from this book, write to trade.permissions@hmhco.com or to Permissions, Houghton Mifflin Harcourt Publishing Company, 3 Park Avenue, 19th Floor, New York, New York 10016.

hmhbooks.com

Library of Congress Cataloging-in-Publication Data is available.

ISBN 978-1-328-46013-4

Book design by Nate Beale/SeeSullivan

Photo research by Maureen Cavanagh

Printed in China

SCP 10 9 8 7 6 5 4 3 2 1

To my team — Allison, Nate, and Annie

FOREWORD

Football defines the city of Green Bay—to itself and to the rest of the world. It is the smallest town in the National Football League, but it is also home to more championships than any other. The seal of the city not only includes its nickname, Titletown, USA, but also the Packers' logo (a *G* in the shape of a football), which is featured prominently in the design. Anyone flying the flag of the city of Green Bay is also flying a flag for the Packers, which, appropriately, makes it handy for tailgating.

In Green Bay, the Packers and their history are everywhere. The cozy two-story brick house where Curly Lambeau was born still stands at 615 North Irwin Avenue, not far from City Stadium, where the Packers played from 1925 through 1956. Over on South Adams Street is St. Willebrord Catholic Church, where Vince Lombardi used to attend weekday Mass. Around the corner is the Brown County Courthouse, a copper-domed beaux arts dreadnought of a building that in 1933 was the site of the near ruination of the franchise, when a disgruntled fan sued it into insolvency. And 315 Cherry Street, the old home of the *Green Bay Press-Gazette,* is the site where, on August 11, 1919, the Packers were born. A bank takes up most of the block now—the original building was razed in 1948—but a green-and-gold historical marker stands near where the entrance to the paper's offices used to be.

There are similar signposts all over Green Bay. Visitors who want to immerse themselves in the legend of the littlest and most illustrious city in pro football can walk the Packers Heritage Trail, a four-and-a-half-mile circuit through downtown that, in stops at 17 different locations, tells the story of the first 50 years of the NFL's only publicly owned team. (There are eight more markers on two separate "spurs" that are more easily visited by bicycle or car.) In Boston you can walk the Freedom Trail, a two-and-a-half-mile red-brick line passing 16 historic sites that tell the story of the American Revolution and the founding of the nation. In Green Bay, the walking tour may be of less national import, but it is no less profound.

The Heritage Trail is the creation of Cliff Christl, who, before he became the Packers' historian, in 2014, spent 36 years covering the team for four different Wisconsin newspapers, including the *Press-Gazette.* It was in that capacity that the Green Bay native played his own crucial role in the history of the Packers. In the spring of 1974, when the paper put the 27-year-old Christl on the beat full-time, managing editor Larry Belonger instructed him to cover the team as aggressively as writers from big cities would cover theirs, and to not be afraid to criticize. It was an abrupt shift for the *Press-Gazette,* which had nursed and

Cliff Christl, a former sports reporter at four Wisconsin newspapers— including the *Green Bay Press-Gazette*— became the Packers' historian in 2014.

coddled the Packers through the first 50 years of their existence — when Green Bay always seemed to be operating on the brink of financial disaster. ("No *Press-Gazette,* no Packers," Christl says.) The young reporter's approach frequently put him at odds with the franchise, which was then an NFL laughingstock. Christl tangled on several occasions with coach Bart Starr, who had been the starting quarterback in the first Packers game that Christl can remember attending — on November 18, 1956, when Green Bay lost 17–16 to the San Francisco 49ers in the final game at old City Stadium.

Now 72, Christl has a face that wears a look of constant skepticism, with pursed lips and eyebrows that seem to always be on the rise. His approach to Packers history is the same as it was to being a beat writer: meticulous, methodical, and scrupulously impartial. Jason Wilde, who covers Green Bay for ESPN Wisconsin but has been shadowing the team for 23 years, the first 13 at Madison's *Wisconsin State Journal,* calls Christl "the godfather" of the Packers beat. "Cliff's approach was never about favors; it was to tell the truth unwaveringly," Wilde says. "It was not to give the players that were sources for him preferential treatment. I think that's why all of us covering the team now have a high level of respect for Cliff and try to emulate him."

There are no ink-stained wretches in the news business anymore, but Christl has been marked by his profession in other ways. The index finger on his right hand is turned 90 degrees toward his pinkie, a condition that, while not painful, has made it extremely difficult for him to hold a pen. A few years ago he visited a hand specialist, who confessed to being baffled and who then told him that his best guess was that it was the result of severe writer's cramp.

It's certainly possible. Christl was writing in notebooks long before he became a reporter. When he was in high school at Green Bay East, his mother and stepfather — Christl's biological father, Clifford H. Christl, died when he was 13 — used to send him to his room in the evenings to do his homework. "But I had no interest in doing homework," he says with a smile. Instead he would keep his own record books for the NFL, the NBA, and Major League Baseball, with the rosters and game-by-game and season stats for every team. He kept track of scoring by position, picked his own all-star teams, and charted every draft. "I don't know if I was ever a fan, even as a kid," he says. "What I was interested in were the players, in studying and learning."

Christl still has the old three-ring notebooks into which he entered everything. He keeps them on the shelves of the floor-to-ceiling cabinet that takes up one wall of his office in the Green Bay condo that he lives in with his wife, Shirley. The room overlooks the eastern side of the Fox River and looks exactly as you would hope the office of the Packers' historian would — all green paint and darkly stained wood. Journalism awards hang from one wall. A program from the last game at old City Stadium sits on a shelf under plastic in a stand next to a program from the first game at the new one. There is a second bookshelf, as well as seven tall file cabinets that fill a walk-in closet and part of another room. "It's the best pro football library outside of Canton, Ohio," Christl says.

His fascination with the early story of the Packers began about 30 years ago, after he read some books on the subject. Christl traces his love of history back to his grandmother, who used to discuss it with him often when he was young. And it was always his favorite subject in school. But as an adult he had never had time to look into Green Bay's history, because he was always so busy reporting on the current team. The researcher in him was impressed by the legwork that had been involved in telling the stories in the books he was reading. Time and again, though, he found that when one author would make a mistake — or, worse yet, jump to a conclusion — another author would repeat the error. And he found a lot of mistakes. Even writers from ESPN and the Wisconsin Historical Society were relying on faulty research. "Some of the books are just almost total BS," he told the *Press-Gazette* in 2018.

Christl now advises the Packers Pro Shop, the team's merchandise outlet at Lambeau Field, about which books it should not carry because they have been discredited. The Packers, for their part, have not always been meticulous about publishing sound information. The team's 1993 book about its 75th anniversary, Christl says, made "an almost incomprehensible number of mistakes."

It was not just the modern histories that were a problem. The seminal work about the history of the Packers is the 1946 book *The Green Bay Packers,* written by Chicago newspaper editor Arch Ward. The book is thorough and engaging. Christl considers it a classic. But Ward was a good friend of Curly Lambeau, a man renowned for exaggerating stories, and not everything in it is true. A definitive history of the team had never really been written.

And so Christl, with the idea that he might someday write such a book, set out not only to correct the record but also to make it. He started compiling oral histories with Packers from the past. He spent hours in the Brown County Library scrolling through microfilm editions of the *Green Bay Press-Gazette;* as the unofficial caretaker of the Packers for nearly a half century, the newspaper is the primary record of the early history of the team. Christl says he has read every edition of the *Press-Gazette* from January 1, 1919, into the spring of 1962.

Christl kept gathering string even after he had retired from the *Milwaukee Journal Sentinel* in 2007. (He had moved to the paper 21 years earlier, when it was still *The Milwaukee Journal.*) His file cabinets filled up. In 2012, with support from the city and the Packers, he created the Heritage Trail. (His companion book for the walking tour is essential reading for those interested in the early history of the team.) Two years later, the Packers hired him full-time to help them finally get their story right. He is a careful and loving custodian of the Green Bay legacy. His columns on the Packers' website are fascinating and essential reading. He has helped correct the official record in several places in the team's annual media guide. Thanks to his efforts, the early history of the Packers is significantly less muddled. "And the true story," says Christl, "is better than the myth."

It is, he says, "the greatest story in sports." Green Bay is important to the NFL for a whole host of reasons. The Packers are from the smallest town in the league. They are the only team owned by their fans. And their 13 NFL championships are a record. But the story of the Packers, the way they grew out of the rivalry between the east and west sides of the city — a city defined much more by the river that divides it than by the bay that it sits on — and the way the people there kept rallying behind them to make sure they could keep playing, makes it much more than a simple record of wins and losses and championships. "I think the Packers," says Christl, "were the one unifying force in this town."

The history of the Green Bay Packers is a tale not only of the single-minded determination of Curly Lambeau, but also of how his dream was kept alive by so many others in Green Bay. It is a story of civic duty and community pride — and glory.

THE PEOPLE'S
TEAM

CHAPTER 1
TWO SIDES OF THE RIVER

Before the Packers, there was Green Bay. Before Curly Lambeau and Vince Lombardi, before Ray Nitschke and Reggie White, before Johnny Blood and Don Hutson, and before Arnie Herber and Bart Starr and Brett Favre and Aaron Rodgers, there was the river and the bay and the forest that surrounded them both. Before the football team that defined the place to the world, there was the place from which it came. And that place defined the team.

The final retreat, about 10,000 years ago, of the glacier that covered much of North America carved—in the soft, reddish soil of what is now northeastern Wisconsin—a river that fed into an estuary of one of the continent's enormous inland seas. For thousands of years after, the valley was home to a number of Native American tribes, which sustained themselves on the rice that flourished in the marshes near the water's edge and thrived on the protein factories of the river and the bay. The water and the land provided life in abundance.

According to most accounts, the first European to lay eyes on Green Bay was a 36-year-old French explorer by the name of Jean Nicolet de Belleborne. The son of a postman from the Norman port city of Cherbourg, Nicolet was one of several adventurous young men recruited by Samuel de Champlain, founder of the city of Quebec, to learn the customs and languages of the native people who lived in the western wilderness of the colony of New France. Nicolet arrived in Quebec in 1618, when he was 20, and Champlain soon sent him into the wild to live among the Algonquin Indians on the Ottawa River.

Champlain had once written to King Louis XIII that, by way of New France, a traveler could easily reach "the Kingdom of China and the East Indies, whence great riches could be drawn." In 1634 he dispatched Nicolet to seek out the "People of the Sea," who lived on the unexplored shores of one of the Great Lakes. It was Champlain's hope that the People of the Sea were the Chinese, but they were actually the Winnebago Indians, who were known to the Algonquin as the Ouinipegou, a derivation of the word *ouinipeg,* which was used by the Algonquin to refer to brackish water. The Ouinipegou were so named because they inhabited an area alongside a large body of water—there was nothing foul-smelling about them. Nicolet met the Winnebago (known today as the Ho-Chunk) when he made landfall, supposedly near the future site of the city of Green Bay.

Nicolet's mission failed in its primary purpose: to make peace between the Winnebago and the Huron, who were then at war. Hostilities between

the two tribes continued, and it was a generation before the French dared to return, at which point Green Bay became an essential way station for fur traders and missionaries. Its location at the mouth of the Fox River made it ideal for the first European settlement in what would eventually be Wisconsin. By traveling southwest on the Fox, traders from Canada could — by way of a marshy two-mile portage to the westward-flowing Wisconsin River — continue on to the Mississippi River, and from there to the Gulf of Mexico.

At first the French trappers and traders who inhabited the area hewed to the Algonquin way of referring to the bay — though with a crucial misinterpretation — calling it "la Baie des Puants," which roughly translates to "the bay of the stinkards." They later began referring to it as simply "la Baie." The name stuck for the next century, through Catholic missions and westward explo-

ration and the French and Indian Wars, near the end of which the area fell under the control of the British, who called it Green Bay, perhaps because of the algae-tinged color of the water.

As settlement of the area increased, the British established Fort Edward Augustus — renaming an armed encampment they had seized from the French — on the western side of the Fox. They had won vast territory but struggled to govern it, and they also failed to establish friendly relations with the local tribes, who began attacking western garrisons. In the early 1760s, the British abandoned Fort Augustus.

The United States took control of the area after the War of 1812 and, in 1816, established a military presence at the deserted fortification. The job of the troops at the woodland outpost, which the Army renamed Fort Howard, was to protect trade routes, construct roads, and negotiate treaties

PREVIOUS SPREAD
Looking south from the mouth of the Fox River in 1867 at the villages of Green Bay (left) and Fort Howard (right), whose rivalry gave birth to the Packers.

ABOVE
The military garrison at Fort Howard, as seen from the eastern side of the Fox River. The fort not only provided security to settlers, but also served as a social and commercial hub for the area.

The industrious, adventurous, inexhaustible Daniel Whitney, son of a minuteman, founder of the city of Green Bay, and great-grandfather of the co-founder of the Packers.

with the local tribes. Among the post's most notable residents was future president Zachary Taylor, who assumed command at Fort Howard in 1817 and served there for about two years.

In 1820 the garrison's commander, Colonel Joseph Lee Smith, moved the fort to the eastern side of the river, situating it on high ground three miles upstream and renaming it Camp Smith. The Army abandoned this new location in 1822, in favor of the fort's original site, but not before a community had begun to grow around Camp Smith. Called Shantytown because of the ramshackle nature of the lodgings constructed by its residents, it marked the beginning of civilian business activity on the eastern bank of the Fox. Not counting soldiers, there were only about 50 adults (primarily farmers and fur traders) living on either side of the river at the time. Conditions were primitive. Most people lived in small huts, and there were

only a handful of proper farms. There were also no roads. There was, though, a distillery on the east side of the river.

The presence of the Army encouraged the arrival of more settlers, who came primarily from New England and western New York. Fort Howard provided not only security but also a place for farmers to sell produce, for people to seek medical care, for children to go to school, and for families to attend organized religious services — as well as the occasional party or dance. Among the first Yankees to arrive, in the summer of 1819, was an adventurous 24-year-old trader from Gilsum, New Hampshire, named Daniel Whitney.

The son of a minuteman, Whitney had a broad face, a high forehead, and a stony countenance that belied the urgency with which he lived his life. He arrived with a small stock of goods and was one of the founding residents of Shantytown. Over the next 25 years he was the driving force behind the development of the region. He was, at various times, an explorer, a fur trader, a shopkeeper, a lumber magnate, a real estate developer, a transportation baron, and the founder of the city of Green Bay. A courageous, clear-eyed businessman, Whitney explored the interior incessantly in search of trading opportunities. He navigated the Fox River all the way to its source in what is now south-central Wisconsin, and he traveled on the Wisconsin River to the Mississippi, along which he established numerous trading posts.

Some of his exploits, as recounted in an 1895 biographical record of the Fox River Valley, read like scenes out of a James Fenimore Cooper adventure tale. On a winter trip to Washington, D.C., his Indian traveling companion balked at crossing the frozen Detroit River. Whitney left his partner on the western bank and crossed with his sled full of supplies. Then he returned, gave the man one end of a long rope, had him lie down flat on the ground, and dragged him safely across the ice to the other side. In the fall of 1824, when a ship carrying provisions for Green Bay became trapped in the ice near Mackinac, Whitney led a party of men and horses over the frozen bay and brought back as many essential items as the team could carry.

Closer to home, Whitney was just as dynamic. He built the first sawmill on the Fox River and was involved in lead-mining operations on the Wisconsin River. He also began purchasing land near the mouth of the Fox, on the east side of the river, directly across from Fort Howard. The terrain — situated along the north and south banks of a tributary of the Fox — was marshy and infested with mosquitoes, and most residents felt that Whitney's acquisition was folly. But the land dried up when he began to clear it. In 1829, Whitney platted the village of Navarino, which he named for the port city in Greece that in 1827 had been the site of a major battle in the Greek War of Independence — a fitting tribute from the son of a minuteman. He built roads in Navarino, as well as a dock, a warehouse, a school, houses for his employees, and a hotel. In 1831, he moved his store from Shantytown to Navarino, which soon after got a post office, a federal land office, and, in 1833, the first newspaper in the Wisconsin territory, the *Green-Bay Intelligencer.*

Whitney's primary rival was New York business magnate John Jacob Astor, who never actually visited Green Bay but whose American Fur Company had arrived shortly after the Army established a presence there. Under the direction of general manager Ramsay Crooks, Astor's operation grew into the dominant business in the area, backing fur trappers in return for the mortgages on their Green Bay properties. It was through foreclosures on those holdings that the American Fur Company became a major landowner in Green Bay. Astor shut down the outfit's operations in 1834, after the inevitable decline of the fur trade, but he maintained a presence in the area by laying out the town of Astor, just to the south of Navarino. Astor became known as "the Hill," and with its large homes it was the primary residential area for local leaders. Hoping to attract businesses, Astor

offered lots to churches and banks, and in 1837 he constructed the luxurious Astor House hotel. The next year, the towns of Astor and Navarino consolidated as the borough of Green Bay, and the east side of the river became a hub of Yankee-dominated commerce.

Progress across the river came more slowly. Unlike on the east side of the Fox, land on the west had been mostly unavailable for development, primarily because of the large amount of area that had been set aside for Fort Howard. Settlement had also been slowed by the presence of the Oneida Indian reservation. The tribe was originally from western New York but had abandoned the region when settlers there started infringing on its territory. The federal government gave the Oneida land on the west side of the Fox River, south of Fort Howard. They were peaceful people, but living near a large number of Native Americans, even with the protection of the Army, was thought to be a risky proposition in the early 19th century, and their mere presence discouraged settlement. It wasn't until 1842, a year after the Army had withdrawn the garrison at Fort Howard, that the town of Howard was laid out. And it still took more than 10 years for development to begin in earnest, chiefly because the government did not release the military land for sale until 1850. According to that year's census, Green Bay, with a population of 1,922, was more than three times the size of Howard. The first brewery in the area, Blesch's Bay Brewery, began operation in Howard in 1851. Three years later, a post office opened up. And in 1856, eight years after the state of Wisconsin had been admitted to the union and two years after Green Bay had become a city, the borough of Fort Howard was established. And a rivalry soon began.

◆ ◆ ◆

Even today, 124 years after the consolidation of Fort Howard and Green Bay, a distinct cultural divide exists between the east and west sides of town. The rest of the world may know Green Bay

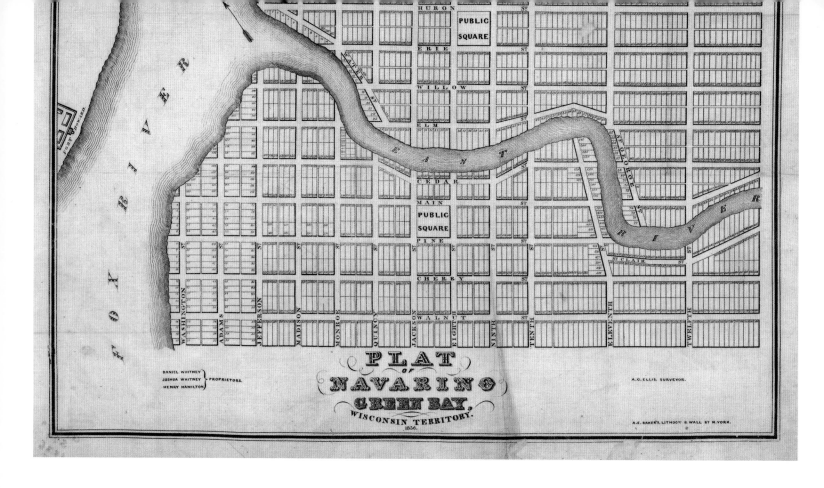

as a city that sits on an arm of Lake Michigan. But the most important body of water to Bayites is not Green Bay itself. It is the Fox River. What side you come from is as much a part of your Green Bay DNA as who your parents are, what you do for a living, or whether or not you have season tickets to Lambeau Field. In some ways the antipathy does not go much deeper than "Our side is better than yours." Ask residents to explain why the rivalry exists and they will be hard-pressed to answer—it is simply self-evident. But the fissure between east and west is so sharp that it is not uncommon for people from one side of the Fox to say that they cannot imagine living on the other.

The animosity, such as it is, goes as far back as 1862, when the Chicago and North Western Railway decided to lay its tracks through Fort Howard instead of Green Bay. The choice made sense. From Fort Howard the railway not only could continue into the northern reaches of Wisconsin, but it could also turn west toward Minnesota without having to bridge the Fox River. After the rail-

way announced its decision, Green Bay immediately began pressing for a bridge to be constructed across the Fox. But Fort Howard, fearful that such a span would harm business on its side of the river, and ambitious to surpass Green Bay in size and influence, refused. So Green Bay went ahead and erected the Walnut Street Bridge on its own, completing the project in 1863. (When a passing schooner damaged the span 12 years later, Fort Howard refused to contribute money or resources for its repair.)

Fort Howard incorporated in 1873, but the town remained at a distinct disadvantage to Green Bay in terms of service professions. Nearly all the doctors and lawyers in the region practiced on the east side of the river. Fort Howard was decidedly blue-collar, which is one of the primary reasons that it stayed significantly smaller. According to census figures, the population of Fort Howard in 1880 was 3,089; the population of Green Bay was 8,555. "The result," according to Jack Rudolph, "was a bitter competition that hung on for years, even after the two communities combined."

The merging of Green Bay and Fort Howard into the single city of Green Bay took place on April 2, 1895. The idea had been floating around since the 1850s but had always gotten hung up on the thorny word *annexation,* which never failed to rile the residents of smaller Fort Howard, who had nixed the proposal in two previous votes. By 1895, the city leaders of Green Bay were restrained enough to go with the word *consolidation,* and the change seemed to help carry the proposal.

The vote to consolidate passed in a landslide, but not before Fort Howard had secured two guarantees: that alcohol could not be sold west of Broadway, and that it would retain its own high school. The liquor law inexplicably stayed on the books in Green Bay for 110 years, until 2005. The high school is still there. And its rivalry with its counterpart on the east side of the river would have an effect on Green Bay—and on professional football—that went far beyond what anyone in the city could have imagined.

· · ·

The year 1895 was a momentous one for Green Bay. Not only did the city expand its boundaries across the Fox River, but it also saw the introduction of two things with which the place is still identified: papermaking and football. Papermaking came in the person of John Hoberg, a German immigrant who moved his struggling paper mill to Green Bay from the Fox River village of Kaukauna, about 27 miles south. With one machine and just a few employees, Hoberg started a steam-power revolution in the industry, which until then had been using waterpower. Six years after Hoberg's mill began operation, the Northern Paper Mills opened for business—the company produced the first splinter-free bathroom tissue—and Green Bay soon became the nation's leading producer of toilet paper. The paper industry helped carry the city into the 20th century.

The first football game in Green Bay (the first on record, at least) took place on the afternoon of Sep-

FOOTBALL TEAM IN GREEN BAY.

WEST SIDE ATHLETIC SOCIETY WILL ORGANIZE AN ELEVEN.

Several Members of the Proposed Organization Begin Training — Games to be Arranged With a Number of Wisconsin Cities—Contests on the Local Gridiron.

tember 21, 1895, at a harness-racing track on the east side of town known as Washington Park. The game was nominally a clash between teams representing Green Bay East and Green Bay West High Schools. In fact, though, both teams used nonstudent players. Green Bay West—the very school that had been the focus of the consolidation vote in the spring—took the field with 10 players. East took the field with only eight. Over two 20-minute halves, the two teams battled to an 8–8 tie, scoring two touchdowns apiece (worth just four points back then) and failing on the conversions after each one. "Football has received its introduction to Green Bay, and henceforth the 'gridiron field' will be the Mecca of the amusement-loving public until snow flies," reported *The Green Bay Gazette* the next day. (The paper also mentioned the "enthusiastic" crowd, which included "a number of ladies.")

The two teams played again a week later on the same field, though this time without any high school affiliations. The game, which was contested in an intermittent drizzle, was purely an east side–west side affair, and ended with the east prevailing 6–4. According to the *Gazette,* "There

The formation of the town's first football team was trumpeted by *The Green Bay Gazette* on August 18, 1895, a little more than four months after the contentious consolidation of Fort Howard and Green Bay into one city.

was a large sprinkling of ladies in the grand stand, and the East and West side colors, black and yellow, and red and yellow, respectively, appeared on many of their costumes." By October 19 the two teams had consolidated into one to represent the city of Green Bay against teams from other towns in northern Wisconsin and the Upper Peninsula of Michigan. Opponents that first season included Stevens Point, Menominee (Michigan), Lawrence University (in Appleton), Oconto, and Fond du Lac (twice, in a home-and-home series that concluded in Green Bay on Thanksgiving Day).

The driving force behind the team, according to the paper, was 24-year-old Chicago native Fred Hulbert, a laundry deliveryman who had graduated in the spring from Wayland Academy, in Beaver Dam, Wisconsin. The blond-haired Hulbert, who had played football at Wayland, lived on the west side of the Fox, on Broadway, and was the trainer of the West Side Athletic Association. The game he introduced to Green Bay that fall was very different from the one played today. The only padding worn by players was a lined canvas uniform called a moleskin, and the only protective gear was a rubber nose guard that was worn strapped to the face like a mask. In an effort to protect their heads, many players, including Hulbert, grew their hair long. Passing was illegal. The ball was made for carrying and kicking only — it was big and rotund, practically round. Most offensive plays involved a ballcarrier trying to "buck," or smash, his way forward behind a gang of blockers.

The game was exceedingly violent. Players locked arms in blocking formations and play advanced in a mass of humanity. Ballcarriers were often buried under hundreds of pounds of tacklers. There was also lots of fighting. The *Gazette*, in a story on the 1896 Green Bay–Oshkosh tilt, found it noteworthy enough to mention that the game had been "free from slugging." Hulbert had actually gotten his nose broken in Green Bay's contested 10–4 victory over Menominee on October 25, 1895. Playing fullback, he had been carrying the ball around end early in the second half when, according to the *Gazette,* "he was struck in the face . . . and knocked senseless" by a player identified only as "Juttner." The game ended in confusion, with Green Bay refusing to continue and officials unable to agree on the outcome.

The chaotic conclusion to the game was appropriate. The first Green Bay town team was little better than a sandlot outfit. Not counting the two games between squads from the east and west sides of the river, it went 1-5, scored only 18 points all season, and lost three games by 30 points or more, including a 66–4 blowout against Lawrence University. Green Bay improved in 1896 with the addition of former Wisconsin tackle T. P. Silverwood. According to his granddaughter, the fledgling attorney had ridden his bike from Madison to Green Bay after graduation to look into establishing a law practice — though that seems unlikely, since he began the fall playing for the town team in Oconto, about 30 miles north of Green Bay. Solidly built and sporting a shock of red hair and a thick handlebar mustache, the 162-pound Silverwood proved to be a more capable player and team organizer than Hulbert. With Silverwood as captain and coach in 1897, Green Bay went 4-0-1 and outscored its opponents 142–6. One of the key additions to the team was fullback Tom Skenandore, a member of the Oneida Nation. Skenandore had previously played football at the Carlisle Indian Industrial School, in Carlisle, Pennsylvania, where he had been listed as "Schanandore." The Carlisle teams of the 1890s included several other prominent Oneida players, including fullback Jonas Metoxen and tackle Martin Wheelock, the latter of whom played for coach Glenn "Pop" Warner and was named second-team All-America in 1899 and 1901 by Walter Camp. In Green Bay in 1897, Skenandore was considered so valuable as a ballcarrier that the team paid him $20 a game, which made him the first professional player in the history of the city.

A sign of how far Silverwood had brought the team by 1897 can be found in its 42–0 thrashing of Lawrence University, the same team that had beaten Green Bay by 62 points just two years before. For one year, at least, the team raised itself above sandlot status. The season ended on Thanksgiving with a 62–0 drubbing of Fond du Lac, which had beaten Green Bay twice in 1895. At the end of the campaign, the team anointed themselves champions — of what, though, is unclear. Such informality and haphazardness were typical for town football teams in Green Bay in those early years. Silverwood, busy with his duties as an attorney, vanished from the scene in 1898, when the town team played only two games. According to Packers team historian Cliff Christl, in the 24 seasons from 1895 to 1918 there were at least five in which Green Bay had no team at all, and another four in which a so-called city team played no more than one or two games. There was no constancy of names, managers, coaches, players, or anything else. There is also scant evidence that games played by town teams attracted many spectators. There were supposedly 1,000 fans at the Thanksgiving victory over Fond du Lac in 1897, but the next day's *Gazette* made no mention of the crowd.

What transformed football into a sensation in Green Bay, and what ultimately gave birth to the Packers, was the rivalry between Green Bay East and Green Bay West High Schools. Both had begun playing football within a few years of the consolidation of Fort Howard and Green Bay, but they did not reach an agreement to play each other until 1905; a game between the two had actually been scheduled four years earlier, only to be canceled by the Board of Education, which felt that it "would not be for the best interests of the city or schools." By the time the two actually met, anticipation was high. The *Gazette* set the stage for the first meeting by describing it as "the most import-

The 1897 city team. Captain T. P. Silverwood is holding the ball. To his left is Tom Skenandore, Green Bay's first professional player. Fred Hulbert, organizer of the 1895 team, is standing in the third row on the far left.

ant ever played in the city." Appropriately enough, the game was contested in bitterly cold weather. Morning temperatures were around nine degrees (they wouldn't rise above 20), and the city had awoken to a frozen Fox River. The game kicked off at 10:30 a.m. at Hagemeister Park, with West beginning at an immediate disadvantage. Right end Walt Spooner had broken his shoulder blade in a streetcar accident on his way to the game—hanging off the edge of a crowded car, he had been struck by another moving in the opposite direction—and was unable to play. Missing one of its starting linemen, West was unable to contain East fullback Fred Schneider, who scored on runs of 10, 30, and 70 yards in a 21–0 victory. There is no record of attendance at the game, but the *Gazette*'s report on the affair noted, "The attendance was about as large as has ever been drawn by a local high school contest and the cheering of the rival delegations of 'rooters' was an important accompaniment of the struggle." Though unspecific in the extreme, it stood in stark contrast to the paper's report on the game played by the town team on the same field later in the day:

> *A disastrous finish to the rather disastrous season for the Green Bay football aggregation directed by "Tod" Burns took place at Hagemeister park yesterday afternoon, when the Company I team of Marinette defeated the local gridiron representatives by a score of 11 to 0. The contest was of a somewhat farcical nature in some respects. The patronage was a disappointment to the promoters. Local football interest yesterday appeared to be centered in the battle between the East and West high schools earlier in the day and as a consequence the box office receipts for the contest of the city teams suffered materially.*
>
> *The shortage of players which has attended previous appearances of the local eleven this season was again experienced by Manager Burns yesterday and there was*

a considerable delay before he could recruit his bunch to the required standard. In the emergency Burns donned a uniform and Marinette substitutes were drafted into service on the Green Bay side of the firing line to appease the clamor of patrons who had paid for the pasteboards at the gate. The contest was short after the Marinette soldiers had scored the second touchdown.

There was no mention in either story about the possible eradication of football—though the prospect was very real. The sport had grown rapidly in popularity on college campuses since the first contest between Princeton and Rutgers in 1869. But revulsion at the violence in the game had been building steadily in the United States for much of the previous decade. In October 1905, President Theodore Roosevelt had told a White House gathering of college officials, "I demand that football change its rules or be abolished. Change the game or forsake it!" Less than a week later, the president's oldest son, Teddy, had gotten his nose broken playing for Harvard in its freshman game against Yale. Near the end of November, shortly after Columbia University had suspended its football program because of safety concerns, the *Chicago Tribune* reported that 19 people had died since January playing college, high school, and sandlot football. The carnage appalled America. Protective equipment still amounted to little more than moleskin and nose guards, and players sometimes sustained gruesome injuries that included wrenched spinal cords and crushed skulls. Newspaper editorials around the country were demanding that colleges and high schools banish the game. In April 1906, the newly created Intercollegiate Athletic Association of the United States (the forerunner of the NCAA) formally adopted new rules for the game, legalizing the forward pass and establishing a neutral zone at the line of scrimmage, as well as prohibiting things like kneeing, punching, and locking hands.

Even with the new rules, the Green Bay school

board banned football four months later. The outcry in town was immediate, with players from East formally petitioning for football to be reinstated. In September the board agreed to lift its ban, provided that the new rules were adhered to and that players from both East and West pledged their commitment to a resolution that stated that the "game goes hand in hand with hard work and manly deportment." While East enjoyed an undefeated season, there are no mentions in the *Gazette* of West ever playing a game that fall. East went 6-0 and defeated Menominee on Thanksgiving Day. There was no game between East and West.

The rivalry truly took off the next year, when the two schools formalized an agreement to meet annually on Thanksgiving. With the field at Hagemeister Park marked off in a checkerboard, and with policemen lining the sidelines to keep spectators back — the proximity of fans sometimes made it hard for offenses to execute end runs — East defeated West 11–0. The star of the game was East's left halfback, Joseph Merrill Hoeffel, who scored on a 35-yard fumble recovery. Four hundred revelers, including students and alumni who had come from as far away as Chicago, took to the streets in celebration. They led a parade up Washington Street, on the east side of the Fox, crossed over to the west side on the Main Street Bridge, paraded south on Broadway, and then crossed back over the river on Walnut Street. "Horns with their noisy din made the down town portion of the city resemble a district besieged by an army of fanatics," read the story in the next day's *Gazette*.

Things took a bitter turn in 1908, when the game was marred by fights between fans on the field while play was going on. The brawling continued at the downtown celebrations later in the day. In 1913 the newspaper put attendance at 3,000; a year later it was nearly 4,000. In 1916 the East-West tilt — played since 1908 at the League Ball Grounds, which was part of Hagemeister Park and included a grandstand and bleachers — drew

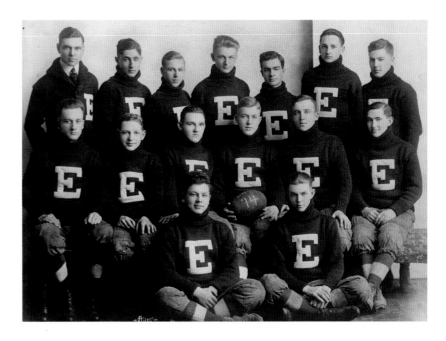

The 1914 Green Bay East football team. Sophomore Curly Lambeau is sitting in the front row, on the left.

5,000 fans, the biggest football crowd in Green Bay's history. The next year, the Green Bay militia patrolled the sidelines with bayonets fixed.

The 1916 game was a momentous one for several reasons. Not only was the size of the crowd a record, but the game also marked the first victory for Green Bay East in eight years. From 1909 through 1915, West had reeled off seven straight wins, by a combined score of 79–17. But in 1916, East was coached by Joe Hoeffel, the hero of the 1907 victory, who had gone on to play end at Wisconsin, where in 1912 he captained the Badgers' unbeaten Big Ten championship team. Against West, Hoeffel's East High captain rolled up nearly two-thirds of his team's total yards. The *Press-Gazette* noted that the 183-pound senior, a three-year starter at fullback, had proved himself the star of the game "by great ground-gaining, heavy booting and hectic defense . . . He was in every play." With West leading 6–0 early in the second quarter — not long after a crush of fans had broken through a sideline fence — the East fullback plunged over the left side from two yards out for the tying touchdown. He then kicked the extra point to give East a lead it would never relinquish.

The fullback's name was Earl Louis Lambeau. But he was better known to everyone in Green Bay as Curly.

CHAPTER 2

CURLY AND CAL

The word *lambeau* is French, meaning a shred or a scrap of cloth. The plural of *lambeau* is *lambeaux*—something that is *en lambeaux* is in tatters. As a surname, Lambeau is exceedingly rare in the French-speaking world, where it appears in that capacity most frequently in Belgium. Of that country's 2017 population of 11.4 million, only 256 shared the name. It was nevertheless from Belgium in the mid-19th century that the first Lambeaus came to Green Bay. In 1853, not long after Daniel Whitney had retired from his highly active business life, a wave of Belgian immigration began to roll into northeastern Wisconsin. At the time, the southern region of Belgium, Wallonia, was fully engaged in the industrial revolution, while the economy of the northern region, Flanders, was dominated by family farms. As more and more people began to seek out manufacturing jobs, migration within the country moved almost exclusively from Flanders to Wallonia—from the farms to the factories. Industrial changes, coupled with multiple disastrous crop failures throughout Europe, sparked a surge of emigration from Wallonia to the United States. From 1847 to 1849, the number of people leaving Belgium for America reached 6,000 to 7,000 a year, and they included almost all walks of blue-collar life, from farmers, miners, carpenters, and masons to glassblowers and lace makers.

In Green Bay in 1853, Belgian immigrants—drawn by the wheat-farming potential of the area, as well as by the presence of Father Edward Daems, a French-speaking priest at Holy Cross Church, on the Door Peninsula—joined a population that was becoming increasingly diverse. Over the next 50 years, in addition to the French, British, and Yankees who had originally settled Green Bay, more recent immigrants from Belgium, Germany, Holland, Ireland, Norway, and Poland established substantial communities in the city. The Belgians settled primarily on the eastern side of the Fox and to the northeast of the city. By 1858, at least 7,500 Belgians resided in Brown, Door, and Kewaunee Counties. And the 44 miles between Green Bay and Sturgeon Bay, to the northeast, were almost exclusively Belgian and included the largest Walloon settlement in the United States.

The Belgian community was already well established when, on April 25, 1873, Victor Joseph Lambeau embarked for the United States on the SS *Victoria*. Just 19 years old, Victor had been born and raised in the village of Hamme-Mille, in north-central Wallonia. He did not depart Belgium alone, traveling with Jean Baptiste Rose and his wife, Marie Adèle — both of whom were about 10 years older than Victor — and their three-month-old son. The Roses were from the neighboring village of Nethen. The four arrived at the port of Detroit in June and from there journeyed on to Green Bay. Victor lived with the Roses for several years after his arrival and, along with Jean (who Americanized his name as John), he started the Rose-Lambeau Mason Contracting Company. One of the projects they worked on was the stately old East High School building, a massive red-brick structure at the corner of Chicago Street and Webster Avenue. The exact date Victor married Marie Adolphine Charlier in Green Bay is unknown, but it was most likely sometime before 1876, which was when their oldest son, Marcel, was born. In the next 14 years, Victor and his wife had five more children — three girls and two boys.

Decades later, Curly Lambeau would become so well known for his explosive temper that he earned the nickname "the Bellicose Belgian." But in the 19th century, the temperaments of the men in the Lambeau family were not a matter of public record — until four o'clock in the afternoon of October 5, 1891, four days before Marcel's 15th birthday. That was when Victor, holding a tin box containing a $3,000 life insurance policy in his left hand, confronted Marie on a Green Bay street corner. With his right hand he drew a .32-caliber revolver from his hip pocket and shot Marie in the neck, just under her chin. Victor then put the revolver to his right temple and killed himself.

Marie survived the shooting and, according to *The Green Bay Gazette,* told people who came to her aid that Victor had shot her because she "would not give him two checks for $100 each." But an acquaintance of Marie's told the *Gazette* that the shooting had been the result of jealousy, and that just a week earlier Victor had threatened to kill his wife. That account agrees with the testimony of John Rose, who told authorities that he had seen Victor not long before the shooting and that it was his conclusion that his business partner not only had been drinking but was also consumed by jealousy. Marie, who spoke only French, insisted to reporters that jealousy had not been the cause. A little more than a week after the shooting, a coroner's jury ruled that Victor had acted while in a fit of temporary insanity.

Marcel, like his father, made his living in the bricklaying and contracting business, though he also later worked as a saloonkeeper. He married Mary Sara Latour in 1897, and the couple had five children. Their oldest, Earl Louis Lambeau, was born at 12:30 p.m. on Saturday, April 9, 1898. He had a burly frame, a broad, handsome face with full lips, and a shock of thick, curly black hair that erupted from the top of his head, inspiring the nickname by which he would be known for the rest of his life.

The Lambeaus lived a somewhat nomadic existence. Between 1898 and 1917, Curly Lambeau's senior year at Green Bay East, the family lived in at least six different homes, including the Michigan House, an east-side tavern where Marcel worked behind the bar and which had rooms he rented out to boarders. According to Green Bay attorney and area history aficionado Ken Calewarts, who in 2003 set out to find Lambeau's birthplace, all the moving may have had something to do with Marcel's work as a contractor. "I think he would live in one house until he built another place that he liked," Calewarts says. "And then he would sell and move into the new place."

Curly Lambeau loved sports, lived life in a hurry — and often by the seat of his pants — and dreamed big from an early age. He grew up on the east side, and when he and the other kids in his neighborhood didn't have a football to play with,

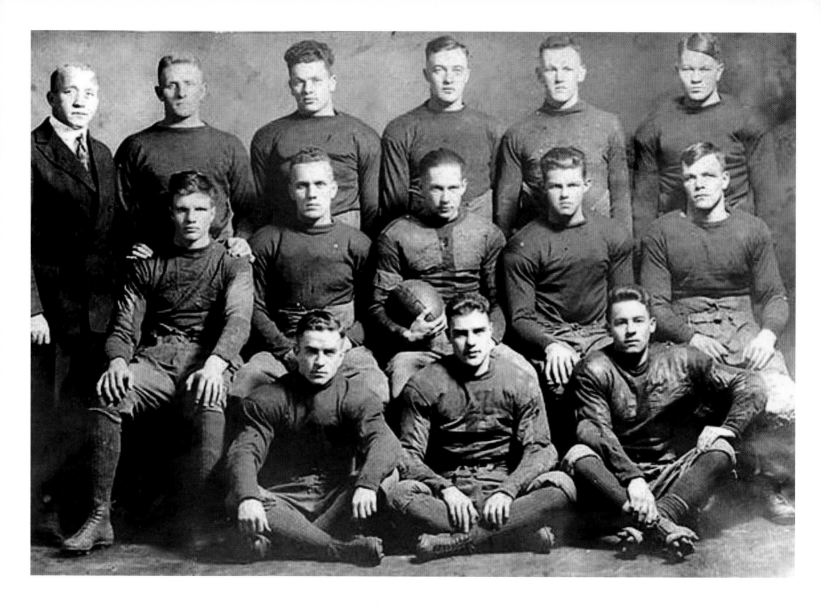

they would make one of their own by filling a salt sack with sand, leaves, and pebbles. The quote that ran next to his senior portrait in the 1917 Green Bay East yearbook read, "When I get thru with athletics I'm going out and conquer the rest of the world." At East, the fast and physical Lambeau not only starred in football, but also excelled as a member of the track-and-field team, competing in the shot put, the hammer and discus throws, and the hurdle and relay events.

Lambeau graduated from East in the spring of 1917, not long after the United States had declared war on Germany. At 19, he was too young

for the draft, which at the time was for men between the ages of 21 and 30.* Most sports fans in town expected him to go on to play football at Wisconsin. On September 26, the *Wisconsin State Journal* identified him as one of four "well-known stars" expected to join the Badgers' freshman team. Two days later, *The Daily Cardinal,* the university's school paper, listed Lambeau among the "new freshmen who appeared" for practice but did not name him as one of the 21 players who participated. Two days after that, the *Green Bay Press-Gazette* reported that Lambeau had left only recently for Madison, before touting him as

_____

* *Lambeau registered for the draft on September 12, 1918, soon after Congress had expanded the range of eligible ages to between 18 and 45.*

"one of the best gridiron prospects that has ever been turned out of a high school."

But Lambeau apparently never enrolled at Wisconsin, which has no record of him in its registry. Indeed, if Lambeau left Green Bay for Wisconsin at all, he seems to have returned in fairly short order and soon after begun playing football for city teams. On October 21 he led a 10-man South Side Skidoos outfit to a 6–0 victory over De Pere. Three weeks later, Lambeau scored two touchdowns and kicked three extra points for the Green Bay All-Stars in a 27–0 shutout of the Marinette Badgers in a benefit game for the Brown County Red Cross. There is some evidence to suggest that the reason Lambeau did not go to college right out of high school had to do with money troubles. On February 17, 1917, when he was still a senior at Green Bay East, Lambeau had sent a letter to Notre Dame football coach Jesse C. Harper. "I am not fixed very well financially," he wrote, "and I would like to know what is the best you can do for me." Apparently nonplussed by the note's blunt tone, Harper waited until March 9 to respond. "If you are willing to work I will be very glad to try to help you," he wrote. "If you are not willing to work and in addition looking for an offer I assure you, you will have to consider some other institution."

Lambeau may have considered other schools, but he nevertheless enrolled at Notre Dame in 1918. By that time the Fighting Irish had a new coach, a former Chicago postal worker by the name of Knute Rockne. Born in Voss, Norway, in 1888, Rockne had come to Chicago with his parents when he was five years old. After graduating high school, he worked in the Chicago Post Office for four years before going to Notre Dame, from which he graduated magna cum laude with a chemistry degree in 1914. Rockne lettered in football during his time in South Bend. As a senior in 1913, he had starred in Notre Dame's 35–13 upset of Army at West Point, during which the Fighting

Irish had introduced the forward pass as a regular feature of their offense. After Rockne finished school, Notre Dame offered him a job — as a graduate assistant in the chemistry department. He accepted the position on the condition that the school would also allow him to help coach the football team. When Harper retired three years later, Notre Dame named Rockne as his successor.

Rockne's first season on the sideline was not an easy one for the Fighting Irish. With the nation at war, enrollment had declined precipitously, and many students left school to enlist in the military. Only four members of Notre Dame's 1917 team returned to South Bend in 1918. The football program that season fell under the jurisdiction of the Student Army Training Corps (SATC), which trained college students to be soldiers, and also limited practice time and banned long road trips. In order to get as many men out for football as possible, the Irish suspended the freshman eligibility rule, which cleared the way for the five-foot-ten, 187-pound Lambeau to become a mainstay of Rockne's first backfield. Lambeau played primarily at fullback, alongside left halfback George Gipp. In Rockne's debut as the Notre Dame coach, a 26–6 victory over Case Tech (now Case Western) in Cleveland on September 28, it was Lambeau who scored the first touchdown.[*] Shortly after the game, the October portion of Notre Dame's schedule was canceled because of the Spanish influenza epidemic — the Irish did not play their second game until November 2. Notre Dame went 3-1-2, suffering its lone defeat against Michigan State by a score of 13–7 on November 16. The Fighting Irish finished the 1918 season on Thanksgiving Day with a scoreless tie against Nebraska on a muddy field in Lincoln.

When Notre Dame broke for the holidays on December 19, Lambeau returned to Green Bay. And that's where his story becomes difficult to nail down. According to the school's records, he

---

* *H. G. McDavitt of* The Indianapolis Star, *in his story on the game, credited George Gipp with this touchdown.*

INDIAN PACKING PLANT SQUAD TO REPRESENT CITY

Great Football Eleven in City This Fall; All Star Team Is Available.

BEST STATE TEAMS WILL BE SEEN HERE

Second Conference of Grid-iron Men At Press-Gazette Thursday Evening.

Lambeau was almost certainly at the first organizational meeting of the Packers, on August 11, 1919, in the offices of the *Green Bay Press-Gazette*. The paper reported on the meeting two days later.

dropped out in December 1918 — receiving no grades in any of his seven first-semester classes — but there is evidence that he spent at least part of the spring semester in South Bend. In 1962, Lambeau would tell *Press-Gazette* reporter Lee Remmel that he had begun having trouble with his tonsils around Christmas but that, despite feeling unwell, he had returned to Notre Dame after the holidays. It is unclear, though, just exactly when he went back to school. Classes resumed on January 7, but the day before, Lambeau had written to Rockne from his residence in Green Bay. He did not mention his health in the letter, instead focusing on his financial difficulties. "It will be hard for me to go back to school as I cannot depend upon receiving money from home, due to ill luck," he wrote. "No doubt all the bunch is back and going to it again. I sure would like to be with them. I

wonder if I could obtain a job so as to make things go along smooth, if I should return." Lambeau also told Remmel in 1962 that, when his health had not improved, he had returned to Green Bay at some point in January.

While Lambeau's whereabouts are uncertain for most of the six weeks after the conclusion of Notre Dame's holiday break, he was definitely in South Bend on Tuesday, February 5, 1919. On that day, he mailed a letter postmarked NOTRE DAME, IND., to his high school sweetheart, Marguerite Van Kessel. In his letter to Van Kessel — reprinted in the 2011 book *Green Bay: A City and Its Team*, by Dr. James Hurly and Thomas Murphy — Lambeau wrote that he had just gotten out of the infirmary after an eight-day stay and that he had been advised by several doctors to have his tonsils taken out immediately. "So the first part of next week I will have them removed," he wrote. "Then I will be minus fifty dollars . . . Its [sic] hell to be sick, especially when it costs so much."

Soon after, Lambeau returned to Green Bay for good and took a job as a shipping clerk at the Indian Packing Company's plant on Morrow Street. Indian Packing was a canned meat concern that had begun operations in Green Bay about two years before. At the time, Indian's business was thriving because of its lucrative agreements with the federal government to supply servicemen with canned meals. There was a family connection to the business for Lambeau. His father had supervised the construction of the plant's original buildings. Indian hired Curly for $250 a month. "I thought," he would tell *Sports Illustrated* in 1962, "that was as much money as any man would want in the world, so I went to work." Assured of an income, Lambeau married Van Kessel on August 16, 1919. He was no longer a student-athlete. He was a working man.

Lambeau could not have known it at the time, but his marriage would not be the most momentous event in his life that month.

◆ ◆ ◆

More than any other team in any other sport, the Green Bay Packers are *of* the place from which they come. They are elemental, a natural outgrowth of the land and the water and the people of their hometown. The Packers would not exist if Green Bay were not so neatly divided in two by the Fox River. The Packers would not exist if the city had not been so passionate about football—the rivalry between Green Bay East and Green Bay West not only produced many of the men who played on the Packers' first team but also, more important, created a football-loving culture. And finally, the Packers would not exist if not for newspaper editor George Whitney Calhoun, a great-grandson of Daniel Whitney, the adventurous minuteman's son who had founded the city. Calhoun's alliance with Lambeau was emblematic of the very essence of the Green Bay community—one was the grand-

Whitney Calhoun, **Manager of the Football Team Representing the Technical High School of Buffalo.**

son of immigrants, the other the great-grandson of an original Yankee settler. Before the franchise that they co-founded came to epitomize a sport and, in many ways, a country, it was created from the same components that had come together to form the city itself. The Packers *are* because Green Bay *is*.

George Whitney Calhoun was born in Green Bay on September 16, 1890, 28 years after the death of his great-grandfather. He was the only child of Walter Calhoun and his wife, Emmeline, a granddaughter of Daniel Whitney. Walter was a civil

Calhoun played center for Buffalo's Technical High School in 1908. He was an active athlete as a young man, playing football, baseball, and hockey. But more than anything, he was a compulsive organizer of teams and leagues.

engineer who had come to town when the Green Bay Water Company was converting its lines from wood to metal piping. As a consulting engineer he moved frequently, going wherever there was work. In the years after George was born, the family moved to Silverwood, Indiana, St. Louis, New Orleans, and then Buffalo, where in 1899 Walter began working on a bridge over the Niagara River. Not long after the family arrived in upstate New York, Walter and Emmeline apparently separated — in April 1901, she was appointed as George's legal guardian. In July 1907, a year after Emmeline died from an unknown ailment, another guardian, who was not Walter, was appointed. And according to the 1910 census, Walter was remarried and living in Buffalo at a different location than his only son, who was living at the same address at which he'd resided since at least 1906. Although specifics are scarce, Walter and George do not appear to have had a close relationship.

As is the case with Curly Lambeau, the details of George Whitney Calhoun's early life are spotty — and often don't match the ones that were eventually put on paper. According to Calhoun's obituary in the December 6, 1963, edition of the *Green Bay Press-Gazette,* the paper for which he was an editor for more than 40 years, he graduated from high school in 1910 and then attended the University of Buffalo. But according to census data, the 19-year-old Calhoun was not in high school in April 1910. He was instead working as a rate clerk for the railroad and had not attended school in more than seven months. His next known job was in 1914, when he was the editor in chief of *High School World,* a weekly devoted to New York high school sports. One year later, in 1915, he moved to Green Bay to work as the telegraph editor at the *Green Bay Review.* Before he left for Wisconsin, he had also apparently worked for a time at the *Buffalo Evening News* — a 1926 story in the *News* said that Calhoun had once been an employee of the paper. But while there is evidence of his working life in Buffalo, there is no record of his hav-

ing spent any time in college there. It is very possible that he attended (or even that he took some classes at) the University of Buffalo, but the school did not become an undergraduate institution until the fall of 1913. And it is hard to see how he would have been a student at the same time he had a full-time job at the *Evening News.*

Something else would have made it difficult for Calhoun to have been in college. On February 25, 1911, he married 21-year-old Marion Gibson in Fort Erie, Ontario, right across the Niagara River from Buffalo. According to the lively team history published in 1983 by John Torinus, a former member of the Packers' executive committee and a longtime colleague of Calhoun's at the *Press-Gazette,* the union was short-lived, and its demise was the result of Calhoun's rheumatoid arthritis. "Cal's wife had divorced him not long after he came down with that terrible case of arthritis, and he was very cynical about women from that time forward," Torinus wrote. "He lived primarily a life among men."

Of Calhoun's disabilities, his obituary said, "It was a football injury in college that crippled him for life. While playing for the University of Buffalo he was tackled and thrown against a goal post, being so severely injured that he was completely paralyzed for some time. He never fully recovered from the accident." But other sources — most notably Torinus — ascribe his ailments to rheumatoid arthritis. Torinus says that Calhoun had been afflicted while still in college, and was badly crippled in his hands, arms, and legs. Either explanation may be true, but since it is unlikely that Calhoun attended Buffalo, the rheumatoid arthritis explanation seems more plausible.

Calhoun had indeed been an athlete as a younger man, when he sported a sneering grin and a thick shock of floppy black hair. He was a first baseman in baseball, a goalie in hockey, and a center in football. There are news reports in the Buffalo papers of his playing hockey as late as 1911, two years after he had graduated from Technical High School, but there is nothing about his playing football beyond his senior season at Tech in 1908. There is likewise nothing about his ever suffering an injury. And the University of Buffalo did not have either a football or hockey team in the years when he might have gone to school there. The athletic department at Buffalo (and the one at Buffalo State, for that matter) has no record of a George Whitney Calhoun lettering in any sport.

The particulars of Calhoun's athletic exploits — and whether his lifelong disabilities were in any way a result of them — are less important than the fact that he also managed most of the teams for which he played. The man was, quite simply, an inveterate organizer. At the age of 11 he was already being listed in Buffalo newspapers as the primary contact for teams interested in scheduling games. In the spring of 1902 he was managing and playing first base for the Elmwood Juniors baseball team. An item (likely written by Calhoun himself) in the May 23 edition of the *Buffalo Evening News* read, "Any challenges from teams not under 12 years old in the Elmwood District, Address Whitney Calhoun, manager, 168 Lexington avenue." Four years later, he was managing the Tashmoo AC baseball team and playing for the club's football team. From 1907 to 1909, he was a hockey goalie and a 145-pound football center (as well as the team manager) at Technical High. He also played goalie for the Tashmoo hockey team. And from the fall of 1909 through the fall of 1911, Calhoun managed the Niagaras, one of Buffalo's numerous town football teams. An entry from the September 28, 1910, edition of the *Buffalo Courier* — again, probably written by Calhoun — manages to be both daring and pleading in the span of 77 words:

WHO WANTS THE NIAGARAS

Any team wishing a game with the Niagara football team of Buffalo for next Sunday can receive a reply from the manager, G.W. Calhoun, No. 224 Ashland Avenue. Phone 13963 Frontier. To-night at the Front band-stand the Niagaras will line up for scrimmage work. All candidates are requested by the management to report on time as important work is to be taken up by the coaches. Practice will start promptly at 8 o'clock.

In May 1917, two years after Calhoun had moved back to Green Bay, he took a job as the telegraph editor at the *Press-Gazette*. That summer, he began writing a semiregular column for the sports page that, in September, was dubbed "Cal's Comment." One of Calhoun's subjects that month was none other than Curly Lambeau.

There is no firm agreement on when or where Calhoun and Lambeau first discussed forming a football team. The most commonly told version of the story is that the idea was hatched during a chance encounter on a downtown street corner in the summer of 1919. Calhoun himself told the story this way in the pages of the *Press-Gazette* in November 1963 and added that the meeting took place in mid-August, when he was on his way back to his office after eating a midday meal at a downtown eatery known as the Baltimore Lunch. The only problem with that embellishment, according to Packers historian Cliff Christl, is that there was no establishment with that name in Green Bay in 1919.

Torinus, who worked for Calhoun when he first started at the *Press-Gazette* in 1934, puts the encounter with Lambeau in generally the same time frame but says that the conversation took place over a glass of beer. According to Torinus, Lambeau told Calhoun that he missed playing football, to which the newspaperman, who the year before had managed the city's semipro team — the same one for which Lambeau had played one game before leaving for South Bend — replied, "Why not get up a team in Green Bay? I'll help you put one together, and I'll give you all the publicity you need."

Lambeau may have missed playing football, but the idea for a team almost certainly didn't materi-

alize simply from a mixture of sentiment and suds —though one or both probably played a role at some point. The prospects for a new team in Green Bay had been publicly bandied about as early in the year as April 29. That was the day that *Press-Gazette* sports columnist Val Schneider mused about the prospects for another town team. "There is considerable comment passed around this city about the prospects of a city football eleven here next autumn," he wrote. "Many of Green Bay's superior grid warriors are now on their way across the Atlantic back to God's country and with their

return the prospects for a state championship eleven are boosted sky high."

Schneider's role in the creation of the Packers is unclear, but there's a good chance that he is the forgotten man in the birth of the franchise. He was certainly in a position to know if something was up with either Calhoun or Lambeau in the summer of 1919, since he not only worked with Calhoun at the newspaper but also knew Lambeau from Green Bay's new eight-team City Industrial Baseball League. There were such teams and leagues all over northeastern Wisconsin at

the time, and with no team sponsored by the Indian Packing Company in 1919, Lambeau was moonlighting for several different outfits. Schneider, a first baseman, played for a team called the Whales, with whom Lambeau played at least two games in the summer of 1919, one at shortstop and the other at third base.

Calhoun and Lambeau had crossed paths several times before that summer, first when Lambeau was playing at Green Bay East and then when he played in the Red Cross charity football game in November 1917. Calhoun had hyped the game in the *Press-Gazette* and Lambeau had been the contest's biggest star, scoring two touchdowns in front of 1,200 paying spectators. The 1918 city team that Calhoun managed, and for which Lambeau played one game, had many of the problems of inconsistency that made town teams such a haphazard tradition in Green Bay—and which make the creation of the Packers such a significant event. It began as a neighborhood organization (another incarnation of the South Side Skidoos), then changed its name to the Green Bay Whales, before finally just calling itself the Bays.

The 1917 city team— probably the Green Bay All-Stars. Lambeau is on the far left in the back. Among his teammates were future Packers Jim Coffeen (second row, second from left), Art Schmael (second row, far right), Jab Murray (first row, third from left), Andy Muldoon (first row, third from right), and Nate Abrams (first row, far right).

In his only appearance before departing for South Bend, Lambeau had helped the Skidoos to a 13–0 victory over De Pere on September 15. Other than the presence of Calhoun and Lambeau, there was little connection between the 1918 town teams and the 1919 Packers.

◆ ◆ ◆

The Green Bay Packers took their first step as a franchise on Monday, August 11, at an evening meeting in the unkempt, ink-stained second-floor editorial offices of the *Press-Gazette*. Calhoun was almost certainly there, and it's likely that Schneider was, too. Lambeau's presence wasn't documented, but it seems fairly certain that he was also in attendance, because the story on the meeting that ran in the *Press-Gazette* on August 13 — the first public mention of the team — made note of the fact that "complete uniforms for eighteen or twenty men will be secured." According to the history of the Packers written in 1946 by Chicago newspaper editor Arch Ward, Lambeau had secured $500 for uniforms from Frank Peck, his boss at the packing plant.

The August 13 story said that the "husky squad" of "pigskin chasers" would play a 10-game schedule. "The Indian Packing corporation will be the representative semipro football team in Green Bay this fall," read the first paragraph. The story went on to refer to the new team as the "Packers" in the third paragraph, and then as the "Indians" in the fourth. It also ran through a list of prospective players, describing the candidates as "former college stars and some veterans who saw service in the gridiron battles overseas." There were 38 names in all. On the evening of August 14, about two dozen players attended a second organizational meeting at the *Press-Gazette* offices. Lambeau was elected captain of the team, and Calhoun was named manager. The first practice was set for September 3, the Wednesday after Labor Day, and practices would thereafter be held three times a week (on Mondays, Wednesdays, and Fridays). The only game confirmed on the schedule was an Oc-

tober 26 date with Marinette, but the plan was to start playing in one month, on Sunday, September 14.

Two days after the Thursday meeting, on the morning of August 16, Lambeau married Marguerite Van Kessel at St. Francis Xavier Cathedral, in downtown Green Bay, just a few blocks from the *Press-Gazette* offices at 315 Cherry Street.

Soon after, the *Press-Gazette* began a steady drumbeat for the Packers, running 15 stories about the team in the 18 days from August 27 through September 13. None of the stories quoted Lambeau — or anybody else for that matter — and many were little more than breathless accounts of upcoming team meetings and prospective opponents. "Footballers on the Indian Packing Corporation squad will hold an important meeting in the editorial rooms of The Press-Gazette on Friday evening at 7:45," reads one story. "It is of utmost importance that every man be on hand as final plans for the season will be outlined." Another promised that "the football public will witness the classiest exhibitions of the gridiron sport, that have ever been seen on a local field."

At the time, the original Packers were just a collection of men from the town who were interested in playing football. But seen through the prism of history, that first team and its players, drawn as they were from the ranks of former players at Green Bay East and Green Bay West, were a symbol of unity. Before the Packers became something that brought people together from all over the country and the world, they were something that brought people together from both sides of the Fox River and forged a bond between generations. Of the 25 men who suited up for Green Bay in 1919, 17 had gone to either East or West High School, including quarterback Jim Coffeen, the son of the doctor who had reset Fred Hulbert's broken nose during the sandlot game against Menominee in 1895. Among the notable imports was Gustav "Gus" Rosenow, a wiry halfback who had coached at Green Bay West in 1918 while also playing for the city team. Rosenow played every game in the Packers' first season despite the fact that his left hand had been mangled in a childhood accident.

For practice, the team met on the hardscrabble athletic field adjacent to the buildings of the Indian Packing plant, which was on the east side of town. Putting the players through their paces was Willard J. "Big Bill" Ryan, a broad-shouldered native of Washburn, Wisconsin, who was also the football coach at Green Bay West. Ryan had been the coach at West in 1916 and 1917 before serving as a private in the U.S. Army's Chemical Warfare Service during World War I. He returned to West after the war. The coach at Green Bay East in 1919 was none other than Curly Lambeau.

The Packers would be playing their games on a field at Hagemeister Park, which had been home to football in the city since the game's debut. Hagemeister was a triangular patch of ground on the east side of town—not far from where Lambeau had played sandlot football as a boy. It was known as Washington Park in 1895, when it had also included the Brown County Fairgrounds and a half-mile harness-racing track. In 1899, the Joannes Brothers wholesale grocery business had purchased Washington Park and then sold the northern portion to the Hagemeister Brewing Company, one of Green Bay's original breweries. Hagemeister Park included fields for football and baseball, as well as an armory, in which the Packers would occasionally practice in inclement weather. Just next door to the armory was the park's terraced, three-story Victorian clubhouse, which was topped with a winsome cupola that rose from the center of the structure. The field at the park was just to the east of the clubhouse and was busy throughout the fall as the home gridiron for both the Packers and East High.

• • •

The Packers opened their season on schedule, against the North End AC team from Menominee, Michigan, on Sunday, September 14. It was a warm, sunny day, with a high temperature of 74 degrees.

There were no police or ushers to maintain order at that first game—there were no stands at all, in fact. There were no entrance gates and there was no fence. The only thing keeping people off the field was a rope that had been stretched around the boundaries. The crowd, which was described only as "large" in the next day's paper, was later set at 1,500, but that seems to have been just a guess. Fans and players alike had gotten to Hagemeister Park that day by taking the Walnut Street trolley, which stopped right next to the field. Spectators stood along the sidelines or, if they had driven,

Lambeau was a shipping clerk at the Indian Packing plant in 1919 when he secured funding for uniforms and equipment from company president Frank Peck. Indian's primary product was marketed under the name "Council Meats."

In 1915, Chicago Cubs right-hander George "Zip" Zabel set the major league record for the longest appearance by a relief pitcher: 18⅓ innings. Four years later he was the referee in the first game the Packers ever lost.

years removed from his senior season at Green Bay West, and the younger brother of left end Rigney Dwyer—ran for the first touchdown in team history, "on a straight line plunge through center." From there, the rout was on.

The Packers' defense was suffocating, allowing Menominee only one first down all day. On offense, Green Bay moved the ball almost at will on the ground and through the air, with Lambeau doing most of the passing. The Packers scored eight touchdowns—including two by Lambeau, who also kicked five extra points—and cruised to a 53–0 victory. More telling, Green Bay used 19 players in the game, while Menominee used just 12. The Packers went two deep at every position but right halfback, which was manned by Lambeau, and right and left guard, which were manned by the Zoll brothers, Carl and Martin, respectively. The brothers were the sons of a west-side stonecutter. Carl, who was 20 in the fall of 1919, was well known around town as a heavyweight wrestler. Professional wrestling was a legitimate sport at the time and was tremendously popular among immigrant communities in the Upper Midwest. Zoll's matches were chronicled in the sports pages of the *Press-Gazette* and drew large crowds to Turner Hall, a German society headquarters that for many years had the largest auditorium in the city.

The 215-pound Zoll was valuable to the Packers in other ways that year. Green Bay opened the season with five straight victories—by a combined score of 331–6—before taking its first road trip, to Ishpeming, Michigan, on October 19. A special overnight Pullman was secured on the Chicago and North Western Railway, but expenses were tight. The team paid for passage for 24 people, but the whole traveling contingent numbered 36 or 37. Zoll, lying on an upper berth, hid two of the extra travelers behind his burly frame when train conductors made their head count. Another stowaway hid in the ladies' restroom.

Despite the adverse travel conditions, the Pack-

watched from atop their cars. Calhoun passed his hat among them for donations. There was no dressing room for the players, who presumably had put on their uniforms at home before heading over to the field—like kids playing Little League. At halftime, the two teams retreated to opposite end zones to rest and go over strategy.

The game began when Lambeau, wearing a new blue jersey, kicked off at three in the afternoon. The details of the contest are few. The story that ran in the next day's *Press-Gazette* was a bare-bones account of the action, and the box score added only a bit more detail, listing the starting lineups for both teams, the players who scored, the names of officials, and the length of the game's four quarters (12 minutes). Menominee's first drive ended with the Lumberjacks turning the ball over on downs. The article did not document the length of the Packers' first drive, only that Green Bay took a few minutes to march down the field into the end zone. Quarterback Clement "Dutch" Dwyer—two

ers beat Ishpeming 33–0 in familiar fashion, mixing the run and the pass to devastating effect. As important, however, was the fact that Green Bay used 20 players in the game, as compared with 13 for Ishpeming. In the Packers' 11 games that year, they never faced a team of more than 14 players. Green Bay won its next four games by a combined score of 217–0, a run that included an 85–0 obliteration of Oshkosh.

And who were the teams the Packers were beating? For the most part, they were hardly teams in the conventional sense. Most of Green Bay's 1919 opponents were organized on the fly and lacked any real credentials. Not that anybody who read the *Press-Gazette* could tell. The paper regularly touted the Packers' opponents as being loaded with former high school and college stars. The *Press-Gazette,* for example, referred to the first game of the season as being against North End AC of Menominee, Michigan. The Menominee *Herald-Leader,* on the other hand, reported that the team was named the Leannah's Colts and that it was badly outmatched—and also that it was actually from across the Menominee River in Marinette, Wisconsin. Three days before the Packers buried New London 54–0 on September 28, the weekly *New London Press* reported that the hometown team had just run through its first practice. After the game, the New London coach told the paper, "We just picked up a bunch, had a few hours practice, went to Green Bay, had a hard game, had a good time and came home." For both Marinette and New London, the game against the Packers seems to have been the only one that either team ever played.

Heading into what was to be the final game of the season, a November 23 road date against Beloit, the Packers were 10-0 and had outscored their opposition 565–6. But Beloit was nothing like the collection of patsies that Green Bay had been playing. The south-central Wisconsin town was home to Fairbanks Morse and Company, an engine-manufacturing concern. Fairbanks Morse sponsored not only a football team but also baseball and basketball teams. And all were state powers. The basketball team played the Original Celtics, a New York-based barnstorming team that introduced the idea of professional basketball to the nation. And more than a dozen former major leaguers played for the company's baseball team over the course of its 14-year existence.

One of those big leaguers was pitcher George Washington "Zip" Zabel, who in 1917 had abandoned his baseball career to go to work for Fairbanks Morse. Zabel had spent only two seasons in the major leagues, both with the Chicago Cubs, but he was there long enough to set a mark that will likely never be broken. On June 17, 1915, with the Cubs trailing the Brooklyn Robins 1–0, with two outs in the top of the first inning, Zabel entered the game for injured starter Bert Humphries, who had been struck on his pitching hand by a batted ball. Eighteen and a third innings later, when Chicago won the game 4–3, the second-year right-hander was still in the game. Zabel's 18⅓ innings pitched remains the major league single-game record for most innings thrown by a relief pitcher. Not surprisingly, the 24-year-old hurler was never quite the same. He lasted only two innings in his next start and soon began to experience arm trouble. Zabel bounced around the minors for the next season and a half, pitching in Los Angeles and Toronto, before hanging up his spikes in July 1917 to go to work for Fairbanks Morse. In his first decade with the company, he played baseball, basketball, and tennis on Fairbanks Morse teams.

But Zabel was no ringer. He was a scientist—and a good one. Originally from Wetmore, Kansas, the quiet and mannerly Zabel had earned a bachelor's degree in chemistry from Baker University, in Baldwin City, Kansas, in 1916. At Fairbanks Morse, he rose to the position of chief metallurgist and continued in various capacities with the company for the next 32 years, conducting well-regarded research on electric plating and spectrograph analysis. He was, in other words, an exceedingly unlikely candidate for corruption.

Corruption, though, was what he was charged with by Calhoun after Beloit ruined Green Bay's perfect season with a 6–0 victory on Fairbanks-Morse Field. In the November 24 edition of the *Press-Gazette,* an irate Calhoun put the blame for the defeat squarely on Zabel, who had been the referee. Near the conclusion of the first half, Beloit had a first down at the Packers' one-yard line when Lyle "Cowboy" Wheeler, who had played end in the Packers' first game and who was keeping time for Green Bay, declared that the half had ended. But the timekeeper from Beloit, team manager D. F. McCarthy, insisted that there were still five seconds left on the clock. "And of course," Calhoun noted bitterly, "Referee Zabell [*sic*] backed him up." Beloit punched the ball into the end zone on the next play. After a missed conversion, the Packers trailed 6–0 at the intermission.

Things got even more contentious after halftime, when Green Bay mounted a third-quarter drive that took the Packers near the Beloit goal line. From the five, Lambeau ran off tackle for "as clean a touchdown as has ever been made on a gridiron," wrote Calhoun. But Zabel ruled that Lambeau's forward progress had been stopped at the two, which was where he spotted the ball. Lambeau then ran for another apparent touchdown. This time, though, Zabel ruled that Green Bay had been offside. He penalized the Packers five yards, effectively ending the scoring threat.

If Zabel was guilty of playing the part of hometown referee, an explanation can perhaps be found in the behavior of the crowd, which, as described by Calhoun, was out of control. When the Packers began the drive that would end with Lambeau's disputed touchdown runs, Calhoun wrote that "the crowd began encircling the field and the gridiron looked more like a mob scene than a football field." And after Lambeau's first touchdown run had been called back, the Green Bay manager noted that "it looked as if there would be a great little free-for-all." In the final quarter the crowd

began actively interfering with the course of play. In the closing minutes, one spectator tripped Green Bay quarterback Orlo "Toody" McLean as he was running downfield.

Was Zabel intimidated by the crowd's behavior? It's possible. There are no records of him ever commenting on his work in the game. At the time, he was only 28 and had been in Beloit for just over two years. It was not uncommon for fans to become unruly when the Packers were on the road. In a 1963 article in the *Press-Gazette,* Carl Zoll recalled how away crowds used to be "pretty tight along the sidelines and once in a while some drunk would come on the field and make some trouble." He also noted that "after every game, a couple of fellows would be laying for you." Fan interference, in other words, was an acknowledged problem. A story in *The Janesville Gazette* on the potential for a December 7 replay of the game noted that Beloit's management was promising that "the field will be roped off five yards behind the side lines." Alas, the rematch was never held. Beloit canceled the game a few days before it was scheduled to be played, saying that a recent sleet storm and the subsequent cold weather had rendered the field unusable.

The letter declining the game was written by Beloit manager D. F. McCarthy and was reprinted in full by Calhoun in the *Press-Gazette* — complete with a final paragraph that was nothing short of out-and-out taunting: "Was interested in reading the account of our game in your Green Bay paper and must say you are all very fortunate in having a class of fans down whose necks you can poke such an unlikely story. However, the story is considered a joke both in Beloit and in Janesville."

• • •

Many of the men from the first Packers team settled in Green Bay. Fullback Wally P. Ladrow, who was 23 when the season began, went on to work in the Green Bay Post Office for 38 years, beginning in 1923. He eventually became superintendent of mails in the city and retired in 1961. Quarterback

Jim Coffeen was the Packers' PA announcer from 1923 to 1953.* Lineman Andy Muldoon became a guard at the Brown County Courthouse in 1925 and stayed on the job — and was a valuable source to newspaper reporters — for 35 years. Fullback Henry J. "Tubby" Bero, a veteran of World War I, went on to be a city electrician and eventually the chief of police. Herman Martell was one of the youngest of the original Packers. He was only 18 in the fall of 1919, when he played in nine games and started one at end. Later in life, Martell was one of the organizers of the Packer Alumni Association.

The very idea of an alumni association for the team that Lambeau and Calhoun had put together would have seemed outlandish in 1919. Town teams had been coming and going in Green Bay for a generation, and there seemed little reason to think that this one was any different. But the Green Bay Packers were built to last.

---

* *Coffeen's obituary in 1955 in the* Press-Gazette *said that he graduated from Green Bay East in 1905. But while the school has a record of his attendance, it has no record of his having graduated—a fact that actually came out in 1910, when Coffeen played well for Beloit College until he was declared ineligible. The* Green Bay Gazette *reported the story at the time, but no mention of Coffeen's academic status was ever made by the paper again.*

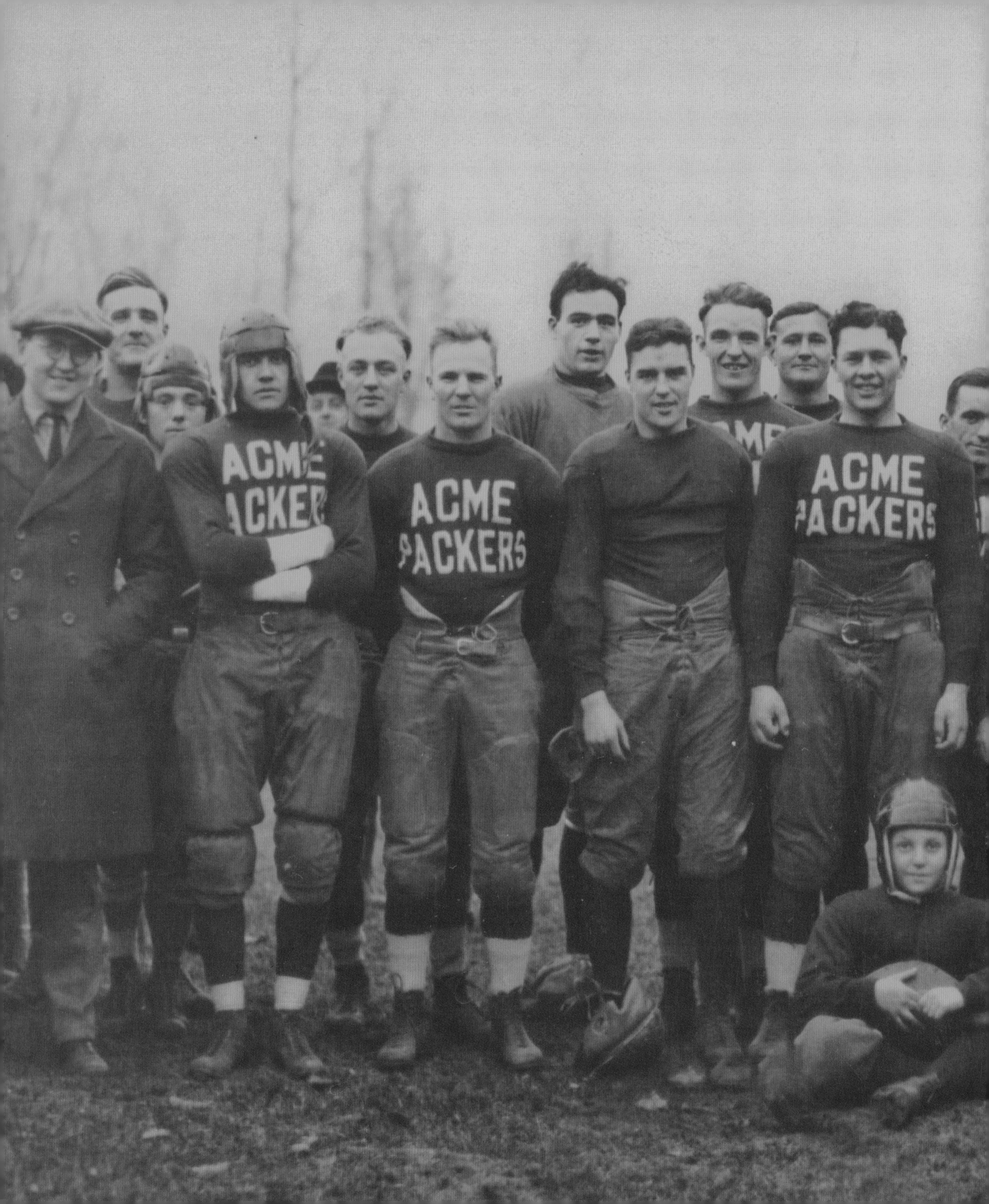
ACME
PACKERS

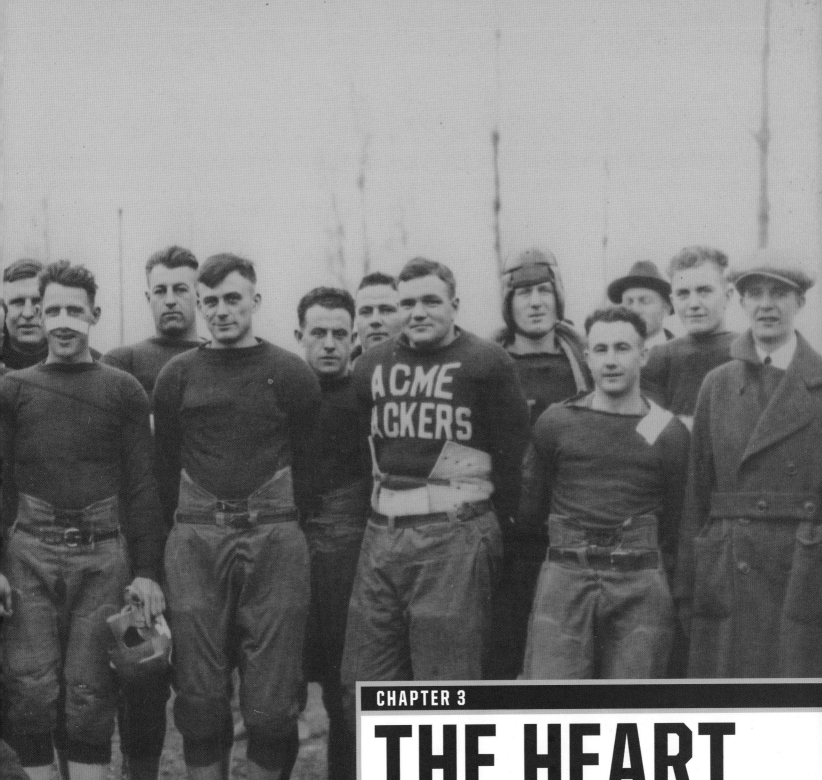

CHAPTER 3

THE HEART OF THE CITY

One of the primary reasons that the Packers became more than just another town team was because they came along at almost the precise moment when the role of sports in the popular culture of the United States was beginning to change dramatically. At the dawn of the 1920s, several factors were converging to make Americans open to the idea of enjoying spectator sports on a much larger scale than they had just a few years before. Foremost among them was the end of World War I, the war to end all wars. It was a moment not only of collective relief but also of a sort of collective euphoria. People were ready to enjoy themselves. The end of the war also coincided with—after a brief economic downturn—what was up to then the most prosperous era in the country's history. Americans had more free time than ever before, and more money with which to enjoy it. The Golden Age of Sports was dawning.

Baseball was the biggest beneficiary. The end of the war came just before the end of the dead ball era, when Babe Ruth of the Boston Red Sox emerged as a superstar by hitting 29 home runs in 1919. Buoyed by the Bambino's talent and charisma, and by the explosion of offense in the game in general, baseball took off as a spectator sport. In one year, from 1919 to 1920, attendance at major league games jumped from 6.5 million to 9.1 million, and attendance for Ruth's Yankees more than doubled, rising from 619,164 to 1.3 million.* College football realized an attendance boom, too, as evidenced by the building explosion that took place on campuses around the country. Massive concrete stadiums—55 in all—went up in such places as Pasadena and Baton Rouge and Philadelphia. And the men who were to become the fathers of pro football took note.

The first meeting of what would one day be the preeminent sports league in the United States

---

* *The big sports news in Green Bay in the fall of 1919 was not the birth of the Packers. It was the World Series between the Cincinnati Reds and the Chicago White Sox. All eight games of the Series were front-page news in the* Press-Gazette. *News about the city's new football team never made it off the paper's inside pages.*

convened in Canton, Ohio, on September 17, 1920. Much like the organizational meeting for the Packers had been the year before, it was decidedly inauspicious. The setting was the showroom of an automobile dealership — flashier than the dingy editorial offices of the *Green Bay Press-Gazette,* but amenities were hard to come by just the same. There weren't enough chairs for the representatives from 11 professional football teams to sit on, so a few of the 15 men in attendance, including George Halas of the Decatur Staleys, took their seats on the running boards of the four cars that were crowded onto the floor — Hupmobiles and Jordans, according to Halas.

The meeting had been called by Ralph E. Hay, a nattily dressed, cigar-chomping 29-year-old car salesman. In addition to owning the dealership that was hosting the conference, Hay also owned the Canton Bulldogs, the 1919 Ohio League champions. The Ohio League was one of the top circuits in pro football. There were pro teams all over the country, of course, and a handful of reputable leagues, but the Ohio association had added credibility because of the presence of Bulldogs captain Jim Thorpe. Despite being over 30, Thorpe was still one of the most famous athletes in the United States. He had been a college football All-America at the Carlisle Indian School, and then a gold medalist in both the decathlon and the pentathlon at the 1912 Olympics. In 1915, Thorpe was 28 years old and three years into a six-year career in Major League Baseball when he signed with Canton owner Jack Cusack to play for the Bulldogs for the astronomical salary of $250 per game. The six-foot-one, 200-pound halfback was worth every penny. Not only was the broad-shouldered, barrel-chested Thorpe a great player — a swift and powerful runner and a booming kicker — but he was also an unparalleled gate attraction. Canton had been averaging about 1,200 fans a game before he arrived, but drew 8,000 for his home debut, a 6–0 victory over Massillon on November 28, 1915. According to a 1981 article by Bob

Braunwart and Bob Carroll in *The Coffin Corner,* a bimonthly publication of the Professional Football Researchers Association, "Thorpe's continued presence at Canton focused the attention of the whole country on Ohio professional football. More players of quality began arriving and both attendance and salaries went up. Ohio sportswriters — without blushing — began to trumpet the 'world professional championship.' True, pro and semipro teams could be found from New England to Iowa in nearly every town and hamlet with 11 able-bodied men and a flat expanse of 100 yards, but they all took on the aspect of minor leaguers; Ohio held the 'majors.' The annual talk of forming a real pro league — with Thorpe's Canton Bulldogs as the capstone — became more vocal than ever before."

And the need for a real league, as Hay saw it, was urgent. Though the Ohio League had credibility with fans, its organization was haphazard, and its affiliations were loose. Schedules were set by the teams themselves, often on a week-to-week basis. And clubs frequently appeared out of nowhere —

PREVIOUS SPREAD
The 1921 Green Bay Packers pose for one of the most iconic team pictures in sports history.

ABOVE
Decatur Staleys' coach George Halas (left) poses with teammates Paddy Driscoll and "Dutch" Sternaman (right) for a picture taken around 1920, the same year that Halas entered the team in the newly formed APFA.

and then disappeared almost as quickly. There was also no salary structure, which left players free to jump from team to team in search of the fattest paycheck. Canton's signing of Thorpe in 1915 had triggered a rapid inflation of salaries, and with players seemingly on the move after every game,* the cost for their services could get pricey, as much as $2,000 per team per game by 1919. The Massillon Tigers sometimes signed extra players before their annual rivalry game against Canton just to ensure that the men would not be available to play for the Bulldogs. Considering that most teams rarely drew more than a few thousand fans for their biggest games, and that most tickets sold for around a dollar apiece, the financial pinch on owners was acute. In 1919, according to the Professional Football Researchers Association, almost every team in the Ohio League lost money, and Akron and Massillon actually went under. One PFRA article on the 1919 season dryly notes, "Fan loyalty was hard to come by when this week's hero halfback was the same fellow who ran your team ragged last week and would likely be scoring touchdowns against you next week."

The greatest star in the Ohio League in 1919 was Frederick Douglass "Fritz" Pollard. Four years earlier, as a halfback at Brown, he had led the Bears to a berth in the Rose Bowl, and in 1916 he had earned All-America honors from Walter Camp. Pollard had been coaching at Lincoln University, a black college in Chester County, Pennsylvania, when the Akron Indians signed him in early November. He was one of a few African Americans in professional football at the time — unlike in baseball's American and National Leagues, there was no color line in pro football in the early days of the game, primarily because there was no league to enforce one. The five-foot-nine, 165-pound Pollard was a breakaway threat, such a valuable as-

set as a runner, a kick returner, and a gate attraction that, according to Pollard himself, he quickly renegotiated his deal up to $500 per game within a few weeks. The *Akron Beacon Journal* estimated that 8,500 fans had turned out at Goodrich Field to see Pollard play in his first game, a 13–6 loss to Massillon.

That Pollard was not a bigger star was a result, at least in part, of pro football's low-rent reputation. More damning in the eyes of the public than the itinerancy of players was the practice of teams employing college stars who were still enrolled in school. There were several compelling reasons that coaches and promoters indulged in such brazen corruption of the nation's youth. First, college stars were good players, certainly better than could be found among the population at large. Second, they were generally cheaper than the soldiers of fortune who then constituted the professional ranks. And third, a crafty promoter could hype the gate by whispering that a certain college star would be playing for the local team. On Sunday, November 23, 1919, one day after Notre Dame had defeated Purdue 33–13 in West Lafayette, Fighting Irish halfback George Gipp and seven of his teammates earned $100 apiece playing for the Rockford Grands, aka the Rockford Badgers. Playing under the name Baker, Gipp threw a 10-yard touchdown pass and drop-kicked a 35-yard field goal in the Grands' 17–9 victory over another Rockford team called the Amateur Athletic Club. Using college players was a solid shortcut to winning, but the net effect of the subterfuge involved in using Saturday's stars in Sunday's games was that people regarded pro football with disdain. The game and the men who played it were perceived as vulgar and dishonest.

The image-conscious Hay was well aware of pro football's public relations problems and felt that a

---

* *One probably apocryphal story goes that in 1915, the Columbus Panhandles had faced Knute Rockne on five different occasions in five different uniforms. The only documented instances of Rockne playing in the Ohio League, in fact, were in games with Massillon. The Tigers' quarterback was Gus Dorais, who had been Rockne's teammate at Notre Dame and had thrown all those passes to the Rock when the Fighting Irish upset Army in 1913.*

league was the solution, just as it had been for Major League Baseball nearly 50 years before. A real league would allow teams to create a salary structure, enforce contracts, and abolish the use of college players. On August 20, Hay hosted a meeting at his dealership with representatives from teams in Akron, Cleveland, and Dayton. Out of this get-together the American Professional Football Conference (APFC) was formed, and Hay was elected the organization's temporary secretary. The seven men at the meeting, including Thorpe, voted unanimously not to use collegiate players and also agreed to refrain from inducing players to jump from one team to another. They also, according to the *Cleveland Plain Dealer,* placed "a maximum on financial terms for players," i.e., a ceiling on salaries. Hay was tasked with reaching out to the country's other top professional football teams and inviting them to a second meeting.

One of the teams that Hay contacted was the Decatur Staleys, who represented the A. E. Staley Manufacturing Company of Decatur, Illinois. Staley Manufacturing was one of the largest corn refineries in the United States, and the man in charge of it, big and boisterous Augustus Eugene Staley, fielded not only a company football team but also baseball and basketball teams. The Staleys were coached and managed by a 25-year-old civil engineer from Chicago named George Halas. The son of immigrants from the Bohemian city of Pilsen, the handsome, sharp-eyed Halas had worked in his father's grocery store before going on to play halfback and end at Illinois, where he also played basketball and baseball. After enlisting in the Navy in January 1918, he reported for duty to Naval Training Station Great Lakes, in the northern suburbs of Chicago, where he was commissioned as an ensign. But the Navy did not send Halas to war. Instead of hunting for German U-boats, he stayed in Chicago and played football. Halas recruited a few friends he'd made at Great Lakes — including future Pro Football Hall of Famers Jimmy Conzelman and Paddy Driscoll

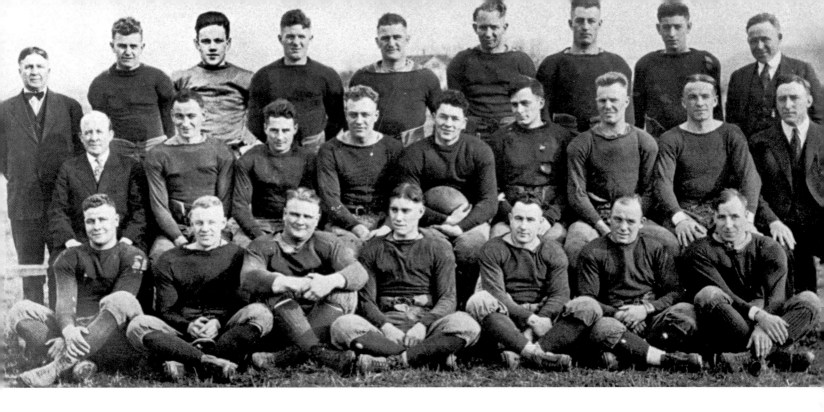

—and helped build a powerhouse that went 5-0-2 in 1918 and defeated unbeaten Navy in its final regular-season game. On January 1, 1919, Great Lakes beat the team from California's Mare Island Naval Shipyard 17–0 in the Rose Bowl. Halas, who scored on a 32-yard pass from Driscoll in the third quarter and returned an interception 77 yards in the fourth, was named the game's MVP.

Halas went to work after the war designing bridges for the Chicago, Burlington and Quincy Railroad. He also kept playing football. In the fall of 1919 he earned $100 a week playing end for the $20,000 Hammond Bobcats—so called because their manager had boasted that he was going to spend that much on his roster. In March 1920, Halas moved to Decatur to coach Staley's football team. "In August," he wrote in his 1979 autobiography, "I set off on probably the first professional football recruiting journey." Halas recruited players by promising them full-time jobs in addition to their football paychecks. Among the men he signed in 1920 were former Notre Dame center George Trafton, halfback Ed "Dutch" Sternaman

(his former teammate at Illinois), and several of his Great Lakes cronies, including Conzelman. Halas also raided the rosters of other pro teams—which was probably among the reasons that Hay invited him to the September 17 meeting. One of the players signed by the Staleys in the summer of 1920 was end Guy Chamberlin, who'd played for Hay in Canton the year before.

Along with Hay and Halas, who had taken the train to Canton accompanied by Staley engineer Morgan O'Brien, there were representatives at that first meeting from eight other pro teams. From Ohio were the Akron Professionals, Cleveland Indians, and Dayton Triangles; from Illinois, the Rock Island Independents and the Racine Cardinals*; from Indiana, the Hammond Professionals and the Muncie Flyers; and from New York, the Rochester Jeffersons. The meeting got under way at 8:15 p.m., and after Hay summed up the details of the August 20 conference, the first order of business was to change the name of the league to the American Professional Football Association (APFA). The teams present also set a membership

OPPOSITE

Eighteen-year-old Rigney Dwyer, a sophomore end at Green Bay West, in the fall of 1914, the year he returned an interception 90 yards for a touchdown in a 12–0 victory over Green Bay East.

ABOVE

After Dwyer was seriously injured in a rail-yard accident, the Packers cropped him into an empty spot in the back row of the 1920 team photo. Business manager Neil Murphy is standing on the far right.

---

* Erroneously listed in the minutes of the meeting as being from Racine, Wisconsin, the Cardinals were actually from Chicago. Their name was derived from that city's Racine Avenue, the address of the team's home field.

BIG BENEFIT
FOOTBALL GAME
—FOR—
REGGIE DWYER
HAGEMEISTER PARK

SUNDAY,
December 5

"LETS
ALL
GO"

Northerns.
—VS.—
Bellevue

Game Called at 2 O'clock

CITY CHAMPIONSHIP

The above two teams will battle for city championship. All of Green Bay's best football men will be seen in action this Sunday. Predictions are that this game will be one of the most exciting of the season. "Cub" Buck will again be seen in action.

Buy Your Tickets Now at

Congress Billiard Hall.
Lynch's.
Neveu & Schweger Drug Store.
Corner Drug.
Stuebe Printing & Binding Co.

The benefit game that the Packers played for Dwyer raised $4,053.09 — more than $50,000 today — and forged an enduring bond between the team and Green Bay.

likely because the minutes of the meeting say that Thorpe appointed officers to a committee to be set up for the drafting of rules and bylaws for the new league. It is more than likely, then, that Thorpe was on hand.

Four other teams joined the APFA that fall: the Buffalo All-Americans, Chicago Tigers, Columbus Panhandles, and Detroit Heralds. On September 26, 1920, Rock Island became the first APFA team to play a game, defeating the St. Paul Ideals 48–0 in a nonleague contest at Douglas Park. The first league game was played one week later in Dayton's Triangle Park, where the home team defeated Columbus 14–0. Rock Island also defeated Muncie 45–0 that same day. The Flyers had a game scheduled the following Sunday against the Staleys, but Halas canceled it because of Muncie's poor showing against the Independents. Decatur instead played a nonleague game against the Kewanee Walworths, winning 25–7. Muncie didn't play another game against an APFA team all season.

Akron, led by Fritz Pollard, was the only team to go undefeated. The Pros outscored their opponents 151–7 and went 8-0-3, including a 10–0 road victory over Canton in front of 10,000 fans on Halloween and a 0–0 tie with the Staleys in Chicago in the season finale for both teams — a game Halas said had been arranged to decide the APFA championship. A crowd of 12,000 turned out to watch the two teams at muddy Wrigley Field (then known as Cubs Park). Decatur's record was 10-1-2, and Halas declared the Staleys world champions. But the APFA awarded the title to the Pros by virtue of their unbeaten record.

Not all the news for the league was encouraging, though. Besides the disaster that was the Muncie Flyers, several other teams were well on their way to extinction. By the first week of December, the Chicago Tigers and the Detroit Heralds had, according to the Pro Football Hall of Fame, disbanded and had their franchises canceled by the league. The APFA was nevertheless eager to expand. The teams that were doing well

fee of $100 — which was never paid, according to Halas — and, in a move endorsed by the promotion-minded Hay, unanimously voted Thorpe to be league president.

Was Thorpe at the meeting? Halas, in his autobiography, said that he was not. Thorpe had played baseball in an International League game in Akron earlier in the day — starting in right field and going 2 for 3 in the Akron Buckeyes' 10–4 loss to the Toronto Maple Leafs at League Park. But Akron is only about 25 miles north of Canton. There was time for him to make the trip. And several researchers put Thorpe in Hay's showroom, most

were bringing in a lot of money — Halas's Staleys made $38,762.49 in 1920, a sizable leap from the $1,950.41 they had earned the year before as a semipro outfit playing mostly local competition. The 11 APFA teams that were still standing at the end of the season were all planning to be back in 1921. But who would join them?

◆ ◆ ◆

Rigney Dwyer was a railroad man, born and raised for a life of iron. His father, Michael, was an engineer for the Chicago, Milwaukee and St. Paul Railroad — better known as the Milwaukee Road. Michael, who had earned the nickname "Pig Iron" because of his toughness, was one of seven railroading brothers, the sons of an original employee of the Milwaukee Road. He and his wife, Mary, lived in Milwaukee, but in the spring of 1896, when the couple were expecting their third child, they rode the rails together. On April 18, Rigney was born in the tiny whistle-stop town of Ontonagon, Michigan, where Mary had gone into labor. Four years later the railroad transferred Michael to Green Bay, where he and Mary and their four sons moved into a house on the west side of town, on South Oakland Avenue, just two blocks north of the yard where he worked.

Thomas, the oldest of the Dwyer boys, started as a fireman on the Milwaukee Road in 1909 and eventually became an engineer. Clement, the youngest, followed suit about a decade later. (The second oldest, Eugene, went to Marquette and became a dentist.) Rigney had begun working in the shops at the yard as a machinist's apprentice. That was the job he held when he registered for the draft on June 5, 1917, two months after the United States had entered World War I, and 10 days before his graduation from Green Bay West High. He was 21 years old, and he already had a wife and a young son to support — he had married Eda Eliason the previous summer, and the couple's first child, Roy, had been born in February 1917.

Being the primary means of support for his wife and child, Rigney might have obtained a deferment from military service, but he had listed himself as single with no dependents on his draft card.[*] Nine months after he registered, he sailed out of New York Harbor for France as a corporal in Battery E of the 121st Field Artillery Regiment. He returned to the United States in May 1919 and was back home in Green Bay just in time to be present at the creation of the Packers.

Dwyer had actually changed jobs not long after he got home from Europe. He had been back in the shops at the Milwaukee Road yard for only a few weeks when a shopmen's strike threw him out of work. He moved quickly to secure employment working outdoors as a switchman, moving railcars around the yard's complicated spiderweb of tracks. It was dangerous work, but with his young family, he needed the paycheck.[**]

The shopmen's strike coincided with the first organizational meetings for Curly Lambeau's football team at the offices of the *Press-Gazette,* and Dwyer's name was among those listed in the paper as one of the players expected to attend the team's gathering on August 14. He had been a standout end at Green Bay West, where his ruggedness had earned him the same nickname that had been given to his father, Pig Iron. As a sophomore in 1914, Dwyer returned an interception 90 yards for a touchdown in West's 12–0 victory over East.

Solidly built at five foot eleven, with brown hair and blue eyes, Rigney Dwyer started at left end in eight of the Packers' 11 games in 1919 — including their first three. (His younger brother, Clement, nicknamed "Dutch," had been the starting quarterback in Green Bay's first game.) A solid tackler and a sure-handed receiver, "Riggie" (who was also

---

[*] *Dwyer also listed himself as single in the 1920 census, giving his primary address as 800 South Oakland Avenue — his parents' house.*

[**] *Dwyer apparently worked both jobs after the strike ended. In the 1920 census (dated January 6) he is listed as a machinist at the railroad, not a switchman.*

known as Rig or Reggie or Reg) was an integral part of the Packers' aerial attack, a favorite target of Lambeau's. In the penultimate game of the 1919 season, a 17–0 victory over the Stambaugh Miners, Dwyer caught two touchdown throws from the Green Bay captain. The next year, Dwyer started the Packers' first nine games. But like every one of his teammates, he was only moonlighting at football. Dwyer still lived on South Oakland Avenue, just a few blocks from the rail yard in which he worked. Eda was eight months pregnant with their second child. He was very much a regular guy. His primary job wasn't playing for the Packers. It was working for the Milwaukee Road.

Mangled hands and missing fingers were badges of honor for a rail-yard switchman, one of the most dangerous occupations in America. The duties of the job included operating the switches that moved railcars from one track to another, as well as pushing cars around the yard to get them into position for loading and unloading, and putting them in sequence in a train. Considering that an unloaded railcar weighs upwards of 20 tons, the smallest misstep could result in catastrophic injury or death. In 1893 Congress passed the Safety Appliance Act, which made air brakes and automatic couplers mandatory on all trains in the United States. Before passage of the act, according to the Federal Railroad Administration, one in every nine trainmen was injured on the job, and one in 115 was killed. Injuries incurred while coupling cars accounted for 44 percent of the total casualties. The measures in the act made the job safer, but only by a few degrees.

Early in the morning of Wednesday, November 24, 1920, less than three days after he had played the entire game in the Packers' 19–7 win over Menominee, Dwyer was working the night shift at the Milwaukee Road yard. It was cold, with temperatures in the mid-thirties, and the moon was nearly full, though its brightness was dimmed somewhat by the clouds that hung in the sky. Dwyer was switching cars sometime around 3 a.m.

when he slipped beneath a moving railcar. Nobody saw it happen. His co-workers in the yard realized that something was wrong only when they heard him screaming for help. When they found him, his left arm and leg were badly mangled and he was bleeding profusely. Clem was also working at the yard that night and was one of the first to reach his brother's side. "I can't feel anything," Rigney told him. He was rushed across the river to St. Vincent Hospital, where doctors declared that his damaged limbs would have to be amputated. Dwyer had lost so much blood, though, that his surgery was put off until he could regain his strength. A November 26 report on his condition in the *Press-Gazette* noted, "According to the doctors, it was only Dwyer's superb physical condition that enabled him to survive injuries that would have quickly killed the average man."

The story went on to note that "Remember Dwyer!" had been the Packers' rallying cry in their 14–0 victory over Stambaugh on Thanksgiving Day, a day after the accident. Scores and updates from the game had been relayed after every quarter to Dwyer's hospital room, where the fallen end had shown, as reported in the *Press-Gazette,* "a keen interest in the game." D. F. McCarthy, the manager of the Beloit Fairies — who had mocked Green Bay in the pages of the paper after the 1919 game — wrote to the Packers to express his sympathy. "We all remember Dwyer as a hard fighting but clean football player," he wrote, "and we sincerely regret that he was the victim of such an awful accident." To that, the *Press-Gazette* added the following observation: "Probably there has been no accident in a long while that has stirred Green Bay to greater sympathy." The paper announced that a benefit game for Dwyer would be played at Hagemeister Park on December 5.

In the 100-year history of the Green Bay Packers, there have been a number of pivotal moments that both forged and strengthened the bond between the team and the community — that truly made the Packers the people's team. But the tragedy that befell Rigney Dwyer stands alone as the first, and by that very fact alone it is one of the most significant. The Packers had begun the fall of 1920 as just another sandlot town team, albeit one that had come back for a second go-round instead of just fading away. But their schedule was still haphazard, with games booked week to week and on the fly, against mostly overmatched ad hoc outfits from nearby towns in northern Wisconsin. The Dwyer benefit game, though, established Lambeau's team as a full-fledged city institution, something for the people of Green Bay to rally around. At halftime of the Packers' final game of the season, against Milwaukee's Lapham AC at Hagemeister Park on November 28, a telegram from Dwyer had been read to the crowd: "Even the nurse is with you guys. So go get 'em."

As halftime speeches go, it was neither a traditional stem-winder nor an emotional appeal. It was short and to the point, with a touch of wry humor. But it was a winner nonetheless. The fans cheered and Green Bay was energized. The Packers led just 6–0 after two quarters, but they ran away in the second half to win 26–0 and run their record to 9-1-1. Dwyer's note is the Green Bay version of Knute Rockne's "Win one for the Gipper" speech. But instead of being delivered in the privacy of a dressing room, Dwyer's message was read to the people and the team at the same time—fitting for a franchise that is defined by people and place more than any other in sports.

And it had an impact beyond the playing field. In the Packers' first two seasons, the number of fans who had come out to watch the team play at Hagemeister Park wasn't much to speak of—and so the *Press-Gazette* rarely did. No attendance figures had been reported in 1919, and the paper documented attendance for only a few games in 1920. The biggest reported crowd had been the 3,500 who turned out to see Green Bay rout local rival De Pere 62–0 on October 24. But the number of people who paid between $1 and $5 for tickets to the December 5 benefit game was 4,000.

On the day tickets went on sale, 3,000 had been sold. Football was secondary. Dwyer wasn't there —he was still recuperating in the hospital—but he was undeniably the draw. "Seats in both bleachers were at a premium long before 2 o'clock and the [late] comers had to be satisfied with standing room along the gridiron edges," was how the *Press-Gazette* began its description of the throng at Hagemeister. "All mingled at the Dwyer game . . . It seemed as if everybody was there. Professional men rubbed shoulders with the mill hands or railroaders and there was a vast sprinkling of women in the throng that packed every seat and stood . . . around the playing field."

The temperature on game day was in the for-

Neil Murphy, an Underwood typewriter salesman, took over for George Whitney Calhoun as the Packers' business manager in 1920 and, for one season at least, turned the Packers into a profitable operation.

ties and, appropriately enough, the sun was shining. The Packers split themselves into two teams, both named for local businesses that had chipped in $100 apiece to start the benefit off: the Bellevue Ice Creams and the Northern Paper Mills. Curly Lambeau captained the Ice Creams, who wore the red-and-white uniforms of Green Bay East, while the Paper Mills, clad in the green jerseys of St. Norbert College, were led by Packers quarterback Jack Dalton. (Lambeau and Dalton were also rival high school coaches, at Green Bay East and Green Bay West, respectively.) Lambeau was the star of Bellevue's 21–13 win, intercepting a pass on defense, throwing for several long gains, and kicking three extra points. He played right halfback, sometimes alongside backup left halfback Dutch Dwyer.

All the money collected at the game went to Riggie. Workers at the gate pinned their tickets to their coats as proof that they had paid their way in. The Meier-Schroeder Company, a local florist, donated flowers that were put on sale to spectators, a gambit that raised an extra $32. And Packers business manager C. M. Murphy secured a tax exemption on the admissions proceeds by naming St. Patrick's Church as the beneficiary of the game. On December 8, Murphy visited Dwyer in his room at St. Vincent's Hospital and presented him with a check for $4,053.02, the equivalent of $52,600 in 2019.

Sometime after the benefit game, Dwyer's oldest brother, Tom, sent an emotional letter to Murphy to express his gratitude. "Complementary thanks for acts of kindness such as the Packers have shown Rig can not be expressed in words," wrote Tom. "I haven't the command of English to do it and you know Rig wasn't handy that way either but you do know the kind of a heart he has and when I say he was deeply touched by what the fellows did you know how he felt. We his father mother wife [and] brothers want to join with Rig in saying 'thank you' to the fellows."

Brought together by the Packers, the people of Green Bay had dug deep. And a love affair had officially begun.

◆ ◆ ◆

Presenting the check to Dwyer was one of the last official acts in the brief career of Packers manager Cornelius Mathew Murphy—known to one and all as Neil—who had taken over from Calhoun before the season. The son of Irish immigrants, the 34-year-old Murphy had grown up in Chicago, selling newspapers on a street corner as a boy. He eventually secured a job as an Underwood typewriter salesman. In 1915, four years after the company had transferred him to Green Bay, he married Elsie Butler, a native of his new hometown.

Like Calhoun, Murphy was a compulsive organizer. He had been active in sports in Chicago as a younger man, managing and playing for several baseball and football teams. He was also friends with former world bantamweight champion Johnny Coulon, with whom he organized a baseball team called, appropriately enough, the Coulons. Murphy continued his involvement in sports after he moved to Wisconsin, umpiring baseball games in the Industrial League and refereeing football games. He had been the referee in the Packers' first game, against Menominee on September 14, 1919, and went on to officiate every one of Green Bay's home games that season. He was also a visiting official in two of the team's three road games, serving as the umpire in the 17–0 defeat of Stambuagh on November 16 and as the head linesman in the bitter 6–0 loss to Beloit one week later. He was quoted in the *Press-Gazette* story on that game: "I wish to go on record as saying that it was the most deliberate steal I have ever seen . . . Green Bay had the ball over the goal line for clear touchdowns on three different occasions, and each time home officials ruled off side. It was a cut and dried deal to give Green Bay the worst of it, and they succeeded one hundred per cent."

Murphy was elected the business manager and president of the Packers on July 16, 1920, at an organizational meeting at city hall. Though not an

CLASS OF SERVICE DESIRED
Fast Day Message
Day Letter
Night Message
Night Letter
Patrons should mark an X opposite the class of service desired; OTHERWISE THE TELEGRAM WILL BE TRANSMITTED AS A FAST DAY MESSAGE.

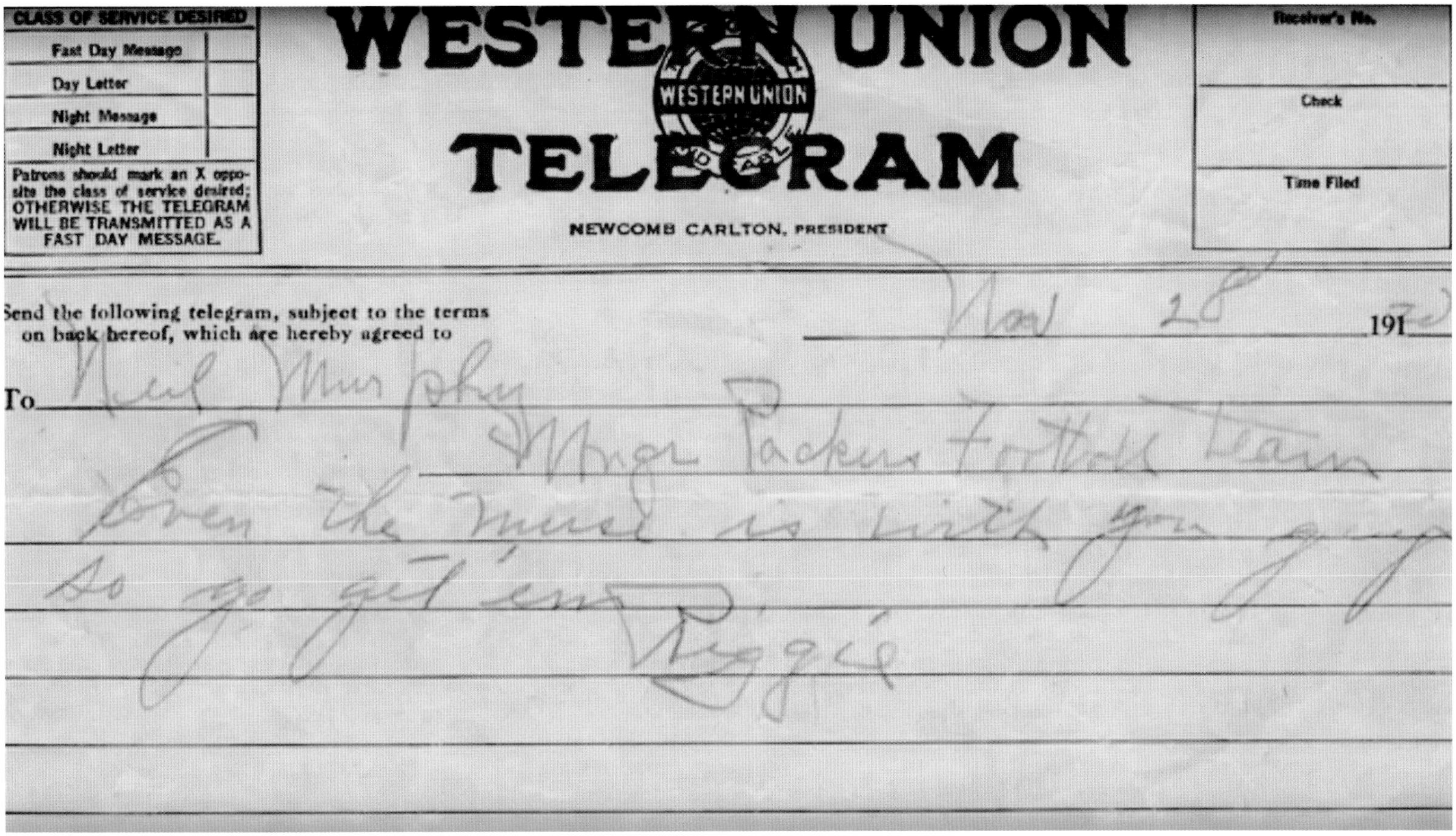

WESTERN UNION TELEGRAM

NEWCOMB CARLTON, PRESIDENT

Receiver's No.
Check
Time Filed

Send the following telegram, subject to the terms on back hereof, which are hereby agreed to

Nov 28 191

To Neil Murphy
Mngr Packers Football team
Even the nurse is with you guys
so go get 'em.
Piggie

Dwyer telegrammed the Packers from his hospital bed during their 26–0 victory over the Milwaukee Lapham Athletic Club. His message is Green Bay's equivalent of the "Win one for the Gipper" speech.

employee of Indian Packing, he had his own company stationery, which listed him as the manager of its football department. It was in this capacity that he accomplished something that was crucial to the Packers' continued survival: he paid $100 to the Hagemeister estate to lease the football field at Hagemeister Park, which allowed the Packers to erect a temporary fence around the gridiron. According to the terms of the lease, the fence could be up from September 1 until December 1, at which point it would have to be taken down.

Construction of the board fence, which enclosed a 400-by-250-foot area, began on August 28, four weeks before the Packers' opening game. The lumber was donated by the Indian Packing plant. The labor, under the direction of local contractors Ludolf Hansen and Marcel Lambeau, Curly's father, was performed by a volunteer workforce made up of Green Bay football fans. "The fellows don't have to have a college education," Murphy told the *Press-Gazette* about the team's call for volunteers. "All we want is a bunch of fellows that aren't afraid of the business end of a hammer when used lawfully." Painted signs were added to the fence in late September, after the Packers opened the season by tying the Chicago Boosters 3–3. A few weeks later, after Green Bay beat Stambaugh 3–0 at Hagemeister Park, the elder Lambeau oversaw the construction of bleachers holding 700 on the north side of the field. The week after that, he added more stands for roughly 800 on the south side of the field.

Murphy estimated the cost of the fence to be about $1,400—and it was worth every penny, significantly improving the Packers' bottom line. No longer were they dependent upon Calhoun passing a hat among a gaggle of spectators standing along the sidelines. Now they could not only charge admission but also keep better control of the crowd. "There will be room galore in side [*sic*] the fence," bragged the *Press-Gazette* before the first game of the season, "because no autos will be given park-

The fence that Murphy had constructed around the playing field at Hagemeister Park in 1920 allowed the Packers to charge admission for the first time.

ing space inside the field." Admission, according to Chicago sportswriter Arch Ward, was 50 cents. The net profits for the season were $6,049.53, and each player received a check for $276 at the end of the year for his services — a stark contrast to the $16.75 that players had reportedly earned in 1919. The fence and bleachers were torn down shortly before the team's end-of-season banquet on December 14. It was no coincidence that the players used the occasion of the party to present Murphy with a diamond stickpin as a gesture of thanks.

On the field, the Packers did well in 1920, going 9-1-1 and playing a few more games against good teams than they had the year before. Lambeau was again the captain, while the coaching duties were taken on by Jack Dalton, who had played in Rockford, Illinois, in 1919 and was the new football coach at West High. A veteran of a machine-gun battalion in Europe during World War I, Dalton was a hard-nosed back who went by the nickname "Leather." He played alongside Lambeau in the Packers' backfield, and the two men shared authority — and an unfriendly relationship. "[Lambeau] was not of the best character," Dalton's son, Maurice Jr., told Cliff Christl in 2001. "He wasn't the greatest guy in the world. He was a womanizer, a boozer. He wasn't the same type of person as my dad. They were complete opposites, I would say."

Calhoun, who was the city editor at the *Press-*

Gazette according to that year's census, was still involved with the Packers — writing about them for the paper — even though he was no longer their manager. Most of the other faces on the team were also familiar. The roster was still composed primarily of veterans of the 1919 season. One of the most visible differences from 1919 to 1920 was that, for the first time, the Packers sported a logo on their uniforms. Council Meats was an Indian Packing brand and, beginning with the Packers' 25–0 defeat of Marinette on October 17, Green Bay's jerseys were emblazoned with a "Council Brand" logo. "The marker sizes up as big as a house," noted the *Press-Gazette,* "and it helps to spot the locals from the opposing gridiron warriors."

It was because of their play, though, and not their logo, that the Packers had begun to attract attention in pro football circles. Former Wisconsin Badgers tackle Howard "Cub" Buck, who had been a second-team All-America selection of Walter Camp's before becoming a star tackle for the Canton Bulldogs, the marquee team of the newly formed APFA, had attended Green Bay's first game of the 1920 season, a 3–3 tie with the Chicago Boosters. The six-foot, 259-pound Buck hailed from Eau Claire, Wisconsin, about 200 miles west of Green Bay, and lived nearby — about 20 miles south, in Kaukauna, where he was a salesman for the Thilmany Pulp and Paper Company. "The Packers look mighty good to me," he told the *Press-Gazette.* "I have heard of 'em before but their class of play surprised me. Lambeau throws forward passes exceptionally well and their ends know how to receive the ball. It was a corking good game of football."

By season's end the ambitious Lambeau was well aware of the new pro league. His team had proven itself to his satisfaction as the class of the northern Midwest, and he aspired to bigger things. The Packers might be from a small town, but Lambeau did not want them to remain small-time.

◆ ◆ ◆

In December 1920, the Acme Packing Company of Chicago bought Indian Packing and retained only one company official, secretary John M. Clair. Frank Peck, the president of Indian Packing and the man who had originally agreed to sponsor Curly Lambeau's football team — and who had continued to sponsor it through the 1920 season — was out. Acme made Clair a vice president of the new company, and his younger brother J. Emmett moved up to Green Bay from Chicago. The Clairs had grown up in an Irish Catholic family on that city's South Side, and though neither of them had been to school beyond the eighth grade, they were fans of Notre Dame football. Both were also willing to listen when Lambeau proposed that they pitch in to sponsor the Packers.

Except for the initial infusion of capital from Frank Peck, Indian Packing's relationship to its football team had never been very close. Fairbanks Morse and Company, in Beloit, sponsored teams in football, basketball, and baseball and gave jobs to the men who played for them. The situation was similar at A. E. Staley, in Decatur, where football coach George Halas used full-time jobs at the starch works as a recruiting tool. In Green Bay, Curly Lambeau worked at Indian Packing, as did the Packers' original fullback, Wally Ladrow. The team also practiced on company grounds, just to the west of the plant. But that was it. It was not a given that Acme would replace Indian as the sponsor of the team, so in the spring of 1921, Lambeau took it upon himself to do something.

"Curly Lambeau asked to meet with my brother John," Emmett said in 1981. "I arranged for him to meet with him, and we had lunch at one of the teapot restaurants in Green Bay. During our meeting, my brother John agreed to finance the club, and it would start that year as a professional team."

On August 27, 1921, two months after he turned 24, Emmett attended the APFA meeting at Chicago's La Salle Hotel and applied for the Packers to join the league. The APFA accepted. The minutes of the meeting read, "Motion made, seconded and carried that Acme Packers of Green Bay, Wisconsin, be admitted to membership."

A month later, on September 25, the Packers played their first game, a nonleague affair against the same Chicago Boosters team that they had opened against in 1920. Instead of another 3–3 tie, Green Bay prevailed 13–0. The team looked similar — with Lambeau starring in the backfield — but also markedly different. Quarterback Buff Wagner and Lambeau were the only starters who had also started the opener the year before.[*] Fifteen of the players who had been on the 1920 roster at the end of the season were back, but there were nine new faces, most notably Cub Buck, previously of the Canton Bulldogs.[**] The *Press-Gazette* had announced the signing of the 29-year-old tackle on September 14. As a collegiate star and an established pro, as well as a former teammate of Jim Thorpe's, Buck lent instant credibility to Green Bay's new APFA team. More important, he also helped coach the offensive and defensive lines. His arrival was a harbinger of things to come. By the end of the season, only about 10 of the 1920 Packers were left, and only a handful remained from the original 1919 team. As Lambeau replaced the Packers' local players with men who had played college football, his roster changed from game to game.

Eventually Lambeau also cut ties with Acme. Even though the Packers wore jerseys with ACME PACKERS emblazoned across the front for the entire season, the team officially distanced itself from the company eight days after playing its first game against an APFA team — Green Bay prevailed 7–6 over the Minneapolis Marines in the final minutes on October 23, on a 10-yard touchdown run by fullback Art Schmaehl and an extra point from Lambeau. On November 2, *The Dope Sheet,* the Packers' official newsletter, ran an editorial note:

> *The Acme Packing Company does not own nor financially back the Packer team. The team is owned and managed and is financially backed by Messrs. J. Emmett and John Clair of the Acme Packing Corp.*
>
> *The Acme Packing Company equipped the team and started it out with uniforms bearing their names but the interest in the team aside from this is none other than that of a progressive Green Bay plant wishing to see a Green Bay team clean up the country.*

No reason was given for the split, but it almost certainly had to do with the fact that the company was in serious financial trouble. Canned meat had been a booming business during World War I, when both Indian and Acme had been providing food to soldiers overseas and were reaping the benefits of large government contracts. But the end of the war had drastically reduced the need for the product. Indian Packing stock had been selling on New York's Curb Market[***] for about $40 a share when it was first offered in the summer of 1919. But by the time Acme bought the company out in December 1920, the price for a share of Indian stock had dropped to a little more than $3. One year later it was reported that the new Acme Packing Company was $3.65 million in debt — more than $53 million in 2019 terms.

Debt and the prospect of economic ruin were becoming familiar to the Green Bay Packers. The departure of Neil Murphy coincided with a return of the team's financial problems. A fenced-in ballpark with seating for 1,800 had been built (again under the supervision of Marcel Lambeau) in the spring of 1921, on the site of the Packers' Hage-

---

[*] *Wagner started at left halfback in the 1920 season opener.*

[**] *Buck played in one game for the Packers in 1920, when he was still a member of the Bulldogs. While on a break from Canton late in the season, he played right guard in Green Bay's 26–0 victory over Milwaukee's Lapham AC on November 28.*

[***] *The forerunner of the American Stock Exchange, the Curb Market was an unregulated and sometimes shady operation that sold equities that didn't meet the standards for trading on the New York Stock Exchange.*

meister playing field. The seating capacity was expanded to 3,500 in late summer, after the team joined the APFA. But the increased cost of paying player salaries and travel expenses took a toll. Cub Buck was a boon on the field and a box office draw, but he was also reportedly costing Green Bay $100 per game. There was also the fact that the Packers had played only one road game during the profitable 1920 season but played three in 1921 — including two trips to Chicago to play the Cardinals and the Staleys, on November 20 and 27, respectively.* The cost for the two trips was reduced a bit because so many players who had been added to the roster lived in or near Chicago, but it was not enough. Green Bay tied the Cardinals 3–3 but lost to the Staleys 20–0, and the Clairs lost $3,800 over the course of the season.

And there were more problems on the horizon.

---

* *The Packers' third game away from Green Bay in 1921 was in Milwaukee on December 4, when they played a nonleague tilt against the Racine Legion.*

With the Packers' entry into the APFA in 1921, the *Green Bay Press-Gazette* ramped up its coverage of the team. The sports section was now a full page in the paper, rather than the partial page that it had been in the team's first two years. And in the autumn, the banner headline that ran across the top of the section was almost always about the Packers. To an extent, this sort of treatment was in line with national trends in sports journalism, which were themselves the result of the country's growing fascination with spectator competition. In 1880 the average daily newspaper dedicated less than 1 percent of its reporting to sports; in the 1920s the average daily paper devoted at least 15 percent of its reporting to sports, which, in the words of University of Illinois journalism professor Robert W. McChesney, "offered the spirit and excitement of conflict and struggle in a politically trivial area." Put another way, sports provided an ideal counterweight for a paper looking to balance the decidedly messier topics covered on its front page.

Sports journalism in the 1920s was as much about mythologizing athletes and events as it was about reporting game scores. There is no better example of this than Grantland Rice's celebrated lead to his story in the *New York Herald Tribune* about Notre Dame's 13–7 victory over Army at the Polo Grounds in 1924: "Outlined against a blue-gray October sky, the Four Horsemen rode again. In dramatic lore they are known as Famine, Pestilence, Destruction and Death. These are only aliases. Their real names are Stuhldreher, Miller, Crowley and Layden."* The *Press-Gazette* didn't have any Grantland Rices on its sports staff—in fact, quite the opposite. The paper's sportswriting was not only uncritical, but also unvarnished. Football was still reflexively referred to in its pages as "pigskin chasing," while teams were "aggregations." George Whitney Calhoun had a reg-

---

* *Jimmy Crowley was a Green Bay native. His coach when he was a star high school halfback at Green Bay East had been Curly Lambeau.*

LAMBEAU   TURNBULL   JOANNES   KELLY   CLIFFORD

ular sports column in 1921, but it was more of a news-and-notes collection of observations than it was any sort of a showcase for muscular prose.

What the *Press-Gazette*'s coverage lacked in ballyhoo, though, was more than made up for by the column inches it devoted to the Packers. Pro football was still regarded as a low-class venture by the wider sporting public, as well as by most of the nation's sports media. But it wasn't regarded that way in Green Bay, even then the smallest town in the league, with a population of just a little more than 31,000. And it certainly wasn't regarded that way by the *Press-Gazette*.

That's not to say that the Packers were the biggest game in town. Coverage of the team was still relegated to the paper's inside pages. Baseball was the top game in the country, and the *Press-Gazette* treated it that way, with World Series results reported on the front page and a "Ruthermometer" that tracked the exploits of New York Yankees outfielder Babe Ruth throughout the summer. In foot-

ball, Green Bay East and Green Bay West were covered at least as extensively as the Packers. But the amount of ink that the paper devoted to the team it had helped to create was unique in the APFA. It was with good reason that Hall of Fame coach Paul Brown once said that Green Bay was the only team in the NFL with its own newspaper.

"In those early years, it wasn't so much that the Packers and the *Press-Gazette* worked hand in hand," says team historian Cliff Christl. "It was more a case of the newspaper serving as guardian angel of a rudderless football franchise." The team had no office building of its own until 1949, and technically no full-time employees besides Lambeau for nearly as long.

The *Press-Gazette* had been founded as a weekly in 1866, when it was known as the *State Gazette*. It morphed into a daily publication five years later (though it didn't start publishing a Sunday edition until September 24, 1961) and eventually changed its name to *The Green Bay Gazette* on August 1, 1894.

PREVIOUS SPREAD
In 1923, the year the Packers became a publicly owned enterprise, the team played its home games at Bellevue Park, a baseball field in the shadow of the Hagemeister Brewery.

ABOVE
Green Bay's "Hungry Five," according to Chicago sports editor Arch Ward, are the men who kept the Packers afloat in 1922 and '23. From left to right: Curly Lambeau, Andrew Turnbull, Leland Joannes, Dr. W. W. Kelly, and Gerald Clifford. Clifford, however, did not become associated with the team until 1929.

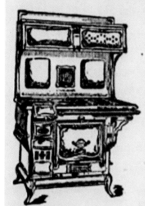
In November 1922, businesses throughout Green Bay, convinced that the Packers were a good marketing tool for the city, rallied to promote and support the team's booster game against the nonleague Duluth K.C.'s.

The paper — "the lonely voice of Republicans in a Democratic town" in the days before 1900, according to local historian (and *Press-Gazette* columnist) Jack Rudolph — withstood several challenges in its first half century, most notably from the *Green Bay Advocate* in the 1890s, and then from the *Green Bay Free Press* beginning in 1914. The competition between the *Gazette* and the *Free Press* nearly broke both publications, and they merged in 1915 to keep from going under.

One of the men most crucial to that merger was Andrew B. Turnbull, who, along with John K. Kline and Victor I. Minahan, had purchased both papers. Turnbull had been born in London, Ontario, in 1884, the son of a conductor on the Grand Trunk Railway. He graduated from high school in Windsor when he was only 15 and soon began working across the Detroit River for $3 a week in the classified advertising department of *The Detroit News*. He subsequently worked on the business side at three other papers in Michigan and Minnesota before he moved to Green Bay in 1915 — one year after he had become a U.S. citizen. Tall and thin, with blond hair and smiling blue eyes, the even-tempered Turnbull was a steadying force at the *Press-Gazette* for four decades. He was the paper's treasurer and business manager in the early years of the Packers, and no man besides Lambeau and Calhoun was as integral to the team's survival in the 1920s.

But before Turnbull could save the Packers for Green Bay, Lambeau had to save the team from itself.

◆ ◆ ◆

On December 12, 1921, Notre Dame barred three football players from participation in athletics and withdrew their varsity letters because the school found that they had played in a professional football game in Milwaukee eight days earlier. The players were guard Heartley "Hunk" Anderson, tackle Arthur "Hec" Garvey, and center Fred "Ojay" Larson. All three had eligibility remaining. Anderson, a Fighting Irish teammate of Lambeau's in 1918, had just completed his senior season, but he was also the captain of the hockey team. Garvey and Larson were both juniors.[*] The news had broken on December 5 in *The Racine Journal-News*, which noted that three current Notre Dame players had been in the lineup

---

* Like Anderson, Larson had also been a Notre Dame teammate of Lambeau's. He was only a junior in 1921, though, because he had played for the freshman team in 1919. According to Kent Stephens, the historian and curator at the College Football Hall of Fame, there were no NCAA rules on eligibility at the time.

for the Packers in their 3–3 tie with a local American Legion team. The game, played 10 days after the Fighting Irish's last game of the 1921 season, was a non-APFA affair that George Whitney Calhoun and his counterparts in Milwaukee and Racine had nonetheless hyped as being for the state championship. It was contested in a light snow in front of 7,000 fans at Milwaukee's Athletic Park — and about the only thing that added up about the contest was the score. The misdirection and obfuscation on the Green Bay lineup card was as complete and effective as anything the Packers tried on the field.

The *Journal-News* identified Anderson and Larson as having played left tackle and center, respectively, for Green Bay. But instead of Garvey, the paper named the third Notre Dame player as tackle Lawrence "Buck" Shaw and put him at left guard. In the *Green Bay Press-Gazette* the players listed at those positions were Warren Smith at center, Emmett Keefe at left guard, and somebody identified only as Oakes at left tackle. Smith had been playing for Green Bay since November 13, the day after his last game at Western Michigan. Keefe had played that season for the APFA Rock Island Independents, whose last game was on November 13. He played two games for the Packers — against the Chicago Staleys on November 27 and against Racine. Oakes hadn't played in any of the Packers' previous 10 games. The *Press-Gazette* also listed a player named Williams at quarterback and another named Sullivan at right guard; as with Oakes, no players by those names had appeared in a Green Bay uniform in any of the Packers' previous 10 games. Two Milwaukee papers put Oakes at left guard, Sullivan at left tackle, and a fourth brand-new member of the team, named Clancy, at center. None of the four names (Clancy, Oakes, Sullivan, or Williams) are in the Packers' record books as having been on the roster in 1921. They are agate type in history — aliases and nothing more.

The outcry was loud over Green Bay's skuldug-gery, playing as it did into pro football's disreputable stereotypes. Notre Dame coach Knute Rockne spoke out two weeks after news of the scandal had broken. "The professional and the gambler have ruined horse racing, boxing, wrestling, and have also given a severe blow to baseball," he said, alluding to the scandal about the 1919 World Series that was then unfolding in Chicago. "We must maintain football strictly within the colleges and high schools and preserve it." *Chicago Tribune* columnist Frank Smith called on the APFA to banish the Packers.

Green Bay never denied the charges. By using collegiate players, the Packers had merely been doing the same as every other team in the league. Calhoun personally addressed the issue in the pages of the *Press-Gazette*. "It is a well-known fact that nearly all of the pro squads make use of the college players while they are still members of varsity teams," he wrote. "We don't defend the action . . . but we can't help but wonder how it is going to be stopped." He also said in another column, "We have a hunch that the alleged scandal will blow over without any fireworks."

But the expulsion of Green Bay from the league became a near certainty on Saturday, January 28, 1922, the first day of the APFA's annual winter meeting. That morning, the *Chicago Tribune* ran an Associated Press story on a scandal surrounding a November 27, 1921, semipro game between teams from the small central Illinois towns of Taylorville and Carlinville. At least eight players from Notre Dame had suited up for Carlinville, while nine from the University of Illinois had played for Taylorville. The APFA had been created in large part to stop the practice of professional teams using college players — the very thing that the general public found most distasteful about pro football. But nothing had changed. Joseph F. Carr, the new league president, had to do something.

Carr had been the head of the APFA for only nine months, having taken over as president the previous April. Born in 1879, Carr was from Colum-

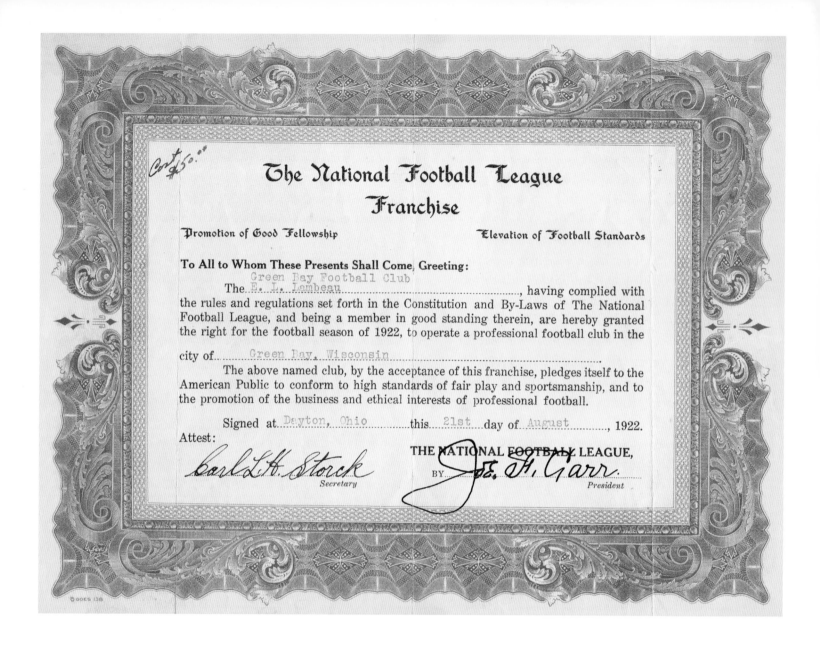

The National Football League
Franchise

Promotion of Good Fellowship   Elevation of Football Standards

To All to Whom These Presents Shall Come, Greeting:

The Green Bay Football Club E. L. Lambeau ...., having complied with
the rules and regulations set forth in the Constitution and By-Laws of The National
Football League, and being a member in good standing therein, are hereby granted
the right for the football season of 1922, to operate a professional football club in the

city of Green Bay, Wisconsin ....
The above named club, by the acceptance of this franchise, pledges itself to the
American Public to conform to high standards of fair play and sportsmanship, and to
the promotion of the business and ethical interests of professional football.

Signed at Dayton, Ohio this 21st day of August, 1922.

Attest:

Carl L. H. Storck
Secretary

THE NATIONAL FOOTBALL LEAGUE,
BY *Joe F. Carr.*
President

Cost $50.00

The 1922 certificate that admitted the Packers back into the NFL. At some point someone scrawled "Cost $50" in the upper left corner, but a record of the actual franchise fee doesn't exist.

bus, Ohio, the sixth of seven children of an Irish immigrant shoemaker. Around the turn of the century, Carr was working as a machinist for the Pennsylvania Railroad when he took a job as an assistant sports editor at the *Ohio State Journal.* Not long after he started at the paper, Carr returned to the railroad's machine shops to recruit men to play on a company baseball team, the Panhandle White Sox. In 1907 he took over as manager of the company's football team, the Columbus Panhandles, which until then had been an on-again, off-again operation. Along with the five Nesser brothers — all of whom worked as boilermakers in the Panhandle shops and all of whom played football

(a sixth brother joined the team in 1910) — Carr turned the Panhandles into a state powerhouse. In addition to his work with the baseball and football teams, Carr later served as secretary and then president of the Ohio State League, a minor league baseball circuit. Though he hadn't been at the APFA's first meetings in August and September 1920, the league admitted the Panhandles at some point during its inaugural season.

The team owners of the APFA had elected Carr to replace Jim Thorpe as president because of Carr's background as a manager and a league administrator. Where Thorpe had been expected to garner publicity, Carr was tasked with actually running things. He promptly moved the APFA's headquarters from Canton to his hometown of Columbus, and then set about drafting a league constitution and bylaws. His most significant new rule stated that any team that harbored or played a player still in college would be barred from the association. At the August 27, 1921, meeting at which the Packers were admitted to the APFA, Carr had said, "No college student, whether engaged in, eligible, or ineligible for athletics, can be contracted for by any member club of the association. Clubs which even attempt to sign up a man still in college will be expelled."

The APFA's winter meeting in January 1922 was held at the Hotel Courtland, in Canton, Ohio. It began at 2:30 in the afternoon and lasted nine hours. Representing the Packers were J. Emmett Clair, Curly Lambeau, and Don Murphy, the son of a wealthy Green Bay lumberman and a friend of Lambeau's. Among the many orders of business conducted—including the establishment of a roster limit of 18 players per team and the transfer of the Chicago Staleys franchise to George Halas, who renamed the team the Chicago Bears—the league kicked the Packers to the curb. The minutes of the meeting are matter-of-fact: "Again the matter of the Green Bay franchise came up and Mr. Clair (J. Emmett) of Green Bay, after a discussion with the club members, asked the Association to consider the withdrawal of the Green Bay franchise with the apology to the Association. A motion to this effect was made by Mr. Halas . . . Carried." The Packers were out. To ensure that the rule banning the use of college players would be strictly observed in the future, the league announced that all remaining member teams would be required to put up a $1,000 guarantee, which would be forfeited if they were found to be in violation of the edict.

There has been speculation that George Halas orchestrated the APFA's ouster of Green Bay. He eventually signed all three players banished by the Fighting Irish (Anderson, Garvey, and Lar-

son) for the 1922 season, and his older brother, Walter Halas, was Rockne's assistant coach at Notre Dame. But besides the Bears' coach being the one who made the motion to accept Clair's offer of withdrawal, there is not much to connect Halas to the discovery of the Packers' rule breaking. A report about the participation of collegiate players in the December 4 game had appeared in *The Racine Journal-News* the following day. The particulars of who was who, and who played where, may have been murky, but what had happened was hardly a secret. And the rivalry that was to become the most storied in the history of pro football had only just begun—Halas's team had played the Packers only once to that point—and there was as yet no heat to it.

Lambeau returned to Green Bay a man without a team—but not without a plan. Before he left for Canton, he had already begun meeting with local businessmen in an effort to reorganize the Packers. And he and those with whom he was in discussions, noted the *Press-Gazette* on January 23, 1922, were "unanimous in their opinion that Green Bay should be represented in the league if not by the Packers—then some other team."

◆ ◆ ◆

Curly Lambeau may have co-founded the Packers and been their captain for three seasons, but they had never been totally his. Three different men had coached the team—Bill Ryan and Jack Dalton in 1919 and 1920, respectively, and former Green Bay East football hero Joe Hoeffel in 1921 —and three different men had run its business affairs: George Whitney Calhoun, Neil Murphy, and J. Emmett Clair. But from the time the Packers were kicked out of the league in January 1922, Lambeau was their driving force—their mainspring and their heartbeat. Primarily because of Curly Lambeau, the Green Bay Packers not only survived but eventually rose to the pinnacle of professional football.

Almost as soon as Clair had withdrawn Green Bay from the APFA, Lambeau applied for the

Packers to be readmitted to the league. The *Press-Gazette* reported that team owners at the January meeting had looked "with favor" on Lambeau's application, but that they were deferring a decision on the matter until June 1. That date came and went, though, without any word from Carr — who was reportedly out of town on an auto tour until the middle of the month. Confusing matters even more was the fact that Clair, who had moved back to Chicago, still held the rights to the franchise, and nobody was certain what he planned to do with it. Some worried that he was going to start a team in Chicago instead of fielding another in Green Bay. A *Press-Gazette* story from April 4, 1922, summed up the situation: "Within the next three weeks, the Clare [*sic*] brothers are expected to make known their decision whether or not they will again assume charge of the franchise in this city. If last year's backers deem it best to withdraw from the promotion field there is no doubt but that other interests will step to the front and take over the team."

Any uncertainty about the intentions of John and J. Emmett Clair vanished when neither showed up at the league's summer meeting, which was held the weekend of June 24–25 at Cleveland's Hollenden Hotel. The conference's most momentous bit of business came when, at the urging of George Halas, the APFA changed its name to the National Football League. But Curly Lambeau, the only representative from Green Bay in attendance, had another matter on his mind. On Saturday afternoon he applied for a new team, apologizing to the other team owners, assuring them that his organization had undergone a thorough housecleaning, and vowing to obey every league rule. A special committee then recommended that Lambeau be granted a new franchise in the NFL, and the other owners agreed unanimously.

"One thing is sure, the football magnates all over the country take their hats off to Green Bay as a football town," Lambeau told the *Press-Gazette* upon his return from Cleveland. "Leaders

of teams that played here last fall told other members of the organization that our city gave them the best treatment of any around the circuit. Joe Dunn of the Minneapolis Marines and Tom Flanagan of the Rock Island Independents were loud in praise of Green Bay. Doc Young of Hammond also gave the town a boost."

According to the Pro Football Hall of Fame, Lambeau paid either $50 or $100 out of his own pocket to buy back the franchise. The cost has been reported at various times and in various places as $50, $100, and $250. The truth is that nobody knows. There was nothing reported about any exchange of money in news accounts at the time, and neither does a purchase price appear anywhere in the NFL's minutes of the meeting. Scrawled by hand in the upper-left corner of Green Bay's 1922 franchise certificate is "Cost $50.00," but it is not clear when that was written or by whom. There is no price for the franchise indicated in the text of the certificate itself. The true cost of the Packers might have been nothing. Nobody knows. Not even the team. And Green Bay's original value isn't the only murky thing about the June 1922 meeting.

The mechanics of how Lambeau secured the franchise have been embellished over the years with a story that falls under the category of too good to check. It first appeared in an abbreviated form in a story in *The Milwaukee Journal* in 1939, and it was drawn out in more detail in Arch Ward's 1946 history of the Packers. The 1939 story simply says that Lambeau asked Don Murphy — the friend who had traveled with him to the January APFA meeting in Canton — to sell his car to raise the funds necessary to buy the team back from the APFA. Ward's story added a few twists, as well as some more detail. According to Ward, Lambeau already had the franchise fee (which Ward put at $50) but lacked the money to travel to Cleveland for the meeting. Murphy, who had played guard for Green Bay in one game in 1920, offered to help on the condition that Lambeau let him play for the team in the first game of the 1922 season. After Lambeau agreed, Murphy sold his cream-colored Marmon Roadster for approximately $1,500 to a bootlegger—in the words of Ward, "a local huckster who was dealing in assorted distillations in those arid times." Lambeau and Murphy then traveled to Cleveland together, bought back the franchise, and returned home. According to Ward, Murphy played for the first minute of the Packers' first game before being lifted by Lambeau—and then never played again.

The story has been told and retold (and amended and embellished) countless times in the 73 years since the publication of Ward's history. But there are problems with it on almost every level. Ward puts the APFA meeting in Canton, not Cleveland. (The *Journal* located the meeting in Akron, and put the franchise fee at $250 instead of $50.) And while Murphy was mentioned in the *Press-Gazette* as having traveled with Lambeau to the league's get-together in Chicago in January, the paper made no mention of Murphy in either of its two stories about Lambeau's trip to Cleveland in June, nor did it mention Murphy in the story it published upon Lambeau's triumphant return to Green Bay. More damning is the fact that, according to the lineups printed in the *Press-Gazette*, Murphy did not appear in a single game for Green Bay in 1922.

When Ward published his book, he was the sports editor of the *Chicago Tribune,* as well as one of the most prominent and colorful figures in the landscape of American sports. In 1933 he had created Major League Baseball's All-Star Game, bringing to fruition an idea that had been kicking around the sport for decades. He badgered the American and National Leagues into staging the first contest at Comiskey Park during the Chicago World's Fair, hyping the event in his popular "In the Wake of the News" column. One year later he came up with the Chicago Charities College All-Star Game, which pitted teams of collegiate standouts against the champions of professional foot-

ball. Ward had also been in on the creation of the Golden Gloves boxing tournament, which had started in Chicago in 1923 as a *Tribune*-sponsored event. In 1941 he had turned down a 10-year, $250,000 offer to become the commissioner of the NFL. Three years later he founded the All-America Football Conference, the first serious challenger to the NFL's hegemony over pro football. At various times Ward was an editor, a writer, an author, a promoter, a founder, and a philanthropist. Few events took place in the world of sports in the first half of the 20th century that he did not document or influence.

But for all his personal achievements, Ward was also a loyal son of Notre Dame, from which he had graduated in 1921, two years after Knute Rockne

Curly Lambeau had been the Packers' best player since their founding, but 1922 was the year he became the driving force behind their very survival.

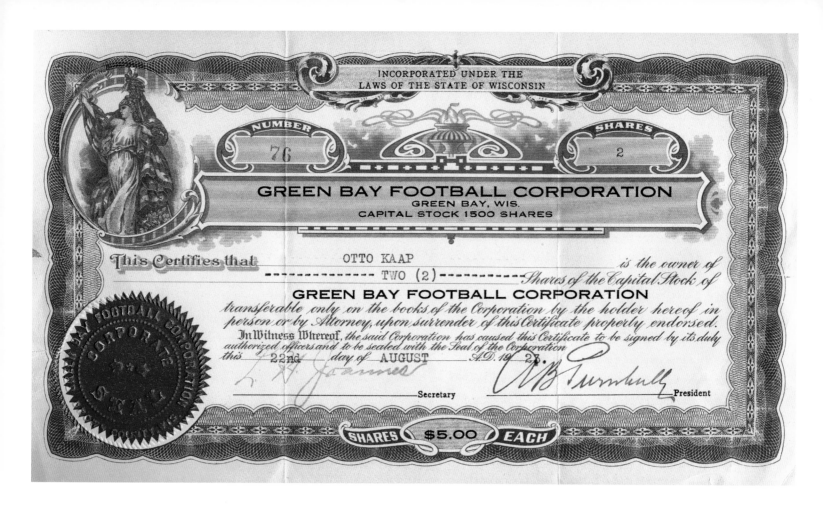

The 1923 stock certificate. Anyone purchasing five shares also got a box seat at every Packers' home game.

hired him to be the school's first director of publicity. Ward and Lambeau later bonded over their intense devotion to the Fighting Irish. Lambeau's teams were stocked with Notre Dame alums, wore blue-and-gold uniforms,* and ran the same Box offense that Rockne had made famous. Ward, who wrote for a publication that had one of the largest weekday circulations of any newspaper in the United States, spilled gallons of ink covering Notre Dame football and hyping the team to the rest of the country.

The title of his book is *The Green Bay Packers: The Story of Professional Football,* and there can be little doubt that — though the Packers weren't the oldest team in the NFL — both Lambeau and Ward wanted Green Bay to be seen as the league's iconic franchise. And the story of Don Murphy has many

of the earmarks of a creation myth. The tale went untold for nearly two decades after it supposedly happened, and then suddenly it was drilled down to such crucial details as the color, make, and model of Murphy's car. The whole story, in the words of Christl, "hardly seems credible."

That's a shame, because the story of the Packers is incredible enough — especially in 1922. The team from the smallest town in the league had been saved through the efforts of one man: Curly Lambeau. He had been the one who immediately appealed to the APFA for Green Bay to be granted a new franchise. He had been the one (with the help of George Whitney Calhoun) who kept up the pressure on league president Joe Carr through the spring and summer. He had been the one who traveled to Cleveland and returned home with a new

---

* *According to team historian Cliff Christl, the Packers first wore green jerseys in 1935, but green did not become a regular color until the 1950s — and even then there were blue-and-gold variations. Green Bay's current green-and-gold color scheme dates back to 1959, Vince Lombardi's first season.*

franchise. And he had been the one who worked tirelessly for the rest of the summer to sign players to fill out his 18-man roster. It is a lot of effort keeping a dream alive. Lambeau's story about the saving of the team may have been apocryphal, but who can blame him for wanting a legend to call his own? Every other small-town team from the Midwest that played in the NFL in those early days blossomed and fell away like leaves from a tree. But the Packers hung on. And they hung on because Curly Lambeau willed it.

◆ ◆ ◆

On September 14, 1922, the articles of incorporation for the Green Bay Football Club were filed with the Brown County Register of Deeds Office. According to the certificate that George Whitney Calhoun submitted four days later to the Wisconsin secretary of state, the *Press-Gazette* editor was the corporation's secretary. The other officers were E. L. Lambeau, president, Joseph M. Ordens, vice president, and Nathan Abrams, treasurer. Each of the men had invested his own money in the team —though there is no record of how much that was. Abrams, a cattle buyer by trade, had been a teammate of Lambeau's at Green Bay East, and the two had played together in Lambeau's one game with the South Side Skidoos in 1918. Abrams joined the Packers the next year and played with them again in 1920 and in four games in 1921. It is likely that he brought aboard Ordens, who had had no public affiliation with the team in any of the previous three seasons. Ordens was a co-owner of the Congress Billiard Room, a downtown poolroom on the east side of the Fox River. (The establishment's slogan was "Clean sport for regular fellows.") His only connection to the Packers had been that the Congress sold tickets to the Rigney Dwyer benefit game, in December 1920. The other owner of the Congress was Harry Levitas, whose sister, Frances, was married to Abrams's older brother, Isadore, who had also played on some of Green Bay's town teams with Lambeau. Two months before Calhoun filed the new team's articles of incorpora-

tion, Ordens had sold his interest in the Congress to Levitas, which may explain why Ordens had extra cash on hand to invest in the Packers.

Lambeau spent the summer recruiting and signing players, several of whom had played for Green Bay the year before. In July, he re-signed Cub Buck, an important transaction, since the affable tackle was as valuable to Lambeau as an assistant coach as he was as a player. Indeed, Buck turned down an offer in early September to become the coach at Indiana. That was around the same time that center Jab Murray agreed to a deal with Lambeau. Murray, a practicing lawyer in Marinette who was running on the Republican ticket for district attorney, had impressed Lambeau during the 1921 season when he played with a broken hand in a 20–0 loss to the Staleys on November 27. (Murray wasn't elected district attorney, but four years later he was appointed city attorney of Marinette, the beginning of a three-decade career in politics.) Lambeau also signed quarterback Charlie Mathys, a former standout at Green Bay West who had gone on to play in college at Ripon and Indiana and then played in the APFA with the Hammond Pros in 1921.

Several other players signed deals that stipulated they had to live in Green Bay during the football season, and the *Press-Gazette* ran ads on September 8–9 looking for work for two of them. "If they are to play with the Green Bay Packers they must find work and move to Green Bay," read the bulletins, which also added a caveat: "Not particular. Labor or office work. Can do anything well."

The ads in the paper may have said "Packers," but Lambeau and his three partners were actively trying to distance themselves from the team's packing plant history. The new franchise's letterhead read GREEN BAY FOOTBALL CLUB at the top and (FORMERLY PACKERS) on the line underneath. Many stories about the team in the *Press-Gazette* in 1922 made no mention of the nickname. The team was called, at one time or another, the Bays, the Badgers, the Big Bay Blues, or simply the Big

Blue Team. On one occasion, they were even "the Green Bay Professional Team." But the nickname "Packers" still crept into the paper's copy—even Calhoun's—and most other dailies covering pro football eschewed the alternate monikers in favor of the old one.

No matter how the team referred to itself, though, or in what other ways it tried to distance itself from the declining fortunes of its meatpacking roots, nothing could hide the fact that it was barely scraping by. The expenses were too much. And a combination of bad weather and poor attendance made the situation dire. Green Bay went 0-3-2 to begin the 1922 season, with all three losses coming against NFL competition. Of those three defeats, only the October 8 game, against the Racine Legion, had been played in Green Bay, and it had drawn just 3,603 fans, only slightly more than the minimum required for the Packers to break even.

Things got worse four weeks later when Green Bay hosted the Columbus Panhandles. A driving rainstorm that began about 30 minutes before kickoff turned the field into a muddy bog and held attendance down to around 1,500. The Packers had taken out rain insurance that would have covered their losses on the game, but the total rainfall for the day was three one-hundredths of an inch short of the amount needed for the team to collect. Green Bay lost $1,500 on the game—exactly the guarantee demanded by Columbus for making the road trip—and, according to a story that ran in the *Press-Gazette* on November 7, was $3,400 in debt for the season. In response the Packers raised ticket prices: from $1.10 to $1.65 for grandstand, bleacher, and standing-room tickets, and from $1.65 to $2.20 for reserved seats.

The only bright side to the Columbus game had been Green Bay's 3–0 victory—its first of the season—the three points coming on Cub Buck's 25-yard field goal in the fourth quarter. Columbus, owned by league president Joe Carr, was one of the NFL's marquee teams. Carr had made the

trip to Green Bay to see the game, and he publicly backed the Packers' plan to raise ticket prices while he was in town. "Your field here is limited," Carr matter-of-factly told the *Press-Gazette*. "At the outset, you probably can't get over 3,500 in your park. Other cities in the league, remember Green Bay is the smallest, are drawing from 8,000 to 15,000 crowds every Sunday and what's more, with but three exceptions, their admission prices are higher than at Green Bay. It is an unfortunate situation here because I consider Green Bay is the best 'little' football city in the country."

Several businesses in the little city did their best to stanch the bleeding. An affiliation of football boosters organized a game in Green Bay on November 30, Thanksgiving Day. The boosters, who were led by local restaurateur and civic paladin George De Lair, originally tried to get George Halas to bring the Bears up from Chicago. But Halas demanded a guarantee that was too expensive for Green Bay. The boosters instead arranged a game with the nonleague Duluth K.C.'s, who had beaten Lambeau's team 6–2 in an exhibition on September 24. The Association of Commerce got behind the game, as did the Rotary Club. Booster tickets sold for $2 and $5 and could be bought at a number of downtown businesses, several of which ran ads promoting the event in the *Press-Gazette* the day before Thanksgiving. The paper itself, in the person of editor John Kline, devoted an editorial to the game. "The fact that these men have interested themselves in the aid of the football team . . . ought to satisfy the public at large that what they are attempting to do is a good thing and that it ought to get back of them," Kline wrote of the boosters. "The Packers team . . . is certainly a civic asset. It has placed Green Bay more prominently than ever on the national sport map. It has 'broken' Green Bay in to the leading papers of the nation and the team has made many thousands of persons in the middle west feel that Green Bay is a live community."

But five hours of steady, soaking rain made a

mess of the playing field and ruined the plans of the boosters. In a morning meeting in the offices of the *Press-Gazette,* Lambeau, Calhoun, and Ordens discussed canceling the game. While they were talking, they were joined by Andrew Turnbull, the paper's business manager. With the rain falling outside and winds gusting up to 46 miles per hour, Turnbull advised the three men to go ahead with the game as a matter of good business practice — a way, in the words of Calhoun's story on the game, "to keep faith with the fans." Turnbull also told them that he would personally see what he could do about solving the team's financial problems. The Packers, behind a third-quarter touchdown plunge by Lambeau and a fourth-quarter field goal by Cub Buck, won the game 10–0. They also lost money — the crowd in attendance was one of the smallest of the season. But there was hope. Writing in the *Press-Gazette* in 1946, Calhoun said that that Thanksgiving Day "marked a turning point in the history of the Packers."

One week later, more than 150 men met at the Green Bay Elks Lodge to discuss how to ensure the financial stability of the team. It was decided by those in attendance to form a five-man committee — which would include De Lair and Turnbull — to incorporate the franchise as a nonprofit and sell stock to fund it. Five days later, at a smaller meeting in the Beaumont Hotel, 42 men made the decision to create the Green Bay Football Corporation, for which 1,000 shares of stock would be sold at $10 a share. The first $1,300 was raised when 14 of the men in attendance purchased stock. The framework had been put in place for a professional sports franchise that was unique in North America. One month later, the NFL transferred ownership of the Packers to the new corporation.

When the franchise filed its articles of incorporation in August 1923, it set the price of its stock at $5. Purchasing a share was basically the same as making a donation to the Packers. Stock in the team couldn't be resold and didn't pay dividends. Its only benefit was voting rights, but anyone buy-

The 1922 document that designated the officers of the privately owned (and short-lived) Green Bay Football Club. Vice president Joe Ordens ran a local pool hall. Treasurer Nate Abrams had been an end on the original Packers.

ing at least five shares was also entitled to a box seat at every home game. At the time, the team had more support from the businesses in the community, particularly from the *Press-Gazette,* than it did from among the general population of the city. Boosters targeted their sales efforts in the downtown business district. The paper ran stock coupons on the sports page in every issue from August 20 to August 30 to encourage readers to purchase shares, and staffed its offices every weeknight from 7 to 9:30 to take subscriptions.

On September 14, the same night that Jack Dempsey fought Luis Firpo for the heavyweight championship at the Polo Grounds in New York City, 450 boosters met at the Elks Lodge to hear the returns from the bout and hold a football "pep meeting" with Curly Lambeau, quarterback Charlie Mathys, and fullback Buck Gavin, a recent signee from Rock Island. And since Dempsey, after having gotten famously knocked out of the ring in the first round, scored a knockout over Firpo in the second, there was plenty of time to discuss the upcoming season and sell a few more shares of stock. The meeting was led by John Kittell, a prominent attorney in town. Kittell, who was in his early fifties, had presided over the meeting on December 7, 1922, at which the Packers' financial future had first been discussed, and he had appointed the five-man committee tasked with incorporating the franchise and organizing the sale of its stock. He was also one of the team's original investors, having ponied up a portion of the $1,300 raised at the meeting on December 12. (He held 20 shares in the team, the maximum allowed for one person.) In his opening remarks to the boosters, Kittell outlined the structure of the new organization, discussed the progress of the stock sale, and promised that none of the officers —when they were finally elected—would be paid a salary.

It is almost certain that Kittell was the author of the original articles of the Green Bay Football Corporation. He was the only attorney to sign the document, which established the team as a non-profit and dictated that no stockholder would receive any dividends or other financial benefit, and that any earnings "shall be donated to the Sullivan Post of the American Legion, Green Bay, Wisconsin."

Three nights after the Elks Lodge get-together, the Packers held their first stockholders' meeting in the assembly room of the Brown County Courthouse. Kittel named a three-man committee to nominate 15 shareholders for the board of directors. While the nominating committee was selecting the board, the rest of the stockholders ratified the corporation's bylaws. They then unanimously approved the men named by the nominating committee to the board of directors. After the larger meeting dispersed, the board then met privately to elect a five-man executive committee. Turnbull was voted president of the corporation, and Kittell was voted vice president. Green Bay grocery baron Leland Joannes was elected secretary and treasurer, while George De Lair and Dr. W. Webber Kelly were made at-large members. In all, 204 shareholders had purchased 1,109 shares, and the sale netted $5,545.

At last, after all the papers had been filed and

the money was in the bank and the organization of the corporation was complete, Lambeau's team finally became the people's team. In the words of Arch Ward, "The Packers were Green Bay, and Green Bay was the town behind them."

• • •

Ward's 1946 history of the Packers has been the primary source for almost all that is known about Green Bay's NFL story. His astute characterization of the fidgety, chain-smoking Lambeau is especially memorable. "Curly has, in his time on the Packer side lines, traveled thousands of miles, by the count of witnesses," Ward writes. "He seldom sits in the inviting brown leather armchair or lounge in his office, preferring to stand, worry a cigarette, and peer out at the courthouse and post office across Walnut Street when you're talking

football with him." And to be sure, the broad-strokes portrait that the book paints of the franchise is accurate. But a number of crucial details cited as fact by Ward are off, or — as was the case with Don Murphy's cream-colored Marmon Roadster — simply too good to be true. A couple of the things that Ward got wrong include dating football's debut in Green Bay to 1897 when it was actually 1895, and locating the team's first practice field at Hagemeister Park instead of on the grounds of the Indian Packing plant. Ward also said that Green Bay held no annual stockholders' meetings when, with one exception, the team has held one every year since 1923.

"Ward was not from Green Bay and had to rely on the distant memories of others to tell the early history of the Packers," says Christl. "His con-nection to the team was its co-founder, Curly Lambeau, who never let the facts get in the way of a good story." Christl also says that longtime *Press-Gazette* writer and former Packers public re-lations chief Lee Remmel once summed up Curly another way: "He was a congenital liar."

Perhaps the most enduring piece of the Packers' legend crafted by Ward was his enumeration of a group he called "the Hungry Five" — the five men who were, in his telling, most responsible for sav-ing football in Green Bay. He traces the Hungry Five (a name he perhaps took from the title of a popular radio show in Chicago in the late 1920s and early '30s) back to Andrew Turnbull and the initial concerned-citizens meetings of 1922 and '23. Ward's Hungry Five consists of Turnbull, Lambeau, Lee Joannes, Dr. W. W. Kelly, and attorney Gerald Clifford. But while all five men certainly played a major role in the continued survival of the Packers, only four of them had been there for the transformation of the franchise into a community-owned source of civic pride. Clifford, who became the team's attorney in 1929, did not attend any of the initial booster meetings, was not involved in any of the early efforts to sell stock, and did not even become a shareholder in the team until 1931.

A mostly forgotten candidate for membership in the Hungry Five would have been Kittell, who died at the age of 61 in 1932, 14 years before Ward published his team history. Kittell was a respected member of the legal community in Green Bay, having organized the formation of several local corporations besides the Packers. He was also a major player in Republican politics in the state and a noted civic booster. Indeed, Kittell was one of the first prominent members of the city's professional community to speak up on the team's behalf. On November 20, 1922, 10 days before Turnbull urged Lambeau and Calhoun to go on with the Booster Day game, Kittell had joined Lambeau at a Kiwanis Club luncheon to try to spur interest in the team. Three days later, Kittell spoke to the Rotary Club about the importance of supporting the Packers, insisting that Lambeau's team was one of the best advertisements for Green Bay that the city had.

Another outspoken supporter whose name is often overlooked because he was not an official member of the Hungry Five is George De Lair. De Lair was the colorful proprietor of the eclectic De Lair's Café, which was dubbed by its owner "the café of a thousand dishes." (A less exotic motto for the café was "A place to eat," which appeared in ads that ran in the *Press-Gazette*.) He was one of the Packers' biggest fans during the team's first four seasons. In November 1921, he had gotten together with a few musicians in town to form the Lumberjack Band, a loosely organized affiliation of 20 or so rooters who descended upon Chicago as part of a contingent of about 500 Green Bay fans for the first game between the Packers and the Bears, who were then still called the Staleys. Anyone with a horn and a drum could join De Lair's roster of tooters, provided that they also wore high boots, corduroy pants, lumberjack shirts, mackinaw jackets, and hunting caps—and could afford train fare to Chicago. The band departed for that first game at 12:50 on Sunday morning and arrived in Chicago several hours later. The crew then marched through the Loop and out to Cubs Park while performing a playlist that included "How Dry I Am" and "On, Wisconsin!"

But like Kittell, De Lair was not around when Ward was writing his book. In February 1924 he entered a sanatorium in Milwaukee to recover from a nervous breakdown. On the morning of June 26, one day after having been discharged—and three days before his 44th birthday—De Lair put a gun to his left temple and took his own life. A story in the *Wausau Daily Herald* attributed his suicide to "despondency over ill health," and the *Press-Gazette* noted that there would be no official inquest into his death.

Even without De Lair, Ward's Hungry Five was a colorful group. Leland Joannes was just 30, tall and dignified, a member of one of the city's oldest families. The Joannes Brothers wholesale grocery business had been an institution in Green Bay since 1872, and Lee was running the operation along with his cousin Harold when he became involved with the Packers. Dr. W. W. Kelly was not only Green Bay's first team doctor, but also one of the Packers' original boosters, making trips to away games and serving as a toastmaster at end-of-season banquets. Born in 1875 in Kingston, Jamaica, Kelly was the son of an Irish captain in the British Army. He grew up in Nottingham, England, earned his undergraduate degree in Bruges, Belgium, and eventually got his medical degree in Montreal, before moving to Green Bay in 1904. He was enormously popular with the players. According to former Packers board member Fred Leicht,

"Dr. Kelly's strong point was psychiatry ... He could pick up a player who wasn't so good, talk to him and put that fire back in him."

But there could be no doubt that the only reason a team existed to save in the first place was Curly Lambeau — the hungriest of the Hungry Five. And any resources used to continue and sustain it were being used to further his vision. Lambeau had not yet conquered the rest of the world, as he had vowed to do as a boy, but as a man he had made the city of Green Bay his own in a very specific way. Next up for him was to conquer the NFL.

CHAPTER 5
A WIDE-OPEN TOWN

For the Packers, a crucial way in which Green Bay was unlike most other cities in the country in the 1920s was how it dealt with Prohibition. Simply put, the city ignored the law. Green Bay in the Roaring Twenties was a wide-open city, a town where the flow of booze never stopped. But not in the manner of Chicago, where bootlegging gangsters kept order with tommy guns and blood money was the city's true currency. In Green Bay the lawbreaking was tacitly endorsed by business leaders and the city fathers. The local breweries may have downshifted into the manufacture of soft drinks and other libations after Prohibition took effect in 1920 — Milwaukee's Schlitz brewery marketed a "cereal beverage," i.e. a near beer called Famo, as "food and drink" — but that didn't mean that Green Bay became any less of a drinking town. Speakeasies and a bustling red-light district just outside the city limits flourished. The Union Hotel in nearby De Pere never completed its basement speakeasy rooms for the simple reason that it did not have to — the cozy bar upstairs never stopped serving alcohol. An unintended and auspicious consequence of all this civic malfeasance was the continued existence of the Packers. "Prohibition," says Cliff Christl, "is one of the main reasons the team survived."

Congress passed the 18th Amendment, which outlawed the manufacture, transportation, and sale of intoxicants, on December 18, 1917. Nineteen months later, it passed the Volstead Act, which provided for the enforcement of the amendment — setting aside funds to establish a "dry enforcement force" of 1,500 agents. Prohibition officially took effect on January 16, 1920. From that day forward, no one in America could legally buy anything stronger than near beer. John F. Kramer, the first Prohibition commissioner, insisted that the law would be "obeyed in cities large and small, and in villages, and where it is not obeyed it will be enforced." Optimism was high. Chicago's Cook County Hospital closed its alcoholic ward on the theory that it would no longer be needed.

But optimism was not the sentiment that greeted Prohibition in northeastern Wisconsin. The attitude there was more like contempt. In the words of Green Bay historian Jack Rudolph, "Brown County practically seceded from the Union as far as enforcement went." For most of Green Bay's history — dating back to the distillery that had been set up in the 1820s on the east side of the Fox River — the town had been known as one that enjoyed a drink. In 1919 it was home to three breweries and more than 100 saloons. The staunchly Republican *Press-Gazette* denounced the new law's attempt to purify American morals as meddling in personal affairs. The paper would later call the law "in large part a farce." A significant portion of the city's population consisted of immigrant families from Germany and other countries in Europe, and because of Prohibition many of them began to warm to the Republican suspicion of federal meddling in local matters. That Green Bay remained a conservative enclave in a progressive state for so long was due at least in part to the overreach of Prohibition.

In truth, the citizens of Green Bay were no different from most other ordinary Americans, many of whom were disquieted by federal efforts to strictly enforce the new law. In 1928 a mother of 10 in Detroit was caught selling two pints of liquor — her fourth offense — and received a life sentence in prison. (It was later commuted to 15 months.) In Chicago, a janitor who had made some home brew for an American Legion social was put in jail. And stories abounded in newspapers throughout the country about bootlegging farmers who had been shot and killed by deputies searching for liquor. Juries began refusing to convict people who had been caught breaking the law.

In the fall of 1928, federal agents descended upon Green Bay on a Saturday night and arrested about 40 men for violation of dry law charges. The agents took a break for the Sabbath, then continued to raid soft drink parlors in the area on Monday, Tuesday, and Wednesday night. By the time they were done, more than 100 men had been arraigned and around 50 "establishments" had been padlocked. The Green Bay City Council attracted nationwide attention because it passed a resolution after the raids protesting the federal government's intervention in local matters. The council, in its wording of the resolution, admitted that saloons were operating within the city under the watchful eye of the local police department. But it also captured the sentiment around the country by calling Prohibition "largely an unpopular law."

In Green Bay could be found the fundamental reason for Prohibition's ultimate failure: men and women who were otherwise upstanding citizens simply refused to obey the statute. Tellingly, Congress never made the purchase of alcoholic beverages a crime. By the time the 18th Amendment was repealed, in 1933, five states, including Wisconsin, were refusing to enforce it.

Bootlegging was big business during the 1920s and operated in parallel with the boom on Wall Street. The manufacture and sale of liquor is estimated to have put $2 billion a year into the pockets of those who dealt in contraband. Chicago was a wide-open city in the 1920s, but it was essentially run by Al Capone. Gangsters never really got a toehold in Green Bay, because they just were not needed — alcohol was everywhere and readily available. Saloons simply converted to "soft drink parlors" and went right on dispensing "spiked" beer and bootleg liquor. Breweries transitioned into the manufacture of legal near beer, which was easy to recharge with wood alcohol, added either to the cask or to the glass. They also made and sold unfermented mash, which yielded wort that could be turned into home brew. There were large numbers of speakeasies on Main Street and throughout the downtown business section. Impending raids were usually tipped off in plenty of time for speakeasy operators to close down before raiders arrived. With no regular agents located in Green Bay (the closest ones were in Milwaukee), it was not hard to evade the law. Roadhouses were located beyond the city limits, on the routes leading into Green Bay, including on Highway 141 from

Though Bellevue Park was "not a good football field," according to George Whitney Calhoun — who said one end zone was about three yards short — its confines were friendly to the Packers. Green Bay went 9-2-1 there.

Manitowoc, and on Cedar Creek Road, address of the notorious Green Mill Garden, a "dance hall" owned and operated by Mrs. Pauline Pierre — known to her customers as Mother Pierre.

◆ ◆ ◆

For all the problems Prohibition caused locally and around the country, the law was without question a boon to the Packers. In their first year as a publicly owned corporation, the team had actually lost money — $147.74 to be exact. Gate receipts in Green Bay were minimal, and teams that made the trip to northeastern Wisconsin had little hope of making more than their guarantee for playing a road game. The Packers, in fact, were a better draw away from Green Bay in the 1920s than they were at home. The 1927 game between Green

Bay East and Green Bay West attracted an estimated 10,000 fans. By contrast, the Packers' 7–6 home loss to the Bears that year drew only about 5,500. But few in the NFL seemed to mind. "Green Bay in the '20s was the most popular stop in the league," wrote Dan Daly and Bob O'Donnell in *The Pro Football Chronicle,* the rollicking history of the game they co-authored in 1990. "Visiting players loved the place. Teams made it a point to schedule several days there. It had a bustling bar scene, and its red-light district in the northeast section was famous."

Visiting players loved the place so much, it seems, that a few of them actually moved there — another way that Prohibition helped the team to survive. In 1921, four players who had begun the season with the Rock Island Independents joined the Packers in midseason: Frank Coughlin, Dave Hayes, Emmett Keefe, and Grover Malone, all of whom had lettered at Notre Dame. The Independents released Hayes, Malone, and Coughlin (who was also the team's coach) on October 18, with the explanation that because the team held daily practices, all of its players had to live in Rock Island. Hayes and Malone lived in Chicago, while Coughlin resided in South Bend. J. L. Hughes, the sports columnist for *The Rock Island Argus,* noted that Coughlin had been a "big disappointment," and added, "His work in three games indicated he had no intentions of risking injury if it could be avoided."

The attitude in Green Bay was much different. Hayes, Malone, and Coughlin had all been released in time for the Packers' first APFA game, a 7–6 home victory over the Minneapolis Marines, and Hayes and Malone were in the starting lineup, at right end and left halfback, respectively. They would remain there for the rest of the season. Coughlin, a tackle, was called "one of the greatest footballers in the country" by the *Press-Gazette.* He joined the team and was in the starting lineup in time for its next game — a 13–3 home loss to Rock Island.

At the time, the Independents were one of the more stable franchises in the APFA. They were a charter member of the league in 1920 and had been playing every year since 1912. Rock Island, with a population of 35,177, was not much bigger than Green Bay, though the Quad Cities (Rock Island and Moline in Illinois, Bettendorf and Davenport in Iowa) had a combined population of 115,574. And, like the Packers, the Independents had solid support from their local newspaper. When Rock Island was on the road, the *Argus* wired the play-by-play back home to a public gathering — an innovation that the *Press-Gazette* copied. But where the Packers' wires were announced to crowds of 1,000 or so in Green Bay, the Independents' play-by-play call would draw a crowd

of around 4,000. The Packers finished with winning records in both of their first two seasons in the APFA/NFL, but Rock Island finished ahead of them both years. In 1922, Calhoun called the Independents "the best supported professional football team in the middle west."

Hometown support or not, a significant number of Rock Island's players preferred playing in Green Bay. Prohibition had taken on a more conventional appearance in the Quad Cities. Alcohol was available, but it was not as out in the open as it was in northeastern Wisconsin. The region was run in the early days of the 18th Amendment by the notorious gangster John Looney, a grim, gaunt man who wore the same dirty suit every day, ate raw liver on toast, and controlled an estimated 150 gambling and prostitution establishments. In the early 1920s, Looney was in the midst of a war with a few rival Quad Cities gangs — and the region was notoriously violent. It's possible that the Independents' players wanted out of Rock Island simply to find some peace and quiet.

Relations between the Packers and the Independents soon became testy. In 1922, four more Rock Island players moved to northeastern Wisconsin to play for the Packers. The first was Francis "Jug" Earp, who was released by the Independents on October 10. The six-foot, 236-pound lineman —a second cousin once removed of Wyatt Earp —would become a mainstay of the Green Bay line (first at tackle and then at center) for much of the next 11 years. When he was released by Rock Island, Hughes wrote that Earp had grown "heavy and fat during the off-season and after nearly a month showed no promise of return to the form which characterized his playing last season." But the *Press-Gazette* said that Earp had asked for his release from the Independents and alleged that there were internal problems on the team. Hughes responded in the *Argus* that "picking up discards seems to be the favorite sport of the Green Bay management."

On October 29, the Independents and the Packers battled to a scoreless tie in Green Bay. After the game, Rock Island halfback Eddie Usher — a Toledo native who had starred for coach Fielding Yost at Michigan from 1918 to '20 — became the second defector of the season to ask for his release. When it was granted, Usher promptly signed with Green Bay. The *Argus* hadn't covered the game in Green Bay, but Hughes later noted that fans who had made the trip were suspicious of the home-town team, which was on an extended tour of northeastern Wisconsin. The Independents stayed in De Pere the night before their game against the Packers, and then remained there for three more nights before heading 45 minutes south to Manitowoc to get ready for their November 5 game against the Milwaukee Badgers. "Ugly rumors are being circulated," Hughes wrote in the *Argus* on October 30. "It is said some of the members of the team are finding late hours and 'soda pop' poor physical conditioners. If this is true, it's time for reckoning."

Rock Island played for three more seasons in the NFL, then jumped ship in July 1926 to joined Red Grange's new American Football League. But the team didn't last one season, folding for good after nine games. Pro football was dead in Rock Island.

But not in Green Bay. In 1927, the NFL cut out most of its small-town teams in the process of downsizing from 22 to 12 franchises. Green Bay made the cut — and in July hosted one of that year's three league meetings. The gathering remains the only meeting the NFL has ever held in Green Bay.

And not surprisingly, according to league president Joe Carr, the visit was delightful. "I knew when the league meeting was arranged for Green Bay that we would have an enjoyable time," Carr said, "but the hospitality of everybody has exceeded my fondest expectations."

◆ ◆ ◆

The Packers' improved financial outlook freed Curly Lambeau to go after better football talent from major colleges or other professional teams. And it was then, when he was liberated from the constant worry about survival, that Lambeau's true genius revealed itself. Though he didn't get the title of general manager until 1946, he was perhaps the greatest player personnel man of the pro game's first 25 years. His energy, combined with Green Bay's wide-open reputation, began to attract talent from far beyond Rock Island. Green Bay had muddled along in its first two NFL seasons, winning seven of 16 games while tying four. But in 1923 the Packers went 7-2-1 and finished third in the league. As the decade went on, the Packers kept winning (finishing above .500 every year) and Lambeau kept signing good players, among them center Bernard "Boob" Darling, quarterback Joseph "Red" Dunn, and end LaVern "Lavvie" Dilweg. And in August 1925, Lambeau signed Green Bay's first African American player, six-foot, 230-pound lineman Walter Jean* — though it's likely the coach had no idea that Jean was black.

Jean, who had previously suited up for the Akron Pros and Milwaukee Badgers, appeared in 19 games for the Packers in 1925 and '26, playing center, guard, and tackle. By the time he got to Green Bay, he had been living for nearly a decade as something of a football nomad. The *Press-*

---

* *There are several permutations of Jean's name—some of which he used at various points in his life—and there is quite a bit of uncertainty over what exactly to call him in the record books. He is listed as "Walt LeJeune (aka Walt Jean)" in* Total Football, *and as "Walt LeJeune (Walter LeArmand LeJean)" by* Pro Football Reference, *and as just "Walt LeJeune" in* The Pro Football Encyclopedia. *But there is no record that he ever called himself LeJeune. According to pro football researcher Steve Jubyna, Jean changed his place of birth from Chillicothe, Ohio, to New Orleans in the 1940 census, and he says that that may explain why he began calling himself Le Jean. But the former lineman had been using that name since at least 1935, when he listed himself as "Walter Le Jean" on his application for a marriage license in Wayne County, Indiana. He also changed his birthday, from January 12, 1898, to the same date in 1896, perhaps so that he would be a month older than his wife, who had been born in February 1896. That would explain why he was listed as 65 instead of 63 at the time of his death, in March 1961.*

Gazette noted that he had "roved a bit during his college career as he played football for the University of Missouri, West Virginia U., and Bethany and Heidelberg colleges. He coached for one year at the Bowling Green State College in Ohio." Jean had indeed played for a few seasons at Heidelberg College, in Tiffin, Ohio, beginning in 1916, and later at Bethany College, in Bethany, West Virginia, in 1921. He did not graduate from Heidelberg. He was also the coach at Bowling Green in 1920. There is no record of him at either Missouri or West Virginia. One obituary for Jean said that he had graduated from Marquette, but that school has no record of him.

Jean's background, much like his football CV, is full of contradictions. He was born on January 12, 1898, in Chillicothe, Ohio, and recorded in the 1900 census as black. The same survey listed his father, Marcel, as black, and his mother, Elizabeth, as white. Walter was listed as "mulatto" in the censuses of 1910 and 1920, but then listed as white in 1930 and 1940. Jean's 1917 draft card gives his full name as Walter LeArmond Jean—the 1900 census had him down as Walter M. Jean—and lists him as white with brown hair and blue eyes. But in a roster of Ohio soldiers who served in World War I, Jean is listed as Walter M. Jean, and his race is recorded as "colored."

"All my evidence points to him being half black," says Karen Schaffer, a great-niece of Jean's who has spent the last dozen years researching her family's genealogy. "The family lore was that we had Cherokee blood—I assume to explain the dark skin. Walter left Chillicothe after the war, and then seems to have decided to filter into society as white. He lived as a white man. He lived in white neighborhoods. He married a white woman."*

Lambeau and the Packers almost certainly thought that Jean was white. In 29 years as Green Bay's coach, Lambeau never had an African American player on his roster. Neither did he employ black players during his stints in the early 1950s as coach of the Chicago Cardinals and the Washington Redskins. Though there is no record of him ever commenting on the subject of race in the NFL, he appears to have adhered to the league's soft ban on blacks in pro football. According to Jubyna, Jean is one of 13 African American players to have played in the league from 1920 to 1933, the year before black players disappeared from the game altogether. The NFL only began a slow process of reintegration in 1946, when former UCLA tailback Kenny Washington signed with the Los Angeles Rams. League officials of the time always claimed that the disappearance of black players from pro football was not intentional and that the NFL had no written or unwritten agreement among the owners not to sign African Americans—a claim that seems extremely dubious. For all the bootstrap brilliance of the NFL's rise from the sandlots to the summit of America's sporting mountaintop, the league's treatment of African American players in the 1930s and '40s is a stain on its legacy. And the story of Walter Jean is a reminder that Lambeau and the Packers played a part in it.

To Green Bay's credit, though, the franchise's commitment to getting its history right has made something positive of the whole affair—of the story of a man who hid his true identity in part so that he could play for a team that would not otherwise have given him the chance. Jean's status as the Packers' first African American player is known to more than just Jubyna and Schaffer because Green Bay dug up the information itself and published the story on its website. Christl, a dogged reporter, found research first done by Jubyna and reported it out in January 2016. Green Bay had always listed Bob Mann, an end who

---

* As part of her research, Schaffer took two DNA tests in 2014. Both tests came up 0 percent for Native American ancestry, while her percentage of African American DNA was about 4 percent. Considering how far removed she is from Walter on her family tree, that amount, she says, "is about right."

THE 1925 PACKER FOOTBALL TEAM.

NORTON   BUCK   CAPT. LAMBEAU   GARDNER   MATHYS

VERGERA   O'DONNELL   LEWELLYN   JEAN   BASING   LARSON

In the middle row of this montage of the 1925 Packers are Walter Jean (third from right), the team's first African American player, and Verne Lewellen (third from left), its first great one.

signed with the team in 1950, as its first African American player. But Walter Jean preceded him by a generation. And Jean's story might have been nothing more than a footnote in history, known only to a few researchers and archivists, if not for the efforts of Christl and the Packers.

◆ ◆ ◆

In 1924, Curly Lambeau signed the Packers' first great player. Verne Clark Lewellen was the youngest of six children of rancher Joseph Lewellen and his wife, Mary Ella. Born in 1901 in Garland, Nebraska, Verne was a star in basketball, football, and track at Lincoln High. The teams he played on won four state titles, and he won two individual state championships in the high hurdles. But

it was on the gridiron—where at various times he played halfback, quarterback, end, and punter—that he truly stood out. As the quarterback and team captain his junior year, he led the Red and Black in scoring, drop-kicked field goals of 41 and 47 yards, and helped Lincoln to a 9-0-2 record. He was named the all-state quarterback that year and was an all-state end the next.

Lewellen stayed in Lincoln to attend Nebraska, where he earned a law degree and starred for the Cornhuskers as a quarterback, halfback, and punter from 1921 through '23, when he was the team captain. On November 10, 1923, Lewellen and Nebraska upset undefeated Notre Dame 14–7 in Lincoln in front of 30,000 fans, many of whom spilled out of the stands of unfinished Memorial Stadium in celebration when the game was over. Lewellen didn't score that day, but he was invaluable as a punter, repeatedly setting the Fighting Irish back deep in their own territory. His first boot of the game went for 70 yards. Notre Dame, led by its Four Horsemen backfield of Harry Stuhldreher, Jimmy Crowley, Elmer Layden, and Don Miller, were considered unbeatable. But 1923 was the second year in a row that the Cornhuskers had defeated coach Knute Rockne's juggernaut. The Irish went 27-2-1 from 1922 through '24, but both losses came in Lincoln, to Lewellen and Nebraska.

It was Crowley, a Green Bay native who had starred for Lambeau at East High in 1921, who tipped his former coach off to the versatile Lewellen. Lambeau subsequently outbid the Milwaukee Badgers and the Kansas City Blues to sign him. As Lewellen told the story, one way that Lambeau had clinched the deal was by promising to find him a job with a Green Bay law firm. Lewellen was available to sign with the Packers because he had flopped in a tryout with baseball's Pittsburgh Pirates earlier in the summer. A lanky six-foot-one, 185-pound right-hander, he threw a devastating pitch that, according to *The Lincoln Star,* was "a speedy cross-fire curveball that generally nets him ten to fifteen strikeouts in every start on the slab." He signed with Pittsburgh in January 1924. But after missing spring training and joining the club following Nebraska's June 7 graduation, he lasted less than a month. He also, according to his son Verne Jr., injured his shoulder in a train accident sometime between the end of his senior season at Nebraska and his June tryout with the Bucs. Pittsburgh cut him loose on the Fourth of July, and Lewellen returned to Lincoln, where he was reported to be joining the Western League's Lincoln Links. But *The Lincoln Star* reported on July 24 that Lewellen had contracted smallpox, and there is no record of his ever appearing in a game for Lincoln.

Baseball's loss was pro football's gain. Lewellen's versatility as a runner, passer, and kicker made him an invaluable part of the Packers' backfield, and it is something of a mystery that he isn't in the Pro Football Hall of Fame. During his nine-year career, the studious and dignified halfback scored 51 touchdowns, more than any other player in the NFL, and was the league's second-leading scorer, with 307 points. According to unofficial statistics for the seasons 1920 through 1932, compiled in *The Football Encyclopedia,* he was also the league's second-leading rusher, sixth-leading receiver, and 12th-leading passer — despite the fact that he was never Green Bay's featured thrower. But for all his offensive prowess, it was as a punter that he was most highly regarded. "No one who ever saw Lewellen kick could ever forget him," wrote Arthur Daley in *The New York Times* in 1962. "He was the finest punter these eyes ever saw."

In Lewellen's day, teams averaged fewer than 10 points a game, and almost two-thirds of all NFL contests from 1920 through 1932 were shutouts. Field position was paramount, and punters were some of the most important players in the game. Teams stuck deep in their own territory often quick-kicked the ball away on early downs rather than make a crucial mistake. The strategy was less risky than it would be today, in part because the ball was rounder. With no punt returner in position to field an early-down kick, the ball was free to roll. Another important factor was that field goals were exceedingly rare — the kicking game was infinitely less refined, and going for three was a very risky proposition. It wasn't unusual for a team to punt from well inside its opponent's half of the field. Cub Buck punted 19 times in a 1923 game against the St. Louis All-Stars at muddy Sportsman's Park. According to unofficial records, Lewellen punted an incredible 136 times in 13 games in 1928, while teammate Harry O'Boyle led the league with three field goals. According to *The Pro Football Chronicle,* one NFL scribe referred to the game in this era as "paid punting."

Lewellen was also a master of the coffin-corner kick and was renowned for his ability to pin opponents deep in their own territory. And since he was often punting from inside his opponent's half of the field, his coffin-corner prowess is one reason that his unofficial average of 39.5 yards a punt is so low. Numbers aside, though, Lewellen is widely considered the first great punter in NFL history and, along with Sammy Baugh, one of the two best punters in the league's first 35 years. In the 1920s and early '30s, Packers games centered on Lewellen as much as they did on Brett Favre from 1992 through 2007, and as much as they do on Aaron Rodgers today. Considering how the game was played in Lewellen's day, a case could be made for him not only as a candidate for the Pro Football Hall of Fame, but also as a candidate for the greatest player in the history of the Packers.

The men who played alongside him certainly thought so. Four charter members of the Pro Football Hall of Fame in 1963 were former Packers: halfback Johnny Blood, tackle Cal Hubbard, end Don Hutson, and Curly Lambeau. Blood, for one, was emphatic that Lewellen belonged in Canton. "Verne Lewellen should have been in there in front of me and Hubbard," he said.

Former Green Bay quarterback Charlie Mathys agreed. "Defensively, offensively—of the players we had in the old days, he was number one. And I'm not alone in saying that . . . He was way ahead of his time in ability. If he doesn't get in the Hall of Fame, it's a joke."

◆ ◆ ◆

The versatile Lewellen was the ideal back for Lambeau's favorite offense, the Notre Dame Box. The mechanics of the Box are simple by today's standards, but the motion it employed made it dynamic for its time, and the opportunities it provided for deception made it tricky to defend. The way Lambeau used it was anything but vanilla. The basic version of the scheme, which was first made popular by Knute Rockne at Notre Dame —another way in which the history of the Pack-

ers is inextricably tied to that of the Fighting Irish —begins with the backfield (quarterback, fullback, and right and left halfbacks) in a T formation behind a balanced line, with the ends split a yard outside the tackles. Just before the snap, all four backs would shift left or right together into an alignment that, viewed from above, resembled a box, with the quarterback sliding from under center to behind a guard, and the halfback to the side of the shift moving forward and stationing himself either directly behind or to one side of the end. The snap might go to the quarterback or to either one of the deep backs.

Lambeau preferred the Box not only because it was adaptable to either running or passing, but also because, as he said, his backs could shift left or right "without destroying their effectiveness or

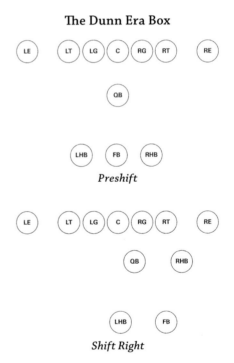

The Dunn Era Box

Preshift

Shift Right

limiting the attack's deception." In his version of the offense, the left halfback did most of the passing, but not all of it. Lambeau's best backs were proficient runners, passers, kickers, and receivers, whom he could use interchangeably at different positions. "Our best teams have been those with at least three better-than-average all-around men

Packer Season Ticket Campaign Is Huge Success

3,390 Pledges Received in One-Day Drive; Total Sales Will Set New All-Time Mark

By RAY PAGEL

Green Bay Packer fans made a most practical demonstration of their interest in the fate and fortunes of the 1943 eleven by a highly enthusiastic response to Tuesday's season ticket drive.

Nearly 125 campaign workers assembled at the Beaumont hotel for a 6:30 report dinner to hear that the one-day drive had netted a total of 3,390 pledges for tickets to the two home games this season. This considerably exceeds the goal of 3,000 which the workers had set for themselves.

Last year, the first time an organized one-day drive was sponsored by the Green Bay Association of Commerce, 1,381 tickets were taken by fans. The entire season ticket sale last year, including out-of-town s a d e l l, amounted to approximately 3,000, the all-time high, Earl S. Ward, Association of Commerce secretary, and Bob Gage retail secre-

Ducats on Way

Ralph C. Smith, Packer ticket director, said today that the tickets for the Packers' games this year are expected from the printer within several days. After delivery fans who pledged to buy tickets in Tuesday's drive will be contacted by ticket office representatives.

Liked by Harry Masse, Kelly

teamed up in one backfield," Lambeau once said.

For most of Lewellen's career, quarterback Red Dunn did the majority of the throwing. He was, unofficially, the second most prolific passer in the NFL during the league's pre-stats era, throwing for 4,641 yards in his eight-year career. But the wiry five-foot-eleven, 177-pound Milwaukee native and Marquette graduate was also valuable as a runner, punter, and kicker, and he was an asset on defense and special teams too. He scored 114 points on field goals and extra points, intercepted 19 passes from the safety position, and returned more than 200 punts. He was, quite literally, all over the field. When Dunn retired after the 1931 season, Lambeau made halfback Arnie Herber — a deep-ball specialist who was not as cagey or as rugged or as strong a rusher as Dunn — his featured passer. The Green Bay quarterbacks became mostly blocking backs after that. Larry Craig, the Packers' quarterback from 1939 to '46, did not attempt a single pass in his eight-year Packers career.

Passing had been the hallmark of Lambeau's team since its days as a town outfit in 1919 and 1920, and he claimed that the Packers were the first NFL team to make "the forward pass their basic attack," as well as the first team to "pass on first, second, third or fourth down . . . regardless of our position on the field." Before he signed Dunn — who had won an NFL championship as the quarterback for the Chicago Cardinals in 1925 — in August 1927, Lambeau had been Green Bay's primary passer. According to Eric Goska, author of the comprehensive record book *Green Bay Packers: A Measure of Greatness,* Lambeau put the ball in the air 136 times in 1924 and threw for 903 yards. He was, of course, not the only passer on the team, and Goska's meticulous scrutiny of the play-by-plays of each game in the *Press-Gazette* and in other papers has revealed that Green Bay attempted 47 additional passes that season that were not attributed to any specific player. It is probable that more than a few of those additional 47 passes were thrown by Lambeau, and, depending on how many he completed, there is a good chance that he was the first NFL player to throw for more than 1,000 yards in a single season.* No team lived and died by the pass more than the Packers.

Green Bay's affinity for the pass stood in stark

---

* According to David S. Neft, Richard Cohen, and Rich Korch's The Football Encyclopedia, *which was published in 1994, Lambeau's 1924 season was the first in which a player surpassed 1,000 yards throwing the ball. The authors attributed 179 passes to Lambeau for 1,094 yards. Goska says that Neft, Cohen, and Korch must have counted "some or all" of his nameless 47 passes in Lambeau's total.*

With its wooden bleachers and board fence, City Stadium was a simple structure that was nonetheless home to history. In 32 seasons there, Green Bay won six league championships and boasted eleven Pro Football Hall of Famers.

contrast to the way the game was played by most other teams in the NFL, who relied on brute force to score points. Pro football was still very much a three-yards-and-a-cloud-of-dust game. Passing was legal, but officially discouraged. The ball, which was fatter and rounder than it is today, had to be thrown from at least five yards behind the line of scrimmage, and at various times during the decade the penalties for incompletions were severe, ranging from five yards to loss of possession—a pass into the end zone that fell incomplete was a turnover. There were no hash marks to guide the restart of play, so the ball was placed at the spot where it had been declared dead, even if that meant it was right up against the sideline. (When the ball went out of bounds, play was restarted 15 yards in from the sideline.) Offenses often avoided running plays that might put the ball near a boundary. In 1924, the year Lambeau threw 136 passes, the Packers ranked second in the league with nine passing touchdowns and rushed for only three scores. The Frankford Yellow

Jackets, on the other hand, ran for an NFL-best 34 touchdowns and threw for only four.

In addition to playing a more wide-open, entertaining style of football, the team from the littlest town in the league was also pretty good. The Packers won 61 of the 99 NFL games they played in the 1920s and were one of the best road draws in the league. Green Bay drew a crowd of 7,000 to Cubs Park in 1921 for its first matchup against the Chicago Bears (then the Staleys) and, in five road games against George Halas's team between 1924 and 1927, never failed to draw fewer than 6,000 spectators—10,000 came out to see the teams play to a 3–3 tie on December 19, 1926. Halas liked the Packers so much as a gate attraction, in fact, that he scheduled three games a year against them — with two home dates — every season from 1928 through 1933, the year the league divided itself into divisions. The games that Green Bay and Chicago played at Wrigley Field in 1928 drew 15,000 and 14,000. The Bears-Cardinals game at Wrigley that year attracted only 10,000. Halas was willing

to endure the Bears' break-even visits to Green Bay because when the Packers came to Chicago, the fans came to Wrigley.

◆ ◆ ◆

In the Packers' early years as a publicly owned franchise, the team received more support from Green Bay's business leaders than from the community as a whole. For the average resident of the city, the annual rivalry tilt between Green Bay East and Green Bay West High Schools was still the biggest game in town. In 1925, the Green Bay derby pulled in a crowd of 7,000, while the Packers' home game against the Bears drew only about 5,400. Two years later, the high schools attracted a crowd of 10,000. The Packers-Bears game, on the other hand, drew only about 5,500. Far from being united behind its NFL team, the city was still defined by the river that divided it. "The East and West personally hated one another," said Ken Kaye, a 1929 graduate of East High, in the 2005 souvenir program for the 100th meeting between the two schools. "Businessmen would almost

have duels. It was really vicious . . . This drifted down from the very civilized upper class to the know-nothings. They all felt the same."

But the Packers were changing that, gradually becoming part of the fabric of the city's everyday life. This happened partly by virtue of the team's survival — every fall meant Packers football. But part of it was the team itself. One way that was evident was in the Packers' new home field: City Stadium.

Construction had begun on a new East High School building in 1923. The site was Hagemeister Park, the original home of the Packers. Lambeau's team had to find a new home. In 1923 and '24, Green Bay played its games at Bellevue Park, a bandbox baseball stadium with a capacity of only about 4,000 people. Built in less than 21 days in the spring of 1923, Bellevue — named for Bellevue Ice Cream and home to a semipro baseball team and the East High football team — was constructed in part out of the stands and bleachers from Hagemeister Park, which had been cut into sections and moved to the new site. "It was not a good football field," wrote George Whitney Calhoun 40 years later. "One of the end zones was about three yards short and the gates at the park were a bit too wide open."

Calhoun would have known something about wide-open gates. The man who had passed the hat at Hagemeister Park for donations during the Packers' first season had become, after Green Bay began charging admission, the guardian of the pass gate, checking for proper press credentials and ensuring that nobody was admitted for free who was not on his list. He was so zealous in his duties, especially in dispensing complimentary tickets to the press, that he became known throughout the NFL as "Gates Ajar" Calhoun.

By the mid-1920s, the man who had co-founded the Packers had aged from the floppy-haired, athletic teenager he'd been at Buffalo's Technical High School into a cigar-smoking, profanity-spewing, finger-typing cynic with a penchant for malapropisms and a taste for Limburger cheese. Calhoun's butchering of the English language around the *Press-Gazette* offices was legendary. Among other things, he referred to Alcoholics Anonymous as "Alcoholics Unanimous" and said that good fortune was "being born under a silver spoon." Former Packers board member John Torinus—who worked for Calhoun during his summers off from Dartmouth in the early 1930s, and then when he started at the *Press-Gazette* in 1934—wrote that the paper had erected a partition in its offices to separate the gruff Calhoun from the rest of the newsroom, and that his workspace had been dubbed "the Black Hole" by the newspaper's staff. Because his arthritis made it difficult for him to get around, Calhoun stayed in the Black Hole most of the time, sending out to a nearby tavern for his lunch, which frequently consisted of a Limburger-on-rye sandwich and a pickle.

"Calhoun's gruff exterior was an attempt on his part to keep people from feeling sorry for him," wrote Torinus, who dedicated his history of the franchise to the man he called his mentor and friend. "He adopted an outer crust of terrible temper to protect what on the inside was a very warm and emotional person. He spoke in streams of profanity, chewed and ate cigars instead of smoking them, and spit the juice into a brass spittoon always handy at his desk."

Evidence of Calhoun's true nature could be found in the way he dealt with the Packers' youngest fans. His normal demeanor with gate crashers was, in the words of Arch Ward, "a beauty to watch." If somebody persisted in trying to bluff their way past him, "Mr. Calhoun [would] read him out of the city with a terse sermon which a night-court magistrate would include in his memoirs." But children were another story, especially after the Packers moved to City Stadium, the place that would be their home field for the next 31 years. At the urging of Mayor Wenzel Wiesner, one of the team's biggest fans, the Green Bay school board built the stadium, located behind the new East High School, for the city's high school teams and allowed the Green Bay Football Corporation to use it on Sundays. When it opened (for an exhibition game against the Iron Mountain All-Stars on September 13, 1925), City Stadium only had seating for about 5,700 in its wooden bleachers, with standing room for around 1,300 more—not counting kids. At the front gate, children accompanied by a parent with a ticket were allowed to walk in free of charge. And kids without an adult to accompany them to the game would gather at the stadium's southeast gate, where players leaving their locker room inside the new East High School would take them by the hand and escort them inside. Children were encouraged to watch games from the grassy area behind the south end zone. It was the continuation of a tradition that had begun in 1921 at Hagemeister Park, where the Packers set aside the grass behind one of the end zones for "the Knothole Gang." It was in this way that Calhoun and Lambeau cultivated a legion of future fans.

The team was becoming a part of the community in other ways too. In 1922, Rigney Dwyer, the end who had been mangled beneath a train car in the Milwaukee Road yard two years earlier, won the election to be Brown County register of deeds. A Democrat, Dwyer would be reelected to the post nine more times, serving in that capacity until his death, in 1944. When he died, he was the longest-tenured elected official in the county. Dwyer wasn't the only Packer elected to public office. In 1928, while still in the prime of his career, Verne Lewellen ran as a Republican for the office of Brown County district attorney. One of his Democratic opponents for that office was teammate Lavvie Dilweg. The six-foot-three, 200-pound end didn't make it out of the primary, but Lewellen secured the Republican nomination and then won the popular vote. On December 2, less than a month after he'd prevailed in the general election, Lewellen played quarterback in place of the injured Red Dunn and guided the Packers to a 7–7 tie with the Providence Steam Roller. In his story on the game, Calhoun wrote, "One of the Providence scribes admitted that if that punting district attorney was as good in the legal game as he was on the gridiron, he should be a world beater even up in Wisconsin."

With the decade drawing to a close, the team from the smallest town in the NFL was making an impression both at home and on the road. When the league downsized from 22 to 12 teams in 1927, it had done so in an attempt to stabilize its finances. The NFL eliminated most of its weaker teams that year and consolidated its best players on its more successful clubs. The hub of the league left the Midwest, where it had started, and centered itself in the large cities of the East. Gone were many of the small-town teams that had defined most of the NFL's first decade, including the Canton Bulldogs, Hammond Pros, and Dayton Triangles. Gone, too, were some of the teams from bigger towns that just hadn't been earning enough money, including the Detroit Panthers, Los Angeles Buccaneers, and Milwaukee Badgers.

The Packers were surviving, and in some ways actually thriving by the end of the 1920s. League president Joe Carr himself had called Green Bay "the best football town of its size in the country." But the best was yet to come. Just around the corner was glory beyond even Lambeau's wildest dreams.

A FIRST DRAFT OF HISTORY

BY

DAVID S. NEFT

**Producing the first extensive en-
cyclopedia of pro football was a
breeze compared with compiling
the first edition of *The Baseball Encyclopedia*.** When I started my research into Major League Baseball,
in 1965, the history of the game
stretched back almost 90 years, to
1876, and there were around 5,000
players (out of more than 11,000
altogether) for whom statistical profiles had to be painstak-
ingly re-created. Added to that was
the fact that teams played several games every week. I had 32
researchers working for me, and
I sent them all across the United
States in search of records and
documentation, visiting librar-
ies and graveyards in every corner of the country and reading as
many newspaper accounts of every game as they could find. When
they brought their information
back to me in New York, we entered the data on computer punch
cards that we then fed into an
IBM System/360 mainframe computer, a very large machine that
was slower — and had less capacity — than most of today's desk-
top computers. The history of pro

football that I edited in 1974, on
the other hand, went back to only
1920, the first season of the American Professional Football Association, which two years later would
rename itself the National Football
League. Teams played, for the most
part, just once a week, and there
were only about 2,000 men (out of
around 9,000 total) for whom we
had to compile statistical profiles.
My research staff shrank to five, including me.

The book that resulted from our
work was *The Sports Encyclopedia:
Pro Football*. It was just 496 pages,
whereas *The Baseball Encyclopedia* was 2,337.

So less work, but no less pains-
taking. The process was much the
same: visiting small towns and
mining local newspapers for detail
and fact. Pro football in the early
years was struggling for public attention with the college game, and
the quality of the coverage of the
sport varied widely, even among
the more heralded publications in
New York and Chicago. But we did
find a few standouts — and in some
unlikely places. *The Rock Island Argus,* which covered the Indepen-

dents in Rock Island, Illinois, was
very good. The daily newspaper in
Canton, Ohio, *The Repository,* was,
as you might expect, pretty reliable. The *Staten Island Advance*
was very good when the Stapletons were in the league. And a now
defunct broadsheet in Philadelphia,
the *Public Ledger,* which wasn't
even the number-three paper in the
city, was quite thorough in its coverage of the Frankford Yellow Jackets. Outside of those four newspapers, details could be pretty thin.

But there was one extraordinary
exception. In the early days of the
NFL, the pro football coverage in
the *Green Bay Press-Gazette* was
far and away the best in any paper
in the country. The sheer amount of
it was what was immediately impressive. The *Press-Gazette* basically wrote about the Packers every
day from September through December, announcing player signings, giving updates on practice, reporting on out-of-town news about
upcoming opponents, and publishing play-by-plays for almost every
game that Green Bay played. For
every angle on the team, the paper
gave readers a superabundance of

information. And what became obvious to us as we did our research was that it also cared about getting its stories right. That was a wonderful combination: the quantity of the coverage and the quality of it. The *Press-Gazette* really set the standard for how to cover a pro football team. The things that we take for granted today — everything from transaction reports to game stories — the Packers' hometown paper was producing in voluminous detail in the early 1920s.

The man most responsible for this was George Whitney Calhoun, who co-founded the Packers along with Curly Lambeau in 1919. Over the next 28 years, Calhoun was, at various times, the team's manager, press agent, and first beat writer. He was even briefly a co-owner for a season, in 1922, before Green Bay became a publicly funded corporation. Being the public relations director of an NFL team and an editor at the paper that covered the team amounted to a totally unique

circumstance in the history of pro football. In keeping one foot firmly planted in both worlds for nearly three decades, Calhoun was an embodiment of the relationship between the team and the town, of the civic nature of being a fan of the Packers.

To give just one example of what I'm talking about, I like to go back to my days at Gannett, when I was in charge of market research for some 80 to 100 papers, one of which was the *Press-Gazette.* Green

George Whitney Calhoun (center, in tam) is honored at halftime of the final game at old City Stadium, on November 18, 1956.

Bay in the 1970s, '80s, and '90s was like a lot of other football markets in the United States, where 80 percent or more of the men were interested in reading about the home team. But in Green Bay, more than 80 percent of the women were also interested in reading about the team. No other market in the country was even within hailing distance of that. The people and the Packers are profoundly intertwined.

Calhoun, a great-grandson of the founder of Green Bay, was a classic newspaperman, hard-bitten and cynical. But he was also a remarkably sentimental keeper of the Packers' legacy. In addition to the copy he contributed to the newspaper, he was the primary writer of *The Dope Sheet,* the team's first official newsletter. And he saved everything. He clipped articles about the Packers out of the *Press-Ga-*

zette (many of which he had authored himself) and pasted them into notebooks — every daily news item, every game story — which he then tucked away at his home or in his office. He did the same with *The Dope Sheet.* The history of sports encyclopedias in the United States started in 1922, when Ernie Lanigan published the *Baseball Cyclopedia,* and took a leap forward in 1951, when Hy Turkin and S. C.

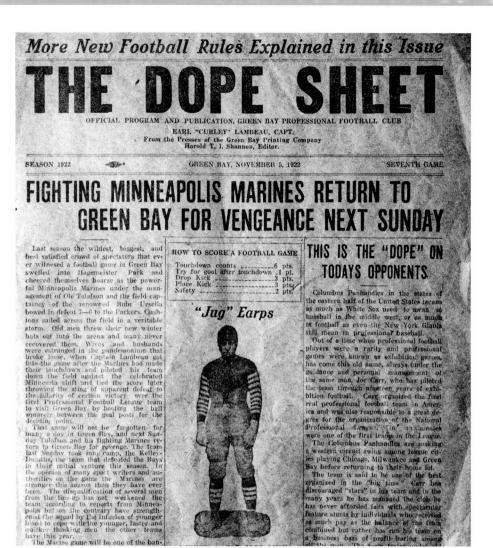

Thompson came out with *The Official Encyclopedia of Baseball.* One year later, Roger Treat published *The Encyclopedia of Football.* Treat used a lot of Calhoun's stuff, and his book was the foundation that I built on when I was writing *The Sports Encyclopedia: Pro Football.* Because of Treat, I knew about Calhoun when I started. But I didn't know how much of the record Calhoun actually kept, or how much was still lying around the offices of the *Press-Gazette* even years after he had passed. That was amazing. On one of my visits to Green Bay for Gannett in the 1980s, I saved a couple of boxes of his scrapbooks from being thrown out by taking them home with me.

You have to remember that nobody in Calhoun's day really saw *The Baseball Encyclopedia* coming. For most of the 20th century, books and newspapers were printed using manual type or linotype machines, both of which were cumbersome and labor-intensive. There's a reason Turkin and Thompson's *Official Encyclopedia of Baseball* listed only a few statistics per player. *The Baseball Encyclopedia* listed 17 stats for batters and 19 for pitchers. And it was 2,337 pages long.

It just couldn't have been done if we'd had to typeset and proofread everything. It had to be done electronically, with a computer. Electronic printing was what made it possible for so many good sports encyclopedias to come out in the late 20th century. But Calhoun didn't know that. He was preserving the record in the best — and only — way he knew how. And every NFL fan owes him a huge debt.

Calhoun lived the history of pro football, and he preserved it for future generations. Every time you hear about a player breaking an

NFL record, remember that a small piece of that record probably belongs to George Whitney Calhoun. In preserving the legacy for a team, he also left a pretty huge one for himself.

CHAPTER 6

CHAMPIONS

Every journey has a starting point, and Green Bay's journey to Titletown, USA, began on a muggy afternoon in late July 1929. Over five weeks that summer, Curly Lambeau forever changed the trajectory of the Green Bay Packers. Up to that point, the team had been good but not great, compiling a winning record every season it had been in the NFL and finishing as high as second (in a 12-team league in 1927) and never worse than ninth (of 22 teams in 1925). But beginning in 1929, the Packers became synonymous with championship football. The glory began here.

Green Bay had gone 6-4-3 in 1928, and while the team was inconsistent — starting 0-2-1, and then winning five of six games before losing two of its last four — there had been several hopeful signs. In Providence on December 2, the Packers tied the eventual NFL champion Steam Roller 7–7. The next week, Green Bay ended the season by beating the Bears 6–0 at sunny Wrigley Field, the Packers' second road win of the year over Chicago. The team's performance convinced Lambeau that, with the addition of a few more good players, Green Bay could break into the NFL's elite. It was shortly after season's end that Lambeau, according to Arch Ward, met with the franchise's board of directors to secure permission to pursue top-tier talent.

"Capt. Lambeau already has started negotiations for a few new men to add to his roster," wrote Arthur W. Bystrom in the *Press-Gazette* on December 18. "He will keep the nucleus of this year's squad and with just a few additional players expects to wield a team that will have little if any weakness."

On July 31, 1929, the *Press-Gazette* announced that Lambeau had landed his first big fish, purchasing tackle Cal Hubbard outright from the New York Giants. The paper described the six-foot-two, 253-pound Hubbard — who was listed in various places at anywhere from six foot two to six foot six, and from 238 to 280 pounds — as a "man-mountain." More important than his size, though, was the fact that Hubbard was one of the finest players of his era. He was so athletic that he could play either end or tackle on defense. He was also one of the first defensive linemen to stand just off the line of scrimmage, almost like a linebacker. In the Giants' 6–0 win over the Packers at City Stadium on October 7, 1928, Hubbard had played end on both offense and defense, and had also occasionally dropped into the defensive secondary. "The big end . . . was in every play," the *Press-*

Gazette noted the next day, "always plugging up holes in the Giant line."

Hubbard was also one of the most intimidating players in the NFL. "You see those two holes over the ears in the helmet?" Hubbard once asked a young teammate. "Well, they're not to hear through. They're for you to stick your fingers in . . . and jerk his face down when you raise your knee up."

Born on a farm in north-central Missouri, Hubbard weighed nearly 200 pounds by the time he was 14. He went to high school in the town of Glasgow and played football there in 1916, but then transferred to the high school in nearby Keytesville, which did not have a team. Hubbard quit Keytesville in March 1919 without graduating. He attempted to enlist in the Army that spring, but the military rejected him because of a foot problem.

In the fall he entered the now defunct Chillicothe Business College, a school close to home where he could continue to play football while also working on his family's farm. He was at a track meet at the University of Missouri in the spring of 1922 when he met Bo McMillin, the coach of the team from tiny Centre College, of Danville, Kentucky. Six months earlier, McMillin had quarterbacked the Praying Colonels to a 6–0 defeat of powerful Harvard, an upset that electrified college football. By the time he met Hubbard, McMillin had already been hired to be the new football coach at Centenary College, in Shreveport, Louisiana. A few months later, Hubbard followed McMillin down to Centenary.

Hubbard was fast enough to return kicks and play end on offense, and in the first game of his college career he brought a kickoff back 65 yards

Cal Hubbard was fast enough to play end for the Giants as a rookie in 1927. But Lambeau made him a tackle after the Packers acquired him in 1929, and Hubbard became one of the most feared linemen in pro football.

Hubbard signed with the New York Giants in 1927 for $150 a game. With the rookie leading the charge, the New York defense surrendered only 20 points the entire season as the Giants went 11-1-1 and won their first championship. Hubbard played all but two minutes of the season, leaving late in the fourth quarter of a 28–7 victory over the Chicago Cardinals on November 20 because of a cracked bone in his foot. He nevertheless played the next week when New York clinched the title at the Polo Grounds with a 13–7 win over the Bears. "It was the toughest, most vicious game I ever was in," Hubbard said of the Bears game years later. "I never saw so many beat-up guys in my life."

Scheduling was still very much an ad hoc affair, often contingent on whether home teams were capable of matching the guarantees demanded by visitors. The Giants, who had been founded in 1925, did not travel to northeastern Wisconsin for the first time until October 7, 1928, when Hubbard starred for them in their 6–0 victory over the Packers. New York had arrived in town the Saturday before the game and, as was typical for teams visiting wide-open Green Bay, stayed there for a full week before departing for Chicago on October 13 for their game the next day against the Bears. The seven days in Green Bay made an impression on Hubbard. "A small-town boy himself, he liked the placid, friendly surroundings," sportswriter Arthur Daley wrote in his 1963 book *Pro Football's Hall of Fame,* which was published in conjunction with the Hall's announcement of its first class of 17 honorees. "It was so different from the hurly-burly of New York. Green Bay was the place for him."

After the season, Hubbard delivered an ultimatum to the Giants: "Trade me to Green Bay or I quit." Before winter turned to spring, Lambeau had reached out to Hubbard—and to a few other players, as well.

Four weeks after the Packers had acquired Hubbard, the *Press-Gazette* announced their signing of Pottsville Maroons halfback Johnny Blood.

down the left sideline for a touchdown, bowling over several tacklers on his way to the end zone. He played three years in Shreveport, until January 1925, when McMillin accepted the coaching job at Geneva College, in Beaver Falls, Pennsylvania. Hubbard again followed McMillin, despite the fact that he was a senior and transferring meant that he would have to sit out the 1925 season. He was on the field for Geneva the next fall, though, when the Covenanters beat Harvard in Cambridge, 16–7. One of Geneva's most effective plays that day was quarterback Leland Schachern running behind Hubbard around right end. "Look, little boy," Hubbard reportedly told Schachern, "just get the ball and follow me."

Lambeau knew Blood fairly well. The six-foot-two, 195-pound veteran was a dynamic runner and receiver. In the Maroons' 26–0 victory over Green Bay in Pottsville on November 25, 1928, he had returned an interception 35 yards for a touchdown. According to the paper, at the time he signed with Lambeau, Blood had been "reading law" in his hometown of New Richmond, Wisconsin. He had since moved to Green Bay, "to get the lay of the land," and was working on a road-building crew with the Schuster Construction Company "to put him in shape." Blood would later say that he had made the trip to Green Bay by hopping two trains, traveling part of the way in a Soo Line boxcar. The oft-repeated story earned him the nickname "the Vagabond Halfback."

The picaresque details surrounding Blood's signing were a harbinger of what was to come. He had been playing in the NFL for four years by that time, but his signing with the Packers marked the true beginning of one of the more unique careers in NFL history—one marked on the field by brilliance, and off the field by equal parts quirky roguishness and infuriating dissipation, as well as pure bunkum. The parallels are not exact, but nearly 40 years before "Broadway" Joe Namath made headlines in New York for his exploits on Saturday nights and Sunday afternoons, Johnny Blood was doing the same in Green Bay.

Blood was born John Victor McNally Jr. on November 27, 1903, one of six children of the general manager of the New Richmond Roller Mills Company. The McNally family was one of the most prominent in St. Croix County, composed of bankers, lawyers, newspaper publishers, and paper-mill owners. John was a precocious youth. He graduated from New Richmond High when he was just 14, too scrawny and young to have ever participated in sports. Instead of going to work or to college, he spent the next two years living at home, where, as he told *Sports Illustrated* in 1963, he "read a good deal" and "learned to type and studied commercial subjects." In *Pro Football's Hall of Fame,* Daley says that McNally "took a whirl" at the River Falls Normal School, a teachers college that today is known as the University of Wisconsin–River Falls. The school has no record of a John V. McNally ever attending or graduating, but a John McNally, a junior studying math and science, did turn up in a student directory in the fall of 1919. (McNally's transcripts from Minnesota, where he attended summer school in 1922 and '23, indicate that he did indeed attend River Falls.)

Around the time McNally was 15 or 16, his father, John Victor McNally Sr., left for a trip to California, and Daley says that young John used John Sr.'s checkbook to pay for several escapades, which according to legend included a failed attempt to enlist in the Navy and a spell working on a farm in North Dakota. John Sr. returned to River Falls sometime before the summer of 1921, when he died under unusual circumstances. On August 23, he drove his family to the trolley station in Stillwater, Minnesota, 20 miles west of New Richmond. But instead of returning home, he disappeared. Police began searching for him not long after he failed to show up at his office for a business meeting. The only things they found, though, were his car and his cap, which were by the side of the road near Apple River Falls, in Somerset, Wisconsin. Two days after McNally disappeared, his body was found floating in the water near a dam on the same river.

The death was ruled an accident—the official story was that McNally had been trying to take pictures when he lost his footing and fell into the water. But more than 50 years later, John McNally Jr. acknowledged that his father's death had been a suicide. The elder McNally had always been a boisterous and athletic man. Along with his three brothers, he had played on the town baseball team in River Falls, and he was an avid fan of boxer John L. Sullivan. But he was also, apparently, very unhappy. According to an account of the search for McNally in *The Eau Claire Leader,* he had previously suffered a nervous breakdown, and had only recently begun to resume some of his duties at the mill. "He simply didn't know how to cope with depression," his son told biographer Ralph Hickok years later. "He couldn't understand what was happening to him."

A year before his father's suicide, when John Jr. was not yet 17, he had enrolled at Saint John's University, in Minnesota. And it was at the tiny Benedictine school that his athletic career began in earnest. He shot up to six-one and 190 pounds and cut a slender, dashingly handsome figure on campus, where he was famous for his combination of sleek athleticism and erudite polymathy. McNally wrote poetry and was recognized by his classmates for his skills as an orator. He was also a regular in school productions. In 1923, his last year at Saint John's, he edited the Saint John's annual, *Sagatagan,* and wrote for the student newspaper, *The Record.* In a 1923 essay for the paper titled "Strength of Character," he wrote prophetically, "Great characters have by the very gift of greatness the power of much evil or of much good."

McNally also—despite having arrived at Saint John's, according to *The Record,* "entirely unacquainted with athletics"—became the first student in the history of the school to letter in four sports: football, basketball, baseball, and track. For this distinction the school's "moderator" of athletics presented him in June 1923 with a silver loving cup. "[Father Albert] felicited him for being not only an all-around athlete, but also an all-around student, a star in the classroom as well as on the campus," read an account of the ceremony in *The Record.* McNally was an outfielder on the baseball team and a guard on the basketball team. In track he was a hurdler, a sprinter, a middle-distance runner, a jumper, and a discus thrower. And on the football field he played halfback and quarterback. He did it all, and he did it well. His middle initial, noted the school newspaper, "stands for versatile."

McNally left Saint John's in the spring of 1923 and completed two semesters of summer school at

Minnesota before entering Notre Dame on September 12. He was a day student in South Bend, meaning that he lived off-campus. McNally told writers years later that he had gone out for the freshman team but quit after coach George Keogan insisted that he play tackle instead of quarterback or halfback. McNally's name, though, does not appear among the football team's "Freshman Numeral Men" listed in Notre Dame's 1924 yearbook, and he was a senior academically—though still only 19 years old. The school has no records of his academic performance. On that count there is only one anecdote, and it comes from McNally himself. He said that he was the ghostwriter for Fighting Irish quarterback Harry Stuhldreher in a poetry class that the two took together.

According to Daley, McNally went AWOL from Notre Dame on March 17 to celebrate St. Patrick's Day, and he was subsequently suspended by the school's disciplinary board for 60 days. According to McNally, though, the suspension was for having been part of a group of revelers that tipped over a streetcar. Notre Dame policy does not allow for the release of his disciplinary records until 2035, but the school's archives do confirm that he left Notre Dame for good on March 18, 1924.

McNally told *Sports Illustrated* in 1963 that he then bought a motorcycle and set out for New York to see his sister. On the return trip, the bike broke down in Amherst Junction, Wisconsin, and he rode the rest of the way to New Richmond on a freight train. "I rode the blinds," he said. "Older hoboes will remember the blinds as the space between the coal tender and the baggage car." He then went to work—along with Ralph Hanson, a friend from Saint John's—as a stereotyper at *The Minneapolis Morning Tribune,* where McNally's uncle, W. J. Murphy, had been the publisher until his death, in 1918, and in which his family maintained a controlling interest. At some point in the fall of 1924, according to McNally, he and Hanson (who hadn't played football at Saint John's) went together to a tryout for a semipro football team

called the East 26th Street Liberties. Since McNally still had college eligibility remaining, the two decided to try out under aliases. On their way to the workout, they passed a movie theater with a marquee touting the Rudolph Valentino film then showing: RUDOLPH VALENTINO STAR OF BLOOD AND SAND IN MONSIEUR BEAUCAIRE. "I'll be Blood and you be Sand," McNally told Hanson.

From that day forward, McNally played professional football only under the surname Blood — though he went by Melvin Blood that first season. (There is no record of Ralph Hanson playing for the Liberties in 1924 and, more important, no rec-

ord of anybody named Sand.) McNally played for $6 a game for the Liberties. In 1925 he played for two teams, earning $60 a game for the Ironwood Miners on the Upper Peninsula of Michigan — where he played for less than a month — and for $75 a game for the Milwaukee Badgers of the NFL. Milwaukee was terrible that season, going winless in six games and scoring only seven points.

In 1926, Blood moved on to a better team, signing with the NFL's Duluth Eskimos, who had played in the league from 1923 to '25 as the Duluth Kelleys. The Eskimos' star player in 1926 was rookie fullback Ernie Nevers, an All-America from

Stanford, where he had played for legendary coach Pop Warner. Nevers, an excellent all-around athlete with blond hair and a square jaw, was a multisport wonder, having also signed pro basketball and baseball contracts—he had actually appeared in 11 games that summer as a pitcher for the St. Louis Browns, going 2-4 with a 4.46 earned run average—but football was where he was destined to make his mark. Warner, who had become famous at Carlisle nearly two decades before, when Jim Thorpe was the biggest star in college football, called Nevers the greatest player he had ever coached. The speedy Nevers was big for his day, standing six feet tall and weighing more than 200 pounds, and was a talented kicker, passer, and runner. He was so famous that, when the NFL announced in July 1926 that Duluth had signed him, the league also announced that the team's nickname was going to be changed to the Nevers. He reportedly made $15,000 plus a percentage of gate proceeds that fall.

Duluth was a traveling team. The Eskimos played 14 NFL games in 1926 (going 6-5-3) but played 29 altogether, all but one of them on the road. Nevers, according to legend, played 1,711 out of 1,740 minutes that season. Blood—who appeared as both Bill and, for the first time, John, in news stories—was part of the Eskimos' backfield rotation and sometimes backed Nevers up at fullback. Duluth continued its road show in 1927 but won only one of nine NFL games, and after the season Blood moved on to Pottsville. In 22 league games with the Eskimos, he had scored only three touchdowns (one rushing, two receiving), but he scored that many in 10 games with the Maroons in 1928, including two in their snowy 26–0 victory over the Packers in Pottsville on November 25. Blood's performance obviously made an impression on Lambeau, who went after him in the off-season. When the Green Bay coach was negotiating Blood's contract, the back asked for $100 a game. Lambeau, aware of Blood's carousing reputation, countered with an offer of $110, on the

condition that Blood stop drinking on Tuesday each week during the season. Blood stuck to his original demand for $100 if he was allowed to drink through Wednesday. Lambeau agreed.

One week after Blood signed with Green Bay, Lambeau landed the final catch of his epic off-season. On September 4, the *Press-Gazette* announced the Packers' acquisition of August "Mike" Michalske, a guard who had been playing for the New York Yankees, first in the American Football League and then in the NFL. Michalske had played for three years at Penn State, seeing time at both guard and fullback. According to the Pro Football Hall of Fame, he was an All-America for the Nittany Lions in 1925, but the school does not count him among its all-time All-America players. He signed with the Yankees in 1926 and stayed with the team when it moved to the NFL after the AFL folded. Michalske was no stranger to the Packers, having played road games in Green Bay in 1927 and '28. When his signing was announced, the paper called him "the best guard in the National Football league."

The son of German immigrants, Michalske stood out on the field not because of his size—at six feet and 210 pounds, he wasn't much bigger than Blood—but because of his speed and intelligence. He'd been fast enough to play fullback in college, and he used his fleetness of foot to his advantage on both offense, where he would pull from the line as the lead blocker on running plays, and defense, where, instead of trying to beat bigger players head-on, he took angles to break into the backfield and pursue the ball along the line of scrimmage. He was also intense. Blood described him as a "holler guy." And in the days of iron-man football, Michalske was revered by his peers for his durability. His nickname, Iron Mike, wasn't so much a testament to his status as a 60-minute man but to the fact that he almost never missed a game. He had been absent from only one contest in his first two years in the league, and had started 25 of the 27 in which he played. "I just didn't get hurt," he said years later. "The players used to say I must have been getting paid by the minute."

There is no greater testament to the eye for talent possessed by Curly Lambeau than his acquisitions of Hubbard, Blood, and Michalske in the summer of 1929. In Blood he'd picked up an excellent runner and a supremely talented receiver, who would soon become the first big-play threat in the history of pro football. And in Hubbard and Michalske the coach had found two anchors for his offensive and defensive lines, one capable of dominating a game with his brawn and brute strength, the other with his brains and bravado. All four men are now in the Pro Football Hall of Fame. Blood, Hubbard, and Lambeau were in the Hall's first class of inductees, in 1963; Michalske joined them one year later. The Packers' off-season haul of 1929 stands as the single greatest in NFL history. It made Green Bay not only the launching point for three of the greatest careers in the early years of the game but also, in relatively short order, the epicenter of the NFL.

That's the sort of thing that's easy to say in retrospect, but there was more than an inkling in Green Bay in the fall of 1929 that big things might be in store. On August 1, the day after the Packers had signed Hubbard, Dr. W. W. Kelly, one of Arch Ward's Hungry Five, replaced former Brown County district attorney Ray Evrard as the team's president. "We have gone out and purchased several players to strengthen the club," Kelly said upon his election. "This has been an added expense but we feel confident that the fans will show their approval by the way they support the team financially and every other way."

An editorial in the *Press-Gazette* a few days later made the case for the team. "Football and the Packer team have been a large part of our community life," the paper said. "They afford the best public entertainment that can be provided, and they are a fine civic and business asset. Let us get back of the team this year as never before."

The people of Green Bay were ready to do just that. A little more than a month later, at 1:30 p.m. on September 8, the Packers held their first practice of the new season at Joannes Park, across Walnut Street from the new Green Bay East High School. Lambeau put his men through a three-hour workout in the blazing Sunday afternoon sunshine before a crowd of 2,000. Expectations were high.

◆ ◆ ◆

Tim Mara was a gambler, and lucky for the NFL that he was. The son of Irish immigrants, Mara had been just a boy when he went to work selling newspapers and ushering at a local theater near his home on Manhattan's Lower East Side. His jobs kept him so busy that he quit school after he turned 13. While delivering newspapers, he made friends with several prominent bookmakers — taking bets was a legitimate profession in those days — and he soon began working for them as a runner, collecting debts and delivering winnings. By the time he was 18, Mara was running his own book, and in 1921 he opened a betting operation at Belmont Park, setting odds and taking wagers on the races. Tall and ruddy, he was known for his honesty and good nature, and for the way he would winkingly taunt prospective bettors, saying such things as "If that animal wins, I'll give you my watch." Mara was popular and well connected, and he hobnobbed with Governor Al Smith and Mayor Jimmy Walker.

In 1925, Mara was interested in purchasing part of the contract of boxer Gene Tunney, who the next year would defeat Jack Dempsey for the world's heavyweight championship. At a meeting with Tunney's manager, former New York City restaurateur Billy Gibson, Mara was introduced to NFL president Joe Carr and Ohio football promoter Dr. Harry March. Both men were trying to convince Gibson to invest in a pro team in the nation's largest city. Carr was convinced that the NFL would remain small-time unless it established itself in New York. Gibson was hesitant, but he suggested to Carr and March that Mara might be interested.

The cost was only $500. Mara didn't know a goal-post from a lamppost, but he was a shrewd tout, and the buy-in was low enough to make a wager on the NFL an enticing proposition. "The Giants were founded on a combination of brute strength and ignorance," he liked to say. "The players supplied the brute strength. I supplied the ignorance."

At first his bet seemed like a loser. Mara named his new franchise the New York Giants and made Gibson the team's president and March its secretary and treasurer. After laying out the money to hire players and a coach and to rent out the Polo Grounds, the Giants began the season $25,000 in the red—and things went downhill from there. For publicity, New York signed 37-year-old Jim

Thorpe to one of the most unusual contracts in NFL history, agreeing to pay him and his gimpy left knee $200 per half game, while not playing him more than 30 minutes a game until later in the season. But Thorpe lasted only three games before injury and exhaustion ended his Giants career. By early December, Mara's team was more than $45,000 underwater. The attendance numbers were not atrocious, but many who came out to New York's home games that season were there on complimentary tickets, which Mara was giving away as a marketing ploy. When he was urged to sell the team and cut his losses, Mara responded, "Where could I find anyone crazy enough to buy it?" The Giants were a financial lemon. But then

Giants' owner Tim Mara (in hat, with former heavyweight champ Jack Dempsey in 1933) was well known in New York as a bookmaker when he spent $500 in 1925 to put an NFL team in the Polo Grounds.

Red Grange and the Chicago Bears came to town.

The impact that Harold "Red" Grange had on professional football in the 1920s has been somewhat oversold. The popular version of the story is that his decision to play for the Bears saved the NFL and started it on a path to becoming the dominant sports league in the United States. But, as was pointed out in *The Pro Football Chronicle,* the well-researched history of the game written by Dan Daly and Bob O'Donnell, the legacy of the red-haired kid from Wheaton, Illinois, is not quite so grand. "At best," they write, "the pro game might have been nudged ahead half a decade because 'The Galloping Ghost' joined up." Daly and O'Donnell quote no less an authority on the matter than George Halas, Grange's coach in Chicago—and one of the founding fathers of the NFL. "We had been doing well in professional football and making money for several seasons," Halas said. "We were gaining ground steadily but slowly."

But it is no exaggeration to describe Grange as one of the greatest gate attractions of the 1920s. The only sports figures who outshone him during the Golden Age were Babe Ruth and Jack Dempsey —and perhaps also Man o' War. "The Galloping Ghost" had been an All-America as a sophomore at Illinois in 1923, but he shot to stardom as a junior when he scored four touchdowns (on runs of 95, 67, 56, and 45 yards) in the first 12 minutes of a 39–14 upset of a powerful Michigan team that was riding a 20-game unbeaten streak. University of Chicago coach Amos Alonzo Stagg called it "the most spectacular single-handed performance ever made in a major game." In Grange's 20-game college career, he scored 31 touchdowns. His last game with Illinois, a 14–9 victory over Ohio State in Columbus on November 21, 1925, drew 84,295 fans, at that point the largest crowd in college football history.[*]

And then, assisted by his agent, C. C. "Cash and Carry" Pyle, Grange abruptly turned pro, signing with Halas and the Bears two days later. Three days after that, Grange played in his first professional game, a scoreless tie with the Chicago Cardinals at Cubs Park on Thanksgiving Day. Thus began a barnstorming schedule of 10 games in 17 days. Grange had agreed to appear in every contest, for which he received a 50-50 split of the gate, with Pyle then taking home 40 percent of Grange's share. The 20,000 tickets printed for the Bears-Cardinals game sold out in three hours, and the official attendance on that snowy Thanksgiving was 36,000—the highest in the history of the league. According to legend, Halas was weeping as he counted the gate receipts. When the tour stopped in Philadelphia on December 5 for a Saturday game at Shibe Park against the Frankford Yellow Jackets, 36,000 showed up to see Grange play in a downpour. In the words of *Sports Illustrated*'s John Underwood, "Grange was an event, a happening so stupendous that the curiosity to see him seemed insatiable."

An appearance by Grange was indeed a happening, and his arrival in Gotham was a godsend for Tim Mara. On Sunday, December 6, with the Bears wearing the same muddy jerseys they had worn in Philadelphia the day before, 73,651 fans turned out to see him play at the Polo Grounds—and got their money's worth. Grange returned an interception 30 yards for a touchdown as Chicago beat the Giants 19–7. More than 125 reporters covered the game, and the *New York World* positively gushed about the exhibition. "The game was fast and beautifully open," the paper said. "The widening out of the game by virtue of the forward pass has put football in the class of fine spectacles so it can be professionalized for profit. Grange was the drawing card, but the game itself was the hold-

Red Grange (right) and Chicago Bears player-coach George Halas (18) watch from the bench at Cubs Park on November 26, 1925, during Grange's professional debut.

There may have been more fans at the Cal-Stanford game in Berkeley in 1924, but there's no way to be sure. The capacity of California Memorial Stadium at the time was, according to Cal, about 80,000, but thousands more watched from the grass on Tightwad Hill, above the eastern stands. The total number of people who watched the Cardinal rally from 14 points down to tie the Bears 20–20 may have been upwards of 90,000.

ing card." The most important takeaway from the game, though, was the $130,000 gate, which saved the Giants. "My worries," Mara said, "are over."

Rescued from financial ruin, New York became the NFL's marquee franchise. With Cal Hubbard leading the charge for the Giants' defense, they had won an NFL title in 1927. A down season in 1928 left Mara $40,000 in the red, but he nevertheless went all out to put New York back on top. He released or traded 18 veterans and fired his coach. He then purchased the Detroit Wolverines for $10,000, acquiring several of their players as well as the team's promoter and coach, Leroy Andrews, whom Mara installed as the new coach of the Giants. The key to the deal was Wolverines tailback Benny Friedman. At only five foot ten and 180 pounds, he was on the small side even in his day, but the two-time All-America from Michigan was a deadly accurate passer who had thrown for nine touchdowns in 1928. With his good looks and outsized personality — as well as a trademark follow-through that made him appear at times to be pitching in the major leagues — Friedman was a star. He was also Jewish, which can't have hurt him as a box office draw in a city where the Jewish population was nearly two million.

In 1929, after a scoreless tie with the Orange Tornadoes on opening day, Friedman and the Giants reeled off eight straight victories, outscoring their opponents 204–29. They seemed well on their way to winning a second NFL championship. A game against the Packers at the Polo Grounds on November 24 was the only thing standing in their way. Curly Lambeau's team was undefeated, too. The NFL crown was still decided by the standings in 1929, so the showdown between Green Bay and New York was that year's championship contest in all but name.

◆ ◆ ◆

In 1929, Curly Lambeau was the Packers' only true full-time employee. His title was coach, but he was in effect the captain, coach, general manager, and front office, with nobody to answer to but himself.

The team had no ticket office, no official publicity department (though, in his unofficial capacity as press agent, George Whitney Calhoun was the best PR man in the game), and nobody else but Lambeau to send out on the road in search of new talent. At the age of 31, Curly Lambeau *was* the Green Bay Packers. But, like every one of his players, he also had a second job. The meatpacking plant had shuttered for good in 1927, but it had ceased to be any sort of profitable business five years before that. For most of the 1920s, Lambeau worked as a salesman at a men's clothing store called Stiefel's. It was a fitting sidelight, because a salesman is what Lambeau truly was. For most of the decade he had been convincing men to come to the smallest city in the NFL to play football for a franchise that, in its early days, had been just barely scraping by — and, even after it had gained a measure of financial stability, still struggled to attract fans at home. The Packers finished the 1928 season on a five-game road trip and were scheduled to play their last *eight* games of the 1929 season away from home.

The fall of 1929 was when Lambeau finally made the transition from being a player-coach to being just a coach. In 1928 he had played in eight of 13 games, the first time he had not played in 10 or more since 1921 and 1922, when the team had played just six and 10 games, respectively. In 1929, Lambeau played in just one game, appearing in a 12–0 victory over the Chicago Cardinals at Comiskey Park on November 17. Green Bay's backfield rotation was shorthanded that day — quarterback Red Dunn and halfback Eddie Kotal had both suffered shoulder injuries in a 14–0 defeat of the Bears the week before. Lambeau had come in as a substitute in the first half against the Cardinals but had been forced out of the game in the third quarter when he cracked several ribs while trying to throw a block. It was his final appearance as a professional football player.

Lambeau's sideline legacy is perhaps the most unique of any man who ever led a team to mul-

Led by quarterback Benny Friedman, who threw for 20 touchdowns, the 1929 New York Giants had the most prolific offense in football. They entered their game against the Packers having outscored their opponents 204–29.

tiple NFL titles. He was a pioneer of the forward pass—liable, as he often said, to attempt one at any moment from anywhere on the field. More than anybody else, he led the way in making the passing game the calling card of professional football. But there are not any passing-game concepts or strategies that bear his imprimatur. And while he was a coach of coaches, the Lambeau coaching tree is not a conventional one—at least as coaching trees are thought of in 2019. Mike Holmgren's first coaching staff in Green Bay, in 1992, produced five future NFL head coaches: Jon Gruden, Dick Jauron, Steve Mariucci, Andy Reid, and Ray Rhodes. Curly Lambeau never had a staff like that, though, to be fair, neither did anybody else in the

NFL in those days. The rise of the coaching staff in pro football did not begin until after World War II, when the NFL relaxed its substitution rules and football became more specialized. For more than a decade, Lambeau was the only formal coach the Packers had. According to the team's media guide, only nine men worked for him as assistant coaches in 29 NFL seasons, and the first, former Packers halfback Red Smith, didn't arrive until 1935. Only two men who coached under Lambeau in Green Bay ever went on to become professional head coaches, and neither of them won a championship.

Lambeau's assistants in the early days came from the ranks of his players. Cub Buck helped coach the line while he was playing in Green Bay, and so did Mike Michalske. Buck went on to coach at Miami (Florida) in 1927 and '28, while Michalske coached at Iowa State in the 1940s. Former fullback Rex Enright coached football and basketball at South Carolina, where he was also the athletic director. Johnny Blood coached the Pittsburgh Pirates (forerunners of the Steelers) in the late 1930s and later in life returned to coach at Saint John's, his alma mater. The list goes on and on. The men who played for Lambeau are the ones who make up his coaching tree.

And Lambeau depended on his player-coaches as completely as a modern NFL coach depends on his offensive and defensive coordinators. His sideline demeanor was fiery and demonstrative — and not always helpful. "He was a very fine coach, I think, during the week," said Charley Brock, who played center for the Packers and Lambeau from 1939 to '47. "But on Sunday you could just as well forget he was there because he absolutely was just . . . he didn't know what was happening." Hubbard concurred. As he told author Ralph Hickok in *Vagabond Halfback*:

> To be frank, Curly really didn't know all that much about football. After all, he spent just that one year at Notre Dame — how much did he learn? Most of us knew more because we spent more time learning, four years of college and then, for most of us, some professional experience too. Why, sometimes Curly would design a new play, draw it up on the blackboard, and we just knew it wouldn't work the way he drew it. He'd have impossible blocking assignments, or the play would just take too long to develop, the defense would mess it up before it got going. And we'd have to tell him that, and one of the veterans would go right up to the blackboard and change it around. Most of the time, Johnny Blood was the spokesman, because he was always ready to speak up to Curly, or anybody.

Rather than X's and O's, Lambeau's greatest talent was in knowing how to pick football players and then convincing them to come to Green Bay. Nothing better demonstrates this than the Packers' 1929 season. By the time Green Bay shut out the Cardinals on November 17, the Packers were 9-0 and well on their way to putting together one of the most dominant seasons in the history of the early NFL. In the first nine games, the defense, spearheaded by a front line that included Hubbard and Michalske, surrendered only 16 points, holding five opponents scoreless. The offense, led by the impeccable play of Lewellen and the swashbuckling receiving of Johnny Blood, wasn't quite as overpowering, scoring 14.2 points per game — a far cry from the 22.7 averaged by the Giants through their first nine contests — but it was still the second best in the league. Outside of the Giants and the Packers, the rest of the NFL averaged a meager 7.3 points per game in 1929.

But even though Green Bay led New York by a half game in the standings, bookmakers installed the relatively healthy Giants as 5-3 favorites over the beaten-up Packers — who would be without Dunn and Kotal. The big city of seven million would certainly beat the small town of 37,000. It just made sense.

But that wasn't how people in Green Bay saw it, and they gave their team a hero's send-off. The Packers left for New York on a train that chugged out of the Milwaukee Road station at 12:50 p.m. on November 21. According to the account of the departure in that day's *Press-Gazette*, they were seen off by "hundreds of fans who cheered long and lustily as the American Legion band played." The train stopped briefly in Milwaukee that afternoon, and the team was feted at the Schroeder Hotel by railroad officials. It was the players' second banquet in as many nights — the board of directors of the Green Bay Football Corporation had held a testimonial dinner at the Beaumont Hotel to honor them the night before they left. "Red Dunn warned [guard] Whitey Woodin that he must keep his manly form even if it was at the

expense of the second helping of chicken," Calhoun noted wryly in his account of the dinner in the *Press-Gazette.* "So far as [fullback] Bo Molenda was concerned this bit of advice fell on deaf ears."

This wasn't Green Bay's first visit to New York. On November 18, 1928, the Packers had beaten the Giants 7–0 on a one-yard touchdown plunge by Lewellen. Attendance at that game had been pegged by the *Press-Gazette* at "some 12,000 fans, together with about 2,000 guests of the management."

But the 1929 date at the Polo Grounds drew a more robust 25,000—attendance may even have been held down a bit by drizzling rain, gray skies, and temperatures that hovered around 40 degrees. The Packers were big. Their line averaged around 220 pounds, end to end. New York's averaged about 210, but only one Giant was over six feet tall. All seven men on the Green Bay line stood at least six feet. As New York's backup center, Saul Mielziner—who at six foot one and 245 pounds was no lightweight—watched Green Bay's players running onto the field before kickoff, he sidled over to Benny Friedman, near midfield, and said wonderingly, "Benny, will you look at those big guys?"

◆ ◆ ◆

The story of Green Bay's first championship is of the little guys versus the big guys, of the small town versus the big city, of David versus Goliath. But the reality is that the Packers were the *real* giants of New York on November 24, 1929. Green Bay's big men were bigger than New York's, and they controlled the game—from the opening play. The Giants' line was no match physically for the Packers' front seven. In the words of Harold C. Burr of the *Brooklyn Eagle,* the Green Bay front "punched holes and pried through the Giant line like a steel cutting tin." New York gained no yards from three running plays in its first series and punted the ball

to the Packers' 25-yard line. Lambeau didn't even attempt to run a play on the muddy field, instead giving the ball to Lewellen, his game changer. On first down, the Brown County district attorney booted a 75-yard punt that went for a touchback. The Giants took over on their own 20-yard line. On first down, right halfback Tony Plansky picked up 10 yards on a run around right end but fumbled the ball away to Johnny Blood, who fell on it near the New York 38.

Now Lambeau turned to his offense. A pass from Blood to Lewellen gave the Packers a first down at the Giants' 20.* Runs by fullback Bo Molenda, who had been Friedman's college teammate at Michigan, and rookie left halfback Herdis McCrary, a product of the University of Georgia, took the ball all the way down to the New York three-yard line. On fourth-and-goal, Lewellen faked a plunge into the line to draw the defense in and then stepped back and fired a quick touchdown pass to McCrary, who was being covered by Friedman. Molenda's extra point was good. Midway through the first quarter, Green Bay led 7–0.

After that, the game settled down into a duel for field position, a struggle in which Lewellen's kicking gave the Packers a decided advantage. Before the third quarter was over, he had punted six more times—only one of his boots covered less than 40 yards, and two of them went for more than 60. The Giants were pinned at their own 24 midway through the third quarter when Plansky connected on a pass over the middle to 200-pound fullback Elwin "Tiny" Feather, who ran the ball all the way to the Green Bay 35. A pass from Friedman to left end Ray Flaherty gave New York a first down at the Packers' 25. A few more runs and a Packers offside penalty moved the Giants to the 15. On second down, Friedman faked a kick and lofted an arching pass toward the end zone, where Plansky made an over-the-shoulder catch at the

Filling in for injured Red Dunn as quarterback, Verne Lewellen played the entire sixty minutes in the 20–6 defeat of the Giants in 1929, throwing a touchdown pass and twice booming punts of more than 60 yards.

---

* *The play-by-play in the* Press-Gazette *recorded this pass as being from Blood to Lewellen, but several other papers said that it was from Lewellen to end Tom Nash.*

goal line. Friedman missed the extra point. Green Bay's lead had been cut to 7–6.

The game then became a brutal, grimy stalemate. Both teams' jerseys — the Packers' were a golden yellow — were smeared with mud. The third quarter ended with Blood saving the day. Plansky punted the ball to McCrary, who muffed the catch at the Green Bay 35-yard line. As a roar went up from the crowd, the ball began to roll toward the Packers' goal line. It made it all the way back to the 20, players from both teams scrambling madly after it, before Blood fell on top of it. It was his second fumble recovery of the game.

The drama seemed to give Green Bay's stagnant offense a boost. On the first play of the fourth quarter, Lewellen faked a punt and circled around right end for a pickup of 11 yards. Three plays later, he threw to McCrary for a first down at the Giants' 42, and on the next, McCrary threw to Lewellen

for another first down, at the New York 27. From there, the Packers ran the ball 10 times before Molenda crashed into the end zone from less than a yard out. After he kicked the extra point, Green Bay led 14–6.

There were still eight minutes left, but the momentum now belonged completely to the Packers. On New York's second play after Green Bay had kicked off, Friedman threw an interception to Jug Earp. From the Giants' 37, the Packers needed nine plays (only one of which was a pass, which picked up three yards) to get down to the four-yard line. When the officials called timeout for a measurement, it was getting dark, making it difficult to see players from the stands. During the stoppage in play, Lambeau made his only substitution of the game, sending in Paul Minick, a second-year player out of Iowa, to replace Jim Bowdoin at right guard. On the next play, Blood ran over left tackle for the final touchdown of the game, screaming "Make 'em like it!" as he crossed the goal line. Molenda missed the extra point, but it hardly mattered. There were only about 30 seconds remaining, and the Packers led 20–6.

Without its starting quarterback and one of its halfbacks, Green Bay had thoroughly dominated the team thought to be the best in the league, and the Packers had done it with 10 men playing the full 60 minutes and an 11th who played 59. New York, on the other hand, had used 19 players. Green Bay's supremacy reached its zenith in the fourth quarter, when the Packers ran 26 plays to the Giants' two. David had slain Goliath, and the New York papers took note. Ken Smith of the New York *Graphic* wrote, "They are all stars — every one of them, not just a few. The whole blamed team is an All-American eleven, to my mind the greatest football team in the world today." And Arthur Daley of *The New York Times* made it a point to single out Lewellen, who had been the best player on the field.

> The hard running, hard fighting Green Bay Packers punctured the bubbles of the Giants invincibility Sunday by tramping roughshod over the hitherto unbeaten New Yorkers. The Packers had weapons that the local outfit could not match. They had a magnificent kicker in Lewellen whose zooming 60 and 70 yard punts with a wet, sodden ball ever kept the Wisconsin eleven in scoring territory; they had a line of 200-pounders, a line that outcharged and outrushed the highly touted New York forwards; they had a fast, deceptive attack with a set of backs running viciously from well screened formations behind wall-like interference.

Green Bay still had three games to play, but the response to the Packers' victory in the NFL's littlest city was euphoric nevertheless. A "Grid-Graph" had tracked the action for fans at the Columbus Club, and Milwaukee radio station WTMJ had broadcast a wire report of the game. People sent more than 500 telegrams to the team from wire offices in Green Bay. Packers treasurer Lee Joannes cabled to the team president, Dr. W. W. Kelly, "Stay with the team. Will hold my appendix till you get back." And the *Press-Gazette* started a $5,000 "Championship Fund" to raise money for player bonuses. "In distinguishing themselves the Packers have distinguished Green Bay," read the announcement of the fund. "All subscriptions, no matter how small, will be welcomed. Let's all do our share." The people of Green Bay dug deep. Donations included $1.00 from Eddie Krippner Jr., $5.00 from William Haslam, $28.20 from Brown County Motors, and $103.50 from the employees and executives of the Green Bay Foundry and Machine Works. The Packers' 1923 stock sale had been supported primarily by the businessmen of Green Bay. But while the ownership of the team was decidedly white-collar, support for the Packers came from everywhere. The benefit game for Rigney Dwyer had begun the special relationship between the team and the town. And the Championship Fund continued it. Membership in Green Bay's gentry class was not a prerequisite for having a stake in the Packers' success. In that they belonged to everyone.

◆ ◆ ◆

Lambeau and his players didn't have much time to celebrate their victory over the Giants. They were due to play the third-place Frankford Yellow Jackets in Philadelphia on Thanksgiving Day — which gave them all of three days to recuperate. Green Bay had beaten Frankford 14–2 at City Stadium back on October 13. But even with Dunn and Kotal back in the lineup, the best the exhausted Packers could do was fight the Yellow Jackets to a scoreless draw. And they had to put up with abuse from the Frankford fans while they did so — apparently Philadelphia has always been a tough place for visiting teams to play.

"Green Bay never played before a more hostile audience," wrote an indignant Calhoun in his story on the game. "From the moment the Bays stepped on the field until the final whistle blew and a near fight developed, these Frankforders were on Capt. Lambeau and his men nearly everywhere. Some of the sideline coaches went to the heights of sarcasm to express their views and the players on the bench had to stand plenty with a smile."

From the City of Brotherly Love, the Packers were off to Providence for a Sunday game against the Steam Roller—Green Bay's third game in eight days. But at 4-5-2, Providence wasn't as good as the Giants or the Yellow Jackets, and the Packers beat them easily, 25–0. On defense, they never let the Steam Roller get within 25 yards of the end zone. On offense, Green Bay was led by Johnny Blood, who scored two touchdowns, one on a 29-yard pass from Dunn and the other on a 73-yard punt return after he took a lateral from Dunn. "Not once," wrote Calhoun, "did the Steamrollers stand any more of a chance than a dry agent at a bootlegger's blowout."

Green Bay went from Providence to Atlantic City, where the Packers practiced until Friday, December 6, then hopped a train to Chicago for their season finale against the Bears. The Packers had outscored the Bears 37–0 in their two previous meetings in 1929, and the third game was no different. Green Bay overwhelmed Chicago, 25–0, as Lewellen ran for a touchdown, threw for another, and boomed punts of 85 and 75 yards. The defense held the Bears to three first downs and picked off five passes. With the victory, the Packers clinched their first championship. The Giants won their final five games to finish with a record of 13-1-1, but they were .071 percentage points behind 12-0-1 Green Bay. The little city that would someday become known as Titletown, USA, had its first honest-to-goodness title.

The Packers took a train home from Chicago the next day, arriving in Green Bay at around 8:30 p.m. on December 9. As the train approached the Chicago and North Western depot, the players could hardly believe their eyes. An estimated 20,000 people—more than half the town's population of 37,000*—had turned out in 20-degree weather to welcome them. People lined the tracks and the streets around the station and stood on the rooftops of surrounding buildings and atop nearby boxcars. According to the *Press-Gazette,* it had been impossible to even approach the station 30 minutes before the train arrived. The throng was so thick along the tracks that the train had to slow to a crawl a few blocks from the depot. The night was dark, with only a half-moon in the sky, and fuses were lit to mark the tracks. A solitary brakeman and several police officers walked ahead of the engine to clear the track of fans. When the train finally pulled into the station, the awestruck players could see that it was decorated in blue and gold bunting. "I hesitated about playing pro football, but now I am glad I played, and I am particularly pleased I signed with Green Bay," said right tackle Bill Kern, a rookie out of Pittsburgh. "It has been a great experience in a great town."

"It is pretty hard to say anything," said a stunned Lambeau. "This welcome is something that we didn't expect and is a complete surprise."

From the station the players were escorted aboard special buses that, following the same American Legion band that had seen them off nearly three weeks before, paraded them to city hall—west on Dousman to Broadway, south on Broadway to Walnut, east on Walnut and across the Fox River to Washington, north on Washington to Main Street, east on Main to Adams, and finally south on Adams back to Walnut. Not quite a mile and a half. At city hall, the mayor gave the players "freedom of the city" for 24 hours. The players were then put back on the special buses and taken home.

The next night, 400 people attended a banquet in the team's honor at the Beaumont Hotel. Thou-

---

* *According to the U.S. Census of 1930, the population of Green Bay was 37,407—up from 31,643 in 1920.*

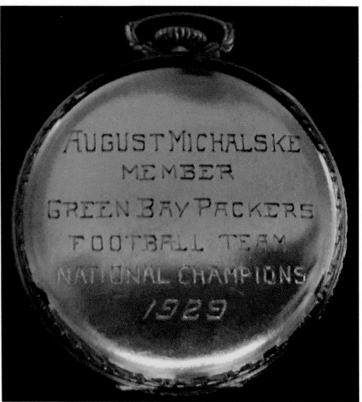

sands more listened to the event on the radio on station WHBY. The Championship Fund had raised $5,073.60, with donations from more than 1,000 people. Andrew Turnbull presented each player with a check for $220, which was from the division of the fund, along with a Hamilton pocket watch and a leather wallet — gifts from the corporation. The watches were silver, inscribed on the back with each player's name and the following:

MEMBER

GREEN BAY PACKERS

FOOTBALL TEAM

NATIONAL CHAMPIONS

1929

When Curly Lambeau was introduced to the crowd, a thunderous ovation several minutes long ensued. Finally he rose and began to speak. At that moment he was no longer just the coach and co-founder of the Green Bay Packers, no longer just a former high school star, no longer just a local hero. He was the man who, by gumption, nerve, and the sheer force of his own will, had made his hometown nationally famous.

"I was given two of the greatest thrills of my life last night and tonight by the welcome tendered by Green Bay fans," he said. "Other teams that won the championship always finished in the second division the following year, but we are going to do our best to break that precedent and if the fans are behind us, we think we can do it."

An estimated 20,000 people met the Packers' train when the team returned to Green Bay from its season-ending road trip as NFL champions. At a banquet the next night, each player received a pocket watch and a bonus check for $220.

CHAPTER 7

FROM CHAMPIONSHIPS TO RECEIVERSHIP

Arnie Herber was only 19 when he returned to Green Bay from the University of Wisconsin in the spring of 1930, but it seemed as though his best days might already be behind him. He had just washed out academically at Madison for the second time in a year and, along with his wife, Lois, and their four-month-old daughter, Jean, he was living in the home of his father-in-law at 605 South Oakland Avenue, on Green Bay's west side. He had no job, and—with the Great Depression just beginning—few prospects. His father had been a switchman for the Chicago and North Western Railway, and his wife's father was a conductor on the Milwaukee Road, but a life on the rails may not have had much appeal to him. His father, Peter Herber Jr., had been killed in the Chicago and North Western yard when Arnie was only seven, nearly ripped in half when he got caught between cars at two in the morning on December 14, 1917.

Arnie had been a standout athlete at Green Bay West High, where he captained the football and basketball teams as a senior and also starred for the track team in the throwing events. Sturdily built, with a thatch of thick black hair, soft eyes, and a cherubic face, Herber won 10 letters at Green Bay West and, more important, led the Wildcats to consecutive victories over Green Bay East in 1926 and '27. In the 1926 game, which ended a string of eight straight losses to East, his twisting 25-yard punt return set up the winning touchdown in a 7–2 victory. The next year, with West trailing 6–0 late in the fourth quarter—and playing in front of a crowd of 10,000 at City Stadium—the 17-year-old Herber led a dramatic drive that culminated with his touchdown pass to halfback Ar-

non Adams with less than two minutes left in the game. Herber then drop-kicked the extra point to give West a 7–6 victory. The Wildcats went 8-0 that season and outscored their opponents 203–12. In Herber's three years at West, the Wildcats went 24-1-1, suffering their lone defeat in the rivalry game against East in 1925. Playing quarterback, Herber did it all: passing, running, punting (he averaged 45 yards a kick), and placekicking, drop-kicking, and returning kickoffs and punts. Stoney McGlynn, the sports editor of the *Milwaukee Sentinel,* called him "the greatest high school player in the nation."

Herber graduated from West in the spring of 1928 and then married Lois Lefevre, who was nearly eight months his senior. He enrolled that fall at Wisconsin, where he captained the Badgers' freshman team and played right halfback in the spring game in May 1929. But in August he was ruled academically ineligible and left Madison for Regis College, a small Jesuit school in Denver, where he played football in the fall. Soon after the birth of his daughter, Jean, on December 6, Herber returned to Wisconsin, where he enrolled in February 1930. But he soon flunked out. "His exposure to higher education was strictly a football experience," Herber's former West High teammate Miles McMillin wrote in Madison's *Capital Times* after Herber died of stomach cancer in 1969. "The brevity of his stay at Wisconsin was predicted by all who knew anything of his interest in studies."

The five-foot-eleven Herber's talents as a passer had caught the eye of Lambeau. The Packers' coach was on the lookout for help in the backfield after the retirement in March of halfback Eddie Kotal, who had left Green Bay to take over as the coach at Lawrence College, in Appleton. Herber signed with Green Bay on August 9. He was at the first practice of the season on Sunday, September 7, when 2,500 fans showed up at Joannes Park to watch Lambeau put the team through its paces. Ten players did not return, but the nucleus of the 1929 champions — Johnny Blood, Lavvie Dilweg, Red Dunn, Cal Hubbard, Verne Lewellen, and Mike Michalske — was back. One week later, Herber started at quarterback ahead of Dunn in the Packers' 46–0 defeat of the Oshkosh All-Stars in a preseason contest at City Stadium. In the home opener on September 21, Herber again started over Dunn in a 14–0 defeat of the Chicago Cardinals. In the third quarter, Herber threw a 50-yard scoring pass to Dilweg for the Packers' second touchdown of the afternoon. Herber started again in a 7–0 win over the Bears the next Sunday.

But after Herber's 2-0 start, Lambeau chose to return to the more experienced Dunn as his primary signal caller for the rest of the season. Herber started two more games in 1930, but they were both at left halfback, and he threw only two more touchdown passes all season. It was a halting beginning, but one of the greatest passing careers in the NFL's first 50 years had begun.

◆ ◆ ◆

The Packers of 1930 were not as dominant as they had been the season before, but they were still impressive as they charged to a 10-3-1 record and their second straight NFL championship — again nosing out the New York Giants (13-4) in the standings, this time by four percentage points. Green Bay scored 234 points, 36 more than it had in 1929, and gave up 111, an increase of 89. But the Packers also shut out four opponents. And they split their season series with the Giants and went 2-1 against the third-place Bears. Almost as important, Green Bay enhanced its reputation as a road attraction. A crowd of 22,000 came to Wrigley Field on November 9 to see the Packers beat the Bears 13–12 in a thriller. Two weeks later, 37,000 filled the Polo Grounds to watch the Giants defeat Green Bay 13–6. And on December 7, a crowd of 20,000 at Wrigley cheered the Bears as they drubbed the Packers 27–0, a victory that ended an eight-game winless streak against Green Bay. All around the NFL, fans wanted to see the Packers, whose visits were becoming must-see events. The team from the littlest town in the league had supplanted the teams from the biggest cities as the NFL's marquee franchise.

That status only became more pronounced in 1931, when Green Bay went 12-2 and won its third league championship in a row. The team went 4-1 against the Bears and the Giants that season, drawing 35,000 to the Polo Grounds and a total of 48,000 to their two games at Wrigley Field. (Green Bay's games at City Stadium against the Bears and Giants drew well, too, with 13,500 coming to the Chicago game and 14,000 to the Giants game.) According to Packers historian Cliff Christl, only 44 of the 203 NFL games played from 1929 through 1931 were attended by more than 12,000 people. Green Bay played in 11 of them, eight of those in New York and Chicago.

The Packers' success was not the only reason for their popularity throughout the NFL. Yes, they were the best team in the league for three straight years, and their games against the Bears and the Giants were almost always high-stakes affairs. But the Packers had also developed a certain aura, a David and Goliath mystique that was irresistible to big-city sportswriters — especially when David kept winning.

The day after the Packers had clinched the 1929 championship, the *Green Bay Press-Gazette* had opined in an editorial, "The battle with the Giants engaged national attention. The country's best football experts and sports writers witnessed it, hundreds of thousands of persons heard it described over radio. Today, Green Bay is in the headlines of metropolitan newspapers. Ever more and better advertising.

"What is all this worth to Green Bay? We say it is worth plenty."

And it was. The Packers — "the team from the obscure Wisconsin village," in the words of the New York *Daily News* — were the darlings of the Gotham press. Not only was Green Bay playing and winning hugely momentous victories in New York, but it was doing so with its own small-town flair. In 1928, the first time the Packers visited New York, Lambeau got his team settled at its Manhattan hotel and then told George Whitney Calhoun that he wanted to practice in Central Park. Calhoun dutifully arranged for a bus to take the players to the park, but he had no idea where to go after that. "I guess Central Park is a pretty big area," Calhoun said in 1961. "The bus driver let us out at the first entrance we came to. We got out and started to practice — and it turned out to be a children's playground. The kids came on later and we tried to dodge 'em. They were romping all over. A whole squad of motor cops came along and threatened to arrest us, so we moved farther out in the park."

Nobody did more to hype the Packers — to keep them at the forefront of the mind of every sports-writer at every newspaper in every town in the NFL — than Calhoun. The keys to his sales pitch were the evening parties he hosted in his hotel room whenever the Packers played in New York. Upon arrival, Calhoun would order cases of beer and a block of ice, and then he would fill his bathtub with ice water and beer bottles. He also, according to John Torinus, used to bring along "a daisy of Wisconsin cheddar cheese." With beer in the tub and cheese on the dresser, he would then get on the telephone to his friends in the press corps and invite them over for a drink and some conversation. Then he would sit back and play host. Calhoun, a bachelor with no children of his own, made the Green Bay Packers his babies, his favorite sons. And he bragged on them accordingly. "Cal could talk newspapermen's language," wrote Torinus in his history of the team. "[He] got more ink for the Packers than any other team in the league could muster."

Calhoun also kept meticulous track of games and statistics, not only for the Packers but also for the rest of the league, cutting out box scores each week from every NFL game and pasting them into notebooks. When author Roger Treat was doing research for his 1952 reference book *The Encyclopedia of Football,* Calhoun's records became his primary resource. "The dynamo of the Packers, other than Lambeau, was a man whose name is never printed in the programs, but who has been from the beginning, and still is, the senior advisor, the patriarchal statesman, the father confessor, the defender of the faith, the only official Monday morning quarterback and the historian of all things Packer," wrote Treat. "George Whitney Calhoun is his name and he is known wherever major league football has been played, from Boston to San Francisco."

Johnny Blood was known in every one of those towns, too, but for different reasons. The adventures of the Vagabond Halfback — some apocryphal, some true, and some a mixture of both — were beginning to take on a mythic quality.

Take two stories that supposedly occurred during the Packers' extended road trip at the end of the 1929 season. Following Green Bay's triumph over the Giants at the Polo Grounds on November 24, Blood and a few of his teammates began partying in their rooms on the 18th floor of the Lincoln Hotel. The revelry continued until the wee hours of the morning and included Blood carrying a 150-pound block of ice through the lobby of the Lincoln at three in the morning and, even more improbably, a visit from heavyweight challenger Primo Carnera, who was also staying on 18. Blood told biographer Ralph Hickok that he had invited Carnera to the festivities after running into him in the hallway. "He looked like a pretty good lineman to me," Blood said, "so I invited him to the party, and we offered to teach him how to play football."

There's only one problem: Carnera was still in Europe. On November 18, the six-foot-six, 280-pound Venetian carpenter had defeated American heavyweight William L. "Young" Stribling at London's Royal Albert Hall after Stribling was disqualified in the fourth round for a low blow. The two fought a rematch in Paris less than three weeks later, on December 7, with Carnera the loser this time—he was disqualified for punching Stribling in the back of the head after the bell ending the seventh round had sounded. It's certainly possible that Carnera crossed and recrossed the Atlantic in the 18 days between his two fights with Stribling. But it seems unlikely, especially given that the Ambling Alp's official arrival in America didn't take place until the last day of the year, December 31, 1929. That was the day that Carnera arrived in New York City after a seven-day voyage aboard the RMS *Berengaria*. The journey had been well covered in the press, with one widely circulated report noting that the Cu-

NATIONAL LEAGUE FOOTBALL

Final Game of the Season at Home

See the Team that beat The BEARS

PORTSMOUTH SPARTANS
vs.
GREEN BAY PACKERS

ALL STAR BACKFIELD -- Portsmouth has a backfield second to none. Lumpkin of Georgia Tech, Eby of Ohio State, Tiny Lewis of Northwestern, Bennett of Indiana and Glassgow & McLain of Iowa are topnotch gridders. Bennett and Glassgow were picked as the best players in the Big Ten in 1928 and 1929 respectively.

CITY STADIUM - GREEN BAY
Admission Prices; $1, $1.25, $1.50, $2 · · Kickoff 2:00 o'clock · · Get Your Tickets Early and Be Sure of a Seat

SUNDAY - NOVEMBER 2

By the time the Packers welcomed Portsmouth to City Stadium in 1930, they were already 6–0 and cruising to a second straight NFL championship.

nard line had furnished Carnera's room with a specially made eight-foot bed.

But as with almost all good Johnny Blood stories, there is an element of truth to the otherwise tall tale. Two years later, in November 1931, Carnera did indeed stay at the Lincoln at the same time as the Packers.[*] But a story in the *Press-Gazette* noted that he had kept to himself when the Green Bay players tried to engage him in conversation. As for Blood's 150-pound block of ice, the first time he appears to have told the story in public was after the Packers' 1930 title, and Carnera was not mentioned.

Blood's second story took place on the train back to Green Bay from Chicago after the championship-clinching victory over the Bears. There are a handful of tales about Blood that involve him snapping teammates with a wet towel.[**] He was apparently doing this to Lavvie Dilweg when Dilweg began chasing Blood through several cars to the rear of the train. Cornered on the platform at the back of the caboose, Blood evaded Dilweg by

---

[*] *This was shortly before Carnera's second-round knockout of six-foot-ten Argentine heavyweight Vittorio Campolo at Madison Square Garden on November 27.*

[**] *There is even one from a train trip in November 1930 in which Blood, in the cryptic words of the* Press-Gazette, *"cold toweled several of the late sleepers." Lesson: Keep Blood away from towels.*

climbing up to the roof and racing forward seven or eight cars in the cold night air before coming down and slipping inside. The source of the story? Johnny Blood. There is no record of Dilweg ever mentioning it.

Sometimes Blood stepped in to correct the record—which only makes his bunkum harder to spot. There was the story about his going tonsil-to-tonsil with actor John Barrymore one night in a bar, the two men quoting Shakespeare to each other. Not true, said Blood. He never met Barrymore. In another—this one from the field during a game at City Stadium—Blood told Arnie Herber to throw the ball "in the direction of Mother Pierre's whorehouse." Herber knew enough about his hometown to know where Blood was heading. According to *The Pro Football Chronicle,* "The pass was there and so was Blood." There was another story—vouched for by both Blood and Curly Lambeau—about Blood crawling out onto an eighth-floor ledge at a Los Angeles hotel and entering Lambeau's room through the window. The reason? To ask the coach for a cash advance—which he got. When the story appeared in *Sports Illustrated* in 1963, writer Gerald Holland noted, "The legend that has grown up around Johnny Blood is so filled with truths and half-truths and no truth at all that it is necessary to try to grasp a few facts of record and hold fast to them."

The facts that everyone can hold fast to are the things Blood accomplished on the field. He was of course surrounded by a host of wonderful players in 1929, '30, and '31—in particular Dunn, Hubbard, Lewellen, and Michalske, as well as center Boob Darling, end Lavvie Dilweg, and halfback Bo Molenda. But Johnny Blood was the heartbeat of Green Bay's three-peat.

A fast, elusive runner with sure hands, Blood was the NFL's first great receiving threat, and his 1931 season stands out as perhaps the finest individual campaign in the early history of pro football. The 78 points he scored led the NFL, and his 10 receiving touchdowns are still the most in league history for a running back. He also rushed for two scores and returned one of his six interceptions for a touchdown. Blood set the pace for a team that scored 291 points, leading the NFL by a wide margin. The next closest team was the Portsmouth Spartans, with 175 points. Amazingly, Blood didn't catch his first touchdown pass in 1931 until the fourth game of the season. Seven of them went for more than 20 yards, with the longest going for 53. He caught passes in traffic. He made marvelous broken-field runs. He also threw for another score. Years after Blood had retired, George Halas said, "The Packers had a lot of great players, but until [Don] Hutson came along, Johnny Blood was the one guy who could beat you with one big play."

◆ ◆ ◆

Things in Green Bay were not quite as euphoric in 1930, after the Packers' second straight title, as they had been in 1929, but there were still big crowds, banquets, and bonuses. An estimated 3,000 fans jammed the Chicago and North Western depot when the Packers returned on December 15 after clinching the championship with a 6–6 tie against Portsmouth. And some 10,000 to 15,000 lined the parade route from the station, though even the *Press-Gazette* allowed that "perhaps the turnout wasn't quite as large as a year ago." But the Championship Fund fell short of its $5,000 goal, pulling in only $4,294—$2,500 of which had been contributed by the Green Bay Football Corporation. The team's 22 players got bonus checks of $200.

In 1931, the Packers wrapped up the championship in the penultimate game of the season, a 7–0 victory over the Brooklyn Dodgers at Ebbets Field, and the celebration in Green Bay was muted. With one game still to play—and that against the Bears in Chicago—a crowd of only 3,500 met the team at the Milwaukee Road depot at 10:30 p.m. on December 1. Bonus checks were $100, but the team canceled a public reception scheduled for the Friday before the Bears game. The rivalry with Chi-

Halfback Arnie Herber (shown here throwing a jump pass during a practice at New York's Travers Island) was a graduate of Green Bay West High School—and the first great deep-ball passer in NFL history.

cago mattered too much to Lambeau for him to let his team be distracted. (Chicago nevertheless prevailed, 7–6, helped in part by a late interception by Red Grange.)

But the mood in Green Bay was more positive in general than it was in the rest of the United States, where the disastrous ripple effects of the stock market crash of 1929 were still being felt. Although the Great Depression had an impact on the Fox River Valley, the region did very well compared with much of the rest of the country. To be sure, there were problems. Banks closed, farm prices declined, and unemployment increased. But few in the area were heavily invested in the market, and the region's leading industry, the manufacture of paper—especially toilet paper—actually expanded. Between 1925 and 1935, production of toilet tissue in the United States doubled, and Northern Paper, which was headquartered in Green Bay, was the largest producer of toilet paper in the country. It was with good reason that the city was known as the Toilet Paper Capital of the World. By 1934, Green Bay's three large paper mills, as well as their satellite operations devoted to converting raw paper rolls into finished products, employed 20 percent of the working population of the city.

The economy of Green Bay also got a boost during the Depression from two other sources: cheese making and railroads. The dairy industry remained relatively strong because people still had to eat. And the railroads endured because they were the primary means of shipping for all the paper and dairy products being produced in Brown County. Financially, Brown ranked in the top 20 percent of Wisconsin counties in 1934. *Press-Gazette* columnist Jack Rudolph, in his 1976 book on the history of Brown County, *Birthplace of a Commonwealth,* wrote that during the Depression the area "never

saw any bread lines or soup kitchens."

The comparative health of the Green Bay economy during the Depression was, of course, good for the Packers, who were able to not only pay championship bonuses but also keep the core of their title-winning teams together for several years. But there was little margin for error. Throughout the 1920s, the NFL had consisted of as few as 10 (in 1928) and as many as 22 (in 1926) teams — 44 different franchises in 35 cities* played in the league from 1920 to 1929. But by 1932 the NFL was down to just eight teams. Two that disappeared around this time, the Pottsville Maroons and the Portsmouth Spartans, were similar to the Packers in a few significant ways. Both were from small towns. The population of Portsmouth was around 33,000 in 1920, while Pottsville's was nearly 22,000. (For the four years that the Maroons were in the league, from 1925 to 1928, they, and not the Packers, were from the smallest town in the NFL.) Also, both the Pottsville and Portsmouth franchises had, like the Packers, turned to their local communities for financial assistance. The Green Bay Football Corporation wasn't the NFL's only public enterprise in the 1920s and '30s.

The Maroons joined the NFL in 1925 after having played for several years as a semipro outfit. The team was managed by John G. "Doc" Striegel, a local physician who, when Pottsville made the jump to the NFL, was the largest investor in the club. Beginning in January 1925, Striegel raised $1,500 for league fees through the sale of $5 memberships. But by October, the Maroons needed $5,000 more. That additional money came from the public sale of stock, which raised more than $2,000 in its first two days on the block. But Pottsville, located in eastern Pennsylvania, about 100 miles from Philadelphia, was centered around the production of anthracite coal, once the preferred fuel for domestic heating. Anthracite mining peaked

---

* This is with the teams from the boroughs of Brooklyn and Staten Island counted as New York City teams. The city had a total of five teams in the 1920s: the Brooklyn Lions, New York Giants (1921), New York Giants (1925), New York Yankees, and Staten Island Stapletons. Only the 1925 incarnation of the Giants survived.

in the early 1920s but then began a steady decline as oil and other fuels became more popular. By 1930, the output of anthracite coal in Schuylkill County had dropped by nearly 19 percent. And between 1924 and 1935, employment in the anthracite coal industry declined by nearly 46 percent. The effect on the town was devastating. The population of Pottsville grew by about 2,500 people between 1920 and 1930, but in the next decade it grew by just 230. Even before the Depression began, Pottsville could no longer support the Maroons. They moved to Boston in 1929 and became the Bulldogs. The team folded one year later.

The Portsmouth Spartans held their first stock sale in 1930, with the goal of selling 250 shares for $100 each. Unlike Green Bay's stock, the Portsmouth shares were intended to pay dividends — the Spartans, in other words, had been organized as a for-profit enterprise. While only 158 of the 250 shares on offer were sold, the team began operations with $15,800 in the bank. The Spartans did well on the field, going 16-9-3 in their first two seasons. Indeed, Portsmouth almost prevailed over Green Bay for the 1931 NFL championship, finishing 11-3 while the Packers went 12-2. The Spartans actually protested that they should have had a chance to play the Packers for the title on December 13. The two teams had not met that season, though they had tentatively scheduled a game for the second Sunday in December. But the Packers refused to play — for obvious reasons — and league commissioner Joe Carr took their side.

Of more immediate concern to Harry Snyder — the Spartans' original owner, as well as the owner and general manager of the Universal Construction Company — was that his team was deeply in debt. In 1931 he had tried all sorts of things to save money and cut costs. He made his players take the bus instead of the train to league games, packed box lunches rather than give players a meal allowance, and even gave them IOUs instead of paychecks. By the end of the season, Portsmouth owed 21 players and coaches money. Coach George

EXHIBIT IN COURT TRIAL HERE

A section of bleachers from the Packer stadium was expected to be one of the exhibits in the suit of Willard J. Bent vs. the Green Bay Football corporation, which went on trial in Circuit court this morning. Bent is suing to recover for injuries allegedly received in a fall from the bleachers at a Packer game. Above, the bleachers are shown partially erected in the courthouse rotunda.

"Potsy" Clark had an annual salary of more than $5,000, but the team paid him just $1,130.15. All told, the Spartans were more than $44,000 in the red in their first two seasons. The franchise reorganized and held another stock sale in 1932, but it fell short of its goals for fund-raising.

The team had enough cash to play in 1932 and '33, but after that there was no more money left for it in Portsmouth. The town was a center for the production of shoes and steel, and both industries experienced steep declines during the Depression. Also, in the spring of 1933 the Ohio River flooded, putting an additional financial burden on the community and driving some employers away. When the Spartans' board of directors met early in 1934, it made the decision to move the team. In April, the Portsmouth stockholders approved the sale of the franchise to a group led by George Richards, the owner of a Detroit radio station. Richards moved the Spartans to his hometown and renamed them the Lions.

That left only one small-town, publicly owned team: the Green Bay Packers. At the end of the

In 1933 a fan who had fallen from his seat at City Stadium two years before successfully sued the Packers and almost broke the team. During the trial, a section of the bleachers was constructed in the rotunda of the Brown County Courthouse.

1931 season, the Packers were relatively healthy. Because of Curly Lambeau and his eye for talent, they were winners on the field — the best team of the NFL's first dozen seasons. Because of northeastern Wisconsin's lax approach to Prohibition and the lack of organized crime in the area, Green Bay was an attractive place to live and play for players throughout the NFL. And because of strong support from the Green Bay community, which on the whole was doing better than other towns in the NFL at the time — as well as the fiscal responsibility of the team's board of directors — the Packers had been able to avoid the sort of debt problems that had consumed the Maroons and would eventually overwhelm the Spartans. But the Depression, which limited the amount of cash that could be spread around, meant that they were never very far from disaster. And they were headed for a fall.

◆ ◆ ◆

There were few civic boosters in Green Bay in the 1920s and '30s more enthusiastic than Gordon Bent, the proprietor of the Gordon Bent Company, the city's largest sporting goods outlet. Born in Nova Scotia in 1884, Bent was the fourth of Charles and Annie Bent's eight children. The family moved to Marinette, on the northwestern side of Green Bay, when Gordon was young, and he later moved to the mouth of the Fox River to take a job with the Morley-Murphy Hardware Company, for whom he sold sporting goods. Bent started his own business in 1909 and gradually expanded his store over the next 30 years from a small retail space to a three-story building that took up an entire city block. Part of his success can be attributed to his talent for self-promotion. His business sponsored numerous events in town, including trapshooting tournaments and bicycle races, and also supported a number of athletic teams, most of which played under his name. From youth sports on up, the Gordon Bents competed in basketball, baseball, softball, and bowling leagues. And many days the pages of the *Press-Gazette* were filled not only

with ads for his store but also with news about the teams that competed under its banner. The jump headline on one story about a game in the Municipal Basketball League, was simply GORDON BENT. In Green Bay in the first 50 years of the 20th century, the man's name was everywhere.

Bent also traveled extensively throughout the country, visiting trade shows and sporting equipment manufacturers and spreading the gospel of Green Bay far and wide. He knew firsthand the value of the Packers' special brand of national advertising, and he closely associated his business with the team. He'd outfitted the original Packers in 1919 and continued to supply gear to Lambeau for years after — a fact he touted in newspaper ads for his store. In December 1922, when Andrew Turnbull was getting ready to turn the team into a publicly held corporation, the committee to organize the stock sale selected Bent and 37 other Green Bay businessmen to be the team's salesmen. He was one of the 204 original stockholders of the Green Bay Football Corporation.

It is nothing less than supremely ironic, then, that Gordon Bent's oldest brother, Willard, was the man responsible for the near death of the Packers. Willard had been in attendance at City Stadium on September 20, 1931, when Green Bay trounced the Brooklyn Dodgers 32–6. Bent paid one dollar for a seat in the top row of the wooden bleachers at the northwest end of the field. During an exciting play, he rose with the crowd to watch the action. As he was standing, the plank on which he had been sitting was somehow jarred loose. Bent's end of the board fell to the ground while the other end remained connected to the bleachers. When he went to sit back down, Bent fell backwards, plummeting 10 to 12 feet and fracturing his spine. He was taken in an ambulance to St. Mary's Hospital, where he spent 53 days in a body cast. Claiming he had been disabled ever since the fall, Bent filed suit against the Packers for $20,000.

The case of *Willard J. Bent vs. Green Bay Football Corporation* went to trial in a third-floor courtroom of the stately Brown County Courthouse in late February 1933. Presiding over the hearing was circuit judge Henry Graass, a Packers fan and local character. Recognizable around town for his looming size and flowing mane of white hair, the 53-year-old Graass had a habit of eschewing a hat and overcoat in even the coldest weather. He was also, in his own way, as much of a civic booster as any businessman invested in Curly Lambeau's team. He was a conservationist. He loved to hunt and fish, though he never caught or killed anything, preferring instead to help his friends by rowing their boats or cooking their meals over a campfire. He was a charter member of both the Kiwanis and Rotary Clubs and a frequent speaker at war-loan fund-raisers. In 1919 he was part of a five-man delegation from the city that went to Boston to meet Green Bay soldiers returning from France aboard the USS *George Washington*.

Representing Willard Bent was another prominent citizen of the city: Arthur Fontaine, 57, a leader in the state's Republican Party and the law partner of none other than T. P. Silverwood, the captain of Green Bay's undefeated town football team in 1897.

The Packers were represented by 43-year-old Gerald Clifford, a prominent Democrat and the pugnacious vice president of the Green Bay Football Corporation.* The son of a former mayor of Iron Mountain, Michigan, Clifford had moved to Green Bay shortly after getting his law degree in Ann Arbor in 1912. During Prohibition he established a formidable reputation as a defense counsel in liquor cases, winning a high number of acquittals — a fact chalked up by the *Press-Gazette* to his extensive study of search-and-seizure law. The paper also described the sharp-eyed litigator as "a hard two-fisted fighter." In his 1946 history of the Packers, journalist Arch Ward named Clifford as one of the "Hungry Five," the group of influential Green Bay boosters who had kept the

team going beginning in the early 1920s. But according to team historian Cliff Christl, there's no evidence that Clifford had anything to do with the Packers or their affairs until he became the team's attorney in 1929, whereas the other four members had been involved from the beginning. From 1929 forward, though, says Christl, Clifford "became as actively involved as any of the other 'Hungry Five' members."

Because of the names involved, the trial garnered considerable local interest. It also caused a bit of a sensation when Marcel Lambeau, who had built the bleachers at City Stadium, erected a section of seats, like the ones from which Bent had fallen, inside the ornate, colonnaded courthouse rotunda. The facts of Bent's fall were not in question at the trial; everybody agreed on what had happened. But the Packers contended that they were not liable because the field was owned by the City of Green Bay and was under the control of the Board of Education. They also argued that Bent had been negligent and that his health problems were his own fault. Clifford took a shot at the plaintiff in his opening statement, saying, "We will concede that if we could have put him in a hammock and given him a nurse to hold his hand, it might have been safer."

The trial, as recounted in the pages of its transcript, painted a sad picture of the 54-year-old Bent, an alcoholic with a sixth-grade education, a heart condition, and an advanced case of syphilis. He had no teeth; they had all been pulled because of, in his words, "rotten gums." He mumbled his way through his testimony as Fontaine led him through a litany of his injuries. Bent had suffered numerous fractures in eight falls or accidents since 1916. Besides his tumble at City Stadium, he had fractured a shoulder in a motorcycle accident, broken his wrist while roller-skating, fractured his breastbone in a car accident, fractured his ribs while breaking up wood behind his broth-

---

* One of the attorneys at Clifford's firm was Packers end Lavvie Dilweg.

er's store, and fractured an elbow while unloading a lawn mower off a truck. He had also fallen in front of his own house while walking home from a movie. He had been hospitalized twice for excessive drinking and had been placed in a straitjacket on at least one occasion. He labored as a motorcycle repairman at the Gordon Bent Company, but beyond the family name, he had little in common with his younger brother. Willard Bent was, in just about every way imaginable, the opposite of Gordon Bent.

Clifford, in his opening statement, made sure to note the disparity. "We will show you that this man never worked except for his brother," Clifford said. "And knowing Gordon Bent as well as I do, that employment comes out of his good heart rather than out of his desire for steady employment and ability to work."

Arguing for Bent, Fontaine countered that the bleachers were unsafe because they had no rear guardrails. He also told the jury that the seating planks were not affixed to the bleachers permanently but were instead slotted into grooves on the side railings. This made them easy to remove, but it also left them susceptible to being jostled loose. Fontaine found a witness who said that something similar had happened to him at a Packers game in 1930. To testify to Bent's lost wages, Fontaine called Gordon Bent to the stand. Willard had been making around $700 a year through 1931 at the Gordon Bent Company, but the year after his fall he made only $150. Willard testified that he had been able to go to his job for only two months during the summer of 1932 before he had to give it up. "I couldn't stand the work," he said. He was unemployed at the time of the trial.

On February 28, after deliberating for more than five hours, the jury found against the Packers, saying that the bleachers were unsafe and that their condition was the primary cause of Bent's in-

jury. The jury awarded Bent $5,544.14 for medical bills, lost wages, and pain and suffering. That amount was reduced by 10 percent, though, because the jury also found that Bent's negligence was a contributing factor in the accident. The total award was $4,989.73. The Green Bay Football Corporation had had liability insurance with the Southern Surety Company of New York, but the company had failed in March 1932. The Packers could not afford to both pay Bent and play football. On August 15, with no tangible assets and debts of more than $10,000, the Packers entered receivership to protect themselves from their creditors, primarily Willard Bent. Receivership is a form of bankruptcy in which a court-appointed trustee, or receiver, reorganizes a destitute business. The business avoids going under but is controlled completely by the receiver. Judge Graass named Frank Jonet, a 50-year-old Green Bay accountant and the former office manager of the Indian Packing Company, as the receiver of the Green Bay Football Corporation. For the third time in 15 years, the Packers were on the verge of going under. Jonet recalled years later that when Graass told him that he had been appointed receiver,[*] the judge handed him $76.18 in cash, as well as a stack of judgments and unpaid bills totaling more than $15,000.

The Packers were in receivership for more than 17 months, run on a shoestring by Jonet and a board of directors headed by team president Leland Joannes. Other board members included Clifford, former presidents Andrew Turnbull and Dr. W. W. Kelly, and former Green Bay quarterback Charlie Mathys, who had been elected to the executive committee following his retirement in 1926. It's hardly a coincidence that in 1933—with the team in financial turmoil and legal jeopardy—the Packers endured the first losing season in their history, going 5-7-1. The team survived mostly because of a $6,000 loan from Joannes. Green Bay

---

Jonet gave the date of his appointment as August 13, 1933, but the official court filing designating him as receiver is dated August 15.

lost money in 1933 and again in 1934 and was in danger of being ordered into bankruptcy by the court. The strain was starting to show. In New York in November 1933, after the Packers had lost three games in a row, Lambeau was stricken with severe abdominal pain. Fearing that it was appendicitis, he sought out a doctor, who diagnosed him with, in the words of the *Press-Gazette,* "a stomach disorder brought on by nervousness." He was put on a strict diet "with some sure cure powders thrown in to hasten a quick recovery."

More troubling than Lambeau's stomach was

Green Bay's inability to afford to keep some of its best players. In 1933, Lambeau sold the contract of end Tom Nash—a first-team All-Pro in 1932 and a mainstay of the Packers' first three championship teams—to the Brooklyn Dodgers. Cal Hubbard abruptly retired from pro football in January 1934 to take a job as the line coach at Texas A&M. (Hubbard was also a minor league umpire.*) Johnny Blood was gone, too—sold to the Pittsburgh Pirates in August 1934 for an undisclosed amount of cash. Blood had run afoul of Lambeau twice in 1933. The first time was when he missed

On October 21, 1933, the 2-2-1 Packers boarded a train for Chicago to play the Bears. Green Bay fell to Chicago 10–7 and went on to finish 5-7-1, the first losing season in team history.

---

* *Hubbard was promoted to the American League in 1936. A hunting accident 15 years later damaged his eyesight, and three years later he became the AL's supervisor of umpires, a position he held until 1970. He was elected to the Baseball Hall of Fame in 1976. Hubbard is the only man to be a member of both the Pro Football Hall of Fame and the Baseball Hall of Fame.*

the 47–0 defeat of the Pirates at City Stadium on October 15. The day after the game, the *Press-Gazette* reported that he was suffering from a hand injury. But on October 19 the paper said that he had been suspended for "breaking team rules." Considering that his presence at a party on the night of October 14 had been touted in the paper, it's not a stretch to assume that alcohol, as it often was with Blood, had been at least part of the problem.

That was certainly the case in New York near the end of the season. On November 25, 1933, the *Press-Gazette* reported that the coach had suspended Blood after the back had "reported unfit for practice" to DeWitt Clinton Field the day before the Packers were to play the Giants at the Polo Grounds. The truth was, according to Blood, that he had shown up drunk. "When I tried a punt, I missed the ball completely and fell flat on my ass," he told biographer Ralph Hickok. "Curly sent me back to the hotel." Blood missed the next two games before returning for the finale against the Bears in Chicago on December 10. He did not play. According to his biography, he hopped a train to California after the season and worked at various times as a bartender, a ditchdigger, and a seaman on a freighter that sailed to, among other places, Hawaii, Yokohama, and Hong Kong. Blood said that it was when he was at sea on the Pacific Ocean that Lambeau had sold his contract to Pittsburgh.

In his later years, Blood would confess that he had had a serious drinking problem. He was, by almost all accounts, a good-natured drunk. "He was a little eccentric, a little weird, particularly if he got a little giggle juice in him," Green Bay fullback Clarke Hinkle said in Richard Whittingham's boisterous 1984 oral history of pro football's early days, *What a Game They Played*. But behavior that had been endearing when Blood was a younger man and the Packers were winning was regarded very differently with the team losing and on its financial deathbed. Lambeau appears to have been fed up. "We are going to miss Johnny Blood

this fall," read an unsigned editorial in the *Press-Gazette* on August 7. "Blood was an 'on and off' performer last year but we believe that if he gets down to business and quits a lot of his foolishness he still has a year or two of good football in him."

With the team selling off its stars and losing games, something had to be done. On December 14, 1934, Joannes announced another stock sale. "We cannot go on operating when the club is losing money — the court will not permit it," he told a meeting of 25 business and industrial leaders when the sale was announced. "We have been negotiating with those who have claims against the corporation and we feel confident that if we can raise $10,000 we can make a settlement with our creditors and have some money left to start rebuilding our team for next year."

In a meeting at the Brown County Courthouse on January 29, 1935, the Green Bay Football Corporation was reorganized as "The Green Bay Packers Inc.," with the articles of incorporation drafted by Clifford and notarized by Lavvie Dilweg. (With one minor change — the word "The" was dropped in 1997 — this is the organization that endures to this day.) By the end of the month the sale had raised $12,000, enough to settle Green Bay's debts and lift the team out of receivership. It was a remarkable feat. And the Packers (for that was now the team's official name) had the industry of Green Bay to thank — the cheese makers, the paper mills, and the railroads, all of which put money in the pockets of both its blue-collar fans and its white-collar benefactors.

The Packers sold 484 shares of stock in the 1935 sale, but to only 113 shareholders. In the words of Christl, "It was almost a closed sale." Basically, Green Bay's wealthiest business and industrial leaders stepped up to save Lambeau's team. Both the Hoberg and Northern paper mills were among the leading shareholders, as were the transportation companies, especially the Northern Transportation Company, of which Packers board member Fred Leicht was general manager. But even more stock was owned by the community's food-related industries, including the Joannes Brothers wholesale grocery operation and the cold storage businesses run by board member Emil Fischer.

Just as important to the survival of the team, though, were the unceasing efforts of Lambeau, the man who kept it going. And with the organization once again on firm financial ground, he was free to do what he did best: find talented players and convince them to come to Green Bay. Less than a month later, on February 22, 1935, he did just that, signing Alabama's All-America end Don Hutson. Pro football would never be the same.

CHAPTER 8

HUTSON

Before Don Hutson there was Clarke Hinkle. In the six years after Curly Lambeau had signed three Hall of Famers in 1929, the Packers' coach found three more: Hinkle, Hutson, and Arnie Herber. Herber and Hutson were transcendent players in the evolution of the forward pass. Hinkle could throw and catch too, but his impact on the game was more elemental than esoteric. Fast, physical, and, in the words of one teammate, "meaner than a rattlesnake," he was the most complete player in the early history of the Green Bay franchise — a ferocious hitter, a punishing runner, and a formidable competitor. The legacy of Hutson might be greater, but no Packers player better defined the era than Hinkle.

The youngest of three sons of mill worker Charles Hinkle, William Clarke Hinkle was born in Toronto, Ohio, on April 10, 1909. (His oldest brother, Gordie, played minor league baseball for 10 years and saw action in 27 games for the Boston Red Sox in 1934.) Clarke played halfback and kicker at Toronto High — where he also starred in basketball and baseball. In 1928 he went to Bucknell, where he majored in, in his words, "coeds and football." After one season on the freshman team he moved up to the varsity and quickly established himself as one of the best backs in college football. In the Bison's last game of the 1929 season, against Dickinson College on Thanksgiving Day, Hinkle scored eight touchdowns and ran for two extra points in a 78–0 victory. In three seasons

with Hinkle at fullback, Bucknell went 20-5-3.

Hinkle may have been from a tiny town in eastern Ohio, but he had been a Packers fan since before he ever signed a contract with Green Bay. In all three of his seasons at Bucknell, Hinkle and the Bison had played Fordham at the Polo Grounds the day before the Packers played the Giants on the same field. Those Green Bay–New York games had had enormous import in the NFL, of course, with the Packers in the midst of their run of three straight championships. New York had actually invited Hinkle to attend the 1931 game as a guest of the team, and he spent part of the second half watching from the Packers' bench. Green Bay won 14–10 that day, in front of 35,000 fans, and both touchdowns had come through the air — one on a

53-yard catch-and-run from Red Dunn to Johnny Blood. Said Hinkle years later, "I was more impressed with the Green Bay Packers than I was with the New York Giants."

Hinkle did not get to meet Lambeau that afternoon. But 40 days later, on New Year's Day 1932, the Green Bay coach was at San Francisco's Kezar Stadium for the East-West Shrine Game, where Hinkle starred for the East in a 6–0 victory. The fullback led all rushers with 62 yards on the ground, and this time it was Lambeau who watched the action from the sidelines, sitting on the East bench. Not long after the game, Hinkle was relaxing back in his hotel room when he heard a knock on his door. "There was Curly Lambeau with a contract in his hands," Hinkle said in *What a Game They Played*.

Lambeau knew how to make a house call. Less than two years earlier, he had left his job as a salesman at Stiefel's clothing store in Green Bay to go to work for the Massachusetts Mutual Life In-surance Company, for whom he was a district sales manager. In San Francisco he sold Hinkle, a small-town boy, on the idea of playing in the smallest outpost in the NFL. "[I] liked the idea of playing in a small town," Hinkle said. "I figured with a small town like that, everybody knew everybody. They would have pretty good spirit, like a college."

Ten days later, after Lambeau returned to Green Bay from the West Coast, he announced that he had signed Hinkle, who had accepted the coach's offer of $125 a game over other deals from the Giants, Boston, and Portsmouth. "I wanted to play so badly," Hinkle said, "that I would have signed for nothing."

At five foot eleven and 202 pounds, Hinkle was a smooth, nifty runner when the occasion called for it, but he was best known as a blunt instrument —a smashing rusher as a fullback and a vicious tackler as a linebacker—who almost never ran out of bounds or dragged a ballcarrier down when he had a chance to initiate contact. "He was the

hardest runner I ever tried to tackle," said Bears Hall of Fame linebacker and center Clyde "Bulldog" Turner. "When you hit him, it would just pop every joint all the way down to your toes." And Hinkle was renowned by teammates and opponents alike for his intensity. "I've never known a man who wanted to win like Hink did," said Cecil Isbell, who played quarterback for the Packers alongside Hinkle from 1938 to 1941. "Before the game, he'd get glassy-eyed, he'd be so fired up and eager to play. After the game, if we lost, he'd sit at his locker and cry like a baby."

Hinkle had played well as a rookie in 1932, rushing for a team-high 331 yards as the Packers went 10-3-1 and nearly won their fourth NFL crown in a row, finishing second to the 7-1-6 Bears. Chicago was led by a punishing fullback of its own: Bronko Nagurski. The son of Ukrainian immigrants from Rainy River, Ontario, Bronislau Nagurski was the premier power runner of his era, a devastating, straight-ahead force of nature. In college at Minnesota, he had been an All-America as both a tackle and a fullback. At six foot two and 230 pounds, he outweighed most linemen by about 20 pounds, and the irresistible power with which he ran made him the most feared player of his day. "Tacklers to the Bronk," said New York Giants coach Steve Owen, "were like flies on the flank of a horse — a nuisance but not serious."

Clarke Hinkle, though, refused to be cowed, especially after the rookie took seven stitches in his chin the first time he tried to tackle Nagurski. From that moment forward, Hinkle's strategy against the big Canadian was "to get to the Bronk before he gets to me." With Nagurski as his foil, Hinkle became a legend.

It all began on the clear and warm afternoon of September 24, 1933, when Green Bay hosted Chicago at City Stadium in front of 10,000 fans. Hinkle had gotten his tonsils taken out just thirteen days earlier, six days before the season opener against the Boston Redskins at City Stadium. He had played well in the 7–7 tie with the Redskins, but he had had to wear heavy bandages around his neck. The wraps were off for the Bears game, though, and Hinkle was ready. On third down late in the first quarter, he lined up in the backfield in punt formation.[*] He took the snap, kept the ball, and, according to the account of the game in the *Press-Gazette,* carried around left end for a yard — and ran straight into Nagurski. "I got through a hole," Hinkle told Myron Cope in his 1970 book *The Game That Was,* "I started upfield, and out of the corner of my eye I could see Nagurski coming over to really nail me to the cross. He was edging me to the sideline . . . and what he would do instead of tackling you was run right through you . . .

"So just before I got to the sideline I cut abruptly right back into him. I thought I might as well get it now as any other time. I caught him wide open and met him head-on."

Hinkle lowered his shoulder just before the two collided with, in the words of the *Press-Gazette,* "a thud." The hit broke Nagurski's nose and knocked him out of the game. He left the field on a stretcher. Hinkle kept on playing. The Bears scored two late touchdowns to win 14–7, en route to a 10-2-1 record and their second straight NFL championship. (Chicago beat the Giants 23–21 in the league's first official championship playoff, on December 17, 1933.[**]) But the story of the game was Hinkle's battering of Nagurski. In their 1997 book about the rivalry between the Packers and the Bears, *Mudbaths & Bloodbaths,* authors Cliff Christl and

Hutson tries to corral a pass from Arnie Herber in the Packers' 23–17 loss to the New York Giants in the 1938 NFL Championship Game.

---

*The Chicago Tribune *said that the hit occurred in the second quarter.*

** *A prelude to this first Championship Game had actually been played one year before, when the league crown was still decided by the standings. The Bears finished the 1932 season in a tie for first with the Portsmouth Spartans. At 6-1-4, the Spartans actually had a better record than Chicago's 6-1-6, but the NFL did not count ties when figuring a team's winning percentage—tie games might as well have never been played. A playoff was used to determine the champion, and the Bears won 9–0 on December 18, 1932, in a game played indoors at Chicago Stadium because of inclement weather.*

PACKERS RIP BOSTON, 21-6, FOR PRO TITLE

———Story on page 56.

PACKERS CRUSH REDSKINS.—Leaving no doubt that they are the best gang of pro footballers in the country, the Green Bay Packers yesterday beat Boston Redskins, 21—6 at Polo Grounds. Example: Stalwart champs stop Irwin (arrow) of Boston.

A bit of the stuff that gave Packers the pro crown. Hinkle gets away for five yards. That stretching Redskin seems to be longing for rubber arms.

Hockey Line-Up at Garden

AMERICANS	Position	BOSTON
(1) Worters	Goal	Thompson (1)
(2) Shields	R. D.	Portland (8)
(3) Murray	L. D.	Smith (6)
(7) Chapman	Center	Cowley (17)
(9) Carr	R. W.	Getliffe (16)
(11) Schriner	L. W.	Sands (18)

American alternates—Cotton (6), Oliver (10), Wiseman (12), Lamb (14), Emms (15), Anderson (16), Doran (17), Kalbfleisch, Klein.

Boston alternates—Shore (2), Jerwa (4), Clapper (5), Goldsworthy (9), Bun Cook (10), Beattie (11), Hollett (12), Stewart, Schmidt.

The Packers almost always drew a big crowd when they played in New York—and sometimes were front-page news. The Daily News gave Green Bay's NFL title-game defeat of Boston at the Polo Grounds the Page One treatment.

Gary D'Amato say of the hit, "Old-timers who witnessed the play still refer to it with reverence as the most brutal collision they have seen."

Hinkle would play eight more seasons and finish his career as the NFL's all-time leading rusher, with 3,860 yards. But he is remembered most for his wide-eyed, all-out style of play—and for his physical combat with Nagurski, which did as much as anything to stoke the fires of the greatest rivalry in the history of the NFL. Hinkle and Nagurski were such ferocious belligerents, it was almost inevitable that each would earn the respect of the

other. Hinkle went into the Pro Football Hall of Fame in 1964, one year after Nagurski, who had been in the Hall's original class. Hinkle chose Nagurski to be his presenter. Years later Nagurski said, "The guy who bruised me the most was Clarke Hinkle of Green Bay."

Despite Hinkle's all-around excellence, he was not a game-breaker, not a threat to score from anywhere on the field at any moment. Arnie Herber had taken over as the Packers' primary passer after Red Dunn's retirement, and the Green Bay native had led the NFL in both passing yards and passing touchdowns in 1932 and 1934. He had also proven himself to be a deep-ball artist. "He throws them pretty accurately up to 35 yards, but he has no equal when it comes to heaving 'em from 35 to 60 yards," Lambeau said of Herber. "His accuracy is uncanny." What Lambeau needed was a field-stretching complement to both Herber and Hinkle. And he was about to find him in an unlikely spot.

❖ ❖ ❖

Like any good salesman, Curly Lambeau had a network, and that network consisted of coaches and players with Notre Dame connections. Lambeau had spent only one semester in South Bend, but the influence of Notre Dame football could be found all over the Packers. Their primary colors were blue and gold. They ran the Notre Dame Box offense. Everything had started with Knute Rockne, of course, but it also eventually came to include the legendary coach's peers and disciples. Lambeau's informal Fighting Irish network extended his reach into almost every corner of the country—and continued to do so for years, even after Rockne was killed in a plane crash on March 31, 1931. Pick a prominent Green Bay player from the 1920s and '30s and there's a good chance that there was a Notre Dame connection somewhere in his background. Tackle Tiny Cahoon played for the Packers from 1926 to '29. He was from Baraboo, Wisconsin, but he came to Green Bay via Gonzaga University, out in eastern Washington, where his coach had been former Notre Dame quarterback Gus Dorais. Fullback Herdis McCrary was a mainstay of the backfield on Lambeau's first three championship teams. He'd gone to college at Georgia, where he was coached by former Fighting Irish center Harry Mehre. Verne Lewellen was at Nebraska when he was brought to Lambeau's attention by Jim Crowley, who had played for Lambeau at Green Bay East before going on to South Bend and becoming one of Rockne's Four Horsemen. And finally, there was Alabama coach Frank Thomas, who had played for the Fighting Irish from 1920 to '22. It was Thomas who would connect Lambeau with one of the greatest players in the history of pro football.

Donald Montgomery Hutson was born on January 31, 1913, in Pine Bluff, Arkansas, the oldest of three sons of a conductor on the St. Louis Southwestern Railway, more commonly known as the Cotton Belt. Don was seven years older than his twin brothers, Robert and Raymond.* He was active as a Boy Scout for several years, reaching the rank of Eagle Scout. To qualify for one of his merit badges, he gathered a collection of 35 to 40 snakes of all different kinds, which he kept in cages in his backyard—and which he later released back into the woods near his house.

As Hutson's fame in pro football grew, so, too, did the temptation for sportswriters to mythologize his origins. The story of his serpents was embellished until it had him owning a collection of rattlesnakes. His roots in the game of football received similar treatment—and it is sometimes hard to untangle fact from fiction.

Hutson did not play football until his senior year at Pine Bluff High in 1930, but contrary to much of what has been written about him, he was a standout athlete. His father, Roy, had been an infielder for Pine Bluff's town baseball team, the White Sox, in the early 1920s. In 1989, Don told the *Los Angeles Times* that he had played outfield

on the Pine Bluff town team when he was 15, and that he had also been named to the all-state basketball team as a senior. According to former *New York Times* writer Arthur Daley, the only reason Hutson went out for football in his final year at Pine Bluff was because the Zebras were going to a preseason training camp in the Ozark Mountains, a place he wanted to visit.

But an alternate version of the legend goes—in the words of both Hutson and countless journalists over the years—that Hutson had been convinced to play high school football by his friend and neighbor from Pine Bluff, Bob Seawell. Hutson confirmed this story to the *Press-Gazette* in 1942. Seawell, while being recruited by Alabama, insisted that he would go to Tuscaloosa only if the Crimson Tide took the lightly regarded Hutson in a package deal. Seawell then played two years for Bama before dropping out of school to become a state policeman in Pennsylvania, while Hutson went on to become the South's top receiver.

But there are a few problems with that story. There was a Bob Seawell who played halfback at Pine Bluff in 1928, but he was several years older than Hutson, having been born in 1909. That in itself does not mean that he was not classmates with Hutson at Pine Bluff—plenty of people, for plenty of reasons, had to put off high school in those days. And in 1930 a 20-year-old Robert M. Seawell was a neighbor of Hutson's in Pine Bluff, living across the street at 1205 Sixth Avenue. But when Hutson and the Zebras went to Texas in 1930 to play the Marshall High Mavericks, there was no player named Seawell listed on the Pine Bluff roster published in *The Marshall Morning News*. And according to census data that had been taken a few months earlier, in April 1930, the Robert M. Seawell who lived across the street from Hutson was a railroad coach appraiser, not a student. There is also no record of anybody named Seawell ever lettering in football for the Crimson

---

* *According to* The Scribner Encyclopedia of American Lives, *Hutson also had one sister, who died in infancy.*

Tide. Seawell did indeed attend Alabama from 1930 to 1933.

However Hutson came to the game of football, he appears to have been a natural receiver from the start. He weighed only 145 pounds as a senior at Pine Bluff, but with his speed and shiftiness, he played much bigger. In one game he caught five touchdown passes, which is still tied for the state record. It seems unlikely that that sort of accomplishment would have escaped the eyes of college football recruiters in the South.

Author Allen Barra, in his thorough biography of Paul "Bear" Bryant, *The Last Coach,* says that Hutson was recruited to play for the Crimson Tide through the same pipeline as Bryant, who hailed from nearby Fordyce, Arkansas, and would play end opposite Hutson in Tuscaloosa. The Palace Recreation poolroom was a hangout in Pine Bluff for both football players and coaches, and the manager there was a man named Jimmy Harland, an Alabama native. Harland tipped off Bama assistant coach Hank Crisp to Hutson's football prowess, and Crisp did the rest. It was an easy sell. "For Bryant and numerous other top players [in Arkansas], the University of Alabama was what football was all about," wrote Barra. The Rose Bowl was at that time the only postseason bowl game in college football, and Bama had played in it three times, winning in 1926 and 1931 and tying 7–7 with Stanford in 1927.

In Tuscaloosa, Hutson grew to six foot one, bulked up to about 180 pounds, earned three varsity letters, and became a star. The Crimson Tide went 25-3-1 in his three years, and "the Alabama Antelope" was named first-team All-America in 1934. He also became good friends with Bryant, who in high school used to make the 40-mile trek north from Fordyce to Pine Bluff to watch Hutson play.

Their coach was a short, beefy midwesterner from Muncie, Indiana, a former Notre Dame quarterback who rarely smiled and who, in the words of Barra, "inspired respect from his players but not love." There were former Fighting Irish players leading football programs at colleges all over the country, but Frank Thomas was one of the first disciples of Knute Rockne to coach at a major southern school. Harry Mehre, who had been Thomas's center in South Bend, had been coaching at Georgia since 1928, and Thomas had been one of Mehre's assistants in Athens when Alabama hired him in 1931. He replaced Wallace Wade, who had left the Crimson Tide to take over as the coach at Duke. In his letter of resignation to Alabama president George H. Denny, Wade had actually recommended Thomas as his successor. "There was a young backfield coach at Georgia who should become one of the greatest coaches in the country," Wade wrote. "He played football under Rockne at Notre Dame. Rock called him one of the smartest players he ever coached. He is Frank Thomas, and I don't believe you could pick a better man."

Thomas ran his team with tough efficiency—and little emotion. Bryant once described him as aloof and imperious. In that way, Thomas was the opposite of the passionate Rockne and the tempestuous Lambeau. But he was like them in one very important way: he ran the Notre Dame Box offense. The Box, which emphasized speed and deception, was ideally suited to Hutson, one of the fastest men in the college game.

In addition to football, Hutson also played three years of varsity baseball for the Crimson Tide. He was known for his speed, of course—he stole 15 bases in the first 12 games of his junior season, in 1934—but he could also hit. Hutson was batting .457 midway through the '34 season. As a senior, he slugged a homer in a 6–0 defeat of LSU. He also ran track that spring. He is frequently credited with running a 9.7-second 100-yard dash at the Southeastern Conference meet. In reality, though, he finished outside of the top three in the 100 at the SECs, and the winning time in the race was 9.8 seconds. (He finished second in the 220-yard dash.) "While Hutson claimed at one point he could consistently run a 9.7 100," says Packers his-

torian Cliff Christl, "his times in the SEC meet as a junior and senior, along with other evidence, suggests he was more of a 10-flat sprinter."

The technical details of Hutson's speed may be murky, but there was nothing inscrutable about what he did on the football field. In Alabama's 29–13 victory over Stanford in the Rose Bowl on January 1, 1935, he was unstoppable, getting behind the defense time after time and gashing the Indians for long gains. He caught six passes for more than 160 yards and scored two touchdowns. The first came just seconds before halftime, with Alabama already leading 16–7. Stanford had domi-

nated the first quarter, holding the Crimson Tide to just four plays and taking a 7–0 lead on a one-yard plunge by fullback Bobby Grayson. The Indians' defense had given up just 14 points all season, and things looked bleak for Bama, but Thomas, who was renowned as a master of in-game adjustments, revised his attack. He began mixing passes to Bryant and Hutson with runs by senior halfback Millard "Dixie" Howell. In the second quarter, Howell took over, scoring on runs of five and 67 yards. But on his second scoring run, a weaving scamper through the entire Stanford defense, he hurt his ankle and was replaced by sandy-haired,

Hinkle carries the ball around right end against the Bears at Wrigley Field in 1939. When he retired following the 1941 season, he was the NFL's all-time leading rusher, with 3,860 yards.

150-pound sophomore Joe Riley. Nicknamed "Little Joe," Riley was the son of a policeman from Dothan, Alabama, and had been singled out by Thomas before the season as "the most promising backfield man to come up from the freshmen since I've been at Tuscaloosa."

Alabama wasn't expecting to get the ball back before halftime—according to the game story in the *Los Angeles Times,* there was "only time for a few plays." But on second down, Crimson Tide safety Riley Smith intercepted a pass on the Bama 46-yard line. The Tide wasted no time. Receiving the first-down snap from five yards deep in the backfield, Joe Riley retreated a few steps and, throwing off his back foot, launched the ball over the middle. Hutson, who had been lined up tight

to the tackle as the left end, was streaking straight downfield and had blown past two Indians defensive backs, junior safety Bob Maentz and cornerback Bob "Bones" Hamilton. Hutson had to reach behind himself slightly to catch the ball, but he never really broke stride and sprinted 30 yards untouched into the end zone for a 54-yard touchdown. He was pulling away as he crossed the goal line. The pass electrified the crowd of 84,474 and effectively put the game away.

Early in the fourth quarter, with the Crimson Tide in front 22–13, Hutson struck again. Howell was the passer this time, but the play was similar to Hutson's first score—with the end running as fast as he could down the middle of the field and sprinting past two Indians defensive backs. From

the Alabama 41-yard line, Howell uncorked a high, arching bomb that dropped over Hutson's right shoulder just inside the Stanford 15. The Indians' Elzo "Buck" Van Dellen grasped at Hutson's ankles. The Bama flier staggered and kept churning. Hamilton dove in vain as Hutson crossed the goal line for a 59-yard touchdown. "It was as great a passing combination as football had ever known," wrote Grantland Rice of the Howell-to-Hutson connection. "And you can go all the way back to Dorais and Rockne—to Gipp and Riley—to Friedman and Osterbaan [sic]. They had nothing on this dazzling combination from the deep south. The timing, the accuracy and the mechanical perfection were the finest I have ever seen in football."

Curly Lambeau agreed. He visited the Pacific Coast every year after the Packers' season was over, and he had been in San Francisco since late December scouting players at the East-West Shrine Game. After watching the West defeat the East 19–13 on New Year's Day, Lambeau called Thomas, who recommended Hutson to the Green Bay coach. Hutson signed a contract with Lambeau on February 19, 1935, for $175 per game. Three days later, the *Press-Gazette* announced the signing, describing Hutson as "the greatest end the south has seen in the last 10 years."

Hutson, who never graduated from Alabama, later told the story that he had signed two contracts after the Rose Bowl: one with the Packers and the other with the Brooklyn Dodgers. According to the Pro Football Hall of Fame, NFL commissioner Joe Carr ruled that the contract that reached his office in Columbus, Ohio, with the earliest postmark would be the one that received official recognition. The two contracts arrived on the same day, but the Packers' deal was postmarked 17 minutes earlier. There is no evidence to support the story, though. Hutson later said his agreement with the Packers was for $300 a game. Lambeau told versions of this story, too, and even claimed to have seen Hutson at L.A.'s Occidental College during Bama's final Rose Bowl practice. The Crimson Tide had indeed worked out at Occidental, but according to news reports at the time, Lambeau was in San Francisco for the East-West game. As for Hutson's claim to have signed for $300 a game, that doesn't agree with the $175 figure in his NFL personnel file.

Hutson later claimed—as did several other players—that he actually signed two contracts with the Packers, which together totaled $300. Hutson said Lambeau had done it that way so that nobody would know how much he was making. "Things were done a bit differently in those days," he told Richard Whittingham in *What a Game They Played*. His teammates claimed that, during contract negotiations, Lambeau would pull out one of Hutson's agreements and ask them how they could expect to be paid so much if Hutson was making only $150. Said one, "After some of [Lambeau's] hocus-pocus you were happy to get what you got the year before, or maybe just a little bit more."

Regardless of the particulars, in acquiring Hutson, Lambeau had set the Packers on the path to more glory.

◆ ◆ ◆

The Don Hutson era officially began in Green Bay on September 22, 1935, in a game at City Stadium against the Chicago Bears. Until that point, Lambeau had kept the speedy end under wraps. On September 15, in the season opener at City Stadium, Hutson had not started and gained no yards on one rushing attempt in a 7–6 loss to the Chicago Cardinals. He did not catch a pass. The Packers had played four preseason games before that, but Hutson had not started any of those either, nor had he caught any scoring passes. Now, with the hated Bears coming to town, Lambeau saw a chance to jump-start his team and give it some confidence. The Packers had lost six straight games to the Bears since beating them 2–0 at Wrigley Field on October 16, 1932. The losing streak was actually seven, counting a midweek exhibition game that the two teams had played in Milwaukee on October 17, 1934. Lambeau liked to go after the Bears right away. With Herber doing the passing, the Packers had thrown deep against Chicago on the first play from scrimmage twice in 1934. Both throws had fallen incomplete. But now Green Bay had Hutson.

The September 22 game was the 31st in the history of the Packers-Bears rivalry,* which was already the NFL's longest. Led by fullback Bronko Nagurski and running back Beattie Feathers, the Bears had supplanted Green Bay as the best team in the NFL. They had gone 13-0 in 1934 but were upset by the 8-5 New York Giants 30–13 in the NFL Championship Game, a defeat that denied Chicago its third straight NFL title.** Coming into the game at City Stadium, George Halas's team had won 17 straight regular-season games, and 18 of its last 19. The day the Packers opened the 1935 season against the Cardinals, the Bears—who had been in training camp for much of the month at St. John's Military Academy, in Delafield, Wisconsin—had beaten an American Legion team in Kenosha 41–0.

The Packers were in considerably better shape than they had been in 1933 or '34. Cal Hubbard had been re-signed in July. And Johnny Blood came back to Green Bay two months later, after proving to Lambeau that he could still play by appearing against the Packers in two exhibition games—with the Chippewa Marines and the La Crosse Old Style Lagers. "Every time we went into play, Blood was on the other team and was the star of the game," said back Herm Schneidman. "So we got back to Green Bay and Blood was back on the team."

"I think Curly rehired me partly because he could see that Hutson and I could be a really devastating combination, with Herber throwing the ball," Blood said years later. "I was 31, going on 32 now, but I really hadn't slowed down much, if at all."

Some in Green Bay, however, were sure that the Monsters of the Midway would be too much for Hutson, who was also going to have to play defensive end. On game day, Emmett Platten, a Packers fan who every weekend paid for airtime on a local radio station, took Lambeau to task for spending money on the Alabama Antelope. "What's Lam-

---

* Until 1974, when the NFL corrected the record, the game was counted as the 32nd. The Packers' 5–0 victory over the Bears at Bellevue Park on September 21, 1924—Green Bay's first victory in the series—was actually an exhibition contest and did not count in that season's NFL standings. The error, though, stayed in the record books for 50 years.

** The game became famous as "the Sneakers Game." Rain and freezing temperatures had turned the field at the Polo Grounds into an icy mess. The Giants backs and ends exchanged their cleats for basketball shoes at halftime to improve their footing on the slippery turf. New York erased a 13–3 Bears lead with four touchdowns in the final quarter.

beau thinking of signing a little guy like that?" Platten said, according to *The Milwaukee Journal's* Oliver Kuechle, in a story that ran several years after the game. "What's he thinking of starting him today? Those Bears will kill him. Let's get some size in there."

Under cloudy skies and with the temperature in the low sixties, Bears fullback Jack Manders kicked off to quarterback Hank Bruder, who, after catching the ball at the five-yard line, took it out to the Green Bay 17, where he was tackled by Chicago right tackle George Musso. Hutson was the starting left end, and when Green Bay lined up for the opening play, he split one yard from left tackle Cal Hubbard, with halfback Johnny Blood split wide from right end Milt Gantenbein. Arnie Herber, the other halfback, was lined up about three yards behind center Frank Butler and was flanked by Bruder and quarterback/guard Charles "Buckets" Goldenberg. On the short snap to Herber, Hutson took off on a fly route and Blood sprinted a few yards into the flat on the opposite side of the field. Herber looked to Blood and faded back to his right as if he was going to throw to him. The Bears — who, in the words of Halas, "never wanted Johnny Blood to beat us" — cheated to their left. But Blood was just a decoy.

Watching all this unfold from his safety position near midfield was Chicago halfback Beattie Feathers, who, until the arrival of Hutson, could have made an excellent case for himself as the fastest man in pro football. In 1934, Feathers had enjoyed the finest season of any ballcarrier in the history of the NFL. In 11 games, the five-foot-ten, 185-pound rookie out of Tennessee had rushed for 1,004 yards on 119 carries, making him the first back in the history of pro football to surpass 1,000 yards on the ground in a single season. His 8.4 yards per carry that year was a record for 72 years.[*] Feathers was so good running around end

that Halas actually ditched his beloved T formation for the single wing to make better use of his ability.

The son of an illiterate laborer from Bristol, Virginia, Feathers was known for his speed and for his hatred of socks, which he never wore — he instead wrapped his feet and ankles in athletic tape.[**] It helped, of course, that the blocking back for Feathers was Bronko Nagurski. But even the Bronk could not keep Feathers from wearing down in 1934. Early in the first half of a 17–6 defeat of the Cardinals on November 25, Feathers ran around right end for 20 yards before, in the words of the *Chicago Tribune,* he was "thrown at the sidelines by three Cardinal players." He left the game and went for X-rays.

The injury was a dislocated shoulder, and it kept Feathers out for the last month of the season, including the NFL Championship Game. The ailment was the first in a debilitating string for Feathers. He would play only eight games in 1935, primarily because of an injured ankle, and he never again came close to his 1934 numbers. His best season was 1936, when he ran for 350 yards. In 1938, Halas traded Feathers to Brooklyn. He played one game with the Packers in 1940 and then was out of football for good. Nobody knew it on September 22, 1935, but Beattie Feathers was already on the downward side of his career.

Halas had warned Feathers before the game to be careful of Hutson's speed. But while Feathers had one eye fixed on Blood, Hutson blew past him. Feathers, Halas would later say in his autobiography, "considered Hutson was already out of passing range." Herber let the ball go from about his own four-yard line. It dropped over Hutson's right shoulder at midfield. He caught the pass in stride and left Feathers grasping at the air. The game was less than a minute old; Green Bay led 7–0. The touchdown electrified the crowd of 13,600 at City

---

[*] *The record was finally tied in 2006 by Atlanta Falcons quarterback Michael Vick, who rushed for 1,039 yards on 123 carries.*

[**] *The practice was not unheard of. Socks did not become mandatory in the league until 1945.*

GREEN BAY PACKERS

HOME GAMES

at City Stadium · Green Bay

Sept. 15	Philadelphia Eagles
Sept. 22	Chicago Bears
Oct. 13	Cleveland Rams
Oct. 20	Detroit Lions

at State Fair Park · Milwaukee, Wis.

Sept. 2	Washington Redskins
Sept. 29	Chicago Cardinals
Oct. 27	Pittsburgh Steelers

MAIN TICKET OFFICE

American Legion Building · 319 East Walnut St.
Telephone Adams 6180 · Green Bay

OUT OF TOWN GAMES

Aug. 2 - College All Stars
Soldiers Field - Chicago
Oct. 6 - Open
Nov. 3 - Chicago Bears
Wrigley Field - Chicago
Nov. 10 - Chicago Cardinals
Comiskey Park - Chicago
Nov. 17 - N. Y. Giants - Polo Grounds - N. Y.
Nov. 24 - Detroit Lions
Briggs Stadium - Detroit
Dec. 1 - Cleveland Rams
Cleveland Stadium - Cleveland

1940 FOOTBALL  SCHEDULE

Stadium, and the Packers made it stand up, holding on to win the game by that same score. A legend had been born. Pro football would never be the same.

"That was a very, very important game for me, because there were some people around town that thought Lambeau made a mistake by paying me," Hutson said years later. "So that took care of that."

◆ ◆ ◆

With Hinkle grinding out yards on the ground, and Herber, Hutson, and Blood (who led the team with 25 catches) stretching defenses, the Packers finished 8-4 in 1935, their best record since 1932, the year before they went into receivership. It was telling that Green Bay won three of four games against the teams who would play that year for the NFL title—the Packers beat the runner-up New York Giants 16–7 at City Stadium on September 29, edged the champion Lions 13–9 in Milwaukee on October 20, and then pounded Detroit 31–7 at City Stadium three weeks later. In the November

meeting, Herber put the game away with three second-half touchdown passes—two to Blood, covering 26 and 70 yards, and a 44-yard bomb to Hutson. Green Bay also won a thriller at Wrigley Field in its second meeting with the Bears. Trailing 14–3 with just two and a half minutes to play, Hutson scored on a 69-yard pass from Herber. After a Chicago fumble, Herber threw to Hutson for another four-yard score and a 17–14 victory. Hutson was not only the fastest man in the NFL but also the shiftiest, frequently faking out defensive backs by changing speeds and directions in an instant. He had a deceptively relaxed-looking running style, one that eschewed high knees and pumping arms. "Hutson is the only man I ever saw who could feint in three different directions at the same time," said Greasy Neale, the coach of the Philadelphia Eagles from 1941 to 1950.

Green Bay and Hutson were even better in 1936. After squeaking past the Cardinals 10–7 in the home opener on September 13, the Packers were

drubbed 30–3 at City Stadium one week later by Halas and a Bears team that was bent on revenge. But Green Bay scored 235 points in its next nine games — all wins — and clinched the Western Division championship with a 26–17 victory over Detroit before playing the Cardinals to a scoreless tie in the final game of the year. Hutson set single-season records for catches (34) and receiving yards (534), and Herber became the first player to officially throw for more than 1,000 yards in a season, leading the league in passing for the third time in five years. Johnny Blood, playing in his final season in Green Bay, caught just seven passes, but two of them went for long touchdowns.

The Packers played the Boston Redskins for the NFL title on December 13, 1936 — the first playoff game in Green Bay's history. The game, which alternated locations every year between the home stadiums of the Eastern and Western Divisions, was supposed to be at Fenway Park in Boston. But Redskins owner George Preston Marshall, frustrated that he could not draw fans to Fenway, wanted to move his team to Washington, D.C. League commissioner Joe Carr had been on hand on November 15 when only 11,200 had turned out to see 4-4 Boston take on the 6-1 Chicago Bears. It was the smallest crowd that the Bears had played in front of all season. Marshall asked Carr to move the championship game to the Polo Grounds in New York. Carr agreed.

So, on a cold and sunny Sunday, a mostly non-partisan crowd of 29,545 watched from the stands in the Polo Grounds as Green Bay beat Boston 21–6. The Packers scored on their second possession of the game, after Redskins quarterback Riley Smith — Hutson's former Alabama teammate — fumbled a lateral from fullback Don Irwin and Green Bay tackle Lou Gordon recovered the ball at the Boston 47-yard line. After runs by

halfback George Sauer and Hinkle took the ball to the Washington 44, Hutson struck.[*] With Green Bay in its Box formation to the left side, Herber received the short snap from center Paul "Tiny" Engebretson and faked a handoff to Hinkle, who crossed behind him and charged toward the right end. Herber then began dropping back to his left, against the flow of the play, all the while looking downfield. Hutson, who was listed as the right end in the official starting lineup but who on this play was positioned about two yards wide of left tackle Ernie Smith, took off on what was basically a corner route, charging into the heart of the secondary on the snap and getting lost in traffic before cutting back to his left. Herber, still backpedaling away from the rush, let the ball go from the Packers' 45-yard line. It traced a high, wobbly arc toward Hutson's left shoulder. The end jumped up to snag the ball at about the Boston 28 and came down just outside the 25. Redskins defensive back Ed Justice had kept Hutson in front of him on the play and was about three yards away from the Packers' end when he came down with the ball. He seemed to have an angle to make the tackle, but Hutson sped by him in a dozen or so quick, graceful strides and it was all Justice could do to push the Alabama Antelope in the back as he accelerated toward the end zone. Green Bay had a lead it would never relinquish.

The game's other highlight came right after halftime, when Herber, from his own 40-yard line, dropped back to his left, stepped up a few yards, and loosed a long pass to Johnny Blood. The ball came down over the halfback's left shoulder and he caught it in stride near the sideline at the Boston 20. Blood ran the ball down to the nine before he was dragged down and out of bounds by Irwin. The Packers scored their second touchdown of the game three plays later, with Herber throw-

Lambeau drafted Larry Craig in 1939 and immediately inserted him at quarterback on offense and at end on defense. Nicknamed "Superman" because of his sculpted physique, Craig was a devastating blocker and a fearsome pass rusher.

[*] *This touchdown has officially been recorded as a 48-yard pass, presumably based on information in the account of the game and the accompanying play-by-play in the normally infallible* Green Bay Press-Gazette. *But careful examination of the film clearly shows that the play began on the Boston 44-yard line. This jibes with two other excellent stories on the game, the first by Stan Baumgartner in the* Philadelphia Inquirer *and the other by the Associated Press.*

ing to end Milt Gantenbein for a 14–6 lead. It was Blood's second-to-last catch as a Packer. In February 1937, Pittsburgh Pirates president Art Rooney signed him to be his team's player-coach.

◆ ◆ ◆

For all his many gifts as a receiver, Don Hutson was not built for pro football—at least not the way it was played in the 1930s and '40s. The NFL was still in its iron-man days, when the rules that limited substitutions forced players to play both offense and defense. And the custom was that a player's position on one side of the ball was generally the same as his position on the other. An end was an end, for the most part, whether his team had the ball or not. So Hutson, who weighed all of 183 pounds and bore more than a passing resemblance to Ichabod Crane, wasn't just a receiver. He was also a defensive end.

According to Cliff Christl, only one other end in the league weighed less than Hutson in 1935, and the other 44 averaged almost 200 pounds. And the builds of Lambeau's ends fell into two basic categories: stocky and strapping. The wispy Hutson was neither, and it wasn't as though playing offense was any easier. The ends in Lambeau's Notre Dame Box typically split one yard from the left and right tackles. Hutson, who averaged only a little more than four catches a game, was essentially a tight end and often had to duke it out in the trenches against opposing linemen. He dealt with the physicality of the game by avoiding as much of it as he could, which made him something of a liability as both a blocker and a tackler. It is hardly a coincidence that the men who played alongside him in Green Bay—including Buckets Goldenberg and Mike Michalske—regarded Clarke Hinkle as the better all-around football player. Even Verne Lewellen, who lived in Green Bay long after he hung up his cleats in 1932, called Hinkle "the greatest all-around ballplayer I've seen." Michalske, in the course of designating Hinkle "the best player the Packers ever had" during a 1977 interview, paused to note that Hutson's idea of playing

defense was to let somebody else make the tackle. Arthur Daley of *The New York Times* added that, by 1938, "every team ran Hutson's end with impunity."

It was in 1938 that the pounding that Hutson was enduring may have cost Green Bay the NFL championship. He hurt his knee in the penultimate regular-season game, a 28–7 drubbing of the Lions on November 13 at Detroit's Briggs Stadium, and then missed Green Bay's 15–3 loss to the Giants at the Polo Grounds a week later. In the Championship Game, against New York on the same site on December 11, Hutson played sparingly. The morning before the game, the *Chicago Tribune*'s George Strickler reported that Hutson's knee was still "too sore and weak to pivot or cut." He caught no passes in the 23–17 loss and played only a few minutes in the second quarter before limping off. He returned in the final minute for, in the words of the *Press-Gazette*, "a last desperate pass attempt, which failed." His only contribution was picking up 10 yards on a lateral from end Carl Mulleneaux on the second-to-last play of the game.

Hutson's injury spurred Curly Lambeau to do what he did best: turn to his Notre Dame network to help him find talent in unlikely places. The NFL had held the fourth draft in its history two days before the 1938 Championship Game, at the New Yorker Hotel in New York City. With the 49th pick, the Packers selected South Carolina end Larry Craig. Powerfully built at six foot one and 211 pounds, Craig had been co-captain of the Gamecocks as a senior, when his coach was former Packers fullback Rex Enright, who had played for Knute Rockne—and been teammates with Jim Crowley—in South Bend in 1923 and 1925. It was Enright who had recommended Craig to Lambeau before the draft.

Craig had grown up one of eight children on a farm in the tiny cotton burg of Six Mile, South Carolina. All the Craig boys were athletes. Edward, the oldest, had run track for the Gamecocks.

Johnson, who was two years younger, played football at Clemson. Tom, the next oldest, had been a co-captain as a senior at South Carolina in 1934. Larry played his first snaps for the Gamecocks the next season, and one of his teammates in Columbia was his brother Tom, who was older by one year. Strong and bruising, Larry was a standout on defense. One North Carolina sports editor referred to him as "a wagonload of football player." Craig was named first-team All–Southern Conference in 1938, but South Carolina went 6-4-1 and he flew under the radar, earning only honorable mention plaudits as an All-America. He was virtually unknown when Lambeau picked him in the sixth round.

In Green Bay, Craig played end only when the Packers were on defense. On offense he was a quarterback, and in that role he was almost exclusively a blocking back. He played in every game during the 1939 regular season, starting eight of them. But he did not throw a pass, and carried only twice, for six yards, and had three receptions for 44 more. On paper he hardly counted. And yet no player was more important to the Packers' fifth NFL championship. Just as he had been at South Carolina, Craig was a fierce pass rusher. And as a lead blocker he was devastating. His nickname on the team was "Superman," because of both his strength and his chiseled frame. "He was one of the most perfectly built human beings I've ever seen," former teammate Clyde Goodnight, who joined the Packers in 1945, once said. "He looked like Hercules. He was just tough."

With the addition of Craig, Lambeau moved Hutson to the defensive backfield, where he was a game-breaker of a different sort. He intercepted only one pass in 1939, but one year later he led the league with six. He would retire after the 1945 season with 30. Most important, though, the move spared him from the physical punishment of playing defensive end. In 1939, Hutson again led the NFL in receiving, and he averaged nearly 25 yards a catch. "In other words," wrote author

Eric Goska, "he moved the ball nearly a quarter of the length of the field every time he touched it." Green Bay left halfback Cecil Isbell, who threw 33 of his 61 career regular-season touchdown passes to Hutson, summed up the impact of Craig perfectly: "Don [Hutson] lasted 11 years, but I don't think he would have survived more than a couple if the Packers had not latched on to Larry Craig."

Green Bay was not dominant in Craig's rookie

Rookie Chicago Bears halfback Beattie Feathers (48) posing with guard Joe Kopcha in 1934, when Feathers became the first player to rush for more than 1,000 yards in a season.

Packers halfback Cecil Isbell carries the ball against the New York Giants in the 1939 NFL Championship Game at Milwaukee's State Fair Park. Green Bay defeated New York 27–0 to win a fifth league title.

season, but with Hutson leading the way, the Packers cruised to the Western Division championship with a record of 9-2. They then drubbed the Giants 27–0 in Milwaukee on December 10 in an NFL title-game rematch. It was sweet revenge for 1938, but it came with a measure of acrimony. Green Bay was supposed to host the championship, but the NFL had decreed that the game had to be played at Milwaukee's State Fair Park, because it held 7,000 more people than City Stadium. Fans in Green Bay were understandably dismayed, while

the New York sportswriters—who were no longer so enamored of the David versus Goliath story line when it came to the Packers and the Giants—grumbled for another reason. Green Bay, they said, was too small-time for the NFL. The town's most vociferous doubter was Bill Corum, columnist for the *New York Journal-American*, who before the game wrote that it was time for the league to drop its smallest outpost. Defending his argument in another column the weekend of the game, Corum acknowledged Green Bay as a special place in the history of pro football, but then said, "Cooperstown was the cradle of baseball. It can't have a team in the major leagues just because of that."

It was a tortured analogy—among other things, Cooperstown had never even fielded a major league team—but it was cutting all the same. Speaking up on behalf of the Packers, though, was none other than the leader of their greatest rival, Bears coach George Halas. "Let Mr. Corum confine his activities to Times Square," Halas said. "We'll take care of the Western division. Green Bay will retain its franchise as long as I have anything to say about it."

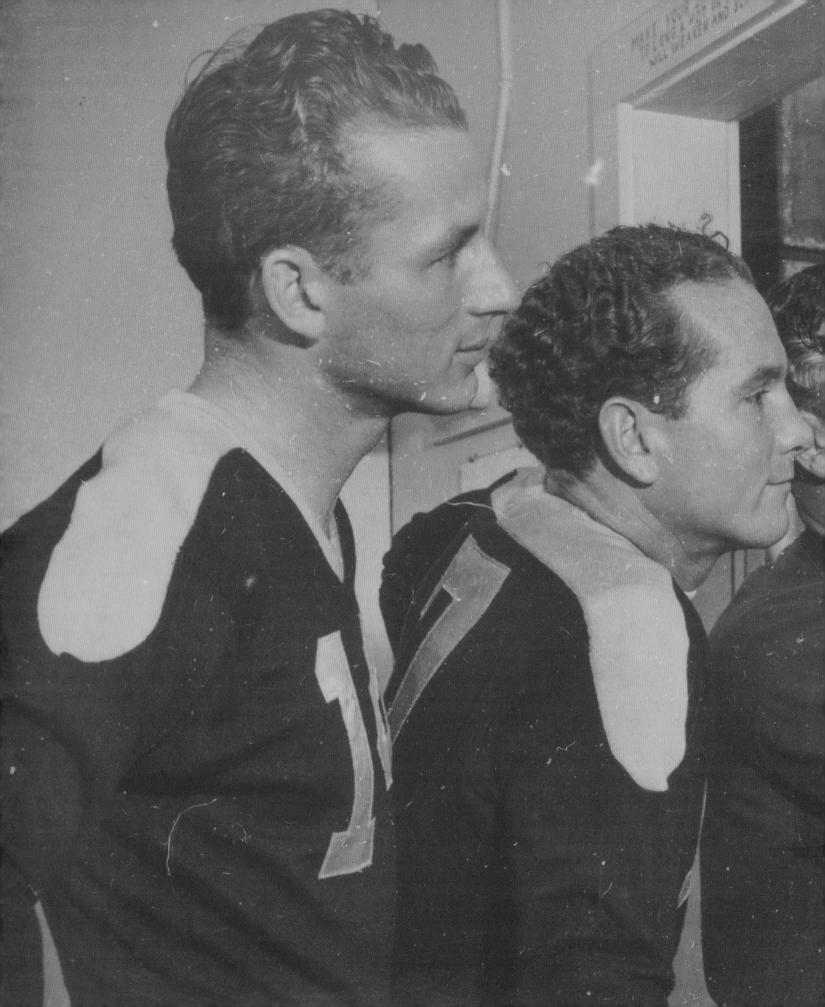

CHAPTER 9

WAR, AND A LAST HURRAH

Unlike Prohibition, which Green Bay largely ignored, and the Great Depression, which the city came through in relatively robust financial shape, there was no getting around the pain and hardship of World War II. In addition to manpower shortages, rationing, and travel restrictions, Brown County sent nearly 8,500 men and women into service between 1940 and 1945, and 185 military personnel from the county were killed in action or died of combat wounds. The first to fall was Marine Private First Class Earl Wallen, who had been struck down during the attack on Pearl Harbor while manning an antiaircraft gun in the crow's nest of the USS *California*. Wallen was the son of Sue Wallen, an assistant manager at the downtown Astor Hotel, where many of Green Bay's unmarried players lived during the season. She was so well known to so many on the team that the *Press-Gazette* dubbed her the "Mother of the Green Bay Packers." In 1944, the members of the Sullivan Legion Post, which was named in honor of Sergeant William Sullivan, the city's first casualty in World War I—and which had been the Packers' beneficiary since 1923—voted to rename their organization the Sullivan-Wallen American Legion Post.

In 1940 the population of Green Bay was 46,205. Only a small fraction of that number were Packers past and present. In the neighborhood of 300 men had played for the team since 1919, but a resident of the city could be forgiven for thinking that there were current and former players everywhere. Men who had played for Green Bay tended to stay in Green Bay, some because it was their hometown and others because they liked it there. Tubby Bero was a police inspector. Dutch Dwyer was the assis- tant city attorney, and his younger brother Rigney was the register of deeds for Brown County. Wally Ladrow was a mailman, and Andy Muldoon was a guard at the courthouse. Dave Zuidmulder was a city fireman. Verne Lewellen and Lavvie Dilweg were both lawyers in private practice. Mike Mi- chalske was the line coach at St. Norbert College. Brothers Carl and Martin Zoll were continuing in their family's building-stone business. Boob Dar- ling was selling insurance in Allouez, and Jug Earp was a car salesman in Green Bay. Hank Bruder ran a tire shop. Arnie Herber had his own clothing store in De Pere. And Don Hutson and Buckets Goldenberg were only a year away from opening the Packers Playdium, a bowling alley and bar that would be in operation for the next 25 years (though Hutson sold the place in the early 1950s). Players lived down the street and around the corner, shopped at the same supermarkets, and ate at the same restaurants. They played in bowling leagues and on basketball teams in the off-season. The unmarried players spent their downtime hanging out in front of the Astor Hotel and eating meals across the street in the first-floor cafeteria of the YWCA. It seemed like they were everywhere because they *were* everywhere.

And almost all of them had families. Their wives were active in social clubs and their children went to city schools. One of those kids was Donald Earl Lambeau, Curly and Marguerite Lambeau's only child. Born on September 16, 1920, Don Lambeau grew up on Green Bay's east side. He attended Green Bay East High and, just like his father, was a star fullback. In the annual rivalry game against Green Bay West in 1937, his senior season, Don carried six times for 49 yards and scored on a two-yard touchdown run in the third quarter of East's 33–6 victory. After graduation, he left for Fordham, in the Bronx, to play for coach Jim Crowley, Curly Lambeau's former East High halfback. Don had the same mass of dark hair and handsome features as his father, but he was heavier, beefier, and not quite as good an athlete. He played for the Rams' freshman team in the fall of 1938, but he never earned a varsity letter.

By the time Don left for Fordham, his family had already broken apart. On May 22, 1934, Marguerite Lambeau was granted a decree of divorce from Curly by circuit judge Henry Graass — the same jurist who had overseen Willard Bent's successful lawsuit against the Packers one year earlier. The grounds were cruel and inhuman treatment. In her complaint, Marguerite claimed that

Lambeau had quarreled with her repeatedly from the earliest days of their marriage and that he had informed her that he no longer cared for her. The *Press-Gazette* story on the case was careful to note that, for legal reasons, the charges were "largely perfunctory in nature."

Left unmentioned in the story was that another example of cruel and inhuman treatment is the flaunting of a relationship outside the marriage. And Curly Lambeau had a reputation as a ladies' man — a fact of which Marguerite was well aware. "She said it really wasn't his fault," Patricia Vandeveld, a longtime friend of Marguerite's, said in 2011. "Women used to call him all the time. She said she'd answer the telephone, and somebody would hang up. She knew who it probably was, and she listened in a few times. She was amazed at how the women would call him and ask to meet for a drink or something. Even people she knew real well."

Vandeveld attributed the end of the Lambeaus' marriage to the marathon road trip the Packers took at the end of the 1932 season. On November 10, the team departed Green Bay for Boston, the first stop on a six-game, 32-day road swing. The Packers were 7-0-1 and seemingly marching to their fourth straight NFL championship. Green Bay won three of the first four games on the trip and, at 10-1-1, was ahead of the second-place Portsmouth Spartans (5-1-4) and the third-place Chicago Bears (4-1-6). But the Packers dropped the last two games of the season, losing 19–0 to the Spartans and then 9–0 to the Bears. And because the league did not count ties when calculating winning percentage, Portsmouth and Chicago finished the season in a dead heat for first place and played for the championship on December 18. Green Bay returned home.

Most of the Packers did not stay for long, though. Two days after the loss to the Bears, Lambeau and 17 of his players departed on a barnstorming tour that began in Honolulu, continued with games on the West Coast, and did not end

PREVIOUS SPREAD
Don Hutson and left halfback Cecil Isbell look on as Curly Lambeau diagrams a play. Before he abruptly retired following the 1942 season, Isbell (center) was on his way to becoming one of the greatest passers of pro football's first fifty years.

With World War II robbing the NFL of its best players, Don Hutson went from being the best receiver in pro football to something even more unapproachable.

until the second week of February. Johnny Blood, who said that he wanted to get away from the cold Green Bay winters — on the day the Packers left, the high temperature in the city was 16 degrees — had arranged the Hawaiian leg of the trip on his own initiative. In early December, Blood had taken it upon himself to cable the sports editor of the *Honolulu Star-Bulletin,* saying that the Packers would like to play in a game in Hawaii and adding, "Please wire name of responsible promoter." Fifteen days later, Blood, Lambeau, and 16 other players boarded the SS *Mariposa* in Los Angeles, bound for Honolulu.

Also aboard the *Mariposa* was Billie John Copeland, a 24-year-old starlet from Los Angeles. On August 2, 1927, Copeland, whose real first name was Willie, had won the Miss California pageant in San Francisco, punching her ticket to Atlantic City to compete in the Miss America competition. But she never made the trip to New Jersey. Seventeen days after her victory, the *San Francisco Chronicle* announced that Copeland had been disqualified on charges of "professionalism." Pageant rules dictated that a girl was ineligible if she had had any stage, screen, or modeling experience. And according to the paper, Copeland — who had been described at the pageant as a student from Ventura—had "appeared in a revue at two theaters in this state, playing at least a week in each."

There are no details about just what happened between Lambeau and Copeland aboard the *Mariposa*, or in Honolulu, but according to Vandeveld it was not long after Lambeau returned to Green Bay that he asked Marguerite for a divorce. It wasn't until May 18, 1934, though, that the *Press-Gazette* reported that Marguerite was seeking to legally terminate her marriage. She won her suit and gained possession of the family home on Miramar Drive and the Nash car, as well as full custody of Don, who was 13. A little over a year later, on June 26, 1935, Curly married Copeland in a civil ceremony in Waukegan, Illinois.

Don and his father maintained a relatively close relationship after the divorce. He and his mother went to Chicago together to attend the Packers' 17–14 victory over the Bears on October 27, 1935. And in November 1938, during the Packers' visit to New York to play the Giants, Lambeau and several of his players attended the Fordham freshman team's game against the Army plebes at West Point. (According to the *Press-Gazette,* Don played only a few minutes before being forced from the game because of an injured shoulder.) Curly, according to the divorce ruling, was responsible for paying all of his son's expenses through college.

Don attended Fordham for almost two years before he withdrew from school on February 13, 1940. One year later he enlisted in the Army. He went into the Signal Corps and was stationed at Fort Lewis, Washington, and then was reassigned in late 1941 to duty in the Philippines. On December 7, 1941, the day of the Japanese attack on the U.S. Pacific Fleet at Pearl Harbor, he was on a ship sailing out of San Francisco Bay. With Japanese submarines rumored to be operating off the coast of California, Lambeau's ship was abruptly ordered to return to San Francisco. He would find himself in the fight soon enough. Within two years, Lambeau was in the mountainous jungles of New Guinea, in the middle of what became known as the Green War, General Douglas MacArthur's western advance along the island's northern coastline.

Lambeau was assigned to a small team of surveyors marking out a route for 100 miles of telephone line in the Markham River Valley, a flat, steamy expanse of land that lies between two ranges of mountains. For five grueling months, Lambeau and his team worked in 90-degree heat, crossing fetid swamps, farmland with razor-sharp tall grass, and dangerously fast rivers swollen by monsoon rains. As they worked in advance of the main construction crew, the men's only company at times was the flies and gnats that constantly swarmed about them. Swatting away bugs was such a fundamental part of life on the island that soldiers came to refer to it as "the New Guinea salute."

Encountering enemy soldiers was a concern, to be sure, but the primary threat to a soldier's life in New Guinea was disease. "It was a rare infantryman who wasn't afflicted with yaws, scrub typhus, blackwater fever, ringworm, malaria, amoebic dysentery, or bacillary dysentery," William Manchester wrote in *American Caesar,* his epic biography of MacArthur. "For every man suffering from a gunshot wound, five were laid low with illness." Sure enough, not long after Staff Sergeant Lambeau and his team finished their survey, on April 8, 1944, he fell seriously ill with scrub typhus and was hospitalized, meaning that his fever must have risen above 102 degrees, the standard for hospitalization for American troops in New Guinea.

The War Department notified Marguerite of her son's illness on April 28, and she and Curly kept up a worried vigil for him, briefly reconnecting to share news and give each other moral support. More than two weeks later, the paper reported that Don was improving but still laid up in an island hospital. He ultimately recovered from his illness and finished up his war service in the Philippines. Don Lambeau was discharged from the Army 55 days after V-J Day, on October 27, 1945. The next day he watched from the bench at City Stadium as his father's team rolled over the Chicago Cardinals 33–14.

◆ ◆ ◆

According to *The Pro Football Chronicle,* a total of 638 people from the NFL — players, coaches, and management — served in World War II. The *Press-Gazette* referred several times during the war to what it called the league's manpower shortage, but that undersold the gravity of the situation. Starting in 1942, military service took away so many players, including most of the game's stars, that the NFL actually considered shutting down. It continued on through the use of overage and draft-deferred manpower, as well as a shortened roster of teams. The Cleveland Rams did not play in 1943, and the Brooklyn Dodgers shut down in 1945. The Pittsburgh Steelers carried on by merging with two teams in consecutive years — first the Philadelphia Eagles, in 1943, and then the Chicago Cardinals, in 1944. According to David S. Neft and Richard M. Cohen's encyclopedic *Pro Football: The Early Years,* 31 Packers players (defined as anyone who had appeared in at least one league game before being inducted) entered military service during the years 1941–1945. Among them were veteran stalwarts Clarke Hinkle and his primary backup at fullback, Ed Jankowski, as well as breakaway halfback Andy Uram, who in 1939 had set an NFL record for the longest run from scrimmage when he raced 97 yards for a touchdown during a victory over the Chicago Cardinals. Also departing for the military were starting center George Svendsen and guard Russ Letlow, the first draft pick in the history of the franchise. To replace them, Lambeau cast a wide net, breaking out of his Notre Dame network and signing players off the street.

One of them was six-foot-four, 222-pound guard Fred Vant Hull, whom the *Press-Gazette* announced as a new Packer on June 6, 1942. Vant Hull had played at Minnesota in 1939 and '40, when the Golden Gophers won the national championship, but he left school before his senior season to transfer to Navy. He spent less than a year at Annapolis, though, missing the plebe football season with a foot injury and resigning from the academy. Despite not having played a down of competitive football in nearly two years, Vant Hull came off the bench as a tackle for Green Bay in the Packers' 1942 season opener, a 44–28 loss to the Bears at City Stadium.

Another curious signing of Lambeau's in 1942 was Bob Flowers, a six-foot-one, 205-pound center who, like Vant Hull, was several years removed from having suited up in a live game. The blond-haired Flowers had been a star high school quarterback in Big Spring, Texas, but he never earned a varsity letter in college, despite attempts to catch on at Tulane, Texas, and Texas Tech. He played briefly with the Big Spring Spartans, an independent town team, in 1937, but according to the Big Spring directory, he was working one year later as a laborer at the Cosden Petroleum Corporation. By then he was already married with a young daughter. On the draft card that he completed in October 1940, he listed himself as a student at Texas Tech, but the school's alumni association, which maintains enrollment records, has nothing on Flowers in its files. When Lambeau announced his signing in August 1942, he said that Flowers — who was, and still is, listed by the Packers as a product of Texas Tech — had been working in California. That may be so. His wife, Patricia, had lived in Hollywood for a time before her marriage. But there is no record of Flowers living anywhere else but Big Spring. He didn't see action for Green Bay in 1942 until he came in as a substitute in a 38–7 defeat of the Lions in week three — nearly five years after his last documented appearance in a football game. Flowers would play for the Packers through the 1949 season, so his NFL career was hardly a fluke. But it remains very likely that he never would have made an NFL roster if not for World War II.

Lambeau tried to put the best face possible on the situation. "With this player shortage staring at us, we jumped at the chance to give [Vant Hull] a chance," he told the *Chicago Tribune* when he was in town for the NFL meetings in April 1943. "A lot of good boys like Flowers and Vant Hull slipped away from us [in the past] . . . A football player might be a trifle rusty after a two or three year layoff, but he'll come back quicker than you think. There are any number of Flowers and Vant Hulls who'll welcome the chance to play. It's up to us to find 'em."

With the seriously diluted NFL as context, Don Hutson's 1942 season bears some clear-eyed scrutiny. He played in all 11 of the Packers' games that season — though he started only four of them — and dominated the league, setting single-season records for catches (74), receiving yards (1,211), touchdown catches (17), and points scored (138).* In each of those categories, Hutson more than doubled the numbers of his next closest competitor. Writer George Will's line about Babe Ruth, "like an Everest in Kansas," comes to mind. And the Babe's 1920 season, when he hit 54 homers while nobody else in the major leagues hit more than 19, may be the closest analogue in sports to Hutson's 1942. Other comparable performances would be Wayne Gretzky's 92-goal NHL season in 1981–82 and Stephen Curry's 402 three-pointers in the NBA in 2015–16 — numbers that were so much greater than those of their peers that they forever changed the way their sport was played. But Hutson wasn't competing in a league that was at full strength. He was lining up against silhouettes.

Before the war, Hutson had been far and away the best receiver in the NFL. In the first seven years of his career, he did more to change the game than any man in the history of the sport. But with

World War II robbing the league of its best players, Hutson went from being the best receiver ever to something even more unapproachable. In the seven seasons before 1942, he caught 262 passes, 53 of them for touchdowns. In the four years from 1942 to 1945, though, he caught 226 passes, 46 of them for touchdowns. Some of his career numbers would not be approached for more than a generation.

In addition to being the NFL's marquee player, Hutson supported the war effort back home by doing such things as chairing a war-fund drive for the Red Cross and serving on a civilian advisory committee for the recruiting efforts of the Green

Thirty-one Packers players served in World War II. The only one killed in action was guard Howard "Smiley" Johnson, a Marine first lieutenant who lost his life in February 1945 during the fight for Iwo Jima.

---

* *The low number of starts wasn't unusual for Hutson. Perhaps because of his smaller stature, he started only 60 of 117 games in his career.*

Bay chapter of the Benevolent and Protective Order of Elks. In 1989, Hutson told a reporter from the *Los Angeles Times* that he hadn't gone into the service during the war because his draft number never came up. "I was I-A the last year," Hutson said, referring to the Selective Service classification for men deemed eligible for military service. "But I had three daughters, and I was never called."* Julia Hutson, named for her mother, was three when the war began. Her sisters, Martha and Jane, were born in 1943 and 1944, respectively.

Jane Robert Hutson was named after one of her father's younger brothers, Robert Porter Hutson, who had been killed in action eight and a half months before she was born. Along with his twin brother, Raymond, Robert had enlisted in the Army before Pearl Harbor, in early September 1941. Nearly two years later he was a 23-year-old flight officer in the Army Air Force, serving with the 46th Troop Carrier Squadron of the 317th Troop Carrier Group, which at the time was supporting Allied operations on New Guinea. On the morning of August 27, 1943, Robert was piloting a Douglas C-47 Skytrain loaded with bombs and ammunition from Port Moresby to the village of Wau, about 150 densely jungled miles to the north. Flying with him were three other American crew members and three soldiers from the Royal

---

Through 1944, Hutson was presumably classified as III-A, which was for men who were ineligible for service because they had dependents at home.

Australian Air Force. At approximately 10:25 a.m., Hutson's plane slammed into the side of one of the green mountains in New Guinea's Owen Stanley Range. The ordnance on board exploded on impact, scattering pieces of the fiery wreckage and its shattered crew over a wide area. Australian troops reached the crash site on foot a few weeks later. The men who had been on the plane were not identifiable from the remains that were recovered.

Don had been aware since early September that Robert was missing, but in a phone call with his mother, Mabel, on Thursday, September 23, he learned the awful truth—and more. According to the *Press-Gazette,* in addition to giving him the news about Robert, his mother also informed him that his 56-year-old father, Roy, had died suddenly and unexpectedly of a stroke shortly after hearing of Robert's death. It was shock upon shock. Roy Hutson had been in perfect health. Don had toyed with the idea of retirement earlier in the year, before signing with the Packers on August 7. "Don feels he owes it to football to continue," Lambeau said at the time. "Most of his success in his off-the-field life has resulted from his work on the gridiron. The game needs Hutson and we feel that Don, besides being a definite help to the Packers, will play a big part in building home-front morale."

But after Hutson got the news about his brother and his father, nobody was sure whether he was going to be available for Green Bay's opening-day game against the Bears at City Stadium on September 26. It was only after he received permission from his mother that Hutson agreed to play. He would leave for his father's funeral in Pine Bluff, Arkansas, immediately after the game.

Sixty years later, in December 2003, Packers quarterback Brett Favre threw for 399 yards and four touchdowns the day after he learned that his father had died. It was an emotional, bittersweet tribute to the man who had raised him. But it was, in a sense, not nearly on the same level as what Hutson did against Chicago—and not merely because of the dual shocks of having lost his brother

and his father. Favre did his work against the 4-12 Oakland Raiders, who finished the season with the third-worst defense in football. The Bears team that Hutson and the Packers were facing had won NFL championships in 1940 and '41 and had gone 11-0 in 1942 before losing to the Redskins in the league title game. Chicago had not lost or tied a regular-season game in almost two years.

On a sunny, warm day at City Stadium, the stands were packed with 23,675 fans, the largest crowd in Packers history. But with the Bears leading 21–14 midway through the fourth quarter, there seemed to be little to cheer about. Chicago had held Hutson without a catch—his only contributions on the score sheet had been his two conversion kicks after Green Bay's first two scores. But a 25-yard run by halfback Tony Canadeo put the ball on the Chicago 40-yard line, and from there Hutson, as was his custom, struck quickly. Three plays later, on third-and-10, he snared a low throw from Canadeo to give Green Bay a first down at the Chicago 26. After two more incomplete passes, Canadeo found him again at the 11. Hutson squeezed between Bears defensive backs Ray "Scooter" McLean and Harry Clarke to make the catch, and then he wheeled around and loped over the goal line for the final touchdown of the game. He then kicked his third extra point of the day to make the score 21–21. The crowd, keenly aware of what was going on, gave him a long and loud ovation. The game ended with no more scoring, and the legend of Don Hutson grew even larger. "There was melodrama in that touchdown and the point after," wrote Dave Yuenger in the *Press-Gazette.* "The seven points not only tied the Bears at 21 to 21 but brought into relief the sacrifice which Hutson had made to remain here to play despite the tragedy which struck his private life last week."

Hutson did not stay after the game to celebrate with his teammates. He left City Stadium, hopped a Milwaukee Road train to Chicago, and caught a flight to Memphis, where friends met him and drove him the 150 miles back to Pine Bluff. The next day he stood by his mother while they put his father in the ground.

· · ·

Eighteen active or former NFL players lost their lives in World War II. The only Packer to die in the conflict was affable reserve guard Howard "Smiley" Johnson, a Marine first lieutenant who was killed by an exploding artillery shell on Iwo Jima on February 19, 1945. Johnson was an orphan from Nashville. His father had died suddenly of a heart condition in 1923, when Howard was only six years old. After his father's death, Johnson's mother moved about an hour away, to Clarksville, where she went to work as a maid at the Hotel Montgomery. While their mother lived and worked at the hotel, Howard and his older brother and two younger sisters went to live in a nearby orphanage, the Independent Order of Odd Fellows Home, in New Providence. While living at the home, Howard played football at Clarksville High, and from there he went on to play at Georgia, where the coach through his sophomore year was Harry Mehre, one of Lambeau's most valuable Notre Dame contacts. Another of Lambeau's Fighting Irish cronies in Athens was Rex Enright, the former Green Bay fullback, who was the Bulldogs' basketball coach. According to Lambeau, it was Enright who told him about the six-foot-one, 210-pound Johnson. "Enright rarely leans over backwards in describing a player," Lambeau told the *Press-Gazette* when Johnson's signing was announced on April 30, 1940. "But when he visited us in California last January he couldn't say enough about this man."

Near the end of Johnson's second season with the Packers, he, Lambeau, and the rest of his teammates watched from the second deck of Comiskey Park—above the south end zone and beneath the press box—as the Bears beat the Cardinals 34–24

to force a playoff with Green Bay for the Western Division championship. It was December 7, 1941. Lambeau had taken his boys to Chicago's South Side that day to scout the Bears, but all anybody could talk about was the news that the Japanese had attacked Pearl Harbor. The accounts of people who were at the game differ as to whether an announcement was made over the public address system or whether word spread through the crowd on its own—though neither the *Chicago Tribune* nor the *Press-Gazette* made any mention of an announcement being made in their coverage of the game. Years later, Green Bay halfback Tony Canadeo, who was a 22-year-old rookie in 1941, said, "Everybody was saying, 'Pearl Harbor? Where the hell is that?'"

Everyone would find out soon enough, including Canadeo. He would go on to become one of the greatest Packers ever, but not until after World War II had put his career on hold for a significant number of years—though not enough to keep him out of the Hall of Fame.

Canadeo's connection with the Packers began early, while he was still in high school. The son of a streetcar motorman from Chicago's West Side, he had been a standout at Steinmetz High, in Chicago, but did not have any scholarship offers to play ball in college. His older brother, Savior, was a welterweight boxer at St. Norbert College, in De Pere.* Savior knew Tiny Cahoon, the former Packers tackle who had retired from the NFL to become a high school coach, first at West De Pere and then, in 1933, at Green Bay West. Cahoon had played at Gonzaga, in Spokane, Washington, for Gus Dorais, and had come to Green Bay via Lambeau's extensive Notre Dame network. The balding, portly Cahoon functioned as Gonzaga's primary recruiting contact in northeastern Wisconsin. "I went up to St. Norbert to see my brother and the school, and I got acquainted with these guys who were going

---

* *Before the NCAA discontinued it in 1960, college boxing was a major sport going back to the years after World War I, and in few places was it a bigger deal than in Wisconsin. The Badgers won eight national championships, beginning in 1939, and used to draw crowds of 12,000 to 15,000 to the Wisconsin Field House.*

out [to Gonzaga] and learned about the school," Tony told author Richard Whittingham in *What a Game They Played*. "I didn't have any other offers, and I actually didn't have one from Gonzaga either. But I was told if you went out there and made the team, you would be given a full scholarship."

It was not much to go on — and if he didn't make the team, Canadeo would have had to either go back home or get a job in Spokane — but he made the trip that summer nonetheless. And he made the team. It was with the Bulldogs that Canadeo earned the nickname "the Gray Ghost of Gonzaga" because his hair had gone prematurely silver even before he arrived on campus as a freshman. A powerful runner, Canadeo was five foot eleven and 190 pounds, with a thick frame that rested atop a pair of legs so muscular they could have been

carved by Michelangelo. He was also versatile, more than capable as a kicker and a passer. Lambeau, who coveted multipurpose backs, picked Canadeo in the ninth round of the NFL draft, on December 10, 1940. He played one season alongside fullback Clarke Hinkle, though Canadeo was little more than a backup. Hinkle rushed a league-high 129 times that season for 393 yards and five touchdowns. But on June 2, 1942, less than six months after the Packers lost the 1941 Western Division playoff to the Bears, 33–14, Hinkle was commissioned as a lieutenant junior grade in the Coast Guard. He had opted for the commission rather than wait to be inducted into the Army. He never played football again.

According to the *Press-Gazette*, the Selective Service board in Green Bay had reclassified Hin-

The Packers beat the New York Giants to win their sixth NFL championship — and their last under Lambeau — on December 17, 1944. Fullback Ted Fritsch (64) was the star of the day, scoring both touchdowns in a 14–7 victory.

kle, who was married with no children, from III-A to I-A—from deferred for service to available for service—sometime in early 1942. Canadeo was single with no dependents in the spring of 1943, when he was called to duty and sent to naval pre-flight training at DePauw University, in Green-castle, Indiana. On August 5, the *Press-Gazette* reported that Canadeo had logged more than 25 hours of flying time and had passed all of his pre-flight tests, but 16 days later the paper reported that he had been honorably discharged from the Navy and had signed a contract to play for the Packers in 1943. No reason was given for his dis-

charge. Robert Canadeo, Tony's oldest son, says that it is possible his father washed out of flight school, but he does not know for sure.

Canadeo played in all 10 games that season for 7-2-1 Green Bay, and his versatility was never more evident. He was like the Packers' Swiss Army knife, leading them in rushing and kick returns and ranking second to Hutson in scoring. Most important, he also led them in passing, throw-ing for 875 yards and nine touchdowns—the first one going to Hutson in the emotional tie with the Bears in week one.

Canadeo's emergence as a passer was fortuitous

for Lambeau, coming as it did on the heels of the abrupt retirement of Cecil Isbell, who had left Green Bay in July 1943 to become the backfield coach at Purdue, his alma mater. A first-round pick in 1938, the wiry-haired Texan replaced Arnie Herber in 1940 as the primary passer in Lambeau's Box offense. Herber, whose play had declined precipitously while he struggled with both his weight and a knee injury, had been cut loose on the eve of the 1941 season. Isbell was a wonderful runner, and an even better passer. In 1945, Lambeau told the United Press that he considered Isbell the greatest passer in the history of pro football. "Isbell was a master at any range," he said. "He could throw soft passes, bullet passes or long passes." Had Isbell played longer, it is almost certain that he would be not only in the Hall of Fame but also in the discussion as one of the great passers of pro football's first 50 years. The 1942 season was just his fifth in the NFL. It was also his last—and his finest. He led the league in passing for the second straight year, with 2,021 yards and 24 touchdowns, both NFL records. And then he walked away for good. Few players in NFL history have ever left on a higher note. "I hadn't been up in Green Bay long when I saw Lambeau go around the locker room and tell players like Herber and [end Milt] Gantenbein and [quarterback] Hank Bruder that they were all done," Isbell later said. "I sat there and watched and then I vowed that it would never happen to me. I'd quit before they came around to tell me."

But even Canadeo's status as the Packers' new primary passer—as well as his marriage on October 11, 1943, one day after he had thrown three touchdown passes in a 35–14 victory over the Lions at City Stadium—could not keep him out of World War II. He was recalled to active duty by the Army in late December. He played in three games for the Packers in midseason in 1944, when he was back home in Green Bay on furlough for the birth of his first son. But Canadeo, who was eventually stationed in England with an antiaircraft unit, missed the Packers' run to their sixth NFL championship. He would also miss all of the 1945 season.

◆ ◆ ◆

The Packers' championship season in 1944, the last of the Curly Lambeau era, was unlike any other in the club's history. Without Canadeo for all but three games, Lambeau divided the rushing duties. Four backs, led by third-year fullback Ted Fritsch, each ran for 200 yards or more. And for the first time since 1933 the team actually scored more rushing touchdowns (16) than receiving touchdowns (15). The Packers were also shut out twice for the first time in 10 years. Their rushing and passing offense both ranked fourth in the 10-team NFL, while their defense was fifth. "On paper, Green Bay appeared little better than average," wrote Eric Goska in his 2004 record book, *Green Bay Packers: A Measure of Greatness*. "But the Packers still had Don Hutson."

Before the season, Hutson had again mused publicly about retirement, and he did not sign with Lambeau until September 2. His business interests had by this time expanded beyond the Packers Playdium. "I went into the finance business as well," Hutson told Richard Whittingham in *What a Game They Played*. "There was a lot going on as a result of my off-season business activities and as a result, for several years, I kept announcing that I was going to retire from football and devote my entire time to my business interests. But I kept coming back . . . It was damn near impossible for me to quit football in Green Bay. You know what the Packers meant to the town and I'd been having some good years. I got the feeling they wanted me to play forever."

Hutson might not have been as enthusiastic about football as he once was, but even at 31 he was still far and away the best receiver in the game, still a sleek, fast, change-of-pace marvel, still capable of breaking a game wide open. In Green Bay's 34–7 drubbing of the combined Cardinals-Steelers team—affectionately known as the Card-Pitt Carpets — at City Stadium on October 8, Hutson caught 11 passes for 207 yards and two touchdowns, the first on a 55-yard bomb after he had sped into the clear past Carpets linebacker John Grigas. After the game, Card-Pitt coach Phil Handler had a neat summary for what had just happened to his team: "Too much Hutson."*

Both of Hutson's touchdown catches against the Carpets had come on passes thrown by halfback Irv Comp, who was in his second season out of tiny St. Benedict's College (now Benedictine College), in Atchison, Kansas. With the loss of Canadeo to military service, Comp had become the Packers' primary passer. A lanky six foot three, with a shock of thick black hair and an angular, smiling face, Comp was legally blind in his right eye because of a cataract he had developed as a teenager, when he was a four-sport star at Milwaukee's Bay View High. He had done well as a rookie in 1943, ranking second on the team in passing and third in rushing. But he had made his biggest impact on defense, intercepting 10 passes. Hutson took Comp under his wing, catching passes from him after every practice and dispensing pointers about avoiding the rush and throwing the long ball. Hutson's tutelage made such an impact that in 1944 the duo represented the most devastating passing combination in the NFL. Comp led the league in passing, with 1,159 yards — ahead of such hurlers as Sammy Baugh and Sid Luckman — while Hutson was tops in every major receiving category, with 58 catches (no other Green Bay receiver had more than nine) for 886 yards and nine touchdowns. He also led the league with 85 points, converting on 31 of 33 extra points.

Green Bay won its first six games that season on

its way to a record of 8-2, and finished comfortably atop the Western Division. The championship would pit the Packers against the Giants at the Polo Grounds on December 17, the third time that the two old rivals had been matched up against each other in the title game since 1938. New York in 1944 was an almost perfect example of the NFL during World War II, a mix of castoffs, over-the-hill veterans, and young players short on experience — a team capable of thrilling play but also inept and boring much of the time. The Giants' quarterback was former Packers great Arnie Herber, who had been out of football for three years and was so overweight when he arrived at training camp that one writer called him a "tub of lard." Herber was 34. Kicker Ken Strong, who had not played in the league since 1939, came out of retirement at the age of 37. And 35-year-old center Mel Hein played for New York on Sundays after coaching the Union College Dutchmen, in Schenectady, New York, on Saturdays.

Herber and the Giants had shut out Green Bay 24–0 at the Polo Grounds on November 19. The big play for New York that day had come on Herber's — and the Giants' — only completion of the game, a 36-yard scoring pass to Frank Liebel that gave New York a 14–0 second-quarter lead. The game got so out of hand that Lambeau sat Hutson in the fourth quarter. "What was the use of using him up in that kind of a game?" Lambeau said.

To prepare for the Championship Game, the coach took his team from Green Bay — where on December 6 there were four inches of snow on the Packers' practice field — to Charlottesville, Virginia, where the team practiced on Lambeth Field, the colonnaded stadium at the University

---

*The "too much Hutson" quote has a tangled history. Though Handler supposedly uttered it after the October 8 game in Green Bay, it was not attributed to him until November 27, 1944, the day after the Packers had drilled the winless Carpets 35–20 in Chicago. "Co-coach Phil Handler of the Card-Pitt combine made exactly the same comment after the game that he did after the earlier engagement in Green Bay," wrote Don Hickok in the Press-Gazette. "Caught at the foot of the ramp leading to the Cardinal dressing room, he declared: 'Too much Hutson, that's all—I hope to live to see the day when we can play the Packers without Hutson.'" In 1945 the quote was also attributed to Handler by junior Press-Gazette reporter Lee Remmel, who later became the Packers' public relations director. In a guest column that he wrote for the Press-Gazette in 1993, Remmel attributed a similar quote to Detroit Lions coach Gus Dorais.

of Virginia. The Cavaliers' coach was Frank Murray, who, as the coach at Marquette from 1922 to 1936, had mentored future Packers greats Lavvie Dilweg and Red Dunn. Green Bay drilled in Charlottesville for nine days before leaving for New York on Friday, December 15. By then, Lambeau had his plan all set.

Against the Giants, Lambeau deployed Hutson primarily as a decoy. He had one reception in the entire game, which came on a pass from Comp in the first quarter that went for 22 yards. With New York focusing on Hutson, fullback Ted Fritsch scored two touchdowns in the second quarter, the first on a one-yard plunge and the second on a 28-yard pass from Comp. Fritsch was all alone on the Giants' 10-yard line when he caught the ball because, according to Comp, Hutson unwittingly sold New York that he was Comp's intended target. "The thing was that Ted and I talked about the play without telling Hutson," Comp told *The Milwaukee Journal* in 1978. "Near the end [of his career], Hutson had a tendency to loaf a little if a pass wasn't supposed to go to him. Since he didn't know he wasn't the primary receiver, he ran a crossing pattern and took both the defensive back and a linebacker with him. Fritsch ran a flair [*sic*] pattern into the left flat, and he was all alone." Green Bay won its sixth NFL championship, 14–7.

Not that many people took notice. The day before the game, the German army had launched a massive offensive against the Allies in the Ardennes Forest. The Battle of the Bulge had begun. Nobody in the United States was thinking much about football. The crowd for the Championship Game was 46,016, more than 10,000 fewer than had come out one month earlier to see the same two teams play on the same field.

Curly Lambeau didn't even return to Green Bay with his team after the game. He stayed behind in New York to attend an NFL meeting. The Packers' trip to Charlottesville had been telling. More and more, Lambeau seemed to prefer life away from his hometown. Since his divorce from Marguerite, the cords that connected him to Green Bay had begun to fray. Very soon, they would start to snap.

CHAPTER 10

THE EARL OF HOLLYWOOD

By the end of World War II, Curly Lambeau had been a fixture on the national sporting scene for more than two decades. Along with the fame that he had brought to the NFL's littlest city, he had also built up a fair amount for himself. He hung out at Toots Shor's and Jack Dempsey's when the Packers were in New York, hobnobbing with the biggest sports stars of the era. He spent his winters in California, befriending a number of well-known Hollywood entertainers. He had a home in Malibu and eventually purchased a ranch in Thousand Oaks. He drove big cars. He always carried a wad of cash. He was burly and handsome and dressed in fancy clothes. He liked to douse himself in cologne. His womanizing and his marriage to a former beauty queen were of a piece with the trajectory of his life. Years before people in Green Bay were saying it derisively, Curly Lambeau had gone Hollywood.

His family life did indeed resemble that of a movie star—which is to say it was a philandering shambles. Lambeau's second marriage had not lasted long. According to the *Press-Gazette* story on the divorce granted to Sue Lambeau (née Billie John Copeland) in circuit court on March 25, 1940 —once again by Judge Henry Graass—Curly and the former Miss California had been separated since September 1937, a little over two years after their wedding. Sue had been pregnant when they separated, and on January 13, 1938, at Queen of Angels Hospital in Los Angeles, she gave birth to a son, whom she christened Earl Louis Lambeau II.

Wisconsin law stipulates that before asking for a divorce, a petitioning spouse needs to have been a resident of the state for at least six months, and a resident of the county in which he or she files for

at least 30 days. The law in 1940 wasn't nearly as clear, but establishing some sort of residency may have been Sue's motivation for moving with Earl from Los Angeles to Green Bay in October 1939. She also, of course, might have simply been trying to save her marriage. Since she had been in town, Curly had been paying her $100 a month in support—an amount that she insisted was not enough. Curly had actually been the first to begin divorce proceedings, on March 18, but she had immediately filed a counterclaim, and it was on her assertions that Judge Graass granted the divorce. The court ordered Curly to pay her $6,875, plus $25 a month in childcare.

Beyond the money, there is no evidence that Curly Lambeau had any relationship with his second child. Sue returned to California after the divorce, and in December 1945 she married Gerald Duryea. She and her son then moved with him to Michigan—first to Detroit and then to the tiny town of Hillsdale. Earl graduated from the University of Michigan in 1959, the same year he legally changed his name to Earl Louis Duryea, the name he had already been using for several years. He then went to the Naval Officer Candidate School in Newport, Rhode Island. After a stint in the Navy, he moved to San Francisco and began working at the Cow Palace, in Daly City. When Curly died, on June 1, 1965, Earl did not return to Green Bay to attend the funeral, nor did his name appear in any of his father's obituaries. Earl went on to a long career as a sports promoter, managing several arenas—including the Cow Palace, the Salt Palace, in Salt Lake City, and the Nassau Veterans Memorial Coliseum, on Long Island—and working for Ringling Bros., Disney's Ice Capades, and the U.S. Olympic Committee, as well as serving as the president of the Harlem Globetrotters in the mid-1980s. But his relationship to his famous father was never publicly mentioned. He had four children of his own. He and his family are part of the Packers' legacy. They are Lambeaus. But their role is unofficial. Unacknowledged.

On July 16, 1945, Curly got married for a third time, to Hollywood socialite Grace Nicholls. The marriage was the fourth for Nicholls, a small, thin, dark-haired beauty who bore a passing resemblance to actress Gene Tierney. Her most recent husband had been Gregory La Cava, the director behind the popular 1930s comedies *My Man Godfrey* and *Stage Door*. Nicholls, who was born in Cleveland in May 1894, was 19 when she got married for the first time and 38 when she got married for the second, to William J. Garland, one of the two sons of Los Angeles railroad and real estate tycoon William Garland, who had left his family an estate estimated at $2.6 million when he died, in 1928.

In May 1933, Grace gave birth to a baby girl named Jane, who soon became the subject of a

sensational inheritance squabble. The five other grandchildren of the late William Garland alleged that Jane was actually the daughter of Grace's first husband, a man named Warren Hoyt, and wanted her cut out of their grandfather's will. For three years the battle raged in the courts, until August 1937, when a judge determined Jane to be the legitimate child of Grace and William J. Garland. The court awarded the four-year-old an equal share in her grandfather's estate.

William J. Garland died in July 1940. His home in Malibu, a tiered, Spanish-style house that faced the beach, was close to one owned by La Cava, and five months after William's death, Grace and the filmmaker wed in a secret ceremony in Las Vegas. But in November 1943, Grace sued La Cava for divorce. Twenty months later she married Curly Lambeau.

Lambeau did not let his third marriage keep him from living up to his reputation as a notorious wolf. "He . . . had a way with women," Lyla Hoyt, Grace's daughter-in-law, said of Lambeau in *West of Eden*, author Jean Stein's 2016 oral history of

Lambeau intended Rockwood Lodge, situated on a bluff overlooking Green Bay, to be pro football's first all-in-one training facility—a place for his players to live and practice.

five Los Angeles families in the mid-20th century. "He had a lady in every place that the Green Bay Packers played football."

In Green Bay, Lambeau's character was well known—his reputation was such that if you were out on a date with a woman, you did not leave her alone in the coach's presence. He had met his second wife, according to rumor, on the way to Honolulu aboard the SS *Mariposa* in December 1932 when he had broken up a fight over her between two of his players. And he was notorious among the men who played on his teams for making advances on their wives and girlfriends. Ward Cuff was a 10-year NFL veteran when he joined the Packers in 1947. He and Lambeau did not get along, partly because of disagreements over money but also because Cuff did not care for his coach's low personal conduct. "A lot of the players didn't like Curly and there was a pretty good reason for it," Cuff said in 2001, the year before he died at age 90. "He was taking their money, trying to date their wives. I'll tell you, he was bad."

Lambeau's womanizing and marriage to a Hollywood socialite who had been married three times before—and who had been at the center of a high-profile paternity case—were sources of gossip in Green Bay, if not of concern. The Packers were still winning, after all. But that was about to change.

◆ ◆ ◆

The All-America Football Conference was founded on June 4, 1944, two days before D-Day, at the Jefferson Hotel, in St. Louis. The league—the first serious challenger to the NFL since Red Grange and C. C. Pyle's short-lived American Football League in 1926—was the brainchild of *Chicago Tribune* editor Arch Ward, who had turned down an offer to be the commissioner of the NFL only a few years before. Ward felt that, between players then in the military and those on the rosters of college and NFL teams, there was going to be ample opportunity for the expansion of pro football in postwar America. He was not the only one who saw things that way. Several of the wealthy men who met with him in St. Louis had already had their applications for new franchises denied by the NFL. There were representatives at that first meeting from six cities: Buffalo, Chicago,

Cleveland, Los Angeles, New York, and San Francisco. Applications for teams in Baltimore, Boston, Detroit, and Philadelphia were made at a second organizational meeting in Chicago three months later.* It was at that time that the applicants for the new league also made an official decision not to pursue any player who was under contract to a team in the NFL or who still had college eligibility remaining. On September 5, 1944, Ward wrote in his *Tribune* column, "In the Wake of the News":

> *We feel an obligation to the owners of teams in the National Football league . . . Wildcat promoters could cause them embarrassment no end by raiding their talent ranks, even tho such unsportsmanlike actions eventually wrecked their leagues . . . There will be none of that from the owners of the teams in the All-America Conference . . . They will try, of course, to get the best possible material . . . They will spend liberally to attain that end, but they are not going to plunge their properties into debt simply to hire two or three name players or coaches . . . National league owners certainly would prefer competition of that type to what they might expect from less responsible rivals.*

Ward wanted the AAFC to coexist with the NFL and envisioned a World Series–type championship game between the two leagues. But the NFL was not interested. "All I know of new leagues is what I read in the newspapers," NFL commissioner Elmer Layden said in April 1945. "There is nothing for the National Football League to talk about as far as new leagues are concerned until someone gets a football and plays a game."

Nine months later, league owners replaced Layden with Pittsburgh Steelers co-owner Bert Bell. The son of a former attorney general of Penn-sylvania, De Benneville "Bert" Bell may have been from one of Philadelphia's most prominent Main Line families, but he was inexorably drawn to the working-class game of pro football. He was the sport's blue-blooded, broad-shouldered champion. He had played quarterback at Penn, where in 1916 he led the Quakers to a 7-6-1 record and their only appearance in the Rose Bowl. After serving in World War I he returned to Penn, where he was an assistant coach for nine seasons, the first three under John Heisman. In 1933, Bell and five partners bought the Frankford Yellow Jackets, moved the team to Philadelphia, and renamed it the Eagles. In Philadelphia, Bell was almost as much of a one-man operation as Curly Lambeau was in Green Bay—in addition to owning the Eagles, Bell was also, at various times, their coach, general manager, and ticket sales department—and his financial struggles were so great that he never lost a soft spot for the team from the littlest city in the NFL. It was Bell who, in 1935, had proposed the plan for a draft of college players as a way to make the distribution of talent throughout the league more equal. The league held its first draft less than a year later.

The florid Bell was a better steward and a savvier leader as commissioner than the acerbic Layden, but he was not any more welcoming to the AAFC.** He refused to refer to the upstart outfit by its name right through the merger of the two leagues in 1950.

The AAFC began play in 1946, and its impact on the NFL was immediate and profound. The competition for players between the two leagues was fierce. On August 23, 1946, the NFL's Los Angeles Rams—who had won the '45 championship as the Cleveland Rams—lost the Chicago Charities College All-Star Game, 16–0. Thirty-five of the 67 players on the college roster printed in the

---

* *None of the cities at the second meeting wound up having a team in the AAFC in its inaugural season in 1946. The league did, however, include teams in Brooklyn and Miami, neither of which had been represented at the AAFC's first two organizational meetings.*

** *The first commissioner of the AAFC was the personable Jim Crowley, Layden's former Four Horsemen teammate at Notre Dame.*

Chicago Tribune the day before the game were on AAFC rosters in the fall, including eight of the 11 starters. Half of the other 32 players did not go on to play professional football in either league. And contrary to the pledge that Arch Ward had made two years earlier, AAFC teams went hard after NFL talent. To be fair, though, most NFL players were on single-game contracts that they renewed every week.

According to a 1980 article written by Stan Grosshandler of the Professional Football Researchers Association, roughly 100 NFL players jumped to the AAFC in the four years that the leagues were in competition. One of the first to bolt was Chicago Bears tackle Lee Artoe, who signed for a reported $15,000 with the Los Angeles Dons, the team owned by Metro-Goldwyn-Mayer Studios chief Louis B. Mayer and actors Don Ameche, Bing Crosby, and Bob Hope. Artoe said that the Dons tripled his salary, and Bears owner and coach George Halas advised him to accept the offer, saying, "Artoe is not worth that kind of money to a team which must pay its players' salaries out of money taken in at the gate." Also hightailing it from the Bears to the Dons were halfback Harry Clarke and quarterback Charlie O'Rourke, both of whom were technically free agents because they were returning from service in World War II. Salaries began to climb. In 1946, the Philadelphia Eagles' payroll nearly doubled from the year before, to $190,000. Two years later it was more than $250,000.

A happier consequence of the war between the two leagues was that it spurred the reintegration of professional football, which had been exclusively a white man's game since 1934. As a testament to how pro football compared to baseball in the eyes of American sports fans, it's hard to think of more glaring examples than the men who broke the color barriers in the major leagues and in the NFL. Jackie Robinson was justly hailed as a hero when he took over at first base for the Brooklyn Dodgers in 1947. But the year before, to considerably less fanfare, and for the first time since 1933, four black men played pro football: halfback Kenny Washington and end Woody Strode, with the Los Angeles Rams in the NFL, and fullback Marion Motley and guard Bill Willis, with the Cleveland Browns in the AAFC.

Motley and Willis were anchors of the Browns' dynasty of the 1940s and '50s — Cleveland won all four AAFC championships before the league merged with the NFL in 1950, at which point the Browns won a fifth straight title by beating the Rams in the NFL Championship Game. Both men are now in the Pro Football Hall of Fame. The athletic 25-year-old Willis, who had played for Cleveland coach Paul Brown at Ohio State, played guard on offense and middle guard on the defensive line. In the latter capacity he was a devastating pass rusher, often leapfrogging opposing blockers to get into the backfield.

But even at six foot two and 213 pounds, Willis wasn't as big or as fearsome as Motley. Originally from Canton, the six-foot-one, 232-pound fullback had played in college at Nevada before entering the Navy during the war. It was during the war that he met Brown at Naval Training Station Great Lakes,[*] where the latter was coaching the base's football team. Motley was 26 by the time he got to Cleveland. Explosive and fast, he played the game like a boxcar on rails — straight ahead and with terrifying momentum. He was almost immediately one of the best players in the AAFC. But even though the new league had helped to smash the racial barriers in pro football, it was not unaffected by the divisions that still existed in the country. Neither Willis nor Motley made the trip to Miami for the Browns' final regular-season game in 1946 — state law in Florida barred mixed-race sporting events.

The Packers' role in the integration of pro foot-

---

* *Great Lakes changed its name to Naval Training Center Great Lakes in 1945.*

ball was, at best, a passive one — but not insignificant. Fullback Ted Fritsch had signed with the
Browns in April 1946 for a reported $10,000. The
five-foot-ten, 210-pound native of tiny Spencer,
Wisconsin, had been with Green Bay since 1942,
when he signed as an undrafted free agent out of
Central State Teachers College, in Stevens Point.
Despite his lack of credentials, he became a regular in the Packers' lineup. He had been the hero of
the 1944 NFL Championship Game victory over
the Giants, when he scored both of Green Bay's
touchdowns in a 14–7 victory, and he was still one
of the team's most popular players.

Fritsch apparently loved Green Bay as much as
the city loved him. He got cold feet not long after
he signed with the Browns — his mother, for one,
was not happy with the deal and told Art Daley of
the *Press-Gazette* (not to be confused with Arthur
Daley of *The New York Times*) that she felt "just terrible about it" and that she hoped her son would
"stick with Curly." In August 1946, after Cleveland had already begun training camp, Fritsch
begged out of his AAFC deal in order to return to
the Packers. "I just made a mistake, that's all," he
said when he re-signed with Lambeau. Desperate
for a fullback, the Browns signed Motley, who was
working in a steel mill and had a family to support. According to Dan Daly and Bob O'Donnell in
The Pro Football Chronicle, "Had Fritsch stayed, it
stands to reason there would have been no Motley
— at least not that season."

Lambeau, who had not employed a single black
player — save for Walter Jean, who identified himself as white — from 1919 to 1933, made no apparent effort to integrate his team at a time when
the player war between the NFL and the AAFC
was at its hottest. The number of blacks in pro
football grew steadily in the next few years — by
1949 there were 16 in both the NFL and the AAFC
— but there was never a one in Green Bay.

◆ ◆ ◆

The Packers' ninth-round selection in the 1946
NFL draft was six-foot-one, 220-pound Texas

Fullback Ted Fritsch
(64) was one of
the Packers' most
popular players
when he signed with
the AAFC's Cleveland
Browns in 1946.
But he returned to
Green Bay before the
season, clearing the
way for the Browns
to sign Hall of Fame
fullback Marion
Motley.

A&M guard Grant Darnell. Lambeau sent Darnell a contract offer that stipulated $150 per pre-
season game, $300 per regular-season game, and
no insurance, and also noted that he would be on
his own if he was injured. Darnell countered with
$500 per regular-season game. Lambeau never re-
sponded, and Darnell never played pro football,
instead embarking on a long and successful career
in the oil industry and as a college and high school
football referee.

Green Bay's failure to sign a ninth-round pick
was telling. The Packers couldn't even sign their
first-round picks. In 1946, Lambeau took Marquette halfback Johnny Strzykalski with the sixth
pick in the first round. But the Milwaukee native,
who played one season of college ball for the Hilltoppers before starring for an Army Air Force
team during the war, spurned Green Bay for the
Cleveland Browns. A few weeks later, when it was
discovered that the San Francisco 49ers actually
held his AAFC rights, he went west. The next year,
Lambeau's top pick was left-handed UCLA quarterback Ernie Case, who instead of signing with
the Packers agreed to a three-year deal with the
AAFC's Baltimore Colts. Case was 26 when Green

The inventor of baseball's All-Star Game, *Chicago Tribune* sports editor Arch Ward also wrote the first history of the Packers, which was published in 1946, two years after he had founded the All-America Football Conference.

Bay drafted him. He had played for the Bruins as a sophomore in 1941 and then gone to war as a B-26 pilot in the Army Air Force. While fighting in the North Africa Campaign, he had sustained severe leg and hip injuries when his plane was shot down and the German army took him prisoner and transferred him to a detention camp in Italy. After 11 months as a prisoner of war, Case and a fellow POW escaped during the invasion of Italy by cutting a hole in a fence. Case, while still suffering from his wounds, was on the run for 31 days before he was rescued by a Canadian infantry unit near Trivento. He returned to UCLA in 1945, and in 1946 he led the Bruins to one of the best seasons in school history. UCLA went 10-0 in the regular season before getting trounced 45–14 by Illinois in the Rose Bowl. Case passed for a then-record 165 yards in the game, ran for a touchdown, and kicked both of the Bruins' extra points. Lambeau had been on hand in Pasadena for the game and was apparently undeterred by UCLA's poor showing. Not only did he draft Case in the first round, but his third-round pick was Case's teammate Burr Baldwin, an All-America end. But Baldwin was not

any keener on playing for the Packers than Case was — he signed with the Los Angeles Dons.

Lambeau spent his first two draft picks in 1947 on one of the top passing combinations in college football because, with Don Hutson having finally retired after the 1945 season, the Packers' aerial game had gone from the best in pro football to the worst, ranking last in the league in completions, passing yards, and passing first downs. The Los Angeles Rams' Jim Benton led all of pro football in receiving in 1946, catching 63 passes for 981 yards and six touchdowns, which bested the entire Packers receiving corps by nine catches, 140 yards, and two touchdowns.

In the absence of a passing attack, Lambeau had turned the offense over to a running game led by Canadeo and Fritsch. No team in the NFL ran as many times in 1946, or for as many yards, as Green Bay. And in 1947, when Lambeau finally adopted a variation of the T formation as part of his offense, the Packers' ground attack got even better. Canadeo led the second-best rushing offense in the NFL.

With a future Hall of Famer leading the way, Green Bay finished with winning records in 1946 and '47, going 6-5 and 6-5-1, respectively. But the team could only paper over the fact that it was not replenishing its roster at a sustainable rate. Finding gems in far-flung places had once been Lambeau's specialty, but no longer. Only three of the 32 players drafted by the Packers in 1946 signed their first NFL contracts with Lambeau. The next year was a little better, with five of 32 signing — but seven others signed with AAFC teams. Lambeau began signing castoffs and over-the-hill veterans to fill out his roster. The player war was breaking Green Bay. Arch Ward may have written the history of the Packers, but now his AAFC was threatening to end them.

In 1948, the bottom finally fell out. Green Bay went 3-9, its first losing season since 1933 and only the second in franchise history. Four of the nine losses were by more than 30 points, and the

Packers ended the season on a seven-game losing streak, which followed on the heels of a motivational trick that backfired on Lambeau. On October 10, Green Bay lost 17–7 at City Stadium to the defending NFL champion Chicago Cardinals, who ran for a whopping 320 yards. After the game, an embarrassed Lambeau promised to impose a "penalty for losing." When players received their paychecks on Tuesday, half of their money had been withheld. Lambeau told the *Press-Gazette* that the fine was for his team's "spiritless performance."

Lambeau also told the paper that he was reserving final judgment on the fines until after the Packers played the Los Angeles Rams in Milwaukee the following Sunday. The general feeling was that a good showing would compel Lambeau to return the money. But after Green Bay beat the Rams 16–0 to boost their record to 3-2, Lambeau refused to comment on the fines — and morale plummeted. The Washington Redskins upset the Packers 23–7 in Milwaukee the next week, and the team went into a death spiral. Green Bay scored just 60 points in its last seven games, while its opponents scored 207. All the hallmarks of a team in disarray began to appear. Players were cut. Fights broke out within the team — specifically between assistant coaches Walt Kiesling and Bo Molenda. (Both would be gone in a staff shake-up after the season.) Lambeau accused his players of refusing to try and delivered locker room tirades. Nothing worked.

Lambeau had lost the team and had no idea how to win it back. "We're in a definite slump, but we could come out of it in 10 minutes — if everybody made up their mind to do their level best the rest of the season," he told the *Press-Gazette*. "Too many of the boys are worrying about the other players; they should worry about nobody but themselves."

Lambeau had never been popular among the men who played for him. Not once had they ever borne him off the field on their shoulders after a victory. He motivated his teams with fear and fiery oratory. "He'd come in at halftime and say,

'Some of you are playing, some of you aren't,'" Herm Schneidman, a back from 1935 to '39, told team historian Cliff Christl. "'Either get in there and get this game won or we're going to fire somebody.' He'd get them all pepped up. He'd walk out of the dressing room and the boys would go out and play twice as hard."

Some of Green Bay's most prominent stars, including Johnny Blood, Clarke Hinkle, and Tony Canadeo, all confessed at one time or another to not really liking Lambeau. And disputes over money were common. "I remember a deal once where Michalske and Hubbard backed him against the wall one time over some money or something," said Howie Levitas, a former Packers board member, who had started working with the team in 1928 as a water boy. "They literally backed him against the wall in the dressing room."

The player who got along with Lambeau best was Don Hutson, but even the Alabama Antelope, who was also a Green Bay assistant for several years before and after his retirement, was careful to note that the relationship did not become a warm one until after his playing days were over. "He was a stern coach and there was a big gap between Curly and the players," Hutson said in *What a Game They Played*. "He didn't mingle with them. He was the coach and that was that."

As the losses mounted, more and more people began to warm to the notion that Lambeau was not the man to lead the Packers into the 1950s. He was no longer attracting top talent to Green Bay. He had lost the confidence of his team. And even though the Packers had adopted a variation of the T formation, Lambeau still retained elements of his beloved Notre Dame Box in the offense, which kept it from being as refined as the attacks of teams that had been using the T for years. There was also evidence that the overall coaching of the team was lacking in sophistication. As a member of the New York Giants in 1948, Ken Keuper, who had been a halfback in Green Bay from 1945 to 1947, played against his old team at State Fair

Park, in Milwaukee. New York trounced the Packers 49–3, and Keuper said that the lopsided score could be credited in large part to the coaching of Lambeau. "Playing as a line backer on defense, I naturally expected that Lambeau would be smart enough to change his offensive signals against us, rather than use the same ones with which I was thoroughly familiar," he told an Elks banquet in Manitowoc during an off-season speaking engagement in 1949. "But no, there came the Packers up to the line with the quarterback calling the same signals that had been used for the past four years —and perhaps longer. Naturally, I was able to tip off the Giants on most of the Green Bay plays, giving us a great advantage."

Ominously, some of the people in town who had taken the firmest set against Lambeau were members of the Packers' board, including former president and team doctor W. W. Kelly, whom Lambeau had had replaced before the 1945 season, and legal counsel Gerald Clifford. More significant was the enmity of George Whitney Calhoun, the man with whom Lambeau had founded the team in 1919. On St. Patrick's Day 1947, former *Chicago Tribune* columnist George Strickler had abruptly resigned his duties as the director of publicity for the NFL, where he had been working for six years. One week later, Lambeau announced that he had signed Strickler to a three-year contract to be Green Bay's assistant general manager and public relations director. The story on Strickler's hiring in the *Press-Gazette* was careful to note that Lambeau had said that the "addition of Strickler to the staff does not affect the status of George W. Calhoun, veteran Packer publicist and director of press ticket arrangements." But there was no comment in the story from Calhoun, who submitted his letter of resignation to team president Lee Joannes.

"From past and present experiences, I know it would be impossible for me to function with Lambeau's Strickler," Calhoun wrote to Joannes. "He has been gunning for me ever since he stepped into the National League job under Elmer Layden and rather than let him completely cut my throat I am beating him to the punch and filing my resignation with you."

Why did Lambeau cut out Calhoun? Strickler's hiring came four months after the publication of Arch Ward's history of the Packers. Ward had painted a delightful portrait of the cantankerous Calhoun and correctly placed him in the heritage of the team, but the central figure in the book, the man portrayed as the prime mover behind the existence and continued success of the Green Bay Packers, is Curly Lambeau. It is possible that Lambeau objected to the credit given to Calhoun by Ward, but there is no evidence for it. And a thorough reading of Ward's book does not make it seem any more likely. A more plausible explanation was that Lambeau and Strickler were friends and that the relationship between the coach and Calhoun had lost whatever congeniality it had had in the summer of 1919.

The urbane Strickler and Lambeau were close enough that Lambeau had been the best man at Strickler's wedding, in Menominee, Michigan, on May 31, 1940. Like so many of Lambeau's cronies, Strickler was a Notre Dame man. He had been a student press assistant to the football team in 1924, when Grantland Rice dubbed the Fighting Irish backfield "the Four Horsemen." It had been Strickler's idea to pose Jim Crowley, Elmer Layden, Don Miller, and Harry Stuhldreher on horseback for a publicity stunt that turned into a genuine artifact of Americana. According to the book *Notre Dame Golden Moments: 20 Memorable Events That Shaped Notre Dame Football*, Strickler secured copyrights to the photo and sold 8-by-11 copies of it on campus. "I made about $10,000 that year as a publicity man for Rockne," Strickler said later. "Most of it was on that picture."

Strickler was decidedly more sophisticated than Calhoun, whose crusty appearance and demeanor were the antithesis of the dapper Lambeau's. Twenty-eight years is a long time to work closely with anybody, and Lambeau and Calhoun were leading increasingly different lives. Calhoun could certainly never have been accused of having gone Hollywood. He swore with abandon. He chewed cigars. He ate Limburger sandwiches. He frequented a downtown Green Bay pub called Sham O'Brien's Emerald Isle Tavern. "Crabbiest bitch on earth — miserable," one of O'Brien's sons told Cliff Christl in 2001. "He'd bring his bone dog in every night. He had a bulldog and I think he looked better than Cal did."

But as former Packers board member John Torinus noted in his history of the team, Calhoun had adopted his gruff manner to protect a sensitive soul. According to Torinus, Calhoun had found out that Strickler was replacing him while he was at work in the offices of the *Press-Gazette*. He was scanning the wire copy that came over the newsroom's teletype machine when he read a story saying that Strickler had been hired to replace George Whitney Calhoun, who had recently retired. (There was indeed a March 24 report from the United Press — a news service used by the *Press-Gazette* — that put the news exactly that way.) "That was the way Cal learned that his old pal Curly Lambeau had dumped him," wrote Torinus. "He was a bitter enemy of Lambeau from that day forward."

Lambeau's bonds to the city were beginning to disintegrate. He had lost his players. He had lost several longtime allies on the Packers' board of directors. And after the disastrous 1948 season, he was beginning to lose the fans. The relationship would only get worse.

◆ ◆ ◆

The bulging bend of the Niagara Escarpment traces a jagged curve for more than 650 miles across the upper half of the North American continent. From its origin in western New York it extends north and west through Ontario and Lake Huron and the Upper Peninsula of Michigan before turning to the south and plunging down the Door Peninsula, on the eastern shore of Green Bay. Formed five million years ago, the escarp-

ment's cliffs of limestone and dolomite were once at the bottom of an ancient ocean but now rise as high as 250 feet above sea level. The escarpment's most famous feature is Niagara Falls, at its eastern end, where the Niagara River cascades spectacularly over the precipice on its northward route from Lake Erie to Lake Ontario. But the falls are not the ridgeline's only imposing landmass — throughout its length it is one of the most prominent geological formations in the Upper Midwest. The cliffs of the escarpment face outward from the arc it describes so that, as it descends down into Wisconsin, it rises from the water of Green Bay in a series of wooded bluffs and rocky palisades.

It was on one of these promontories, about 18 miles northeast of Green Bay, that, in 1937, the Norbertine Fathers, who operated the downtown Columbus Community Club, constructed a recreation house for the use of club members. Designed by the Green Bay architecture firm of Foeller, Schober & Berners, the brick-and-fieldstone structure was laid out roughly in the shape of a *T*, with a lounge area — complete with a high, raftered ceiling, a large stone fireplace, and a small stage — taking up most of the long end, and the cross section overstuffed with a dining room, a kitchen, offices, men's and women's locker rooms, and living quarters for the lodge's caretaker. The interior design was decidedly North Woods cabin, with walls of knotty pine and chandeliers and light fixtures of wrought iron. The Knights of Columbus christened the place, nestled amid a forest of birch and cedar, Rockwood Lodge.

But for all its rustic ambience and aesthetic charm, Rockwood Lodge was a financial albatross. Less than two years after it had begun operations as a private club in the fall of 1937, the Norbertines opened it to the general public. And when local restaurateur Fred DeMeuse bought it in the summer of 1944, with the intention of transforming it into a supper club, Rockwood had already been vacant for about two years. DeMeuse's supper club experiment did not last long. In May

1946, he sold Rockwood Lodge to the Green Bay Packers Inc. for $32,000.

Lambeau was behind the purchase, convincing the board of directors to put up the money for the lodge and the 50 or so acres that surrounded it. He envisioned Rockwood as an all-in-one football facility — the first of its kind — a place where his players and coaches and their families would live and train throughout the season, from training camp through the end of the playoffs. Lambeau was a visionary, a man who had seen the possibilities for pro football in Green Bay before anyone else — and who had made those possibilities into reality through the force of his own will. The cost of purchasing the lodge (roughly $435,000 today) was steep, and while a few board members may have had doubts about the wisdom of spending so much money, they nevertheless acquiesced to Lambeau and his formidable salesmanship. Dr. W. W. Kelly had seconded the motion to purchase the site, and not one dissenting vote was cast against Lambeau's proposal.

To be sure, there were also practical reasons for the team to buy Rockwood Lodge. Home building had lagged during both the Great Depression and World War II, and when millions of soldiers, sailors, and airmen returned to the United States in 1945, the country experienced the worst housing shortage in its history. The governor of Ohio gave over an apartment in his mansion to a veteran and his wife who needed a place to live. A family of seven in De Pere took up residence in a tent along the banks of the Fox River. Lambeau felt that Rockwood would free the players from worry about where they were going to live. The plan was for every player except those who already had homes in Green Bay to reside rent-free at the lodge. Lambeau called Rockwood the team's "permanent home" and explained that by that he meant that the Packers would do everything at the lodge except play exhibition or league games. Lambeau also boasted that he felt that the setup would allow him to get the "absolute maxi-

mum" from his players, and he got the board to approve the disbursement of $8,000 so that he could make upgrades toward that end. A football field was laid out on Rockwood's front lawn, and the lodge's large common room was used for film sessions and chalk talks. The kitchen was upgraded to restaurant quality, and a chef from a local eatery, Melvin Flagstad, was brought in to be the cook and caretaker of the facility. Consultants from the Chicago department store Marshall Field's assisted with the decorating of the place. Lambeau also spent $17,500 on five prefabricated cottages to house married players and staff. On the eve of the 1946 season, *Press-Gazette* writer Sara Lou Du Pont noted, "To those of you who are busily house-cleaning and cooking three meals a day plus snacks, the life of a Packers wife sounds a little like paradise."

There was just one problem: the site was not suited to be a football facility. The soil of the practice field at Rockwood was very thin or nearly absent. The most recent glaciation — roughly 10,000 years before Lambeau and the Packers arrived — had scraped or eroded away the topsoil above the escarpment, leaving bedrock at the surface. The Packers were basically practicing on a field of limestone. And the limestone in this particular area was massive, formed in large, unbroken slabs, like pavement in a parking lot. Players began referring to the field as "the Rock" and started coming down with shin splints and sore knees and feet. The team began busing from Rockwood to their old practice field near City Stadium. Charley Brock, a center for the Packers from 1939 to 1947, trained at the lodge for two years. In 1981 he told the *Press-Gazette* that one summer a detail of high school students had spent two weeks doing nothing but picking rocks from the field before players reported for practice. Dick Wildung was a rookie guard in 1946 when he arrived in Green Bay for his first training camp. "Rockwood Lodge was a beautiful place," he later said. "But it was just no good for football because of that damn rock."

According to John Torinus, who joined the Packers' executive committee in 1949, it was not long before the purchase of Rockwood Lodge began to anger committee members. To make matters worse, Torinus says, Lambeau's wife was in charge of decorating the lodge — and expenses were mounting. "At one meeting of the Executive Committee, the financial committee threatened to resign over the bills which were being presented by Lambeau for decorating the cottage that he and his wife were occupying," Torinus wrote in his book *The Packer Legend: An Inside Look*. In 1947, the executive committee began to strip Lambeau of his authority by, among other things, forming subcommittees to supervise everything from business matters to publicity and requiring him to report to them every Monday at noon.

To make matter worse, all the money that the team was spending on Lambeau's vision was not being rewarded with victories and championships. In fact, Green Bay was getting *worse*. That was the real problem — the problem that gave rise to all other problems — and Rockwood Lodge was getting a healthy share of the blame. Former fullback Clarke Hinkle, speaking at an Elks Club football banquet in November 1946, did not mince words. "When I was here, we played for the Green Bay public because we knew everybody by their first names," he said. "We played for our friends or somebody we knew. But that isn't the case today. The team is quartered out at Rockwood Lodge, isolated from the community and the players don't know anybody. These boys nowadays are just playing for the check. They don't know what the Green Bay spirit is."

The ground beneath Rockwood Lodge may have been solid rock, but the ground beneath Lambeau's feet was beginning to crumble.

Rockwood Lodge was undone as a football Valhalla primarily because of the ground on which it stood. The Packers were practicing on limestone slab covered by a thin layer of topsoil. Players took to calling it "the Rock."

CHAPTER 11

UP IN FLAMES

Ever since the rainy Thanksgiving Day in 1922 when he promised Curly Lambeau and George Calhoun to help figure out a way to make the Packers a financially viable enterprise, Andrew Turnbull had acted as the franchise's guardian angel. He was the team's first president, serving from 1923 to 1928. In 1927, when the NFL was paring its membership from 22 teams down to 12 by eliminating most of its small-town clubs, he and Lambeau represented Green Bay at two crucial league meetings — the first in New York in February and the second in Cleveland in April — at which the decisions were being made about who would stay and who would go. The Packers made the cut, while such iconic teams as the Canton Bulldogs and the Hammond Pros disappeared from pro football forever. Two years later, Turnbull administered the Packers' "Championship Fund," which raised more than $5,000 for gifts and cash bonuses to be given to every coach and player. He also encouraged his *Press-Gazette* writers to take it easy on the home team. When longtime writer and editor Art Daley came to the paper in 1941, Turnbull told him, "Just remember: Don't say anything real bad about our team because if we lose 'em, we'll never get 'em back." In all, Turnbull served on Green Bay's executive committee and board of directors for more than 25 years, through the near financial ruin of the franchise in the wake of Willard Bent's lawsuit in 1933, as well as through the Great Depression and World War II.

Sometimes his assistance was direct. On November 28, 1926, the Packers beat the Detroit Panthers 7–0 on a muddy field before a crowd estimated at only about 1,000 in 30,000-seat Navin Field (later Tiger Stadium). In the *Press-Gazette* story on the game, Calhoun noted dryly that the affair had "failed to draw what might be termed a corporal's guard." When Calhoun went to secure the guaranteed money that the Packers were due for playing the road game, he was told that the Panthers had none to give. Green Bay, which needed the cash to pay its hotel bill, give its players meal money, and pay for a Pullman car for the train trip home, promptly called Turnbull, who wired the team $500. It's no coincidence that Turnbull was once introduced at a team banquet as the godfather of the Packers. "I'm sure there were three or four times, if it wasn't for Andy and a few of his close associates giving money, the Packers would have had to fold up," George Nau Burridge, a Green Bay businessman and neighbor of Turnbull's, told team historian Cliff Christl in 2001.

In addition to being partners of a kind for over a quarter century, Lambeau and Turnbull were also friends. When Turnbull's wife, Susan, died from the effects of a heart condition in 1944, Lambeau was one of her pallbearers. When the 65-year-old Turnbull remarried in Los Angeles in April 1949, Lambeau and his wife, Grace, were in attendance.*

Nearly four months after the wedding, on August 8, 1949, Turnbull submitted his letter of resignation to the Packers' executive committee. The newspaperman had long been a reliable ally for Lambeau. But the team's troubled financial situation, the fiasco of the purchase of Rockwood Lodge, and the moves of the committee to strip Lambeau of much of his authority had made being the coach's ally much more difficult. Lambeau was becoming more and more isolated.

◆ ◆ ◆

It did not help Lambeau with the board of directors that Green Bay was once again one of the worst teams in the NFL. The Packers opened the 1949 season on September 25 against the Bears at City Stadium and were soundly beaten, 17–0. Chicago outgained Green Bay 403 yards to 187, and the Packers didn't complete one throw outside of the four interceptions that passers Jug Girard, Stan Heath, and Jack Jacobs tossed to the Bears. The *Press-Gazette*'s story on the game, written by Art Daley, was a model of Turnbullian spin.

The 1949 Green Bay Packers have recaptured the flaming spirit of other years.

This return to the blood-and-guts brand of football — missing for most of the 1948 season — flared brilliantly despite a bitter 17 to 0 defeat at the hands of the Chicago

Bears before 25,571 fans at City Stadium Sunday afternoon.

The final score doesn't begin to tell the tale of fire and brimstone that left the sellout crowd weak and limp as the gladiators moved out of the arena.

The truth is that Green Bay's performance had been so pitiful that Lambeau called a special session of the executive committee on Monday night to announce that he was turning over all coaching duties to his three assistants: defensive coach Charley Brock, backfield coach Bob Snyder, and line coach Tom Stidham. Lambeau, who was also Green Bay's vice president and general manager, told the committee that he planned to continue with his remaining duties and oversee the rebuilding of the franchise. His only role as a coach going forward, he said, would be in an advisory capacity. "It was a complete surprise to the executive committee," team president Emil R. Fischer told the *Press-Gazette*. "But Curly feels he can be of greater service to the club under present circumstances, and we therefore were in no position to demur."

The move did little to boost the Packers on the field. They were drubbed 48–7 at City Stadium by the Los Angeles Rams the next week and won only two games the rest of the season. Running out of the wing T, Tony Canadeo enjoyed the finest campaign of his Hall of Fame career, running for 1,052 yards on 208 carries, an average of 5.1 yards per rush, but it wasn't enough to make up for an anemic passing offense that completed only 91 throws all season. Green Bay's 2-10 record was the worst in franchise history. Not surprisingly, Lambeau's three-man coaching committee did not work out. Players and coaches alike groused about it, and so did fans. To settle disagreements on football matters, Brock, Snyder, and Stidham would resort to verbal votes. Confusion reigned. In a 41–21 loss to the Cardinals at Comiskey Park in Chicago on

PREVIOUS SPREAD
Rockwood Lodge was consumed by fire on January 24, 1950. Curly Lambeau abruptly resigned eight days later to become the coach of the Chicago Cardinals.

---

* *Turnbull's best man was bullfrog-voiced character actor Eugene Pallette.*

Curly Lambeau's Contract Renewed for Another Two Years

Board Authorizes Issuance of $200,000 in Packer Stock

Founder To Serve as Coach and Manager

Board's Decision Vote of Confidence To Mentor; Stock Sells for $10 Share

By ART DALEY

Earl L. (Curly) Lambeau, who founded the Green Bay Packers back in 1919, will lead our town's professional football forces another two years.

Lambeau's contract as general manager and head coach—the center-point of rumblings for many weeks—was renewed at a four-hour meeting of the board of directors of Green Bay Packers, Inc., at the courthouse last night.

The decision stands as a vote of confidence to the 31-year football veteran who has been under fire by various factions since the club started losing games in 1948 and worsened this season when the financial condition of the corporation grew precarious.

In another action aimed at bolstering the financial condition, the board of directors recommended to the stockholders authorization of the issuance of $200,000 additional shares of stock in the corporation at $10 per share.

The board of directors added the following statement:

"Purpose of this issuance of stock is not only to increase the working capital of the corporation but also to permit the broadening of the base of ownership in the Packer football team—to be more truly representative of the people interested in the Packers in this year of 1949 as contrasted with the smaller group originally incorporated back in 1934."

This will enable everyone in Packerland, who desires, to become an owner in the Packer team, the directors pointed out, adding that "this move likewise would permit the more active participation of more interested people in the affairs of the Packer corporation."

Despite early reports of a "hot session," directors said that the meeting was conducted in a "most businesslike fashion" — especially on the matter of Lambeau's contract.

About 25 interested fans and representatives of the press and radio gathered in the corridors of the courthouse. A large number of them watched the meeting through the glass door. The session started at 7:40 and was officially over at 11:25. It was midnight when the last of the directors left.

Twenty-one of the 25 directors were present to vote on Lambeau's contract and make financial recommendations. Absent were Charles Mathys, Edward Bedore, Russ Bogda, and Fred L. Cobb. Directors attending were Emil R. Fischer, president of the corporation, H. J. Bero, Milan Boex, G. W. Calhoun, Gerald F. Clifford, L. H. Joannes, Leslie J. Kelly, Dr. W. W. Kelly, F. J. Jonet, Fred Leicht, Harvey Lhost, John D. Moffatt, John E. Paeps, Gus Rosner, Arthur Schumacher, Ed Schuster, William Servotte, John Torinus, H. G. Wintgens and Lambeau. The vote was not announced.

Directors announced that Lambeau will return to the head coaching position he gave up last Sept. 30 in order to move to the front office. At that time, Lambeau became advisory coach — at his own suggestion — and placed his three assistants, Charley Brock, Bob Snyder and Tom Stidham, in charge of the club's field operations.

Directors declined to comment on terms of the contract. His current five-year pact expires Dec.

championships in 1929, 1930 and 1931. The three in a row still stands as a league record.

Lambeau-coached teams later took three more championships and never finished out of the league's first division until 1948 when the club had a 3-9 record. Thus far this year, the Packers won two and lost eight.

The Packers' troubles started in 1948 when, after winning three impressive non-league games and a 31-0 league opener over the Boston Yanks, the Packers were trounced by the Bears here but whipped Detroit the following Sunday. The next Sunday, the Bays lost to the Cardinals, 17-7, and Lambeau fined the entire squad one-half of a game's pay for the showing against the Cards.

After the fine, the Packers whipped Los Angeles, 16-0, but then lost every game. The losses included a 7-6 struggle with the Bears in Chicago.

The 1949 season started with new optimism as the new assistants were added to replace Walt Kiesling and Bo Molenda. The club won two out of five non-league contests but then lost to the Bears and Los Angeles Rams in league play, the loss to the Rams coming two days after Lambeau became advisory coach.

A victory over the New York Bulldogs followed, but then came losses to the Cardinals and Rams. The team snapped back to beat Detroit but then lost to the Bears, New York Giants, Pittsburgh and Cardinals last Sunday. The team has two more games left — at Washington and Detroit.

Though the Packers have lost eight games this season, the spirit of the squad was considered generally better than it was in 1948. At least three of the defeats were the result of defensive lapses made possible by inexperienced men who had to be used because of injuries to regulars such as Irv Comp and Jack Jacobs.

Lambeau stepped into the picture last Sunday, for instance, before the Cardinal game and asked the players to overlook the "reports of dissatisfaction" in Green Bay and "play to win this one for the good fans of Green Bay."

Lambeau, of course, was referring to the thousands of fans who contributed $50,000 in the 10-day drive to save the Packers. The money was obtained in the sale of tickets to a Packer All Star game played at City stadium Thanksgiving day and attended by 15,000 fans despite freezing weather.

On the field Sunday, the Packers ran into a red-hot Cardinal team which scored 24 points in the first 20 minutes. Then the Packer spirit caught fire and the Bays counted 21 points in less than 10 minutes. During the last half, Green Bay battled the stronger Cards to a standstill.

With all rumors and "reports of dissatisfaction" ending with last night's meeting, the 1949 Packer squad is free, so to speak, to keep its collective mind on the next opponent.

Lambeau was on the practice field this afternoon as the team prepared for its game with Washington. The squad will leave Friday morning and next week will train at Hershey, Pa., in preparation for the finale against Detroit.

Lambeau To Appear At QB Meet Tonight

E. L. (Curly) Lambeau, the Packer head coach, will appear at the 10th meeting of the Quarterback club in the Vocational school tonight. The meeting will start at 7:30.

Lambeau will answer questions in the question-answer session which will close the meeting and will narrate the film of the Packer-Chicago Cardinal game at Chicago last Sunday.

Three phases of the historical session of the Green Bay Packers, Inc., board of directors, at the courthouse last night are shown above. At the top, Curly Lambeau (left) smiles with four members of the board after the directors renewed his contract as general manager and head coach for two years and authorized issuance of another $200,000 worth of stock. With Lambeau are John D. Moffatt, Harvey Lhost, Bill Servotte and H. J. Wintgens. The center view shows Lambeau (light hat) stepping out of the meeting room door while radio and press representatives are given a statement by Director John Torinus (with glasses at extreme right). Emil R. Fischer, president of the Packers, is shown ahead of Lambeau. Below, reporters and sportscasters sweat outside the meeting room—for four hours. The group includes (left to right) Lee Remmel, Art Daley and Dave Yuenger of the Press-Gazette; George Strickler, director of publicity for the Packers; Michael Griffin of WBAY; Don Arthur of WDUZ; Bob Savage of WBAY; and Earl Gillespie of Press-Gazette Radio Station WJPG.

Appleton Signs Pact With Browns

APPLETON, Wis. —(P)— The Appleton Baseball club announced today it had signed a working agreement with the St. Louis Browns for the 1950 season.

Andrew Parnell, Appleton president, said the Wisconsin State league club would work through

Central Drills

conference season next Friday night, Dec. 8, at St. Mary's Springs, Fond du Lac. A return

[illegible] and little Bob Bender, have scored 21 points each. Forward Bob Charneski has 19, his running mate, Larry Smits, 18, and

Fox Valley Basketball Season Opens Friday

West at Home to Oshkosh; Devils Visit Fond du Lac

By LEE REMMEL

Each having displayed their wares for popular appraisal in non-conference games, the basketball disciples of East and West will debut in Fox River Valley conference competition Friday night.

Their appearances will help mark inauguration of the loop's 27th cage season, which will see all eight members in action.

The Wildcats will be the first to show at home, launching their conference play against Oshkosh at West gymnasium Friday night while East opens away from home at Fond du Lac against the Cardinals of Coach Exner Menzel, former University of Wisconsin performer.

Although neither the Wildcats or Red Devils have championships hopes, their initial 1949-50 outings have indicated that both clubs are at least slightly improved over last season and that they may cause rivals more trouble than they did in 1948-49 activity.

The Wildcats, despite losing to St. Norbert High Tuesday night in their opener, flashed promise of better things, particularly if Hurdis McCrary can remember the scoring formula he possessed in counting 205 points a year ago. The rangy center's inability to hit from the field was largely responsible for the Purple and White's loss to the Squires. He was held to three free throws by an excellent defensive job by St. Norbert center Jack Jansky.

Better Later In Season

The rest of the cast seems to be adequate—Malone has capable guards in Don Rondou, looking better than he did last season, and Dick Purath; and enough scoring punch at forward in the fiery John Thune and Bruce Anderson, a conscientious worker.

Across the river, Jake Schaffer, veteran East mentor, has had something of a rebuilding situation and it appears that the Red Devils will be better, at least in the season, than their supporters previously had a right to expect.

Starting with but two lettermen, Forward Dave Weihaupt and Guard Gene Mead, Shaffer has fashioned a team that promises to be interesting and one that could conceivably become obnoxious to the pacesetters about midseason.

To go with Weihaupt and Metoxen, Jake has a -foot, 1-inch center, Jack Ebert, Gordon Metoxen, considerably improved over last season when he made a few brief varsity appearances, and diminutive Bill Maguren. Metoxen is teaming with Weihaupt at forward while Maguren is paired with Mead, a mercurial fellow with a good shooting eye, at guard.

Rathburn To Be Badgers' Fullback Next Fall, Odell

"I feel that Stony's going to be our fullback next fall," Backfield Coach Bob Odell of the University of Wisconsin told the approximately 300 persons who attended the 27th annual West High football banquet at Kutsch's in Kellnersville Wednesday night.

The "Stony" he referred to was Floyd Rathburn, for three years a star on West High grid teams and now considered a top-flight varsity prospect for 1950 as a member of the current UW freshman squad.

Rathburn

Odell went on to say that he thought Rathburn was just the man the Badgers need in the fullback slot, commenting, "He's the likes of which we didn't have this fall." Later, in mentioning that he wished that the UW could have Gene Evans,

PRESS-GAZETTE Sports

Green Bay, Wis., Thursday Evening, Dec. 1, 1949

St. Norbert Host to Muskie '5' Tonight

St. Norbert Eyes First Victory of 1949-50 Campaign

St. Norbert college's first basketball victory of the season is the target for tonight at Van Dyke gymnasium when the Green Knights meet Mission House starting at 8 o'clock.

So far this season St. Norbert has lost to Allen Bradley of Milwaukee and the classy De Paul university five of Chicago. Tonight's game is actually the first Norbertine encounter of the season where the Knights have a chance for victory. The Bradley and De Paul fives were superior in height and experience, but Mission House will field a team with no great height or experience advantage. Both the Norbertine and Mission House starting fives will average a shade under the six foot mark.

Swamped Muskies, 87-40

Last year St. Norbert turned in its most powerful scoring game at Mission House and swamped the Muskies 87 to 40. The Knight score represents a single game scoring record for the Norbertines and it also broke the one game scoring high for the Mission House gymnasium. In a return game on the local court St. Norbert had to work much harder for their second win. The Knights were held to a slender 6 point lead at halftime, but caught fire late in the final half and won 69 to 44.

Coach Orv Dermody expressed dissatisfaction with the Knight floor game against De Paul and will be trying out several players not used before. Jim Mazaner, giant 6 foot 6 inch sophomore who has little court experience, will probably see considerable action. Another player scheduled to play a big part in the Norbertine attack is Chuck Holton. The pencil thin forward was a star in the De Paul game and gave indications of great scoring power. He starred along with Dick Lenss and Roman Kosnar in defensive roles against the sky high Demons.

Name Parker Coach For Senior Bowl

JACKSONVILLE, Fla. —(P)— Buddy Parker, coach of the Chicago Cardinals professional football team, was named today one of the four coaches for the Senior bowl football game.

Parker will team with Steve Owen of the New York Giants in leading one of the all-star squads of college seniors in the Jan. 7 game. Coaches of the other team will be Bo McMillin of the Detroit Lions and Clarence (Biggie) Munn of Michigan State.

'Frisco 49ers Call Off Strike

Decide Obligation to Fans More Important Than Bonus, Claim

SAN FRANCISCO —(P)— The San Francisco 49ers pro football squad called off a threatened strike today.

A team spokesman said the 32 players decided their obligation to fans who want to see them play the New York Yankees here Sunday was more important than their demand for a $500 bonus per player for the game. Sunday's affair is a semi-final playoff in the All America conference.

Earlier team Captain Norman Standlee, 245 pound fullback and onetime Stanford great, and Halfback Len Eshmont, former Fordham flash, speaking as "elder spokesmen" said the men wouldn't show up for the game unless they were promised the bonus.

Tony Morabito, one of the club owners, said nothing doing. He told the 49ers to turn out for practice this morning or the season would be over as far as they were concerned.

The squad of 32 went into a huddle last night. They came out of it at midnight with the announcement there would be no strike. Their spokesman handed out a statement saying:

Still Feel Request Was Fair

"It is the unanimous decision of the team that our first and most important loyalty is to the fans who have supported us so loyally. We feel the same obligation to the coaching staff.

"We therefore have decided to enter next Sunday's contest with a most determined will to win. We still feel our principle involved in requesting remuneration for next Sunday's game was most fair and sound, since all of us were under the impression at the time we signed our 1949 contracts that compensation for this game would be forthcoming."

The 49ers won second place last Sunday in final All America conference standings by beating the Yankees 35-14. The Yanks wound up third and the two teams are scheduled to open the playoff here.

Morabito said player contracts specifically called for appearances in all exhibitions, training camp, conference and playoff games without additional compensation and that conference rules prohibit player bonuses for playoffs.

November 27, there were several occasions where the Packers' sideline sent two or three plays onto the field at the same time. It was at that game that Lambeau—the "advisory" coach—delivered pre-game and halftime pep talks to his bemused players. For a man who was chafing at having to answer to committees about how to run his team, Lambeau seemed oblivious to the fact that he was making the same mistake himself. Everybody was in charge in 1949—and thus nobody was.

To make matters worse, the NFL's bidding war with the AAFC and the money pit at Rockwood Lodge were combining with the Packers' declining fortunes to make their financial position a perilous one. Since Green Bay had begun to lose on a regular basis, it had not been drawing well at the box office—a problem that was especially acute when the Packers played home games in Milwaukee, as they had done at least once a season since 1933. Green Bay was in receivership at the time and had gone to the bigger city in search of money—and found it. Milwaukee was a valuable source of revenue for the team during the 1930s, with the games there sometimes drawing more fans than the games at City Stadium. In seven contests at Milwaukee's State Fair Park (which seated around 30,000) in 1945, '46, and '47, the Packers drew an average of 26,026, a little more than the average of 23,149 for the nine games in Green Bay in those seasons. But in six games in Milwaukee in 1948 and '49, when the Packers went a combined 5-19, attendance dropped dramatically, to an average of 15,874. (Attendance for six games at City Stadium actually increased slightly in those years, to an average of 24,150.) The low point came on November 20, 1949, when only 5,483 came out to State Fair Park to see the 4-3-1 Pittsburgh Steelers drub 2-6 Green Bay 30–0.

According to John Torinus, the board of directors, looking to save money, ordered Lambeau in November to "drop several players from the roster and renegotiate the salaries of all other players." Beginning with the release of end Clyde Good-night—the franchise's second-leading career receiver—after the season-opening loss to the Bears, Lambeau kept his roster in a constant state of flux, cutting veteran players and signing new ones every week. And toward the end of the year he began to do more cutting than signing. When the Packers waived end Ted Cook after a 30–0 loss to the Redskins in Washington on December 4, there were just 27 men on the roster, "its lowest level in years," according to the Press-Gazette. Green Bay had started training camp at Rockwood Lodge on August 1 with 44 players, but only 28 were left at the end of the season. The NFL roster limit was 32. Torinus says that the board also decided to fire George Strickler (who had been stripped of the title of assistant general manager one year earlier) and put Rockwood Lodge up for sale—though neither of those two things happened before the end of the year.

But the board's most momentous decision was to schedule an intrasquad exhibition game on Thanksgiving Day. At a breakfast meeting of 100 boosters (a group who referred to themselves as the Packer Backers) at the downtown Hotel Northland on November 14, the team announced the exhibition as the centerpiece of a $50,000 fund-raising drive. The team still had three road games left to play—and to pay for—and $50,000 was the amount needed, according to Fischer, for the team to "stand a chance of breaking even." Fischer told the gathering that the Packers were facing as much as $90,000 in red ink and that the main problem was that the team just wasn't drawing well. "Our biggest losses naturally resulted from smaller attendance," Fischer told the Press-Gazette. "Our losses last year amounted to $33,000 but we had resources to cover it."

Lambeau addressed the crowd and noted that the rise in salaries that had resulted from the player war with the AAFC was the major cause of the Packers' problems. "It would not be necessary to hold a meeting of this kind if things were normal," he said. Lambeau went on to tell the story of a "well-known coach in the other circuit" who came to Green Bay in 1946 and offered to double the salary of every player on the roster. Fischer added, for good measure, that Green Bay was in danger of losing the Packers if its fund-raising goals were not met.

For the next 10 days, the game was promoted ceaselessly and at length in the pages of the *Press-Gazette*. There were 500 volunteers out selling tickets (priced at $3.60, $2.40, and $1.20) and collecting donations from throughout northeastern Wisconsin. But on the morning of the game, the Packers were still short — campaign chairman Jerry Atkinson said that the total amount raised was more than $40,000 but that there were 8,800 tickets to the game still available. The Packer Backers pulled out all the stops to entice the people of Green Bay to come out. More than 1,000 merchandise items had been donated for giveaways, including motor oil, boxes of cheese, tailor-made suits, winter coats, and bologna bags. In addition, the paper said that "a noted personage" was due to arrive at halftime by helicopter. "The sky visitor's identity will remain anonymous until he steps from the plane," wrote the *Press-Gazette*'s Lee Remmel.

The real attraction, of course, was football, and the roster of former Packers in attendance was long and distinguished. A dozen members of the original 1919 team, including Lambeau, were on hand. Four members of the champions of 1929, '30, and '31 were there, including Johnny Blood and Verne Lewellen, as well as four members of the 1939 championship team, including Arnie Herber and Don Hutson. The affair was dubbed the Packer Backers' All-Star Game, and — before the first induction ceremony at the Pro Football Hall of Fame in 1963 — it was the greatest assemblage of early stars in the history of the sport. Five future members of the Hall — Lambeau, Blood, Herber, Hutson, and Tony Canadeo — made appearances, and two, Canadeo and Hutson, actually played. Remmel described the gathering of team alumni as "a million dollars worth of football talent." The people of Green Bay may have been tiring of Lambeau as the Packers' coach, but there was no denying that the franchise he built had become something greater than anybody ever anticipated. If the All-Star Game was Lambeau's last hurrah, it was a glorious one.

And it was a totally Green Bay affair, right down to the weather. Temperatures were in the twenties, an icy wind was blowing, and the field was covered by a half inch of snow, making the footing, in the words of the *Press-Gazette*'s Art Daley, "buttery." The weather was so bad that it prevented the arrival of two special guests: 1920s lineman Cub Buck — the Packers' first big star — who became snowbound in Monroe, Wisconsin, en route from his home in Rock Island, Illinois; and the nameless "noted personage" who was supposed to have arrived in a helicopter at halftime. With the bitter, blustery conditions holding down attendance, City Stadium wasn't sold out. But an eye-popping 15,000 fans showed up anyway, and their contributions were enough to lift the team to its $50,000 goal. (The *Press-Gazette* was careful to note, though, that the count included $42,174 in cash and "more than $7,826 in pledges.") It hardly mattered that most of the players admitted that they had not gone all out, or that the Blue team had beaten the Gold, 35–31. The money raised did not put Green Bay in the black, but it did allow the team to finish the season. The legacy of the Packers was what put fans in the stands, and what saved the team from going under.

◆ ◆ ◆

When Emil Fischer died at the age of 70, in January 1958, his obituary in the *Press-Gazette* noted that his tenure as president of the Packers did not represent his most significant contribution to the city of Green Bay. Instead, the paper lauded him for "the development of Green Bay's expanding cheese industry, which he helped bring to the forefront until the city is known today as the 'cheese capital of the world.'"

In the mid-19th century, immigrant farmers from Europe had briefly turned the land around Green Bay into one of the country's most important producers of wheat. But the cultivation of wheat was hard on the soil, and as it became depleted of nutrients, farmers converted from growing grain to raising cattle — not for meat, but for the production of dairy products. By 1895, Brown County was churning out nearly 960,000 pounds of cheese, and by 1910 it had 48 cheese factories and 18 creameries within its borders. In the first two decades of the 20th century, Green Bay grew into the largest cheese distribution center in the world, shipping some 60,000 tons of cheese every year.

At the center of this expansion was Fischer, the short, ruddy son of a German-born shoe salesman. Fischer was born on August 15, 1887, in the southeastern Wisconsin town of Plymouth, one of the epicenters of the state's cheese-making industry. He began working for a cheese-manufacturing company there after he graduated from high school, then moved to Green Bay in 1908, the year he turned 21. Over the next 13 years, Fischer worked for several cheese-making-and-distributing concerns in the city before striking out on his own and establishing the Northern Cold Storage Company, "literally the first step in Green Bay's expansion into a major cheese center," according to the *Press-Gazette*. It was while he was at Northern that he traveled the country in the interest of persuading major cheese companies, including Kraft, to establish operations in Green Bay. In 1926 he and several partners established Atlas Cold Storage, purchasing the old Acme Packing plant — formerly the Indian Packing plant, the original sponsor of the Packers — for their headquarters.

During his travels in support of the Green Bay cheese industry, Fischer had seen firsthand the impact made on the rest of the country by Lambeau's team, and it had impressed him. In 1935, Fischer joined the Packers' executive committee. He ascended to the presidency on July 25, 1947, replacing wholesale grocery magnate Lee Joannes, who had served as the team's president since 1930. "My father enjoyed the arts, shooting and horse racing," his son, Emil Fischer Jr., told the *Milwaukee Journal Sentinel* in 2013. "But his main interest was the Green Bay Packers. He was one of a group of businessmen who thought that the Packers were a good thing for the city and [the businessmen] helped hold the franchise together financially during some tough times."

Few times were tougher than the one faced by Fischer and the executive committee in November 1949. The $50,000 or so that had been raised by the Thanksgiving Day exhibition game was a temporary fix, enough to allow the Packers to finish the season. But the long-term health of the franchise was still in doubt. NFL commissioner Bert Bell openly supported keeping a team in Green Bay. "The National League wouldn't be the same without a Green Bay," Bell said in 1946, in response to rumors that the Packers were going to be moved to a new city. "I would say that the Green Bay Packers, after 26 years in the league, are here to stay." But the media and several officials in both pro football leagues questioned why little Green Bay deserved a franchise. "The case of Green Bay is ridiculous," wrote nationally renowned sportswriter Dan Parker in an article titled "See Here, Bert Bell," for the August 1947 issue of *Sport* magazine. "Granted that for its size this is one of the hottest football centers in America, but it doesn't belong in the National Professional Football League any more than Kalamazoo... It is not a Major League City." There was concern in Green Bay that, with the impending peace agreement between the NFL and the AAFC, the Packers would be left out of the new pro football landscape — a very real possibility if the team was unable to meet its financial obligations.

And that was just what was in danger of happening. For the third time in their history, the Packers were on their deathbed. On November 30, 1949, six days after the frigid exhibition fundraiser, Fischer presided over an evening meeting of the board of directors at the Brown County Courthouse. On the agenda were two things: the financial health of the franchise and the contract of Green Bay's vice president and general manager, Curly Lambeau. It was already dark outside, with the temperature dropping into the twenties, when the meeting got under way at 7:40 in the Board of Supervisors Room on the first floor. Outside the room's closed doors, about 25 fans and members of the press mingled and waited for news. There was a reason for the interest: Oliver Kuechle of *The Milwaukee Journal* had reported nine days earlier that a faction of the board was going to try to oust Lambeau. It wasn't long before those gathered in the hallway heard shouting coming from inside the room.

The tensions were the result of the board's anti-Lambeau bloc — George Whitney Calhoun, Dr. W. W. Kelly, and Gerald Clifford — officially declaring itself. Until now the three men had mostly aired their grievances in the privacy of Clifford's sixth-floor corner office in the downtown Bellin Building, a gleaming white, nine-floor Chicago School structure on the corner of South Washington and East Walnut Streets. Calhoun's animosity toward Lambeau could be traced to the latter's decision, in 1947, to replace him with George Strickler as the team's director of publicity. As for Kelly and Clifford, their opposition was rooted in a variety of issues, among them the downward trend of the Packers both on the field and on the balance sheet, as exemplified by the boondoggle that Rockwood Lodge had become, as well as Lambeau's $25,000 salary and his insistence on spending months at a time in California. Even though

Lambeau had summarily removed the aging Kelly from his post as team physician in 1945, the doctor was still in his corner one year later when he seconded the motion to purchase Rockwood Lodge. Clifford had also been on board with the acquisition of Rockwood—the motion had carried unanimously—but in 1947 the attorney was behind the machinations that stripped Lambeau of much of his authority.

Calhoun, Clifford, and Kelly made their bid to oust Lambeau by asking for a secret ballot on the extension of the coach's contract, which was due to expire on New Year's Eve. Twenty-one of the board's 25 members were present that night, and the motion was narrowly defeated on a 12–9 vote. A voice vote to extend Lambeau's deal followed and passed 18–3, with the only three votes against coming from Calhoun, Clifford, and Kelly. For the moment, Lambeau had won.

But the simple mechanics of the proceedings belie the acrimonious nature of the meeting, which lasted for nearly four hours. Clifford, who was renowned for his fiery courtroom demeanor, was especially animated. He leaped out of his seat to demand a secret ballot when the subject of Lambeau's extension was first raised. And when Lee Joannes—the board's president from 1930 to 1947, who had become an outspoken critic of Lambeau's spending, as well as a frequent visitor to Clifford's office—cast a voice vote in favor of Lambeau's extension, Clifford jumped to his feet again and shouted, "What?" He sat down, shaking his head, after Joannes repeated his vote. Outside the meeting room doors, reporters slumped on the wooden benches in the hallway and filled brass spittoons on the floor with the butts of their cigarettes. The affair did not end until 11:25, but some board members stayed in the Supervisors Room until midnight. Twenty years later, one attendee told the *Press-Gazette*'s Jack Rudolph that he had left the meeting physically sick over, in Rudolph's words, "the vicious exchange of charges and personalities that erupted."

Lambeau and Fischer put things in a more positive light after it was all over. "I am satisfied we now will have complete harmony in the organization for the first time in four years," Lambeau said two days later. "Wednesday's meeting cleared the air. All major points in connection with our operation and my contract were settled on the floor and only a few minor details need to be clarified." Fischer echoed those comments, saying that the Packers "have successfully passed another crisis and are back on a sound footing."

But both men were putting their best spin on what had taken place. Lambeau had not signed an extension at the meeting, and Fischer's "sound financial footing" was just speculation. The other order of business to come out of the marathon conference was that the board had passed a motion asking shareholders to authorize the sale of $200,000 additional shares of stock for $10 each. No stock had yet been sold. No money had yet been raised. And there was no more "harmony" than there had been before. Kelly resigned from the board in December. The remaining members, said Kelly in his letter of resignation, "should not in any way be hampered by my divergent ideas and views."

Lambeau did not endear himself to anyone in Green Bay when, soon after, he floated a proposal that was antithetical to the community spirit of the Packers. According to Torinus, the coach told members of the special committee tasked with drafting the stock plan that "he knew of four investors who would put up $50,000 for stock in the Packers if the corporation was converted to a for-profit rather than a nonprofit corporation." Lambeau also publicly recommended a reorganization of the franchise—with him having authority over the executive committee—and the statewide sale of for-profit stock. This was after the board had already touted its stock proposal as a way to not only raise money but also broaden "the base of ownership in the Packer football team—to be more truly representative of the people interested

Fischer the president of the league's new National Conference, further enmeshing Green Bay in the fabric of the reconfigured landscape of pro football. In his story on the merger in the *Press-Gazette,* Art Daley asked, "What does it mean—the new peace—to the Packers? What does it mean to the fan?

"Chiefly, it means that the Packers will remain in Green Bay."

December came and went. The new year began. Lambeau left for the league meetings in Philadelphia on January 17. He still had not signed his new contract. In fact, a new contract hadn't even been offered to him.

◆ ◆ ◆

The afternoon of Tuesday, January 24, 1950, was warmer than usual for Green Bay. It was cloudy, and the wind was gusting up to 25 miles per hour out of the northeast, but the temperature was right around 34 degrees. There were about three inches of snow on the ground. A storm was blowing in, and there were occasional bursts of thunder and lightning, unusual for that time of year. It was the sort of day that made life at Rockwood Lodge—situated on a bluff overlooking Green Bay, and some 200 yards off Highway 57—seem more remote than usual. This effect was heightened by the fact that the lodge's only occupants were the family of caretaker Melvin Flagstad. During the season, Flagstad lived with his wife, Helen, and their four children—teenagers Ellyn and Melville, 12-year-old Daniel, and nine-year-old Sandra—in a cottage adjacent to the lodge. But after the players left in December, the family moved into the more spacious main building.

A mix of sleet and rain had forced the cancellation of school that day, so Daniel and Sandra Flagstad were at home with their mother and father. The children were playing with two young friends—12-year-old Sandy Agamiate and her nine-year-old brother, Don—who lived across Highway 57 from the lodge. At around 2 p.m., the four children were in a second-floor room, jumping on mat-

in the Packers in this year of 1949 as contrasted with the smaller group originally incorporated back in 1934."

Lambeau was adamant. "Stock should be voting stock and profit sharing," he said in January. "I would like a setup similar to the one we had previous to 1947 or before my authority was decentralized. I believe that the present situation is unworkable and we cannot exist under the present arrangement of operation through committees and subcommittees." What he did not say was that a conversion of the corporation to a for-profit enterprise would mean that it could be moved away from Green Bay—which was just what so many in the city feared.

Lambeau also said, "No group of 12 men can get together once a week for the football season for only an hour and a half, including lunch, and run a professional football team."

Bert Bell was more of a fan of the stock sale than Lambeau was. On December 9, when the NFL announced that it had merged with the AAFC into a new 13-team league, Green Bay was included on the roster of teams, along with franchises in New York, Chicago, Philadelphia, Washington, D.C., Pittsburgh, Los Angeles, San Francisco, Cleveland, Detroit, and Baltimore. The NFL also appointed

tresses and getting ready to play blindman's bluff. Daniel was dispatched to look for a blindfold, and when he stepped into the hallway, according to the *Press-Gazette,* he smelled smoke coming from the attic. He yelled for his father, who ran upstairs and found the attic in flames. Melvin Flagstad ordered the children out of the house, told his wife to call the fire department, and then rushed upstairs with a fire extinguisher. Helen, after calling for help, ran the 200 yards from the lodge to the highway in her housecoat and began flagging down cars. Her children ran into the snow without any shoes.

Her husband, meanwhile, was no match for a blaze that was threatening to engulf the entire roof. Trapped on the second floor, Flagstad suffered a three-inch gash on his left hand when he broke a window and jumped to safety. He then, along with a passing motorist who had been signaled to stop by his wife, pulled a 100-pound gas tank away from the north side of the house, which was the one closest to Rockwood's cluster of five cottages. The two men then ran in through the lodge's front door and came back out with a green couch. After they set it down in the snow on the front drive, Flagstad ran back inside. He made a few such trips, saving his collection of violins, as well as a charcoal portrait of Lambeau.

According to the story in the *Press-Gazette,* which described the fire as a "howling inferno," flames shot through the roof of the lodge at 2:15. By 3:15 the entire roof had caved in. And 15 minutes after that, "two of the walls buckled crazily and then tumbled down." Flames leaped 50 feet into the air. The fire was so out of control that those who arrived to fight it could only stand and watch. The only organized crew on-site was a four-man outfit from the Duquaine Lumber Company, located in nearby New Franken. They arrived shortly after 2:15 with a pumping unit and 600 feet of hose—which they did not even use. "Our job was to save the five adjacent cottages," one of the crew told the *Press-Gazette.* "But we didn't

have to because the wind was in the other direction. As for the lodge itself, nothing could have been done to keep that fire down."

About 40 onlookers, including Tony Canadeo and Ted Fritsch, watched Curly Lambeau's dream get reduced to ashes. All that remained of Rockwood Lodge after the fire had burned itself out was two crumbling walls and a chimney. Canadeo, who was not a fan of Rockwood's practice field, made a joke about the Packers' old home in downtown Green Bay. "Well," he said, "I guess it's back to the Astor Hotel." Three weeks later, Canadeo echoed the sentiments of many Green Bay fans when he joked at a church breakfast, "I didn't set the Rockwood Lodge fire, but I was sure fanning it."

Melvin Flagstad, who lost nearly everything he owned in the blaze, was adamant that faulty wiring had caused the fire. He told reporters at the scene that he had recently seen the lodge's interior lights flickering. Flagstad's older daughter, Ellyn, who was 19 at the time of the fire, later confirmed that Rockwood had a problem with its wiring. "I think it was an electrical fire," she said in 2008. "I was standing there outside a linen closet at the end of the season in '49 when the fire chief was making an inspection. He said, 'I'm going to report this . . . This has to be fixed or you're going to have a problem here. These are all bare wires.'"

No official report on the blaze has ever been found, but apparently nobody—no fire department officials, police officers, or insurance company investigators—saw any reason to argue with Flagstad's suspicion. There were no news reports of any investigation, and the Packers collected, according to executive committee member John Torinus, $75,000 from their insurance coverage—and they collected it in about two weeks. In early February, Fischer said that the team had between $40,000 and $50,000 in cash on hand, including "a settlement on Rockwood Lodge." Years later Torinus wrote, "There was a lot of friendly kidding in the community of Packer board members as to which one had put the torch to the lodge."

The $75,000 windfall has been seized upon several times over the years as evidence that somebody from the Packers lit the match that burned Rockwood Lodge to the ground. Even some former players have been more than happy to play along with the conspiracy theory. In 2013, 90-year-old Ken Kranz, a defensive back on the 1949 team, did not mince words. "They torched it," he told *ESPN the Magazine*. But to fully buy in to the notion that the fire was deliberate means buying in to some very improbable scenarios. First, that an arsonist would strike a structure fronted by more than 200 yards of mostly open ground in the middle of the afternoon. Second, that someone who did manage to sneak up to the lodge unseen (perhaps from the woods that flanked its north and south sides) would then climb up to the attic to do his work. And third, that a member of the executive committee would set, or hire somebody to set, a fire in a home that housed a family with young children. The apparent absence of any sort of investigation into the fire is devastating to this point. To deliberately set a fire that kills someone is murder, and to accept that Rockwood was torched on purpose, you have to accept that whoever did so was willing to kill another human being, possibly a child. It is, of course, possible that the fire at Rockwood Lodge was set on purpose — but it is not probable.

The destruction of Rockwood had the effect of eliminating Lambeau's last physical tie to Green Bay. His friend Andrew Turnbull had retired from the board of directors and the executive committee. Some of his oldest allies on the board had become his bitter enemies. He lived at least half the year in California and had little to no relationship with his first wife. Most significantly, he had been stripped of much of his authority over the franchise he had co-founded, promoted, nursed, and led to greatness. All he was left with after the immolation of his football Shangri-la was . . . nothing. He still had not even signed a contract extension.

Lambeau was returning to Green Bay from Philadelphia when Rockwood Lodge went up in flames. He had left the city accompanied by Strickler on the Broadway Limited on Monday evening — the night before the fire — and didn't get into Green Bay until Wednesday after dark. Eight days after the blaze, Lambeau abruptly resigned and announced that he was leaving the Packers to become the new coach of the Chicago Cardinals. In his letter of resignation to Fischer, Lambeau wrote that his "differences of opinion" with members of the executive committee had "brought about a dangerous disunity of purpose with the corporation, one which in my opinion threatens the existence of the club." Fischer said that Lambeau's resignation "was not entirely unexpected."

According to a report by Oliver Kuechle — a Lambeau confidant — in *The Milwaukee Journal* the day after the coach resigned, Fischer had not presented Lambeau with a contract extension until the two were at the NFL meeting in Philadelphia. "Lambeau took one quick look at it, then tossed it back," wrote Kuechle. "It was a two-year contract all right, but it was not an extension of his old. And it still left intact the galling authority of the executive committee [and] subcommittees."

Lambeau, finally, was done with Green Bay. And there were many in Green Bay who were done with him. "We've had two breaks in Green Bay the last two weeks," Clifford said. "We lost Rockwood Lodge and Lambeau."

But former Green Bay guard Buckets Goldenberg spoke for many when he lamented the loss of Lambeau, "We're through. I don't see how the Packers can last without him. He was the Packers."

On the last count, Goldenberg was mistaken. Curly Lambeau had been the Packers for nearly 30 years, but he wasn't anymore. The man and the team were no longer one and the same. Nobody in Green Bay knew for sure what the Packers were going to be moving forward — or even if they *would* be, for very long.

A MONUMENT TO TITLETOWN

BY

AUSTIN MURPHY

Outside the stadium bearing his name is a sculpture of Earl "Curly" Lambeau, a co-founder, captain, and coach of the Packers—the man most responsible for ensuring that the team survived, then thrived. In this bronze rendering, he appears to be pointing at the nearby statue of Vince Lombardi, although, from what we know of Lambeau, he may have been calling attention to an attractive woman strolling down South Oneida Street.

So central was Lambeau to the founding and early survival of this franchise that it's tempting to describe him as its patron saint. But Curly, a man of large appetites and larger alimony payments, fell markedly short of sainthood. At the time of his fatal heart attack, the thrice-divorced 67-year-old was dating a woman roughly half his age, "Golden Girl" Mary Jane Van Duyse, who served as drum majorette in the team's marching band (and who in 2013 auctioned off a collection of love letters from the big lug). Two months after Lambeau's death, in 1965, the city council voted to change the name of eight-year-old Green Bay City Sta-

dium to Lambeau Field. Among the distinct minority of citizens opposed to the name change was Lombardi, a devout, daily communicant who disapproved of his libertine predecessor and had not attended his funeral.

It could not have been easy for Curly, in the twilight of his life, looking on as Lombardi became the face of the franchise that he had midwifed and led to six NFL championships. While he may have felt shortchanged by fate, Lambeau has been amply compensated in the 54 years since his death. The stadium named after him is one of the most unique, iconic, and charming in the NFL, if not the world.

It's not the architecture of Lambeau Field that leaves one awestruck and yearning to return so much as it is the sum of the game-day experience. One result of the stadium's eight face-lifts since its dedication, notes the architecture critic and author Aaron Betsky, is that it's now "impossible to discern the hand of a single author, let alone a clear plan to the stadium. The result of this history is a circle of brick façades that barely cover

the concrete and steel innards of the original structure . . . There is little to no landscaping, no grand arrival sequence, and no sense that the building fits into the context in any manner. In any other city, it would have been torn down."

And that, he goes on, "has remained part of its charm."

Exactly. What Lambeau lacks in architectural coherence, it makes up for tenfold in character. In three-plus decades with *Sports Illustrated,* I visited this venue a score or so of times. It never failed to thrill. After months or years away, there was always a "Whoa!" moment when the building came into view, looming like an optical illusion, rising incongruously above the rooflines of the surrounding duplexes and ranch-style homes. While a ring of Packers-related enterprises has sprung up around it — hotels, restaurants, gastropubs, parking lots, and, in wintertime, a skating rink and tubing hill — the vibe remains old school, small town.

That, in a shot glass, is Green Bay's brand. Going to battle in a stadium plunked down in a neigh-

borhood rife with their own season-ticket holders is one way the Packers forge extraordinarily close bonds with their fans. Another, of course, is the Lambeau Leap. The half dozen strides it takes the celebrating Packer to reach the wall — post-touchdown, pre-Leap — gives fans just enough time to set down their beers before welcoming him into their embrace.

With no principal owner, there is no owner's ego to feed. In January 2015, I arrived in Green Bay from Dallas–Fort Worth, where I'd debriefed various Cowboys (including Dez Bryant, on whose acrobatic noncatch the game would turn) on their upcoming divisional playoff against the Packers. Upon arriving in Wisconsin, I was struck by both the 50-degree temperature swing — the mercury sank to minus 12 in Green Bay that week — and the contrast between the ballparks.

At the $1.2 billion, three-million-square-foot AT&T Stadium, aka Jerry World, aka the Jones Mahal, with its helipad, art gallery, and Death Star–size digital media board, the football sometimes feels incidental. At Lambeau, it is everything. It is also out of doors. The team that might as well have been called the Gypsies during its first 38 years — the Packers hosted home games at seven different venues, from an open pitch owned by the Hagemeister Brewery to State Fair Park, in Milwaukee — has now played in the same building for an NFL record 63 years. That building has no roof, nor will it ever.

This goes far beyond nostalgia. In a way that no other NFL stadium does (Arrowhead comes closest), Lambeau reveres its past while serving as a direct link to it, a portal to a bygone epoch marked by the breath steaming through the face masks of Starr and Hornung and Nitschke and Wood, set to a soundtrack of kettledrums and the stentorian narration of John "the Voice of God" Facenda on NFL Films.

Fans here are forced to share — actually, they take pride in sharing — the hardships of the players. As with the Lambeau Leap, and the sublime preseason custom of local kids loaning their bikes to the Packers for the two-block journey to the practice field, it binds them closer. Yes, the stadium now features some luxury suites and 7,000 seats in the south end zone, added in 2013, equipped with actual seat backs and armrests. But the vast

majority of butts in this 81,441-seat colossus are parked on aluminum bleachers.

"Yes, they are heated," the Lambeau tour guides like to say, before delivering the punch line: "With *solar* power."

The tour's highlight arrives when Packers pilgrims are permitted to run (or walk) down the tunnel to the field. Crowd noise is piped in. Gooseflesh appears. During this passage, the tourists cross over three concrete slabs outlined in red bricks. Those slabs, from a previous tunnel razed in a renovation, were dug up at the request of ex–Packers head coach Mike Sherman. They now serve as touchstones, reminders of the great players — and coaches — who have gone before.

Two of those larger-than-life characters now stand sentinel outside the building. Yes, Lombardi pushed this club to its pinnacle. But it was Lambeau who got it off the ground.

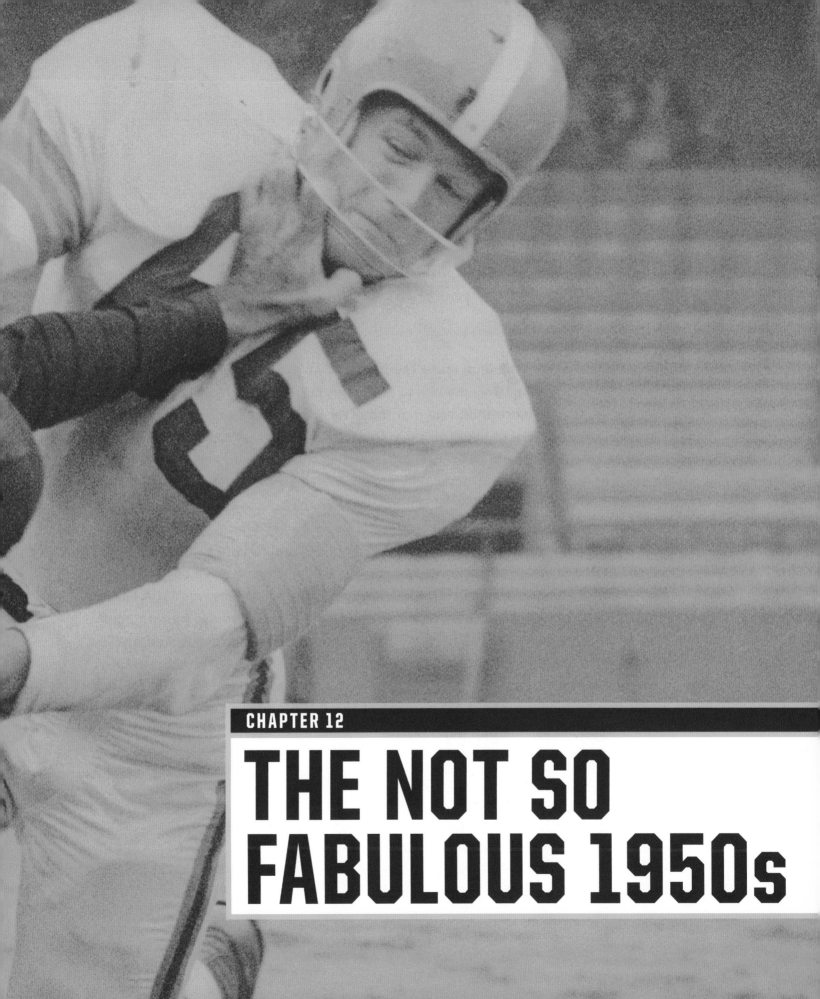

CHAPTER 12

THE NOT SO FABULOUS 1950s

The year the Packers became more the property of the citizens of Green Bay and less a plaything of the businessmen of Green Bay can be traced to the team's 1950 stock sale. A little more than two months after Curly Lambeau had resigned, the Packers held the third stock offering in their history and saved their franchise for the third time in 27 years. In early February, when the team had less than $50,000 in cash on hand—and that after collecting a $75,000 insurance settlement for the loss of Rockwood Lodge—the franchise announced plans to go ahead with the sale of approximately 9,500 shares of stock at $25 per share. At the time, only 468 shares of stock in Green Bay were owned. The goal for the sale was to raise $200,000. Led by sale chairman Lee Joannes, the fund-raising drive began in April, and by May 23 it had brought in $89,800. The final tally for the sale was $104,137.50 —not $200,000, but more than enough to put the team on sound footing again. One of the franchise's new owners was Fred Miller, president of Milwaukee's Miller Brewing Company, who had purchased the maximum 200 shares. The same amount was purchased by the *Press-Gazette* and by Packers president Emil Fischer. But according to Joannes, about 60 percent of the 4,165½ shares of stock sold had been purchased by "the $25 guy."

For most of their existence, the Packers had received more financial support from the business leaders of Green Bay, who saw the team as a civic asset, than from the working population of the city. But suddenly the base of their ownership was much broader, more diverse. They were no longer just a civic asset; they were a civic heirloom. One woman came to the team's offices on Washington Street and bought a single share of stock with $25 in quarters. A civil engineer from Eau Claire, who was careful to note that he was glad to see the team had moved back to town from Rockwood Lodge, subscribed to one share. Another went to an Army wife from Green Bay who was stationed with her husband in Guam and who had read about the stock sale in *The Stars and Stripes*. An employee of the Allis-Chalmers machine manufacturing company, in Milwaukee, purchased four shares. Other

single-share buyers included a 92-year-old woman from Green Bay who had been to only one game at City Stadium but never missed the Packers on the radio and a nun who was teaching grade school in Muskogee, Oklahoma. "Thus, the Packers, backed by workers, the thousands of fans who purchased stock and other worthy fans who contributed their moral support, gave the answer to the rest of the sports world," crowed the *Press-Gazette*. "That the greatest, biggest little town in the country can compete in major league professional football!"

But at the same time that the long-term future of the franchise was being secured, more immediate issues were also playing out. The last traces of Curly Lambeau's final tumultuous years were erased on February 6, five days after the coach's resignation, when the *Press-Gazette* announced

that publicity head George Strickler had been fired. The bad blood was being wrung out of the organization — to make way for the new blood that was coming in.

◆ ◆ ◆

The same day that Strickler was let go, the Packers announced the hiring of Gene Ronzani as the second coach in team history. The 40-year-old Ronzani had won an NFL championship as a rookie member of the Bears' backfield in 1933, and after his six-season career was over, he had come up through the coaching ranks in the Chicago organization — briefly returning to play again for the Bears during World War II. Ronzani had led American Association farm teams in Newark and in Akron, Ohio, before he returned to Chicago in 1947 as the Bears' backfield and quarterbacks coach. He

PREVIOUS SPREAD
Packers quarterback Tobin Rote stiff-arms Browns linebacker Chuck Noll in Cleveland's 41–10 drubbing of Green Bay at Municipal Stadium on October 23, 1955.

ABOVE
In the words of one Eastern writer, City Stadium — with its wooden bleachers, board fence, and lack of amenities — was little more than a "chicken coop" by the early 1950s.

had a gifted offensive mind and was, according to Halas, Chicago's chief strategist. "I think Ronzani will revitalize the entire Green Bay scene," said Halas, who was sometimes given to hyperbole when it came to extolling the virtues of his team's biggest rival. "When Lambeau quit, I figured we'd win both games next fall. But Gene'll have those Packers right back at the old stand, and I'm saying I'll settle for a split with the Packers right now."

Ronzani, with his shock of thick black hair and broad smiling face, should have appealed to fans from all reaches of the "Packerland" region, which the club had defined during the stock drive as the entire state of Wisconsin and the Upper Peninsula of Michigan. The coach actually hailed from the U.P.—from Iron Mountain, to be exact. His father, Giovanni (who had Americanized his name to John when he immigrated to the United States just before the turn of the century, from Lusiana, in Northern Italy) worked in the mines that

produced the ore for which the town had been named. Gene won eight letters in football, basketball, and track at Iron Mountain High, where he played football with Frosty Ferzacca, who went on to become the coach at Green Bay West. After high school, Ronzani headed south to Marquette, where he won nine letters and was captain of the football team as a senior in 1932. At five foot nine and 200 pounds, he was a sturdy runner and a gifted receiver out of the backfield.

But Ronzani was also a Bear, which meant that he was never able to endear himself to the people of Green Bay. It did not help that he had a habit of picking up Chicago players off the waiver wire, and that most of the assistant coaches he hired were also ex-Bears, including John "Tarzan" Taylor and Ray "Scooter" McLean.

Still, fans were indisputably happy to have the Packers back home after four years at Rockwood Lodge. An estimated 2,000 (many of them shareholders, noted the *Press-Gazette*) showed up to the practice field just east of City Stadium on July 22 for the first training session of the season. And for the Packers' home opener, against the Detroit Lions on September 17, a contingent of Iron Mountain fans—including the mayor of the town—were on hand at City Stadium. The U.P. crew presented Ronzani with a set of luggage to commemorate "Gene Ronzani Day." It would be the high point of the afternoon: the Lions proceeded to intercept Green Bay seven times and won 45–7. Afterwards, Ronzani attributed the thrashing to the vagaries of football and not to Detroit's being better than the Packers. "I think the team with the best breaks won the ball game," he said. "We were there, but we weren't there enough—fumbles, pass interceptions, men in the open. The team that was alert won."

But the truth was that Ronzani had inherited an aging, broken-down team. Tony Canadeo, who had begun training camp as a holdout, was 31. Ted Fritsch was 30. Quarterback Tobin Rote showed flashes of promise, but he was a rookie. Rote's inconsistency (he threw 24 interceptions) seeped into the rest of the offense, which gave the ball away 57 times in 12 games. The Packers beat the Redskins 35–21 in Milwaukee in week two—the only game all season in which Green Bay did not commit a turnover—and then improved to 2-1 by upsetting the Bears 31–21 at City Stadium on October 1. But Ronzani's team went 1-8 the rest of the way. The defense gave up nearly 400 yards per game and surrendered 41 or more points five times. Things got no better in 1951, when the Packers finished 3-9 again.

Some of Ronzani's problems were self-inflicted. If Lambeau had lost his team in his last few years in Green Bay, Ronzani had a hard time making it his in the first place. He was a friendly man by most accounts, but that is a tough line to walk for a football coach. Discipline was lax. Ronzani once skipped a day of training camp in Grand Rapids, Minnesota, to go fishing. He would talk to journalists during practice. He was also known to jump into drills with his players, and would hold footraces between them after practice, with the winner treated to a cold beer in the coach's office. He also had a conspicuous habit of not looking players in the eye when he addressed them in meetings. "He'd look up at the ceiling, down at the floor, out the window," says former end Dan Orlich, who played for the Packers from 1949 to 1951. "Everywhere but at you."[*]

Ronzani was also secretive about his game plans, to the point of being neurotic—a tic that became especially pronounced when the Packers were preparing to play the Bears, his former team. Ronzani did not give his players playbooks, for fear that the information would fall into enemy hands. Instead he would show the plays at team meetings and expect players to learn and memorize their assignments for each one. And when the Packers practiced at Bluejay Stadium, a minor league ballpark across Walnut Street from City Stadium, Ronzani would have the injured players stand in front of the knotholes and gaps in the wooden fence so that nobody could see what was going on inside. "An airplane would fly over, he'd stop practice," former linebacker Deral Teteak told Cliff Christl and co-author Gary D'Amato in the 1997 book *Mudbaths & Bloodbaths: The Inside Story of the Packers-Bears Rivalry*. "He was really paranoid. He used to say, 'They're around here somewhere. I know they are. They always [spied on the Packers] when I was there.'"

Ronzani was also afraid to fly over the Rocky Mountains, so his team rode the train on road trips to the West Coast, which took two days. When the train made scheduled stops in the western states, the players would get off to stretch their legs and

---

* *Born December 21, 1924, in Chisholm, Minnesota, Orlich played college ball at Nevada. Green Bay selected him in the eighth round of the 1949 draft after having taken quarterback Stan Heath, his Wolf Pack teammate, in the first round. Orlich was the last living Packer to have played for Curly Lambeau. He passed away in January 2019.*

go through an informal workout. "I didn't appreciate those train rides too much," says Orlich. "We'd get out and just start running around and throwing passes. There was nothing organized. It was just getting exercise because we were cooped up in the train all day."

Despite his quirks, Ronzani was generally well liked by his players. Unlike the combustible and authoritarian Lambeau, Ronzani had actually been carried off the field on their shoulders after a victory: With Green Bay limping along at 1-4 in 1953 and amid rampant rumors that Ronzani would be fired, the team rallied around him in a 35–24 defeat of the expansion Colts in Baltimore on Halloween. He was not afraid to try new things, at various times employing more of a spread-out, single-back set, as well as sometimes putting Rote in the shotgun. The Packers had the second-best passing offense in the NFL in 1951, one year after having had the second worst. But the wins never came. Ronzani went 14-31-1 in nearly four seasons on the sidelines, never finishing with a winning record and never making the playoffs. With a 2-7-1 record and two games left to go in the 1953 season, he was informed by the executive committee that he could resign or be fired. Ronzani chose to resign.

◆ ◆ ◆

It is clear from the record books that Gene Ronzani knew what he was up against in Green Bay. He spent much of his first season trying every which way to upgrade his roster. According to author Eric Goska, only 12 of the 35 players who dressed for one game in 1950 had connections to Lambeau. The rest had been added through the draft or other means. It was while Ronzani was turning over personnel at a rapid rate that he made one of the most important changes in the history of the team. One of the free agents he signed was end Bob Mann, the first African American to play for the Packers since the reintegration of pro football.

Robert Mann was born on April 8, 1924, in New Bern, North Carolina, the youngest of William and

Clara Mann's three children. In the modern era, his combination of academic and athletic prowess would be celebrated. But since he came out of the segregated, Jim Crow South, there is not much record of him until he left his hometown. William was a family doctor with his own practice. Clara was the supervisor of elementary schools in Craven County. Bob was a sleek, 150-pound halfback and team captain at all-black West Street High, where he graduated second in his class in 1941. From there he moved on to Hampton Institute, in Virginia, playing end and earning All–Central Intercollegiate Athletic Association honors in 1943.

The next year he transferred to Michigan. After sitting out most of the 1944 season with an injury and then serving a year in the Navy, he starred for the Wolverines in 1946 and '47, leading the team in receiving yards both seasons. The five-foot-eleven, 167-pound Mann was never on scholarship in Ann Arbor—his parents paid his tuition. And according to the university registrar, he never graduated from Michigan. In April 1948 he signed with the Detroit Lions as an undrafted free agent.

Mann's time in Detroit was momentous, tumultuous, and brief. As a rookie in 1948, he caught 33 passes for 560 yards, second best on the team in both categories. The next season he led the NFL in receiving yards, with 1,014, and ranked second in catches, with 66. Cerebral and handsome, Mann was also a salesman for the Goebel Brewing Company, which was owned by Lions president Edwin J. Anderson. But during the off-season in 1950, Lions coach Bo McMillin—who said that at 170 pounds Mann was "totally ineffective as a blocker" —asked Mann to take a $1,500 cut in salary. Mann refused, and in early August, right after his most recent contract with Goebel had ended, Detroit traded him to the New York Yanks in exchange for quarterback Bobby Layne. But Mann was not in

New York for long—the Yanks released him outright less than a week after he had caught a 44-yard touchdown pass in a 24–7 preseason loss to the Redskins on September 7. He returned to Detroit and sold real estate. He also played basketball to keep himself fit. On November 25, the Packers announced that they had signed him. Mann practiced with the team that morning and then played for Green Bay the next day at City Stadium, catching one pass for eight yards in a 25–21 victory over the San Francisco 49ers that was played during a blizzard—the *Press-Gazette* called it "the worst winter-game weather conditions in the history of Packer competition anywhere."

Though he was the first African American since the reintegration of pro football to play in a game for the Packers, Mann was not actually the first black player signed by Green Bay after the departure of Lambeau. Ronzani never said so publicly, but he showed early in his tenure that he was determined to integrate the team. On July 21, 1950, the Packers announced the signings of guard James "Shag" Thomas and halfback James Clark, both of whom had been members of Ohio State's Rose Bowl–winning 1949 team. Neither player had been drafted. The five-foot-seven, 235-pound Thomas had played for the Buckeyes after serving in the Army during World War II. Clark, a six-foot-one, 185-pound speedster, had spent nearly three years in the Marines. Green Bay cut both players on September 6, before its final preseason game.[*]

In 2001, Mann told Cliff Christl, who was then writing for the *Milwaukee Journal Sentinel,* that the only two blacks in Green Bay during his career with the Packers had been a porter at the Hotel Northland and a cook for the railroad. That was an exaggeration—but not by much. The population of Green Bay in 1950 was 52,735, an increase of more than 15,300 from 1930, when, according to census data, there had been just 21 blacks (nine males and 12 females) living in the city. When

Mann arrived, 20 years later, there were 17 African Americans (11 males and six females). Coming to Green Bay from Detroit in 1950, Mann must have felt conspicuous—not just a stranger in a strange land, but also a stranger with no place to hide. That he played for the Packers only made him stand out more. "In Green Bay, everybody knew the players," he said. "You couldn't get away from being a Green Bay Packer. No way in the world."

As white as the city was, it was nothing like the Jim Crow South. Mann called the fans at City Stadium the greatest in the world and said that everybody on the team was friendly to him when he first arrived. But racial prejudice was a fact of life in the United States and the NFL—and sometimes even in a hamlet in northeastern Wisconsin, where it was more a function of benightedness than of bigotry. On road trips to Baltimore, Mann had to stay in separate lodgings from the rest of the Packers. Once, after a meeting at the team hotel, a cabbie refused him a ride home. Guard Dick Afflis—a six-foot, 252-pound bodybuilding devotee who went on to a pro wrestling career as Dick the Bruiser—grabbed the cabbie through the driver's-side window, pulled him out, and ordered him to take Mann where he wanted to go. Back in Green Bay, where housing was not readily available for blacks, Mann said that he lived at a motel rather than trying to get an apartment. After *Press-Gazette* writer Art Daley had referred to him on several occasions as "colored," Mann pulled Daley aside and explained that the proper term was "Negro."

It was not that the town itself was overtly hostile to African Americans, but there was enough unpleasantness that black players simply were not comfortable in a place where few blacks had chosen to live. Nate Borden played defensive end for the Packers from 1955 to 1959. Unable to find housing within the city limits, he lived in a run-down home outside of town. Mann used to head

---

* *Shag Thomas, who died in 1982, went on to a long career as a professional wrestler.*

south in his Chrysler to Milwaukee or Chicago when he wanted to get a haircut, or to enjoy nightlife that was a bit more urban than what could be found at the Packers Playdium. It would be nearly a decade before Green Bay carried more than two or three black players on its roster. Still, the color line on the team had been broken. In its own way, it was a simple first step toward the revival of the franchise — though nobody felt that way at the time.

◆ ◆ ◆

If there was one thing in Green Bay that defined the town as home to the NFL's smallest-market team, it was City Stadium. Even when it was built, in 1925 it had been a second-rate structure, hardly on a par with the concrete cathedrals that were then going up on campuses all over the country. It held only about 25,000 in its heyday. The Packers had no locker room at City Stadium until 1936, when a small wooden one was built under the south stands, but even that had only a dressing area, showers, a training room, and a storage area. And its "lockers," at least initially, were nothing more than hooks and nails in the walls. Visiting players used the locker rooms at Green Bay East High, but only at halftime. They changed into their uniforms before games — and showered and changed after games — in their rooms at the Hotel Northland.

For spectators, there weren't adequate toilet facilities until 1937, when the seating capacity was increased to 17,500. That was the same year that a press box finally went up atop the south stands. Before that, journalists covering games used to sit at card tables set up along the sidelines. The place was made mostly of wood, from its bleacher seats to the board fence that surrounded it on three sides. According to former board member John Torinus, the area underneath the skeletal structure was a favorite spot for unsavory patrons to attempt to look up the skirts of women attending games. City Stadium had seen an amazing amount of NFL history — the Packers won six league championships when it was their home field, and 87 Hall of Famers played in a regular-season or a preseason game on its turf — but the fact remained that by the early 1950s, many in the league agreed with the take of one visiting journalist who described it years later as something like "a chicken coop."

There's a better metaphor for the place, of course. "City Stadium," says Cliff Christl, "was the Packers' log cabin." From its humble confines, Green Bay rose from the sandlot to the top of the NFL. City Stadium was home for 32 years to the greatest team in what became America's greatest sports league. Before the Packers epitomized America, they embodied the hardscrabble roots of pro football. And City Stadium was the physical manifestation of the league's blue-collar origins.

But to the south, the Milwaukee Braves were leading Major League Baseball in attendance every season playing in brand-new County Stadium, which had opened in 1953. And even though the Packers did not draw as well in Milwaukee as they did at City Stadium, other NFL owners, even George Halas, had begun to make it known that they preferred to play in a more modern stadium with at least the prospect of a bigger payday. The push for a new home for the Packers had begun not long after the 1950 stock sale returned the franchise to financial health. Mayor Dominic Olejniczak, who was also a member of the board of directors, had said as early as 1951 that Green Bay "must give serious consideration to a new stadium."

Even though the Packers had shored up their finances, there was still a fear that the team might move somewhere else. The personification of that fear — justly or not — was Fred Miller. As much as anyone, he had been responsible for the success of the 1950 stock sale, having purchased the maximum 200 shares on behalf of his family business. Miller was actually one of the few stockholders from outside of the Green Bay area. The team had originally planned to raise $200,000 — $100,000 from greater Green Bay and another $100,000 from the rest of the state and the Upper Peninsula of Michigan. But in the final accounting, almost all of the money raised by the sale came from the Green Bay area. On May 23, the *Press-Gazette* made its final report on sales numbers, trumpeting Miller's purchase of 200 shares and saying that the team had gone "over the top" in greater Green Bay. The paper said that $105,825 had been pledged and that $89,800 of that was cash in the bank. On June 9, the paper said that "close to $110,000" had been sold in the Green Bay area and quoted NFL commissioner Bert Bell as saying, "And the rest of the state including Milwaukee hasn't even been touched yet." Since the final tally from the sale was actually $104,137.50 — more than $1,000 less than the *Press-Gazette*'s "over the top" amount — it seems clear that the paper and the Packers were putting the best possible spin on the results. What is also clear is that Miller's $5,000 purchase had provided the team with a significant boost. His sudden importance to the fortunes of the team made people in Green Bay nervous. And rightly so.

The darkly handsome grandson of the founder of the Miller Brewing Company, Fred Miller was a sportsman. He'd been a three-year starter as a six-foot, 200-pound tackle at Notre Dame from 1926 to 1928 and was team captain and a first-team All-America as a senior. He graduated cum laude from South Bend and was only 41 when he ascended to the presidency of the family business. Miller spoke openly of his desire to bring big-league sports to Milwaukee, and in 1950 he tried to buy baseball's St. Louis Browns. A year later, he sponsored Milwaukee's entry into the newly formed NBA, the Hawks. And in 1953 he was integral in helping convince Boston Braves owner Lou Perini to move his team to Milwaukee. Miller's purchase of Packers stock coincided with his decision to sponsor the team's radio broadcasts. Green Bay returned his largesse by naming him an honorary line coach — a title he also held with the Fighting Irish. Miller, a pilot, used to fly his company plane to South Bend to participate in Notre Dame practices.

Miller was always careful to say that the Packers should stay in Green Bay, but people in town couldn't help but be suspicious — and the runaway popularity of the Braves only made them more nervous. Art Daley wrote in the *Press-Gazette* that Miller actually refrained from visiting the city too frequently. "Miller was well aware of the undertone of feeling in Green Bay," wrote Daley. "Writers in various sections of the country predicted that Miller someday hoped to move the Packers to Milwaukee." But whatever misgivings Green Bay had about Miller vanished when he died in a plane crash on December 17, 1954. The uncertainty over the permanence of the Packers, however, remained.

At a meeting with a citizens' group in January 1956, Fred Leicht, the Packers' grounds committee chairman, put it bluntly: "There is no use kidding ourselves. We are doing more than deciding on a stadium. We are deciding whether we want to keep the Packers in Green Bay." The team, Leicht said, "was depending entirely on the road schedule to stay in the black," and he pointedly told the group that opposing teams were pressing to have their games with Green Bay played in Milwaukee. Leicht said that the league average attendance in 1955 was 35,000, with box office receipts of $103,000. But games at City Stadium averaged just 22,000 and $74,000. He also said that the Packers had made about $261,000 in 1955 from their share of gate receipts on the road. But teams visiting Green Bay and Milwaukee had earned a total of $161,000. For the 11 other teams in the NFL in 1955, playing the Packers did not pay.

There was a real fear that the city's most ancient rivalry, the one between the east and west sides of town — the very rivalry that had helped to create the Packers in the first place — might doom the project. East-siders, for the most part, wanted any new stadium to be built on the site of the original City Stadium. In all of the Packers' 37 years of ex-

istence, they had never played a game on the western side of the Fox River. West-siders wanted to change that. Three of the four proposals for a new stadium were for the City Stadium site, and one was for Perkins Park, on the northwest side, just a few miles west of the site of the old Fort Howard Army post.

There were some people, though, who just wanted the new stadium to go up where it made the most sense. Even Curly Lambeau—who by 1956 was out of coaching, having flopped in stints with both the Chicago Cardinals and the Washington Redskins—chimed in as a voice of reason. Lambeau was a lifelong east-sider, but he said that it made better business sense for a new stadium to go on the west side of town. "I'm an east sider, strictly," he told the *Press-Gazette*. "But I firmly believe that a stadium on the west side is the best answer to bigger attendance and easy access to the stadium . . . That superhighway [U.S. Highway 41] is a temptation for fans in Milwaukee south of there and in the valley to come. Same for fans coming from the north and west."

The rivalry between the two sides of town, as exemplified by the annual gridiron showdowns between Green Bay East and Green Bay West, had never really cooled off. In the 1940s, tensions had occasionally boiled over. The night before the 1942 East-West game, a mob of about 500 students went on a rampage through town, on both sides of the river. Things began innocently enough. The first report of a disturbance, according to the *Press-Gazette,* was when a gang of 40 to 50 boys marched into a Walgreens drugstore and "took everything off a candy display counter." But over the next few hours the crowd began to grow—and grow more unruly, starting bonfires, smashing bottles, and destroying property. But even as it increased in menace, the mob also, improbably, retained something of a provincial charm, continuing to loot mostly candy counters. At one point, several rioters—presumably hopped up on Flipsticks and Atomic Fireballs—ran into an ice cream parlor

and, according to the paper, "scooped ice cream out of the freezers with their hands." The night of lawlessness may have been fueled as much by a collective sugar high as by school spirit.

The citizens of Green Bay were horrified. The fire department finally dispersed the horde using fire hoses. Police inspector H. J. "Tubby" Bero, who had played fullback for the original 1919 Packers, called the riot the worst in the city's history. Six years later, though, things got a little more serious. After West beat East 13–0, a mob estimated at between 500 and 800 people rocked Wisconsin Public Service buses, damaged property, and vandalized cars. Police arrested 19 people, and school officials briefly considered discontinuing the rivalry. But East-West endured and remained one of the most important games in town. In 1952, East-West drew a record crowd of 14,047 to City Stadium. The attendance record rose in 1953, when the game brought out 15,071 fans.

With the prospect for a serious—and potentially ruinous—territorial battle, city leaders wisely decided to put only the money issue to a vote. And then they decided to leave nothing to chance. On March 31, 1956, a "pep rally" was staged at the downtown Columbus Club, on South Jefferson Street. Among the guests were Curly Lambeau, Johnny Blood, and Tony Canadeo, as well as Bears coach George Halas, who made his feelings clear. "Let's consider this matter from the viewpoint of an owner of another club in the National Football League," he told the crowd of more than 1,000. "If you can draw 35,000 to 45,000 at home against the Packers, you naturally feel you should be able to draw a comparable crowd at Green Bay. And when this becomes impossible it is inevitable that you look forward to playing at Green Bay with less enthusiasm . . . This isn't selfishness—just reasonable and necessary business prudence."

Halas wasn't speaking hypothetically. Six years earlier, at the 1950 NFL meetings in Philadelphia, he had actually been in favor of ditching one of the games in the Bears' home-and-home rivalry with the Packers. In absorbing three teams from the AAFC—the Baltimore Colts, Cleveland Browns, and San Francisco 49ers—the NFL was going to realign itself into two new conferences, which it eventually named the American and the National. With the new league at 13 teams instead of an even 10, seven were going to be in one conference and six in the other. More important, one of the Bears' traditional Western Division rivals, the Cardinals or the Packers, was going to have to play in a different conference. That was going to mean an end to one of the two oldest rivalries in the NFL. The Bears had played the Packers 60 times in the regular season and once in the postseason, and they had played the Cardinals 59 times in the regular season and never in the playoffs.

A visit from the Bears could almost always be counted on to sell out City Stadium, but the biggest crowd there in the three years before the 1950 league meetings had been the 25,571 who had shown up to see Chicago trounce Green Bay 17–0 on September 25, 1949. None of the three Bears-Cardinals game at Comiskey Park during that time had drawn fewer than 51,123. Losing a second game against his South Side rival was going to be costly to Halas—and that didn't sit well with him. "It was learned that Ray Bennigsen, president of the Cardinals, fought like blazes in the meeting room to retain the two-game rivalry" with the Bears, wrote Art Daley in the *Press-Gazette* on January 21, 1950. "Bear owner George Halas also wants to keep it."

One of Lambeau's last acts as the leader of the Packers was also one of his most important. He argued that the league should keep the Bears-Packers rivalry intact. The owners were unable to reach an agreement, and came to a decision only after Bell threatened to divvy up the teams himself. On the final day of the meetings, January 23, 1950, the owners voted to put Green Bay and the Bears together in one conference, while the Cardinals would be in the other.

Perhaps the owners finally came to that agreement because they knew that Bell was likely to support keeping the Packers and the Bears together. Three days before the conference issue was decided, Bell had told reporters, "We certainly can't break up a 30-year traditional rivalry." The commissioner—who had suffered through financial difficulties of his own as the owner of the Philadelphia Eagles in the 1930s—had a soft spot for Green Bay. He had been a vocal supporter of the 1950 stock sale, for example. Both Halas and Bennigsen seemed to acknowledge as much after the meeting was over, telling Art Daley that the agreed-upon setup was the only way forward. In a twist, Halas himself had made the motion that was finally approved.

Bell might have been sentimental about the Packers, but he could not justify carrying them forever. In his telegraphed remarks to the March 1956 pep rally, the commissioner was blunt. "We have firm offers for a franchise from many cities whose stadiums can accommodate large crowds," he wrote. "There is no doubt in my mind that the Green Bay Packers could sell their franchise (God forbid) for a maximum of three quarters of a million dollars."

On April 3, 1956, by a greater than two-to-one margin, Green Bay voters approved a $960,000 bond issue (about $9 million today) for construction of a new stadium.

◆ ◆ ◆

To help decide where to put the new stadium, the Packers hired the Cleveland-based Osborn Engineering Company—the same outfit that had done the site survey for Milwaukee's County Stadium—to study possible locations. It was, in the words of John Torinus, "a brilliant idea." The Osborn engineers surveyed 15 prospective sites around Green Bay and on July 10 recommended a spot on the undeveloped far southwestern side of town, a sloping parcel of pasture grazed by the Guernsey cows owned by dairy farmers Victor and Florence Vannieuwenhoven. The site offered plenty of

When it was built in 1957, Green Bay City Stadium sat on a parcel of land next to the farmhouse (bottom right) of the couple who had sold the property to the city the year before.

space for parking and future expansion, as well as proximity to U.S. Highway 41. The soil was also better suited to supporting the weight of a large structure, and the grade of the terrain, which descended from west to east, made it ideal for the construction of a bowl, in which the level of the field would be below the level of the land that surrounded it. The city council took all of six days to approve Osborn's recommendations, with the vote passing 17–7. (Every dissenting vote had been cast by aldermen from the east side of town.) One month later, the city purchased the 48.87-acre site from the Vannieuwenhovens for $73,305.

The bowl of the stadium was shaped before the year was out, with contractors taking dirt from the upper hillside on the west and moving it to the lower side on the east, in a circuit that traced the same oval as the stadium would. The earthen concavity allowed contractors to put 21 rows of poured-in-place concrete directly on the compacted dirt on the east and west sides of the bowl. At the same time that the concrete was being placed, construction was also taking place outside the bowl, where support structures were going up for the additional 39 rows of seats that would rise above the concrete stands on the east and west sides of the field. Concrete stands were cheaper than support structures, which helped to keep costs under control. San Francisco's Candlestick Park, the eventual home of the 49ers, was built for baseball, had a capacity of 43,765, and took nearly two years to build. It was finished in 1960 at a cost $15 million. Green Bay City Stadium could accommodate 32,154, cost $960,000, and took less than a year to complete.

At the time, the place was the only arena in the NFL built exclusively for football. It was thoroughly modern, but still endearingly small town.

The Vannieuwenhovens' original farmhouse stood just off the stadium's southwest corner for six more years, inhabited by Victor and Florence's only son, Don, who sold it to the Packers in 1963 when the team needed more parking.

Green Bay celebrated the opening of the new stadium on September 29, 1957, with a 21–17 win over the Chicago Bears. The victory was the culmination of a weekend of festivities. George Halas sponsored a float in the Stadium Dedication Parade on Saturday afternoon — "the greatest and most colorful in the city's history," according to the *Press-Gazette* — as did the Detroit Lions and the New York Giants. The parade was attended by an estimated 70,000 people. It included 17 marching bands and started on the west side of the Walnut Street Bridge and ended inside the old City Stadium, where a farewell program was held that featured Miss America and actor James Arness, the star of the CBS television series *Gunsmoke*. The program had to be halted several times because children from the stands kept coming onto the field and mobbing the actor. "No one was arrested," noted the *Press-Gazette*, "but neither was the field ever really cleared."

Vice President Richard Nixon attended the game, as did Bert Bell. "The dedication of this stadium today is the greatest thing that has ever happened in professional football," Bell said. "I have been watching teams in this league for more years than I care to remember but I have never seen such fine spirit as I saw today. The facilities as they stand right now are the finest in the league. Attending the game today has been one of my biggest thrills in pro ball."

The only problem was that the Packers were still not a winning team. Green Bay won just twice more all season and finished last in the Western Conference. It was the 10th straight year that the team had failed to achieve a winning record.

◆ ◆ ◆

Gene Ronzani had been replaced by Lisle W. "Liz" Blackbourn on January 7, 1954. The 54-year-old Blackbourn, the son of a farmer from Beetown, Wisconsin, was a football lifer. After graduating from Lawrence College, in Appleton, he had won 140 of 176 games as the coach at Milwaukee's Washington High from 1925 to 1947, and then had gone 18-17-4 in four years at Marquette. Blackbourn was strict with his players, who derisively referred to him as "the Lizard," and he could be blunt in his evaluation of their talent. On November 26, 1955, two days before the NFL draft,* he had told Bud Lea of the *Milwaukee Sentinel* that only eight of the 33 players on his roster could make a championship team — and, even worse, he named the players who he thought weren't performing. "We've got only one halfback who is a real football player," Blackbourn said, referring to rookie Veryl Switzer. "I'm disappointed in [guard Joe] Skibinski and [defensive tackle Bill] Lucky. I thought they could handle themselves better . . . We've been skating on some pretty thin ice all season."

His players were not amused. According to Christl, "Some never forgave him for divulging those thoughts."

Blackbourn's players may not have liked it, but the coach's eye for talent was formidable. And his legacy in Green Bay comes from more than just his coaching record. It also has to do with the men he brought in to play for the Packers — men

---

* *The 1956 NFL draft was held in two stages, with the first three rounds taking place on November 28, 1955, in Philadelphia, and the last 27 over two days in January 1956 in Los Angeles. The league had previously held the draft at its January meeting but changed its schedule to deal with competition from teams in the Canadian Football League. "The Canadians finish their season in early November and almost immediately come south of the border to sign up as many college aces as they can lay their hands on," read a November 28, 1955, report from the Associated Press. The NFL continued with its two-tiered draft for three more years, then began holding the whole event in either November or December through 1966, after which it moved the event to after the New Year. The draft would not become an annual rite of spring until the mid-1970s.*

who would go on to define a team, a league, and a country. In the four-plus drafts that Blackbourn oversaw (1954–1957 and the first four rounds of the 1958 draft, which were held on December 2, 1957, one month before he was fired), he made the decisions to draft six players who would go on to be enshrined in the Pro Football Hall of Fame: Bart Starr, guard Forrest Gregg, halfback Paul Hornung, fullback Jim Taylor, linebacker Ray Nitschke, and guard Jerry Kramer. Blackbourn had been the first to publicly laud Starr during training camp in 1956, and he continued to praise and encourage the quarterback during the next few years. Starr made his first NFL start for Blackbourn as a rookie in Green Bay's final game at old City Stadium, a 17–16 loss to the San Francisco 49ers on November 18, 1956. Blackbourn's skill as an evaluator of players was so formidable that Vince Lombardi hired him as a scout in 1964, six years after he'd been shown the door in Green Bay.

But Blackbourn did not do it alone. He could not have. The early rounds of his last three drafts as coach of the Packers (1956, '57, and '58) occurred during the season, when he was busy with other things. He thus leaned heavily on Green Bay's one-man personnel department, Jack Vainisi. The young front-office man, who would die of a heart attack in 1960 at the age of 33, left a legacy as one of the first truly great scouts in the history of pro football—an NFL draftnik decades before the draft became a major event. In 1979, Blackbourn told Bob Wolf of *The Milwaukee Journal* that when it came to selecting players out of college, "We very rarely went against his opinion."

Vainisi's forte lay in his organization and preparation. He maintained extensive files on college players. But unlike Eddie Kotal, the former Packers halfback who'd become a legendary bird-dog scout for the Los Angeles Rams, Vainisi did not travel extensively. He certainly went out on the road—for their honeymoon in 1952, Vainisi's new bride, Jackie, traveled through Oklahoma, Texas, and Alabama with him while he signed new players—but he was primarily an office rat, haunting the corridors of the team's headquarters on South Washington Street. From there he maintained an extensive network of college coaches who fed him information on players, information that Vainisi alone organized and consolidated into something coherent that could be used on draft day. At the 1952 draft in New York, Vainisi had material on players that was so well organized that other teams frequently checked with Packers brass on questions of eligibility. In the days before the world went digital, Vainisi's collection of files and three-ring notebooks was the Packers' very own supercomputer, with Vainisi himself the central processing unit.

Like Blackbourn, Vainisi was a football lifer, having grown up surrounded by Bears on Chicago's North Side. He was a grammar school classmate of George Halas Jr., the son of the Chicago coach. And Bears players helped coach the eighth-grade team on which Vainisi played. His father ran Tony's Fine Foods, a combination delicatessen and grocery store that was frequented during the NFL season by Chicago players, particularly those who lived across Wilson Avenue at the Sheridan Plaza Hotel. And his mother used to cook five-course Italian meals for Bears players at least once a season. It was through these connections that Vainisi met Gene Ronzani, who hired him in 1950 after Ronzani became the coach in Green Bay.

Vainisi played freshman football at Notre Dame in 1945 but was drafted into the Army after only one year of college. He was stationed in occupied Japan, where he worked in the headquarters of General Douglas MacArthur and played service football. He became ill while he was overseas, and doctors originally diagnosed his sickness as scarlet fever. After a brief recuperation, they allowed him to continue playing football. But Vainisi had actually been sick with rheumatic fever, a more dangerous disease by far, and the strain of playing did permanent damage to his heart. He returned to Notre Dame and earned his degree, but he never played football again. Instead he dedicated himself to finding work in the front office of a professional team.

According to Blackbourn, Vainisi hadn't been a salaried employee under Ronzani. "When I came here, I put him on the same basis as the assistant coaches," Blackbourn said in 1979. "I realized what a valuable man he was."

There is now a movement afoot to enshrine Vainisi in the Pro Football Hall of Fame as a contributor to the game — the same category used to honor influential owners and general managers. Vainisi certainly deserves consideration, but some of the claims that have been made on his behalf oversell his credentials, especially the assertion that Vainisi was responsible for making all of the Packers' draft picks during his 11 years with the team. There is little evidence for that. Indeed, Blackbourn's endorsement of Vainisi — "We very rarely went against his opinion" — is telling. Sometimes, Blackbourn was also saying, he *did* go against Vainisi's recommendations. Vainisi's titles with the Packers in the 1950s were scout, game and talent scout, and administrative assistant and talent scout. He was never the team's general manager. From 1954 to 1958, that role was filled by former Green Bay star Verne Lewellen, whose responsibilities did not include preparing for and running the Packers' draft operations.

Vainisi's influence on Green Bay in the 1950s and beyond was enormous. The Packers would not have chosen many of the players they did if not for Vainisi's efforts. But he did not have the ultimate authority to say yes or no to drafting a player. From 1954 to 1958, that authority rested with Lisle Blackbourn.

But even with his formidable eye for talent, Blackbourn was, for whatever reason, unable to put it to good use on the field. In his authoritative biography of Vince Lombardi, *When Pride Still Mattered,* author David Maraniss asks, "Which is more important, the talent of the troops or the skill of the leader?" The Packers were about to find out the answer.

But first they were going to have to hit rock bottom.

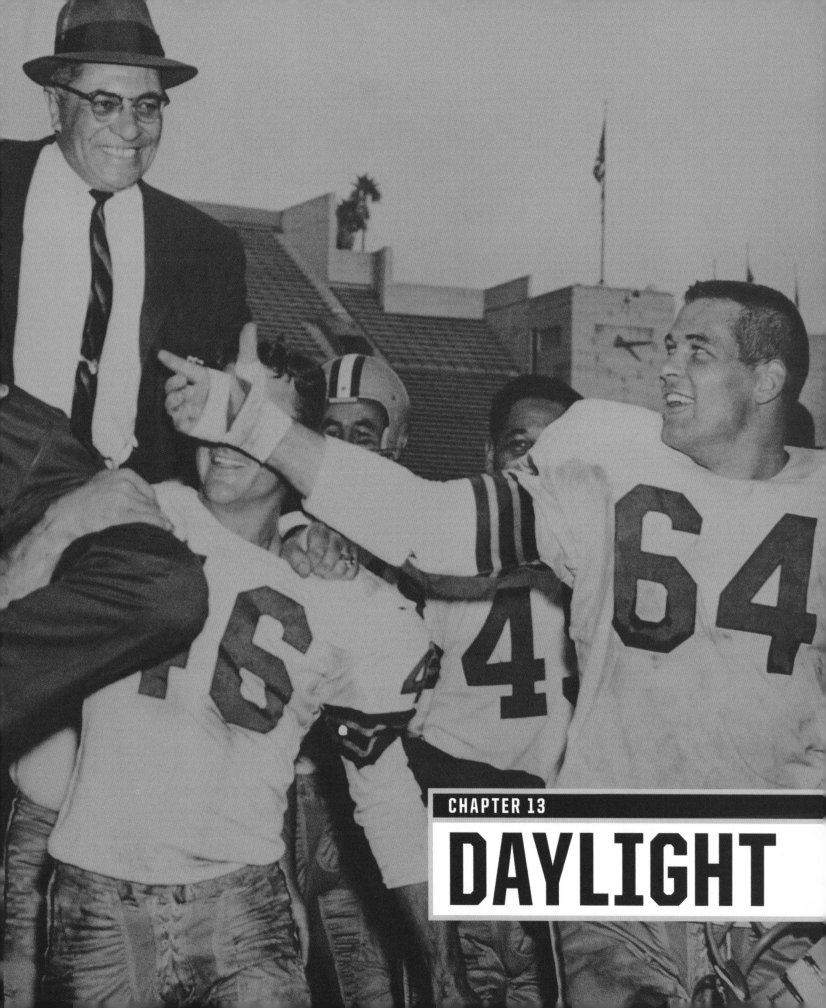

CHAPTER 13

DAYLIGHT

John Reinhart was just going for a haircut. In the late summer of 1959, the 29-year-old investment broker was a manager in the Green Bay office of the Chicago firm of Link, Gorman, Peck & Co. He worked on the fifth floor of the six-story Northern Building, on the northeast corner of Adams and Walnut. The block-long Northern was one of downtown Green Bay's biggest office structures and had claimed to be as modern as any in the state when it opened in 1930. The lobby was trimmed in imported marble and decorated with hand-carved walnut paneling. Among the Northern's original tenants had been Curly Lambeau, who kept an office in the building for nearly 20 years as the Green Bay representative of the Massachusetts Mutual Life Insurance Company. Lambeau occupied a few different offices during his time in the Northern. He had started on the fourth floor in 1930, then moved to the third in 1933. By the time he resigned as the Packers' coach, in 1950, his office was in room 206, on the second floor — right next door to the barbershop owned by Joe Gryboski. In the morning, before his workday began, Lambeau used to mingle with customers and other visitors at Gryboski's shop. The Northern was across the street from both the courthouse and city hall, and the place was a meeting spot for city leaders — mayors, judges, city councilmen, and the coach of the Green Bay Packers.

Gryboski himself was one of those city leaders. A longtime alderman for the city's Eighth Ward, he had been at the forefront of the drive in 1958 to build the Brown County Golf Course. A scratch golfer, the 50-year-old Gryboski was the father of eight children and an usher at St. Willebrord Catholic Church, the downtown parish where George Halas used to attend Mass whenever the Bears were in town. Gryboski was also a prominent supporter of the Packers. He had been a vocal proponent of the new stadium, serving on a citizens' committee that advocated for the bond proposal to fund construction. And since the mid-1940s he had been a member of the Packers' "chain gang," the five-man crew that moved and positioned the down-and-distance markers at Packers games.

Having a side job with the Packers wasn't unusual in Green Bay. They got passed around the way such jobs do in every town — because somebody knew somebody, or somebody had been in the right place at the right time. The only difference in Green Bay was that the city was small enough that *everybody* knew somebody. Gryboski knew Lambeau. James Manci, a local supper-club owner and sports promoter—who was giving up his job holding the down marker—knew Gene Ronzani. Burel Nielsen, a machinist at Northwest Engineering Company and one of the other members of the crew, lived next door to Gryboski and occasionally golfed with him. Not only did the men who played for the Packers seem to be everywhere, but the people who had some sort of connection to them seemed to be everywhere, too.

On the day in 1959 that Reinhart had been looking for a trim, the barber asked the broker if he wanted Manci's old job on the chain gang, and the younger man said yes. Simple as that. There would be no paycheck for the day's work, just free game tickets. The job seemed interesting, though. The Packers were putrid, but they had a new coach. Nobody knew quite what to expect.

◆ ◆ ◆

Things had gone from bad to worse after the Packers fired Lisle Blackbourn. The team's preferred choice to replace him probably would have been defensive assistant Tom Hearden, who had starred at halfback for Curly Lambeau at Green Bay East before playing for Knute Rockne at Notre Dame from 1923 to 1926. After an injury-plagued three-year NFL career, Hearden had gone into coaching, taking over as the head football coach at Green Bay East in 1936. He led the Hilltoppers to six Fox River Valley Conference titles, and then he moved on to coach at St. Norbert College, in De Pere, where he won 41 of 54 games. His résumé was impeccable. But Hearden suffered a stroke in May 1957 and was unable to coach that season. He was still incapacitated when Blackbourn's job opened up.[*] So instead of Hearden, Green Bay went with an-

other member of the coaching staff: Ray "Scooter" McLean.

McLean had been an assistant with the Packers since 1951, when Gene Ronzani brought him north from Lewis College, in Romeoville, Illinois, where he had been the head coach. As a diminutive, pass-catching halfback for the Bears from 1940 to 1947, the five-foot-ten, 168-pound McLean had won four NFL championships.[**] After he retired, he had gone on to Lewis, where he coached the Flyers for three seasons before coming to Green Bay.

The balding McLean, with his gregarious personality and charming, gap-toothed grin, was popular with everybody—a favorite of both George Halas and Packers management, as well as fans and players. Everyone liked him. And Scooter liked to be liked. Therein was the problem. He had been a favorite as an assistant because he was an

---

[*] *The stroke forced Hearden, who never fully recovered, to give up coaching. He died on December 27, 1964, after suffering a heart attack at his home in Green Bay.*

[**] *McLean also held the distinction of having booted the last drop-kicked extra point in NFL history—until New England Patriots quarterback Doug Flutie converted one on January 1, 2006, in the final game of his career.*

Lombardi in the mid-1930s, when he was a guard at Fordham—one of the Rams' famous "Seven Blocks of Granite."

agreeable, understanding conduit between Green Bay's head coaches and the players. But when he became the man in charge, McLean never dropped his assistant's demeanor. He was not demanding, sometimes cutting drills short if players complained that they were gassed. He put a committee of players in charge of levying fines and enforcing discipline—and then did nothing when the group let him down. Even curfew was a flexible concept. Worse still, he never stopped being one of the boys. He played poker on the road and in training camp with his players—and often lost. McLean repeated Ronzani's mistake of being a nice guy, and then compounded it by putting himself in the position of owing his players money. They took advantage of him at almost every turn.

The results on the field were disastrous. There was never really a point in the 1958 season when the Packers looked like a winning football team. They fell to the Bears at the new City Stadium on opening day, then tied the defending NFL champion Lions on the same field the next week—and that was as close to decent as they came all year. They blew a 17–0 lead in a 24–17 loss to the Colts in Milwaukee. They got overpowered by the Redskins on October 19, trailing by 34 before they scored their first points. In Green Bay's only win, a 38–35 defeat of the Eagles at City Stadium on October 26, a crowd of 31,043 looked on in horror as the Packers almost blew a 38–14 fourth-quarter lead. The nadir came in week six, when Green Bay went into Baltimore and got destroyed by the Colts 56–0, still the worst defeat in the history of the franchise. The game got so out of hand, and some Packers let up so obviously, that even the habitually supportive *Press-Gazette* took notice. Art Daley, writing in the paper the next day, noted the "almost complete lack of effort" by some of the players and called the game "the biggest quit in Packer history."

McLean couldn't argue, and he promised that changes were coming—but in a way that was almost comical. "We've got to cut out some bad roots," he said. "They're getting to be a problem because they're starting to affect the rest of the team. We know who some of them are and we're going to do something about it . . . There is no use being a good guy. Good guys always get it in the neck. I'm not going to be a good guy anymore."

But nothing was done, and the Packers continued to lose. The defense blamed the offense, and vice versa. Players were critical of other players, but few were critical of McLean. "A lot of us feel real bad about Scooter," tackle Dave Hanner said. Green Bay finished 1-10-1, the worst record in team history. Only one offense in the NFL gained fewer yards than Green Bay, and only one defense gave up more. The Packers not only scored the fewest points of any team in the league, but they also surrendered the most.

After the season-ending 34–20 loss to the Rams in Los Angeles on December 14, it was time for McLean to get it in the neck. He was told that he could either resign on his own or be fired. Three days later, Scooter resigned. He had lasted less than a year.

In nearly two decades in local politics, first as an alderman for Green Bay's Fifth Ward and then as the five-term mayor of the city from 1945 to 1955, Dominic Olejniczak was accustomed to sharp public disagreements and the vitriol that sometimes went along with them. But he had been president of the Packers for only a little more than seven months when it was made clear to him that being a local politician was not nearly as bruising an enterprise as running a professional football team—especially one that came with a sense of communal entitlement that was practically written into the franchise's articles of incorporation. On the night of December 9, 1958, two days after the Packers had been creamed 48–21 by the 49ers in San Francisco in the penultimate game of the season, somebody hung Olejniczak (*Oh-la-NEE-chick*) in effigy from a lamppost in front of the team's offices on South Washington Street. The headless dummy could have been anybody, but whoever strung it up had made sure there was no doubt about who it was supposed to represent. The sign that hung from its neck was inscribed with Olejniczak's nickname: OLE.

The short and stocky Olejniczak may not have approved of the threatening message, but he certainly sympathized with the frustration that had inspired it. The youngest of nine children born to immigrants from the western Polish town of Poznań, Olejniczak was a lifelong east-sider. He had grown up on Crooks Street, less than a half mile from Hagemeister Park and the old City Stadium. After he graduated from Green Bay East High, his first job had been working in his father's real estate office over a corner drugstore. The soft-spoken Olejniczak had come of age when the Packers were essentially a one-man show—and the best team in pro football. But since he'd been named to the board of directors in 1950, at the age of 41, Green Bay had become a joke in the NFL. Including the results of the disastrous 1958 season, the Packers had won just 32 of 108 games. College players dreaded being drafted by Green Bay, which was known around the league as "the salt mines of Siberia." Olejniczak had been one of the leaders in the drive to get Green Bay City Stadium built on the west side, but the Packers' new field had not done anything to reverse the failing fortunes of the franchise.[*]

There was a growing consensus in Green Bay that the 13-member executive committee and the 45-man board of directors were the Packers' real problems. They had become too meddlesome and too controlling, both on the field and in the locker room. Lisle Blackbourn's relationship with the executive committee had soured in 1957 after the coach took umbrage at being questioned about why he wasn't giving more playing time to high-priced rookie back Paul Hornung, who had won the Heisman Trophy the year before at Notre Dame. The next season, McLean had to answer for how he was disciplining—or not disciplining—his players. One member of the committee who could see the problems from both sides was former Packers star Tony Canadeo, who had been elected to the body in April 1958. "When you haven't won a goldarn game, you want to know what's going on," he told author David Maraniss in *When Pride Still Mattered*. "If you don't ask, you're being a jackass."

Writing in *The Milwaukee Journal* on Novem-

---

[*] *Olejniczak's role in the construction of the new stadium would have raised eyebrows today—and raised at least one at the time. He had pushed for the stadium in the early 1950s in his dual roles as mayor and member of the board of directors, and he continued to advocate for it after he was no longer mayor. On April 8, 1956, five days after voters had passed the stadium bond and two months before the Osborn company recommended Victor Vannieuwenhoven's cow pasture to the city council, Olejniczak purchased from Vannieuwenhoven 20 acres of land adjacent to his pasture. In January 1957, Olejniczak sold 19 of the acres to the county, for $28,500. He then sold the last acre to the Packers for an undisclosed sum. "I resent this," Brown County Board superintendent A. B. Pinkerton said of the complicated mechanics of the deal. "I think the city . . . has bent over backward to make a millionaire out of a certain individual."*

ber 4, 1958, two days after the debacle in Baltimore, Oliver Kuechle, a Lambeau acolyte familiar with committee interference going back more than a decade, summed up the problem:

> There are the weekly reports that the executive committee demands at its Monday noon luncheons from the coach and general manager and the "whys" and "wherefors" of this and that.
>
> There are the "friendly" hints that [Vito "Babe"] Parilli, not Starr, ought to be the starting quarterback. There are the meetings with players, without the coaches present, which Liz Blackbourn experienced in his onerous season a year ago—and isn't that a fine way to engender morale among players? . . .
>
> The Packers are in the big leagues, but in a lot of ways they don't show it. How can there be a winner? They themselves invite a lot of their ills. The day that the executive committee clipped Curly Lambeau of absolute authority in the mid-forties and substituted administration by soviet, that day the team's troubles began—off the field and on. And look back. There hasn't been a winning season since.

Kuechle may have omitted the reasons why the board had stripped Lambeau of authority in the first place—but he was not wrong. And Olejniczak knew it. On December 16, two days after the Packers concluded the worst season in franchise history, Olejniczak announced a front-office shake-up. The executive committee was going to be essentially cut in half, from 13 members down to seven. But more important than that, Green Bay was going to hire a general manager and give him responsibility for the team's entire football operation. No longer would the coach have to meet weekly with the committee and the board's many subcommittees. He would instead deal directly with the general manager—or he would be the general manager, too. And the general manager would answer only to the president and the board of directors. Whoever got the job (or jobs, if the decision was made to hire somebody to fill both roles) was going to be in complete command of the team in much the same way that Curly Lambeau had run the show for nearly 30 years.

But who would that man be? There was no shortage of candidates, including Kentucky coach Blanton Collier, former Cleveland Browns quarterback Otto Graham, and Jim Trimble, the coach of the Hamilton Tiger-Cats in the Canadian Football League. One of the hopefuls was more prominent around town than any other: Curly Lambeau. He had been out of coaching for five years at that point, having flamed out in two-year stints with the Cardinals and the Redskins. He'd won 209 of 334 games with Green Bay, but only 17 of 46 in his last four seasons on the sidelines. He was living in California full-time by 1958 and had wired the Packers from Palm Springs about his interest in the general manager's job. He met with Olejniczak in Green Bay over the holidays, and in January 1959 he moved back to town, saying that he was through with California and that he planned to live in Green Bay during the winter and in Door County during the summer. The man who had spent a good chunk of his later career disassociating himself from Green Bay was suddenly eager to reconnect with his hometown.

And many in town were ready to welcome him back. Local radio personality Fritz Van publicly stumped for Lambeau, and a city appliance store conducted its own informal "Lambeau Poll," touting the results as being 7–1 in favor of Curly returning to become the general manager of the Packers. In a city where reminders of the glory days were everywhere, there was no shortage of sentiment for the Bellicose Belgian.

But Olejniczak and other members of the committee remembered all too well why Green Bay had parted ways with Lambeau in the first place. Sentiment in town might have been for Curly, but Olejniczak was not. And Ole was going to do

things his own way. Shortly after McLean's resignation, Olejniczak tasked Jack Vainisi, the Packers' well-connected administrative assistant and talent scout, with seeking out suitable coaching prospects. Nobody in the organization knew the league as well as Vainisi, who had grown tired of watching the players he scouted being wasted on one of the worst teams in the NFL. (That, as much as his personal ambition, probably explains why he was one of the applicants for the general manager's job.)

Vainisi had watched the playoffs closely in December and had also spoken to several men in the league whose opinions he trusted, including Cleveland coach Paul Brown, Chicago Bears coach George Halas, and Bert Bell. The league commissioner was a vocal proponent of Vince Lombardi, the 45-year-old backfield coach of the New York Giants. The Giants had one of the top offenses

in the NFL, and Lombardi was highly regarded around the league for his command of the game, his organized way of working, and his authoritative presence. Before the 1958 season, Bell had tried to convince him to become coach of the Philadelphia Eagles, the commissioner's old team. But New York's owners—Tim Mara's sons, Jack and Wellington—convinced Lombardi to stay.

Vainisi had Olejniczak speak to Bell, Brown, and Halas. "I shouldn't tell you this because you're liable to kick the crap out of us," Halas told Olejniczak about Lombardi, "but he'll be a good one." Bell also said that Lombardi was the right man for the job. In his biography of Bell, *On Any Given Sunday*, author Robert S. Lyons writes that the commissioner told Olejniczak "in no uncertain terms that he wanted Lombardi to run the Packers."

But there was no broad consensus in Green Bay

One of the few bright spots during the disastrous 1958 season came when the Packers tied the defending champion Lions 13–13 at new City Stadium on October 5. Bart Starr (15), here being pressured by Detroit defensive end Darris McCord (78), started at quarterback and connected with wide receiver Max McGee on a 40-yard touchdown pass.

Halfback Paul
Hornung (5) follows
guard Jerry Kramer
(64) around the
end of the line on
Red Right 49—the
power sweep—the
signature play of the
Lombardi era.

for Lombardi, who was not even Olejniczak's first choice for the job. That was actually Iowa's Forest Evashevski, the hottest coach in the Big 10. Evashevski, fresh off the Hawkeyes' drubbing of Cal in the Rose Bowl, had visited Green Bay on January 19, a month and a half after the Packers had selected Iowa quarterback Randy Duncan with the top pick in the 1959 draft. If Evashevski came to Green Bay, he would be reunited with his best player. But on January 23, when Olejniczak offered him the dual positions of coach and general manager, the Hawkeyes' coach turned the Packers down. "They offered me the job," Evashevski told Packers historian Cliff Christl in 2003, six years before he died, at the age of 91. "I think the fellow's name was Olejniczak. When I turned it down, he said, 'I thought you were all set. We don't know where to go.'"

That may be so, but the day before Evashevski supposedly turned the Packers down, on January 22, Olejniczak and Canadeo had met with Lombardi at the NFL league meeting in Philadelphia. Lombardi impressed both men with his confidence and with his plan for how he would handle the job, from how he would deal with the executive committee to what he would expect from his players and assistants. Four days later, the Packers flew him to Green Bay to meet with Olejniczak, Canadeo, and two other members of the executive committee: Dick Bourguignon, a gruff, straightforward real estate man, and Jerry Atkinson, the chairman of H. C. Prange's Department Store. The meeting took place at Prange's, where the four men made Lombardi an offer to be coach and general manager. Lombardi told them he needed a higher salary than they were proposing, and they met his demand for $36,000 per year for five years. They also promised that the board of directors would stay out of his way. He would be in complete command.

Lombardi did not accept the job at the meeting. He left Green Bay to take the offer back to the Giants and to his family, both of whom signed off on the move. All that remained was for Olejniczak to sell Lombardi to the board of directors.

◆ ◆ ◆

"Who the hell is Vince Lombardi?" The question, from *Press-Gazette* managing editor John Torinus, was put to Dominic Olejniczak at a meeting of the Green Bay executive committee at the Hotel Northland on January 28, 1959. The nine-story, red-brick Northland not only was a hub of downtown social life, but it had also played its own important part in the history of the Packers. Visiting teams had been staying there since shortly after its opening in 1924, and the only NFL meeting ever held in Green Bay had taken place there in 1927. Curly Lambeau had even lived at the Northland for a while.

The executive committee meeting had actually begun as an assembly of the full board of directors, but Olejniczak and Jerry Atkinson had explained to the board that serious candidates for the job of coach and general manager were put off by the notion of having their fate decided by 45 men. The board quickly voted to adjourn and to leave the hiring process to the executive committee. That was when Olejniczak introduced Lombardi's name — and when Torinus asked his question.

Vincent Thomas Lombardi was not a midwesterner. He was an Italian American from the East Coast. He had been born on the second floor of his family's home in Brooklyn's Sheepshead Bay on June 11, 1913, the son of a butcher so stocky and barrel-chested that he was known by the nickname "Old Five by Five." Lombardi began playing football when he was 12, joining a local team that played in a Brooklyn league. He continued to play sandlot ball during the four years he spent study-

ing at a preparatory seminary called Cathedral College of the Immaculate Conception — Cathedral Prep — which did not have a football team of its own because the school was opposed to the sport. Lombardi left Cathedral Prep in 1932 in part because he wanted to win a scholarship to play football in college. From an early age he had been enamored with the game's physical contact and demand for toughness, and he was a devoted fan, poring over the sports pages and making the trip to Coogan's Bluff, in upper Manhattan, to watch pro and college games at the Polo Grounds. He was a burly five foot eight and 175 pounds, muscled not from lifting weights but from toting 225-pound half steers at his father's butcher shop on Manhattan's Lower West Side. He repeated his senior year of high school at Brooklyn's St. Francis Prep, played fullback on the 5-1 Catholic school champions, and won a scholarship to Fordham.

The Fordham campus, on Rose Hill in the Bronx, was where Lombardi's connection to Green Bay began. The Rams' new coach was "Sleepy" Jim Crowley, one of Notre Dame's fabled Four Horsemen and the most famous player from Green Bay East High outside of Curly Lambeau. At Lombardi's first practice, Crowley had ordered the slow-footed freshman moved to the line. Lombardi was undersized for a guard, and somewhat comically built — long arms hung off his short-stack frame, which itself rested atop a pair of stout legs and big feet. But in Crowley's version of the Notre Dame Box offense, none of that was a negative if a man was quick off the ball and tenacious in the trenches. That suited Lombardi fine. Despite struggling with injuries in his first three years at Fordham, Lombardi became an important part of the rotation at right guard. He was a fiery and demanding leader, a live wire charged through with relentless aggression. On defense, Lombardi and the other linemen became known as "the Seven Blocks of Granite." The Rams were 5-0-2 and ranked number eight by the Associated Press heading into the final game of Lombardi's senior season, against New York University in Yankee Stadium on Thanksgiving Day 1936. A victory would earn the Rams a trip to the Rose Bowl. But the Violets upset them 7–6. The legend of that Fordham team has nevertheless endured because of the legend Lombardi would build for himself. The Seven Blocks of Granite were the cornerstones of his career.

Lombardi kicked around a bit after he graduated from Fordham in 1937. He was a bill collector. He played semipro football, first for the Brooklyn Eagles of the American Professional Football Association and then for the Wilmington Clippers. He lived at home. He worked in his father's butcher shop. He even went to law school for a semester at Fordham, in 1938. Nothing stuck. Finally, he got a call from Andy Palau, the quarterback at Fordham when Lombardi had been the right guard. Palau had just been hired to be the new head football coach at St. Cecilia High, in Englewood, New Jersey. Did Lombardi want to be his assistant? The pay would be $1,700 for the year. He jumped at the chance.

Lombardi took to coaching as if he had been born to it. He enjoyed delivering guidance and instruction, and St. Cecilia's—where he also taught biology, chemistry, physics, and Latin—was where he developed, in the words of author David Maraniss, "the pedagogical skills that later allowed him to stand apart from the coaching multitudes." The job also gave Lombardi an outlet for his passionate personality. Before the third game of the season, he delivered a pep talk so stirring that Palau said of it years later, "I was shaking in my boots." Lombardi stayed at St. Cecilia's for eight years, taking over as the head coach in 1942 when Palau left to become the backfield coach at Fordham. Lombardi lost his first game and then didn't lose again for three years, a streak of 32 games during which the Saints went 29-0-3. At one point they won 25 games in a row. In 1947, Lombardi, now married with two small children, returned to his alma ma-

ter as the freshman coach for $3,500 a year.

But Fordham, which had suspended its football team for three years during World War II, was de-emphasizing the program. Lombardi loved the school, but he was also anxious to advance his career, and Rose Hill was no longer a place where he could do that. In 1949 he moved up the Hudson River to West Point, where he took over as the offensive line coach on the staff of Army's Earl "Red" Blaik.

At West Point, Lombardi found a culture that meshed with his own personal philosophy, not only about football but also about life: that success was the result of toughness, discipline, organization, accountability, teamwork, and sacrifice. And in Blaik, whose favorite aphorism was "You have to pay the price," he found the embodiment of those virtues. A West Point graduate and former Army football player, Blaik had been commissioned in the cavalry in 1920 but had served only two years before resigning from the Army and entering his family's construction business. He'd gotten into coaching soon after, then was an assistant at West Point from 1927 to 1933, before taking over as the head coach at Dartmouth. He'd been hired as the coach at Army in 1941 and had proceeded to lead the already storied program to the greatest heights in its history. Like Lombardi at St. Cecilia's, Blaik and the Cadets enjoyed a 32-game unbeaten streak—which included two national championships and two Heisman Trophies —from 1944 to 1947. Blaik had been recommissioned as a colonel in the reserves during World War II, but even after the war was over, his stature was such that he was known to one and all in and around the Army program as simply "the Colonel."

More than any man Lombardi had ever met, Blaik was obsessed with football, his life's work and seemingly his only interest. He was engrossed with preparedness and the intricacies of the game. His job interview with Lombardi had been a detailed interrogation on the latter's coaching beliefs and methods. Blaik subscribed wholeheartedly to

Lombardi watches Starr warm up at Wrigley Field on November 12, 1961, before the Packers' 31–28 defeat of the Bears. The symbiotic relationship between the coach and the quarterback — Starr was regarded as an extension of Lombardi on the field — was one of the defining traits of the Green Bay dynasty of the 1960s.

the military's emphasis on attention to detail. The Army playbook was a slim volume. Because cadets faced such heavy demands on their time, Blaik preferred a small number of plays that his team could execute with violent precision, rather than an extensive and complex offensive system. He watched film compulsively, often dragging his assistants with him during off-hours to sit together in a darkened room and dissect old game footage. Army had been undefeated when it lost 14–2 to Navy in 1950, and Blaik could not stop watching the movie of the defeat. "All right," he would say whenever there was a pause in the workday, "let's get out that Navy film."

"You could see the other coaches sneak looks at one another, and although you couldn't hear the groans you could feel them in the room," Lombardi and sportswriter W. C. Heinz wrote in the 1963 book *Run to Daylight!*, the coach's diary of one week from the Packers' 1962 season. "Then we'd all file out and into the projection room once more."

In truth, Lombardi loved the round-the-clock devotion to football in Blaik's program. From the Colonel he learned how to put film study to effective use, how to set a workday schedule, and how to draw up a plan for a crisp 90-minute practice. Years later he liked to tell people that everything he knew about organizing and preparing a team to win he'd learned from Red Blaik, whom he called "the greatest coach I have ever known." Blaik hated losing. One of his axioms was that there is a vast difference between a good sport and a good loser, and in it can be found the spirit behind Lombardi's most famous quote: "Winning isn't everything; it's the only thing."*

The two men were alike as coaches in so many ways, but vastly different in temperament. Blaik was the personification of dignified cool. He held himself aloof at practices. Lombardi — in part be-

---

* *Lombardi was not actually the first person to say this, but it has widely been attributed to him. The quote appears in the 1953 John Wayne movie* Trouble Along the Way. *In the film, the Duke plays a divorced father named Steve Williams who moves with his tomboy daughter to a New York City Catholic college to take over as the football coach. The line is actually spoken by 10-year-old actress Sherry Jackson, who says, "Like Steve says, 'Winning isn't everything; it's the only thing!'"* Trouble *screenwriter Melville Shavelson told David Maraniss that he got the line from his agent, who also represented UCLA coach Red Sanders. It is Sanders who appears to be actual source of the quote.*

cause his role as an assistant demanded it, but also because he could not help himself—was more hands-on. He was also more explosive. In the words of Blaik, he was "like a thoroughbred—with a vile temper."

Lombardi later said of Blaik, "He toned down my temper, or tried to. When I'd get too intense and explosive on the field, he'd call me into the office the next day and sit there and look at me and twirl his class ring—West Point 1920—and say, 'Vince, we just don't do it that way at West Point. You can't talk that way to cadets. You can't drive them that way because they're being driven all day.'"

In December 1953, the New York Giants tried to hire Blaik to be their coach. He turned them down and suggested Lombardi instead, but the Giants chose Jim Lee Howell for the head job and asked Lombardi to be their new offensive backfield coach. Lombardi was 40 and was anxious to become a head coach, but Blaik—who was rebuilding his program after it had been devastated by a cheating scandal in 1951—was not leaving West Point anytime soon. If Lombardi wanted to move up, he had to move on. He accepted New York's offer and went to work for Howell.

Also joining Lombardi on the staff at the Polo Grounds that fall was defensive assistant Tom Landry, a 30-year-old defensive back who functioned as a player-coach in 1954 and '55. The quietly intense Landry, with his lean frame and handsome features, was the polar opposite of the loud, explosive Lombardi, whose jack-o'-lantern grin was impossible to miss. The only commonality between the two men—the outspoken New Yorker and the taciturn Texan—was a burning desire to win. And in their six years together in New York, the Giants never had a losing season. The hallmark of Lombardi's offense was the power running game, defined by a rugged offensive line and an end sweep that, when run correctly, was virtually unstoppable. Landry's base defense was the 4-3, a relatively new concept that used four down

linemen and three linebackers. Howell used to joke that with two such talented assistants, all he had to do was make sure the footballs were filled with air. New York won the NFL championship in 1956, routing the Bears in the title game 47–7, and then lost the 1958 Championship Game in overtime to the Baltimore Colts, in what came to be called "the greatest game ever played."

So who in the hell *was* Vince Lombardi in January 1959? A lot of people in Green Bay were wondering just that. He had never been a head coach above the high school level, and he was not a household name. The *Press-Gazette* published an editorial on January 30 applauding his hiring, under the headline WELCOME, MR. LOMBARDI. The column relied on information from the coach's résumé that did not totally check out. "He was a brilliant student," read the editorial. "During his four years at Fordham University he was on the dean's list and he graduated cum laude. Following his graduation, he entered law school and studied for two years." While Lombardi had made the dean's list as a freshman at Rose Hill, he did not graduate cum laude. And he had spent only one semester in law school before giving it up.

But his credentials from Army—Vainisi had reached out to Blaik when he was doing his research—and from the Giants were unimpeachable. Outside of Landry, there was no NFL assistant who was more accomplished. The name Vince Lombardi was not known to most followers of the game, but it was known to many *inside* the game. He was an ambitious man who knew what he wanted to do and how he wanted to go about doing it. The executive committee, including Torinus, voted unanimously to authorize Olejniczak to make the best possible deal with him.

At 3 p.m., Olejniczak entered a small, smoke-filled room at the Northland, crammed with 16 anxious reporters, and announced Vince Lombardi as the fifth coach in the history of the Green Bay Packers. It was official.

◆ ◆ ◆

Lombardi's first months on the job were spent settling in and making the sorts of changes befitting a new man in charge. Many of his tweaks were cosmetic, focused on remaking the culture of a losing organization. He remodeled and redecorated the Packers' offices on South Washington Street, which, he had told his secretary, Ruth McKloskey, were "a disgrace." Walls got fresh coats of paint, were torn down, or were covered with wallpaper. Workspaces were moved around. He also instituted policy changes about how the team would travel. Not only would his players fly in better planes and stay in better hotels, but they would also follow a dress code: neckties and green blazers. "Our No. 1 job in Green Bay is doing away with the defeatist attitude I know is there," he said. "Defeatists won't be with the club very long."

Lombardi was also remaking things on the football field. Before his first week as coach had ended, he had hired two assistants: defensive line coach Phil Bengtson, the San Francisco 49ers' top defensive assistant since 1951, and offensive backfield coach Red Cochran, who had held the same job for the Detroit Lions the previous three seasons. In June, Lombardi purchased the contract of 34-year-old safety Emlen Tunnell from the Giants. Lombardi knew Tunnell, New York's first African American player, from their days together in Gotham, and the coach respected his abilities as both a player and a leader. Lombardi did not just want Tunnell for his defensive prowess — the future Hall of Famer's 79 interceptions still rank second in the NFL record books — he also wanted him as a de facto assistant coach who could help mentor the young black players he planned to bring to Green Bay.

Lombardi's primary concern, though, was the players who were already there. He had been breaking down film since shortly after getting hired. Every frame from every game in the miserable 1958 season flickered before his eyes. Bright spots were few and far between. But there

was one player who intrigued him more than any other: Paul Hornung.

Hornung, with his blond hair, blue eyes, square jaw, and cantilevered chin, was known to the collective football world as "the Golden Boy." But his background was more blue-collar than gilt-edged. He'd grown up over a grocery store in Louisville's working-class West End, the only child of a single mother who had separated from his hard-drinking father when she was pregnant. He and his mother, a stenographer and administrative assistant for the Works Progress Administration, grew especially close because they did not have much else besides each other — when he was about 10, they slept on two army cots while sharing a room in another family's house. Hornung grew into a peerless football player at Louisville's Flaget High, a split T quarterback who could run, throw, and kick. He could have played college football anywhere. Bear Bryant desperately wanted him to come to Kentucky. But his Catholic mother, Loretta Williams, wanted her six-foot-two, 200-pound son to play at Notre Dame. And Hornung could not say no to his mother.

But there were not many in Green Bay who saw Hornung as golden — to that point he'd been a disappointment. The Packers had chosen him number one in the 1957 draft, with the hope that he could revive the franchise. In South Bend, he had won the Heisman Trophy because of his exploits as a dual-threat quarterback. The Fighting Irish were 2-8 in 1956, and Hornung is still the only player from a losing team to win the Heisman. For all his promise, though, he was better known around Green Bay for carousing off the field than for anything he had done on it. The city had always been wet, and there was no shortage of bars for Hornung to frequent. In the words of Maraniss, they were "the only establishments that outnumbered churches in Green Bay." And Hornung seemed intent not only on visiting each one but also on meeting the ladies who patronized them. The title of Hornung's 1965 autobiography, *Football and*

the Single Man, was a winking nod to the title of Helen Gurley Brown's 1962 bestseller *Sex and the Single Girl.* By 1959, all Hornung had established in Green Bay was a reputation.

On the field, Hornung had spent his first two seasons switching from quarterback to fullback to halfback—and seemingly moving down the depth chart at each position. Neither Lisle Blackbourn nor Scooter McLean, Lombardi's predecessors, seemed to know quite what to do with him.

That was not a problem for Lombardi, who had helped make Frank Gifford a star in New York. Gifford was entering his third season when Lombardi arrived from Army in 1954, and though he had been a Pro Bowler the year before, he was unhappy with his role. Lombardi knew just how to use him. "You're my halfback" were the first words the coach ever spoke to Gifford, and he set about taking advantage of the USC All-America's talents as a runner, passer, and receiver. Gifford won the MVP award in 1956, leading the league in yards from scrimmage and ranking in the top 10 in 14 other offensive categories. That was the same year that the Giants won the NFL title, and by the time Lombardi left, in 1959, Gifford was well on his way to a career that would eventually land him in the Pro Football Hall of Fame.

In Hornung, Lombardi saw a player similar to Gifford, and he seized on the Golden Boy as somebody around whom he could rebuild the Packers' woeful offense. Hornung was a powerful, determined runner gifted with an innate sense of timing. It hardly mattered that he did not have elite speed. He had a knack for gliding along behind his linemen and making decisive cuts upfield at precisely the right moment—perfect for the run-to-daylight style of offense that Lombardi had perfected in New York, with ballcarriers attacking holes that they found in the line rather than blindly following the design of the play. Hornung, who weighed upwards of 220 pounds, seemed to be at his best near the goal line. And he could also throw the option pass, a favorite wrinkle of Red

Blaik's. "You won't have to worry about playing three positions anymore," Lombardi told Hornung that winter. "You are my left halfback. You're my Frank Gifford."

Hornung became the plunging dagger of the Green Bay power sweep, the signature player in the signature play of Lombardi's offense. The look of the sweep was simple: just the left halfback carrying the ball around right end. But under Lombardi's edict of "run to daylight," there were myriad ways for the play to unfold. What Lombardi loved about the power sweep was that it was an almost automatic four yards or more if everybody did his job. "There is nothing spectacular about it," Lombardi once said. "It's just a yard gainer . . . It's my number-one play because it requires all 11 men to play as one to make it succeed."

In the Packers' playbook, the power sweep was Red Right 49. Besides the wide stretch of the play, its most distinctive feature was the way the guards disengaged from the line and pulled in unison to the right, turning upfield only after they got around the right tackle. The right guard ran widest, while the left guard curled inside him to help clear the lane. The center and the right tackle sealed off the middle of the field, while the fullback led the way for the halfback and was responsible for the defensive end. The tight end, split three yards from the right tackle instead of the normal yard or so, held the edge against the outside linebacker—the key block in the whole scheme.

The Packers' tight end in 1959 was six-foot-three, 234-pound Ron Kramer, who had come to Green Bay in 1957 as a first-round pick out of Michigan. According to Red Cochran, Kramer took a wider-than-normal split on the power sweep so that the linebacker playing over him would have to move over, which opened up a gap between himself and the defensive end. "If the linebacker tried to step to the outside to cut off everybody getting outside him, the tight end moved him on out and everybody cut inside," said Cochran. "If the linebacker tried to come across the tight end to jam the play, then the end drove him down the line and the play went outside."

Lombardi, based on what he had learned from Blaik at Army, had no problem running the play 20 or even 30 times in a row at practice. He drilled it endlessly. His players used to joke that how they felt did not matter—they would run the sweep until *Lombardi* got tired.

Lombardi was adamant that his team be in better physical condition than it had been in 1958, and the two-a-day practices that he put the Packers through at training camp were brutal trials for even the most well-conditioned players. On July 24, the first day of practice, his players endured more than 20 minutes of conditioning work—calisthenics and up-down grass drills, in which they would run in place, flop on their bellies, and then pop back up at the sound of a whistle—before beginning work on football. Lombardi did not let up as camp wore on. Beefy defensive tackle Dave "Hawg" Hanner, who had reported nearly 20 pounds above his playing weight of 260, had so much difficulty with the practices that he had to be taken to the emergency room on three separate occasions for intravenous fluids. His teammates began to joke that Hanner had two rooms at camp—one at the Packers' headquarters at St. Norbert College and one at St. Vincent's Hospital in Green Bay.

Lombardi's team got off to a fast start in 1959, winning its first three regular-season games, including a 9–6 victory over the Bears at Green Bay City Stadium on September 27. The elation after the defeat of Chicago was so complete that the Packers carried Lombardi off the field on their shoulders. But a 45–6 loss to the Los Angeles Rams in Milwaukee on October 18 began a five-game losing streak that threatened to turn Lombardi's new beginning into more of the same old story. Still, Lombardi's faith in his system never wavered, and his devotion to conditioning paid off in a four-game winning streak to end the year. The Packers finished 7-5. Green Bay had a winner

again. Center Jim Ringo had been with the Packers since 1953. He had played for Ronzani, Blackbourn, and McLean. His verdict on Lombardi's first season was emphatic: "This is the first time since I've been in Green Bay that guys are talking about next year."

◆ ◆ ◆

The autumn of 1960 was an epochal one for the Packers. On October 17, six days before Green Bay beat the San Francisco 49ers 41–14 in Milwaukee to improve to 3-1, the franchise lost an important part of its past. Former team president Andrew Turnbull, one of Arch Ward's Hungry Five and the man who had saved the team in 1923, died of a heart attack at his home in the Green Bay suburb of Allouez, at the age of 76. Forty-one days later, the franchise lost an important part of its present. On Sunday, November 27, three days after the Packers had lost in Detroit on Thanksgiving, 23–10, Jack Vainisi died at his west-side home. At his funeral, the following Wednesday at the Church of the Annunciation, Hornung asked Vainisi's widow, Jackie, if there was anything he could do. She responded by telling him that he had been Jack's favorite player, and that what he could do was "become the kind of football player Jack knew you could be."

Hornung, who had led the NFL with 94 points in 1959, was already well on his way to doing just that, but he nevertheless took Jackie's admonition to heart. The Golden Boy, like Lombardi and the rest of the team, wanted to beat the Bears in Chicago on December 4 in honor of Vainisi—and they did just that. Hornung ran for a 10-yard touchdown, caught a 17-yard scoring pass from quarterback Bart Starr, and kicked five extra points and two field goals. Green Bay won 41–13, its most lopsided victory in the series to date. Hornung's 23 points gave him a league-high 152 for the season. He finished that year with 176 points, an NFL record that stood for 46 years.

The victory over the Bears helped vault the Packers to the Western Conference championship and a date in Philadelphia with the Eagles on December 26 for the NFL title. Philadelphia's offense, led by quarterback Norm Van Brocklin and five-foot-nine flanker Tommy McDonald, featured the second-best passing attack in the NFL. The Packers' pass defense, by contrast, was ranked ninth. And that was where the game turned. Van Brocklin completed only nine of his 20 passes but threw for 204 yards. Three of his completions went for 25 yards or more, including a 35-yard scoring strike to McDonald in the second quarter that gave the Eagles a 7–6 lead.

On paper, Green Bay was the better team, picking up 22 first downs to Philadelphia's 13, outrushing the Eagles 223 yards to 99, and outgaining them by 105 yards. The Packers ran 77 plays to Philadelphia's 48. But they seemed incapable of actually winning the game. At no time was this more evident than in the opening minutes. Defensive end Bill Quinlan intercepted Van Brocklin's first pass, a screen into the left flat to halfback Billy Ray Barnes. Green Bay ran its first play from

the Eagles' 14-yard line — and could not score. Lombardi chose to go for it on fourth-and-two from the six, but fullback Jim Taylor slipped coming out of his stance on the soggy field and was stuffed for no gain. The Packers spent the rest of the game coming up short, including on their final drive. Philadelphia led 17–13 when Green Bay got the ball for the last time, with just a minute and 20 seconds left. Starr moved the Packers efficiently downfield, but they could get no closer than the Eagles' nine-yard line, which was where Taylor was brought down after catching a pass from Starr. The final gun sounded. The title belonged to Philadelphia.

In the locker room, Lombardi set the tone for the off-season — and the rest of the decade.

"Perhaps you didn't realize that you could have won this game," he said to his players. "But I think there's no doubt in your minds now. And that's why you will win it all next year. This will never happen again. You will never lose another championship."

CHAPTER 14

GREATER GLORY

Navy Lieutenant Commander John S. McCain flew his 23rd bombing mission over North Vietnam on Thursday, October 26, 1967, taking off shortly before noon from the deck of the USS *Oriskany*, an aircraft carrier cruising the waters of the Gulf of Tonkin. McCain's target that morning was a thermal power plant in downtown Hanoi, less than a half mile from the presidential palace. As his 20-plane squadron approached the center of the city, it came under heavy antiaircraft fire. McCain stayed on course, diving from 9,000 feet to about 3,500 before releasing his payload. But just as he was beginning to make the climb back to cruising altitude in his single-engine A-4 Skyhawk jet, a Soviet-made surface-to-air missile—"a flying telephone pole," as he later described it—blew off his right wing.

McCain immediately radioed that he had been hit and then, with his plane inverted and falling fast, reached up behind his head and pulled the handle of his ejection seat. He was still traveling faster than 500 miles per hour, and the force of the ejection knocked him out cold. He struck part of the airplane, breaking his right knee and both of his arms. His parachute opened as it was supposed to, though, and he regained consciousness just as he was hitting the water of Trúc Bạch Lake, in the center of the North Vietnamese capital. He was wearing more than 50 pounds of gear, and he sank twice to the shallow bottom before he was able to inflate his life vest by pulling the toggle with his teeth. Several Hanoi residents hauled him to shore, and then some of them beat him se-

verely. McCain said that his right shoulder was broken by a strike from the butt of a rifle, and that he was also bayoneted in the groin and the ankle. The locals eventually took him to a nearby police station, and from there he was transported to Hỏa Lò Prison, better known to U.S. prisoners of war as the Hanoi Hilton. McCain would spend the next five and a half years of his life as a prisoner of the North Vietnamese.

During his first four days in captivity, McCain drifted in and out of consciousness while he was subjected to frequent interrogations. He held out at first, giving just his name, rank, serial number, and date of birth. His captors, though, refused him medical treatment unless he answered their questions. He eventually told them the name of his

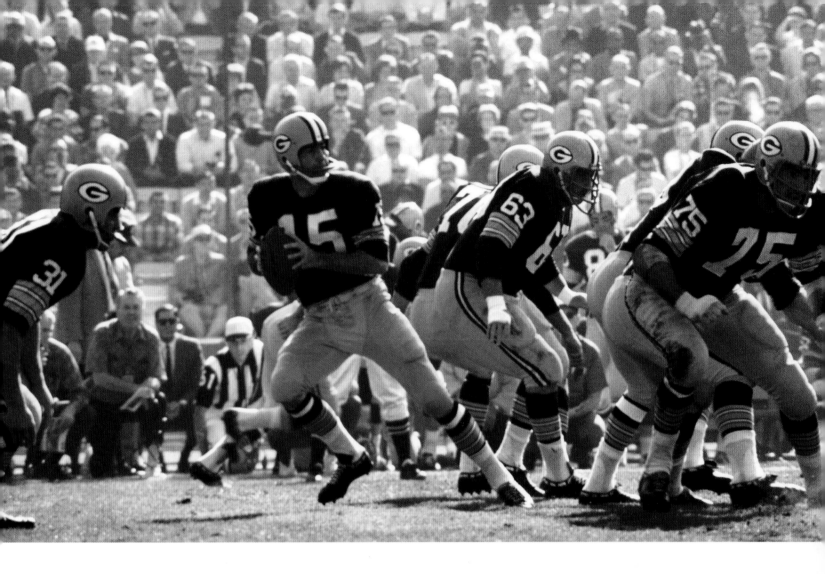

ship and his squadron number, but he also mixed in some fiction with the truth. When asked for a list of future targets, he rattled off the names of towns that had already been bombed. And when asked for the names of the men in his squadron, McCain gave five to his captors: Ken Bowman, Gale Gillingham, Forrest Gregg, Jerry Kramer, and Bob Skoronski. The men weren't in Attack Squadron 46. They weren't even in Vietnam. They were in Green Bay, Wisconsin, 7,600 miles east of Hanoi. They were the starting five members of the Packers' offensive line.

* * *

How did the names of Green Bay's offensive linemen find their way into the interrogation logbooks of the Hanoi Hilton? It had a lot to do with the moment in American history and culture. The Packers under Vince Lombardi rose to the pinnacle of

the NFL at the same time that the NFL was rising to the pinnacle of sports in America. The United States' involvement in the Vietnam War divided the country and made taking pride in being an American more complicated than it had been just a decade before. But there was nothing complicated about being proud of the Packers. Their five NFL championships and two Super Bowl victories in the 1960s were won with qualities that most Americans—whether they were for or against the war—considered emblematic of the nation at its best: honest effort and sacrifice, individual skill and teamwork, toughness in the face of hardship and pain, pride in a job well done, and small-town, no-frills excellence. Like the minutemen of the Revolution or the settlers of the American West, Lombardi's Packers were icons of an era—grimy, calloused, battle-scarred, and unbeatable.

This sack of Raiders quarterback Daryle Lamonica was one of seven unassisted tackles for Packers end Willie Davis in Green Bay's 33–14 victory over Oakland in Super Bowl II. Davis was one of six Hall of Famers on the Packers' defense in 1967.

John McCain wasn't from Green Bay. He was a Navy brat—the son and grandson of Annapolis graduates—and had no real hometown. He had been born in the Panama Canal Zone and raised on naval bases around the United States and the world. He had gone to the Naval Academy from a private prep school in the leafy suburbs of Washington, D.C. He wasn't from Arizona and he wasn't from Green Bay—he was best defined as just an American. And in so many important ways, the Green Bay Packers of the 1960s helped define Americans to themselves. The country might have seemed to be coming apart, with assassinations and protests, political upheaval and endless war, but every American could look to the Packers with pride. The United States came to identify itself

with the game of pro football in the 1960s, and the Green Bay Packers were the very best in that game.

The NFL became the nation's preeminent sports league because of one thing: television. No sport fit the parameters of the new medium so well. And the Packers began their rise to the top of the league just as it was securing the broadcast deal that would cement its place in American popular culture. TV was a local thing in the NFL in the late 1950s and early '60s, with broadcast deals being negotiated between networks and individual teams for hundreds of thousands of dollars. The Packers, for example, had a regional deal with CBS in 1961 that paid them around $100,000. (At various times, the *Press-Gazette* reported this amount to be as much as $120,000 and as little as $75,000.) Ten of the team's 14 games in 1961 (the three games in Milwaukee and all seven road contests) were broadcast on the network's Green Bay affiliate, WBAY-TV. Such local arrangements were the rule because of federal antitrust laws, which held that the league could not eliminate competition—via a package deal with one network—among its member clubs for television contracts.

But eliminating that competition was exactly what the NFL, led by its young new commissioner, Pete Rozelle, wanted to do. The Colts' victory over the Giants in the 1958 NFL Championship Game had attracted a national audience of 45 million to NBC and convinced the former public relations man that pro football could be a profitable television venture—provided the league held together.* In April 1961 the 35-year-old Rozelle reached a two-year deal with CBS worth $9.3 million to televise the NFL's entire 98-game schedule, with the revenue to be shared equally among the league's 14 franchises. The Packers stood to make about $332,000 per season—a huge boost to their bottom line. But three months later, a federal judge in Philadelphia struck the agreement down, ruling that it violated federal antitrust law.

Rozelle was undaunted, and he went before Congress in late August to advocate for a bill that would legalize single-network contracts for professional sports leagues. Testifying before the House antitrust subcommittee, Rozelle painted a bleak picture of a world in which the NFL couldn't negotiate a package TV deal. "Only those fans in the large metropolitan centers and favored by their geographical locations, such as New York, Los Angeles and Chicago, will be assured of seeing the games of their home team on television," Rozelle said. "I don't think I have to tell this committee what the response of fans in Green Bay, Minneapolis–St. Paul, Dallas, St. Louis, Detroit and even such cities as San Francisco and Philadelphia

will be when they are informed that they will no longer be able to follow the road games of their home teams on television."

But circumstances were not nearly so dire—at least not in Green Bay. The only games that Packers fans couldn't watch from the comfort of their own living rooms in 1961 were the four played at Green Bay City Stadium. What the NFL was primarily concerned with was not how often fans would be able to see their local teams, but how much money there was to be made. And making more money was just fine with the Packers. President John F. Kennedy cleared the way for the NFL to pool television rights on September 30, 1961, when he signed the Sports Broadcasting Act into law. The next year, the Packers got their $332,000.

TV turned the NFL into a colossus. Two years later, CBS re-upped with the league for $14 million per year, and NBC outbid ABC for broadcast rights to the American Football League for five years and $36 million. By decade's end, broadcast rights for the NFL were worth $46.25 million—and America was hooked.

◆ ◆ ◆

Thousands of porch lights flickering on and off in the darkness. That was the first thing the Packers saw as their silver-and-blue United Airlines DC-6B banked over Austin Straubel Field at 8:06 p.m. on December 18, 1961. The 63,000 people of Green Bay were welcoming the champions of the NFL's Western Conference home, taking their cues from former fullback Ted Fritsch, who was announcing the team's arrival over the radio. Then came the fireworks, courtesy of the Chamber of Commerce. It wasn't a ticker-tape parade through the Canyon of Heroes, but there was snow on the ground and the sun had set nearly four hours before—and besides, their victory was not yet complete.

The Packers had been gone from Green Bay for more than two weeks, ever since they had locked up the conference title—and the right to host the

---

* The 1958 title game was shown in Green Bay on NBC affiliate WMBV-TV.

NFL Championship Game — on December 3 with a 20–17 victory over the New York Giants in Milwaukee. They had then flown from there to the West Coast for the last two games of the season. Anticipation for their return was high. There were only 500 people at the airport to greet the team's charter from Los Angeles, but Chamber of Commerce officials insisted that that was due to uncertainty over the plane's landing time. (The players had been forced to lay over briefly in Denver because of winter weather in the Midwest, and the flight's arrival had been pushed back multiple times after an initial estimate of 6:35.) But the planning for the Championship Game had begun almost as soon as the Giants were defeated on December 3. Temporary seats were going to be added to Green Bay City Stadium, which had been expanded before the season to 38,669. The Packers had sold 54,000 season tickets between their venues in Green Bay and Milwaukee, so the team had to use a complicated formula to determine how tickets would be distributed. Groundskeepers placed a tarp and a knee-deep bedding of straw over the turf at the stadium in an effort to ensure a fast field for New Year's Eve.

That Green Bay hosted the first title game in its history in the last year of its regional television arrangement is wholly appropriate. In 1961, the team still belonged to the city, both legally — since most of the shares purchased in the 1950 stock sale had been bought right there — and in spirit. But of the six championships Green Bay had won since 1929, none had been decided there, and only one, the 1939 title-game victory over the Giants in Milwaukee, had been played in the state of Wisconsin. After 42 years, the smallest outpost in the NFL was about to become the league's capital. "This is the biggest event ever to hit Green Bay," Frank Shekore, the president of the Chamber of Commerce, said on December 9 at a meeting of more than 200 boosters at the Beaumont Hotel, where plans were being made for the Championship Game celebration.

It was at the Beaumont three days earlier that 110 men and women — representing, in the words of the *Press-Gazette,* "all phases of the city's business and civic life" — had gathered for breakfast and adopted a nickname for the city that has endured ever since: Titletown, USA. The moniker would become ubiquitous for the next 25 days, adorning banners and shop windows all over downtown and providing a theme for the civic celebration that city leaders were planning for the week of the game. The festivities opened on the afternoon of December 23, when the Chamber of Commerce hosted a giant Christmas party for the Packers and their families at the Brown County Veterans Memorial Arena. More than 3,500 fans attended, and the guest list included Tony Canadeo and Curly Lambeau. Every player and coach received a sterling silver tray, paid for with the proceeds from ticket sales for the event ($1 for adults, 50 cents for children under 12), and under a 50-foot Christmas tree were gifts from city merchants for Packers wives and children. Honorees walked a red carpet provided by the Chemstrand Corporation that was, the *Press-Gazette* was careful to note, "the same luxurious carpet . . . that is used at all formal White House functions."

Lombardi, who loathed the name Titletown and worried about overconfidence, was the real guest of honor at the party. Not only did the crowd give him a standing ovation when he rose to speak, but so, too, did his players. "We should all be proud of this team because of its singleness of purpose, its dedication to winning," he said in his remarks. "This team overcame many adversities during the season — it is a team that would not be beaten. It overcame illness, an appendectomy, the Army and injuries."

Lombardi wasn't exaggerating. The 1961 Packers had faced a unique combination of obstacles on the way to their seventh championship in 32 years. Besides the usual illness and injuries that every team faces — right guard Jerry Kramer had been lost for the year after severely injuring his

A ferocious runner, Jim Taylor surpassed 1,000 yards rushing every season from 1960 through '64, and led the NFL with 1,474 yards on the ground in 1962, the year he was named MVP.

Hornung, linebacker Ray Nitschke, and wide receiver Boyd Dowler. Hornung and Nitschke got their notices on October 17, two days after Green Bay had beaten the Browns to jump out to a 4-1 start. Dowler got his on October 26.

The losses were more a problem of fitness than they were of manpower. Hornung, who was assigned to the 896th Engineer Floating Bridge Company in Fort Riley, Kansas, missed only two games, as did Nitschke, who was in the 32nd Infantry Division at Fort Lewis, Washington, along with Dowler — who didn't miss any. In all three cases, the players were eventually able to secure weekend passes that allowed them to play on Sundays. The trick was for them to stay in shape during the workweek. Lombardi couldn't supervise them as closely as he could have if they'd been in Green Bay, but he did what he could, mailing the Packers' offensive game plans every week to Private Hornung.

The absences of the three may have worried Lombardi, but the players took them mostly in stride. Hornung's housemates — tight end Ron Kramer and cornerback Jesse Whittenton — put a star in the front window of their rented home, a winking parody of the service flags displayed by families of members of the armed forces. The double duty didn't seem to faze Hornung. He led the league in scoring (with 146 points) for a third straight season and was named MVP by the Associated Press.

But for the Championship Game, Lombardi took no chances. According to David Maraniss in *When Pride Still Mattered*, the coach got President Kennedy (or one of his aides) to intervene in the case of Hornung to make sure that the halfback was available not only for the game but also for practice the week before. Nitschke and Dowler got 14-day passes and reported to the Packers on December 22. "The returning prodigals!" Lombardi roared when he greeted them, before telling them to skip the team workout and just run and loosen up for 30 minutes. "Don't overdo it," he in-

right ankle in a 28–10 victory over the expansion Minnesota Vikings in Milwaukee on October 29 — Green Bay also had had to contend with the loss of defensive tackle Dave Hanner for 10 days after he underwent an emergency appendectomy on September 19.

But the most difficult challenge for Lombardi by far had been the loss of three of his top players to military service. The construction of the Berlin Wall, which had begun on August 13, prompted a massive mobilization of the nation's armed forces. President Kennedy ordered thousands of reservists and national guardsmen to active duty that fall. Two dozen of the NFL's 500 or so players got called up, including three from the Packers: Paul

structed. Hornung reported for practice the day after Christmas, giving Lombardi a full squad for the first time in eight weeks.

If Lombardi was happy to have his whole team back together in pursuit of his first championship, Green Bay itself was absolutely ecstatic to be hosting its first title game. Operators at St. Norbert College answered telephones by saying, "Beat the Giants"—a practice that was catching on all over town. And five days before the game, more than 500 fans turned out in 20-degree weather to watch Lombardi put his team through its paces on its Oneida Street practice field. Team co-founder George Whitney Calhoun took to the pages of the *Press-Gazette* to write daily columns on the early history of the Packers. (Calhoun had been retired for several years but still wrote a "Cal's Comments" column that typically ran on Sunday.) His first effort of championship week was titled simply "(1919)"—a reminder not only of how old the Packers were but also of how integral a part they had played in the growth of pro football. About 150 members of the national sports media descended upon the city for the title game. By kickoff, at 1 p.m. on New Year's Eve, even Chris Schenkel, announcing the game on NBC for a record audience of 55 million, was calling Green Bay "the cradle city of the National Football League."

Game day had begun at Green Bay City Stadium at five in the morning, when workers started clearing the field. First the grounds crew carried away the 14 inches of snow that was on top, shoveling it into baskets rather than moving it with a snowplow, which might put ruts in the turf. Next, the thick layer of hay was removed, put into a baling machine, and taken away. And then, finally, the tarp was rolled off, exposing a field that was in good condition. Game-time temperature was about 20 degrees, and many in the crowd of 39,029 were bundled up in red hunting caps and coats. "Like church service on the morning that deer season opens," joked Lindsey Nelson, Schenkel's NBC broadcast partner. In the words of Maraniss, "The

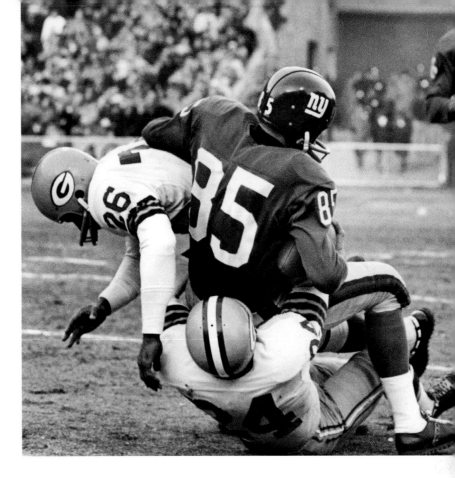

citizen owners of Titletown were ready to claim their due."

Over the next two and a half hours, that's just what the Packers did, winning 37–0. Green Bay dominated the Giants so completely that the game was essentially over at halftime. The first quarter had ended with neither team having scored. But Hornung went over from six yards out on the first play of the second to begin an onslaught that ended with the Packers leading 24–0 by the time the two teams headed for their dressing rooms at intermission. Hornung was brilliant. The Golden Boy—the workhorse on this day because fullback Jim Taylor, the NFL's second-leading rusher, was still hobbled by the leg injury he had suffered against the Rams in the final game of the season—was by far the best player on the field. He rushed 20 times for 89 yards and hauled in three passes for 47 more, including a 26-yard catch-and-run on Green Bay's first scoring drive. Flaring out into the flat from his spot at left halfback, Hornung snared a short lob from quarterback Bart

Hall of Fame defensive backs Herb Adderley (26) and Willie Wood (24) join forces to bring down Giants receiver Del Shofner in the Packers' 16–7 win over New York in the 1962 NFL Championship Game.

Starr and then rumbled to midfield through the heart of the New York secondary. He kicked three field goals and four extra points to go along with his touchdown, giving him 19 points for the game. As the prize for being named the championship MVP, he took home a red Corvette convertible. Ever the good son, he gave the car to his mother.

Led by cornerbacks Hank Gremminger and Jesse Whittenton, as well as a physical defensive line, the Packers held the Giants to just six first downs and 130 yards of offense, and limited quarterback Y. A. Tittle to six completions in 20 pass attempts.* Tittle also threw four interceptions, including one each to Gremminger and Whittenton. "They didn't want to play," Hornung told Maraniss. "It was too cold for them. Not too cold for us." After the game, New York dressed quickly and fled for home. The Giants "beat the New Year east," wrote one *New York Times* columnist. "It was the only thing they beat today."

Lombardi loved to preach to his players about perfection and how it could never be attained, but how the pursuit of perfection could yield excellence. On this day, his team came as close to perfect as any Green Bay team ever has. With about three minutes left in the game, Lombardi began to acknowledge the achievement, pulling his offensive stars from the field one at a time. First Hornung, who got a standing ovation, and then wide receiver Max McGee, Dowler, and Starr, who got a standing O of his own.

When the final gun sounded, the stadium erupted in bedlam. Fans stormed the field and, with the Lumberjack Band playing "Auld Lang Syne," began the process of tearing down the steel goalposts in the south end zone. The goalposts in the north end zone eventually came down, too. A set of uprights was then hitched to the back of a station wagon and dragged through downtown, with people riding atop the four-inch pipes and sparks flying as they made countless loops on the one-and-a-half-mile circuit formed by Washington and Adams Streets. For hours the procession went on, long after the sun had set, with people honking horns, shouting out of windows, hitching rides on bumpers, and riding in convertibles with the tops down. It was, in the words of the special edition New Year's Day *Press-Gazette,* "the most spectacular traffic jam in the city's history."

The smallest town in the NFL was once again home to the best team in pro football.

◆ ◆ ◆

For all the joy it engendered in Green Bay, there was one sad note to Titletown Week. On Christmas morning, 65-year-old Tubby Bero, a halfback on the original 1919 Packers — the backup to Lambeau at right half in the first game the team had ever played — died at a local hospital after an extended illness. He had gone on to a long career in the city's police department after his playing days were over, eventually rising to chief of police, a position he held from 1946 until a stroke in September 1960 forced him into retirement.

Bero's death came as members of his generation began to depart the scene — and as the legend of the Lambeau-era Packers was supplanted in the popular imagination by that of Lombardi's team, which went on to win its second straight NFL championship with a 16–7 victory over the Giants in New York on December 30, 1962. Tackle Andy Muldoon had died in 1960, just a few months before the passing of Andrew Turnbull, the team's first president. And in December 1963, Green Bay's co-founder, George Whitney Calhoun, died at the age of 73.

Calhoun had retired as the telegraph editor at the *Press-Gazette* in 1957 but stayed on for a short time after as a special assistant to the managing editor — his old newsroom aide, John Torinus — until health problems forced him to fully retire. From that point on, the arthritic Calhoun rarely left the room he rented in the boardinghouse at

---

* In the parlance of the Packers' defense, Gremminger and Whittenton were officially halfbacks.

601 West Walnut Street, just across the river from the paper's offices. It was in his home that Calhoun wrote his "Cal's Comments" column on Packers history. It was also where he used to reminisce about the old days with a steady stream of regular visitors, including George Halas on Saturday nights when the Bears came to town. In a room reeking of cigar smoke and cluttered with books about football and piles of old newspapers and magazines, Calhoun would receive his old rival and greet him with, in the words of *Press-Gazette* writer Lee Remmel, "profane cordiality."

One of the things Calhoun used to tell his visitors was that he was working on a book about the history of the Packers, going so far as to tell Torinus that he was in the process of correcting proofs that had come back from the publisher. "A frantic search of all of his papers and belongings after he died failed to reveal any trace of such a book," Torinus wrote years later. "I think such a book was a dream which Cal had had for a long time but never realized."

Halas sent a floral arrangement in the shape of a goalpost to Calhoun's funeral, which was attended by 75 people, including former players Jug Earp, Joe Laws, and Ted Fritsch. Not in attendance was Curly Lambeau, whose relationship with Calhoun had all but ended in 1947 — and had never been repaired.

Less than two years later, Lambeau himself would be gone. On Tuesday, June 1, 1965, he was in the Door Peninsula town of Sturgeon Bay to see his 32-year-old girlfriend, Mary Jane Van Duyse, the baton-twirling drum majorette for the Packers' band. The two had met in 1960, five years after his divorce from his third wife, and Lambeau had since become a regular visitor at the Van Duyse family home. It was just before 7:30 p.m. on a cool spring evening that the 67-year-old Lambeau, joking that he needed a little exercise, helped Francis Van Duyse, Mary Jane's father, cut part of his lawn. After giving the power mower back to Francis, Lambeau crossed the yard to talk to Herb

Reynolds, the Van Duyses' neighbor, who commented on how sweaty Lambeau was. "I feel kind of sick," he replied. And then he collapsed on the freshly cut grass. Lambeau had suffered a massive heart attack. "I knew he was dead as I held him in my arms," Francis Van Duyse told the *Press-Gazette*.

Lambeau was laid to rest the following Saturday in a ceremony befitting a man who had done as much to put Green Bay on the map as Jean Nicolet or Daniel Whitney. A soft rain was falling as his casket, draped in an American flag, was taken from a downtown funeral home to his family's plot in the Allouez Catholic Cemetery, which sits on a hill overlooking the eastern bank of the Fox River. The casket was attended by an honor guard from the Sullivan-Wallen American Legion Post, which also provided a bugler to sound taps by Lambeau's grave. Among his pallbearers were six of his former players — Don Hutson, Johnny Blood, Arnie Herber, Buckets Goldenberg, Charley Brock, and Dick Weisgerber — and his old friend George Strickler, who was by then the assistant sports editor of the *Chicago Tribune*. The large crowd at the service also included Bears coach George Halas, who had flown in the night before from the NFL meetings in New York.

Lombardi had also been at the meetings in New York, but he did not return for the funeral. The coaching staff was represented at the service by Phil Bengtson, with the head coach only providing a comment to the Associated Press. "Curly Lambeau's death is a loss not only to Green Bay and the state of Wisconsin, but to all of professional football," Lombardi said. Privately, though, he resented Lambeau. Curly's death gave new life to a long-simmering sentiment to name City Stadium in honor of the Packers' co-founder — a sentiment that Lombardi did not share. At Lambeau's funeral, Monsignor John Gehl, of St. Francis Xavier Cathedral, had used the occasion to advocate for just such a change. "I do think that our stadium or arena should be called by his

name," Gehl said. "This would be proper."

When the 1965 Packers yearbook came out in late July, *Press-Gazette* writer Art Daley, who edited and published the annual along with newspaper colleague Jack Yuenger, chose for the cover a picture of Lambeau and Lombardi shaking hands on the field at City Stadium. Lombardi, a former seminary student and a daily communicant at Green Bay's St. Willebrord Catholic Church, did not care for the flashy, womanizing Lambeau. And more than that, according to Maraniss, "he wanted to be regarded separately and better." The Packers were Lombardi's team now. He called Daley to complain. "What do you mean putting me on the cover with him?" Lombardi asked. "That was the worst yearbook you ever put out." He hung up on Daley and then refused to speak to him for nearly a year. He later confided to Daley that he

did not want himself or his team to be taken out of the spotlight. But despite Lombardi's opposition, the City Council voted unanimously to rename Green Bay City Stadium on August 3. The new name of the place would be Lambeau Field.

Today it's clear that Lombardi's obsession with his primacy won out. The popular image of the history of the Green Bay Packers is more a muddy, bloody Ray Nitschke calling out defensive signals against the Bears than it is a posed black-and-white portrait of Johnny Blood standing in front of a hedge. The ascension of the NFL into the preeminent sports league in the United States has made Lombardi's teams the historical icons of the franchise. While the stadium being called Lambeau Field does force some acknowledgment of the Packers' distant past, it has not been able to prevent its namesake or his teams — and the sto-

The 1967 NFL Championship Game— the "Ice Bowl" — as seen from the Cessna 140 flown by pilot Richard Jerow. The temperature at kickoff was -13 degrees—still the coldest game in NFL history.

ries of their glory and their struggle for survival —from being largely forgotten. Lambeau and Calhoun were not around to do anything about it. And Lombardi's teams simply won too much. Green Bay won 96 games in the 1960s, more than any other team in pro football. The Packers won two championships in a row in 1961 and '62, and then two more in 1965 and '66—the latter coming in Super Bowl I, where they pounded the AFL's Kansas City Chiefs 35–10. And as the fall of 1967 began, Lombardi's team was poised to do something that only Curly Lambeau's had in the history of pro football: win three championships in a row.

◆ ◆ ◆

Lombardi and his boys had come up short of a three-peat in 1963, when Hornung missed the entire season because Commissioner Pete Rozelle suspended him indefinitely for betting on NFL games. Green Bay finished 11-2-1, but both losses were to the Chicago Bears, who went 11-1-2 and won the Western Conference and eventually the NFL championship. The title was Halas's sixth and last as the coach of the Bears. Still, the Packers' .846 winning percentage remains the best in franchise history for a non-playoff team. Even when they weren't winning championships, Lombardi's Packers set themselves apart.

And in many ways, Green Bay never distinguished itself more than it did in 1967. By that fall, the Packers were aging and on the verge of decline. For the first time in the Lombardi era, they were without Paul Hornung and Jim Taylor, both of whom had gone to the newly formed New Orleans Saints—Green Bay traded Taylor there in July, five months after the Saints had picked Hornung in the expansion draft. Hornung and Taylor were both 31. Of the teammates they left behind in Green Bay, several were getting long in the tooth, including some of the Packers' most important players. Defensive end Willie Davis was 33 when the season began, and tackle Forrest Gregg turned 34 in October. Defensive tackle Henry Jordan was 32, and wide receiver Max McGee was 35. Fuzzy

Thurston, Bart Starr, Bob Skoronski, Willie Wood, Jerry Kramer, and Ray Nitschke were all at least 30. This wasn't roster depth. In every case but McGee's and Thurston's, these players were starters.

Nevertheless, they were starters coming off a 12-2 season and a second straight championship. And the Green Bay defense, with standout players at so many positions, was even better than it had been in the championship seasons of 1961 and '62. Six of the 11 starters are now in the Pro Football Hall of Fame: defensive backs Herb Adderley and Willie Wood, linebackers Ray Nitschke and Dave Robinson, defensive end Willie Davis, and defensive tackle Henry Jordan. In the championship-winning seasons of 1965 and '66, the unit had allowed the third-fewest yards in the league, and just about all of its stars were at or near the top of their game in 1967. Lombardi meant it before the season when he said that the Packers were capable of winning a third straight league title. But he didn't plan to go about "facing the greatest test we have ever faced" in the usual way. "I think that in the past we have tried to defend our title," he said. "I think possibly this was the negative approach. This year we are going to take the positive approach—we're going to fight for the title."

Fight is just what the team had to do. Starr, the reigning MVP, struggled with several injuries, including to the thumb on his throwing hand, his ribs, and his shoulder. He missed two starts and threw 17 interceptions in 210 pass attempts, one year after having thrown just three in 251. He didn't complete his first touchdown pass— he would finish with only nine—until week six. Green Bay also used six different running backs and lost first-stringers Jim Grabowski (knee) and Elijah Pitts (Achilles tendon) to injuries. By the end of the year, Chuck Mercein, a fullback who had spent part of the season playing semipro ball in Mount Vernon, New York, was getting meaningful carries. Green Bay's offense ranked ninth in the NFL in total yards and points—and it had to scratch and claw for every one of them.

In 1967, the Packers relied on their defense—which was the best in the NFL, and deserves mention as one of the best of all time. Green Bay held six opponents to 13 points or fewer, shut out both the San Francisco 49ers and the Atlanta Falcons (who gained only 58 yards in 50 plays), and hammered the Cleveland Browns 55–7. The pass defense gave up fewer than 100 yards per game. Cornerback Bob Jeter intercepted eight passes, the second most in the league, and Adderley picked off four more. Robinson was a first-team All-Pro, as were Davis, Jeter, and Wood. The Packers surrendered 209 points in 14 games, good for the third fewest in the NFL, and allowed only 3,300 yards, the fewest in the league. "In those days quarterbacks called their own plays, and since most of those guys were right-handed, most of their play calls went to the right," says Robinson. "So our defense loaded up on our left side. As a quarterback, when you looked to your right, there were five future Hall of Famers out there. Teams stopped running plays that way. I had 27 interceptions as a linebacker. I would have had a lot more if they had thrown my way more often."

No matter how formidable the defense, though, when the Packers lost 10–7 to the Minnesota Vikings on October 15 to fall to 4-1-1, their legion of vociferous doubters found the courage to speak up. *What's wrong with Green Bay? Are the Packers too old?* After the season, right guard Jerry Kramer published a memoir of the 1967 campaign titled *Instant Replay,* which he co-authored with sportswriter Dick Schaap. The book is an eloquent, honest account of a year in the life of an NFL player. Kramer had been a fixture of the Packers' offensive line since not long after he was drafted in the fourth round out of Idaho in 1958, but injuries had plagued him. He played the 1960 Championship Game against the Eagles with a detached retina. And he'd missed the 1961 title-winning shutout of New York because he'd injured his ankle midway through the season. He then missed all but two games in 1964 while dealing with a mysterious abdominal ailment that doctors eventually found was caused by wood splinters that had been embedded in his body 11½ years earlier, the result of an accident he'd suffered on his family's ranch.

Now, though, he was plagued not by injuries but by uncertainty. "The writers remind me of a bunch of vultures circling around, hoping the carcass won't turn over and get back up on its feet," he wrote in *Instant Replay* of the journalists asking him if the Packers were finished. "But the questions are getting to me . . . and now I'm starting to have my own questions, my own doubts."

So many of the most important victories in Packers history have come in New York against the Giants, all the way back to 1928, when Curly Lambeau's team won 7–0 in its first visit to the Polo Grounds. Green Bay's first game after the October 15 loss to Minnesota was against New York at Yankee Stadium. And once again, a game in Gotham proved to be just the tonic that the Packers needed. Left tackle Bob Skoronski gave a pregame speech to the team that spoke directly to the doubts that Kramer and his teammates were feeling. "He said that he's tired of hearing how old our offensive line is, how we're too old to win anymore, that all the talk makes him sick," Kramer wrote in *Replay.* "And that's my feelings exactly. For the first time in a long time, I'd built up a real hate for our opponents. The New York writers had helped me with all their talk about the old offensive line. I was just filled with hate, the perfect attitude for a good game."

Green Bay went out and buried the Giants 48–21. The Packers never looked back after that, wrapping up the championship of the Central Division—the NFL had divided its Eastern and Western Conferences into two divisions apiece before the season—with a 17–13 victory over the Bears in Chicago a little more than a month later. Green Bay lost its final two games of the season after everything had already been decided and finished the regular season with a record of 9-4-1, setting up a Western Conference playoff game in Milwau-

Fullback Chuck Mercein (30) raises his arms to show that he gave no assistance to Bart Starr (15) on the quarterback's game-winning one-yard touchdown dive in the Packers' 21–17 victory over the Cowboys in the Ice Bowl.

kee on December 23 against the Coastal Division champion Los Angeles Rams.

In Las Vegas, the 11-1-2 Rams were three-point favorites to beat the Packers. Los Angeles entered the postseason on an eight-game winning streak that included a 27–24 home victory over Green Bay on December 9. Led by their "Fearsome Foursome" defensive front of ends Deacon Jones and Lamar Lundy and tackles Merlin Olsen and Roger Brown, the Rams had given up a league-low 196 points, while their offense, led by quarterback Roman Gabriel and his 25 touchdown passes, was the number-one scoring attack in the NFL. "It might just be the greatest challenge we've ever faced," Starr

said before the game. "There never has been a bigger one. There's no doubt about that."

Through most of the first 15 minutes, it appeared that the Vegas oddsmakers might have been right. On a gray, 20-degree Saturday afternoon at County Stadium, neither team was able to sustain a drive until, with less than two minutes to go in the first quarter, Green Bay receiver Carroll Dale fumbled near midfield when he was hit by cornerback Irv Cross. L.A. strong safety Chuck Lamson recovered at the Rams' 48-yard line. Four plays later, Gabriel found flanker Bernie Casey in the right corner of the end zone for a 28-yard touchdown and a 7–0 lead. On the ensuing possession, Green Bay lost seven yards on two carries by rookie halfback Travis Williams before the quarter ended. The Packers began the second facing third-and-17 from their own 23-yard line. On the first play, Lamson intercepted Starr's pass to Dale and returned the ball all the way to the Green Bay 10. The game seemed to be spinning out of control.

But then the Green Bay defense took over. On third down from the Packers' five, Henry Jordan sacked Gabriel for a loss of seven yards. L.A. attempted a field goal, but Dave Robinson charged through the line and got his right hand on the ball to block the kick. Two possessions later, Green Bay tied the game when Williams, running behind Kramer and Forrest Gregg, tore through the Fearsome Foursome and sprinted 46 yards for a touchdown. The tide of the game had turned. The Packers led 14–7 at halftime and won going away, 28–7. The defense sacked Gabriel five times, with Jordan accounting for three and a half all by himself.

Jubilant fans carried Williams off the field on their shoulders. Nicknamed "Roadrunner," the muscular six-foot-one, 210-pound speedster had set a national junior college record with a 9.3 in the 100-yard dash at Contra Costa College. He had gone on from there to Arizona State and was Green Bay's fourth-round pick in 1967. As a rookie, he was perhaps the most exciting player in the game, a threat to score every time he touched the ball. He had returned four kickoffs for touchdowns (including two in the blowout of Cleveland on November 12) and averaged 41.1 yards per return during the regular season, both NFL records that still stand. The only problem for Williams was that he rarely got to touch the ball because he had such a terrible time holding on to it. Lombardi was reluctant to play him. Williams had worked his way into the rotation at halfback against the

Rams only because of all the injuries the Packers had endured in the backfield. He had not even returned his first kick until October 30, when — filling in for an injured Herb Adderley — he ignited a come-from-behind 31–23 victory over the Cardinals in St. Louis with a 93-yard runback straight up the middle to pay dirt in the fourth quarter. Now he was the rushing hero, torching the Rams for 88 yards and two touchdowns on 18 carries. After the game, Williams pinpointed his 46-yard scoring run as the biggest moment of his young career. "[It was] the biggest touchdown because it was a championship game," he said. "I've forgotten about the other ones and now I have to forget about this one and think about the next game."[*]

The next game, of course, was the NFL Championship Game in Green Bay on New Year's Eve.

• • •

The 1958 NFL Championship Game was not actually the greatest game ever played. The Colts' sudden-death victory over the Giants at Yankee Stadium had been a thriller, and it had transformed the league in profound and lasting ways, but it did not define a town, a team, a sport, and an era in the ways that the 1967 Championship Game did. In the history of the NFL, nothing comes close to matching the legacy and the mythology of the Ice Bowl. The coldest game ever played — and the greatest.

In the 52 years since the Packers faced off against the Dallas Cowboys on the "frozen tundra," the game they played has been deconstructed and dissected countless times, in books, in newspapers and magazines, and in documentary films. Chuck Mercein has three books in his home library that are specifically about the Ice Bowl. The game has become a cottage industry for NFL Films, the league's in-house video production

---

Williams's performance against the Rams would prove to be the high point of his NFL career. He played sparingly in the Championship Game one week later, and then didn't touch the ball in Super Bowl II. In 1971, new Green Bay coach Dan Devine traded him to Los Angeles, where he played one more season before blowing out his knee. His career over, Williams's life spiraled out of control. He struggled for the next two decades with homelessness and alcoholism and—save for the dollar bill that was found inside one of the shoes he was wearing—was penniless when he died in Martinez, California, in 1991.

unit, which has made the Ice Bowl into America's home movie. The footage is iconic, the Liturgy of pro football, played repeatedly for the devoted. The game had initially been cut into a 30-minute movie, "A Chilling Championship,"* by 26-year-old NFL Films producer Bob Ryan. "I don't think, in my recollection, that one game has been done and redone so many times," says Ryan, who went on to become the vice president and editor in chief of NFL Films. "We wanted to make Hollywood movies, without the actors but with the music and the drama. That game had everything—great teams, iconic coaches, Hall of Famers on both sides."

Of the three NFL championships decided in Green Bay, the 1967 game was the one that served to define the city to the rest of the world. Until then, Green Bay was known throughout the NFL as "the best little city in America," the place where the people themselves had fought for and preserved the last of pro football's town teams. But after the Ice Bowl, the industrial city on the banks of the Fox became known as something else: the epitome of small-town toughness. And the epitome of champions. December 31, 1967, was and still is the coldest New Year's Eve in the history of Green Bay. The hardiness of the capacity crowd of 50,861—huddled, bundled in red-and-black hunting gear, heads bobbing, steam rising—was nearly as remarkable as the grit of the players. Former Packers tight end Gary Knafelc, who had become the public-address announcer at Lambeau Field, told David Maraniss that looking out on the crowd was "like seeing big buffaloes in an enormous herd on the winter plains . . . It was prehistoric."

It was more than that. It was elemental. Football is a tough game played by tough men, but the minus-13-degree temperatures and the frozen turf combined to turn a sport that likes to make facile comparisons between itself and combat into an actual struggle for survival.

The stories from that day have passed into folklore. Like George Washington chopping down the cherry tree, they seem to straddle the line between anecdote and myth—but the magic of the Ice Bowl is that they all also happen to be true. The wake-up calls for the Cowboys at their Appleton hotel that cheerily announced the temperature. The whistles that froze to the lips of officials and tore off skin. The electrified field—Lombardi's pride and joy—which malfunctioned because the turf had been covered by a tarp overnight and the condensation beneath it turned to ice when exposed to the elements. The cameras that froze and would not work. NFL Films brought 15 cameras to the game, but only eight or nine functioned properly in the cold. "One of our two slow-motion cameras went out," says Ryan. "An end zone camera went out. Either the cameras would freeze or the film kept snapping."

Enough were operating, though, to capture images that, once seen, are unforgettable. Condensation puffing out of face masks like steam from factory whistles. Players half running, half tiptoeing to keep from slipping on the icy field. Dallas coach Tom Landry in a hunting cap and hooded sweatshirt, and Lombardi in a furry Cossack hat with the flaps pulled down over his ears. Cowboys receiver Bob Hayes running routes with his hands in his pants. Packers receiver Boyd Dowler grabbing his head after getting slammed to the rock-hard turf on Green Bay's final drive. Dallas defensive tackle Bob Lilly kicking at the ground on the goal line, trying to scratch out better footing in the game's final seconds. Mercein's arms raised, seemingly in victory, as he falls on top of Bart

---

* Calling the NFL Championship Game "the Ice Bowl" never occurred to Ryan. A game story from the Chicago Tribune by George Strickler on January 1 used the term in a small headline buried on the first page of the sports section. The front-page headline in The Dallas Morning News on the same day referred to the game as "The Icebox Bowl." According to Packers historian Cliff Christl, the first known use of the term occurred one week earlier, after Green Bay's playoff victory over the Rams in Milwaukee, when the temperature was 20 degrees. It appeared in a Washington Post story on the game by sportswriter William Gildea.

Starr on the game-winning quarterback sneak.

The Packers' final drive was the perfect conclusion to the drama that had played out over the preceding two and a half hours—and to the renaissance that had taken place in Green Bay over the preceding nine years. Both teams were worthy champions. The Packers had dominated the first half and taken a 14–0 lead. The Cowboys took over in the second, holding the Green Bay offense to 10 yards in the third quarter as they surged ahead 17–14. But what won out in the end was the Packers' experience and determination—and Vince Lombardi. Every one of the 68 yards that Green Bay covered on its final drive—on the way to its

11th NFL championship—was gained because of everything that the previous nine years had been about: toughness, teamwork, sacrifice, and the unending pursuit of perfection. Lombardi's Packers had confronted the greatest challenge in the history of professional football—and emerged as champions for all time. Green and gold and glorious.

Two weeks later, Green Bay crushed the Oakland Raiders 33–14 in Miami in Super Bowl II. But the game was, in the words of Mercein, "very anticlimactic." On February 1, 1968, Lombardi introduced Phil Bengtson as the new coach of the Packers. And just like that, an era was over.

A MOMENT FROZEN IN TIME

BY
CHUCK MERCEIN

Vince Lombardi saved me. He really did.

I had been playing for the New York Giants before Lombardi brought me to Green Bay midway through the 1967 season. The Giants had picked me in the third round of the 1965 draft — I was the 31st player taken. But they had also selected Auburn's Tucker Frederickson in the first round that year with the number-one pick. Tucker was a fullback, too, so I didn't play a whole lot as a rookie. My big chance came in '66, my second season, when Tucker injured his knee in the preseason and I became the starter. I played well, but I suffered a lacerated kidney midway through the year, which slowed me down. I still led the team in rushing and was looking forward to doing even better in '67. But in training camp, Allie Sherman, New York's coach, made me the backup to Frederickson without ever really giving me a chance to compete for the starting job. That didn't sit well with me, and I let Sherman know that I wasn't happy about it.

Still, he surprised the hell out of me when he called me into his of-

fice just a few days before the season began and told me that he was cutting me to make room for another player. He also told me that it would be a good idea for me to play a few games with the Westchester Bulls in the Atlantic Coast Football League. The Bulls were semipro. They were also an unofficial farm team for the Giants, a place they would send players they had cut so that they could stay in game shape until they got called back up to the NFL. It was pretty bare-bones — patchy fields, small stadiums, bus trips — but I swallowed my pride and sucked it up.

Sure enough, Allie called me back to New York in October. But he wanted me to be a placekicker. I hadn't kicked since my days at Yale, and I really didn't want to be a kicker in the pros. I wanted to be a fullback, and I was sure I was good enough to play in the NFL. But I did as I was told — and it didn't go well. I missed an extra point and a field goal in a 27–24 win over the Steelers in Pittsburgh and Allie cut me again a week later. I really didn't know what I was going to do. I was depressed and discouraged. I was

only 24, but it felt like this might be it. *Is this what the end feels like?* I didn't know. But I did know that my days with the Giants were over.

Thankfully, I landed a tryout with the Redskins in early November, and afterwards Otto Graham, their coach, told me that he was ready to sign me up. But on Sunday, November 5, the night before I was going to drive down to D.C. to sign with the Redskins, New York owner Wellington Mara called me. He had just gotten off the phone with Lombardi, the Giants' old offensive coordinator. Lombardi had told him that he'd lost two running backs — Elijah Pitts and Jim Grabowski — in Green Bay's 13–10 loss to the Colts earlier that day. Mara said that he had recommended me to Lombardi. I'd been packing up my car for the trip to Washington, but I stayed by the phone after I heard that.

It rang a few seconds later. It was Lombardi. He told me that he wanted me, that the Packers needed me, and that if I signed with them I would help them win their third NFL championship in a row. *Are you kidding? The world's*

best coach? The world's best football team? The Giants were not good — they went 7-7 in 1967. The Packers were the defending NFL and Super Bowl champions. It would be like going from the basement to the penthouse. It was very self-affirming — a big boost to my confidence — that Coach Lombardi wanted me over the many other players who I knew were available. Immediately after I hung up the phone, I told my wife to start helping me unpack the car. I was going to the world champion Green Bay Packers!

The Packers were my first favorite football team. I'm from the North Side of Milwaukee. We lived on Bartlett Avenue when I was a

kid. I would have gone to Shorewood High School, but my dad, who was a DJ on the radio and a late-night-movie host on TV, got a big job in Chicago and we moved down there when I was about 12. I grew up on the Packers — but I grew up on the Packers when they were bad. I had only been a year old in 1944, when they won their last NFL championship. They had been so terrible for so long that I really sort of lost touch with them until Lombardi took over, a few years before I left for Yale, in 1961. The 1961 season was his third in Green Bay, and it was his first NFL championship. He transformed that team, right away.

Coach Lombardi was tough,

no-nonsense. He kept his distance from his players. He only had close relationships with Paul Hornung and Max McGee and, of course, Bart Starr. Not that Lombardi wasn't friendly. It's just that he was the boss, the CEO. And that's the way it should be. When people say, "He's a players' coach," I don't know what that means.

After I got to Green Bay, I studied Lombardi's playbook hard. I think the Giants were still using the offense he'd put in back in the 1950s, but the numbering of plays was a little different. As I remember it, even-numbered plays went to the left in New York, but in Green Bay even numbers went to the right. You had to be careful. You didn't want to run a sweep the wrong way! But besides that, his scheme was uncomplicated — basic football. It was technique, it was perfectionism. Lombardi used to say that you could never reach perfection, but you could achieve excellence in the pursuit of perfection. We practiced the Green Bay Sweep constantly, and we would run it against every defense you could possibly imagine: odd defenses, even defenses, stacked defenses. We didn't have many plays, but we ran them really well. There are teams in the NFL now that have 150, 200 plays. We had 10 to 20.

I remember once when Lombardi had me cheating up on the sweep in order to get to the defensive end quicker. I said, "Coach, won't they know it's coming?" And he said, "I don't care if they know it's coming. They have to stop it." That was the kind of confidence he had.

He threw me right into the mix. I got there on a Tuesday and I played that Sunday against the Cleveland Browns. I had six carries for 24 yards, and we won 55–7. And then I carried 12 times and scored a touchdown in our first playoff game, a 28–7 win over the Rams in Milwaukee. That was fun. My mom had a big Italian family, with a lot of brothers and sisters, and all my uncles and aunts came to watch me play.

Family is a perfect metaphor for playing in Green Bay. The Packers were a very close team. I had just come from New York, and the Giants' players were all over the place — some lived in New Jersey,

Lombardi leaves the field after the Packers' victory in Super Bowl I. Among those capturing the moment is team photographer Vernon Biever (center, with camera).

some lived on Long Island, some lived in Westchester County, some lived in Connecticut. They scattered after practice. But in Green Bay we all went out together. We had specific nights. Monday night was boys' night out, and we would often go to Fuzzy Thurston's bar. Sunday night was family night, and all the players and their wives and their families had a dinner together somewhere at some restaurant. This was not like two or three guys going out together. This was the entire team.

And that sense of brotherhood

really came into play in the 1967 NFL Championship Game. The Ice Bowl. It was 13 below at kickoff, and it only got colder. I read somewhere that by the time we started our last drive, the windchill factor was down to minus 57. We were losing, down by three points, 17–14. We hadn't done a damn thing offensively in the second half, and we were freezing. But once an ice cube is an ice cube, it doesn't get any colder. Everybody in that huddle was calm — determined but not desperate. We started that drive with just under five minutes left in

the game and with 68 yards to pay dirt. Donny Anderson had told Bart that he would be open in the right flat if he needed him, and Bart got things going by throwing to him for six yards. I followed with a run off tackle for seven and a first down. I ran out of bounds practically right into the Packers' bench, and I remember Lombardi yelling to me, "Attaboy, Chuck!" What a feeling! I was doing what he had brought me in to do: help Green Bay win a third NFL championship in a row!

I told Bart that I would be open in the left flat and he threw one to me

over there for 19 yards, the biggest play of the drive. Then Bart trusted me enough to give me the ball again, this time on a handoff up the middle that I took another eight yards, all the way to the Cowboys' three-yard line. We tried Anderson on a couple of dives, but the footing was so icy that he slipped. On third down, Bart called our final timeout and went to the sideline to talk to Lombardi. There were only 16 seconds left. I knew in my heart that Bart was going to call my number, 31 wedge. And that's just what he called when he got back to the huddle. What I didn't know — since Bart didn't bother to tell us — was that he was going to keep the ball himself in order to avoid any possible problem with the handoff. He snuck over for the winning touchdown on a play we had never run before and didn't even have in our playbook. It wasn't until afterwards that I found out that I had accounted for half of our yards on that final drive. Winning such an iconic game was a proud moment — for me and for all of us. Winning the Super Bowl was anticlimactic after that.

I played two more seasons with the Packers. Lombardi retired from coaching to become Green Bay's general manager in 1968, but the year after that he left to become the coach of the Redskins. He was a very loyal person. I saw him in New York in the summer of '69 at Winged Foot Golf Club, where I'm a member. He told me that I looked like I was in great shape. And then he said, "How would you like to

come play fullback in Washington for me?" I said that I'd love to, and he told me to give him a call if I was ever free. So after the Packers cut me, about three-quarters of the way through the year in '69, I called Coach Lombardi and he told me to get on the next plane to D.C. There were only four games left in the season, and he said that if I didn't get activated, I'd still get paid and that we'd start over in the spring. But we never got the chance. I went to camp the next summer and he was already very, very sick. He died soon after. I still miss him.

To be a part of the Packers' history is very humbling. I'm so proud. I own a share of Packers stock. I have every book ever written on the 1967 NFL Championship Game. I've done so much in my life, but the high point of my football career was on the frozen tundra of Lambeau Field in the Ice Bowl. It was a moment that defined a team, a league, and an era. And it still defines me in a way. My life changed forever after that game. I thank God every day for all of his blessings, and one of them, for sure, is that I got to play for Vince Lombardi and the Green Bay Packers.

Chuck Mercein ended his six-year NFL career in 1970 with the New York Jets. He spent most of the next four decades working as a broker and investment adviser for several firms on Wall Street. Now retired, Mercein, 76, lives in White Plains, New York.

CHAPTER 15

THE LOST GENERATION

Twenty-four years. It's a long time to be miserable. In 37 of their first 49 seasons of football, from 1919 through 1967, the Packers had been a winning team. But beginning with Vince Lombardi's resignation as coach, Green Bay endured more than two decades in the wilderness of professional football. From 1968 through 1991, the Packers won more games than they lost just five times and reached the postseason only twice. Some of the causes for Green Bay's futility were familiar, including organizational incompetence and a devotion to past glory. But they led to problems that were uncomfortably new, such as racial discord and a rift between team and town.

The problems seemed to build and build, fed by losing that only became more frequent—an endless cycle of defeat and despair. Of the five coaches who led the Packers in those 24 years, none left Green Bay having won more games than he lost. Indeed, each did worse than the man who preceded him, as the winning percentages declined from .488 all the way down to .375. Before it was over, the Packers found themselves once again struggling for survival and having to prove themselves worthy of membership in the NFL. This time, though, it was not a stock sale that saved the franchise—it was something more profound. It was football itself. Winning football. But it was a long time coming.

◆ ◆ ◆

When Lombardi handed the coaching reins to defensive coach Phil Bengtson, there was little reason to think that the greatest team of the era was headed for a free fall. Since 1959, Green Bay had won 89 regular-season games and five championships, including three in a row from 1965 to 1967—something that in the annals of the NFL had been done before only by the Packers themselves, and that in the days when the league was a single division and there were no playoffs. Lombardi's unprecedented success was certainly part of the reason that he was so emotional—tears were rolling down his cheeks—at the press conference at which he announced that he was giving up coaching to focus solely on his job as the team's general manager. "I am positive," Lombardi said of Bengtson, "that under his leadership and direction, Green Bay Packer football will continue to be excellent, continue to grow and be everything you want it to be."

Bengtson, too, sounded sure of the Packers' continued success. "It really doesn't bother me," he said of following in Lombardi's footsteps. "Four in a row . . . that's my ambition. It's unheard of, but we have the greatest group of players ever assembled on a football field. I see no reason why we can't continue winning."

But that is not what happened. Green Bay's roster had been aging in 1967. By 1968 it was getting very close to ancient. More than a dozen players were in their thirties. Quarterback Bart Starr was 34. He led the league in completion percentage, but he also missed part or all of eight games after pulling a muscle in his throwing arm during warm-ups before a 16–14 loss to the Rams in Milwaukee on October 13. Still, all the Packers had to do to win the NFC Central Division that season was go 8-6, but they finished 6-7-1, their first losing record in 10 years. Things never really got better for Bengtson after that. Lombardi resigned as general manager in February 1969 to become coach, vice president, and part owner of the Washington Redskins. When he had stepped down as Green Bay's coach the year before, he had said that it was because being both coach and general manager was too much for one man. But on March 6, 1969, team president Dominic Olejniczak nevertheless promoted Bengtson to both jobs, giving him the dual titles of coach and general manager. The Packers improved to 8-6 that year but missed the playoffs. Two days after the conclusion of a 6-8 season in 1970 — bookended by shutout losses to the Lions — Bengtson abruptly resigned.

Green Bay's journey into the pro football desert had begun.

◆ ◆ ◆

Bryan Bartlett "Bart" Starr was born in Montgomery, Alabama, on January 9, 1934, the oldest son of Benjamin B. Starr, a strict Air Force master sergeant, and his wife, Lula. As a young boy, Bart was a good athlete, though not as gifted as his brother, Hilton, known affectionately as "Bubba," who was younger by two years. Bart was the quieter and more introverted of the two, and he felt it keenly when the more aggressive Bubba seemed to be getting most of the attention and praise from Ben, whose personality was similar to his younger

son's. Bart's need to prove himself and the urge to seek approval from a strong figure of authority were the mainsprings of his life until he was well into his thirties.

The problems between father and son became more pronounced in the summer of 1946. That was when Bubba, running around outside barefoot after church one Sunday morning, stepped on a piece of bone and cut his foot. His mother cleaned the wound but — hoping to spare the boy a painful shot — did not take him to a doctor. The cut became infected and Bubba, who was only 10, died of tetanus three days later, on July 30. The Starr family was devastated. Lula blamed herself. Ben took to belittling Bart, who, at the same time he was grieving for his brother, was also suddenly forced to compete against his ghost for their father's affection. "[Our relationship] deteriorated," Starr wrote of his father years later. "Bubba was no longer around for Dad to point to as an example of what I should strive for. He didn't believe I could excel unless I adopted my brother's personality,

Bart Starr was the most popular player from the Packers' 1960s dynasty. But he was unable to translate his greatness as a quarterback into success as a coach. In nine years under his direction, Green Bay went 52-76-3 and made the playoffs just once.

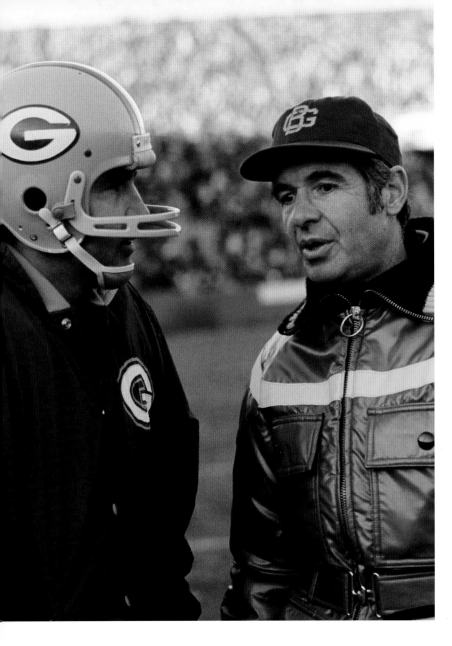

Dan Devine's talent as a coach was his ability to find good players. But that didn't keep him from making one of the worst trades in NFL history in 1974, when he sent five high draft picks to the Rams for 36-year-old quarterback John Hadl (left).

leader of the Packers' dynasty. He used to practice for hours on end in the backyard of his family's home on Montgomery's south side, perfecting his footwork or throwing passes through a tire he had hung from a tree.

As the starter in 1951, Starr led Lanier to a 9-1 record. He also shot up to about six foot one and put on 15 pounds. Several SEC schools wanted him, but the soft-spoken senior with the round face and kind eyes had been an Alabama fan from the time he was a boy, when he idolized Crimson Tide left halfback Harry Gilmer. (In Alabama coach Frank Thomas's version of the Notre Dame Box offense, Gilmer was the primary passer.) As a sophomore at Bama, Starr was the starting quarterback on a 6-3-3 team that earned a berth in the Cotton Bowl. But he injured his back before his junior year and shuffled in and out of the starting lineup for the rest of his college career. He threw just two touchdowns in his last 21 games, and the Crimson Tide went 0-10 in his senior season. His pro prospects were dim.

Starr came to the attention of the Packers only because of the network of collegiate scouts maintained by Green Bay personnel man Jack Vainisi. Just as Curly Lambeau had done years before, Vainisi maintained close ties with the men he had known at Notre Dame, many of whom had scattered to campuses throughout the country. The basketball coach at Alabama in 1956 was Johnny Dee, who had first met Vainisi a decade earlier, when Dee had lettered in both basketball and football in South Bend. In the autumn of 1952, when Starr was a freshman in Tuscaloosa, Dee was pulling double duty as a football assistant. It was Dee who recommended Starr to Vainisi. On January 17, 1956, Lisle Blackbourn took Starr in the 17th round (out of 30) of the NFL draft, with the 200th pick (out of 360). He was such an obscure selection that the *Press-Gazette* listed him in its report on the draft as "Bryan Bartlett."

The Packers muddled through the 1950s with several different quarterbacks, some better than

and constantly prodded me with pointed comments that began, 'Your brother would have . . .'"

Bart ran the scout team as a sophomore quarterback at Montgomery's Sidney Lanier High in 1949. He made the varsity as a junior, but was only a backup until the second quarter of the fourth game of the season, when the first-string quarterback suffered a broken leg. The five-foot-nine, 160-pound Starr took over and led the 3-0 Poets to a 13–0 victory—and then to five more wins and a tie in their last six games. It was an opportunity for which he had prepared himself with the same quiet determination and meticulous attention to detail that would one day make him the

others. The studious and dependable Starr was actually the starter in both the last game at old City Stadium, on November 18, 1956, and the opening game at Green Bay City Stadium the following September. Still, he spent most of his first three seasons shuffling in and out of the lineup before Lombardi arrived—at which point the shuffling continued. Three months after he had been hired, Lombardi traded for Chicago Cardinals quarterback Lamar McHan in an effort to improve his team's depth at the position. Starr was a second- or third-stringer for nearly half of the 1959 season (along with second-year quarterback Joe Francis, who struggled in his only appearance) until shoulder and leg injuries landed McHan on the bench in November. Starr lost to the Colts in his first start for Lombardi, then led the Packers to victory in their last four games of the season. He started against the Bears on opening day in 1960 but completed only eight of 22 passes and threw two interceptions in a 17–14 loss. Lombardi benched him in favor of McHan.

But after four games with the inconsistent McHan under center, Lombardi decided to stick with Starr, who never looked back. In the locker room after the Packers defeated the Giants in the 1961 NFL Championship Game, Ben Starr finally admitted to Bart that he had made him proud, wrapping him in a tearful bear hug and saying, "I was wrong, son."

Starr never really stopped ascending after that, establishing himself as the embodiment of the term *field general*. He thrived under Lombardi's tutelage. In leading Green Bay to five championships in the 1960s, Starr became known as Lombardi's brains on the field. He knew the Packers' playbook as well as the coach, and his judgment and error-free style of play were perfect complements to Lombardi's relentless pursuit of perfection. Starr was not flashy. He could not throw the long ball like Arnie Herber, for example. But he was deliberate, consistent, and unflappable—and a winner. Arm trouble ended his career in 1971,

and when he walked away from the game he was easily the most popular star of the Packers' most glorious era. Green Bay has always been a place where the past is as important as the present, and Starr's popularity did not diminish in the years after he retired from the game. It certainly did not hurt that the Packers had not been able to replace him at quarterback.

Starr's reputation and his popularity were why Green Bay hired him on December 24, 1974, to be the eighth coach in franchise history. It certainly had nothing to do with his coaching experience. Starr had only one season as an NFL assistant under his belt. But optimism was high, and Packers fans were elated. Eight months after his hiring, *Sports Illustrated* put Starr on its cover, beneath the headline DREAMS OF GLORY IN GREEN BAY. Aware of the challenge he was facing, Starr was cautious. "He did not want his picture to appear on the cover . . . because his role as a savior of the Packers is a difficult one and so far he has coached only two exhibition games," wrote the magazine's Edwin Shrake. "It took Moses 40 years to straighten out his mess, but Starr has only a three-year contract."

◆ ◆ ◆

The mess that Starr took charge of in Green Bay was an ugly one. The management of the team had started to disintegrate even before Lombardi left for Washington. Eight days ahead of his departure—but after he had made up his mind to go to the Redskins—Lombardi presided over the Green Bay draft room. But instead of directing the action, he essentially let coach Phil Bengtson run the show, with disastrous results. The Packers had the 12th pick in the first round, and there were a raft of good players still available, including wide receiver Charlie Joiner and cornerback Roger Wehrli, both of whom would go on to become Hall of Famers. But over the objections of his scouts, Bengtson selected six-foot-eight, 280-pound defensive tackle Rich Moore, an intriguing if almost totally unheralded prospect from a 6-4 Villanova team.* According to Lombardi biographer David Maraniss, Green Bay personnel director Pat Peppler bolted from the room when Bengtson made the pick. By the time Lombardi caught up to Peppler in the hallway, he could only plead, "Pat, I'm sorry, but I've got to stay out of it. It's Phil's team."

There had been a sense in Green Bay when Lombardi left that the glory was nearing an end. Peppler wasn't the only one who had pleaded with Lombardi to let him accompany the coach to the nation's capital. But nobody could have guessed how bad things would get. On January 14, 1971, team president Dominic Olejniczak compounded the error of having made Bengtson coach and general manager by hiring Missouri coach Dan Devine for the same two jobs. It was as though nobody had been listening to Lombardi's admonition that the dual roles were too much for one man. And whereas Bengtson at least was an NFL coaching veteran, Devine had never led a team above the collegiate level, though he was a formidable winner, with a career record of 119-41-8. It was a curious pick, though not totally out of left field.

But there was confusion around Devine's hiring, as well as significant dissent. Executive committee members Tony Canadeo and Dick Bourguignon wanted to offer the job to Penn State coach Joe Paterno. But Olejniczak and other members of the committee preferred Devine because he was also the athletic director at Mizzou and they felt that his administrative experience would help him with his duties as general manager. Paterno, they said, was just a football coach. The vote of the board went 5–2 in favor of Devine, with Canadeo and Bourguignon casting the dissenting ballots. The two men were never accepting of Devine, who they felt knew little about football, and they did not keep their opinions to themselves, even when talking to assistant coaches and players.

The undermining of Devine from within the organization is perhaps why those who worked for the team considered a rumor that seems implausible to be completely believable. The story goes that Olejniczak was never supposed to have contacted Devine—whose Mizzou team was coming off a 5-6 season. Ole was actually supposed to reach out to Bob Devaney, the coach of national champion Nebraska, but had confused the names. Devine, in other words, was a mistake.

However Devine came to Green Bay, there can be no doubt that his time with the Packers was marked by discord—in the front office, on his staff, and among his players—and a lack of trust within the organization. The ill will was fostered not only by those who disliked Devine and who dwelt upon his faults but also by Devine himself, a difficult man who never quite fit.

Devine was not a total outsider to the Upper Midwest. He had been born in the tiny west-central Wisconsin town of Augusta on December 23, 1924, and grown up about 175 miles to the north, in Proctor, Minnesota, a suburb of Duluth. He had been a standout athlete at Proctor High before going on to captain the basketball and football teams at Duluth State Teachers College (now Minnesota Duluth). But his childhood had hardly been idyllic—and may help explain the complex personality that made him one of the most divisive figures in the history of the Packers.

Devine's father was the successful manager of a cigar store in Eau Claire, Wisconsin. But when Dan was four, his parents—Jerome and Erma—sent him to Proctor to live with Jerome's sister, Mary, and her husband, Joseph. Dan was the second oldest of three children at the time, and, the way he told the story years later, his parents had sent him away because Jerome had gotten sick and could

---

* *Moore lasted only a season and a half in Green Bay, tearing his Achilles tendon in a 30–17 defeat of the Philadelphia Eagles on October 25, 1970. The Packers traded him to the New England Patriots in July 1971 for outside linebacker John Bramlett, whom they eventually cut. Moore injured his knee in a preseason game against the Bills a month later, went on injured reserve, and never played another down in the NFL.*

not support his family. Gregory Devine, one of Dan's four younger brothers — Jerome and Erma would have six more children beginning in 1929 — says that the move was indeed precipitated by financial difficulties, but that they had nothing to do with illness. Jerome lost everything during the Great Depression. In the 1930 census, Dan was listed as a resident of two places — with his parents in Eau Claire and with his aunt and uncle in Proctor. Ten years later he was listed only as a member of his uncle's household. Of Jerome and Erma's nine children, Dan was the only one who did not live with them, and he felt the pain of the separation acutely.

"Many nights I cried myself to sleep," he wrote in his 2000 memoirs, *Simply Devine*. "I never tried to find out more about why my parents had sent me away. It was a decision that I'm sure affected their lives as well. One aching feeling that never left me was how desperately I missed my family."

The defining trauma of Devine's life — being abandoned by his parents — may help explain the insecurity and mistrust that characterized his tenure as the coach of the Packers. He alienated people inside and outside the organization at almost every turn. He often vanished from the office, without explanation, for several hours at a time. He was openly dismissive of the Lombardi-era veterans. Never known as an X's and O's man — his strength as a college coach had been recruiting — he once diagrammed a 12-man formation on the chalkboard for his assistant coaches. And on more than one occasion he showed his players game film of his Missouri teams. Just days after John Brockington, a rookie fullback out of Ohio State, had run for 142 yards in a 20–17 victory over the Bears, on November 7, 1971, Devine told reporters that Vikings fullback Dave Osborn was his kind of football player and joked that he was "on the wrong team." Brockington, who would rush for more than 1,000 yards that season, took the comment as a slight, as did several of his teammates. "When I played in college, we never thought we were going to lose a football game," says Brockington, whose coach with the Buckeyes had been the fiery Woody Hayes. "With Devine? He'd tell us, 'If you guys don't play your best today, you're not going to win.' It was like he didn't like us. It was messed up, man."

Devine's career in Green Bay did not have a fortuitous beginning. In the third quarter of a rainy 42–40 loss to the Giants in the season opener at Lambeau Field on September 19, 1971, Giants guard Bob Hyland plowed into him. Devine fell awkwardly and broke his left leg. Hobbled by his injury and plagued by an aging roster and an incompetent kicking game — Green Bay cycled through three different kickers, who together made only 14 of 26 field goals — Devine suffered through a miserable season. The Packers went 4-8-2. Things in Green Bay were getting worse, not better.

Starr's chronically injured throwing arm, which had required two preseason operations to repair a torn biceps tendon, kept him off the field until late November and eventually forced his retirement on July 21, 1972, at which point he joined Devine's staff as the quarterbacks coach and offensive play caller. Starr was seen as a steadying presence for second-year quarterback Scott Hunter, who had had to start 10 games as a rookie in 1971, throwing for seven touchdowns, with 17 interceptions, and completing just 46 percent of his passes. "I became an extension of Bart Starr on the field," says Hunter, who threw just nine picks in 14 starts the next season. "I was a lowercase Bart Starr."

The Packers improved greatly in 1972, going 10-4 and winning the NFC Central Division. Devine made several astute personnel moves — player evaluation was his real strength as an NFL coach. In the draft, he took San Diego State cornerback Willie Buchanon in the first round and Hillsdale College kicker Chester Marcol in the second. Buchanon, an All-America in 1971, became a lockdown corner almost immediately, picking off four passes and being named the NFL's Defensive Rookie of the Year. More important, his arrival allowed Devine to shift Al Matthews, who had been playing cornerback despite lacking the necessary speed, to strong safety. Green Bay went from ranking 18th in total defense in 1971 to fourth in 1972 and gave up just seven passing touchdowns. Marcol, a three-time NAIA All-America, led the league with 33 field goals as a rookie and was a first-team All-Pro. Devine also traded Ice Bowl hero Donny Anderson to the Cardinals for six-foot-one, 220-pound halfback MacArthur Lane, who, together with the six-foot-one, 225-pound Brockington, gave the Packers a punishing rushing tandem — Brockington ran for 1,027 yards, Lane for 821. "All we had to do was get close and Chester would kick a field goal," says Brockington. "MacArthur Lane was the cherry on top, but Willie Buchanon and Chester Marcol were the difference between 1971 and '72."

Devine's eye for talent had made the Packers winners once again. But in the divisional playoff game against the Redskins on December 24, the team was undone by his worst instincts. Without explanation, he took over play-calling duties from Starr, who by then was attracting buzz as a future coach and was known to covet the Green Bay job. The Redskins had beaten Green Bay in Washington 21–16 one month earlier by using a five-man line to shut down the running game and force Hunter to pass. On Christmas Eve, Washington did the same — and Green Bay never adjusted. Devine refused to let Hunter throw the ball. Brockington ran 13 times for nine yards. "It was embarrassing," he says. For much of the game, Starr stood by himself on the sideline and referred all inquiries to Devine. The Packers lost 16–3. Trying to convince Devine to let Hunter throw the ball was, Starr wrote years later, the only disagreement he ever had with the head coach. He kept quiet about the dispute afterwards, but it was his last game as a Green Bay assistant.

The good feelings from the run to the postseason quickly dissipated. The Packers went 5-7-2 in 1973 as Devine rotated among three starting quarter-backs: Hunter, Jerry Tagge, and Jim Del Gaizo. Finding a reliable starter — in their Green Bay careers, none of the three completed more than 50 percent of his passes — consumed Devine. He had drafted Hunter and Tagge in 1971 and 1972, respectively, and by the fall of 1974 he had traded away a total of five draft picks for four other signal callers, including Del Gaizo and 40-year-old Zeke Bratkowski, Starr's former backup, who was a Minnesota Vikings assistant when Devine acquired him to shore up the position. Nothing seemed to work — or, really, to make him happy.

That might have been because Devine was decidedly unhappy. Not only was he aware that he was being subverted by people within the Packers organization, but he also believed that the entire city of Green Bay was against him. In early October he was the subject of an article in *Time* magazine titled "Haunted in Green Bay." In the story, Devine claimed that his children were being heckled on the school bus and that his dog had been shot and killed outside his house two years earlier by fans upset over the Packers' losing ways. His wife, Jo, had been diagnosed with multiple sclerosis earlier in the year, but the rumor in town was that her unsteady gait was the result of a drinking problem. "It's been vulgar, malicious and ugly," Devine said of the city's behavior toward him and his family. "It just makes me sick."

In a story that quoted only one Packers coach by name — Dan Devine — it was a comment attributed to an anonymous one that cut the deepest. "People here have only four things to do — eat, sleep, make babies and root for the team."

The shooting of the Devines' dog has been discussed countless times since it first appeared in print. In Green Bay the tale is one of the most enduring legacies of Devine's four years in charge of the Packers, but it is so shopworn that it is regarded as something of an urban legend. The rumor around town was that Devine had a dog that was raiding the livestock of a local farmer, and that it was the farmer — and not a disgruntled

fan—who had shot and killed the dog. In his 2000 autobiography, though, Devine wrote that there had actually been *two* shootings that took place within a few days of each other in 1972. One did indeed involve a farmer shooting and killing one of his family's dogs. The other involved a second dog, this one named Earth, which had been shot outside Devine's house one day at five in the morning. It was this incident that Devine said had been blamed on angry locals. "Rumors circulated that some disgruntled fans or anti-Devine people had shot my dog," Devine wrote. "I honestly don't believe that was what happened. My guess is that some young folks were out joyriding in the country, probably had been drinking, and Earth probably had taken after them chasing their car and they shot him."

But that's not how he told the story in 1974. Back then Devine had had no doubt that angry fans had been responsible. The "rumors" to which

he refers in his autobiography, after all, began with his telling the story to a national publication. So how could he interpret the incident 26 years later in the most generous way possible? Who shoots a dog for chasing a car? Who goes joyriding at 5 a.m.? The only fact that can be derived from the multiple versions of the story is that Devine told it one way to *Time* in 1974—when he was under fire and it made Green Bay look as bad as possible—and another in his autobiography.* In all the years in between, he never spoke up to set the record straight. Why let an incorrect version of the story linger for a quarter century without saying anything? Odd behavior from an odd man.

If the purpose of Devine's comments to *Time* was public relations spin, what he did next can only be described as a last-ditch attempt to save his job. On October 22, 1974, he swung one of the worst trades in NFL history, sending two first- and two second-round picks, as well as a third-round

One of Devine's best acquisitions was when he traded for Baltimore Colts linebacker Ted Hendricks. In 1974, his only season in Green Bay, Hendricks was a dominant defensive force and blocked an NFL-record seven kicks.

---

* *In the 1974 version of the story, the dog had been shot and killed. In Devine's 2000 retelling, though, the dog survived.*

pick, to the Rams for 34-year-old quarterback John Hadl, whom Los Angeles coach Chuck Knox had benched the previous week. Devine, acting in his capacity as general manager, had orchestrated the deal himself and had told nobody in the organization — not even the executive committee or his own coaching staff.

The Packers won Hadl's first three starts, to improve to 6-5, but then imploded and lost his last three, finishing 6-8. Hadl threw three touchdown passes and eight interceptions. The low point came on December 1, when the 4-7 Philadelphia Eagles drubbed Green Bay 36–14 in windy, rainy Veterans Stadium, a loss that mathematically eliminated the Packers from playoff contention. Hadl threw one pick and lost three fumbles. After falling to the 49ers in San Francisco a week later, the Packers' players were so fed up with Devine that they discussed boycotting the last game of the season. He resigned on December 16. "Dan Devine never

seemed to understand Green Bay," Cliff Christl wrote in the *Press-Gazette*. "And Green Bay never seemed to understand Dan Devine."

Devine's futile quest to find a starting quarterback — and the riches he expended in the effort — took the wind out of the Packers. And after he left to become the coach at Notre Dame, it was as though the team never stopped exhaling. It would be nearly two decades before the franchise would breathe fresh air.

◆ ◆ ◆

Before Bart Starr even took over as coach, the Hadl trade had severely compromised the Packers, making it all the more critical that Starr be an outstanding general manager. Unfortunately for them, he was not, and his missteps started before Green Bay ever played a down in 1975. Over the summer, Starr let future Hall of Fame linebacker Ted Hendricks leave rather than re-sign him. Devine had acquired the six-foot-seven, 220-pound Hendricks in a trade with the Baltimore Colts on the eve of the 1974 season, and he had been a dominant force. He intercepted five passes, recovered one fumble, and blocked seven kicks—one extra point, three field goals, and three punts, one of which rolled through the back of the end zone for a safety. Starr made Hendricks an offer but said later that it was futile, because Hendricks wanted out of Green Bay. Other people in the organization have said that money was the issue. But Hendricks says that there was more to it than just dollars and cents. "I started to negotiate with them," he says. "They handed me a contract with no guarantee to it. It was just five contracts with options and no increments. And they said, 'This is it.' And I said, 'I can't sign that.' I knew that I could get a guaranteed contract. And I knew that if I did, I wouldn't have to worry about getting hurt."

Years later, Starr admitted that refusing to budge on negotiations with Hendricks had been a mistake. But by then it was too late. The linebacker eventually signed with the Oakland Raiders. "The GM of the Colts thought he was putting me in cold storage sending me to Green Bay," Hendricks says. "But there were great people there. I was lucky to have gotten to play there. I would have stayed."

Starr's personnel miscues kept piling up. In 1979, he overruled scouts and passed on Notre Dame quarterback Joe Montana in favor of running back Steve Atkins in the second round of the draft. When Montana was still available in the third, Starr passed on him again to take nose tackle Charles Johnson, at which point former assistant coach Red Cochran, who was then Green Bay's chief Midwest scout, stormed out of the draft room in frustration. One year later, Starr drafted Penn State defensive tackle Bruce Clark with the fourth pick in the first round. The Packers' reputation had deteriorated so much by that point that it was one of the reasons Clark spurned Green Bay to sign with the Toronto Argonauts of the CFL. The executive committee stripped Starr of the title of general manager after the season but left him with ultimate authority over trades and draft selections. It was still his show in 1981 when the Packers brought USC safety Ronnie Lott to town two days before the draft for dinner with Starr, linebackers coach John Marshall (who had previously been on the staff at Southern Cal when Lott was an underclassman), and Dick Corrick, Green Bay's director of player personnel. Lott believed that the Packers were going to draft him. But Starr felt he needed a quarterback, and assistant coach Zeke Bratkowski was high on Cal's Rich Campbell. With the sixth pick in the first round, Green Bay took Campbell, a move that Starr later acknowledged was "a colossal blunder."

It was not all bad, though. In April 1976, Starr traded for Houston Oilers backup quarterback Lynn Dickey. The Oilers had taken Dickey in the third round out of Kansas State in 1971, and he was in the mix for the starting job in Houston before he broke his hip in the preseason in 1972. Dickey had been tackled from behind while he was scrambling in a game against the St. Louis Cardinals. His left knee hit the artificial turf in the Astrodome with such force that it popped his hipbone out of its socket, broke off a piece of the socket bone, and tore ligaments, a gruesome injury of the sort associated with head-on auto accidents —a "dashboard injury," in the parlance of emergency room doctors. Dickey missed the entire season while undergoing painful rehab. After he returned, he was never able to supplant starter Dan Pastorini. Dickey asked Houston to trade him. In exchange for the six-foot-four, 220-pound Dickey, Starr gave up cornerback Ken Ellis, plus two draft choices (a fourth-round pick in 1976 and a third-rounder in 1977) and, in an ironic twist, John Hadl. The price was steep, but the trade would prove to be a bargain.

Dickey was from Osawatomie, Kansas, the younger of two sons of a brakeman on the Missouri Pacific Railroad. Carl Dickey's job was to walk the length of a train whenever it made a stop and check for smoke, fire, and other problems. Lynn can still remember Carl coming home at the end of a working day with his face covered in soot. Lynn wanted no part of that. And he was inspired to excel in athletics because of his brother, Larry, who had been crippled by polio when he was six. Lynn had been a teenager when Lombardi's Packers were at the height of their glory, and when he was traded to Green Bay, he still had a healthy reverence for what the place meant to football. When he arrived at Lambeau Field for his introductory press conference on April 2, 1976, the Packers gave him a tour of their facilities, and then he walked out into the stands in the north end zone by himself. "I was all alone," he says. "It was eerie. I could almost hear Coach Lombardi yelling."

Dickey may have played for a lesser version of the Packers than Starr had, but he deserves to be recognized alongside his coach as one of the finest passers ever to play quarterback in Green Bay. Dickey had a cannon for a right arm. But his hip injury, a separated shoulder in 1976, and a badly broken leg that he suffered on the last play of a 24–6 loss to the Rams in Milwaukee on November 13, 1977, robbed him of playing time — he did not play a full season as a starter until his 10th year in the NFL — and rendered him practically immobile. When he got protection, he was brilliant. In 1983, Dickey led the league with 4,458 yards passing and 32 touchdowns. But he was an ineffective statue in the face of a stiff pass rush. In 1981 he was sacked 40 times, the second most in the league. And in his entire career, he never received All-Pro recognition or made a Pro Bowl.

Starr's other superlative personnel decision was his selection of Stanford wide receiver James Lofton with the sixth pick of the 1978 draft. An industrial engineering major with a B-plus average, Lofton had been in Palo Alto on a track schol-

arship. He qualified for the 1978 NCAA Track & Field Championships in the 100-, 200-, and 400-meter dashes and was the national outdoor champion in the long jump. One month after the Packers drafted him, Lofton jumped 27 feet 0 inches at the USA Outdoor Track and Field Championships in Los Angeles, tied for the second-longest legal jump in the world that year.[*] Lofton's parents had divorced when he was seven, and he and his older brother and two older sisters were raised in Los Angeles by his father, Michael, who had retired from the Army as a lieutenant colonel and taken a job as an executive at a bank. James was cool, intelligent, and handsome, the kind of superstar that Green Bay had not had since Paul Hornung. "James came to camp late," says tight end Paul Coffman, who, as an undrafted free agent out of Kansas State, was a rookie along with Lofton in 1978. "When we first got there, he hadn't arrived yet because he was at the Olympic Trials. And then he comes in and it's like he knows everything. He understood coverages and why we were doing what we were doing. He was just so smart. He had that rare combination of intelligence and ability."

The six-foot-three, 198-pound Lofton was the Packers' best receiver since Don Hutson. He caught 46 passes for 818 yards and six touchdowns in 1978 and made the Pro Bowl as Green Bay went 8-7-1, its first winning season since 1972. But the Packers fell back to 5-11 in 1979 and Lofton grew frustrated, getting into an argument with Starr after one loss and giving the finger to fans at Lambeau Field after they booed him for dropping a pass during another. But he soon turned things around. He got married and bought a home in Green Bay. He was the Packers' United Way spokesman and in 1983 was one of five finalists for the NFL's Man of the Year. He was also Green Bay's union representative during the 1982

---

[*] *Lofton was actually outjumped at the meet by event winner Arnie Robinson, who soared 27 feet 4 inches. But Robinson had a 2.2-meters-per-second wind at his back. Lofton had the barely legal 2.0. Wind assistance does not affect the results of a competition, only whether the distance jumped constitutes a record.*

players' strike. His wife, Beverly, had sung the national anthem at the last four home games in 1981. He had also matured into the best receiver in the game, fast and sure-handed. In 1983, he averaged 22.4 yards per reception, tops in the NFL.

It was in 1983 that Lofton, Dickey, and the rest of the Packers' offense won the defining victory of the Bart Starr era, a 48–47 defeat of the defending NFL champion Redskins on October 17, the second-highest-scoring Monday night game of all time. Green Bay and Washington combined for 1,025 total yards. Dickey completed 22 of 31 passes for 387 yards and three touchdowns. Lofton caught four passes for 105 yards. Coffman, left in single coverage against a safety in the first half, hauled in six for 124 and two touchdowns. The Packers won the game in spite of their defense — which seemed to struggle more often than not under Starr. The Redskins ran 33 more plays, picked up 10 more first downs, and held the ball for more than 39 minutes — and lost only because reigning NFL MVP Mark Moseley missed a 39-yard field goal attempt on the last play of the game. "We did not dink and dunk the ball in those days," says Dickey. "We didn't have time. We had to score fast. When I'd come to the sideline, I'd put my helmet under the telephone desk and kick back. I knew I was going to be there awhile."

The Packers had the fifth-most-prolific offense in football in 1983 but finished 8-8, because they also had the third-worst defense. The low point came against the 7-8 Bears at frigid Soldier Field on December 18, in the last game of the season. The temperature at kickoff was two degrees, and by the time the game ended it was approaching zero. Late in the fourth quarter, Dickey and Lofton connected on passes of 19 and 23 yards to lead Green Bay on a 64-yard drive that culminated with Dickey throwing a five-yard touchdown pass to Coffman that gave the Packers a 21–20 lead. After Dickey returned to the bench, he looked up at the scoreboard and saw that the Los Angeles Rams had beaten the New Orleans Saints 26–24, knock-ing New Orleans out of the playoffs. The Packers had already beaten the Rams 27–24 in L.A. on September 18. To eliminate 9-7 Los Angeles and make the postseason as a wild card, all the Packers had to do was hold on for three minutes and 58 seconds. And there was cause for hope: Bears running back Walter Payton, who had run for 148 yards on 30 carries in the game, was sidelined with a rib injury.

But Chicago quarterback Jim McMahon subjected the Packers to an agonizing torture. Opting for short passes to running back Matt Suhey and tight ends Jay Saldi and Emery Moorehead, McMahon led the Bears on a nine-play, 58-yard drive, from their own 38 to the Packers' four. It was excruciating. With 10 seconds left, Bob Thomas kicked a 22-yard field goal. No winning record. No playoffs.

Shortly before eight o'clock the next morning, Judge Robert Parins, who had taken over as president from Dominic Olejniczak the year before, finally did what had to be done and fired Starr. There had been hopeful moments in his nine years on the sideline, but Starr's career record as coach was 52-76-3. He had led Green Bay to the playoffs only once, in the strike-shortened 1982 season. His Packers teams had lost 20 games by 20 points or more and had won only 13 games against teams that finished with winning records. It was a testament to how entrenched Starr was in Green Bay — in addition to being the public face of the Lombardi-era dynasty, he and his family lived in town year-round — and how popular he was personally that the news of his termination came as something of a surprise. It was hard to fire your neighbor, especially when he had been a pillar of the community for more than 20 years. In his *Press-Gazette* column on the press conference at which Starr's firing was announced, Don Langenkamp wrote, "There was, even among this jaundiced crowd, just the briefest moment of shock." Even Starr, who had closed his office door and wept after Parins gave him the news, said that he was stunned by the decision.

He should not have been. Besides his personnel missteps and poor record on the field, Starr never settled the turmoil within the franchise the way he had promised to do on the day he was hired. The turnover on his staff was nearly constant. In nine years, he had had 24 assistant coaches. As of the end of the 1983 season, Minnesota's Bud Grant had had 14 in 17 years, and Miami's Don Shula had had 17 in 14 years. In Dallas, Tom Landry had had as many assistants as Starr in 24 years. Some good coaches came through Green Bay — Monte Kiffin, Dick LeBeau, Tom Lovat — but none of them stayed for very long, and they were outnumbered by others who were unfit. The scouting department was led by three different personnel directors and often seemed at odds with the coaching staff, a problem that frequently came to a head on draft day, when the two factions were pulling in opposite directions.

And while many of his players said then — and say now — that they loved and respected Starr, their admiration did not translate to victories on the field. He was criticized from inside the team and out for being aloof and passionless, as well as inconsistent in his enforcement of discipline. But there are all sorts of examples from around the NFL of coaches who did those things but still won games. In New York in the 1980s, Giants coach Bill Parcells famously let star linebacker Lawrence Taylor do whatever he wanted while enforcing rules for the rest of his team. The problem for Starr on the sidelines was that he never really got beyond his lack of coaching experience. The Green Bay offense did not become a dynamic scoring attack until 1982, when Bob Schnelker took over from Starr as the offensive coordinator.

But beyond his play calling, Starr also never developed a feel for sideline strategy. In a tie game at Minnesota on September 23, 1979, he decided to run out the clock and play for overtime despite having the ball on his own 25-yard line with 1:41 left. The Vikings won the coin toss and promptly drove for the winning touchdown and a 27–21 victory. In the loss to the Bears on the day before he was fired, Starr had not used his timeouts in the final minutes, even after it became a near certainty that Chicago was going to score. It was maddening. Starr's Packers were booed at Lambeau Field, where the sellouts continued but the number of no-shows seemed to be increasing.

The split in Green Bay was almost even between those who still loved Bart Starr and those who were sure that it was time for him to go. "During the last year, I'd get about 100 to 200 letters every Monday morning criticizing me for not firing him," Parins said years later. "The day after I fired him, I got 500 letters, 'Who the hell do you think you are?'"

Despite ample evidence to the contrary, Starr was adamant that he was leaving the Packers better than he found them, saying that they were "now in a position to go on and win." But while the mistrust of the Devine era may have been gone, the incompetence remained — and winning was still a long way off. The wait for victory was starting to fray the bond between team and town.

"Earlier in the season, Bob Schnelker had told us that things were going to end badly," Coffman says. "He said, 'Bart Starr, that man loves you guys. He would do anything for you. Don't screw this up or he's going to get fired. And then they're going to bring in some son of a bitch.' And that's just what happened."

◆ ◆ ◆

Like every team president who came before him, Robert Parins was a prominent member of the Green Bay community. Born in 1918, Parins was the son of a farmer and tavern owner from the town of Preble, which was incorporated into Green Bay in 1964. He graduated from Green Bay East High and then went on to the University of Wisconsin, where he earned his law degree in 1942. After working as an insurance adjuster in Minneapolis, he returned to Green Bay in 1944 and, less than two years later, set up a law prac-

Lynn Dickey is one of the best pure passers ever to play for the Packers, but a litany of injuries—including a broken leg and a dislocated hip—rendered him essentially immobile in the pocket.

tice with fellow attorney Meyer Cohen. He served a two-year term as Brown County district attorney, from 1949 to 1951, and then returned to private practice, earning statewide renown as a special prosecutor before running unopposed for the position of circuit court judge in 1967, the year after he had been elected to the Packers' board of directors. In 1979 he was elected vice president, and three years later, on May 3, 1982, the board voted him the first full-time president in team history. Parins stepped down from the bench to take the job. His salary as a judge had been $49,127. He made more than that with the Packers—the first member of the executive committee ever to draw a salary from the team—though he refused to say how much. He had no extensive experience as a pro football executive, but he told the *Press-Gazette* that a full-time president was "essential to the operation" of the team.

Parins also said that he did not see his lack of football credentials as a problem. But history would prove him wrong. He had been bold enough to fire Starr, but five days later, on Christmas Eve, when he replaced Starr with Forrest Gregg,

another beloved alumnus of Green Bay's 1960s championship teams, he repeated the mistake of giving his new coach the general manager duties. The GM position had been open ever since Starr was demoted in 1980. Now Gregg was getting both titles despite the fact that the Hall of Fame tackle had never before run a draft or made a trade.

Gregg nevertheless seemed like an excellent choice to lead the Packers back to respectability. A six-foot-four, 240-pound second-round pick out of Southern Methodist in 1956, he had been one of the linchpins of the greatest offensive line of his time, a hulking (for his day), technically sound blocker who was practically unbeatable in pass protection. He had retired in 1971, after playing a final season in Dallas, and then gone into coaching, working as an offensive line assistant in San Diego and then in Cleveland, where he became the head coach in 1975. Gregg turned the Browns around in his first two seasons, going from 3-11 to 9-5 and earning NFL Coach of the Year honors in 1976. He went 18-23 in three seasons with Cleveland, then spent a year as the coach of the CFL's Toronto Argonauts before taking over the Cincinnati Bengals in 1980. In Cincinnati, he once again turned a losing team into a winning one, improving from 6-10 in his first year to 12-4 in his second, when the Bengals won the AFC championship. He was not quite as big a hero in Green Bay as Starr was, but he had more coaching chops.

There was more to Gregg's sideline experience, though, than wins and losses. And in the details of his coaching career before he came to the Packers can be found some of the reasons for his failure in Green Bay, where his four years on the sideline would be marked by almost as much turmoil as had prevailed a decade earlier under Dan Devine. Only this time there was a harder, meaner edge to it.

Gregg's tenure in Cleveland had ended with much of his team in open revolt over his abrasive style. One player called the situation a "pathetic mess." But it was not only the players who were lining up against him. Gregg was also being undermined by the Browns' front office. During a team meeting on the Monday after a 9–0 loss to the Rams on November 28, 1977, Gregg caught player personnel director Bob Nussbaumer hiding in a closet, where he was spying for owner Art Modell. The betrayals from above and below forever changed Gregg. He did well in Cincinnati, where he seemed to have matured as a coach, but what had happened to him in Cleveland left him mistrustful of almost everyone. The word most often used to describe his leadership style in Green Bay was *paranoid*. People in the Packers' front office who had known and liked Gregg as a player were taken aback by how much he had changed.

One of Gregg's first moves as coach of the Packers was to get rid of the players' Thursday Night Club, a weekly get-together for most of the team at a local restaurant. "He wanted to be in control of everyone all the time," says Lynn Dickey, who defiantly reinstituted the tradition after Green Bay started 1-7 in 1984. "What was he going to do? Fine the whole team?" Dickey loved Starr, who he thought was a good coach undone by his having to

be his own director of player personnel. But Dickey did not like Gregg, whom he found to be demeaning, belittling, and mean, a sentiment he says was shared by a large majority of his teammates. "We went from one of the finest men I ever met in my life," says Dickey of the coaching change, "to one of the worst."

Many of Gregg's players may not have liked him, but Green Bay took on his hard-nosed personality all the same. In fact, the new attitude went beyond hard-nosed. The Packers became, for the first and only time in their long history, a dirty team. Under Starr in 1983, Green Bay had been the third-least-penalized team in the NFL. By Gregg's fourth season, in 1987, it was tied for the most penalized team in the league. The Packers committed more than 100 penalties a season every year that Gregg was on the sideline, something that Starr's teams had never done.

Green Bay under Gregg was at its chippiest when playing the Bears. In the mid-1980s, the NFL's oldest rivalry became its most acrimonious, defined by trash talking, cheap shots, fines handed down by the league office, and open animosity between Gregg and Bears coach Mike Ditka. The trouble began during a preseason game in Milwaukee's County Stadium on August 11, 1984, the first time the two had met with Gregg in charge of Green Bay. With the Packers leading 14–3 and with the ball on their side of the 50-yard line, Gregg called a timeout with less than two minutes remaining in the first half. Ditka, who was standing just a few yards from Gregg—teams shared the same sideline at County Stadium, which had to be reconfigured to accommodate football—objected loudly. The two began shouting at each other and eventually had to be separated by their players. "Ditka was trying to get it over with and get to the locker room," Dickey says. "Forrest was trying to win the Super Bowl."

Things only got nastier after that. It didn't help that while the Packers were well into their second decade of misery, the Bears were ascending to

the top of the NFL, on their way to winning Super Bowl XX in January 1986. The Bears were big and brilliant, bullies with an intimidating, dominant defense. Green Bay beat Chicago only once in Gregg's four years, and the Packers' attempts to get mean invariably made them look ineffectual and frustrated. In a 16–10 loss at Lambeau Field on November 3, 1985, safety Ken Stills delivered a forearm to the chin of Bears quarterback Jim McMahon on Chicago's first possession, then drilled fullback Matt Suhey long after the whistle on its third. The NFL fined Stills $500, but Gregg said nothing. Things reached a nadir at Soldier Field on November 23, 1986, when Green Bay defensive end Charles Martin picked up an unsuspecting McMahon from behind and body-slammed him to the turf. Martin, one of several Packers defensive players wearing a white towel on his belt with the numbers of Chicago's offensive players scrawled on it, was thrown out of the game. McMahon was lost for the season with a shoulder injury. The Bears were incensed. Ditka called Green Bay's players "thugs" and "hooligans."

To make matters worse, the bad behavior during Gregg's tenure was not confined to the field. In October 1986, Martin got into an argument with a woman at a Green Bay bar and threw a drink on her. He eventually paid her $500 and apologized. In May 1987, cornerback Mossy Cade went on trial for second-degree sexual assault, charged with having forced a woman (an aunt by marriage) to have sex with him at his home in De Pere.[*] He was convicted and sentenced to two years in prison. (He served 15 months.) To make matters worse, on the same day that Cade's trial began, another Packer went on trial on the same charges. This trial, though, was more damaging to the psyche of the town. The defendant was none other than James Lofton.

On the evening of December 17, 1986, Lofton and a few of his teammates had attended a dinner for receivers coach Tom Coughlin and then gone to the Top Shelf, a downtown Green Bay nightclub on the top floor of a three-story office building. It was at the Top Shelf that Lofton, who was married, with a one-year-old son, met a 30-year-old woman who was visiting town from the Upper Peninsula of Michigan. When the bar closed at 1 a.m., Lofton and the woman took the building's glass elevator to the ground floor, where they entered a stairwell and she performed oral sex on him. He was arrested and jailed the next morning. The collective shock in the city was palpable.

No one disputed the basic facts of what had happened on December 17. At issue was whether the woman had performed fellatio willingly — she said Lofton had forced her to her knees and held her by the hair. The case caused such a sensation in town that Lofton's attorney argued that it would be impossible for him to find an impartial jury in Green Bay. Lofton's trial actually began almost three hours to the south, in Janesville, where a jury was selected. It then moved back to Green Bay, to the Brown County Courthouse, where the trials of Cade and Lofton took place across the hall from each other.

The legal drama was a public relations nightmare for the Packers. In an interview a week after Lofton's arrest, Judge Parins admitted to being "embarrassed." Wisconsin attorney general Dave Hanaway joked that the state had chosen Green Bay as the site for its newest prison so that "the Packers could walk to work." The *Press-Gazette* weighed in at the end of the 1986 season, writing in a December 21 editorial that was headlined NO MORE, "Frankly, the community deserves better than it got from the men who wore the town's colors this year . . . Green Bay's history of support for its football team, its proven willingness to dig deep time and again to rescue

* Cade's attorney was former Brown County district attorney Donald Zuidmulder, whose father, Dave Zuidmulder, had played halfback for Green Bay from 1929 through 1931.

Tackle Forrest Gregg was beloved as a player during the Lombardi era, but when he returned to Green Bay as the Packers' coach in 1984, people in the team's front office were taken aback by how much he seemed to have changed.

the Packers, should not go unnoted by today's players."

Lofton's trial took only four days. On May 22, 1987, he was acquitted by a jury of ten men and two women. The district attorney said that several factors made it difficult to build a case against him, including a lack of physical evidence and inconsistencies in the alleged victim's story. One juror later said, "I don't think it's a case that should have been brought to court because they didn't have enough evidence to convict the guy." But there would be no redemption for Lofton in Green Bay. The Packers had traded him one month earlier to the Oakland Raiders.

"When the fans called, we had no excuse," Bob Harlan, who was then the assistant to Judge Parins, wrote in his 2007 memoirs, *Green and Golden Moments,* about the public outcry over the team's off-the-field problems. "We really had to make a move to let them know that we felt as bad about the situation as they did. We told them that we realized that this was very harmful to the organization, and we were going to deal with it. The whole thing had to be cleaned up, and we started cleaning it up by letting Lofton go."

That may be so, but the Packers had had no such problems keeping Cade on the roster long after he was charged in November 1985. In fact, Gregg never suspended him. Cade played in 14 games that season and started 16 the next, and he lost his spot on the depth chart only after he was convicted in 1987. But Lofton was a star, and that made his problems too big to ignore. He would go on to play seven more years, appearing in three Super Bowls with the Buffalo Bills. In 2003, 10 years after he had played his last game, he was inducted into the Pro Football Hall of Fame. He has since made peace with the Packers, returning to the team in 2018 as a television analyst for preseason games.

But in 1987, Lofton's departure was a bitter pill, and what it meant to the franchise was — in a way that went beyond what was happening on the playing field — more misery, more defeat. One of the brightest stars ever to play for Green Bay, a worthy heir to the legacies of Blood and Hutson and Hornung and one of the few good things about an otherwise miserable era, had had to be banished from the city. The boys-will-be-boys exploits of Packers players had always been tolerated before. But Lofton had been accused of a serious crime, one on another level entirely from a charge of merely being drunk and disorderly or even of driving while intoxicated. It was unprecedented in the history of the franchise. But times were very different, and so was the relationship between team and town.

◆ ◆ ◆

One obvious distinction between Lofton and the hard-partying Packers of yesteryear was that the wide receiver was black. And while there is no way of knowing whether his race had anything to do with the accusations against him — there is no evidence to support such a claim — an uncomfortable consequence of the incident was that the matter of race relations in Green Bay was suddenly a subject of national scrutiny. The issue was not an open wound in the city in 1987, but that had more to do with the fact that blacks were only slightly more prevalent than they had been in the days of Bob Mann. About one in 300 people in Brown County was African American, and the saying went, "If you're a black man in Green Bay, you're either a Packer or you're passing through." Former defensive end Willie Davis, a Hall of Famer from the Lombardi era, told *Sports Illustrated* in 1987 that the biggest problem in Green Bay in terms of race was that the people there simply did not know what they did not know. "A lot of fans will say something to black players without realizing it may have racial overtones," he said.

Outright racism may not have been a problem, but discrimination often had been. Dating back to the 1950s, black players had had trouble finding proper housing in the city. Many landlords would not rent to blacks, and African American players often had to make do with substandard homes

or apartments on the outskirts of town. In 1960, Davis and rookie halfback Paul Winslow shared a dilapidated cabin just off an industrial lot. "You would call, and a guy would tell you he's got an apartment for you, so you'd go to see him," says Dave Robinson, who played linebacker in Green Bay from 1963 through 1972. "If he was nice, he'd say, 'Oh, we just rented it out.' If he wasn't, he'd say, 'We don't rent to blacks.'"

Vince Lombardi had done what he could to assimilate his players into the city, and his team was, for the times, a model franchise in the NFL when it came to race relations. "We make no issue over a man's color," Lombardi told *Sports Illustrated* in 1968. "I just won't tolerate anybody in this organization, coach or player, making it an issue. We respect every man's dignity, black or white." Before the 1960 season he informed Green Bay's tavern and restaurant owners that any place that refused to serve to his black players would be designated off-limits to the rest of his team. "Vince integrated the city of Green Bay," says Robinson. "When I got there, there was no place that would refuse you service."

Lombardi may have made things more tolerable for his black players, but the Packers' success and his own personality had a lot to do with that.

After he left and the team became a laughingstock, there was not much about the city that appealed to young African American men. Bruce Clark, the defensive tackle who spurned the Packers after Green Bay had made him its number-one draft choice in 1980, said that he did not want to come to a place with a small black population where "the city and the team don't have that much to offer." Even Lofton, before his legal troubles, had mentioned that he might want out.

In the fishbowl of Green Bay, the Packers' black players struggled to fit in, to blend in — a problem that was exacerbated in the 1970s and '80s by the team's chronic ineptitude. And in that way, the losing made it tough for every Packers player. There seemed to be no escape from their mediocrity in a town where everyone knew who they were and, more significantly, remembered a time when Green Bay had been Titletown. When Vince Lombardi stepped down as coach in 1968, there had been no reason to think that the winning would not continue. But by the time Forrest Gregg finally resigned in 1988 to become the new coach at Southern Methodist, there was really no reason to think that the Packers were going to stop losing anytime soon.

James Lofton celebrates the Packers' 41–16 victory over the St. Louis Cardinals in the first round of the 1982 playoffs with linebacker Mike Douglass (53) and cornerback Mike McCoy (29). It was Green Bay's first postseason win since Super Bowl II.

CHAPTER 16

RESURRECTION

In a clear-eyed look at the sorry state of the Packers in *Sports Illustrated* in May 1987, eminent sportswriter Frank Deford delivered a harsh verdict on Green Bay's place in the NFL. Noting that the next-smallest U.S. cities with major league sports franchises were Hartford and Salt Lake City—and that the metropolitan areas of both were almost six times the size of Green Bay's—Deford said that the Packers should be sold "to Milwaukee for $60 million or whatever," and that the proceeds from the sale should go to the athletic department at the University of Wisconsin-Green Bay. "With that kind of financing, UWGB could bring in recruits from everywhere to play on Lambeau Field, plus build a 20,000-seat basketball arena," Deford wrote. "So, in one fell swoop, Green Bay could trade a lousy football franchise for a first-class basketball and football program."

That was never going to happen, of course, because, as Deford himself acknowledged, all proceeds from a sale would, by law, have to go to the Sullivan-Wallen American Legion Post. There was also the matter of the city selling off its birthright, divesting itself of the very thing that had made it famous. Without the Packers, went the saying, Green Bay was just "Oshkosh with a few more people." The Packers might have been lousy, but they were still inextricably bound to the place that had created them. No amount of losing was going to change that. *Press-Gazette* columnist Don Langenkamp called Deford's proposal "ridiculous."

But some sort of reckoning was due, and nobody knew that better than Bob Harlan. The assistant to team president Robert Parins, Harlan had been with the Packers since 1971, when Dan

Devine hired him to be the assistant general manager. The sandy-haired and genially pleasant Harlan had served in a variety of capacities in several departments in the organization, including ticket sales, public relations, and contract negotiations. He'd had an up-close view of nearly two decades of futility. "We were a stairway just going down," he says of the franchise. "We just kept getting a little worse, and a little worse. And we've got a fan base that is very loyal, very loyal. Fans would call me and say, 'Bob, do you think the league's getting too big for us? Is Green Bay just too small to compete?'"

Even in their darkest days, the Packers had almost always turned a profit—the strike-shortened 1982 season was the first time since 1951 that the team had actually ended a year in the red

—not only because of the money they received from the NFL's television contracts but also because they were notoriously parsimonious when it came to their payroll. Much of the responsibility for that, at least in the mid- to late 1970s, rested with Starr, who had played in an era when players for the most part took what Vince Lombardi offered. Starr frequently held a hard line on contracts, which cost the Packers when other teams were willing to be more generous. Exhibit A for this sort of shortsightedness was the loss of linebacker Ted Hendricks after the 1975 season.

But Starr's problems went beyond being an unreasonable negotiator. Five years after he had lost Hendricks came the botched drafting of Penn State defensive tackle Bruce Clark, whom Nittany Lions coach Joe Paterno had called the most dominant player he'd ever coached. The Packers took Clark with the number-four pick because they wanted him to play nose tackle, something the six-foot-three, 273-pound Clark—who had played the nose in only five games in Happy Valley—was not itching to do. Clark never said no to Green Bay's proposal, but he also intimated that he might sign with a CFL team rather than play for the Packers. Starr was not savvy enough to take that threat seriously, nor does he appear to have ever understood that Clark may not have rejected the notion of playing nose tackle before the draft because of the possibility that it might cost him money. One month after Green Bay had selected him, Clark signed with the Toronto Argonauts.

The incompetence continued after Parins hired Forrest Gregg in December 1983. And beginning soon after the conclusion of the 1984 season, Green Bay became even stingier with player contracts, eliminating all signing and roster bonuses for veterans. From 1981 to 1984, player costs for the Packers had gone up 120 percent, but from 1984 to 1985, the increase was just 2 percent. It was no coincidence that the team reported a record profit of $2,029,154 for fiscal 1985. "We have found a way to get our player costs in line," Parins said. But the Packers paid the price on the field for all the money they were saving in the front office. In 1986 they unceremoniously released a half dozen veterans—and their salaries—before the season, including quarterback Lynn Dickey, tight end Paul Coffman, outside linebacker Mike Douglass, defensive end Mike Butler, and tackle Greg Koch. In their place, Green Bay turned to younger, less experienced players and lost six straight games to start the season. The Packers recovered a bit in the final 10 games to finish 4-12, but their record in 1986 was still the worst since the year before Vince Lombardi had come to town.

Harlan, the man who had negotiated many of the contracts for the departed veterans, knew the situation was getting bleak. "The way we were doing business, we were never going to succeed," he says. "It was just so obvious."

Harlan had been sharp enough to recognize one hopeful sign. In 1985, the Packers became one of the last teams in the NFL to put private "luxury" boxes in their stadium. Before the season, at a cost of $5 million, Green Bay installed 72 private boxes—28 on the west side and 44 on the east—in Lambeau Field. Leases went for $10,000 to $15,000, and Parins put Harlan in charge of selling them. "We were stunned at how fast the boxes went," Harlan later said.

Part of the team's record 1985 profit—$741,000 of it, to be exact—came from its leasing of luxury boxes. Credit for that has to go to Parins. For all his shortcomings as a football man—starting with his failure to hire a general manager when he was elected, and then not going far enough in 1987 when he hired Tom Braatz to be executive vice president of football operations without giving him full authority—Parins also oversaw an era during which Green Bay became rich beyond anything it had ever experienced before, making more than $1 million every year but one, while also stashing away a sizable cash reserve. The Packers had $22.8 million in assets in 1982; by 1989 they had $32.5 million. Parins had grown

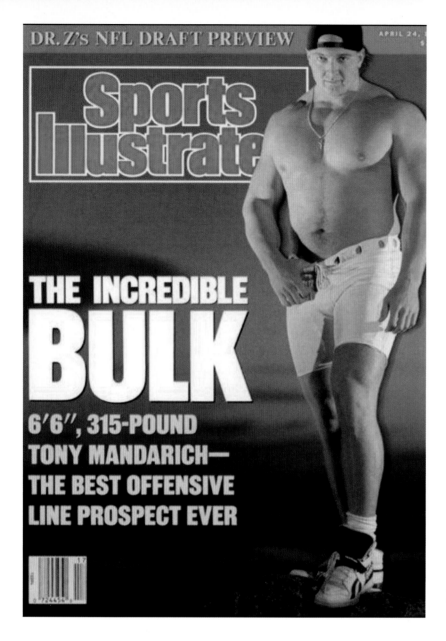

APRIL 24,

Sports Illustrate

THE INCREDIBLE BULK

6'6", 315-POUND TONY MANDARICH— THE BEST OFFENSIVE LINE PROSPECT EVER

The Packers made Tony Mandarich—the most hyped offensive line prospect in NFL history—the number-two pick in the 1989 draft. But he played only three seasons in Green Bay. The team did not renew his contract in February 1993.

up in an era when the franchise always seemed to be on the brink of ruin, and he never stopped running it as though another Great Depression might be right around the corner.

He also saw something special in Bob Harlan, and for that every Packers fan owes him a debt of gratitude.

◆ ◆ ◆

Bob Harlan succeeded Parins as team president on June 5, 1989, after a unanimous vote of the board of directors. In a lot of ways, Harlan was a logical choice, having held positions of responsibility throughout the organization and often serving as its public face. He was popular with fans and

the media, in part because he used to go out of his way to make himself available to both groups—it was his personal policy to, whenever possible, take all of his own telephone calls without any sort of screening. Harlan was not a native of the city, but he had been with the Packers for 18 years and had actually lived in Green Bay longer than Andrew Turnbull had when he became the first president in team history, in 1923. Most important, Harlan was Parins's first choice as a successor because he had the sort of experience that Parins himself had lacked when he ascended to the presidency in 1982. "Bob Harlan," Parins said, "is the consummate football executive."

The son of a trucking company owner from Des Moines, Iowa, Harlan was born in 1936, the year the Packers won their fourth NFL championship. He first became a fan of the team in the 1950s, when he was a journalism major at Marquette and the sports editor of the student newspaper. After a six-month stint in the Army following his graduation in 1958, he took a job as a reporter for United Press International in Milwaukee. But after only a few months, he went back to his alma mater to be the sports information director. After the school dropped football following the 1960 season, Harlan became primarily the public relations contact for the basketball team. In 1964, his final year at Marquette, the 28-year-old Harlan worked closely with the Warriors' new coach, Al McGuire. It was an odd match—the guileless kid from Iowa and the streetwise New Yorker—but even though Marquette went 8-18, Harlan was enthralled. The relentlessly positive McGuire used to advise him, "Bob, always tell people what they want to hear," and Harlan took it to heart. From McGuire he learned lessons about dealing with all sorts of different characters—and he got an up-close look at how to be the public face of a work in progress.

"It was like *Guys and Dolls* working for Al," Harlan says. "He just did unbelievable stuff. I was with him in his office one day when he called this big business executive in town. The guy's secretary answers and asks who's calling, and Al says, 'This is Mayor [Henry W.] Maier.' She put the call through right away, and then when the guy gets on the phone and says, 'Hello, Mr. Mayor,' Al interrupts him and says, "It's not Mayor Maier, it's Al McGuire. I knew if I said it was Al McGuire that I wouldn't get a chance to talk to you.' And then he says, 'I need a private jet to go recruiting this weekend and I need your help.' Al did stuff like that all the time."

In 1965, Harlan left Marquette for Major League Baseball, taking over as the director of community relations for the St. Louis Cardinals. In St. Louis, he not only had a front-row seat during Bob Gibson's heyday and the run to the 1967 pennant, but he also got a behind-the-scenes look at how a first-class organization was run. His job was, as he puts it, to make speaking appearances — as many as 250 a year — which gave him plenty of opportunities to follow McGuire's advice and tell people what they wanted to hear. The Cardinals promoted him to public relations director in 1968, and he was working in that capacity three years later when Devine tabbed him to be the assistant general manager in Green Bay. Harlan did not so much work his way up from the bottom of the organization as he did through and around it, seeing the Packers from all different angles and sides. By the time he was elected president in 1989, nobody in the organization knew the team better.

Harlan's first year in charge of the Packers was a memorable one. Under second-year coach Lindy Infante, the former offensive coordinator of the Cleveland Browns, Green Bay went 10-6 and nearly made the playoffs. The season was highlighted by two things: the emergence of third-year quarterback Don Majkowski and a thrilling victory over the Bears at Lambeau Field. Majkowski, an athletic six-foot-two 10th-round draft choice out of Virginia who sported a blond mullet that flowed out the back of his helmet, went by (and encouraged the use of) the nickname "Majik Man." His arm was not the strongest, but he played with fear-

less abandon. He threw for 27 touchdowns, led the NFL with 4,318 passing yards, was the runner-up for the league's Most Valuable Player award, and was the catalyst in a high-wire act of a season. Green Bay won one game by three points, another by two, and four more by a single point, including a cathartic 14–13 defeat of Chicago on November 5 that was the Packers' first victory in the series since 1984. Trailing 13–7 late in the fourth quarter, Majkowski drove Green Bay 73 yards in 13 plays to the Bears' 14-yard line. On fourth-and-goal with 41 seconds left, he scrambled to his right and threw across his body to wide receiver Sterling Sharpe, who had gotten open in the middle of the end zone. Officials initially threw a flag on the play, ruling that the pass was not a touchdown because Majkowski had crossed the line of scrimmage before he released the ball. But after a lengthy replay review, they overturned the call. Lambeau Field shook. Harlan rewarded Infante with a two-year contract extension in January 1990.

But 1989 had been a mirage. There is a lot of luck involved in winning so many close games, and the Packers seemed to have used up all of theirs in one season. The next year, Majkowski struggled with a

The two men who started the turnaround in Green Bay, Ron Wolf (left) and president Bob Harlan, on November 27, 1991, the day Harlan introduced Wolf as the Packers' new general manager and gave him total control of the team.

torn rotator cuff and Green Bay slid back to 6-10, and then to 4-12 in 1991. Majkowski started just 16 of those 32 games. Among the quarterbacks who started in his place was Anthony Dilweg, a grandson of Lavvie Dilweg, the Packers' star end of the 1920s.

The problems went beyond depth at quarterback. The team lacked talent at almost every position. Wide receiver Sterling Sharpe was the only Packer sent to the Pro Bowl in 1990, and the next year the team had no representatives in the game. Not only was the football bad, but the organization's prestige took a sizable hit when, to great fanfare, Braatz selected hulking Michigan State tackle Tony Mandarich with the second pick in the 1989 draft. Dubbed THE INCREDIBLE BULK on the cover of *Sports Illustrated,* which called him "the best offensive line prospect ever," the brash six-foot-six, 315-pound Mandarich was considered a can't-miss selection. He bench-pressed 545 pounds and ran a 4.65 40-yard dash. Rumors that he was a creation of performance-enhancing drugs went unheeded, as did some telltale warning signs that went along with his 22-inch biceps: he had acne on his back, he was going prematurely bald, and both his frame and his feet seemed too small for all the muscle they were supporting. More telling, when Mandarich finally reported after holding out until five days before Green Bay's opener—he signed a four-year, $4.4 million contract—he was 15 to 20 pounds lighter than he had been at the NFL scouting combine a few months earlier. Mandarich denied taking steroids and insisted that he had lost the weight not because of the NFL's random drug-testing rules but because he wanted to be more nimble for all the pass blocking he was going to have to do.

Mandarich never failed a drug test in the NFL. His real problem was an inability to handle the pro game. His run blocking was serviceable, but he lacked the skills necessary to protect the pocket for a quarterback. He rarely saw the field as a rookie except on special teams, and then alternated between incompetent and average as a starter in 1990 and '91. If he had been drafted in the fifth or sixth round, nobody would have noticed, but Green Bay had taken him at number two.* "Michigan State had been a straight-ahead power team, and that's what kind of player Mandarich was," former Packers scout Charley Armey, who had left Green Bay two years before Mandarich was drafted, said in 1994. "He couldn't go side to side, but you couldn't see that until he was asked to do it. If he had played at Brigham Young, you would have known."

In a desultory 31–0 road loss to the Eagles on December 16, 1990, six-foot-five, 291-pound Philadelphia defensive end Reggie White treated Mandarich like a tackling dummy, getting one and a half sacks, six knockdowns, two tackles, two pass knockdowns, and a forced fumble. "I can't believe how Reggie was throwing Mandarich around," Eagles nose tackle Mike Golic said after the game. "It was amazing. They're basically the same size and Reggie treated him like a toy. I'd start to rush, and I had to watch to keep from tripping over Mandarich. We didn't know where to go because we didn't know where Reggie would throw this guy."

Bears defensive end Dan Hampton was blunt. "Mandarich was all a facade," he told *Sports Illustrated* in 1992. "The Packers got the prize, unwrapped it and saw that he wasn't the same—physically and emotionally—as what they had seen in college. He's pathetic."

On November 20, 1991, at a 7:30 a.m. meeting of the seven-man executive committee, Harlan finally went against the life advice he had been given years before by Al McGuire—he told people something they might not want to hear. Harlan said that he wanted to fire Braatz and bring

---

* *Mandarich played six years in the NFL, for the Packers and the Indianapolis Colts, starting 63 of the 72 games in which he played after his rookie season. In 2008 he admitted to having used anabolic steroids while at Michigan State and said that he had been addicted to alcohol and painkillers when he was playing in Green Bay.*

in a general manager to run the team on his own. The new general manager would answer to the president and to nobody else — not to the executive committee and not to the 45 members of the board of directors. "It simply had to be done," says Harlan. "I said, 'I want permission to hire a full-time, strong football person and give him total authority over the operation.' Tom Braatz had a 50-50 relationship with Lindy Infante. They both had a 50-50 say, and if they couldn't come to a conclusion, then it went to the president. And I said, 'The president isn't capable of making a football decision. You know?' And that's why I wanted a football guy."

After a two-and-a-half-hour meeting, the executive committee unanimously approved Harlan's proposal. The only real resistance he met in selling the committee on his plan was that one member wanted to use a search committee to find the new general manager. Harlan insisted that a search committee would take too much time. "I wanted to hire someone during the season, have him come in and go to practice and be in the locker room, be on the airplanes, be around the coaches, and then come and tell me, 'This is what's wrong with your team,'" says Harlan. One hour later he called Braatz, who was on a scouting trip in Bloomington, Indiana, and informed him that he was out of a job. At 3 p.m., Harlan met the media and announced the change. He said he had not chosen a successor for Braatz. "I would like to have him have a chance to see the team and see the team practice, and have some thoughts on the makeup of this ballclub prior to the draft."

In truth, he had only one man in mind for the job.

◆ ◆ ◆

Bob Harlan had met Ron Wolf before. In January 1987, when Wolf was the personnel director of the Oakland Raiders, he had visited Green Bay to in-

The highlight of the Packers' 10–6 season in 1989 came when quarterback Don Majkowski led Green Bay to a last-minute 14–13 defeat of the Bears at Lambeau Field.

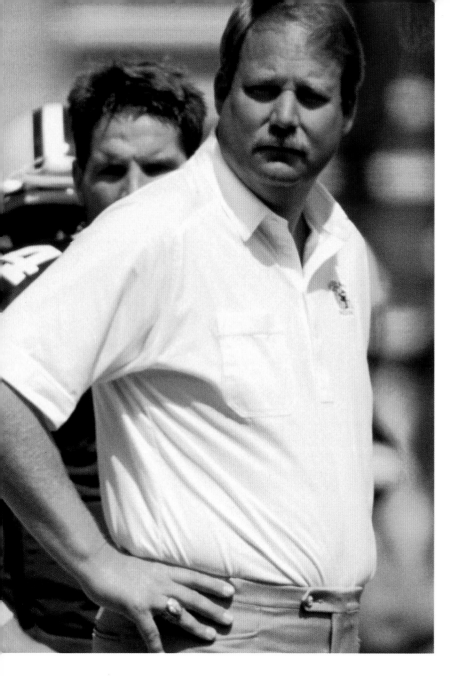

Mike Holmgren had been the quarterbacks coach and offensive coordinator of the San Francisco 49ers for six years when Ron Wolf hired him to be the new coach of the Packers on January 10, 1992.

of college prospects. Wolf was curious about the structure of the Packers' front office, about how Parins fit into the executive committee and how the committee fit into the board of directors. Harlan came away from the meeting impressed by Wolf's organization and attention to detail.

After Wolf interviewed with Judge Parins on Monday morning, Harlan drove him back to the airport. The two did not discuss the meeting, and the next time Harlan heard from Wolf was later the same day when Wolf called to withdraw his name from consideration. Parins was not ready to give someone full control over the Packers. "There was no clear line of authority, and I didn't know how I would make that work," says Wolf, who hides his piercing gaze behind grandfatherly spectacles that belie his shrewd nature. "So when I discovered that—I wasn't going to become a part of that."

That power-sharing setups do not work in the NFL was one of the many lessons that Ron Wolf had learned in 28 years in pro football. The oldest of two sons of a plastics engineer, Wolf was born in 1938 in New Freedom, Pennsylvania, 30 miles north of Baltimore, on the Mason-Dixon line. Unsure of what he wanted to do in life, he enlisted in the Army after graduating from Susquehannock High and spent three years in the service. He was stationed in Berlin, where he was a sergeant in the intelligence office of the U.S. commander. Wolf had known from early on in his time in the Army that a military career was not in his future, but he was impressed by all the smart people with whom he worked in Berlin. He decided then that if he was ever going to get ahead in the world, he needed to go to college. When he returned to the United States he enrolled at Maryville College, a small Presbyterian school near Knoxville, Tennessee, because, he said, "I didn't have to take an entrance exam." He stayed at Maryville for 18 months before transferring to Oklahoma.

Wolf had been fascinated with pro football ever since his first brush with the game, which came in

terview for the job that eventually went to Tom Braatz. Wolf flew into Austin Straubel Field at about 9 p.m. on a cold Sunday night, and Harlan, who was then the assistant to Packers president Robert Parins, picked him up to take him to his hotel. But before they left the airport, Wolf told Harlan that he had not had a chance to get dinner. There was not much open, so Harlan took him to a Denny's on South Oneida Street, two miles south of Lambeau Field. For three hours the two men ate hamburgers and talked football. Harlan wanted to know how Wolf scouted the draft and kept track

1948 courtesy of the Baltimore Colts of the AAFC.[*] While stationed in Berlin, he sent letters to all 12 NFL teams looking for a job. He kept up his letter-writing campaign after his return to the States — and after the AFL formed, in 1959, he had eight more teams to write to. But nobody was interested in a guy with no experience and no connections in the game. "It was," Wolf told the *Milwaukee Journal Sentinel* in 2015, "a closed-door society."

At the same time that he was reaching out to teams in both leagues, Wolf was also corresponding with Ted Elbert, one of the editors of *Pro Football Illustrated,* a weekly publication based in Chicago. In his letters to Elbert, Wolf would point out mistakes and make corrections, and in 1962 Elbert offered him a job. Wolf left Norman and moved to Chicago. At *Pro Football Illustrated* he wrote a few stories and did some editing, but, more important, he also began making contacts throughout the league. He attended a College All-Star Game, an NFL draft, and a few league meetings. He also displayed an amazing capacity for recall, something for which he would become renowned during his long career. But *Pro Football Illustrated* folded after he had been there for six months, and Wolf returned to Oklahoma.

And that was where his career in the game might have ended. But in the spring of 1963, he got a call from the AFL's Oakland Raiders. Al Davis, the Raiders' coach and general manager, had mentioned to Elbert that he needed somebody who knew names for his talent department. Elbert told him that Wolf had an amazing memory and would be perfect for the job. Davis hired him on a trial basis, and Wolf, a history major, left Oklahoma without graduating.

In Oakland, Wolf worked closely with Davis and sat in on every scouting meeting. "There were only eight teams, so you are talking about 264 players — that was it," Wolf says. (The AFL roster limit was 33 in 1963.) "We stayed every night for three hours. Al would go through each position with the coaching staff — which consisted of four people, by the way. We'd watch all the left tackles one night, all the left guards the next, all the right corners, all the left corners, and you could see who was a good player and who wasn't a good player. And that's how I learned."

Wolf matured into one of Davis's most trusted lieutenants, rising to the position of personnel director. He was a road-warrior scout who kept files on — and remembered significant details about — thousands of college football players. And he had a hand in drafting some of the best players on the great Raiders teams of the 1960s and '70s. With Wolf and Davis working together and sticking to Davis's mantra of "size and speed," Oakland not only made excellent first-round draft picks, including cornerback Jack Tatum and tight end Raymond Chester, both Pro Bowlers, but also found such gems in the lower rounds as fullback Marv Hubbard (11th, 1968) and defensive end Horace Jones (12th, 1971). Additionally, Wolf was in on the drafting of Hall of Fame punter Ray Guy in the first round of the 1973 draft.[**] Such a mystique began to build around Wolf, who was widely reputed to have a photographic memory, that his stint with Army intelligence in Berlin in the 1950s became the source of rumors that he had once been a Cold War spy. When the expansion Tampa Bay Buccaneers hired him to be their vice president of operations on April 30, 1975, he was the youngest chief executive of a team in the NFL.

But in Tampa, Wolf learned that titles mean something. He was not the Buccaneers' general manager, with total authority over the football operations of the team. Tampa Bay owner Hugh Culverhouse, who had told Wolf that he could work

---

[*] *The Colts were coached by former Packers halfback Cecil Isbell in 1948.*

[**] *Wolf was not right about every player. In the second round of the 1968 draft, he preferred Heisman Trophy–winning quarterback Gary Beban to the passer the Raiders picked instead: Alabama's Ken Stabler. Beban appeared in five NFL games without ever making a start. Stabler is in the Pro Football Hall of Fame.*

his way up to being general manager, hired USC's John McKay as his coach. McKay was 52, Culverhouse was 56. They had both served in the military in World War II. They played golf together. Wolf was 36 and did not play golf. And he could only watch as McKay's authority over football operations grew while his own was diminishing. The Buccaneers went a combined 2-26 in 1976 and '77, and when the time came for somebody to lose his job, it was Wolf who got the ax, not McKay. Wolf resigned rather than be fired in 1978 because, he wrote years later, "Culverhouse felt McKay knew more than I did about player personnel, my area of expertise."

Culverhouse replaced Wolf with three men, including Dick Beam, a former assistant on McKay's staff at USC, who had come to Tampa Bay in 1975 as the coach's administrative assistant. Beam, whom Wolf refers to as McKay's "driver," took over all administrative duties. It was insult atop indignity.

Wolf returned to Oakland as personnel director and was successful once again, helping the Raiders build Super Bowl winners in 1980 and '83. And when the Packers came calling with their 50-50 offer in 1987, he knew better than to take it. Outside of Judge Parins, who was not a football man, nobody was in charge in Green Bay. "I had been through that before," Wolf says. "I wasn't going to do it again." Wolf stayed in Oakland until 1990, when he moved on — seeking a change of scenery and having reached, as he told the *Milwaukee Journal Sentinel* in 2015, "an impasse" with Davis — to become the personnel director of the New York Jets under general manager Dick Steinberg.

It was when he was with the Jets that the 53-year-old Wolf began to think that the chance to run his own team had probably passed him by. Who exactly was going to hire the guy who had built the worst expansion team in the history of the NFL, anyway? The New York gig felt like it might be his last. He and his wife, Edie, bought a house on Long Island and, with their two young sons, prepared to settle in. But they had been in their new home in Garden City for only four months when Bob Harlan called. And the job that Harlan was offering was very different from the one that Wolf had interviewed for in 1987. Harlan offered Wolf total control of the Packers, with no interference. They came to an agreement on Saturday, November 23, 1991, and four days later Harlan introduced Wolf as Green Bay's new general manager.

When Wolf spoke about his new job to his friends in the NFL, they told him that he was heading into a dead end, to pro football's Siberia. But when Wolf told Davis about the job, his old mentor summed up the arrangement perfectly. "With the power you have," Davis told Wolf, "you're like an owner." An owner of a 3-9 team, true. There was a lot of work to do. But work was always what Ron Wolf had done best.

◆ ◆ ◆

Not long after Harlan had hired him, Wolf got a firsthand look at how far the team had fallen even in its own hometown. He was trying to buy some Packers-themed gifts to send home to his boys, Jonathan and Eliot, who were ten and nine, respectively, but he had a hard time finding any. Just about all he saw, in store after store, was NCAA merchandise, mostly Notre Dame and Wisconsin gear. Baseball hats, stocking caps, jerseys, jackets, footballs, pom-poms, pennants, coffee mugs, plastic cups — no matter what it was, almost none of it came in green and gold or was emblazoned with a G in the shape of a football. Everything seemed to be blue and gold or red and white. "And I thought, *Gee whiz, this is amazing,*" says Wolf.

But if the team's existence was being ignored by the local populace, it was absolutely being taken for granted inside Lambeau Field. The 59,543-seat stadium may have always been sold out on Sundays — Lambeau's sellout streak dates all the way back to 1960 — but there had been almost 29,000 no-shows at the season's last two home games in 1991. And from what Wolf could tell, nobody —

from the players on the field to the people in the front office — was really all that upset about it. He attended his first practice a few days after Green Bay had lost 35–31 to the Falcons in Atlanta on December 1 to fall to 3-10. He then went up to Harlan's Lambeau Field office, sat down, and said, "We got a problem on your practice field. It's like a country club down there. This club is 3-10 and they are walking around like they are 10-3. We are going to make a change."

There were other telling moments. Not long after he was hired, Wolf brought in a few free agents who he thought could help the team. But Infante responded by telling Wolf that he was fine with the roster as it was. That sort of thinking, to Wolf,

characterized the entire organization. Green Bay finished 4-12 in 1991, and as far as the general manager could tell, nobody was angry. "The prevailing atmosphere was, inconceivably, as pleasant as could be," Wolf later wrote in his 1998 management guide, *The Packer Way: Nine Stepping Stones to Building a Winning Organization*. "No one really seemed concerned. No one really reflected a sense of urgency."

On Sunday, December 22, one day after the Packers had beaten the Vikings 27–7 in the last game of the season, Wolf fired Infante and initiated a search for a new coach. He had two candidates in mind: Bill Parcells, who had been out of coaching since 1990 but was still one of the most respected men in the game, and Mike Holmgren, the 43-year-old offensive coordinator of the San Francisco 49ers. Holmgren was, at the time, the hottest coaching prospect in the league. Not only was he the architect of the best offense in the NFL, but he had also shown that he could do something with nothing. In 1986, when Joe Montana missed eight games with a back injury, Holmgren had helped the 49ers go 4-3-1 with undistinguished quarterbacks Jeff Kemp and Mike Moroski under center. "I was really impressed with that," said Wolf.

Parcells, as it turned out, was not yet ready to return to the sidelines. While he wavered, Wolf pursued Holmgren, a six-foot-five bear of a man whose physical presence was only slightly less imposing than his personality, which was forceful and commanding. Wolf was enamored with Holmgren's passing-game pedigree—a former backup quarterback at USC, he had been the offensive coordinator for LaVell Edwards at BYU from 1982 to '85 before going to work for Bill Walsh in San Francisco. Wolf offered Holmgren a five-year contract worth $2.5 million and promised him that if he took the job he would report only to Wolf. When the two agreed on the deal, Wolf told Holmgren, "We're the only two people in America who can mess this up." On January 10, 1992, just 19 days after he had fired Infante, Wolf hired Holmgren as the 11th coach in the history of the Green Bay Packers.

◆ ◆ ◆

Four days before Ron Wolf's first official day on the job, on Sunday, December 1, 1991, he had met Bob Harlan at Atlanta–Fulton County Stadium, where the Packers were getting ready to play the Falcons. About one hour before kickoff, Harlan was sitting in the press box when Wolf came in, sat down next to him, and told him he was going to head down to the field to see Atlanta's third-string quarterback. Before he left, Wolf told Harlan that the kid had had a great arm in college. Harlan did a quick scan of the Falcons' roster, stopping at the name

Brett Favre. *Brett FAV-ray,* Harlan thought to himself. *Who the heck is that?*

Wolf was in a hurry to get to the field because he had been told by his friend Ken Herock, Atlanta's vice president of player personnel, that if he wanted to see Favre throw, it would have to be before the rest of the team came out onto the field. Once the team came out, Herock said, Falcons coach Jerry Glanville would not let Favre participate. Wolf and Herock were old colleagues. When Wolf was the personnel director of the Raiders in the early 1970s, Herock had been his chief scout. And Wolf knew exactly how to read into Herock's advice. "What it told me was, *I've got a chance to get Brett Favre,*" says Wolf.

The Packers' new general manager had been a fan of Favre's ever since the quarterback's days at Southern Mississippi. Wolf had first seen the fearless, rocket-armed kid on tape in the fall of 1990 while he was at Southern Miss on a scouting trip for the Jets. He was finishing up his research when Thamas Coleman, the Golden Eagles' former defensive coordinator—who was then working as an administrative assistant in the athletic department—told him something that made him pause: "You should watch tapes of him when he was a junior and wasn't banged up."

Favre had been seriously injured in a car accident on the evening of July 14, 1990, when he lost control of his speeding Nissan Maxima on a dark road near his home in Kiln, Mississippi. The car flipped several times, hit a telephone pole, and came to rest on its side. In addition to suffering a concussion, lacerations, and cracked vertebrae, Favre had also been injured internally. On August 8, surgeons removed 30 inches of his small intestine.

All the tape that Wolf had watched had been from Favre's senior season. The six-foot-two quarterback missed the Golden Eagles' September 1 opener, a 12–0 defeat of Division II Delta State, and then returned the next week to lead Southern Miss to a 27–24 upset of number 13 Alabama. But he was 30 pounds below his normal playing weight of about 215. On the quarterback's junior-year tape, Wolf saw a stronger, more robust version of Favre, who Wolf became convinced deserved consideration as one of the best quarterbacks in the 1991 NFL draft—worth at least a second-round pick. The next time Wolf saw Favre was in January 1991 at the East-West Shrine Game, in Palo Alto, California. Favre looked even better by then. Wolf flew home certain that Favre was the best player in the draft. Dick Steinberg had been in Palo Alto, too, and he agreed.

But Wolf and his boss never got the chance to draft Favre. The Jets had no first-round selection, having given it up for the number-one pick in the 1990 supplemental draft, when they took Syracuse receiver Rob Moore. Steinberg tried unsuccessfully to trade up into the first round. And then he and Wolf watched helplessly as the Falcons selected Favre with the fifth pick in the second round—one spot before New York's turn. The Jets took Louisville quarterback Browning Nagle instead. Wolf was a veteran of 28 pro football drafts by that point. He was used to filing away his disappointments and moving on. But Favre was an exception. Wolf was convinced that he was a winner, a difference maker. And he resolved that if he ever had a chance to run another team, he was going to pursue Brett Favre to be his quarterback.

Wolf never made it to the field that day in Atlanta. The Packers' new general manager was waylaid by TV reporters from Green Bay and Milwaukee. But he already knew all he really needed to know. When he returned to the press box about 30 minutes later, he sat down next to Harlan and said, "Bob, we're going to make a trade for Brett Favre."

⋄ ⋄ ⋄

More than a few of Green Bay's all-time great players have come from the South. Don Hutson was from Pine Bluff, Arkansas. Paul Hornung was from Louisville, Kentucky. Bart Starr was from Montgomery, Alabama. Willie Davis and Forrest Gregg were both Texans. The Packers may have been a local operation for much of their history, but their reach had been national for a very long time.

Brett Lorenzo Favre fit neatly into Green Bay's southern tradition. Born on October 10, 1969, in Gulfport, Mississippi, he grew up along the Gulf of Mexico in Hancock County, in an area situated between the small towns of Kiln and Diamondhead. His father, Irvin, was the football and baseball coach at Hancock North Central High, where his mother, Bonita, was a special education teacher. Irvin and Bonita raised Brett and his two brothers and one sister in a two-bedroom, one-bathroom house on a dead-end dirt road that terminates on the banks of a backwater called Rotten Bayou. The road was named for Irvin in the early 1980s, but the sign was misspelled: IRVIN FARVE. Irvin was well known in the area—he had turned the North Central football program into a modestly successful one—but it would be up to his second son to make his surname world-famous. By the time Brett was finished in the NFL, nobody would ever misspell the family name again.

Favre was a coach's kid, and his childhood days were filled with youth sports and rough-and-tumble games of all kinds in the yard with his brothers. The Favre house had a deck that extended over the waters of the bayou, which was home to several alligators. Favre had four dogs when he was growing up, and the gators got them all. He enjoyed a fine career playing for his father at Hancock North Central High, but Brett was a passing quarterback in an option offense—he averaged only seven passes a game operating out of the wing T—and was lightly recruited as a college prospect. "Three days before the signing date, I was going to either Pearl River Junior College or Delta State," he told *Sports Illustrated* in 1993. "Southern Miss took me as a defensive back. When I went there as a freshman I worked out both ways at first."

Favre may have been third on the depth chart at the beginning of his freshman season in 1990, but it was not long before he was starting. Against

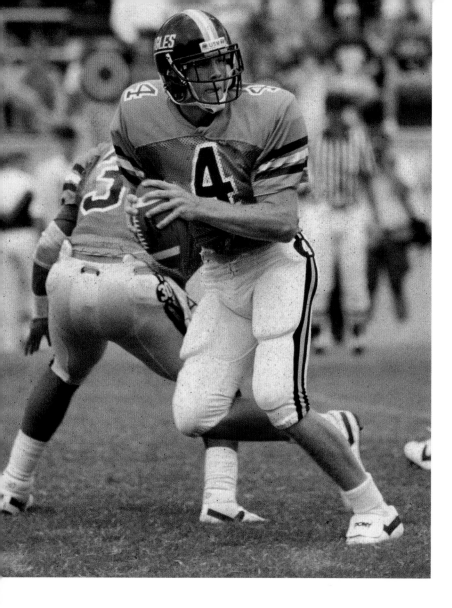

Favre was a winner at Southern Miss, but he flew under the radar of NFL scouts in part because of injuries he suffered in an auto accident the summer before his senior season in 1990.

cons for three years and $1.2 million—and then began running afoul of coach Jerry Glanville at every turn. Glanville and Ken Herock did not get along, and according to Herock, he had had to fight just to draft Favre because Glanville preferred Browning Nagle. "[Glanville] was clearly pissed," Herock told author Jeff Pearlman in the former *Sports Illustrated* writer's rollicking 2016 biography of Favre, *Gunslinger.* "And I think he harbored that resentment for Brett far beyond the draft." Once Favre was on the roster, Herock could not help him—and, by most accounts, the hard-partying Favre needed help. Glanville did not care for his young quarterback's attitude or his professionalism. Among other transgressions, a hungover Favre missed the team photo.

On August 31, Herock traded a fourth-round pick to the Chargers for journeyman quarterback Billy Joe Tolliver. Herock's understanding was that Tolliver would be third string behind Favre and chronically fragile starter Chris Miller. But after two weeks, Glanville made Tolliver his number two. Favre played a grand total of eight snaps that season and threw two interceptions, one of which was returned for a touchdown. Glanville's take on Favre was that the kid just did not care. By the time the Falcons played the Packers in December, Favre was buried further down on the depth chart than he ever had been as a callow freshman at Southern Miss. After the season was over, Herock and Glanville agreed to trade Favre away. Herock promptly called Wolf.

On February 11, Wolf traded for his quarterback, sending the 17th pick in the first round of the 1992 NFL draft to Atlanta for Favre. The Packers had an extra first-round selection that year because they had traded down with the Eagles in the 1991 draft. Wolf and Holmgren explained to reporters that the trade was a good deal because they still had the number-five selection, and because they had planned on using one of their first-round choices to take a quarterback anyway. Green Bay was also getting Favre on the cheap.

Tulane in the second game of the season, he came off the bench in the second half with the Golden Eagles trailing 16–10 and threw two touchdown passes to lead Southern Miss to a 31–24 victory. Three weeks later, on his 18th birthday, he started against sixth-ranked Florida State in Tallahassee. The Seminoles trounced Favre and the Golden Eagles 61–10, but by then he was already entrenched as the number one. Favre started every game until his car accident sidelined him for the opener of his senior season. Southern Miss was a second-tier Division I-A team, but in Favre's four years under center, the Golden Eagles went 30-17 and beat three ranked teams, including number-six Florida State in the first game of his junior year.

After the 1991 draft, Favre signed with the Fal-

The Packers were taking over the final two years of his rookie deal, which paid him a base salary of $260,000 in 1991. By contrast, Seattle Seahawks quarterback Dan McGwire, the 16th pick in the 1991 draft, earned $400,000 as a rookie. Holmgren also went one step beyond the practical explanations for why Favre was worth the risk. "When you get a chance to get a quarterback that you think is a great one, you do it," he said.

The reaction of the team's fans was decidedly less optimistic. Loyalists who had watched helplessly for years as the Packers bungled their draft choices and got taken to the cleaners on the trade market were not happy with the decision to surrender a first-round pick for a complete unknown. "Some of the worst mail I ever got was when Ron made the trade for Favre," says Harlan. "It took guts for Ron to make that move."

◆ ◆ ◆

The Cincinnati Bengals are not traditional rivals of the Green Bay Packers. Green Bay's history stretches all the way back to the predawn of the NFL; Cincinnati's goes back to 1968. A rivalry might have made sense geographically — the driving distance between Green Bay and Cincinnati is about the same as it is between Green Bay and Detroit — but the two teams play in different conferences and rarely encounter each other. Indeed, before they met at Lambeau Field at one o'clock on a sunny 53-degree afternoon on September 20, 1992, they had played each other in the regular season a grand total of six times in 34 years. There was nothing at all special about their week-three matchup, nothing to suggest that it would turn out to be one of the most consequential games in the history of the Packers.

Green Bay–Cincinnati seemed to be a game between one team on the rise and one that was stuck in the same old rut. The Bengals, coming off a 3-13 season, had jumped out to a 2-0 start and were seemingly ready to make some noise in the AFC Central Division. They had a new coach in David Shula. They were led by quarterback Boomer Esia-son, the 1988 NFL MVP. The Packers, on the other hand, had been mired in bad for 24 years, stuck at the bottom of the NFL heap. And though they had a new general manager and a new coach, things did not seem to be much different. Green Bay was 0-2 and was coming into the game off an ugly 31–3 loss to the lowly Buccaneers in Tampa Bay. With Green Bay trailing 17–0 at halftime, Holmgren had benched quarterback Don Majkowski in favor of Favre. After the game, Majkowski vented to reporters. "I didn't agree with the switch," he said. "I was very angry."

To weary Packers fans, it looked like more of the same was in store in 1992. The Bengals game was a pick 'em on the betting line. That in itself seemed sort of like a victory. On Sunday morning, the marquee outside Motor Parts West, in Ashwaubenon, just a few blocks southeast of Lambeau Field, read, GO PACK. BEAT SOMEONE. ANYONE. PLEASE.

The game began slowly, with both teams pushing the ball harmlessly around the middle third of the field on their opening possessions. With about eight and a half minutes to go in the first quarter, on third-and-seven from the Packers' 38, Majkowski dropped back to pass. As the pocket collapsed around him, Bengals defensive tackle Tim Krumrie grabbed hold of Majkowski's left ankle and never let go, dragging the quarterback down to the turf. Majkowski fell forward in a twisting, slow-motion sort of collapse, then remained on the ground, writhing in pain. He had suffered torn ligaments in his ankle and had to be helped off the field by two trainers. Green Bay punted the ball away while Favre warmed up and talked on the phone with quarterbacks coach Steve Mariucci, who was up in the press box. Two plays later, Esiason threw an interception. The Brett Favre era in Green Bay had officially begun.

For the first 40 minutes or so, there was not much to distinguish it, not much for the 57,272 in the stands to cheer. Favre completed his first pass, to wide receiver Sterling Sharpe, and then played poorly. He fumbled four times, losing the ball twice. Forced into duty as the holder for kicker Chris Jacke because of the injury to Majkowski, he mishandled two snaps and was responsible for Jacke missing two of his three field goal attempts. Favre also called some the oddest formations that Holmgren had ever seen. At the end of three quarters, Cincinnati led 17–3 and seemed in control of the game. Green Bay scored its first touchdown when rookie cornerback Terrell Buckley — the player on whom the Packers had used the number-five pick in the 1992 draft — returned a punt 58 yards for a score 2:17 into the fourth quarter. The Bengals responded by driving for a field goal and a 20–10 lead with 8:05 left.

And then, all at once, Favre began to play with a real feel for the game, hitting the kinds of throws and playing with the kind of fearlessness that would define his career. He led the Packers on an 88-yard scoring drive, completing five of six passes for 67 yards and scrambling for another 19. The key play came with about six minutes left. On first down from the Green Bay 49, Sharpe lined up in the slot to Favre's left. The receiver juked cornerback Rod Jones at the line and took off on a corner route. Favre took a five-step drop and lofted a beautiful ball that Sharpe caught in stride at the Bengals' 28. Three plays later, Favre threw the first touchdown pass of his career, a five-yarder through traffic over the middle to Sharpe. The Packers trailed 20–17. Suddenly there was hope.

Green Bay stopped Cincinnati on the Bengals' ensuing possession, but Buckley fumbled the punt and Cincinnati got the ball back on the Packers' 36 with 3:11 left. Green Bay used up both of its remaining timeouts during the short drive that followed, which ended when Jim Breech kicked a 41-yard field goal with just over a minute to go. Cincinnati led 23–17 and seemed to have the game well in hand. The Bengals looked to be even more in control when rookie receiver Robert Brooks fielded a poor kickoff against the sideline and stepped out of bounds at the Green Bay eight-yard line. Had Brooks let the ball go, Cincinnati would

have been penalized and the Packers would have had the ball on their own 35. As it was, with just 1:07 left, Favre had 92 yards to go and no way to stop the clock.

On first down, he threw out of his own end zone into the right flat to fullback Harry Sydney, who stepped out of bounds at the 11-yard line with 1:01 left. On second-and-seven, Favre dropped straight back, looked over the middle to tight end Jackie Harris, and then threw long down the right sideline to Sharpe, over the head of Jones. The ball was slightly above and behind Sharpe, who twisted to his left as he extended himself to make the catch and then kept twisting around as he fell forward. He came down on top of the ball at the Bengals' 46. Sharpe got up clutching his midsection. He had suffered broken ribs. Nobody was really paying attention, though. Favre was hustling the Packers to the line and the clock was still running: 45 seconds, 44, 43 . . .

With 34 seconds left, center James Campen snapped the ball to Favre, who threw over the middle to running back Vince Workman for 11 yards. The situation on the field was frantic. Green Bay again rushed to the line and Favre spiked the ball with 19 seconds to go. He looked like he was out of breath. Sharpe, doubled over in pain, screamed at Holmgren to take him out. The coach subbed in Kitrick Taylor, a journeyman receiver from Washington State. The speedy Taylor was primarily a special teams player for the Packers. He entered the game with all of 33 career receptions — none of them for a touchdown.

Favre did not know any better, though. The call for the next play was "all go," with Green Bay's three wideouts sprinting straight toward the end zone. But Favre didn't put up a Hail Mary. He dropped five steps, looked over the middle to Harris, and pump-faked a throw to him, freezing free safety Fernandus Vinson. Favre then looked back to his right, stepped up in the pocket, and unleashed a bullet in the direction of Taylor, who was streaking all alone ahead of Jones down the right

sideline. The throw was perfect. Taylor caught the ball in stride over his left shoulder at the one-yard line. Vinson, who had bitten on Favre's pump fake, was closing in, but, like Jones, he was behind the ball. He was helpless. Touchdown. Lambeau Field erupted.

Favre ripped off his helmet and, holding it by the face mask in his right hand, thrust both arms into the air in celebration. He ran around the field slapping his linemen on the shoulder pads. He squatted down on the turf, overcome with emotion, burying his face for just a second in his left hand. He held for Jacke's extra point in bizarre fashion, balancing the ball on its point and then taking his hands off it completely. Jacke made the kick anyway and Green Bay won 24–23. The sound inside Lambeau was one loud, long, deafening roar — equal parts exultation and relief. It was a sound 24 years in the making.

Favre was not the only Packer who was emotionally spent. Campen was crying. In the north end zone, Lombardi-era linemen Jerry Kramer and Fuzzy Thurston — on the sidelines with a host of other former Packers for an alumni reunion — embraced in celebration. Holmgren described the victory, his first as an NFL coach, as "the happiest win of my life."

There would be many more to come, but this was the starting point. All the hallmarks of Brett Favre's long and glorious career were there. The fearlessness and brilliance, the questionable decision-making and boneheaded plays, and the thunderbolt right arm that made throws no other quarterback could make. A new era had officially begun. "Favre threw that pass," says Ron Wolf, "and everything changed."

Holmgren worked tirelessly to rein in Favre's impetuous play and soon turned the strong-armed gunslinger into the best quarterback in the NFL.

CHAPTER 17

REGGIE AND A RETURN TO GLORY

More than a year before he hired Ron Wolf, Bob Harlan had done something else that set the Packers up to be successful. In the summer of 1990, Green Bay spent $8.3 million to expand Lambeau Field, adding 36 private boxes and 1,920 theater-style club seats in the south end zone. Just as in 1985, the new seating was immensely popular with fans, selling out before construction was even completed. In the first season, income from private boxes jumped from $745,004 to $1,115,000, and net receipts from home games increased by more than $500,000. The boosts contributed to a record $42.3 million in revenues. About two-thirds of the income came courtesy of the NFL's new four-year, $3.6 billion TV contract with networks ABC, CBS, and NBC and cable networks ESPN and TNT—a deal that would bring in about $128 million to Green Bay through 1993. The Packers had pretty much always turned a profit since the 1950 stock sale rescued them from their deathbed, but now they had never been richer.

Green Bay's robust bottom line came at just the right time, because in 1993 free agency came to the NFL. In September 1992, not long before Brett Favre took over for Don Majkowski, a federal jury in Minneapolis had struck down the league's Plan B free agency system on the grounds that it violated federal antitrust laws.[*] Plan B had been implemented in the wake of the 1987 players' strike, the settlement of which had left the NFL without a collective bargaining agreement. Under the plan's strictures, owners could prevent 37 of the 47 players on their rosters from becoming free agents

---

[*] *The suit had originally been filed in New Jersey in 1990, but the NFL had it moved to Minneapolis because the league felt that the Eighth Circuit U.S. Court of Appeals provided a more favorable venue—in 1989 the same court had ruled that the NFL was exempt from antitrust allegations. The players were fine with the move, because the judge who would be hearing the case, David Doty, had ruled in their favor earlier in the proceedings. The trial had to be held in an area where an NFL team was located.*

—in effect hanging on to their best 37 players. Led by Jets running back Freeman McNeil, eight players (including Majkowski) who had been protected when their contracts expired filed suit claiming that Plan B had unfairly prevented them from negotiating with other teams. Two weeks after Plan B was struck down, three other players, whose contracts were due to end at the conclusion of the 1992 season, filed a class-action suit in the same court, seeking free agency for themselves and about 280 other players. One of the three was Philadelphia Eagles defensive end Reggie White, a perennial All-Pro and the league's 1987 Defensive Player of the Year.

White was about to change the face of the NFL. And the fate of the Packers.

◆ ◆ ◆

Before he died suddenly on the day after Christmas in 2004 from cardiac arrhythmia, Reggie White had left a number of legacies in pro football. On the field, he was the league's all-time sacks leader, one of the most dominant defensive

players in history. He'd won a Super Bowl. He had been a first-team All-Pro eight times and gone to 13 Pro Bowls. Off the field, he had been the lead litigant in the class-action suit that, on January 6, 1993, forced the NFL to accept free agency. Reggie White was going to be remembered one way or another.

An ordained Baptist minister, White was a committed disciple of Jesus Christ. He relished the idea of saving, of redeeming. His primary focus was on the salvation of souls, of course, and, through his ministries in Philadelphia, Green Bay, and his home state of Tennessee, he did plenty of that. But his greatest legacy in Green Bay is as one of the saviors of the Packers.

The sin that most NFL fans associated with Green Bay was losing—the 24-year cycle of defeat that had turned the place into the Siberia of the NFL. It was the kind of place to which Mike Holmgren, when he had been a San Francisco 49ers assistant coach in the late 1980s and early 1990s, used to threaten to exile players who did

Reggie White was the most sought-after player in the first free-agent class in NFL history. On April 6, 1993, the day he signed with the lowly Packers, Jimmy Sexton, White's agent, boasted to reporters, "We shocked the league, didn't we?"

White studies the Bible with Favre in the locker room before the Packers' 38–27 loss to the Cowboys in the 1995 NFC Championship Game.

not perform. *You keep that up and I'll ship your ass to Green Bay.*

Together with Wolf, Holmgren, and Favre, White helped wash that sin away. But there was also another sin, a deeper sin—an original sin that went all the way back to the beginnings of the franchise. Besides Walter Jean, whose father had been black but who had presented himself as a white man, an African American had never played on one of Curly Lambeau's teams. Not before the NFL's soft ban on blacks went into effect in 1934, and not after the color line was finally broken in 1946. It had taken Gene Ronzani, Lambeau's successor, to integrate the Packers, and Vince Lombardi, the greatest coach in franchise history, to make the team one on which

African American players would feel more welcome. That warmth, though, was not necessarily coming from the city of Green Bay itself.

One of the drawbacks to living in Green Bay for African American players was the lack of amenities taken for granted in such NFL towns as Atlanta and Houston, or even nearby Chicago—finding decent restaurants or nightclubs, for example, or getting a decent haircut. The population of the city in 1990 was 96,466, and only 453 of those residents were black, less than 0.5 percent. There simply was not anybody in the area who knew how to shave a proper flat-top or high-top fade. The problem was so acute that in the late 1980s, defensive line coach Greg Blache had started cutting hair for the Packers' black players.

When he was a boy in New Orleans, Blache and his younger brother, C.J., had cut each other's hair as a way of saving money. And when Greg went to Notre Dame, where he was a defensive back before a leg injury cut short his playing career, he used to cut hair for black players in the dorms.* "Back in those days everybody had Afros, so it was easy," says Blache. "You just had to make sure everything was neat and even."

Blache had kept in practice over the years by giving trims to his two sons. He began cutting hair shortly after he arrived in Green Bay because one of the players mentioned to him before a road trip that he was not going to have time to get his hair cleaned up before leaving town. Blache told the player to meet him down in the locker room, where he would be waiting with his clippers. "I didn't do fades and stuff," Blache says. "I could make it look neat."

Before Blache and his clippers came to town, players used to drive two hours south to Milwaukee to find a barber familiar with African American hairstyles. There was also a black barber from Milwaukee who used to make occasional trips north, but the primary reason he used to come, says Blache, was to cut the hair of inmates at the maximum-security Green Bay Correctional Institution.

"Green Bay was a very, very white community," says Blache, who's now retired and lives outside of Green Bay. "If you were a black man, people thought you played for the Packers."

◆ ◆ ◆

Reginald Howard White entered the world on December 19, 1961, in Chattanooga, Tennessee. He weighed only six pounds as a newborn, but he soon began to fill out. By the time he was three months old, he weighed more than 30 pounds—the average weight of a two-and-a-half-year-old. His mother said that Reggie never ate baby food,

but grew big by eating from the table along with everybody else.

Thelma Dodds was 19 when she gave birth to Reggie—three years after his older brother, Julius, had been born. Not long after Reggie's birth, the boys' father, Charles White, moved to California, where he played semipro baseball and softball. He and Thelma never married, and he was not significantly involved in his sons' lives when they were growing up. Years later, Reggie wrote of Charles, "I grew up knowing him, and he claimed me as his son. I didn't see him very much, but I was always proud of him." Thelma, who worked in a nearby hosiery mill, would leave the house—which was in the predominantly white Chattanooga neighborhood of St. Elmo—at 2:30 every afternoon and not return home until close to midnight.

In 1969, Thelma married Leonard Collier, an Army cook stationed at Fort Riley, Kansas. After the wedding, she departed for Kansas with Leonard, leaving Julius and Reggie behind to live with her mother, Mildred Dodds. Mildred lived a few miles east of St. Elmo, in the Emma Wheeler Homes, a network of affordable two-story duplex houses that Mildred considered "the best project around."

Dodds's home, which she ran with the help of an aunt and a cousin, was a loving one, but Reggie nevertheless grew up like a boy who was angry about something. "When a kid wants attention," he wrote in his 1996 autobiography, *Reggie White in the Trenches*, "he's often not too choosy about how he gets it." He set fire to a set of curtains. He punched out a window trying to get to his brother after Julius had locked him out of the house. Once, following a scolding from his Aunt Jeanette, Reggie retaliated by throwing piles of dirt through an open window onto her bed.

Another reason that Reggie was angry may

---

* *Blache never lettered for the Fighting Irish, but he stuck around the football team as an assistant through the 1975 season. He was the inspiration for one of the Notre Dame assistant coaches in the movie* Rudy, *which is about the one-game career of practice-squad stalwart Daniel "Rudy" Ruettiger.*

have had to do with being teased about his size. He learned to fight, sometimes battling with his cousins and sometimes with boys from the neighborhood who wanted to take on the big kid. When there was nobody to spar with and he was mad or depressed, Reggie used to go into the woods that surrounded the Wheeler projects, grab a stick, and beat it against a tree.

Leonard and Thelma moved back to Chattanooga when Reggie was nine—White's half sister, Christie, was born not long after—and he and Julius moved in with them in a new home in St. Elmo. But things had changed for Reggie in the year that Thelma was gone. He had attended nearby Piney Woods Baptist Church every Sunday with Mildred—the niece of two Presbyterian ministers—and he continued to go there after his mother's return. When he was 13, he asked Jesus to come into his life. "Instantly," he wrote in his autobiography, "I was saved." He began carrying a Bible everywhere, and kids who had once teased him for his tremendous size switched to teasing him for his tremendous faith. Reggie responded by becoming something of a bully for Christ. Inspired by Zechariah 13:3, which said that those who speak lies in God's name must be put to death, he began telling kids at school, "Y'all keep lying, I'm gonna kill you." He said that he later saw the error of his ways, but his affinity for a literal interpretation of scripture was a tendency that would never totally leave him.

When he was 17, Reggie earned his minister's license by preaching a sermon on forgiveness at Greater Saint John Baptist Church. At the same time that he was beginning to develop a reputation as a servant of the Lord, he was also beginning to develop another as a football player. He had preordained what would happen—he was 12 or 13 when he responded to a query about what he wanted to be when he grew up by saying, "I want to be a minister and I want to play in the NFL." Reggie was six feet four inches tall and 225 pounds as a sophomore at Chattanooga's mostly black Howard School. By the time he graduated, he

had grown an inch and put on 10 pounds. Playing defensive tackle and tight end, he was all-city as a junior and all-state as a senior, when he was also named Chattanooga's Player of the Year and a *Parade* All-America. (He was also an all-state center in basketball.)

White went on to a four-year career at Tennessee, where he started as a freshman in 1980 and was the Volunteers' captain his senior year, during which he was so dominant (a school record 15 sacks and nine tackles for a loss) that he earned All-America and SEC Player of the Year honors. At six foot five and more than 280 pounds, the freakishly strong White was a holy terror at defensive tackle. The Vols' sports information office dubbed the massive White "the Minister of Defense," a nickname that was catnip to reporters and fans fascinated by a man who preached about God's love while playing with dreadful ferocity. White did not shy away from the notoriety, quoting scripture freely to eager reporters. A favorite was Ecclesiastes 9:10, which reads, "Whatsoever thy hand findeth to do, do it with thy might."

White eschewed the NFL draft and instead signed a five-year, $4 million contract in January 1984 with the Memphis Showboats of the upstart United States Football League. The Showboats were close to home, as well as to his soon-to-be wife, Sara Copeland, whom he had met two years earlier at the First Apostolic Church of Knoxville and who was now a junior at East Tennessee State.

White played for two years in Memphis and was first-team All-USFL in 1985, but at the end of that season, the upstart league ceased operations. On September 20, White signed a four-year, $1.6 million deal with the Eagles, who had taken him with the fourth pick in the 1984 supplemental draft—used by the NFL to determine which teams held the rights to USFL players—and who also spent an additional $1.3 million to buy out the final three years on his contract with the Showboats. He joined the Eagles in week four and was credited with two and a half sacks in Philadelphia's 16–10

loss to the New York Giants at Veterans Stadium. White finished the season with 13 sacks in 13 games.

"He's 6'5", 295 pounds, and runs the 40 in 4.6," Eagles coach Buddy Ryan told *The Philadelphia Inquirer* in 1988. "The good Lord doesn't make them like that. He's the best defensive lineman I've ever been around." As a coordinator, Ryan had coached Hall of Fame defensive linemen Alan Page and Carl Eller of the Minnesota Vikings, as well as Dan Hampton and Richard Dent of the Chicago Bears. "None of those guys could run like [Reggie]," Ryan told the *Inquirer*.

White thrived under the blitz-happy Ryan, perfecting a grab bag of pass-rushing moves made devastatingly effective by his speed and strength: the spin, the rip, the hump, the club, and his favorite, the bull rush. Despite playing only 12 games because of the players' strike in 1987, White had 21 sacks to lead the league — one and a half off the all-time record for a 16-game season. He was so versatile that Ryan used to move him from left end to nose tackle — wherever he could do the most damage — in his vaunted 46 defense. "That way, we can scare the hell out of a whole bunch of people instead of just one," said Ryan. Double teams and triple teams did not seem to matter. White could take over a game all by himself.

He had also matured into one of the most respected players in the league, earning deep regard from peers and coaches for his commitment to Christ and his work in inner-city ministries. When he won the right to become a free agent in 1993, it was more than just his pass-rushing prowess that made him the most coveted player on the market.

As many as eight teams were vying to sign him. Cleveland Browns owner Art Modell sent his private jet to Knoxville to fly Reggie and Sara to Cleveland and put them up in a five-room, $800-a-night suite at the Ritz-Carlton. Modell also banned all cursing at the team's headquarters for the 48 hours that White was in town. Hall of Fame running back Jim Brown called White at the hotel. So,

too, did the mayor of Cleveland. Modell concentrated much of his effort on Sara, who was from the area and still had family there. The Browns' owner had white, red, pink, and yellow roses waiting for her at the hotel room, and he also presented her with a $900 leather coat. White's agent, Jimmy Sexton, had begun free agency thinking he could get his client $2.8 million a year. By the end of the first week, after White's visit to Cleveland, Sexton knew that he was going to be able to get at least $3.5 million a year. Only quarterbacks Warren Moon and Dan Marino made more.

Dubbed "the Reggie Tour" in the papers, White's free agency, which began on March 1, became a 37-day national event. Falcons cornerback Deion Sanders promised to build White a church if he signed with Atlanta. The governor of Georgia gave him a tour of the state capitol building and a Falcons jersey. Lions coach Wayne Fontes took him to the Palace of Auburn Hills to see the Pistons play the Lakers. San Francisco 49ers president Carmen Policy and coach George Seifert took White to dinner at Clark's by the Bay, the restaurant owned by former star receiver Dwight Clark. When White visited the New York Jets, he intimated in his press conference that the team would have a better chance of signing him if it traded for Bengals quarterback Boomer Esiason. Twenty-four hours later, the Jets did just that, dealing a third-round draft pick to Cincinnati for the former NFL MVP. The word of Reggie White was gospel around the NFL.

On March 10, between trips to Detroit and New York, White made a stop in Green Bay. Wolf had gotten the go-ahead to pursue White from Bob Harlan. Thanks to the money from the NFL's television deal and Lambeau Field's luxury seating, the Packers had more cash in the bank than anyone realized. But Wolf, who disdains gaudy displays, did not approach his negotiations with White like a man who was willing to spend extravagantly. Instead he emphasized football. Wolf talked to White not only about Green Bay's current team, which was coming off a 9-7 season, but also about the Packers' rich history. Until White arrived in Green Bay, he had no idea that the team was community-owned. "You're already a great football player," Wolf told White. "Come here and you'll be a legend."

The Packers, like other teams, put a good deal of effort into their courtship of White, but there were some wrinkles that made it a uniquely small-town experience. The weather was terrible on the day of his visit—Green Bay had gotten four inches of snow the night before, with more on the way—and flights were getting canceled. The Packers' chief financial officer, Mike Reinfeldt, made a call to his father-in-law, who owned a plane that happened to be on the ground that day in Pontiac, Michigan. White flew to see the Packers in a borrowed private jet. And instead of a stretch limo, he was picked up from Austin Straubel Field in a Jeep Wrangler. There was no Ritz-Carlton in Green Bay —there still isn't—so White stayed at the Embassy Suites on Main Street. And instead of seafood at Clark's by the Bay, White went out to lunch with Wolf, Holmgren, and defensive coordinator Ray Rhodes at the Red Lobster on Lombardi Avenue, less than a mile west of Lambeau Field.

Green Bay may have hewed to a no-frills approach when White was in town, but it also kept up the pressure after his visit was over. In the only nod the team made to the sorts of outré gestures of Modell and others, Wolf sent Sara White roses every other day for two weeks. Later in the month, Holmgren and Rhodes flew to Knoxville unannounced and attended White's speaking engagement at a local Kiwanis Club. The three men then went back to his house for coffee. The visit was one of the few White received during his free agency, and the fact that Holmgren and Rhodes had gone out of their way impressed him tremendously. And then on March 29, Holmgren called White and got his voicemail. Instead of hanging up or leaving a traditional call-me-back message, Holmgren said, "Reggie, this is God. Go to Green Bay."

White had in fact been waiting for a sign from God. The Packers had not been on his list of prospective teams when he began his search, but he had said publicly from the outset that he wanted to go to a team that could compete for a championship—White had never won a title at any level of football. He had been impressed by Wolf, Holmgren, and Rhodes, and also by Green Bay's history. Just as important, White had been a fan of Brett Favre's ever since the day in November 1992 when the quarterback, playing with a separated left shoulder, had led the Packers to a 27–24 upset victory over White and the Eagles in Milwaukee. Favre had injured the shoulder late in the first quarter when, after he released a pass, White hit him in the chest and fell on top of him. Favre never came out of the game, completing 23 of 33 passes for 275 yards and two touchdowns. "Right there, I knew that this Mississippi country boy had all the stuff of a championship quarterback," White later wrote. "When I left the Philadelphia Eagles . . . the vivid memory of Brett Favre playing straight through the punishment I put on him stuck in my mind."

The most important thing, though—even to a man of God—was whether Green Bay could make a competitive bid. The top offer came from the 49ers, who put together a five-year, $19.5 million package. But the final two years of the deal were not guaranteed. If White got hurt, San Francisco could cut him. He did not like that. The Packers' offer was for four years, but it came with no such catch. It was also slightly richer, at $17.6 million, and included more up-front money than any other deal. White would get a $4.5 million signing bonus and $4.5 million his first year. In his second season, he would earn $3.1 million. If he signed with Green Bay, in other words, White would get more than 51 percent of his money in the first year, and more than 68 percent by the end of his second. The 49ers were hamstrung by restrictions on how much money they could offer up front because they had reached the 1992 NFC Champion-

ship Game. NFL rules dictated that the league's top four teams could sign free agents only after they had lost one first, and that the salary had to be based on the deal signed by the departed free agent. San Francisco was offering a $4 million signing bonus, but only $4.4 million in salary over the first two years. "As it came down to the end, it just came down to money," says Wolf. "And we spent more money than anybody else."

On April 6, 1993, White stunned the NFL by signing with the Packers. "I think every team was shocked that I picked Green Bay," White said at the press conference where he was introduced as the newest member of the Packers. "I think I made the right decision."

◆ ◆ ◆

The Packers' defense had ranked 23rd in the NFL in 1992, but the arrival of White immediately elevated it to one of the best in pro football. In 1993, Green Bay had the number-two defense in the league, and the Packers' 46 sacks were fifth best. White led the way with 11. Wolf believed that building a solid defense began with the line —with stopping the run and pressuring the quarterback. "Otherwise," he wrote in *The Packer Way*, "you have to resort to gimmick defenses, and that ultimately leaves you vulnerable to big plays."

White's presence up front made possible the emergence of strong safety LeRoy Butler, one of the most dynamic defensive players in Green Bay in the past 30 years. He had been drafted in the second round out of Florida State as a cornerback in 1990, but Rhodes moved him to safety in 1992 because he wanted a playmaker in the middle of his defensive secondary—a ball hawk who could both cover receivers and tackle running backs in the open field. The six-foot, 197-pound Butler was an unlikely candidate for pro football stardom. Raised by a single mother in the Blodgett Homes projects on the west side of Jacksonville, he was so severely pigeon-toed as a baby that when he was eight months old, his doctors broke bones in both of his feet in an effort to reposition them. Butler

spent much of his time in a wheelchair and in leg braces until he was eight years old, when he fell out of his wheelchair and took off running. Like in a scene from *Forrest Gump,* his leg braces flew off. He promptly ran outside and started playing kickball. He went on to be a standout at Robert E. Lee High before becoming an All-America for the Seminoles.

After a year spent adjusting to his new position in the Packers' secondary, Butler began to flourish. He intercepted six passes in 1993 and got his first sack on a game-changing play in a 17–3 defeat of the Bears on Halloween at Lambeau Field. With the Packers leading 10–3 early in the fourth quarter, Chicago had the ball at the Green Bay 12-yard line. On third-and-seven, Butler blitzed up the middle, hit quarterback Jim Harbaugh, and knocked the ball into the air. It rolled all the way back to the Packers' 37 before Butler fell on it. It was the sort of dashing, bruising effort that epitomized a career that helped redefine the safety position. In 12 seasons, the versatile Butler had 38 interceptions and 20.5 sacks. Fritz Shurmur, who became the Green Bay defensive coordinator after Rhodes departed in 1994, deployed Butler all over the field. "A lot of safeties in this league are never around the ball," Shurmur told *Sports Illustrated* in 1997. "You hardly know they exist. The best description of LeRoy is that if the ball is there, he's near it."

Of all the Packers who have not been inducted into the Pro Football Hall of Fame, it's Butler, along with Verne Lewellen, who is most deserving. Butler was a first-team All-Pro four times and is widely considered to be the best safety of the 1990s. Of the 318 men enshrined in the Pro Football Hall of Fame, only 11 were exclusively safeties. Four more played both cornerback and safety. Butler deserves to join them. According to Greg Blache, before Butler came along, safeties generally fell into one of two categories: coverage guys and in-the-box guys. Mark Murphy, the strong safety whom Butler replaced, "was an in-the-box safety," says Blache. "It was different if you needed him to cover somebody. LeRoy had the talent of a cornerback, but the range of a safety. And he could play wherever — in the box, deep middle, in the slot."

What Butler's Canton candidacy lacks is a champion, an advocate to make his case over and over again. He was picked in the 1990 draft by executive vice president of football operations Tom Braatz and coach Lindy Infante, both of whom had long but relatively undistinguished careers in pro football, and both of whom have since passed away. In their stead, Butler's banner has been picked up by the men who played with him. "It's crazy that LeRoy Butler is not in the Hall of Fame," Favre said in 2015. "We don't win nearly as many football games as we did or have the kind of success we did without LeRoy Butler."

With his nose for the ball, Butler made his share of indelible plays during the Packers' resurgence. In zero-degree weather on the day after Christmas in 1993, Green Bay clinched its first playoff berth in 11 years — and its first in a full season since 1972 — with a 28–0 beatdown of the Los Angeles Raiders. With the Packers up 14–0 early in the fourth quarter, Butler forced a fumble with a crunching hit on the Raiders' Randy Jordan after the rookie running back had caught a swing pass at the Oakland 38-yard line. As Jordan tumbled to the ground, the ball bounced straight up into White's hands and he carried it down the sideline to the 24, where he was corralled by left guard Steve Wisniewski, who began dragging him out of bounds. Before he went down, White lateraled the ball to the trailing Butler, who caught it at the 25 and galloped, untouched, into the south end zone. He dropped the ball without breaking stride, pointed toward the stands in front of him, and then leaped up the six-foot wall into the waiting arms of the fans in the first row. Butler thereby invented the Lambeau Leap, a touchdown celebration that has become a tradition at Lambeau Field.

Many of the most thrilling moments were be-

ing delivered by Favre. Two weeks after Butler's Lambeau Leap, Favre beat the Lions in the Silverdome in a wild-card playoff game. Losing 24–21 with just 1:05 left to play, he took the snap at the Detroit 40-yard line, dropped back five steps, and then stepped up in the pocket. Unable to find an open receiver, he scrambled a few yards to his left, just beyond the left hash marks — it looked for an instant as if he were going to throw a screen pass to running back Darrell Thompson, who had released to that side. Suddenly Favre stopped, turned back downfield, set his feet, and threw back across his body — and across the whole field — to receiver Sterling Sharpe, who was all by himself in the right corner of the end zone.

Green Bay became a perennial playoff team after that, and the list of defining moments kept growing. The sense began to build, in the city and in the NFL, that a championship was coming. There was the time in 1995 when, playing on a badly sprained left ankle, Favre threw five touchdown passes to beat the Bears 35–28 at Lambeau Field. It was the moment that solidified his reputation for toughness. Six weeks later, on Christmas Eve, the Packers won their first division title in 13 years with a 24–19 victory at Lambeau over the Pittsburgh Steelers — a triumph made possible when Steelers receiver Yancey Thigpen dropped a six-yard touchdown pass from quarterback Neil O'Donnell on fourth down with 11 seconds left in the game. Two weeks after that, Green Bay visited San Francisco in the divisional round of the NFC playoffs. The 49ers, the reigning Super Bowl champions, were 10-point favorites, but the Packers whipped them 27–17. The play of the game came on San Francisco's first offensive snap. On first down, quarterback Steve Young threw to fullback Adam Walker in the right flat. Third-year linebacker Wayne Simmons met Walker head-on, and hit him chest-high. Walker fumbled. Rookie cornerback Craig Newsome scooped up the ball at the 49ers' 31-yard line and raced untouched into the end zone for the game's first score. Green Bay never looked back. Favre, who had just won the first of his three MVP awards, completed 15 of his first 17 passes for 222 yards and a touchdown, and the defense sacked Young three times and forced four turnovers (two interceptions and two fumbles). "It was destiny," said White.

Pro football's axis was again beginning to tilt toward northeastern Wisconsin, not just on the field but off it as well. It was a testament to the awesome power of winning in the NFL—as well as to the outsized influence of Reggie White, who had given Green Bay back its good name. Wolf describes his signing as "landscape-changing," and it really was. To the disbelief of many in the NFL, Green Bay had gone from being a speed bump on the schedule to a force to be reckoned with. White was instrumental not only in reversing a generation's worth of losing but also in changing the perception of the city throughout the league. Where just a few years before black players had openly complained about the quality of life in Green Bay, now prominent black players were suddenly more receptive to playing in the NFL's smallest city. A few of the African American players acquired by Wolf after White's arrival were wide receivers Andre Rison and Desmond Howard, defensive end Sean Jones, and tight end Keith Jackson. White helped each of them to see the upside of living and playing in a place that was all about one team and one game.

At the same time, Wolf was also instituting some policies that helped make life just a little better for the Packers' African American players. He had started by arranging for regular visits from a Milwaukee barber who knew how to cut the hair of black players. When the move proved to be popular, he hired Henry and Bobbie's Bungalow Restaurant, a Milwaukee soul food joint, to cater a meal on Wednesdays at the team's facility. The fare, which included catfish, fried chicken, and barbecue, was immediately popular.

Wolf's homey touches helped ease the transition of the Packers' African American players

into a community that was eager to accept them. "The thing that people have to know is that just because there's a lot of white people, that doesn't make them racist," Sean Jones told *Sports Illustrated*'s Robert Klemko about Green Bay in 2016. "It's probably the least racist place I've ever been in my life.

"That said, they don't know what they don't know. They don't know how to cut a fade with a No. 2, and they don't know how to make fried chicken and cornbread. Where's the black history museum? Where's Chinatown? They didn't have any of that, but they embraced you and they wanted to win."

And oh, did they ever want to win. There had been so many miserable years since 1967 for Packers fans—not only were they long-suffering and patient, but they were also more than a little aware that their pain had come at the expense of teams from bigger cities, with bigger bankrolls and more sophisticated supporters. In those heady early years, with Wolf, Holmgren, Favre, and White leading the way, the feeling among the

On the Packers' second offensive play of Super Bowl XXXI, Favre recognized that the Patriots were blitzing and called an audible at the line of scrimmage that resulted in a 54-yard touchdown pass to wideout Andre Rison.

Green Bay faithful was one of giddy elation. But there was also a nervous edge to it. It was almost as if there was something about what was happening that was not quite real. And to Cheeseheads used to nothing but bad, things like Favre's MVP and the presence of White and the victories in the playoffs were lifelines to hold on to. They conferred a sense of legitimacy on everything that was happening. The slogan "The Pack Is Back!" had been trotted out so many times over the years that it had become more than trite. It had become almost meaningless. But now, suddenly, it was true.

What was happening in Green Bay in the mid-1990s was very different from what had happened in 1989. This was no mirage. And it was more than just delusional optimism. The Packers were good. Really good.

⋯

Until January 12, 1997, there had not been a pro football championship game of any kind in Green Bay for 29 years, since the Ice Bowl on New Year's Eve 1967. That changed when the Packers hosted the Carolina Panthers in the 1996 NFC Championship Game. In each of Ron Wolf's five years at the helm of the franchise, Green Bay had won more than it had lost—but its seasons had always ended in defeat. In 1992, a 27–7 loss to the Vikings in Minnesota had kept the Packers out of the postseason. And in each of the three seasons after, Green Bay had lost in the playoffs to the Dallas Cowboys in Texas Stadium—in the divisional rounds in 1993 and 1994 and in the 1995 conference championship game. Of all those defeats, it was the last one that stung the most. The 38–27 loss was the Packers' seventh in a row to the Cowboys, and the sixth in a row at Texas Stadium. The game had been bruising and nasty, lowlighted by 324-pound Dallas tackle Erik Williams throwing a cut block at the left knee of 295-pound nose tackle John Jurkovic. Williams drove his helmet into the back of Jurkovic's knee, tearing his MCL and putting him out of the game. The play precipitated a run of penalties for late hits, each one intended to make up for the play before. White was incensed. "It was ridiculous," he said after the game, adding that Williams had been punching and scratching him in the face while blocking him. "Guys' careers can get ended like that."

But White also had something else to say. "This team," he promised, "will win a championship."

And the resolve carried over. The Packers of 1996 were a juggernaut, winning 13 games and breezing to the number-one seed in the NFC. Their offense led the NFL in scoring, while their defense surrendered the fewest points in the league. Favre won his second straight MVP award. One of their three defeats had come in a 21–6 loss in Dallas on Monday, November 18. But the loss was deceptive. The defense had not allowed a touchdown; the Cowboys' 21 points came from kicker Chris Boniol, who kicked seven field goals to tie an NFL record. The offense, playing without injured receivers Robert Brooks and Antonio Freeman, and ailing tight end Mark Chmura, was not at full strength. The victory might have been Dallas's eighth in a row over Green Bay, but it was not a telling one. The Packers went on to win their last five games. The Cowboys lost two of their last five and staggered into the postseason off a 37–10 loss to the Redskins in week 17.

As the top seed in the NFC, the Packers had home field advantage throughout the playoffs, and they won their divisional-round game at Lambeau on January 4, spanking San Francisco 35–14. But Dallas, the reigning Super Bowl champion, was upset 26–17 the next day by the upstart Carolina Panthers. Green Bay, instead of playing its fiercest rival for the right to play in Super Bowl XXXI, hosted a team just one year removed from its inception.

The Packers' 30–13 victory over the Panthers on January 26 — played, appropriately enough, in three-degree weather — was gratifying, allowing the citizens of Titletown to celebrate the return of championship football to its rightful home. But it was not the win that everyone was waiting for. There was something more to come. One final box to check. When the Packers had last played in the Super Bowl, nobody really knew what to make of the game — which was not even called the Super Bowl, instead going by the unwieldy moniker "the AFL-NFL World Championship Game." Pro football's marquee event in those days was the NFL title game, not the gimmicky matchup between teams from the rival leagues. But in the 29 years since Green Bay's 33–14 victory over the Oakland Raiders in Super Bowl II, the game had grown into a national event, a showcase watched by more than 100 million people around the world. To the citizens of Green Bay, and to the Packers themselves, the NFC championship was nice, but the Super Bowl was what counted.

All that stood between Green Bay and a return to glory was the New England Patriots, who had defeated the Jacksonville Jaguars 20–6 in the AFC Championship Game a few hours after the Packers had beaten the Panthers.[*] The Patriots were coached by Bill Parcells, who had won Super Bowls in 1986 and 1990 at the helm of the New York Giants. Parcells had retired from coaching after the second championship and started working as a television analyst for NBC. In 1991 he had been one of Ron Wolf's top candidates to become the new coach in Green Bay, but "the Tuna," as Parcells was known, was not yet ready to return to the sidelines. The Packers were not the only team he spurned. He also turned down a five-year, $6.5 million offer to take over all football operations for the Tampa Bay Buccaneers. Ten days later, Parcells, who said that he had felt pressured by Buccaneers owner Hugh Culverhouse to make a quick decision, tried to take back his re-

---

*Like the Panthers, the Jaguars were in their second season in existence.

fusal. But a miffed Culverhouse rescinded the deal. A year later, New England hired Parcells on essentially the same terms, though general manager was never part of his official title.

In the Patriots, Parcells took over a team that had not won a playoff game in eight years and quickly turned it into a winner. Leaning on second-year quarterback Drew Bledsoe, who threw for an NFL-best 4,555 yards, New England won a playoff game in 1994. Two years later, the Patriots went 11-5 and had the number-two scoring offense in the NFL — only the Packers were more prolific — and Parcells was being hailed as a genius. But he was a genius in the final year of his contract. And in New Orleans in the week before Super Bowl XXXI, the news broke that, because of a rift with Patriots owner Robert Kraft, he was going to leave New England after the Super Bowl to become the coach of the New York Jets. The story and the distractions that resulted from it — Kraft and Parcells held a midweek press conference to assure everybody that things were okay — sucked up all the oxygen in the days leading up to the game.

For the media in New Orleans, the focus on Parcells and his job status was an understandable judgment call. It was breaking news. The return of the smallest town in pro football to the pinnacle of the sport was gauzy feature stuff. But the intrigue around the coach and his future was also a very East Coast story — a New York coach who was now in Boston might be moving back to New York. *Stop the presses!* There was an element of elitism to the whole affair — a metaphorical flyover of a team from flyover country — that did not go unnoticed in the Packers' locker room. The tone of the coverage was brought into sharper relief when reporters from around the country began to descend on Favre's hometown of Kiln, Mississippi, which is only about an hour's drive east of New Orleans. The cumulative effect of all the coverage was that Favre and his family came off looking like caricatures out of *Li'l Abner*. Stories were

dutifully recounted about the remoteness of the place, about the local alligators' taste for the Favre family's dogs, and about the quarterback's childhood sleeping habits. (He preferred to sleep on top of his covers so that he would not have to make his bed in the morning.) Twenty-nine years after it had won an afterthought of a game, Green Bay returned to the Super Bowl as an afterthought of a team.

And that made Desmond Howard an afterthought of an afterthought. Wolf had signed the receiver on July 11, 1996, giving him a one-year, $300,000 contract, a show-me deal — the league minimum for fifth-year players was $196,000. Howard had won the Heisman Trophy as a junior at Michigan in 1991, and the Redskins had taken him with the fourth pick in the 1992 NFL draft, but his frame and his hands were not suited to the pro game. He had trouble separating from defensive backs who pressed him at the line of scrimmage and had caught only 92 passes in his first four seasons. Wolf, though, thought he had value as a kick returner. He had returned only one punt for a touchdown in the NFL — as a rookie in 1992 — but in his last two years in Ann Arbor he had brought back three kicks for scores (two kickoffs and a punt). With the Packers in 1996, he was the primary returner for both kickoffs and punts, leading the league in the latter category with three touchdowns and an NFL-record 875 return yards. He was also much more sure-handed as a returner than as a receiver. In 80 kick returns (58 punts and 22 kickoffs), Howard lost just one fumble. In the 35–14 win over the 49ers in the divisional playoff on January 4, he took San Francisco's first punt back 71 yards for Green Bay's opening touchdown. Later in the first quarter, he returned another punt 46 yards to the 49ers' seven-yard line to set up Green Bay's second score. The team's stars were Favre and White, but Howard was the Packers' most potent weapon.

"It's gotten to the point where it's almost ridiculous," said Green Bay receiver Don Beebe after the San Francisco game. "Why kick it to him? If I'm the special teams coach playing the Green Bay Packers, I'd just [punt] it out of bounds."

But as was made clear repeatedly in New Orleans, Parcells's ego was boundless. And in the Super Bowl, on January 26, he and the Patriots kicked to Howard every time, something they had boasted that they were planning to do in the days leading up to the game. On his first touch, just two and a half minutes into the opening quarter, Howard took a 51-yard punt from New England's Tom Tupa and raced 32 yards down the right sideline — in front of the Patriots' bench — to give the Packers the ball at their own 45-yard line. Howard bounced up woofing at the New England sideline. Two plays later, with Green Bay in a two-tight-end set, Favre surveyed the Patriots' defense and, seeing both safeties up at the line, guessed that a blitz was coming — a gambit that would leave the cornerbacks in single coverage. He audibled from a quick-out to the tight end into a downfield blitz beater called 74 Razor. After taking the snap, he dropped five steps and threw off his back foot over the top for a touchdown to receiver Andre Rison, who had sped past cornerback Otis Smith on a deep post route. Favre's pass hit Rison in stride at the Patriots' 22 and he ran untouched into the end zone for the game's first points.

Green Bay seemed to have all the momentum after Bledsoe threw an interception on New England's next possession. Chris Jacke kicked a 37-yard field goal to swell the lead to 10–0. But the Patriots came back, driving 79 yards for a touchdown to cut the Packers' lead to 10–7. After Favre and the offense went three-and-out, New England got the ball back on its own 43. Bledsoe needed only four plays to score from there. The key play was a 44-yard pass to wideout Terry Glenn that put the ball at the Green Bay four-yard line. On the next snap, Bledsoe threw a bootleg pass to the right to tight end Ben Coates for a touchdown. The Patriots led 14–10 before the first quarter was even over. And they seemed to be taking control of the game.

But less than a minute into the second quarter, Favre struck back. On first-and-10 from the 19, he once again recognized that the New England cornerbacks were in single coverage and sensed another blitz. He audibled into a maximum-protection blocking scheme and threw a deep fade down the right sideline to Antonio Freeman, who was running a few steps ahead of strong safety Lawyer Milloy. There was nothing in front of Freeman but open field, and he raced into the end zone for an 81-yard touchdown, the longest scoring pass in Super Bowl history. Green Bay was back in front, 17–14.

Howard set up the Packers' next score, a 31-yard field goal, with a weaving 34-yard punt return to the Patriots' 47. Later in the second quarter, Green Bay increased its lead to 27–14 after picking off Bledsoe for a second time. Favre drove the offense 74 yards in nine plays for a touchdown, finishing things off himself with a scrambling, diving two-yard scoring run around the left side. The game then turned into a stalemate, with neither team mounting much of a threat until late in the third quarter, when New England running back Curtis Martin ran the ball in from 18 yards out and cut the Packers' lead to 27–21. The momentum again seemed to be slipping away from Green Bay.

That was when Howard seized it back. Standing at his own one-yard line, he received the ensuing kickoff with 3:24 left in the third quarter and headed straight up the middle of the field. The blocking for a middle return was perfect, and the Green Bay wedge gave Howard a clear lane. Nobody came close to tackling him until he had crossed the 25, when linebacker Marty Moore dove at Howard from behind. ("I think my hand may have touched his leg," Moore said, "but that was it.") At the 29, Patriots receiver Hason Graham, who had been activated the morning of the game over regular Troy Brown, hit Howard with a diving, glancing blow to his right shoulder. Graham's right hand came down across Howard's face mask and dragged his head down slightly. But while the hit broke Howard's gliding stride, it did not stop his forward momentum — it actually bounced him outside to daylight. He high-stepped for a few yards and then suddenly he was almost all alone.

Running down the left side, in the green between the hash marks and the numbers, Howard sprinted past New England kicker Adam Vinatieri and into the open field at the Packers' 46.* Nobody came close to him after that. When Favre threw to tight end Mark Chmura in the back of the end zone for a two-point conversion, Green Bay led 35–21 and the game was effectively over. The next time New England kicked the ball, with a little more than a minute left in the third quarter, Tupa punted it out of bounds. Lesson learned — but too late.

White had ended the Patriots' next possession after Howard's touchdown with sacks of Bledsoe on second and third down. He would add one more to finish the game with three, a Super Bowl record. He finally had his long-awaited championship. Favre threw for 246 yards and two long touchdown passes. But Howard was the star — an easy choice as the game's MVP. He returned six of the seven punts he caught for a record 90 yards. He took back four kickoffs for 154 yards and a touchdown. His best punt returns led directly to 10 points. He scored six more on his kickoff return, which was followed up by a two-point conversion.

"Desmond Howard," said New England assistant Al Groh, "ruined a perfectly good game."

He had done more than that. He had lifted the Packers back to the top of the NFL.

---

* *Vinatieri complained in* The Boston Globe *the next day that he had been held by defensive end Keith McKenzie. Replays do indeed show McKenzie getting a fistful of the front of Vinatieri's jersey and the kicker struggling to break free. But it happened right in front of umpire Ron Botchan, who did not throw a flag. Howard appears to have been running too wide and too fast for Vinatieri to have caught him.*

A TURNAROUND BUILT ON FAITH

BY

PETER KING

The one thing Green Bay Packers fans have always had is faith. That was hard to have as the 1991 season drew to a close. The 4-12 Packers hadn't had a 500-yard rusher in either 1990 or '91. They also hadn't had a 2,000-yard passer in either season. Ron Wolf, who'd been hired to replace Tom Braatz as general manager on November 27, took a look around and decided that he had to get a new offensive brain to replace conservative coach Lindy Infante, and a new arm to replace the errant ones of Don Majkowski, Mike Tomczak, and Blair Kiel, who had combined that year for 17 touchdown passes and 19 interceptions.

The challenge Wolf faced was this: How to remake a moribund team that had won only four of its last 21 games. Isn't it amazing, looking back 28 years, that the Packers were that awful?

In 1992, I covered the first draft of the Ron Wolf–Mike Holmgren regime, and I remember three things:
1. The optimism in town, and around the team. There was this vibe of trust around Wolf and Holmgren, Wolf's handpicked Bill Walsh disciple of a coach. I went to dinner in Green Bay with Holmgren and his wife, Kathy, the night before the draft and, from the waiter to the neck-craning fans, the good feeling was palpable.

2. The Vince Lombardiness of the place. Remember: There was no lovely Lambeau Field remake yet, no craft-beer-filled atrium, no Don Hutson Center. Brett Favre was just a few months removed from a one-season stint as a pudgy, failed Falcon. Aaron Rodgers was eight years old. I toured the Packers Hall of Fame and heard Lombardi's voice in a cool exhibit on the coach. His portrait hung in the spartan lobby of the team's office. The last time he had been in Green Bay was the last time this franchise had consistently been any good. "There are ghosts of Christmases past in here," Wolf told me the day before the draft. "I feel them. They're here wherever you go."

3. Wolf's confidence. I hadn't known him well before my trip to Green Bay, but I soon got the feeling that he knew what he was doing and he wasn't shy about letting you know it. Ten weeks earlier he'd traded one of the Packers' two first-round picks in the draft to Atlanta for Favre. And before the draft began, Wolf told Holmgren, "We've already had a good draft. We've got Brett Favre."

How preposterous it was back then to think Favre was the answer to every Cheesehead's prayers. (Wait: Cheeseheads weren't even really a thing in the NFL yet!) Wolf knew. He knew Favre had "it" even though he'd ballooned to 248 pounds by the end of his star-crossed 1991 season in Atlanta. Wolf knew because when he'd worked in the front office of the quarterback-needy New York Jets in 1991, he'd graded all the players in the draft and he had Southern Miss

quarterback Brett Favre number one. That's number one. Overall.

I didn't know the full story till I saw Wolf the day before the draft in his Green Bay office. In 1991, the Jets didn't have a first-round pick; they'd used it in the 1990 supplemental draft to pick Syracuse wide receiver Rob Moore. Wolf was convinced that if New York had picked Favre in the first round in 1991, he never would have been an option for the Packers in 1992. As it was, Favre tumbled down the board in

'91 and Jets general manager Dick Steinberg started trying to trade up to get him. But he kept striking out — till he came to this portion of the draft:

32. Phoenix Cardinals
33. Atlanta Falcons
34. New York Jets

Steinberg knew that Falcons general manager Ken Herock liked Favre, and that Atlanta had scouted him a lot. Steinberg made a tentative deal with the Cardinals to leapfrog the Falcons, but when Phoenix's pick came up, the Cards said no dice. There was a player they wanted — North Carolina State defensive end Mike Jones — and they didn't want to risk losing him by moving down two spots. New York was ticked off. Rightfully so. With the 33rd selection, Atlanta picked Favre. The Jets settled for Browning Nagle. Yikes.

Falcons coach Jerry Glanville was down on the cocky kid from Kiln, Mississippi, from the start. Favre never had a chance in Atlanta. Glanville was thrilled when Herock came to him in early 1992 and said that he could get a first-round pick from the Packers, number 19 overall, for Favre. Turns out Glanville was good at burying people. He never gave that 19th pick, Southern Miss running back Tony Smith, much of a shot, either (87 carries in three years). And so that Favre pick didn't work out for anyone — except for Wolf and the Packers.

Now all the Packers had to do was coach Favre, which Holmgren (mostly) and Steve Mariucci did together, overcoming the many, many rough times along the way. The story about Holmgren putting to a vote of his coaching staff whether Favre would remain the quarterback after a rocky stretch in 1994 is absolutely true. But there was another reason why the Packers turned around.

Holmgren trusted Wolf and didn't interfere much in the personnel side of things. Wolf trusted Holmgren and didn't interfere much in the coaching side of things.

My favorite example of this was in 1995. Holmgren gave me inside access to the team to write a story for *Sports Illustrated* about a week in the life of the Packers. I could go anywhere, see anything. On Wednesday that week, Wolf was out scouting someplace and he phoned Holmgren in his office. Wolf told him he was signing tight end Keith Jackson. The Packers didn't need a tight end; Mark Chmura was reliable. He was also one of Favre's best friends. But Jackson was an offensive force, he was available, and Wolf thought it would boost the offense for the playoff stretch.

Holmgren got off the phone. He was not happy. He wasn't angry about it; he simply felt Jackson wasn't needed and could upset the well-balanced chemistry of the team. A coach works hard to make sure that the feeling in his locker room is just right. One of the reasons Holmgren had let me in was that he knew I would be seeing a harmonious team — and I did. He wasn't sure what effect Jackson was going to have on the Packers' mood. But he told me that afternoon, "We'll make it work. That's my job."

I've often thought that a truly underrated aspect of the Packers' transformation into a truly great team was that Holmgren was really good at his job — the coaching, the game planning, the dressing down,

the propping up. And Wolf was also really good (Hall of Fame good) at roster construction, at knowing that the 38th man in the locker room could win a game as well as the third man in the room. And he and Holmgren respected the heck out of each other. Holmgren knew very little about Favre in February 1992 when Wolf traded for him, but he had to trust that Wolf knew what he was doing. They were joined at the hip, and it turned out to be a partnership that started a three-decade run of prominence.

Holmgren got the best out of Favre, who became one of the greatest quarterbacks of all time. Wolf and Holmgren persuaded Reggie White to come to Green Bay, opening the door not only for a remake of the Packers' defense but also for a new way of thinking in the NFL — for free-agent players who might never have considered Green Bay. The faith I saw in the people around Green Bay in early 1992? Very well placed.

That faith has been rewarded over and over since the arrival of Wolf. Wolf begat Mike Sherman, who, after an undistinguished personnel run, begat Ted Thompson, who drafted Aaron Rodgers in 2005. The Packers have had terrific quarterback play for 26 seasons. And now, with the youthful Brian Gutekunst in Wolf's old chair, the pressure will build for him to find the team's next great passer, the man to lead the franchise into the 2030s.

CHAPTER 18

INTO THE FUTURE

It had been a long climb back to the pinnacle of professional football for the Packers, and the feelings of exhilaration and inspiration were palpable not only throughout the organization but also throughout the team's legion of devoted fans. An estimated 250 of them greeted Green Bay's DC-10 charter at Austin Straubel International Airport when it landed at 2:10 in the afternoon on the Monday after Super Bowl XXXI, and 100,000 more lined the streets of downtown in snowy, 20-degree weather for the victory procession to Lambeau Field. Inside the stadium, 60,000 were waiting for a celebration dubbed "Return to Titletown." The mood in the city was giddy—the crush of people was so great that it took the open-air buses more than three hours to travel the 10-mile route that ended at the stadium. And the word "Titletown" was omnipresent. People could not stop saying it. "Doesn't it sound sweet to read that word again and have it mean something?" gushed a January 28 editorial in the *Press-Gazette.*

Six months after Green Bay's Super Bowl victory, the village of Ashwaubenon, a suburb on the west side of the Fox River that borders Lambeau Field on three sides, voted to rename a section of Gross Street—a north–south artery two blocks east of the stadium—for coach Mike Holmgren. Vince Lombardi had won five championships and retired as coach before a street was ever named after him; Highland Avenue did not become Lombardi Avenue until August 1968. This time, though, nobody was waiting around. The Pack really *was* back,

and it was as if the people of Green Bay wanted to make it official before that fact could change.

It was the prudent thing to do, because not long after the Packers won their 12th championship, it became clear that remaining elite in the modern NFL was just as hard as becoming elite. The advent of free agency, the very thing that had helped to transform Green Bay into a winner again, also imposed a kind of self-destruct timer on the team— as it did on any championship team. In the 1990s, the discussion around Super Bowl–winning franchises suddenly included talk of their windows, those finite periods during which the conditions for winning championships were ideal, when a team had enough young stars under contract on both sides of the ball to contend. The Packers' window had opened in 1995, when they reached the NFC title game. By January 1998 it was already starting to close.

Nothing could have seemed more improbable on September 1, 1997, when Green Bay beat the Bears 38–24 at Lambeau Field on opening day. The Packers cruised through the 1997 season like a team that was ready to repeat. For the most part, the offensive and defensive starters were the same as they had been in 1996. Free agency had cost Green Bay only a few significant contributors from its Super Bowl team, including kick returner Desmond Howard, who signed with the Oakland Raiders, and kicker Chris Jacke, who signed with the Washington Redskins. There had been buzz before the season began that the Packers had a chance to go undefeated. That dream died in week two, when they lost 10–9 to the Eagles in Philadelphia after rookie kicker Ryan Longwell missed a 28-yard field goal in the closing seconds. But the loss did not change the fact that the team seemed destined to capture a second straight championship — Green Bay won 12 of its next 14 games. Brett Favre won an unprecedented third straight MVP award. The Packers had the number-two scoring offense in the NFL, and the defense held six regular-season opponents to 11 points or fewer. They defeated the Buccaneers and the 49ers in the playoffs by a combined score of 44–17 and rolled into San Diego for Super Bowl XXXII as 11½-point favorites over the AFC champion Denver Broncos. The headline for a column on the game in the Super Bowl Sunday edition of the *Press-Gazette* read, ANYTHING BUT A "W" SEEMS UNLIKELY.

But it was in San Diego that things finally began to break apart. Reports appeared on the Wednesday before the game that coach Mike Holmgren had been contacted by the Seattle Seahawks about

becoming the team's coach and general manager. Holmgren denied the report, but his interest in a dual role was well known. He had hinted in the past that he was intrigued by such an arrangement, and he had turned down at least one offer to extend his contract with the Packers, which ran through the 1999 season. Unlike Bill Parcells in New England the year before, Holmgren would not admit that there was truth to the rumor, but he also did not dismiss the notion that he might move to Seattle, saying, "I'd rather not deal with anything like that until after the game."

It was the first sign that the championship organization Ron Wolf had built might be in danger of splintering. And it did not bode well. Despite Holmgren's insistence to the contrary, it is hard to avoid the conclusion that the Denver Broncos may not have been the only thing on his mind

Packers' president Bob Harlan celebrates the passage of the Lambeau Field renovation sales tax on September 12, 2000. The tax contributed $160 million to the $295 million renovation plan.

in San Diego. In a crushing 31–24 upset loss, he was clearly outcoached by Denver's Mike Shanahan, whose moves Holmgren never countered. The most glaring example of this was in his refusal to account for the Broncos' high-risk defensive strategy of blitzing Favre relentlessly — specifically by keeping a back in to block instead of sending him out for a pass. With the score tied 7–7 near the end of the first quarter, Denver's pressure induced Favre into throwing an interception that led directly to a Broncos touchdown. On the Packers' next series, free safety Steve Atwater sacked Favre and forced a fumble that was recovered by defensive end Neil Smith. Four plays later, Denver

kicker Jason Elam booted a 51-yard field goal for a 17–7 lead.

"Certain calls were to be made that weren't made," Wolf told the *Milwaukee Journal Sentinel* in 2007. "Mike Holmgren refused those calls . . . There would have been an adjustment on the blocking scheme and it would have been over. One of the great things about playing the game of football is you have to adjust. When you fail to adjust in critical situations you're going to lose, and that's what happened. To be pigheaded about it, I mean, to have the answer and then not apply it, that's a little different."

There were other odd decisions. During the regular season, the Broncos' run defense had allowed a league-high 4.73 yards per rush. On those terms alone, it was the worst run defense ever to appear in a Super Bowl. But Holmgren did not exploit it, especially late in the game. Green Bay running back Dorsey Levens had run for 1,435 yards in 16 regular-season games and had rushed for 226 more in the Packers' two playoff victories. He carried the ball four times for 38 yards on Green Bay's opening possession against Denver. But despite the score being close and the Packers' needing to control the clock, Levens ran the ball only once after the 9:11 mark of the third quarter. Late in the fourth, Holmgren inexplicably lost track of what down it was during the Broncos' winning touchdown drive. And on fourth-and-six from the Denver 31-yard line with 32 seconds left — after a timeout had given him plenty of time to make a decision — Holmgren called for a pass that, according to tight end Mark Chmura, Green Bay had not run since training camp and was not the ideal option against the Broncos' blitz. Sure enough, Denver brought pressure, and linebacker John Mobley broke up Favre's floater to Chmura. Game over.

In the locker room after the game, Wolf bluntly summed up the crushing implications of the defeat: "We're a one-year wonder. Just a fart in the wind."

Favre was more resolute. "I'm 28," he said. "I think I'll be back — hopefully several times."

But it was not to be. Nine starters became free agents after the 1997 season, and Green Bay lost five of them: cornerback Doug Evans, punter Craig Hentrich, safety Eugene Robinson, guard Aaron Taylor, and defensive end Gabe Wilkins. And a month after an 11-5 season in 1998 ended with a disappointing 30–27 wild-card loss to the 49ers in San Francisco, Holmgren left, too. He had never regained the trust of Packers fans after the news of his possible move to Seattle had immediately preceded his questionable coaching decisions in one of the most excruciating losses in

team history. Rumors of a secret deal between the coach and the Seahawks abounded. Things became ugly toward the end. On November 29, 1998, as Holmgren was walking toward the tunnel in the north end zone at Lambeau Field at halftime of a 24–16 victory over the Philadelphia Eagles, a disgruntled fan yelled to him from the stands that he should start focusing on his current job instead of worrying about his next one. Instead of ignoring the heckler, Holmgren responded with what the *Press-Gazette* described the next day as "a few choice words." Holmgren later admitted that he was "embarrassed" by the incident and said that the fan had said some "pretty personal" things about his family, which had "crossed the line with me." The exchange was captured on video by a local television station, but on the tape the fan's only comments were about Holmgren's job.

On January 8, 1999, five days after the playoff loss in San Francisco, Holmgren left Green Bay — left the general manager who had found him the players who helped him turn a losing team into a winning one in his first season, left the city that had revered him so much it had named a street for him, and left a future Hall of Fame quarterback in the prime of his career — to become the coach and general manager of the Seattle Seahawks. The Seahawks had none of what the Packers did. There was no brilliant young quarterback. There was no winning tradition; there was hardly a tradition at all. The franchise was just 23 years old and had been to the playoffs only four times. But not only did Seattle give Holmgren an eight-year contract worth at least $4 million a season, making him by far the highest-paid coach in the NFL, but it also gave him what the Packers would not — and what he coveted most: total control over football operations.

But with much more responsibility than he had ever had in his career, Holmgren struggled to replicate the success he had enjoyed in Green Bay. He led the Seahawks to a 9-7 finish and a wild-card berth in 1999, the team's first postseason appearance in 11 years. But Seattle missed the playoffs in each of the three seasons after that, going 22-26. And his problems went beyond the field. In the summer of 2002, Holmgren released middle linebacker Levon Kirkland, citing concerns over the former All-Pro's weight. The 10-year veteran signed with Philadelphia and became a leader on the Eagles' fourth-ranked defense. On December 31, 2002, Seahawks president Bob Whitsitt announced that Holmgren had agreed to step down as the team's general manager. He was just a coach again. "I think it was a way to free me up to do the things they know I like to do most," Holmgren said after the move.

Holmgren coached in Seattle for six more years and had only one more losing season. He even led the Seahawks to an NFC championship in 2005. But he did it all without the power that he had left Green Bay to get. And if he had just been patient, he would have eventually gotten his chance to take over the Packers' football operations. Wolf had brought former defensive coordinator Ray Rhodes back to Green Bay to replace Holmgren in 1999, making Rhodes the first African American coach in the team's history. But the Packers went 8-8 and missed the playoffs in a season of discontent and underachievement—the lack of a sense of urgency on the practice field reminded Wolf of the atmosphere around the team when he first arrived, and the lack of discipline on the team recalled the worst days of Scooter McLean. Wolf hated to fire the team's first African American coach, but he bit the bullet after one season and replaced Rhodes with Seahawks offensive coordinator Mike Sherman. Sherman, who had been the tight ends coach in Green Bay in 1997 and '98, was on the job for all of two seasons before Wolf retired in 2001. Packers president Bob Harlan then made Sherman, who had not begun coaching in the NFL until 1997, Green Bay's coach and general manager.

Holmgren had been shooting for the stars, trying to see how great he could be on his own. It is the very ambition at the root of the American Dream. Running, reaching, grasping. But money and power are the classic corruptors of all things noble and good, and there was something unseemly about his departure, and it lay in what he was leaving behind. Green Bay was not just anyplace. And Brett Favre was not just any quarterback.

Favre later said that he had been blindsided by Holmgren's departure. With the tempestuous coach on the sideline, Favre had matured from a raw, rocket-armed freelancer into a superstar. But after Holmgren left, Favre's discipline seemed to go, too. The quarterback came to rely too much on his arm strength and talent. In his three MVP seasons, he had averaged 37.3 touchdown passes and 14.0 interceptions. But in the 10 seasons he played in Green Bay after Holmgren's departure, he averaged 26.0 touchdowns and 19.3 interceptions. Favre still remained a formidable winner—in the 16 years that he was under center in Green Bay, the team suffered through just one losing season. But the Packers were never again as great as they had been when Favre and Holmgren were together.

"I just expected us to be together forever," Favre said. "I think that was the first time in my career that my eyes were opened to, *You won't be here forever—neither will the players you play with or the coaches that coach you.*"

⋄ ⋄ ⋄

As the Packers were beginning their drive toward what many assumed would be a second straight championship, they began another drive that was nearly as significant. On October 10, 1997, Green Bay announced that it planned to go ahead with a new stock sale, the fourth in franchise history and the first since the one in 1950 that had saved the team from ruin. This time the goal was not to rescue the organization from financial disaster, but instead to help ensure its continued existence. Packers president Bob Harlan wanted upgrades for Lambeau Field—the official term was "capital im-

the Sullivan-Wallen American Legion Post to the Green Bay Packers Foundation. In the unlikely event that the organization was sold, the foundation would disburse the proceeds to charitable causes throughout the state of Wisconsin.

The sale, which went from November 13, 1997, to March 16, 1998, added 105,989 new owners (who purchased 120,010 shares of stock) and raised more than $24 million. The Packers' existing 1,940 shareholders received a 1,000-to-1 split on their original shares, meaning that a single share multiplied overnight into 1,000 shares.* In the first 11 days of the sale, Green Bay raised $7.8 million. Sales remained brisk through the holidays but slowed dramatically after New Year's. Residents of Wisconsin purchased more than half of the stock, but 46.4 percent of new shareholders came from the 49 other states, Guam, and the U.S. Virgin Islands. Just as it had in 1950, ownership of the team became more diverse, more widespread. And just like in 1950, the stock offering deepened the relationship between the team and the people who supported it. It was a long way from George Whitney Calhoun passing his hat among the spectators at Hagemeister Park in 1919.

And yet—and this is the magic of the Packers—there was still an element of Calhoun's fedora in the whole thing, a spirit and a bond between the team and the people that went well beyond a mostly worthless piece of paper hanging in a frame on the living room wall. Lewis "Louie" Konop had purchased his first share of Green Bay stock in 1950, for $25. Konop had grown up on the east side of town, on Elm Street, just across the East River from old City Stadium—as a boy, he and his friends used to sneak into Packers games by crawling through holes they had dug under the wooden fence that surrounded the place. Konop was the oldest of six children. His father, Charles, was a mechanic at the Nash Motors dealership, on

Running back Dorsey Levens ran for 226 yards on 52 carries in the Packers' two playoff games before Super Bowl XXXII. But he had only 19 carries in the loss to the Broncos—the last with 10:55 left in the game.

provements"—as well as face-lifts for some of the team's other facilities. The target for the 1950 sale had been $200,000, or $1.33 million in 1997 dollars. Now Green Bay was hoping to raise as much as $80 million.

Besides the money, the most significant aspect of the offering was that it gave the franchise a chance to amend its bylaws and other particulars for the first time in more than 60 years. The team dropped the word "The" from the official name of the corporation, which became Green Bay Packers Inc. And the beneficiary was changed from

* As in the past, purchasing Packers stock was basically a way to make a contribution to the team. The stock is not traded on a major exchange, does not appreciate in value, and pays no dividends. The only real privilege associated with owning it is the right to vote on team matters presented at annual stockholders' meetings.

Madison Street. Louie had gone to Green Bay East High, and then into the Navy during World War II. In 1946, he purchased 120 penny peanut-vending machines for $10 each. He soon graduated to vending other merchandise besides peanuts, including cigarettes, coffee, candy, sandwiches, and even disposable swimsuits. By the time of the 1997 stock sale, Konop had built his operation into one of Wisconsin's largest locally owned vending machine operations.

He was also still a fan of the Packers. "My father didn't miss a game for 47 years," says Tom Konop, the younger of his two sons, who is now the president of the business that his father built, as well as the president of the Green Bay Packers Hall of Fame. "My dad knew Vince Lombardi. We're still big Packers fans."

And so, when Green Bay opened the fourth stock sale in its history, Louie Konop knew the perfect Christmas gift for each of his seven grandchildren: a share of the team. And when an eighth grandchild was born, on February 22, 1998, he made one of the final purchases of the sale, buying a single share for his new grandson, Tom's son Ryan. Louie passed away at the age of 94 in 2016. Ryan is now a senior at Butler University. And his share still hangs in a frame on the wall of his bedroom back home in Green Bay.

A family heirloom.

◆ ◆ ◆

The Packers' bottom line had spent most of the 1990s climbing to record highs. Green Bay was so well-off that in October 1994 the team announced that, beginning with the 1995 season, it would no longer be playing four home games (one in the preseason and three in the regular season) in Milwaukee's aging County Stadium. The trips to Milwaukee were, in many ways, road games for the Packers, and the team said that cutting the dates would mean an extra $2.5 million in revenue from concessions, parking, and ticket sales. Ninety new luxury boxes were built above the north end zone in 1995, fully enclosing the field and increasing

Lambeau's capacity to 60,890. The suites added $2.2 million in revenue in their first season of use. Green Bay made a record $6.7 million in fiscal year 1998, which ran from April 1, 1997, to March 31, 1998. The Packers ranked ninth out of 30 teams in the NFL in revenue in 1997, continuing a steady climb that had taken them from 20th (of 28) to 15th to 11th in the preceding three years. In the financial ledger, the team seemed to be doing as well as it was on the field, where it had qualified for the playoffs five years in a row.

But the hard truth that the Packers had to face after the sale was that passing the proverbial hat was no longer enough. Harlan insisted that he was thrilled to have raised $24 million, but it was far short of the $80 million goal the team had set back in November. The Packers reached the playoffs again in 1998 but dropped to 15th in the league in revenue. The next year they fell to 16th (of 31). The problem was something called "locally generated revenue," which was accountant-speak for how much money a team was able to make with its home stadium through concessions, parking, naming rights, ticket sales, luxury boxes, and club seats. The Washington Redskins ranked 17th in the NFL in that category in 1996, the team's final season in aging RFK Stadium. One year later, after moving into brand-new FedEx Field, in Landover, Maryland, the Redskins jumped all the way to number two in local revenue. In 1999, Washington led the league with $83.9 million. The NFL's profit-sharing television deal paid Green Bay the same as every other team in the league, but without a deep-pocketed owner who could dip into savings during lean times, it was crucial for the Packers to be able to make money on their own. And in that regard, they were falling off the pace because of Lambeau Field.

It was not that the stadium was a dump. It was still a great place to watch football. But it was maxed out, basically usable for only 10 days a year between the preseason and the regular season. Once Green Bay was done playing football,

Lambeau Field was shut down, the heat and water turned off. In 1998, the Packers made about $20 million from Lambeau, whereas teams with new or renovated stadiums were making about $36 million. "Every time a team moved into a new stadium, they jumped over us in revenue—and it seemed like everybody was moving," says Harlan. "We needed something that would be open 365 days a year . . . Why would you come to Lambeau in January, February, and March? What, are you going to look at the stadium and then go home? We needed to make it a destination."

Harlan had seen how the opening of Camden Yards, in Baltimore, in 1992 had ushered in a building boom for destination stadiums—not just in Major League Baseball but also in pro football. From 1995 to 2003, 17 new or renovated stadiums opened in the NFL. Harlan scrapped his original plan for a renovation to Lambeau that would have cost between $75 million and $96 million, in part because it became apparent that the plan was too modest, but also because he needed to make sure that he had money on hand to pay free-agent signing bonuses. The Packers were not going to be able to make stadium improvements without outside help.

On January 22, 2000, Harlan announced a plan for a $295 million renovation to Lambeau Field. The design was by the Minneapolis architectural firm Ellerbe Becket Inc., which had planned the 1997 renovation of Notre Dame Stadium. In South Bend, nearly 21,000 seats had been added without spoiling the stadium's classic look. Harlan cited it as the model for what he wanted to do with Lambeau Field. Ellerbe Becket's design for Lambeau, which would increase capacity by 11,600, was industrial and vintage, all red brick and green wrought iron. But there were modern touches, including three stories of luxury boxes that circled the field, a new press box, and a five-story atrium for shopping, entertainment, and team offices.

The retro look came directly from Harlan: "I told them, 'I want a red-brick building with green wrought-iron gates, and I want it to look like it's the fifties. I want black-and-white pictures and elevators that you can see out of. I want pipes showing . . . I wanted to show the history and the tradition of this franchise in this city. It got to the point that they would bring me something and show it to me and say, 'Bob, does this look old enough?'"

But $160 million, more than half of the cost of the renovation, was slated to come from public funding. And unfortunately for Harlan, the people of Wisconsin held a dim view of publicly financed sports stadiums—and with good reason. In 1995, the issue of public financing for a new stadium for Major League Baseball's Milwaukee Brewers had gotten so contentious that it resulted in the only recall of a state legislator in Wisconsin history. Brewers owner Bud Selig had been threatening to move his team if he could not find a replacement for County Stadium, which had opened in 1953. But the proposed 0.1 percent sales tax that would be levied on the 1,690,493 residents of the five-county stadium district caused so much controversy that the vote on the matter was confined to the Wisconsin legislature rather than being left open to a public referendum. Wisconsin voters had already rejected a plan that would have created a special sports lottery to help finance construction of the ballpark.

The fight in the legislature was a bitter one. A stadium financing bill passed the state assembly by a 52–47 vote on September 29, 1995, and then cleared the final hurdle when it passed the state senate one week later by a vote of 16–15. The deciding ballot was cast by George Petak, a Republican state senator from Racine. Petak had been for the new stadium before his county was included in the stadium district, at which point he turned against it. But after a 16-hour session that ended at 4:55 a.m.—during which the bill was defeated on two separate occasions—Petak, realizing that the bill was going to fail for a third and final time, switched his vote at the last second. Voters in Racine were incensed. They removed Petak from office eight months later in a closely contested recall election. "We made 15 trips to Madison to talk to the politicians," says Harlan about his efforts, five years later, to secure funding for Lambeau Field. "They were still upset about it."

There were other things working against Harlan's plan. Chief among them was that the proposed sales tax for the 220,733 people in Brown County — the Lambeau stadium district — was 0.5 percent (a penny for every two dollars spent), meaning that a population base more than seven and a half times smaller than the one in Milwaukee would be paying a levy five times as big on every purchase. The proposed Lambeau Field Atrium was also a major sticking point, with critics protesting that it would compete with local businesses. "Why do the Packers want to put a mall next to the stadium when we've got empty stores in the mall downtown?" one opponent asked.

It was seemingly the complete opposite of what any outsider would have expected — the people's team was telling the people what it needed to survive, and for the first time ever, the people were reluctant to kick in. But this was not a stock drive soliciting voluntary contributions. The renovation tax would compel financial support from everyone in Brown County, whether they wanted — or could afford — to give money to the Packers or not. The Wisconsin Legislative Fiscal Bureau estimated that the tax would cost the average citizen of Brown County 13 cents a day. That worked out to about $47 a year. If you were a season-ticket holder, it was not much. But in a county where more than 42 percent of households had incomes of $30,000 a year or less, neither was it insignificant.

And so the drive for funding was not as sentimentally good-natured as it had been for the stock sale less than three years before. There would be no shares to hang on the wall, to be passed down from parent to child. In February 2000, shortly after Harlan announced the plan for renovation, support for the tax had been at nearly 62 percent in Brown County, but by early May it had dropped to 49 percent, while opposition had increased from 34 percent to 46 percent. Four months later, support for the tax increased to 53 percent, but Harlan went into the September 12 referendum thinking that the vote could go either way. He responded by making himself the public face of the Packers. On the Saturday before the polls opened, Harlan started work at six in the morning, visiting a dozen or so restaurants to talk to prospective voters over breakfast. Then he went to a Walmart and stood in front of the store for an hour, meeting people as they were going in and coming out. He did the same thing at Sam's Club before heading to De Pere and canvassing for votes door-to-door. At one point, Harlan approached a woman who brushed past him and snapped, "Don't you touch me! You people are crazy!"

Harlan was used to such responses. "I could talk to 20 people, and 10 would like it and 10 would hate it," he says. "It was brutal."

On Election Day, the voters of Brown County narrowly rewarded Harlan for his efforts, approving the sales tax 53 percent to 47 percent. It had been close, but the community's support for the Packers won out. "The people are the owners," says Harlan. "I am a caretaker. I tried to take care of the team and to make sure it was healthy and financially stable. If the referendum had failed, I'm not sure the Packers would still be here."

The results — completed on time and on budget — bore out his vision. Green Bay had ranked 20th in the NFL in team revenue in 2001. One year later, with the renovation not yet finished, the Packers jumped up to 10th, based in large part on the early opening of their new gift shop and the sale of several gate sponsorships. One year later, Green Bay ranked 10th again. Today, 16 years later, the team still ranks in the top half of the league's revenue ranking. The sales tax ended on September 30, 2015. The stadium is still sold out on game days, of course, but the Atrium makes Lambeau Field a year-round destination. The Packers Hall of Fame,

a restaurant, a gift shop, and other event spaces have turned the NFL's longest continually occupied stadium into an entertainment district. The Atrium is booked through 2021, and in 2017 Lambeau Field hosted more than 700 events. It is no coincidence that the main entrance to the Atrium, where statues of Curly Lambeau and Vince Lombardi stand sentry, bears the name Harlan Plaza.

"You can argue all day about whether the public should help fund the construction or renovation of venues for professional sports teams," read an editorial in the *Press-Gazette* on September 20, 2015, a little more than a week before the sales tax was set to expire. "What you can't argue about, though, is the outcome of this example of public funding: it has been an unqualified success, doing exactly what it set out to do."

The renovation of Lambeau looks even better when compared with what has happened in Milwaukee with Miller Park. The sales tax used to fund its construction has yet to sunset, even though it has been in effect since 1996. The earliest it could be retired, according to reports, is 2019 or 2020.

Lambeau Field, on the other hand, needs no such help anymore. When it was improved and expanded again between 2011 and 2015, the Packers did it all without any public money. They added more than 8,000 seats — bringing capacity to 81,441 — upgraded the scoreboards and the team's football facilities, and renovated the Atrium, to the tune of $312 million. And, aided in part by the $67,407,750 they raised in a fifth stock sale, in 2011, they did it all themselves.

◆ ◆ ◆

In March 2001, while Lambeau Field was still in the early stages of its renovation, Brett Favre signed a 10-year, $100 million contract that everyone assumed would make him a Packer for life. "I couldn't envision myself playing with another team," he said at the press conference announcing the new deal. "Don't want to. If that was to ever come up, I probably would just retire. I've made enough money to where I don't need to jump ship and go somewhere else."

Why would he ever want to do that? Favre had been the primary catalyst for the resurrection of the franchise, a playmaking savant whose right arm had helped to lift Green Bay back into the NFL's elite. During his rise from being a third-stringer for the Falcons to an MVP for the Packers, he had been consistently brilliant, and he had also become something more than just a local hero. He was the gunslinger who not only had returned the Lombardi Trophy to its rightful home, but also could not be stopped by injury, illness (on the last day of the 1995 season, he vomited on the sideline before throwing the winning touchdown pass against the Steelers to clinch the division title), or Buccaneers All-Pro defensive tackle Warren Sapp, whose trash talk Favre would time and again defuse with a head butt and a smile. He had started every game for Green Bay since the week after he came off the bench to spark the Packers to a comeback win over the Bengals in 1992, a streak that by that time had grown to 154 regular-season games and 14 playoff games.

What made Favre all the more embraceable was his humanity. He was flawed and funny and far from perfect. He loved to hunt, a big deal in Wisconsin. He dared to joke during games with the combustible Holmgren, a famously intense taskmaster. He pantsed players at practice. And before the 1996 season — the one that ended with Green Bay's first championship in 29 years — he tearfully admitted to having been addicted to painkillers. He was not from Wisconsin, but there were a lot of people from the state, and from everywhere else in the United States, who could identify with him. He became larger than life, the marquee player on one of the NFL's marquee teams.

But not long after Green Bay's loss in Super Bowl XXXII and the subsequent departure of Holmgren, Favre's impetuousness — the very quality (besides the winning) that had made him so endearing — began to grate on Cheeseheads, almost imperceptibly at first, and then more and more. After Wolf fired Ray Rhodes following the 1999 season, new coach Mike Sherman was moderately successful at getting Favre to play within himself. In 2001, he came as close to his MVP days as he ever would, throwing for 32 touchdowns, with just 15 interceptions. Green Bay went 12-4, and the glory seemed to have returned. But Wolf had retired three months before the season began, and Harlan made the callow Sherman coach and general manager. It was a stunning decision. The two jobs had been too much for Vince Lombardi in 1968 —and then for Phil Bengtson, Dan Devine, Bart Starr, and Forrest Gregg. Sherman had been a career assistant in college football before becoming the Packers' tight ends coach in 1997. His only other experience as a head coach had been at the high school level, but within just four years he had nevertheless risen to a position of power enjoyed by only two other men in the NFL at the time: Holmgren and Eagles coach Andy Reid, both of whom had won at least one playoff game.* When Sherman became coach and general manager in Green Bay, he had yet to even reach the postseason.

"I made a mistake on Mike Sherman," says Harlan. "Brett had told me that it was the best team chemistry he had seen in Green Bay. This is after two Super Bowls. I was afraid that if I brought somebody in from the outside, he and Mike would clash. And so, even though it went against my philosophy, I did it . . . I didn't want to disrupt the organization, because it looked like we were taking off again, you know?"

Harlan says that the promotion changed Sherman. "Mike became a different person," he says.

"He stopped talking to people." Scouts in the office even began to worry that they might run into the scowling Sherman in the hallway. That may explain why Favre, after two seasons of relatively disciplined play, became increasingly erratic. From 2003 through 2006, he never threw fewer than 17 interceptions, and in 2005 he threw 29. Even worse, he was throwing for fewer and fewer touchdowns, dropping from 32 in 2003 to just 18 in 2006.

To be fair, the Packers had declined significantly. The team that went to two straight Super Bowls had featured a dominant defense. But after Reggie White retired in 1999, and LeRoy Butler did the same in 2002, neither Wolf nor Sherman was able to shore up the unit.** Sherman in particular did poorly in the NFL draft. Of the 21 players he selected in three years, only three ever reached the Pro Bowl. Favre went from being the best player on a great team to being one of the only reasons the Packers were any good.

Even more scarring was that the team began to get a reputation for blowing playoff games. In the second round in 2001, Favre threw six interceptions in an ugly 45–17 loss to the St. Louis Rams. In a snowy wild-card game in 2002, Green Bay lost at Lambeau Field in the postseason for the first time when Michael Vick and the Falcons hammered the Packers 27–7. One year later, they lost in the second round to the Eagles after Philadelphia quarterback Donovan McNabb completed a 28-yard pass to wideout Freddie Mitchell on fourth-and-26 with 1:13 left in the game. Eagles kicker David Akers booted a 37-yard field goal with 10 seconds left to tie the score at 17 and then —after Favre threw a ghastly interception on the

---

*Five other coaches were the de facto general managers for their teams: New England's Bill Belichick, Jacksonville's Tom Coughlin, Minnesota's Dennis Green, Washington's Marty Schottenheimer, and Carolina's George Seifert. All of them had won at least one playoff game, and Seifert had won a Super Bowl as coach of the San Francisco 49ers.

**White retired for the first time on April 19, 1998, but he came back two days later, saying he wanted to honor a promise he had made to play through the 1998 season. He retired again in February 1999 and sat out the next season. But in 2000 he came back for one final year with the Carolina Panthers. He started 16 games for Carolina, adding five and a half more sacks to his career total, giving him a then-record 198. White died in his sleep on December 26, 2004, at the age of 43, due to the effects of cardiac arrhythmia and a respiratory disorder.

Packers' only offensive play of overtime — won it with a 31-yarder. Favre did not talk to reporters after the game.

His frustration at not being able to get back to the Super Bowl was no doubt at the root of his yearly flirtations with retirement. What had begun in November 2002 with an offhand remark in a television interview grew into an annual off-season ritual of will-he-or-won't-he? speculation. The questions about when he would retire became more frequent with each passing year, a constant drumbeat of drama. Green Bay had been through this before, with Don Hutson in the 1940s. Like Hutson, Favre was one of the biggest stars in the game. But the game was much bigger in 2005 than it had been in 1945, when there was no ESPN, no World Wide Web. At the dawn of the age of debate-style sports television — when having a

"take" on the news of the day was almost as important as the news itself — it seemed that everybody had an opinion on Favre's future. And Favre seemed to take pleasure in keeping the conversation going. The man who was renowned throughout the NFL for his toughness became something of a drama queen.

"There was something about the speculation that Favre appeared to enjoy," wrote author Jeff Pearlman. "Which was strange in that Favre wasn't one to chase headlines. He never ran from the media, but he also never seemed to openly crave the spotlight. Now, he was craving it." And some people in Green Bay were beginning to get annoyed, an attitude that only became more pronounced when the Packers went 4-12 in 2005, Favre's only losing season in 16 years in Green Bay.

The Packers were able to turn things around

Former quarterback and coach Bart Starr was an honorary captain for the Packers before their NFC championship game loss to the Giants on January 20, 2008 — Brett Favre's last game in a Green Bay uniform.

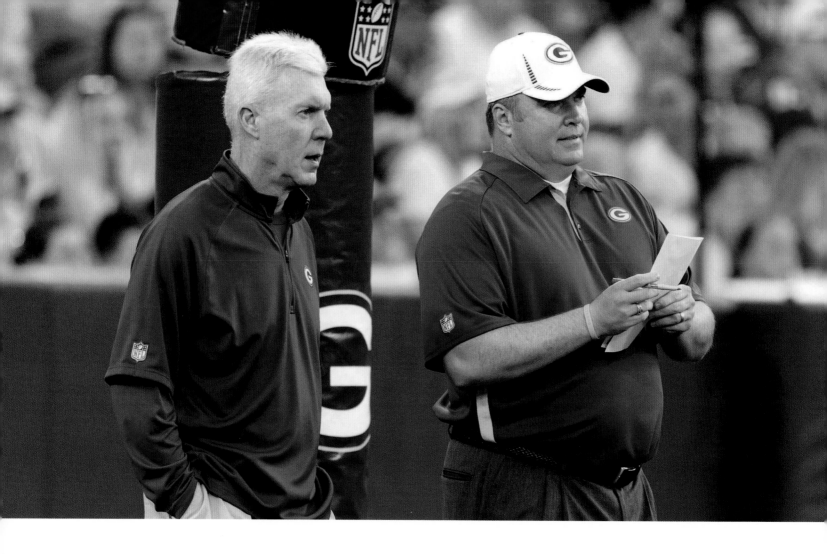

General manager Ted Thompson (left) and coach Mike McCarthy together made the choice to stick with Aaron Rodgers as their quarterback over Brett Favre. The decision caused anguish in 2008, but eventually returned Green Bay to the pinnacle of pro football.

fairly soon, however—in no small part because they were still led by one of the best quarterbacks in the game. But there were other reasons. In January of that year, Harlan had relieved Sherman of his duties as general manager and hired in his place former Green Bay scout and Seahawks vice president of football operations Ted Thompson. Much of the blame for the struggles of 2005 had to do with Thompson's decision not to re-sign starting guards Mike Wahle (whom Thompson actually cut before he was due a $6 million roster bonus) and Marco Rivera. The losses of Wahle and Rivera hurt in the short run, but they eventually proved beneficial—part of a purge of expensive veterans that helped the Packers get under the salary cap. Thompson was often criticized by fans for refusing to go all out in pursuit of free agents, but many of them forget that one of his first moves was to give the Packers the financial

breathing room they needed to go after players at all. And one of Thompson's most important early acquisitions came in April 2006, when he signed 29-year-old Oakland Raiders cornerback Charles Woodson to a seven-year, $39 million deal. The former Heisman Trophy winner soon became the linchpin of the Green Bay secondary, a two-time All-Pro with the Packers, as well as the NFL's Defensive Player of the Year in 2009. No free agent in the team's history outside of Reggie White made the sort of impact on the franchise that Woodson did.

After the debacle of 2005, Thompson fired Sherman in January 2006. The two had never been able to get along, even though it had been Thompson's decision to retain Sherman for at least one year after he was hired. "During the season, I started going down to practice, which I normally don't care to do," says Harlan. "But I wasn't going down to watch the practice; I was going down to watch Mike and Ted. And they hardly spoke to each other. I would see Ted go over and say something to Mike, and Mike would be looking off to the side like Ted's not even there."

To replace Sherman, Thompson hired 49ers offensive coordinator Mike McCarthy. The Packers went 8-8 that season, but in 2007, with Favre leading a team that featured several of Thompson's draftees playing prominent roles, Green Bay improved to 13-3 and seemed more than ready to play in another Super Bowl. But in a frigid NFC Championship Game against the New York Giants at Lambeau Field, where the temperature at kickoff was one below zero, Favre threw his last pass as a Green Bay Packer, in his 275th consecutive start.* With the game tied 20–20 in overtime, he lofted a ball toward receiver Donald Driver down the right sideline. But the throw was nothing like the one that Favre had unloaded 15 years before to Kitrick Taylor. Instead of a laser, the pass was a floater. And instead of hitting his receiver in stride, Favre threw it well inside of Driver, right to Giants cornerback Corey Webster, who jumped the route and corralled the interception. Four plays later, New York's Lawrence Tynes kicked the game-winning field goal. "I just didn't throw it outside enough," Favre said. "It was a shake route and Donald slipped into an out, which is fine — but I just didn't get it out far enough."

And then began what had become a time-honored off-season tradition in Green Bay: speculation about Favre's possible retirement. But this time it was different. It was well known that Favre did not like Thompson, who had infuriated the quarterback by not trading for brilliant but mercurial Raiders wideout Randy Moss at the 2007 draft. Favre complained about it publicly at the time. "[Moss] was going to wipe his contract clean and sign for $3 million guaranteed, plus a fourth-

round pick," Favre told the Jackson (Mississippi) *Clarion-Ledger*. "That would have been a steal. But we were not willing to guarantee part of that $3 million. I even had [Bus Cook, Favre's agent] call up there and tell them I would give up part of my salary to guarantee that part of the money. Apparently, that wasn't enough either."

Favre was also sometimes less than cooperative with McCarthy, who, as the quarterback could never forget, had been hired without any input from him. McCarthy gave Favre wide latitude to change play calls at the line of scrimmage, and the quarterback did not hesitate to do so. "There were some games that were a struggle — or that became a struggle — for Mike with Brett," says receiver Greg Jennings, a second-round draft pick out of Western Michigan in 2006. "I would be in the huddle when Mike would call a play, and we'd hear it in the helmet. I mean, I am standing next to Brett and Brett is like, 'What? We are not running that play.'"

Just beneath the surface of Favre's relationships with both men was the fact that his heir apparent was already on the roster. On April 23, 2005, Thompson had selected Cal quarterback Aaron Rodgers with the 24th pick in the first round of the NFL draft. Rodgers had been expected to be one of the first players taken, but the knock on him was that he was a product of a system in Berkeley that produced good college quarterbacks but not good professional ones. The legacy of highly rated passers who had played for Golden Bears coach Jeff Tedford was long and relatively undistinguished. Dating back to his time as an assistant at Fresno State and Oregon from 1992 through 2001, Tedford had had a hand in the development of Trent Dilfer, Akili Smith, David Carr, and Joey Harrington. All four had gone in the first round. And after Tedford took over at Cal in 2002, it took him just one season to turn Kyle Boller into a first-

---

* Favre started 253 straight regular-season games and 22 straight playoff games for the Packers. His 275 consecutive starts would still be the record for quarterbacks. But by the time Favre retired, after the 2010 season, he had started 322 straight games (298 regular season, 24 playoffs).

rounder, too. But the success of Tedford's protégés in the NFL didn't extend far beyond draft day. Dilfer won a Super Bowl with the Baltimore Ravens in 2000, but he was a game manager on a team with one of the better defenses in recent memory. In a journeyman 13-year career, he never threw more than 21 touchdown passes in a season. Tedford's other four first-round picks never even reached the playoffs. Fair or not, one of the reasons that Rodgers fell so far on draft day in 2005 was that their failures were clinging like lint to his blue pinstripe suit.

It was uncomfortable. For five hours, Rodgers sat backstage in a green room in the Jacob Javits Convention Center, in New York City, waiting . . . and waiting . . . and waiting. Utah quarterback Alex Smith went number one, to the 49ers. The Dolphins took Auburn running back Ronnie Brown next, and then the Browns took Michigan receiver Braylon Edwards. Both of those teams could have used a good quarterback, but both chose to pass on Rodgers. On and on it went like that. Rodgers tried to seem unperturbed, but the tension and dismay were evident on his face.

The most coveted asset for any NFL team is a franchise quarterback. But the 22 teams that picked after San Francisco and before Green Bay all seemed to fall victim to a sort of collective groupthink. Many needed a quarterback, but none took one. Instead, five wide receivers, five linebackers, four defensive backs, three running backs, three defensive linemen, and two tackles came off the board before the Packers got to make their pick at number 24. Thompson did not hesitate. He called Rodgers's cell phone and said, according to Pearlman, "How do you feel about coming to Green Bay?"

Draft day may have been uncomfortable for Rodgers, but it was nothing compared with his relationship with the man he had been brought to Green Bay to replace. Favre and Rodgers had an awkward association at best — a working relationship in which nothing really worked. Favre seemed to go out of his way to make the rookie feel uncomfortable, and even threw a little public shade at him. In an interview with ESPN before the 2005 season, Favre noted that he was not paid to be a coach, and then added, "My contract doesn't say I have to get Aaron Rodgers ready to play." Rodgers carried a clipboard as Favre's primary backup for three seasons, and by the time Favre threw his interception in the 2007 NFC Championship Game, Rodgers was ready to take over. More important, Green Bay was ready for Rodgers to take over.

It was almost a relief when, on March 4, 2008, reports began to circulate that the 38-year-old Favre was finally retiring from professional football. At a press conference two days later, an emotional Favre said, "I know I can play, but I don't think I want to."

But it came as no surprise, four months later, when Favre attempted to come back, saying he felt that the team had pressured him into a hasty decision. Thompson and McCarthy were both emphatic that they had moved on and were preparing for the 2008 season with Rodgers as the quarterback. The situation quickly grew into a public relations disaster for the team, which did not want to cut or trade the most popular player in the history of the franchise. The Packers were already planning to retire Favre's number 4 at Lambeau Field before the team's season opener against the Vikings on September 8. Favre was still under contract, due to make $12 million that year. On July 11, the team received a letter from Favre and his agent, Bus Cook, requesting the quarterback's unconditional release so that he could sign with another team. On July 13, 200 fans held a rally in support of Favre outside Lambeau Field. On July 30, new team president Mark Murphy (not to be confused with the Packers' former safety), who had replaced Harlan in December 2007, flew to Mississippi to visit Favre at his home in Hattiesburg. It was there that Murphy offered Favre a 10-year, $25 million marketing deal to *not* play football.

The endless drama of the previous seven years had, in a way, foretold how things were going to end for Favre in Green Bay — the same way they had for so many of pro football's great quarterbacks, including Johnny Unitas in Baltimore and Joe Montana in San Francisco. There is inevitably a clash between a player who still thinks he can get the job done and a team that needs to move on. The difference with Favre was that it was getting out of hand. And it only got worse. On Sunday, August 3, Favre returned to Green Bay two days before he intended to begin practicing with the Packers. "That training camp was one of the craziest times of my entire career," says Mark Tauscher, who was getting set to begin his ninth season as Green Bay's starting right tackle. "The fans were booing us."

But Favre never made it to the practice field. Late on the night of August 6, Thompson traded him to the Jets for what ultimately became a third-round choice in the 2009 draft.* And just like that, Favre was gone. The man who had done as much as anyone to restore the glory of Titletown was a Packer no longer. The man who had begun the decade saying that he could never imagine playing for another NFL team was soon going to be wearing colors other than green and gold.

In truth, Brett Favre was already gone. He had actually flown out of Green Bay less than 12 hours before he was traded — on a chartered flight back to his home in Mississippi — after it became clear that the Packers had no intention of letting him compete for the starting job. He left behind confusion and uncertainty, as well as a host of angry fans.

The Packers' fate was in the hands of Aaron Rodgers.

---

* *Thompson traded that pick away (along with a second- and another third-round pick) to the Patriots so that the Packers could move up to take USC linebacker Clay Matthews with the 26th selection of the first round.*

CHAPTER 19

THE PEOPLE'S TEAM

As a rule of municipal governance, the renaming of streets is not the most practical civic undertaking. The process is costly, not just for city administrators—requiring changes to maps and road signs, as well as to directories for everything from emergency response to mail delivery—but also for residents and businesses. A new address means new stationery, new sales slips, new shipping labels, and new business cards, as well as updates to mailing lists and billing accounts. Changing the name of a street is a simple enough thing to do, but it leads to an almost infinite array of complications and expenses. "If you vote yes you personally are giving us a bill for $10,000," one business owner told the Ashwaubenon Village Board in 2014 when it was considering changing the name of a street near Lambeau Field.

The names of the streets in downtown Green Bay are mostly still the same as the ones on Daniel Whitney's 1836 plat of the village of Navarino. Whitney named his north–south streets for the U.S. presidents of his time (Washington, Adams, Jefferson, Madison, Monroe, Quincy, and Jackson) and his east–west roads, with the exception of Main Street, for trees (Walnut, Cherry, Pine, Cedar, Elm, and Willow) and four of the five Great Lakes (Erie, Huron, Michigan, and Superior). One hundred and eighty-three years later, the old place still follows almost exactly the same layout.

But the area around Lambeau Field has been in a near constant state of development since construction on what was originally Green Bay City Stadium began in 1956. The neighborhood is dominated by Lambeau Field, of course, as well as by the buildings immediately adjacent to it, including the Packers' indoor practice facility, which is named for Don Hutson, the Brown County Veterans Memorial Arena, and the Resch Center, which is home to the Green Bay Blizzard of the Indoor Football League and the Green Bay Gamblers of the United States Hockey League. The district is more spread out than downtown and also more industrial, dotted with bank branches, car dealerships, chain restaurants, gas stations, hotels, service centers, and strip malls. You don't walk from place to place around Lambeau Field—you drive. And if you are driving, there's a good chance it will be on a street named for one of the Packers.

The major east–west thoroughfare in the area is Lombardi Avenue, which was dedicated on August 7, 1968, six months after Vince Lombardi had re-

signed as Green Bay's coach.* Formerly Highland Avenue, the street is not just the home address of the Packers, but also the major connector in the area to Interstate 41, the north–south highway that's the primary conduit for Lambeau Field traffic. Lombardi Avenue is one of 14 thoroughfares in the Green Bay area named for Packers. Eight of them are in the Lambeau neighborhood: Tony Canadeo Run, Brett Favre Pass, Holmgren Way, Lombardi Avenue, Lombardi Access Road, Mike McCarthy Way, Bart Starr Road, and Reggie White Way. Closer to downtown is Donald Driver Way — named for the leading receiver in team history — on the western side of the Fox River, just across the Ray Nitschke Memorial Bridge from

the old offices of the *Green Bay Press-Gazette*. The Packerland Industrial Park, three miles northwest of Lambeau Field, is home to five more Packers-inspired strands: Hinkle Street, Hutson Road, Isbell Street, Lambeau Street, and Starr Court. Built in the late 1960s, the Packerland site has gone through several redevelopments that did away with a few other streets named for some of the team's early greats: Canadeo Court, and Blood, Herber, and Lewellen Roads.**

But those were exceptions. Thoroughfares in Green Bay that have been named for Packers tend to last. Mike Holmgren ditched the city for Seattle, and yet Holmgren Way endures. Brett Favre left the Packers and went on to play for the hated

Cornerback Charles Woodson breaks up a pass to Steelers wideout Mike Wallace just before halftime in the Packers' 31–25 victory over Pittsburgh in Super Bowl XLV. Woodson broke his collarbone on the play and missed the rest of the game.

---

* *At the ceremony, Green Bay mayor Donald A. Tilleman had said that, as far as he could tell, the renaming of Highland Avenue for Lombardi was the first time that the city had ever named a street for a man who was still alive. When it came time for Lombardi to speak, he turned the mayor's words into a joke. "I just want you to know," he told the crowd, "I'm not dead." The sad twist, of course, was that Lombardi died 25 months later, from the effects of colon cancer.*

** *Some streets that have been reported as being named for Packers, including Hubbard Street and Hampton, and Robinson Avenues, never actually were. Hubbard Street had been mentioned in the weekly* Green Bay Gazette *as far back as September 1869.*

Holmgren Way and Brett Favre Pass are two of the 14 Green Bay thoroughfares named for Packers' players and coaches.

ing seasons. And in one of the most recent, 2017, Rodgers missed the last nine games with a broken collarbone.

But there is more about Rodgers that is miraculous than just his play. The wonder of human life lies not only in the fact that it happens, but also in the incalculable number of times that it does not happen at all. Each one of us exists through a mixture of circumstance and luck that began long before we ever came into the world. It is a more common miracle than Rodgers's talent as a quarterback, but it is a miracle all the same.

On July 7, 1944, First Lieutenant Edward W. Rodgers was piloting his B-24G Liberator, the *Powder Room,* north toward Germany on a long-range bombing run from a U.S. air base in southeastern Italy, his 44th mission in five months. The son of a refrigerator salesman from Dallas, Rodgers had been a copywriter in the advertising department of the Austin *American-Statesman* before the war, but it had become clear in Italy that he was a splendid pilot. During an attack on Vienna on March 17, antiaircraft flak had torn through the left side of his plane, damaging the wing, smashing one engine, setting fire to another, and crippling the plane's rudder. The plane fell out of formation, and Rodgers and his crew were given up for lost. But they nursed the wounded bomber over the Alps of Yugoslavia and made it safely home.

This time, Rodgers was not so fortunate. In the air over western Hungary, the planes in Rodgers's sortie came under attack from enemy aircraft. At about 1:15 p.m., the *Powder Room* went down with one engine on fire. Rodgers and the 10 men in his crew bailed out. The navigator, First Lieutenant John A. Simmons, was killed before he reached the ground. The Germans took Rodgers, who was wounded by shrapnel that hit his arms and his jaw, to Stalag Luft III, a prison camp for Allied airmen about 100 miles southeast of Berlin, in Nazi-occupied Poland. Run by the Luftwaffe, the camp had been the site, almost four months

Vikings, but Brett Favre Pass is still there. "Sometimes people scratch out the *P* once in a while, and we have to replace that," Green Bay mayor Jim Schmitt told the *Press-Gazette* in 2011. In a place where the football team grew out of the land, the streets named for its players and coaches are like seams stitched into the map, holding the place together.

And one day, a street in Green Bay will be named for Aaron Rodgers.

◆ ◆ ◆

Aaron Rodgers is a miraculous quarterback, a perfectionist with an amazing arm and a sense of timing possessed by few other players in the history of pro football. Rodgers at his best plays the game like an original, combining passing wizardry with a gift for improvisation. He can be so good that there is a danger that people in Green Bay might take his play for granted. There is more than a little truth to the city's derisive nickname "Entitledtown." The transition from Brett Favre to Rodgers may not have been smooth, but it has given Green Bay nearly three decades of unbroken Hall of Fame play at the quarterback position. No team in NFL history has enjoyed a run so long. Since 1992, the Packers have endured just four los-

before, of the prison break immortalized in the movie *The Great Escape.* Rodgers was in Stalag Luft III for six months and then was transferred to another POW camp near Nuremberg, 240 miles to the southwest. It was from there that he was liberated by Russian troops in the spring of 1945. He returned home, but he did not return to the newspaper, choosing instead to make a career out of the Air Force.

Rodgers rose to the rank of lieutenant colonel before he retired in 1963. He spent his last two years on active duty at Vandenberg Air Force Base, in central California, and then remained there as the chief engineer for more than 20 years. Along with his wife, Kathryn, he settled in the nearby town of Lompoc, where he raised three girls and a boy, Edward W. Rodgers Jr.

Ed Rodgers played on the offensive line at Lompoc High, and then played right guard at California State University, Chico, a Division II program known informally as Chico State. As a six-foot-three, 220-pound senior, he earned All–Far Western Conference honors in 1976. He then played semipro ball for four years in the California Football League, getting married in 1980 to Darla Pittman, whom he had met when the two were students at Chico State.

The couple had three boys in six years: Luke, in 1982, Aaron, in 1983, and Jordan, in 1988. Save for a brief stint in Oregon in the mid-1990s, when their father was attending Western States Chiropractic College, the Rodgers boys grew up in Chico, 80 miles north of Sacramento. Aaron and Luke competed against each other almost every day, the younger brother always trying to beat the older one. Aaron, a fan of 49ers quarterback Joe Montana, was a pitcher in baseball, a point guard in basketball, and a quarterback when he played football. "I always wanted the ball in my hands when the game was on the line," he said in 2005.

At Pleasant Valley High, Rodgers was a nervy, spectacular passer, leading the Vikings to a 9-3 record and the sectional semifinals as a junior in 2000, and throwing for a combined 4,419 yards in his last two seasons. He was so committed to being a good quarterback that he would spend his free time studying football film instead of going to parties. But he was only 17 as a senior, and he was small, just five foot ten and 165 pounds — though he had exceptionally big feet. He had an A-minus average and had scored 1310 on the SAT. He desperately wanted to play football in college, but he received no Division I scholarship offers. Craig Rigsbee, the coach at Butte College, a two-year school of 13,000 students in the nearby town of Oroville, lived a few streets over from Rodgers and his family. One day in 2002, he crossed a few yards to Rodgers's house and recruited him to play for the Roadrunners. In one season with Rigsbee at Butte, Rodgers threw for 2,408 yards and 28 touchdowns, with only four interceptions, leading the Roadrunners to a 10-1 record and a number-two ranking in the National Junior College Athletic Association. He also grew several inches. His juco gamble paid off with a scholarship to play football at the University of California. By the time Rodgers arrived in Berkeley, he stood six foot two and tipped the scale at 195 pounds.

At Cal, it took the 19-year-old Rodgers all of five games to establish himself as the starting quarterback. On September 11, 2003, he came off the bench in relief of starter Reggie Robertson late in the first quarter of a Thursday night game against Utah in Salt Lake City. Trailing 14–0, Rodgers brought the Golden Bears back, completing 15 of 25 passes for 224 yards and two touchdowns. His 21-yard scoring pass to senior wide receiver Geoff McArthur in the final seconds of the third quarter gave Cal a 24–21 lead. But the Bears were unable to stop the Utes and their sophomore quarterback, Alex Smith, who was making his first college start. Utah scored 10 points in the fourth quarter to prevail, 31–24. Rodgers had lost, but he would not be a backup again until he reached the NFL. He beat Illinois in his first start, then helped Cal to a 34–31 overtime upset of third-ranked USC

—the eventual national champion—in his second.* Rodgers and the Bears won 15 of their next 20 games. He threw for more than 5,400 yards in two years at Cal and was a first-team All-Pac-10 selection as a junior. Saying that he was "fulfilling a childhood dream," Rodgers declared for the NFL draft in January 2005. Along with Smith and Auburn's Jason Campbell, he was one of the top quarterbacks coming out of college and seemed sure to be one of the first players off the board at the April 23 draft.

But his days of being overlooked and having to be patient were far from over.

• • •

The three years that Rodgers spent behind Brett Favre did not magically transform him into the best quarterback in the NFL. The Packers went 6-10 in 2008, his first year as the starter. Rodgers did not play poorly—he threw for 28 touchdowns and 4,038 yards, with 13 interceptions—but there were growing pains. Things had gotten off to a funky start on the night in August that the unretired Favre returned to Green Bay. Not long after Favre's plane had landed at Austin Straubel International Airport, some of the 56,600 fans at Lambeau Field for the Packers' annual Family Night scrimmage actually booed Rodgers during his unofficial debut as the starter. In eight of Green Bay's losses, the quarterback and the offense came up empty when the Packers had the ball with less than five minutes left and a chance to tie or take the lead. When a reporter asked him at the end of the season if he would ever be able to step out of Favre's shadow, Rodgers said, "Not to some people."

But Green Bay's problems in 2008 had more to do with an abysmal defense—which ranked 26th against the run and gave up the 22nd-most points in the NFL—than with Rodgers, who ranked fourth in the league in both passing yards and touchdowns. "We just didn't know how to finish games," says former receiver Greg Jennings. "We lost so many close ones. But we knew eventually we would get it."

Rodgers had already done much to impress his teammates, starting with waiting patiently behind Favre for his chance to start, handling his apprenticeship to the aging gunslinger with class. Favre had showered and dressed apart from the team, in a separate staff locker room, ever since the renovation of Lambeau Field in 2003. Rodgers did not do that. And during the three years he spent carrying a clipboard, Rodgers took his duties as the quarterback of the scout team very seriously. He was so earnest about the role that receiver Donald Driver used to jump in with the scout-team offense just to take reps with him. In 2009, Rodgers and the Packers improved enough to make the playoffs: he finished fourth in the league in passing yards (4,434) and passing touchdowns (30) as the team went 11-5 but lost a 51–45 shootout to the Arizona Cardinals in a wild-card game. Green Bay seemed to be building toward something.

In 2010, all that patience paid off in glory. Despite suffering through a rash of injuries—12 starters, including Rodgers, missed a combined 86 games, and the team placed 15 players on injured reserve—Green Bay went 10-6, with the six losses coming by a combined 20 points. The Packers, with the fifth-best defense in the NFL, qualified for the playoffs as a wild-card team, then proceeded to win three postseason road games in a row to reach Super Bowl XVL, where they would face the Pittsburgh Steelers at Cowboys Stadium in Arlington, Texas. General manager Ted Thompson had completely remade the roster. Only one Green Bay starter, left tackle Chad Clifton, had been acquired by former general manager Mike Sherman.

The Super Bowl was a culmination of everything

---

* Illinois was the only Division I-A team that had shown any interest in Rodgers coming out of high school, but that did not translate to a scholarship offer. The Illini offered him only a chance to walk on in the fall.

that Rodgers had shown to Packers fans since 2008: the uncanny arm strength and accuracy, the ability to extend plays with his feet, and the myriad ways he could dissect defenses from outside the pocket. When Green Bay was on offense, the Super Bowl belonged almost completely to him —he handed the ball off only 11 times. On the first of his three touchdown passes, he hit a leaping Jordy Nelson in stride down the right sideline just in front of Steelers cornerback William Gay for a 29-yard score, giving the Packers a 7–0 lead with 3:44 to go in the opening quarter. On the second, with 2:24 remaining in the first half, Rodgers threw over the middle for a 21-yard touchdown to Jennings, who was running a skinny post from the left slot. The pass was a laser, delivered by Rodgers after a five-step drop and two hops forward. It zoomed over the head of inside linebacker James Farrior and just beyond the outstretched fingertips of free safety Ryan Clark. The touchdown put Green Bay up 21–3.

The performance of Rodgers overshadowed the heroic efforts of the Packers' defense, which forced three Pittsburgh turnovers, including a late-first-quarter interception that free safety Nick Collins returned for Green Bay's second touchdown. In the first 29 minutes of the game, the unit held the Steelers to just three points. But after cornerback Charles Woodson left the field with a broken collarbone late in the first half, the Packers' defense was like a prizefighter without a jab—forced to rely on its ability to take punches while waiting for an opening in which to land a knockout blow. Pittsburgh scored 14 unanswered points to close the deficit to 21–17 before such an opportunity arose. On the first play of the fourth quarter, with the Steelers facing second-and-two from the Packers' 33, linebacker Clay Matthews put his shoulder into a tackle and popped the ball free of the grasp of running back Rashard Mendenhall, whose fumble was scooped up by middle linebacker Desmond Bishop. Just like that, Green Bay went from reeling to redoubtable.

And Rodgers made the Steelers pay. He threw his third scoring pass of the game eight plays later. On second-and-goal from the Steelers' eight-yard line, he took the shotgun snap and, while looking to his left, bounced backwards away from the rush. In an instant he turned back to his right and lofted a pass to Jennings, who was all alone in the corner of the end zone. The Packers' lead swelled to 28–17.

But Rodgers still had not connected on his biggest pass of the day. Pittsburgh answered his touchdown to Jennings with one of its own, on a 25-yard throw from quarterback Ben Roethlisberger to receiver Mike Wallace. Roethlisberger then pitched to wideout Antwaan Randle El for the two-point conversion to cut the Packers' lead to 28–25 with 7:34 left in the game. Green Bay sputtered on its next possession and, with 5:59 left, faced third-and-10 from its own 25. The Steelers were still very much in the game. The outcome was in doubt. And Rodgers, as he had dreamed of all his life, had the game in his hands.

The play call was strong left, trips 27 Tampa. Jennings, lined up in the slot to the left, took off on another skinny-post route. But instead of being covered by a linebacker, this time he was shadowed by nickel cornerback Ike Taylor, who was playing press coverage. Jennings broke slightly to the outside to get around Taylor, then cut back toward the middle of the field. He had a step on Taylor, but the cornerback still seemed to have good coverage—in fact, Jennings did not appear to be open—when Rodgers let loose with a dart. The ball zipped past Taylor's extended left arm and hit Jennings in perfect stride at the Green Bay 45. He was brought down at the Steelers' 44 for a gain of 31 yards. Seven plays later, Mason Crosby kicked a 23-yard field goal to give the Packers a 31–25 lead with 2:07 left. The defense stopped Pittsburgh on downs, and suddenly the Packers were champions of pro football for the 13th time.

"That one throw was all about the last three years of my career," Rodgers said after the game.

"I'm not vindictive, but I'm blessed with a very good memory. You wait, you keep quiet and you take advantage of an opportunity when it comes."

Rodgers was the clear choice as Super Bowl MVP. His stat line was brilliant—he completed 24 of 39 passes for 304 yards and three touchdowns—but it did not tell the full story. He had lifted everyone around him. Indeed, his numbers might have been better if his receivers had not dropped nine passes. Nelson, the breakout star of the game, with nine catches for 140 yards, dropped three. James Jones dropped a sure touchdown. All was forgiven in the delirium of the winning locker room, where Rodgers and several teammates belted out a version of Queen's "We Are the Champions" in the shower.

"I told Ted back in 2005 he wouldn't be sorry," Rodgers said. "I told him in '08 that I was going to repay their trust and get us this opportunity . . . It's named the Lombardi Trophy for a reason. Because we play and live in Titletown."

Two days later, the people of Green Bay got a chance to show their appreciation. More than 56,000 purchased tickets for another "Return to Titletown" celebration at snowy Lambeau Field. In 10-degree weather, the team and its fans celebrated together. Green Bay's birthright was back home.

◆ ◆ ◆

Corey Behnke owns a house on the south side of Shadow Lane in Green Bay, a low-slung ranch home with gold aluminum siding and a backyard that abuts Lombardi Avenue. The view from his porch is of the northern face of Lambeau Field and its Atrium. On game days, the atmosphere on Shadow Lane is very much like that in a college town on a Saturday afternoon, with house bands playing, the smell of grill smoke hanging in the air, and green-and-gold-clad fans—red Solo cups in hand—walking up and down the street. Behnke allows family and friends to park their cars in his front yard and driveway for free —he estimates that he can fit 12 to 14. (Parking in stadium lots is $40 per car.) When the Pack-ers play at Lambeau, he and his girlfriend, Rachel McCutchen, host an ever-changing coterie of family and friends. The couple live primarily in New York, where the 42-year-old Behnke is the lead producer at LiveX, a streaming video enterprise he co-founded, which handles webcast production for such events as the New Year's Eve celebration in Times Square and the U.S. Open golf tournament. He estimates that he spends approximately 35 percent of the year at his Shadow Lane residence. "It's not a party house," Behnke insists. "I hate when people call it that. It's a lake house, where the lake happens to be Lambeau Field."

Packers season tickets have been in his family since his grandfather first purchased them in 1957. Behnke shares them with his relatives, so even though he is in Green Bay on football weekends, he does not always watch the Packers play from his regular seats in section 122, row 16. It is hardly a problem: Lambeau is always sold out, so TV blackouts don't apply and Behnke can watch the games from the comfort of his living room. The setup is ideal. McCutchen keeps a steady flow of tailgate food coming out of the kitchen. And the seven-foot-tall, glass-doored refrigerator in Behnke's single-car garage is always fully stocked with all sorts of Wisconsin beer—with one exception. "It can never *not* have Busch Light," says Behnke. "It's Wisconsin comfort food—33 cents a can."

Behnke was born on Green Bay's east side, but he did not grow up there—his family moved to Los Angeles when he was four. He nevertheless remains devoted to his hometown. He returned often throughout his childhood to see his grandfather, who lived in the tiny village of Brillion, about 30 minutes due south of the mouth of the Fox River. He watches Green Bay City Council meetings on YouTube. He bids on Packers memorabilia in online auctions—he is currently trying to collect every program from every game the team has ever played, a project that he figures is about 40 percent of the way to completion. A Green Bay superfan, he has gone to games in cities all over

the NFL, often wearing a garish outfit that includes a Ray Nitschke jersey, an oversized fabric helmet, a pair of wide receiver gloves, and green-and-gold camouflage pants. For playoff games (he has missed only one since 2007) he hires a professional makeup artist to paint one side of his face green and the other gold. He bought the residence on Shadow Lane in 2016, for $335,000, to indulge his life's passion. "I don't have kids," he says. "This is how I amuse myself."

Behnke's most conspicuous bit of fandom is the blog he and his college buddy Aaron Nagler started in 2007. CheeseheadTV.com has grown in the past decade into something beyond what Behnke ever intended. It was originally a WordPress creation, primarily a platform for a podcast called *Packer Transplants,* which was basically Behnke and Nagler talking about the Packers once a week for 20 minutes. With the podcast, the two friends were merely taking the conversations they had all the time—in their apartments, over the phone, or over beers at Kettle of Fish, New York City's Green Bay headquarters in Greenwich Village—and broadcasting them on the Internet. *Packer Transplants* is now an hour long, frequently has guests from the team and the journalists who cover it, and also has its own production crew, made up primarily of staffers conscripted from LiveX. And the podcast is only one feature. The site has pregame and postgame analysis, draft analysis, and even something that Behnke calls a "game matrix" that breaks down the result of every contest—exhibition, preseason, regular season, and postseason, league and nonleague—that the Packers have ever played. The register not only has Green Bay's record against the Chicago Bears and the Dallas Cowboys, but also against the Kamehameha High School Alumni and Sampson Naval Training Station. Calling it a matrix is fitting: in the same way the red and blue pills determined which version of reality people could see in the 1999 movie *The Matrix,* reading Cheesehead TV is a little like swallowing the green pill.

In a dozen years, the site has grown at an exponential rate. In its first six months of existence, from July through December 2007, it had fewer than 20,000 page views. In the first 11 months of 2018, it had more than 10 million. Not all the numbers are so huge. Cheesehead TV makes zero money. For two seasons, *Packer Transplants* was sponsored by Stillmank Brewing Company, a Green Bay brewery. "We were literally paid in beer," Behnke says. "They would ship us cases and we would drink it on the air."

Behnke handles the design and operations of Cheesehead TV, but he is careful to note, "I'm not a writer." It is Nagler, Behnke's co-founder, who gives Cheesehead TV its voice. The son of a schoolteacher from Appleton, a town 30 minutes southeast of Green Bay, Nagler's first memory in life is attending a game at Lambeau Field with his grandfather when he was three years old. He played football as a kid, first in Pop Warner and then at Appleton West, where he was a JV quarterback. Beyond his own modest playing experience, he remembers always being fascinated with the game. "When I got older," he says, "I sought out coaching manuals and tried to find as many coaching clinic tapes as I could get my hands on." His analysis—in print, on the air, and on Twitter, where he has more than 60,000 followers—is at once wonky and eminently accessible. He loves the nuances of good run blocking and loathes the three-man pass rush. Greg Bedard, who used to cover the Packers for the *Milwaukee Journal Sentinel* before moving on to cover the New England Patriots for *The Boston Globe,* said in 2010, "CheeseheadTV is the best fan blog out there ... Aaron is extremely smart, but I do worry about his sanity and seriously question whether he sleeps."

In addition to being a football wonk, Nagler has

also perfected an engaging deadpan style. When the Packers are losing, he likes to tweet, "Lotta ballgame left." And after a defeat, he is likely to conclude his "Gut Reactions" column, which he files immediately afterwards, with a variation of the line "I need a drink." He has become essential reading for many Green Bay fans, not only because he knows what he is talking about but also because he suffers just like they do.

Nagler met Behnke in 1996, when they were both acting students at the University of North Carolina School of the Arts, a conservatory in Winston-Salem. Nagler was a freshman, and it was early in the first semester when he got up in front of the entire drama school, which at the time numbered about 100, to recite the famous "To be, or not to be" soliloquy from *Hamlet.* Before he began, Nagler mentioned that he was from Appleton. After he finished and was returning to his seat, he heard from the back of the auditorium, "Go, Pack, go!" Behnke, a junior, had just introduced himself. Nagler remembers being embarrassed because Behnke happened to be sitting right next to the dean, but a friendship founded on Packers football had nevertheless been born. It helped, of course, that 1996 was the year the Packers won their first Super Bowl since 1967. The two complement each other well on *Transplants,* with the energetic Behnke hewing to his outsider status, while the composed Nagler gives his considered opinions on the news of the day. There are animated disagreements and the occasional rant, but everything fits within the framework of a common theme: The Packers are awesome.

After drama school, Nagler worked for five years in New York as an actor, during which time he married his wife, Carolyn (the couple have since divorced). It was when their oldest daughter, Madeline, was three years old that he landed a gig on tour with the Broadway production of *The Full Monty.* Nagler was on the road for three months, from September through November 2005, and his moment of clarity came when he ate a lonely Thanksgiving dinner in a Denny's off a highway in Alabama. When he got home to his family in Queens, he promptly retired from acting and found an office job, first at the United Media newspaper syndicate and then, in 2007, in the public affairs office of the Blackstone Group, a private equity investment giant. He had been doing his own football blog, *Aaron Nagler's Football Report,* in his spare time for about a year — "I think my father and two friends read it," he told *The New York Times* — when Behnke (one of those friends) suggested they start a Packers site that would host both a podcast and Nagler's analysis. Five years later, Nagler left Blackstone for the sports website Bleacher Report, which hired him to help cover the NFL. In 2015, he joined the online operation at *Sports Illustrated,* where he worked as an on-camera analyst and wrote scouting reports for coverage of the NFL draft. The next year he went to work for Gannett, augmenting the *Green Bay Press-Gazette*'s digital and social coverage of the Packers. He had gone from Kettle of Fish all the way to Lambeau Field.

But there was a catch: Nagler had to stop working for Cheesehead TV. His hire had not been popular with some members of the pro football beat in Wisconsin, specifically with a few of the writers he would be working with directly — the condensed staff of the *Press-Gazette* and the *Milwaukee Journal Sentinel,* which Gannett had combined in 2016 — who objected to the presence of a blogger in their midst. And after two seasons on the beat, when the man who hired Nagler moved on to another job, Nagler moved on, too — right back to Cheesehead TV. To the millions of Packers fans surfing the Internet, the transition has been seamless.

Covering pro football in Green Bay in 2019 is very different than it was in the 1920s and '30s, when George Whitney Calhoun was both an editor at the *Press-Gazette* and the Packers' press agent. Through most of the 1970s, the local paper was the only outlet that chronicled the team on a daily basis. Curly Lambeau had confidants at the Milwaukee papers — most notably Oliver Kuechle of the *Journal* — but there were no reporters from either the *Journal* or the *Sentinel* who were in Green Bay every day. Today there are sportswriters from publications in both Madison and Milwaukee who are based in the city, and ESPN has a reporter with the Packers year-round. On any given day, there are upwards of 50 people covering the team.

It is an odd circumstance. The transition from paper to digital delivery has forever altered the landscape for print media. Newspapers and magazines have not yet figured out how to sell themselves online. As a result, the news business has become a relentless cycle of downsizing and consolidation. The industry is in decline. But even as writing staffs shrink, the pro football beat has mushroomed into a round-the-clock commitment, with national — even international — implications. Green Bay's most recent stock sale, launched in December 2011, sold a record 269,640 shares to more than 250,000 people, including 2,000 in Canada. With Facebook and Twitter and fan blogs like Cheesehead TV, the churn of news during the season and around events like the draft is constant. Readers on the Internet do not seem to care where the news is coming from, only that it is there. A blogger might not be a journalist, but to a fan base that has gone postmodern, consuming news on smartphones from anywhere in the world, he or she is just as much a part of how it engages with the Packers as any media outlet.

The NFL has noticed. At events such as drafts and playoff games, where the league handles credentialing, fan blogs are treated as equals alongside *Sports Illustrated, The New York Times,* and the *Green Bay Press-Gazette.* Before he ever got to Gannett — or even to Bleacher Report — Nagler had covered playoff games and Super Bowls under the banner of Cheesehead TV. But the NFL does not issue passes for regular-season games at Lambeau Field — the Packers do. The team has never credentialed the site for a regular-season game. Blogs are not professional purveyors of journalism, and the Packers refuse to recognize them.

It is a curious decision, but understandable, given how intertwined Green Bay's history is with that of the *Press-Gazette*. For the Packers' first 50 years of existence, the team and the paper maintained a symbiotic relationship in which the paper pulled double duty as midwife and publicity machine. The Packers were good for Green Bay, went the conventional wisdom, and so the paper helped to ensure that the team continued to exist. Whenever the Packers were on their deathbed, which in those years was almost always, the *Press-Gazette* was there to help nurse them through.

Things changed in 1974, when new beat reporter Cliff Christl was told to start covering the team with a critical eye. Bart Starr clashed with Christl over everything from editorial cartoons to the way the *Press-Gazette* edited team press releases. In October 1978, Starr threatened to ban Christl and three other writers from the Green Bay locker room when they asked why running back Duane Thomas, who had been in town for a tryout the week before, was still hanging around. Thomas's presence was a possible violation of the NFL's rule against stashing away nonroster players, which said that such players could work out for a team only once and that they could not be retained for more than 24 hours.* Vince Lombardi had said of Starr, in *Run to Daylight!*, "You don't criticize him in front of others," and it really was true. The former quarterback could not brook public criticism, which was nearly impossible for reporters to avoid when they were covering a team as bad as the Packers were in those days.

In 1978, Starr also denied several female reporters entrance to the locker room. The next year, in an effort to keep women out, the Packers announced that they were banning all reporters and said that players would answer questions only in a separate "interview room." Starr later relaxed

Green Bay superfans Corey Behnke (left) and Aaron Nagler, the New York City–based co-founders of CheeseheadTV.com, prepare to host another episode of their podcast, *Packer Transplants*.

the policy, and when Sheree Olson became the reporter for WNFL radio in Green Bay in 1981, he kept the locker room open to her. But in 1984, new coach Forrest Gregg banned Olson, who was forced to wait outside a locker room door guarded by police. One year later, the NFL established an equal-access policy—though that still did not mean that teams had to open their locker rooms. There were several more incidents around the league after that, most notoriously in 1990, when several New England Patriots players harassed a female reporter from the *Boston Herald*.

But nothing like that happened in Green Bay— perhaps because in 1990 there still were no female reporters in the state who were covering the Packers on a regular basis. Two years later, Lori Nickel, a 22-year-old reporting intern at *The Milwaukee Journal*, started covering the team occasionally. Beginning in 1997, Nickel—who today is a feature writer for the *Journal Sentinel* (the *Journal* and the *Sentinel* merged in 1995)—wrote about the Packers several times a week. She covered Green Bay regularly during the football season for the next

---

* A league investigation eventually cleared Green Bay of any wrongdoing.

Packers president Mark Murphy, a former Pro Bowl safety for the Washington Redskins, takes a ride down the tubing hill that is part of the team's Titletown District development.

19 years, though she was never the beat writer. While she does remember getting a dirty look once from Reggie White, who was outspoken about not wanting women in the locker room, she says that she has always had confidence that the team supported her right to do her job. She also has always felt that her fellow reporters would have had her back if an issue ever came up. "The Packers have actually been pretty good," Nickel says.

The reason for that is that Green Bay is very much part of the NFL's corporate structure. Equal access is league policy, and the Packers adhere to it in part because being a member of the league has made the team very profitable. The Packers reported record revenue of $454.9 million in the fiscal year that ended on March 31, 2018. That ranked just inside the top 10 in the league, and *Forbes* listed Green Bay as the NFL's 12th most valuable franchise, at $2.625 billion. Not bad for pro football's smallest city. Curly Lambeau was, for many years, the Packers' only full-time employee. Now there are departments for brand and marketing, community outreach, development and hospitality, and — the telltale sign of all corporate hierarchies — human resources.

It is a far cry not only from how things were in the days of Curly Lambeau and Vince Lombardi, but also how they were just a generation ago.

Nickel can remember running into players at local restaurants and driving past them on Interstate 43 on her way back to Milwaukee on Sunday nights after home games. Not anymore. Some small-town traditions have been preserved, including players borrowing bicycles from young fans to ride from the locker room to the practice field during training camp. But the days of players hanging out in front of the Astor Hotel are long gone. Says Nickel, "There's no small-town feel to covering that team anymore."

◆ ◆ ◆

It used to be that the city of Green Bay was what kept the Packers going. But in the past 25 years or so, the roles of team and town have slowly been reversing. Now it is the Packers who are looking out for the health of the city. And not for entirely altruistic reasons. Team president Mark Murphy likes to say that the Packers have two main goals: winning championships and making sure that they remain in Green Bay. What is good for the team is good for the town, and vice versa. The Packers and the people are one.

Around the time of the 2003 stadium renovation, the Packers began buying land to the immediate west of Lambeau Field. They knocked down a Kmart. They bought and razed a number of houses. Through 2018, the team had spent more than $32 million to purchase nearly 45 acres of land, from South Ridge Road, which runs north–south behind the western side of Lambeau Field, all the way to Marlee Lane, a deep out from the Red Lobster that Ron Wolf took Reggie White to when he was wooing him during free agency in 1993. The acquisitions made sense. The stadium's makeover had turned Lambeau Field into a year-round destination. Why not try to entice visitors to extend their trips from two days to four? Why not give fans something else to do besides visit the Atrium?

Green Bay (the team, not the city) began to realize the potential for development in 2013, after it had convinced Nebraska-based outdoor retail giant Cabela's to establish a store on about 21 acres that it owned at the junction of Interstate 41 and Lombardi Avenue, roughly a mile west of the stadium. The Packers had originally approached rival retailer Bass Pro Shops about putting a store on the site,[*] but Bass Pro declined, saying that the population of the area was not big enough. Cabela's was also hesitant — Green Bay would be by far the smallest market for any of its 36 outlets — but the chain ultimately agreed, primarily because of the store's proposed location, which was not only off a major highway close to Lambeau Field but also on the threshold of both the North Woods and Door County, two of the state's premier vacation and recreation destinations. The site has been an unqualified success. In 2017, the Green Bay Cabela's was the chain's fourth-best-performing outlet.

That gave the Packers, in Murphy's words, "the confidence" to proceed with an even more ambitious project. In 2015 the team announced its plan for Titletown, a multipurpose development on the 45 acres between South Ridge Road and Marlee Lane. The site would have residential and retail buildings, dining and entertainment businesses, and 10 acres of land set aside for public use, including a full-size football field, an NFL-combine-themed playground, a tubing hill, and a skating rink. Everything would be anchored by three prominent tenants: Hinterland Brewery, a Green Bay brewpub that would move from its downtown location (appropriately enough, in a former meatpacking plant); a sports medicine clinic run by Bellin Health, the region's leading healthcare service; and Lodge Kohler, a four-diamond hotel owned by the Kohler Company, the Wisconsin-based manufacturing giant best known for its plumbing fixtures. The goal for the Packers was not just to goose their local revenue by enhancing Lambeau Field's newfound appeal as a year-round destination. The team was also making an effort to en-

sure the economic health of Green Bay — specifically that it would continue to be able to support an NFL franchise.

To that end, the hotel, which is directly across South Ridge Road from Lambeau Field, was important. The American Automobile Association annually inspects and approves more than 27,000 hotels in the United States, Canada, Mexico, and the Caribbean, and it assigns each one a rating from one to five diamonds — from budget properties to those that provide the ultimate in luxury and atmosphere. Before Titletown's Lodge Kohler opened in July 2017, Green Bay's top-rated hotels amounted to a handful of three-diamond properties. According to Murphy, the lack of a premier hotel was costing the Packers — and the city — a chance to host conferences and conventions, something the Atrium had been built specifically to do. "We had heard from a lot of different people, 'We really like Green Bay, but it would really be nice if you had a better hotel,'" Murphy told a breakfast meeting of area business leaders in 2018. For all its amenities, Lodge Kohler has no meeting space. It uses the conference rooms at Lambeau Field.

More ambitious than the hotel, though, is a venture called TitletownTech, in which the Packers have partnered with the Microsoft Corporation in an attempt to boost economic growth and job creation in northeastern Wisconsin and ultimately lure young entrepreneurs to the region — or at least convince them to stay. Brown County's population is aging. Spurred by members of the baby boom generation (defined as anyone born between 1946 and 1964), the number of people 65 and over is expected to grow from 28,757 in 2010 to around 40,000 next year, and then to nearly 60,000 by 2030. The effect is noticeable at Lambeau Field, which Behnke describes as one of the least spirited stadiums in the NFL. Packers fans might travel well — a boisterous contingent prac-

---

[*] *Bass Pro Shops later purchased Cabela's, for $4.5 billion, in 2016.*

tically took over the Los Angeles Memorial Coliseum when Green Bay lost 29–27 to the Rams on October 28, 2018 — but at home they can be downright cranky. Behnke would prefer to stand the whole game, or at least at crucial moments, but to do so he has to suffer the opprobrium of the older patrons in his section. "If you want to watch the game in your living room, then do that — you can literally watch any game from anywhere," he says. "But if you are in that stadium, you owe your attention to helping the team win. That means standing as much as appropriate."

But Green Bay's aging fan base is a concern not just on game day. Behnke is the kind of young, educated entrepreneur whom the city is having trouble attracting and retaining. The U.S. Census Bureau estimates that on July 1, 2017, the population of Green Bay was 105,116. Of the residents who were 25 and over, 24.9 percent had a bachelor's degree or higher; the national average is 30.9 percent. Contrast that with Boulder, Colorado, a city of comparable size (107,125) but located in a state that is among the very best for startup activity. The percentage of people in Boulder who were 25 and over and had a bachelor's degree or higher was 73.8. And Wisconsin has been one of the worst states in the country in terms of startup activity since 2015. The hope is that TitletownTech — a gleaming two-story, 46,000-square-foot building that opened in April 2019 — will change that. The Packers and Microsoft have seeded TitletownTech's venture capital fund with $5 million each. The building houses a venture studio that provides resources, advisers, and meeting space to young companies developing and marketing digital products and services. There is also an "innovation lab" staffed by three Microsoft employees who provide support to local businesses dealing with technological issues. "Of all the things we've done in Titletown," Murphy says, "this has the potential to have the biggest impact."

When the plans for Titletown were announced, a member of the Greater Green Bay Chamber of Commerce made a point of saying, "What you're seeing there [in the Titletown District] is what millennials especially are looking for . . . It's a place that is walkable. It's a place where you can live, where you can shop, where you can hang out with your family, your animal, your kids. That's what we're looking for when it comes to talent retention and attraction to the Green Bay area."

It is still too early to tell whether the district will be a success in that regard — the project's second phase, involving the construction of residential and office buildings, began in 2018 — but if it is, then Titletown will be Murphy's greatest legacy.

That is saying something, considering that the former Redskins free safety ended 2018, the Packers' second losing season in a row, by firing longtime coach Mike McCarthy and assuming responsibilities for the football operation himself. It was the 63-year-old Murphy — still boyish, with a full head of red hair and a gap-toothed grin — and not second-year general manager Brian Gutekunst, who on January 7, 2019, selected Matt LaFleur to be the 15th coach in the history of the Green Bay Packers. Having one man in charge of everything, including football operations, is a setup that has not worked for the Packers since the days of Curly Lambeau. It is what Bob Harlan, Murphy's predecessor, worked hard to avoid. But as the organization's president and chief executive officer, there is nothing in 2019 that Murphy does not oversee. He has a wealth of experience not only in the NFL, where he was a Pro Bowl player as well as Washington's union representative during the 1982 players' strike, but also in administration. Before he came to the Packers, Murphy was the athletic director at Colgate, his alma mater, from 1992 to 2003, and then at Northwestern from 2003 to 2007. He earned his MBA during his playing career. He graduated from law school at Georgetown University in 1988 and went to work as a trial attorney at the Department of Justice a year later. He is smart, successful, and versatile. But can he

do everything? The success or failure of the Green Bay Packers, on the field and on the balance sheet, is now his responsibility.

It is a curious situation — so much control over the fortunes of the people's team resting in the hands of one man — but not an unprecedented one. The Packers, after all, were willed into existence, and then into the best team in football, by one man. But times are different. Green Bay might still operate in a small town, but it has long since moved beyond being a small-town operation.

· · ·

In July 2008, ESPN ginned up a series on *SportsCenter*, its flagship news program, to find "the true TitleTown, USA." The network named 20 "finalists," and considered all sports, not just football. The show then visited each one, stopping in big cities, including Boston, Detroit, and Pittsburgh, and smaller towns like Gainesville, Florida; Massillon, Ohio; and Parkersburg, West Virginia. Green Bay made the list, but never really had a chance. ESPN, as the network is wont to do, was just trying to spur debate and create controversy during a

slow time on the sports calendar. The triviality of the contest annoyed Packers fans (as did the network's funky spelling of "TitleTown"), but the fact that it existed at all was telling. Some people, it seemed, just could not fathom how a little city in northeastern Wisconsin could have such a hold on the nickname. Certainly there were other places in the country deserving of the name Titletown.

The winner of the contest was decided by an online fan ballot, and after more than three weeks of "competition," Green Bay finished third, behind runner-up Parkersburg and champion Valdosta, Georgia, which prevailed on the basis of its strong high school football tradition. Both towns are smaller than Green Bay, and neither supports a professional team — and neither can lay historical claim to the nickname. Eleven years later, nobody refers to either one as Titletown. There are more than 19,000 cities and towns in the United States, but there is only one Titletown, USA. And everyone knows where it is.

The name belongs to Green Bay — and so do the Packers.

The Titletown District represents a reversal of roles in Green Bay, with the team as benefactors of the town. The Packers want the development to not only enhance Lambeau Field's status as a year-round destination, but also spur economic development in the area.

ACKNOWLEDGMENTS

The first call I made when I started writing this book in the spring of 2017 was to Cliff Christl. For a variety of reasons, the early history of the Green Bay Packers has become muddled over the past century, twisted and stretched to fit all manner of embellishments and conspiracy theories until it bore only a faint resemblance to how things actually happened. There were simply no decent books that were readily available about the origins and early history of the team — or even about Curly Lambeau. Vast acres of American forests have been harvested to tell the team's story during the Vince Lombardi era. But there is precious little about anything that happened before. So I went straight to the source.

The Packers, to their great credit, hired Christl to be their full-time historian in 2014. In 36 years as a sportswriter at four Wisconsin newspapers — including as the football beat writer at the *Green Bay Press-Gazette* — he earned a reputation as an honest reporter, a dogged researcher, and a fearless teller of the truth. In his new role, nothing has changed. His columns for the Packers' website, where he regularly debunks dubious claims and retells forgotten tales, are essential reading for anybody interested in the history of the team. The record that I was researching had, to a great extent, already been set straight. And that is thanks solely to Cliff and his lifetime of diligent and enlightening work. This book is not an authorized history, but neither Cliff nor Green Bay director of public affairs Aaron Popkey ever refused to answer one of my questions. I am indebted to both.

My agent, Rob Kirkpatrick, was a believer in this project from the very beginning. I have known him for more than a decade, and his contributions have always been invaluable. His advice and guidance helped me turn an unformed idea into something much more ambitious.

At Houghton Mifflin Harcourt, my editor, Susan Canavan, was amazing throughout the process of turning a somewhat vague idea into a full-fledged book. Her thoughtful edits and sage advice sustained me through many long days and nights. I also received tremendous help from her assistants, Jenny Xu and Mary Cait Milliff. Will Palmer did the copyediting and — as all good copy editors do — he made my writing better. In many cases, much better. My designer was Nate Beale, who was a creative, supportive, and flexible resource through everything. Thank you.

I also received invaluable support from members of the Green Bay community. Peter Reinhart told me the story of how his father, John, came to be a longtime member of the chain gang at Lambeau Field. Debra Anderson opened up the Archives and Area Research Center at the University of Wisconsin–Green Bay for me. She also connected me with Dr. Jerrold Rodesch, an emeritus professor at the school, who guided me through the early history of the region and the city. At the Neville Public Museum of Brown County, Louise Pfotenhauer and Lisa M. Cain provided an immeasurable amount of assistance by giving me access to their amazing collections of photographs and artifacts. And finally, Mary Jane Herber at the Brown County Library helped me with research assistance, advice, insight, and good humor.

At the archives of the University of Buffalo, Scott Hollander was a hero at helping me dig into the past of Packers co-founder George Whitney Calhoun, who went to high school in the city and worked there as a younger man.

This book would not have been possible without the amazing people with whom I work every day at *The Players' Tribune*. Derek Jeter and Jaymee Messler created and built a place that allows me to do what I love so much — share the stories of the people who play the games that we all watch. I am so lucky to be part of this team. I also received valuable guidance and advice from five of the smartest people I know: Gary Hoenig, Jessica Robertson, Jim Gorant, Rich O'Brien, and Carl Scott. Help also came from Jeff Levick, Sofia Check, Guillermo Hernández Martínez, Megan McNally, Nate Gordon, Alex Rose, Lisa Phillips, Eugenia Chow, and Taylor Baucom, as well as from Sean Conboy, Sam Donsky, Seamus McKiernan, Matthew Malady, Paul Mueller, Dan Treadway, and Michael Blundell.

Among my former colleagues at *Sports Illustrated* whom I want to thank for their advice, assistance, and friendship are Mark Bechtel, Stephen Cannella, Richard Demak, Tim Layden, Peter King, Robert Klemko, Gabe Miller, Mark Mravic, Austin Murphy, and Susan Szeliga. And, for his inspiration, thank you to William Nack. Miss you always, Bill.

The beautiful pictures in this book were found and selected by Maureen Cavanagh. She is not only one of the best photo editors in the business, but she is also one of the best friends I've ever had. She has been my colleague for many years, and I hope for many more. Thank you, Moe.

I received endless support — morale and otherwise — from an amazing roster of friends. Thank you to Maura Concannon, Richard Deutsch, Corban Goble, Barak Klarfeld, Cheryl Marciano, Rich Ryan, Annemarie Warek, Gianluca and Cheryl Cotugno, and Devon and Caroline Nagle.

For most of the past two years — for most of my life, really — Gregg Chabot has been there for me with advice, guidance, and friendship, frequently all at the same time. Gregg is a thoughtful reader, a great listener, and one of the best writers I know. He's also my best friend.

To my mother and father, who started me down this road by moving me to Wisconsin all those years ago, thank you. Thanks, too, to my sister, Cynthia. Among my extended family, thank you to Mary Anne Keane, Bill and Kelly Gildea, Bo and Sue Keane, and Phil and Ali Keane.

Finally, to my family — Allison, Nate, Annie, and Maddy. Nobody gave me more help, or provided me more freedom to work, than all of you. Thank you, from the bottom of my heart. Vince Lombardi's famous trinity of life was, in order, "God, family, and the Green Bay Packers." I know that for much of the past two years the Packers have come first more often than they should have. I assure you, though, that I never forgot my real priority. This book is for you.

BIBLIOGRAPHY

Barker, John S., ed. *The Flight of the Liberators.* Rochester, NY: Du Bois Press, 1946.

Barra, Allen. *The Last Coach: A Life of Paul "Bear" Bryant.* New York: W. W. Norton, 2005.

Beech, Mark. *When Saturday Mattered Most: The Last Golden Season of Army Football.* New York: Thomas Dunne Books, 2012.

Blaik, Earl "Red." *You Have to Pay the Price.* New York: Holt, Rinehart and Winston, 1960.

Bohn, Michael K. *Heroes and Ballyhoo: How the Golden Age of the 1920s Transformed American Sports.* Lincoln, NE: Potomac Books, 2009.

Butler, LeRoy, and James J. Keller. *The LeRoy Butler Story: From Wheelchair to the Lambeau Leap.* Neenah, WI: JJK Sports Entertainment, 2011.

Christl, Cliff. *Packers Heritage Trail.* Stevens Point, WI: KCI Sports, 2017.

Coenen, Craig R. *From Sandlots to the Super Bowl: The National Football League, 1920–1967.* Knoxville: University of Tennessee Press, 2005.

Cook, Bernard A. *Belgians in Michigan.* East Lansing: Michigan State University Press, 2007.

Daley, Arthur. *Pro Football's Hall of Fame.* Chicago: Quadrangle Books, 1963.

Daly, Dan, and Bob O'Donnell. *The Pro Football Chronicle.* New York: Collier Books, 1990.

D'Amato, Gary, and Cliff Christl. *Mudbaths and Bloodbaths: The Inside Story of the Bears-Packers Rivalry.* Madison, WI: Prairie Oak Press, 1997.

Davis, Jeff. *Papa Bear: The Life and Legacy of George Halas.* New York: McGraw-Hill, 2005.

Devine, Dan, with Michael R. Steele. *Simply Devine: Memoirs of a Hall of Fame Coach.* Champaign, IL: Sports Publishing, 2000.

Eisenberg, John. *That First Season: How Vince Lombardi Took the Worst Team in the NFL and Set It on the Path to Glory.* New York: Houghton Mifflin Harcourt, 2009.

Evans, William L. *The Military History of Green Bay.* Madison: State Historical Society of Wisconsin, 1900.

Favre, Brett, with Chris Havel. *Favre: For the Record.* New York: Doubleday, 1997.

Goska, Eric. *Green Bay Packers: A Measure of Greatness.* 2nd ed. Iola, WI: Krause Publications, 2004.

Gottehrer, Barry. *The Giants of New York.* New York: G. P. Putnam's Sons, 1963.

Green Bay Press-Gazette. *Titletown's Team: A Photographic History of the Green Bay Packers.* Battle Ground, WA: Pediment, 2009.

Gullickson, Denis J., and Carl Hanson. *Before They Were the Packers: Green Bay's Town Team Days.* Black Earth, WI: Trails Books, 2004.

Halas, George, with Gwen Morgan and Arthur Veysey. *Halas by Halas: The Autobiography of George Halas.* New York: McGraw-Hill, 1979.

Harlan, Bob, with Dale Hoffman. *Green and Golden Moments: Bob Harlan and the Green Bay Packers.* Stevens Point, WI: KCI Sports, 2007.

Hickok, Ralph. *Vagabond Halfback: The Saga of Johnny Blood McNally*. Self-published, CreateSpace, 2017.

Howard, Needles, Tammen and Bergendoff, in association with Timothy L. Heggland. *City of Green Bay Intensive Resource Survey: Final Report*. Milwaukee: Howard, Needles, Tammen and Bergendoff, 1988.

Hurly, Dr. James, and Thomas Murphy. *Green Bay: A City and Its Team*. Green Bay: Hurly Investments, 2011.

Ives, Gail, in association with On Broadway, Inc. *Green Bay's West Side: The Fort Howard Neighborhood*. Charleston, SC: Arcadia, 2003.

Kellogg, Louise Phelps. *Early Narratives of the Northwest, 1634–1699*. New York: Charles Scribner's Sons, 1917.

Kestly, Steve, ed. *East vs. West: A Rivalry 100 Years in the Making*. Green Bay: Green Bay East High School and Green Bay West High School, 2005.

Kramer, Jerry, and Dick Schaap. *Instant Replay: The Green Bay Diary of Jerry Kramer*. New York: New American Library, 1968.

Layden, Tim. *Blood, Sweat, and Chalk*. New York: Sports Illustrated Books, 2010.

Lombardi, Vince, with W. C. Heinz. *Run to Daylight: Vince Lombardi's Diary of One Week with the Green Bay Packers*. New York: Simon and Schuster, 1963.

Lyons, Robert S. *On Any Given Sunday: A Life of Bert Bell*. Philadelphia: Temple University Press, 2010.

Manchester, William. *American Caesar: Douglas MacArthur, 1880–1964*. New York: Little, Brown, 1978.

Maraniss, David. *When Pride Still Mattered: A Life of Vince Lombardi*. New York: Simon and Schuster, 1999.

Martin, Deborah Beaumont. *History of Brown County, Wisconsin: Past and Present*. Vol. 2. Chicago: S. J. Clarke, 1913.

McCain, John, with Mark Salter. *Faith of My Fathers: A Family Memoir*. New York: Random House, 1999.

Miller, Nathan. *New World Coming: The 1920s and the Making of Modern America*. New York: Scribner, 2003.

Mnookin, Robert, and Alain Verbeke. "Persistent Nonviolent Conflict with No Reconciliation: The Flemish and Walloons in Belgium." *Law and Contemporary Problems* 72, no. 2 (2009): 151–86.

Neft, David S., and Richard M. Cohen. *Pro Football: The Early Years*. Ridgefield, CT: Sports Products, 1978.

Neft, David S., Richard M. Cohen, and Rick Korch. *The Football Encyclopedia*. New York: St. Martin's, 1994.

Pearlman, Jeff. *Gunslinger: The Remarkable, Improbable, Iconic Life of Brett Favre*. Boston: Houghton Mifflin Harcourt, 2016.

Rudolph, Jack. *Birthplace of a Commonwealth (A Short History of Brown County, Wisconsin)*. Green Bay: Brown County Historical Society, 1976.

———. *Green Bay: A Pictorial History*. Virginia Beach, VA: Donning, 1983.

———. *The Green Bay Area in History and Legend: Green Bay Press-Gazette Articles*. Edited by Betsy Foley. Green Bay: Brown County Historical Society, 2004.

Schwarz, Alan. *The Numbers Game: Baseball's Lifelong Fascination with Statistics*. New York: Thomas Dunne Books, 2004.

Severance, Frank H., ed. *Publications of the Buffalo Historical Society*. Buffalo: Buffalo Historical Society, 1915.

Smith, Alice E. *The History of Wisconsin*. Vol. 1. Madison: State Historical Society of Wisconsin, 1973.

Starr, Bart, with Murray Olderman. *Starr: My Life in Football*. New York: William Morrow, 1987.

Stein, Jean. *West of Eden: An American Place.* New York: Random House, 2016.

Syken, Bill, ed. *Packers: Green, Gold and Glory.* New York: Sports Illustrated, 2013.

Torinus, John B. *The Packer Legend: An Inside Look.* Neshkoro, WI: Laranmark Press, 1983.

Walter, Tony. *Baptism by Football: The Year Green Bay and the Packers Forged Their Futures.* Green Bay: M&B Global Solutions, 2017.

Ward, Arch. *The Green Bay Packers: The Story of Professional Football.* New York: G. P. Putnam's Sons, 1946.

White, Reggie, with Jim Denney. *Reggie White in the Trenches.* Nashville: Thomas Nelson, 1997.

Whittingham, Richard. *What a Game They Played.* New York: Harper and Row, 1984.

Willis, Chris. *The Man Who Built the National Football League: Joe F. Carr.* Lanham, MD: Scarecrow Press, 2010.

Wolf, Ron, and Paul Attner. *The Packer Way: Nine Stepping Stones to Building a Winning Organization.* New York: St. Martin's, 1998.

NOTES

1: TWO SIDES OF THE RIVER

page

2 *The final retreat:* Interviews with Ken Bradbury and Eric Carson, Wisconsin Geological & Natural History Survey, June 19, 2017.

2 *For thousands of years after:* Collections of the Neville Public Museum.

2 *Nicolet's mission failed:* Interview with Emeritus Professor Jerrold Rodesch, University of Wisconsin–Green Bay, September 22, 2017.

3 *algae-tinged color:* Ibid.

4 *only about 50 adults:* Green Bay Press-Gazette, July 1, 1934.

5 *Navarino, which he named:* Milwaukee Sentinel, August 11, 1895.

7 *intermittent drizzle:* Green Bay Gazette, September 29, 1895.

8 *"large sprinkling of ladies":* Ibid.

8 *force behind the team:* Green Bay Gazette, August 18, 1895.

8 *trainer of the West Side Athletic Association:* Ibid.

8 *"free from slugging":* Green Bay Gazette, October 19, 1896.

8 *"he was struck in the face":* Green Bay Gazette, October 27, 1895.

8 *The game ended in confusion:* Ibid.

8 *playing for the town team:* Green Bay Gazette, October 7, 1896.

8 *"Schanandore":* Cliff Christl's History, https://www.packers.com/news/cliff-christl-history, August 9, 2018.

9 *There was no constancy:* Christl, packers.com, November 19, 2014.

9 *"best interests of the city":* Green Bay Gazette, November 2, 1901.

10 *"most important ever played":* Green Bay Gazette, November 29, 1905.

10 *frozen Fox River:* Green Bay Gazette, December 1, 1905.

10 *streetcar accident:* Green Bay Gazette, December 1, 1905.

10 *"important accompaniment of the struggle":* Ibid.

10 *"A disastrous finish":* Green Bay Gazette, December 1, 1905.

10 *19 people had died:* Chicago Tribune, November 26, 1905.

11 *school board banned football:* Green Bay Gazette, August 20, 1906.

11 *formally petitioning:* Green Bay Gazette, 1906.

11 *"hard work and manly deportment":* Ibid.

11 *formalized an agreement:* Green Bay Gazette, November 20, 1907.

11 *marked off in a checkerboard:* Green Bay Gazette, November 27, 1907.

11 *Four hundred revelers:* Green Bay Gazette, November 29, 1907.

11 *"Horns with their noisy din":* Ibid.

11 *"He was in every play":* Press-Gazette, December 1, 1916.

2: CURLY AND CAL

14 *only 256 shared the name:* Interview with Statbel, the official statistical office of the Belgian government, May 7, 2018.

15 *embarked for the United States:* Collections, University of Wisconsin–Green Bay Archives and Area Research Center.

15 *One of the projects:* Press-Gazette, January 16, 1930.

15 *four o'clock in the afternoon:* Green Bay Gazette, October 5, 1891.

15 *testimony of John Rose:* Green Bay Gazette, October 14, 1891.

15 *temporary insanity:* Ibid.

15 *an east-side tavern:* Wright's Directory of Green Bay, 1903.

15 *rented out to boarders:* Green Bay Gazette, September 29, 1903.

15 *"I think he would live":* Interview with Ken Calewarts, December 11, 2018.

16 *track-and-field team:* Yearbooks for 1914–1917, Green Bay East High School.

17 *never enrolled at Wisconsin:* Christl, packers.com, May 4, 2017.

17 *South Side Skidoos:* Press-Gazette, October 23, 1917.

17 *in a benefit game:* Press-Gazette, November 12, 1917.

17 *"not fixed very well financially":* Christl, packers.com, June 25, 2015.

17 *Only four members:* Notre Dame Scholastic Football Review, 1918, Digital Collections, University of Notre Dame, http://archives.nd.edu/Football/.

17 *freshman eligibility rule:* Notre Dame Scholastic Football Review, 1918.

17 *scored the first touchdown:* Associated Press, September 29, 1918.

17 *schedule was canceled:* Notre Dame Scholastic Football Review, 1918.

17 *muddy field in Lincoln:* Indianapolis Star, November 29, 1918.

18 *receiving no grades:* Christl, packers.com, June 25, 2015.

18 *had written to Rockne:* Ibid.

19 *supervised the construction:* Press-Gazette, April 12, 1939.

20 *wood to metal piping:* Press-Gazette, December 6, 1963.

20 *bridge over the Niagara River:* Buffalo Evening News, June 24, 1899.

20 *George's legal guardian:* Buffalo Express, July 29, 1907.

20 *another guardian:* Ibid.

20 *employee of the paper:* Buffalo Evening News, November 27, 1926.

20 *On February 25, 1911:* Marriage record, Welland County, Ontario, February 25, 1911.

23 *calling itself the Bays:* Christl, packers.com, November 29, 2014.

24 *helped the Skidoos:* Press-Gazette, September 16, 1918.

24 *second organizational meeting:* Press-Gazette, August 15, 1919.

24 *Hulbert's broken nose:* Green Bay Gazette, October 27, 1895.

25 *hand had been mangled:* Gustav Rosenow, World War I and World War II draft registration cards.

25 *high temperature of 74:* Press-Gazette, September 15, 1919.

26 *two of the extra travelers:* Press-Gazette, November 30, 1963.

27 *any real credentials:* Christl, packers.com, October 29, 2015.

27 *the Leannah's Colts:* Ibid.

27 *only one that either team ever played:* Ibid.

27 *baseball and basketball teams:* Christl, packers.com, November 20, 2014.

27 *more than a dozen former major leaguers:* Christl, packers.com, October 29, 2015.

27 *abandoned his baseball career:* Bill Lamb, "George Zabel," Society for American Baseball Research, sabr.org.

27 *struck on his pitching hand:* Chicago Tribune, June 18, 1915.

27 *experience arm trouble:* Lamb, "George Zabel," sabr.org.

27 *baseball, basketball, and tennis:* Ibid.

27 *degree in chemistry:* Ibid.

27 *various capacities:* Janesville Daily Gazette, March 5, 1966.

28   *replay of the game: Janesville Gazette,* December 2, 1919.

28   *who was 23:* Wally P. Ladrow, World War I draft registration card.

28   *the Green Bay Post Office: Press-Gazette,* January 3, 1971.

29   *at the Brown County Courthouse: Press-Gazette,* July 1, 1960.

29   *chief of police: Press-Gazette,* December 26, 1961.

29   *Herman Martell: Press-Gazette,* October 28, 1957.

3: THE HEART OF THE CITY

33   *cigar-chomping:* Chris Willis, "Ralph Hay: A Forgotten Pioneer, an Interview with Dr. James F. King," *The Coffin Corner* 26, no. 4 (2004).

33   *added credibility:* Bob Braunwart and Bob Carroll, "The Ohio League," *The Coffin Corner* 3, no. 7 (1981).

33   *$250 per game:* Pro Football Hall of Fame.

35   *a rapid inflation:* "Twilight: 1919," PFRA Research, www.profootballresearchers.org.

35   *as much as $2,000:* Ibid.

35   *signed extra players:* Ibid.

35   *signed him in early November:* Ibid.

35   *On Sunday, November 23: Sports Illustrated,* January 29, 1968.

36   *Hay hosted a meeting:* Pro Football Hall of Fame.

36   *temporary secretary: Canton Evening Repository,* August 21, 1920.

36   *a second meeting:* Willis, "Ralph Hay: A Forgotten Pioneer," *Coffin Corner.*

36   *big and boisterous:* Staley Museum.

37   *the $20,000 Hammond Bobcats:* "Twilight: 1919," PFRA Research, www.profootballresearchers.org.

38   *Thorpe had played baseball: Akron Beacon Journal,* September 18, 1920.

38   *Four other teams:* Pro Football Hall of Fame.

38   *Halas canceled it:* Roy Sye, "Muncie Flyers — 1920," *The Coffin Corner* 24, no. 3 (2002).

38   *muddy Wrigley Field: Quad-City Times,* December 13, 1920.

39   *was an engineer: Press-Gazette,* November 3, 1933.

39   *sons of an original employee: Green Bay Gazette,* November 28, 1905.

39   *rode the rails together:* Interview with Patrick Dwyer, April 25, 2018.

39   *transferred Michael to Green Bay: Press-Gazette,* November 3, 1933.

39   *on South Oakland Avenue:* 1900 U.S. Census, Brown County, WI, June 7, 1900.

39   *started as a fireman: Press-Gazette,* December 28, 1946.

39   *became a dentist: Press-Gazette,* October 1, 1923.

39   *a machinist's apprentice: Press-Gazette,* August 3, 1944.

39   *10 days before: Press-Gazette,* June 15, 1917.

39   *married Eda Eliason: Press-Gazette,* February 1, 1991.

39   *the couple's first child, Roy: Press-Gazette,* February 27, 2005.

39   *121st Field Artillery Regiment:* U.S. Army Transport Passenger Lists.

39   *shopmen's strike: Press-Gazette,* August 6, 1919.

39   *working outdoors as a switchman: Press-Gazette,* August 3, 1944.

39   *Pig Iron:* Christl, packers.com, November 24, 2016.

40   *eight months pregnant: Press-Gazette,* November 17, 1971.

40   *in the mid-thirties: Press-Gazette,* November 24, 1920.

40   *"I can't feel anything":* Interview with Patrick Dwyer, April 25, 2018.

40   *"We all remember Dwyer":* Dennis McCarthy to C. M. Murphy, November 30, 1920.

41   *Green Bay was energized: Press-Gazette,* November 29, 1920.

41   *between $1 and $5: Press-Gazette,* December 1, 1920.

41   *was 4,000: Press-Gazette,* December 6, 1920.

41   *3,000 had been sold: Press-Gazette,* November 30, 1920.

42   *in the forties:* Ibid.

42   *chipped in $100 apiece: Press-Gazette,* November 29, 1920.

42   *Workers at the gate: Press-Gazette,* December 6, 1920.

42   *raised an extra $32:* Ibid.

42   *St. Patrick's Church:* Certificate of Exemption from Federal Tax on Admissions, Treasury Department, December 5, 1920.

42   *presented him with a check: Press-Gazette,* December 9, 1920.

42   *taken over from Calhoun: Press-Gazette,* July 17, 1920.

42   *son of Irish immigrants:* 1920 U.S. Census, Brown County, WI, January 18, 1920.

42   *selling newspapers:* Interview with Patricia (Murphy) Sullivan, "Neil the Family Man," YouTube.com, December 14, 2016, https://www.youtube.com/watch?v=fqhrBU-egRY&t=285s.

42   *four years after the company:* Ibid.

42   *the Coulons:* Interview with Cornelius Murphy Jr., "Neil's Team — Acme Packers (Green Bay Packers)," YouTube, January 30, 2011, https://www.youtube.com/watch?v=xpwX0FwIQ7Q.

43   *manager of its football department:* Christl, packers.com, March 23, 2017.

43   *until December 1:* Interview with Cornelius Murphy Jr., "Neil's Team — Acme Packers (Green Bay Packers)," YouTube, January 30, 2011, https://www.youtube.com/watch?v=xpwX0FwIQ7Q.

43   *began on August 28: Press-Gazette,* August 27, 1920.

43   *Painted signs were added: Press-Gazette,* September 29, 1920.

43   *bleachers holding 700: Press-Gazette,* October 15, 1920.

43   *more stands for roughly 800:* Christl, packers.com, June 26, 2014.

43   *the cost of the fence: Press-Gazette,* August 21, 1920.

44   *net profits for the season: Press-Gazette,* December 15, 1920.

44   *were torn down: Press-Gazette,* December 13, 1920.

44   *diamond stickpin: Press-Gazette,* December 15, 1920.

44   *machine-gun battalion:* World War I U.S. Army passenger list, July 6, 1918.

44   *the nickname "Leather": Janesville Daily Gazette,* January 30, 1957.

45   *"a corking good game": Press-Gazette,* September 27, 1920.

45   *only one company official: Press-Gazette,* December 23, 1920.

45   *Clair a vice president:* Ibid.

45   *that city's South Side:* 1910 U.S. Census, Cook County, IL, April 16, 1910.

45   *"a professional team":* Christl, *Packers Heritage Trail.*

46   *offensive and defensive lines: Press-Gazette,* September 14, 1921.

46   *about $40 a share: New York Tribune,* August 5, 1919.

46   *a little more than $3: New York Tribune,* December 23, 1920.

47   *$100 per game: Chicago Tribune,* August 19, 1937.

4: SAVED

52   *they merged in 1915: Press-Gazette,* June 27, 1965.

52   *son of a conductor: Press-Gazette,* October 17, 1960.

52   *soon began working:* Ibid.

52   *after he had become a U.S. citizen:* Ibid.

53   *"The professional and the gambler": Decatur Herald,* December 29, 1921.

53   *banish the Packers: Chicago Tribune,* December 15, 1921.

54   *the previous April: Dayton Herald,* May 2, 1921.

54 *Irish immigrant shoemaker:* 1880 U.S. Census, Franklin County, OH, June 3, 1880.

54 *working as a machinist:* 1900 U.S. Census, Franklin County, OH, June 1–2, 1900.

54 *Pennsylvania Railroad: Chicago Tribune,* May 21, 1939.

54 *admitted the Panhandles:* Pro Football Hall of Fame.

55 *"Clubs which even attempt":* United Press, August 28, 1921.

55 *Hotel Courtland: Akron Beacon Journal,* January 9, 1922.

55 *a $1,000 guarantee: New York Herald,* January 30, 1922.

56 *on an auto tour: Press-Gazette,* June 2, 1922.

56 *moved back to Chicago: Press-Gazette,* January 10, 1922.

56 *Cleveland's Hollenden Hotel: Press-Gazette,* June 24, 1922.

56 *APFA changed its name:* Associated Press, June 26, 1922.

56 *vowing to obey: Press-Gazette,* June 26, 1922.

56 *"One thing is sure": Press-Gazette,* June 27, 1922.

58 *first director of publicity: Notre Dame Alumnus,* September 1955.

59 *cattle buyer: Press-Gazette,* April 30, 1941.

59 *Congress Billiard Room: Press-Gazette,* September 5, 1919.

59 *Congress sold tickets: Press-Gazette,* December 4, 1920.

59 *Harry Levitas: Press-Gazette,* January 23, 1920.

59 *whose sister, Frances: Press-Gazette,* February 4, 1975.

59 *sold his interest: Press-Gazette,* July 11, 1922.

59 *re-signed Cub Buck: Press-Gazette,* July 25, 1922.

59 *Buck turned down an offer: Press-Gazette,* September 13, 1922.

59 *lawyer in Marinette: Press-Gazette,* October 7, 1922.

59 *Republican ticket for district attorney: Press-Gazette,* September 5, 1922.

59 *played with a broken hand: Press-Gazette,* November 29, 1921.

59 *appointed city attorney:* Associated Press, February 18, 1926.

59 *three-decade career: Press-Gazette,* April 28, 1958.

59 *letterhead:* Christl, packers.com, July 29, 2016.

60 *slightly more than the minimum: Green Bay Packers Media Guide,* 2017.

60 *rain insurance:* Ibid.

60 *raised ticket prices: Press-Gazette,* November 7, 1922.

60 *"Your field here is limited":* Ibid.

60 *George De Lair: Press-Gazette,* November 22, 1922.

60 *demanded a guarantee: Press-Gazette,* November 28, 1922.

60 *Booster tickets sold for:* Ibid.

60 *"get back of them":* Ibid.

61 *more than 150 men: Press-Gazette,* December 8, 1922.

61 *The first $1,300: Press-Gazette,* December 13, 1922.

61 *NFL transferred ownership:* Minutes of NFL meeting, January 20, 1923.

61 *entitled to a box seat: Press-Gazette,* August 18, 1923.

61 *downtown business district:* Ibid.

61 *"pep meeting": Press-Gazette,* September 15, 1923.

61 *John Kittell: Press-Gazette,* December 8, 1922.

62 *appointed the five-man committee: Press-Gazette,* December 8, 1922.

62 *one of the team's original investors: Press-Gazette,* December 13, 1922.

62 *20 shares in the team:* Christl, *Packers Heritage Trail.*

62 *his opening remarks: Press-Gazette,* September 15, 1923.

62 *It is almost certain:* Christl, packers.com, May 26, 2016.

62 *first stockholders' meeting: Press-Gazette,* September 18, 1923.

62 *204 shareholders:* Christl, packers.com, December 31, 2015.

62 *sale netted $5,545: Green Bay Packers Media Guide,* 2017.

63 *things that Ward got wrong:* Christl, packers.com, May 26, 2016.

63 *"Ward was not from Green Bay":* Ibid.

64 *did not attend:* Ibid.

64 *organized the formation: Press-Gazette,* September 21, 1932.

64 *On November 20, 1922:* Christl, packers.com, May 26, 2016.

64 *Three days later: Press-Gazette,* November 23, 1922.

64 *12:50 on Sunday morning: Press-Gazette,* November 26, 1921.

64 *a playlist that included: Press-Gazette,* November 28, 1921.

64 *entered a sanatorium: Wausau Daily Herald,* June 26, 1924.

64 *before his 44th birthday:* George De Lair, World War I draft registration card, September 12, 1918.

64 *an institution in Green Bay: Press-Gazette,* July 18, 1934.

64 *Born in 1875: Press-Gazette,* August 4, 1951.

64 *moving to Green Bay in 1904:* Ibid.

5: A WIDE-OPEN TOWN

68 *never stopped serving:* Interview with McKim Boyd, March 9, 2018.

69 *three breweries: Press-Gazette,* November 7, 1982.

69 *more than 100 saloons: Press-Gazette,* October 16, 2011.

69 *"in large part a farce": Press-Gazette,* July 18, 1934.

69 *a life sentence: Lansing State Journal,* December 12, 1928.

69 *commuted to 15 months: Detroit Free Press,* March 12, 1930.

69 *made some home brew: Chicago Tribune,* November 5, 1931.

69 *federal agents descended: Press-Gazette,* July 18, 1934.

69 *attracted nationwide attention:* Ibid.

69 *no regular agents:* Ibid.

70 *had actually lost money: Green Bay Packers Media Guide,* 2017.

71 *four players who had begun the season:* Christl, packers.com, March 30, 2017.

71 *also the team's coach: Rock Island Argus,* September 19, 1921.

71 *had to live in Rock Island: Rock Island Argus,* October 19, 1921.

71 *wired the play-by-play:* Christl, packers.com, March 30, 2017.

71 *"the best supported": Press-Gazette,* October 25, 1922.

71 *150 gambling and prostitution: The Dispatch* (Moline, IL), December 17, 1993.

71 *notoriously violent:* Ibid.

71 *four more Rock Island players:* Christl, packers.com, March 30, 2017.

71 *who was released: Rock Island Argus,* October 11, 1922.

71 *"heavy and fat": Rock Island Argus,* October 12, 1922.

71 *internal problems: Press-Gazette,* October 17, 1922.

71 *"picking up discards": Rock Island Argus,* October 20, 1922.

72 *promptly signed with Green Bay: Press-Gazette,* October 31, 1922.

72 *stayed in De Pere:* Christl, packers.com, March 30, 2017.

72 *"hospitality of everybody": Press-Gazette,* July 18, 1927.

73 *"roved a bit": Press-Gazette,* August 5, 1925.

73 *did not graduate from Heidelberg:* Christl, packers.com, January 28, 2016.

73 *There is no record of him:* Ibid.

74 *youngest of six:* 1910 U.S. Census, Lancaster County, NE, April 18, 1910.

74 *rancher Joseph Lewellen:* Interview with Verne C. Lewellen Jr., January 17, 2018.

74 *Verne was a star:* Lincoln High Athletic Hall of Fame.

74 *four state titles:* Ibid.

74 *in the high hurdles:* Ibid.

74 *all-state quarterback:* Ibid.

75 *spilled out of the stands: Nebraska State Journal,* November 11, 1923.

75 *went for 70 yards:* Ibid.

75 *tipped his former coach off:* Christl, packers.com, n.d.

75 *subsequently outbid:* Press-Gazette, July 31, 1924.

75 *job with a Green Bay law firm:* Christl, packers.com, n.d.

75 *tryout with baseball's Pittsburgh Pirates:* Pittsburgh Post-Gazette, July 5, 1924.

75 *"a speedy cross-fire curveball":* Lincoln Star, December 2, 1923.

75 *signed with Pittsburgh:* Daily Republican (Monongahela, PA), January 19, 1924.

75 *missing spring training:* Pittsburgh Daily Post, February 21, 1924.

75 *lasted less than a month:* Pittsburgh Post-Gazette, July 5, 1924.

75 *train accident:* Interview with Verne C. Lewellen Jr., January 17, 2018.

75 *an incredible 136 times:* Bob Carroll, "Verne Lewellen," *The Coffin Corner* 12, no. 1 (1990).

76 *unofficial average of 39.5 yards:* Ibid.

76 *"in front of me and Hubbard":* Press-Gazette, February 3, 1963.

76 *"it's a joke":* Press-Gazette, April 21, 1967.

76 *would shift left or right:* Christl, packers.com, March 17, 2016.

77 *"Our best teams have been":* Ibid.

77 *more than 200 punts:* Christl, packers.com, n.d.

77 *"their basic attack":* Christl, packers.com, March 17, 2016.

80 *"not a good football field":* Press-Gazette, September 15, 1963.

81 *longest-tenured elected official:* Press-Gazette, August 3, 1944.

81 *"best football town of its size":* Press-Gazette, November 29, 1922.

6: CHAMPIONS

88 *began on a muggy afternoon:* Press-Gazette, July 31, 1929.

88 *sunny Wrigley Field:* Press-Gazette, December 10, 1928.

88 *"man-mountain":* Press-Gazette, July 31, 1929.

89 *town of Glasgow:* Archives of Keytesville High School.

89 *without graduating:* Archives of Keytesville High School.

89 *a foot problem:* Chariton Courier, May 30, 1919.

89 *continue to play football:* Chariton Courier, October 21, 1921.

89 *tiny Centre College:* Columbia Missourian, May 4, 1922.

89 *a kickoff back 65 yards:* Shreveport Times, October 1, 1922.

90 *One of Geneva's most effective plays:* Sports Illustrated, September 5, 1994.

90 *stayed there for a full week:* Press-Gazette, October 8, 1928.

91 *Schuster Construction Company:* Press-Gazette, August 27, 1929.

91 *too scrawny and young:* Interview with Casey Eckardt, athletic director at New Richmond High, January 30, 2018.

91 *school has no record:* Interview with registrar, University of Wisconsin–River Falls, January 31, 2018.

91 *did indeed attend River Falls:* Interview with registrar, University of Minnesota, February 12, 2018.

91 *Stillwater, Minnesota:* Eau Claire Leader, August 25, 1921.

91 *failed to show up at his office:* Ibid.

91 *his car and his cap:* Eau Claire Leader, August 25, 1921.

91 *body was found floating:* Eau Claire Leader, August 26, 1921.

91 *ruled an accident:* Minneapolis Tribune, August 26, 1921.

92 *edited the Saint John's annual:* Sagatagan, 1923.

92 *wrote for the student newspaper:* Ibid.

92 *"or of much good":* St. John's Record, June 1923.

92 *letter in four sports:* Ibid.

92 *"stands for versatile":* St. John's Record, May 1923.

92 *two semesters of summer school:* Registrar records, University of Minnesota.

92 *a day student in South Bend:* Archives of the University of Notre Dame.

92 *was the ghostwriter:* Sports Illustrated, September 2, 1963.

92 *"I rode the blinds":* Ibid.

92 *a stereotyper:* Ibid.

94 *went by Melvin Blood:* Minneapolis Tribune, November 27, 1924.

95 *nickname was going to be changed:* Minneapolis Tribune, July 12, 1926.

95 *road games in Green Bay:* Press-Gazette, September 4, 1929.

95 *son of German immigrants:* 1920 U.S. Census, Cuyahoga County, OH, January 9, 1920.

95 *to play fullback in college:* Harrisburg Telegraph, October 27, 1925.

95 *"holler guy":* Post-Crescent (Appleton, WI), October 26, 1983.

96 *"We have gone out":* Press-Gazette, August 2, 1929.

96 *"large part of our community life":* Press-Gazette, August 6, 1929.

96 *three-hour workout:* Press-Gazette, September 9, 1929.

96 *hobnobbed with:* Interview with Maura Concannon, January 27, 2018.

99 *appear in every contest:* Sports Illustrated, September 4, 1985.

99 *Halas was weeping:* Ibid.

99 *"Grange was an event":* John Underwood, "Was He the Greatest of All Time?" *Sports Illustrated*, September 4, 1985.

100 *had both suffered shoulder injuries:* Press-Gazette, November 13, 1929.

100 *forced out of the game:* Press-Gazette, November 18, 1929.

100 *cracked several ribs:* Press-Gazette, November 19, 1929.

102 *Holmgren's first coaching staff:* Green Bay Packers Media Guide, 2017.

102 *neither of them won a championship:* Interview with Andrew Fast, NFLCoachingTrees.com, February 12, 2018.

103 *"he didn't know what was happening":* Charley Brock, interviewed in *Green Bay Packers: The Grandstand Franchise*, WPNE-TV, Wisconsin Educational Television Network, University of Wisconsin–Green Bay Center for Television Production, 1983.

103 *5-3 favorites:* Press-Gazette, November 23, 1929.

103 *stopped briefly in Milwaukee:* Press-Gazette, November 21, 1929.

103 *a testimonial dinner:* Ibid.

105 *around 40 degrees:* Brooklyn Daily Eagle, November 25, 1929.

105 *"like a steel cutting tin":* Ibid.

105 *75-yard punt:* Press-Gazette, November 25, 1929.

105 *fumbled the ball away:* Ibid.

105 *quick touchdown pass to McCrary:* Ibid.

106 *over-the-shoulder catch:* Chicago Tribune, November 25, 1929.

106 *golden yellow:* Ibid.

106 *smeared with mud:* Ibid.

106 *Blood fell on top of it:* Press-Gazette, November 25, 1929.

106 *crashed into the end zone:* Ibid.

106 *interception to Jug Earp:* Ibid.

106 *difficult to see:* Ibid.

106 *sending in Paul Minick:* Ibid.

107 *"Make 'em like it!":* Ibid.

107 *"Grid-Graph":* Press-Gazette, November 23, 1929.

107 *WTMJ had broadcast a wire report:* Milwaukee Journal, November 24, 1929.

107 *more than 500 telegrams:* Press-Gazette, November 25, 1929.

107 *"Will hold my appendix":* Press-Gazette, November 27, 1929.

107 *"In distinguishing themselves":* Press-Gazette, November 25, 1929.

108 *"Not once":* Press-Gazette, December 2, 1929.

108 *"I hesitated about playing":* Press-Gazette, December 10, 1929.

108   *"pretty hard to say anything"*: Ibid.

108   *"freedom of the city"*: Ibid.

109   *on station WHBY*: *Press-Gazette*, December 11, 1929.

109   *check for $220*: Ibid.

109   *"greatest thrills of my life"*: Ibid.

7: FROM CHAMPIONSHIPS TO RECEIVERSHIP

112   *washed out academically*: Interview with registrar, University of Wisconsin, April 5, 2018.

112   *He had no job*: 1930 U.S. Census, Brown County, WI, April 4, 1930.

112   *conductor on the Milwaukee Road*: *Green Bay Gazette*, July 7, 1906.

112   *caught between cars*: *Press-Gazette*, December 14, 1917.

112   *married Lois Lefevre*: *Press-Gazette*, December 27, 1987.

113   *right halfback in the spring game*: *Press-Gazette*, May 15, 1929.

113   *ruled academically ineligible*: *Press-Gazette*, August 27, 1929.

113   *enrolled in February 1930*: *Press-Gazette*, February 11, 1930.

113   *retirement in March*: *Press-Gazette*, March 27, 1930.

113   *put the team through its paces*: *Press-Gazette*, September 8, 1930.

114   *practice in Central Park*: *Press-Gazette*, December 3, 1961.

115   *150-pound block of ice*: *Press-Gazette*, December 16, 1930.

115   *seven-day voyage*: Associated Press, December 21, 1929.

115   *eight-foot bed*: Associated Press, December 30, 1929.

115   *he had kept to himself*: *Press-Gazette*, November 24, 1931.

117   *entering Lambeau's room*: Gerald Holland, "Is That You Up There, Johnny Blood?," *Sports Illustrated*, September 1, 1963.

117   *Bonus checks were $100*: Christl, packers.com, June 22, 2017.

118   *interception by Red Grange*: *Press-Gazette*, December 7, 1931.

118   *actually expanded*: Craig Richard Coenen, "The Survival of Professional Football in Green Bay, Wisconsin, 1921–1959," MA thesis, Lehigh University, 1994.

118   *production of toilet tissue*: Craig Richard Coenen, "The Survival of Professional Football in Green Bay, Wisconsin, 1921–1959," MA thesis, Lehigh University, 1994.

118   *20 percent of the working population*: *Press-Gazette*, July 18, 1934.

118   *cheese making and railroads*: Interview with Mary Jane Herber, March 8, 2018.

118   *top 20 percent*: Craig Richard Coenen, "The Survival of Professional Football in Green Bay, Wisconsin, 1921–1959," MA thesis, Lehigh University, 1994.

118   *a local physician*: 1920 U.S. Census, Schuylkill County, PA, January 9, 1920.

118   *$1,500 for league fees*: *Mount Carmel Item*, January 8, 1925.

118   *needed $5,000 more*: *Lebanon Daily News*, October 15, 1925.

118   *more than $2,000*: *Pottsville Republican*, October 17, 1925.

119   *dropped by nearly 19 percent*: Craig Richard Coenen, "The Survival of Professional Football in Green Bay, Wisconsin, 1921–1959," MA thesis, Lehigh University, 1994.

119   *declined by nearly 46 percent*: Ibid.

119   *250 shares for $100 each*: C. Robert Barnett, "The Portsmouth Spartans," *The Coffin Corner* 2, no. 10 (1980).

119   *only 158 of the 250 shares*: Ibid.

119   *$15,800 in the bank*: Craig Richard Coenen, "The Survival of Professional Football in Green Bay, Wisconsin, 1921–1959," MA thesis, Lehigh University, 1994.

119   *IOUs instead of paychecks*: Ibid.

119   *Coach George "Potsy" Clark*: *Portsmouth Times*, December 23, 1931.

119   *short of its goals*: Craig Richard Coenen, "The Survival of Professional Football in Green Bay, Wisconsin, 1921–1959," MA thesis, Lehigh University, 1994.

119   *shoes and steel*: Ibid.

119   *decision to move the team*: Associated Press, March 27, 1934.

119   *stockholders approved the sale*: *Portsmouth Times*, April 6, 1934.

120   *Born in Nova Scotia*: *Press-Gazette*, May 31, 1952.

120   *Charles and Annie Bent's*: 1900 U.S. Census, Marinette County, WI, June 7, 1900.

120   *sold sporting goods*: *Press-Gazette*, December 16, 1938.

120   *started his own business in 1909*: *Green Bay Gazette*, March 18, 1909.

120   *entire city block*: *Press-Gazette*, August 9, 1938.

120   *jump headline*: *Press-Gazette*, March 31, 1941.

120   *outfitted the original Packers*: *Press-Gazette*, December 16, 1938.

120   *to be the team's salesmen*: Christl, packers.com, May 26, 2016.

120   *one of the 204 original stockholders*: Interview with Cliff Christl, March 7, 2018.

120   *fracturing his spine*: Trial transcript, *Bent vs. Green Bay Football Corp.*, Brown County Circuit Court, 1933.

120   *taken in an ambulance*: Ibid.

120   *53 days in a body cast*: Ibid.

121   *even the coldest weather*: *Press-Gazette*, March 8, 1946.

121   *He was a conservationist*: *Press-Gazette*, March 13, 1946.

121   *He loved to hunt and fish*: *Press-Gazette*, March 8, 1946.

121   *He was a charter member*: Ibid.

121   *soldiers returning from France*: Ibid.

121   *Arthur Fontaine*: Trial transcript, *Bent vs. Green Bay Football Corp.*, Brown County Circuit Court, 1933.

121   *son of a former mayor*: *Press-Gazette*, February 25, 1952.

121   *"hard two-fisted fighter"*: *Press-Gazette*, February 26, 1952.

121   *erected a section of seats*: *Press-Gazette*, February 23, 1933.

121   *"a nurse to hold his hand"*: Trial transcript, *Bent vs. Green Bay Football Corp.*, Brown County Circuit Court, 1933.

122   *"except for his brother"*: Ibid.

122   *something similar had happened to him*: Ibid.

122   *He was unemployed*: Ibid.

122   *deliberating for more than five hours*: Ibid.

122   *Southern Surety Company of New York*: *Press-Gazette*, March 6, 1934.

122   *failed in March 1932*: *Hartford Courant*, March 24, 1932.

122   *judgments and unpaid bills*: *Press-Gazette*, March 23, 1950.

122   *Other board members*: *Press-Gazette*, January 4, 1935.

123   *Green Bay lost money*: *Press-Gazette*, December 15, 1934.

123   *severe abdominal pain*: *Press-Gazette*, November 29, 1933.

123   *"sure cure powders"*: Ibid.

123   *the contract of end Tom Nash*: *Press-Gazette*, October 11, 1933.

123   *line coach at Texas A&M*: *Press-Gazette*, January 27, 1934.

123   *sold to the Pittsburgh Pirates*: *Press-Gazette*, August 6, 1934.

124   *"if we can raise $10,000"*: *Press-Gazette*, December 15, 1934.

124   *the sale had raised $12,000*: *Press-Gazette*, December 30, 1935.

124   *leading shareholders*: Interview with Cliff Christl, July 2, 2018.

8: HUTSON

128   *"meaner than a rattlesnake"*: Christl, packers.com, n.d.

128   *youngest of three sons*: 1930 U.S. Census, Jefferson County, OH, April 14, 1930.

128   *minor league baseball for 10 years*: Bill Nowlin, Society for American Baseball Research.

129   *53-yard catch-and-run:* Press-Gazette, November 23, 1931.

129   *62 yards on the ground:* San Francisco Examiner, January 2, 1932.

129   *sitting on the East bench:* Press-Gazette, January 11, 1932.

129   *over other deals from:* Christl, packers.com, n.d.

131   *"He was the hardest runner":* Ibid.

131   *"never known a man who wanted to win":* Ibid.

131   *clear and warm afternoon:* Press-Gazette, September 25, 1933.

131   *tonsils taken out:* Press-Gazette, September 11, 1933.

131   *heavy bandages:* Press-Gazette, September 18, 1933.

131   *on a stretcher:* Christl, packers.com, n.d.

132   *chose Nagurski:* Associated Press, September 2, 1964.

132   *"The guy who bruised me":* Paul Zimmerman, "The Bronk and the Gazelle," Sports Illustrated, September 11, 1989.

132   *"He throws them pretty accurately":* United Press, February 8, 1939.

133   *sons of a conductor:* Roy B. Hutson, World War I draft registration card.

133   *his twin brothers:* Robert and Raymond Hutson, World War II draft registration cards.

133   *rank of Eagle Scout:* Boys' Life, February 1935.

133   *35 to 40 snakes:* Press-Gazette, September 30, 1942.

133   *until his senior year:* Marshall Morning News, October 8, 1930.

133   *all-state basketball team:* Los Angeles Times, April 30, 1989.

133   *There was a Bob Seawell:* The Zebra, Pine Bluff High School, May 1929.

133   *born in 1909:* 1910 U.S. Census, Cook County, TX, May 11, 1910.

133   *a neighbor of Hutson's:* 1930 U.S. Census, Jefferson County, AR, April 12, 1930.

134   *did indeed attend Alabama:* Interview with registrar, University of Alabama, March 26, 2018.

134   *weighed only 145 pounds:* Marshall Morning News, October 8, 1930.

134   *tied for the state record:* Arkansas Activities Association.

134   *man named Jimmy Harland:* 1931 Pine Bluff City Directory; 1930 U.S. Census, Jefferson County, AR, April 5, 1930.

134   *stole 15 bases:* Anniston Star, April 28, 1934.

134   *batting .457:* Anniston Star, April 20, 1934.

134   *slugged a homer:* Anniston Star, April 13, 1935.

134   *outside of the top three:* Christl, packers.com, n.d.

134   *the winning time:* Anniston Star, May 19, 1935.

135   *caught six passes:* Rose Bowl play-by-play, Los Angeles Times, January 2, 1935.

135   *he hurt his ankle:* Ibid.

136   *sandy-haired, 150-pound:* Anniston Star, September 6, 1934.

136   *son of a policeman:* 1930 U.S. Census, Houston County, AL, April 14, 1930.

136   *"most promising backfield man":* Dothan Eagle, July 26, 1934.

136   *junior safety Bob Maentz:* Oakland Tribune, January 2, 1935.

136   *Bob "Bones" Hamilton:* Oakland Tribune, October 15, 1935.

137   *59-yard touchdown:* Oakland Tribune, January 2, 1935.

137   *"as great a passing combination":* Atlanta Constitution, January 2, 1935.

137   *in San Francisco since late December:* Press-Gazette, December 28, 1934.

137   *Lambeau called Thomas:* Christl, packers.com, n.d.

137   *$175 per game:* Ibid.

137   *never graduated from Alabama:* Interview with registrar, University of Alabama, March 26, 2018.

138   *to jump-start his team:* San Bernardino County Sun, September 18, 1936.

138   *already the NFL's longest:* Press-Gazette, September 18, 1935.

138   *"Blood was on the other team":* Christl, packers.com, August 8, 2014.

140   *Under cloudy skies:* Press-Gazette, September 23, 1935.

140   *son of an illiterate laborer:* 1920 U.S. Census, Sullivan County, TN, January 2–3, 1920.

140   *an injured ankle:* Chicago Tribune, December 7, 1935.

143   *cold and sunny Sunday:* Chicago Tribune, December 14, 1936.

143   *fumbled a lateral:* Associated Press, December 14, 1936.

143   *Redskins defensive back Ed Justice:* Chicago Tribune, December 14, 1936.

143   *out of bounds by Irwin:* Associated Press, December 14, 1936.

144   *second-to-last catch:* Press-Gazette, December 14, 1936.

144   *Art Rooney signed him:* Press-Gazette, February 22, 1937.

144   *It was Enright:* Christl, packers.com, n.d.

144   *one of eight children:* 1920, 1930, and 1940 U.S. Census, Pickens County, SC.

144   *All the Craig boys:* Greenville News, November 2, 1938.

145   *"a wagonload":* Greenville News, October 16, 1938.

145   *"looked like Hercules":* Christl, packers.com, September 14, 2017.

145   *"latched on to Larry Craig":* Christl, packers.com, June 30, 2016.

146   *NFL had decreed:* Press-Gazette, November 29, 1939.

146   *drop its smallest outpost:* Christl, packers.com, January 5, 2017.

147   *"cradle of baseball":* Press-Gazette, December 12, 1939.

147   *"will retain its franchise":* Press-Gazette, December 11, 1939.

9: WAR, AND A LAST HURRAH

150   *in honor of Sergeant William Sullivan:* Press-Gazette, August 22, 1919.

150   *voted to rename:* Press-Gazette, March 15, 1944.

150   *a city fireman:* 1940 U.S. Census, Brown County, WI, April 15, 1940.

150   *Brothers Carl and Martin Zoll:* Ibid.

151   *in Allouez, and Jug Earp:* Ibid.

151   *Don carried six times:* Press-Gazette, November 12, 1937.

151   *Rams' freshman team:* Press-Gazette, November 17, 1938.

151   *a decree of divorce:* Press-Gazette, May 22, 1934.

151   *"largely perfunctory":* Press-Gazette, May 23, 1934.

151   *"really wasn't his fault":* Christl, packers.com, March 16, 2017.

152   *second week of February:* Press-Gazette, February 9, 1933.

152   *high temperature:* Press-Gazette, December 14, 1932.

152   *"Please wire name":* Honolulu Star-Bulletin, December 1, 1932.

152   *bound for Honolulu:* Manifest of outward-bound passengers, SS Mariposa, December 16, 1932.

152   *Also aboard the* Mariposa: Ibid.

152   *Miss California pageant:* Oakland Tribune, August 3, 1927.

153   *not long after Lambeau returned:* Christl, packers.com, March 16, 2017.

153   *went to Chicago together:* Press-Gazette, October 28, 1935.

153   *against the Army plebes:* Press-Gazette, November 17, 1938.

153   *all of his son's expenses:* Press-Gazette, May 23, 1934.

153   *withdrew from school:* Interview with registrar, Fordham University, April 6, 2018.

153   *enlisted in the Army:* Press-Gazette, November 14, 1942.

153   *He went into the Signal Corps:* Ibid.

153   *ordered to return to San Francisco:* Ibid.

153   *100 miles of telephone line:* Press-Gazette, February 17, 1945.

153   *five grueling months:* Ibid.

153   *on April 8, 1944:* Ibid.

153   *The War Department notified:* Press-Gazette, April 29, 1944.

153   *still laid up in an island hospital:* Press-Gazette, May 18, 1944.

154   *finished up his war service:* Press-Gazette, February 17, 1944.

154   *discharged from the Army:* Press-Gazette, October 29, 1945.

154   *watched from the bench:* Ibid.

154   *to transfer to Navy:* Minneapolis Tribune, June 19, 1941.

154   *with a foot injury:* Asbury Park Press, November 26, 1941.

154   *resigning from the academy:* The Capital (Annapolis, MD), February 17, 1942.

154   *came off the bench:* Press-Gazette, September 28, 1942.

154   *star high school quarterback:* Big Spring Daily Herald, December 17, 1934.

154   *with the Big Spring Spartans:* Big Spring Daily Herald, December 29, 1936.

154   *already married:* Big Spring Daily Herald, February 21, 1937.

154   *young daughter:* 1937 births, Bureau of Vital Statistics, Texas Department of Health.

154   *had lived in Hollywood:* Big Spring Daily Herald, February 21, 1937.

154   *came in as a substitute:* Press-Gazette, October 12, 1942.

155   *"With this player shortage":* Chicago Tribune, April 6, 1943.

155   *war-fund drive:* Press-Gazette, January 20, 1943.

155   *civilian advisory committee:* Press-Gazette, October 12, 1943.

156   *"I was I-A":* Los Angeles Times, April 30, 1989.

156   *in early September 1941:* Associated Press, September 8, 1941.

156   *23-year-old flight officer:* Military Application for Headstone or Marker for Robert Porter Hutson, Graceland Cemetery, Pine Bluff, AR, September 3, 1949.

156   *the morning of August 27, 1943:* Royal Australian Air Force casualty records, National Archives of Australia, 2018.

157   *aware since early September:* Press-Gazette, September 8, 1943.

157   *before signing with the Packers:* Press-Gazette, August 7, 1943.

157   *"feels he owes it to football":* Ibid.

157   *permission from his mother:* Press-Gazette, September 24, 1943.

157   *largest crowd in Packers history:* Press-Gazette, September 27, 1943.

157   *25-yard run:* Ibid.

157   *low throw from Canadeo:* Chicago Tribune, September 27, 1943.

157   *final touchdown of the game:* Ibid.

157   *long and loud ovation:* Press-Gazette, September 27, 1943.

158   *Milwaukee Road train to Chicago:* Press-Gazette, September 25, 1943.

158   *His father had died suddenly:* Tennessee Death Certificate, Alex Johnson, April 9, 1923.

158   *maid at the Hotel Montgomery:* 1930 U.S. Census, Montgomery County, TN, April 12, 1930.

158   *nearby orphanage:* Ibid.

158   *beneath the press box:* Chicago Tribune, December 9, 1941.

158   *son of a streetcar motorman:* 1920 U.S. Census, Cook County, IL, January 13, 1920.

159   *prematurely silver:* Gonzaga Athletic Hall of Fame.

159   *opted for the commission:* Press-Gazette, May 23, 1942.

160   *from III-A to I-A:* Ibid.

160   *naval preflight training:* Press-Gazette, April 22, 1943.

160   *washed out of flight school:* Interview with Robert Canadeo, April 13, 2018.

161   *as well as his marriage:* Press-Gazette, October 11, 1943.

161   *recalled to active duty:* Press-Gazette, December 31, 1943.

161   *in Green Bay on furlough:* Press-Gazette, October 17, 1944.

161   *did not sign with Lambeau:* Press-Gazette, September 2, 1944.

162   *Carpets linebacker John Grigas:* Press-Gazette, October 9, 1944.

162   *a cataract:* Milwaukee Journal Sentinel, December 20, 2007.

162   *four-sport star:* Bay View High School Oracle, 1937.

162   *took Comp under his wing:* Associated Press, August 24, 1944.

162   *only completion of the game:* Press-Gazette, November 20, 1944.

162   *"What was the use":* Brooklyn Daily Eagle, November 20, 1944.

162   *four inches of snow:* Press-Gazette, December 6, 1944.

162   *on Lambeth Field:* Press-Gazette, December 13, 1944.

163   *"The thing was":* Milwaukee Journal Sentinel, December 20, 2007.

163   *stayed behind in New York:* Press-Gazette, December 18, 1944.

10: THE EARL OF HOLLYWOOD

166   *Hollywood entertainers:* Cliff Christl, "Lambeau: More Than a Name," Voyageur: Northeast Wisconsin's Historical Review, Brown County Historical Society, December 2001.

166   *He drove big cars:* Ibid.

166   *Queen of Angels Hospital:* Los Angeles Times, January 16, 1938.

166   *Wisconsin law stipulates:* Wisconsin statute 767.301: Residence Requirements.

166   *from Los Angeles to Green Bay:* Press-Gazette, March 26, 1940.

166   *$100 a month in support:* Press-Gazette, March 18, 1940.

166   *on March 18:* Ibid.

166   *it was on her assertions:* Press-Gazette, March 26, 1940.

166   *The court ordered Curly to pay:* Ibid.

167   *in December 1945 she married:* Marriage Index, Orange County, CA, December 22, 1945.

167   *University of Michigan:* The Sea Chest, U.S. Navy Officer Candidate School, February 5, 1960.

167   *legally changed his name:* Hillsdale Daily News, June 24, 1959.

167   *name he had already been using:* The Hornet, Hillsdale High School, 1954 and 1955.

167   *married for a third time:* Press-Gazette, November 5, 1945.

167   *born in Cleveland in May 1894:* 1900 U.S. Census, Cuyahoga County, OH, June 12, 1900.

167   *when she got married for the second:* Los Angeles Times, August 14, 1935.

167   *estimated at $2.6 million:* Ibid.

167   *In May 1933:* Ibid.

167   *the legitimate child:* Los Angeles Times, August 18, 1937.

167   *died in July 1940:* Los Angeles Times, July 27, 1940.

167   *secret ceremony in Las Vegas:* Los Angeles Times, April 12, 1941.

167   *Grace sued La Cava:* Associated Press, November 18, 1943.

167   *Twenty months later:* Los Angeles Times, November 5, 1945.

168   *you did not leave her alone:* David Fleming, "Blaze of Glory," ESPN the Magazine, September 19, 2013.

168   *broken up a fight:* Christl, packers.com, March 16, 2017.

168   *"A lot of the players":* Christl, packers.com, June 21, 2018.

169   *"All I know of the new leagues":* Associated Press, April 20, 1945.

170   *roughly 100 NFL players:* Stan Grosshandler, "All-America Football Conference," The Coffin Corner 2, no. 7 (1980).

170   *tripled his salary:* Des Moines Tribune, February 11, 1946.

170   *"not worth that kind of money":* Chicago Tribune, January 5, 1946.

171   *a reported $10,000:* Press-Gazette, April 23, 1946.

171   *"stick with Curly":* Press-Gazette, May 16, 1946.

171   *"I just made a mistake":* Associated Press, August 11, 1946.

171   *a contract offer:* Interview with Grant S. Darnell II, May 8, 2018.

171 *Darnell countered:* Ibid.

171 *never played pro football: Tulsa World,* April 17, 2010.

172 *49ers actually held his AAFC rights: Press-Gazette,* January 30, 1946.

172 *three-year deal: Baltimore Sun,* February 12, 1947.

172 *B-26 pilot:* Ibid.

172 *took him prisoner: New York Herald Tribune* News Service, October 10, 1954.

172 *After 11 months: Baltimore Sun,* February 12, 1947.

172 *Case and a fellow POW: Los Angeles Times,* December 23, 1946.

172 *cutting a hole in a fence: Honolulu Advertiser,* December 17, 1946.

172 *Canadian infantry unit:* UCLA Athletics Hall of Fame, July 6, 2011.

172 *Lambeau had been on hand: Press-Gazette,* January 2, 1947.

172 *variation of the T formation: Press-Gazette,* January 11, 1947.

173 *"penalty for losing": Press-Gazette,* October 11, 1948.

173 *their paychecks on Tuesday: Press-Gazette,* October 13, 1948.

173 *"spiritless performance":* Ibid.

173 *Walt Kiesling and Bo Molenda: Milwaukee Journal,* November 30, 1948.

173 *staff shake-up: Milwaukee Journal,* January 24, 1949.

173 *refusing to try: Milwaukee Journal,* November 21, 1948.

173 *locker room tirades: Milwaukee Sentinel,* November 16, 1948.

173 *"We're in a definite slump": Press-Gazette,* November 4, 1948.

173 *borne him off the field:* Cliff Christl, "Lambeau: More than a Name," *Voyageur: Northeast Wisconsin's Historical Review,* Brown County Historical Society, December 2001.

173 *"backed him against the wall":* Ibid.

174 *"change his offensive signals": Press-Gazette,* December 14, 1949.

174 *St. Patrick's Day 1947: Press-Gazette,* March 17, 1947.

174 *three-year contract: Press-Gazette,* March 24, 1947.

174 *best man at Strickler's wedding:* Marriage License for George Strickler and Amy McKay, Menominee County, MI, May 31, 1940.

175 *bottom of an ancient ocean:* R. D. Stieglitz, ed., "Wisconsin's Niagara Escarpment," *Geoscience Wisconsin* 22 (2016).

175 *brick-and-fieldstone:* Blueprints for Rockwood Lodge, Berner-Schobers Associates Inc.

175 *the cross section: Press-Gazette,* November 2, 1937.

175 *The interior design:* Ibid.

175 *forest of birch and cedar: Press-Gazette,* May 13, 1937.

176 *opened it to the general public: Press-Gazette,* April 29, 1939.

176 *vacant for about two years: Press-Gazette,* July 31, 1944.

176 *for $32,000: Green Bay Packers Media Guide,* 2017.

176 *behind the purchase:* Christl, packers.com, November 16, 2017.

176 *roughly $435,000 today:* CPI Inflation Calculator, Bureau of Labor Statistics, bls.gov.

176 *not one dissenting vote: Press-Gazette,* May 25, 1946.

176 *an apartment in his mansion: Press-Gazette,* January 3, 1946.

176 *tent along the banks: Press-Gazette,* July 22, 1946.

176 *to reside rent-free:* David Fleming, "Blaze of Glory," *ESPN the Magazine,* September 19, 2013.

176 *do everything at the lodge: Press-Gazette,* May 25, 1946.

176 *disbursement of $8,000: Green Bay Packers Media Guide,* 2017.

176 *Melvin Flagstad:* Fleming, "Blaze of Glory."

176 *Marshall Field's:* Ibid.

176 *spent $17,500: Green Bay Packers Media Guide,* 2017.

176 *"busily house-cleaning": Press-Gazette,* August 16, 1946.

176 *scraped or eroded away:* Interview with Ken Bradbury, Wisconsin Geological & Natural History Survey, May 16, 2018.

176 *pavement in a parking lot:* Ibid.

176 *high school students: Press-Gazette,* September 6, 1981.

177 *"that damn rock":* Fleming, "Blaze of Glory."

177 *"When I was here": Press-Gazette,* November 26, 1946.

11: UP IN FLAMES

180 *New York in February: Press-Gazette,* February 10, 1927.

180 *Cleveland in April: Press-Gazette,* April 20, 1927.

180 *on a muddy field: Detroit Free Press,* November 29, 1926.

181 *one of her pallbearers: Press-Gazette,* August 9, 1944.

181 *Turnbull remarried: Los Angeles Times,* April 19, 1949.

181 *his letter of resignation: Press-Gazette,* August 9, 1949.

181 *special session: Press-Gazette,* September 30, 1949.

181 *"It was a complete surprise":* Ibid.

183 *verbal votes: Press-Gazette,* November 29, 1949.

183 *sent two or three plays:* Ibid.

183 *pregame and halftime pep talks: Press-Gazette,* November 28, 1949.

183 *27 men on the roster: Press-Gazette,* December 5, 1949.

183 *with 44 players: Press-Gazette,* August 1, 1949.

183 *only 28 were left: Press-Gazette,* December 14, 1949.

183 *NFL roster limit was 32: Press-Gazette,* August 6, 1949.

183 *$90,000 in red ink: Press-Gazette,* November 14, 1949.

183 *"Our biggest losses":* Ibid.

184 *500 volunteers: Press-Gazette,* November 22, 1949.

184 *8,800 tickets to the game: Press-Gazette,* November 24, 1949.

184 *1,000 merchandise items:* Ibid.

184 *"sky visitor's identity":* Ibid.

184 *A dozen members: Press-Gazette,* November 25, 1949.

184 *Packer Backers' All-Star Game: Press-Gazette,* November 24, 1949.

184 *"a million dollars worth":* Ibid.

184 *"buttery": Press-Gazette,* November 25, 1949.

184 *lineman Cub Buck:* Ibid.

184 *"more than $7,826 in pledges":* Ibid.

184 *did not put Green Bay in the black:* Ibid.

184 *"expanding cheese industry": Press-Gazette,* January 2, 1958.

185 *German-born shoe salesman:* 1900 U.S. Census, Sheboygan County, WI, June 7, 1900.

185 *moved to Green Bay in 1908: Press-Gazette,* October 28, 1929.

185 *"literally the first step": Press-Gazette,* January 2, 1958.

185 *Acme Packing plant: Press-Gazette,* March 26, 1926.

186 *"My father enjoyed the arts": Milwaukee Journal Sentinel,* July 23, 2013.

186 *"here to stay": Chicago Tribune,* December 12, 1946.

186 *On the agenda: Press-Gazette,* November 29, 1949.

186 *the temperature dropping: Press-Gazette,* December 1, 1949.

186 *Outside the room's closed doors:* Ibid.

186 *anti-Lambeau bloc: Milwaukee Journal,* November 21, 1949.

186 *$25,000 salary: Press-Gazette,* September 21, 1969.

187 *seconded the motion: Press-Gazette,* May 25, 1946.

187 *expire on New Year's Eve: Press-Gazette,* November 22, 1949.

187 *Twenty-one of the board's: Press-Gazette,* December 1, 1949.

187 *leaped out of his seat: Milwaukee Journal,* December 23, 1949.

187 *jumped to his feet:* Ibid.

187 *"I am satisfied": Press-Gazette,* December 2, 1949.

187 *"back on a sound footing":* Ibid.

187   *"my divergent ideas and views"*: Press-Gazette, December 15, 1949.

187   *reorganization of the franchise*: Press-Gazette, January 13, 1950.

187   *"more truly representative"*: Press-Gazette, December 1, 1949.

188   *"through committees and subcommittees"*: Press-Gazette, January 13, 1950.

188   *could be moved away*: Press-Gazette, February 7, 1950.

188   *"No group of 12 men"*: Milwaukee Journal, February 1, 1950.

188   *"the Packers will remain in Green Bay"*: Press-Gazette, December 10, 1949.

188   *left for the league meetings*: Press-Gazette, January 17, 1950.

188   *25 miles per hour out of the northeast*: Press-Gazette, January 25, 1950.

188   *34 degrees*: Press-Gazette, January 24, 1950.

188   *three inches of snow*: Press-Gazette, January 25, 1950.

188   *thunder and lightning*: Milwaukee Journal Sentinel, August 18, 2016.

188   *lodge's only occupants*: Press-Gazette, January 25, 1950.

188   *cottage adjacent to the lodge*: Milwaukee Journal Sentinel, August 18, 2016.

188   *cancellation of school*: Ibid.

188   *lived across Highway 57*: Ibid.

189   *in her housecoat*: Press-Gazette, January 25, 1950.

189   *without any shoes*: Ibid.

189   *three-inch gash*: Ibid.

189   *100-pound gas tank*: Ibid.

189   *green couch*: Ibid.

189   *his collection of violins*: Milwaukee Journal Sentinel, August 18, 2016.

189   *The only organized crew*: Press-Gazette, January 25, 1950.

189   *"back to the Astor Hotel"*: Ibid.

189   *"I was sure fanning it"*: Press-Gazette, February 13, 1950.

189   *faulty wiring had caused the fire*: Press-Gazette, January 25, 1950.

189   *"'These are all bare wires'"*: Cliff Christl, "Interview with Ellyn Katch Kehoe," Voyageur: Northeast Wisconsin's Historical Review, Brown County Historical Society, Summer/Fall 2008.

189   *cash on hand*: Press-Gazette, February 11, 1950.

190   *the Broadway Limited*: Press-Gazette, January 25, 1950.

190   *"not entirely unexpected"*: Press-Gazette, February 1, 1950.

190   *"galling authority"*: Milwaukee Journal, February 2, 1950.

190   *"We've had two breaks"*: United Press, February 1, 1950.

190   *"We're through"*: Milwaukee Journal, February 2, 1950.

12: THE NOT SO FABULOUS 1950S

196   *less than $50,000*: Press-Gazette, February 11, 1950.

196   *only 468 shares*: Press-Gazette, April 5, 1950.

196   *Fred Miller*: Press-Gazette, May 23, 1950.

196   *same amount was purchased*: Press-Gazette, April 11, 1950.

196   *"the $25 guy"*: Press-Gazette, May 23, 1950.

196   *civil engineer*: Press-Gazette, April 14, 1950.

196   *an Army wife*: Press-Gazette, April 13, 1950.

196   *purchased four shares*: Press-Gazette, April 14, 1950.

197   *Other single-share buyers*: Press-Gazette, April 18, 1950.

197   *"greatest, biggest little town"*: Press-Gazette, May 23, 1950.

198   *Chicago's chief strategist*: Los Angeles Examiner, February 13, 1950.

198   *"back at the old stand"*: Press-Gazette, February 8, 1950.

198   *before the turn of the century*: 1920 and 1930 U.S. Censuses, Dickinson County, MI.

198   *from Lusiana*: Manifest of the SS L'Aquitane, passenger Caterina Broglio, May 9, 1905.

198   *with Frosty Ferzacca*: Press-Gazette, February 6, 1950.

198   *won nine letters*: Marquette "M Club" Hall of Fame.

199   *An estimated 2,000*: Press-Gazette, July 24, 1950.

199   *set of luggage*: Press-Gazette, September 18, 1950.

199   *"team that was alert"*: Ibid.

199   *training camp as a holdout*: Press-Gazette, August 3, 1950.

199   *skipped a day of training camp*: Christl, packers.com, July 6, 2017.

199   *talk to journalists*: Christl, packers.com, March 23, 2017.

199   *jump into drills*: Ibid.

199   *footraces between them*: Ibid.

199   *not looking players in the eye*: Interview with Dan Orlich, June 15, 2018.

199   *afraid to fly over*: Christl, packers.com, December 14, 2017.

200   *"didn't appreciate those train rides"*: Interview with Dan Orlich, June 15, 2018.

200   *carried off the field*: Press-Gazette, November 2, 1953.

200   *resign or be fired*: Christl, packers.com, June 29, 2017.

200   *William and Clara Mann's*: 1930 U.S. Census, Craven County, NC, April 2, 1930.

200   *halfback and team captain*: Pittsburgh Courier, December 13, 1947.

200   *second in his class*: Sun Journal (New Bern, NC), May 27, 1941.

200   *playing end and earning*: Hampton University Football: 2017 Media Guide.

201   *parents paid his tuition*: Interview with Marjorie Mann, January 5, 2019.

201   *"ineffective as a blocker"*: United Press, October 31, 1950.

201   *$1,500 cut in salary*: Ibid.

201   *contract with Goebel*: Detroit Free Press, November 2, 1950.

202   *sold real estate*: Press-Gazette, December 2, 1950.

202   *practiced with the team*: Press-Gazette, November 25, 1950.

202   *"worst winter-game weather"*: Press-Gazette, November 27, 1950.

202   *only two blacks in Green Bay*: Christl, packers.com, July 12, 2014.

202   *"everybody knew the players"*: Ibid.

202   *greatest in the world*: Ibid.

202   *On road trips to Baltimore*: Ibid.

202   *Dick Afflis*: Ibid.

202   *lived at a motel*: Ibid.

203   *head south in his Chrysler*: Ibid.

203   *only at halftime*: Interview with Cliff Christl, August 12, 2018.

203   *"a chicken coop"*: Christl, Packers Heritage Trail.

203   *even George Halas*: Milwaukee Sentinel, September 22, 1957.

203   *Mayor Dominic Olejniczak*: Press-Gazette, October 5, 1951.

203   *planned to raise $200,000*: Press-Gazette, April 17, 1950.

204   *big-league sports to Milwaukee*: Press-Gazette, September 14, 1951.

204   *baseball's St. Louis Browns*: Akron Beacon Journal, December 31, 1950.

204   *sponsored Milwaukee's entry*: Press-Gazette, September 14, 1951.

204   *integral in helping convince*: Press-Gazette, April 9, 1953.

204   *the team's radio broadcasts*: Press-Gazette, May 23, 1950.

204   *honorary line coach*: Ibid.

204   *fly his company plane*: Associated Press, October 27, 1950.

204   *"Writers in various sections"*: Press-Gazette, December 18, 1954.

204   *pressing to have their games*: Press-Gazette, January 12, 1956.

206   *"I'm an east sider"*: Press-Gazette, February 2, 1956.

206   *"off a candy display counter"*: Press-Gazette, November 4, 1942.

206 "scooped ice cream": Ibid.
206 worst in the city's history: Ibid.
206 "business prudence": Press-Gazette, March 31, 1956.
207 argued that the league: Press-Gazette, February 2, 1950.
207 threatened to divvy up: Press-Gazette, January 24, 1950.
207 On the final day: Ibid.
207 "We certainly can't break up": Ibid.
207 Halas himself had made: Ibid.
207 Osborn Engineering Company: Press-Gazette, April 21, 1956.
207 recommended a spot: Press-Gazette, July 11, 1956.
207 Guernsey cows: Christl, packers.com, September 28, 2017.
208 Every dissenting vote: Press-Gazette, July 17, 1956.
208 the city purchased: Press-Gazette, August 21, 1956.
208 before the year was out: Press-Gazette, November 30, 1956.
208 dirt from the upper hillside: Press-Gazette, October 5, 1997.
208 support structures were going up: Ibid.
209 sold it to the Packers: Christl, packers.com, September 28, 2017.
209 Halas sponsored a float: Milwaukee Sentinel, September 22, 1957.
209 as did the Detroit Lions: Press-Gazette, September 30, 1957.
209 inside the old City Stadium: Ibid.
209 "No one was arrested": Ibid.
209 "facilities as they stand right now": Ibid.
209 a farmer from Beetown: 1900 U.S. Census, Grant County, WI, June 4, 1900.
209 Milwaukee's Washington High: Wisconsin Football Coaches Association Hall of Fame.
209 "never forgave him": Christl, packers.com, March 23, 2017.
210 praise and encourage the quarterback: Ibid.
210 "very rarely went against his opinion": Milwaukee Journal, May 2, 1979.
210 did not travel extensively: Christl, packers.com, October 27, 2016.
210 an extensive network: Ibid.
210 so well organized: Press-Gazette, January 19, 1952.
211 "I put him on the same basis": Milwaukee Journal, May 2, 1979.
211 Vainisi's titles: Christl, packers.com, October 27, 2016.

13: DAYLIGHT
214 worked on the fifth floor: Press-Gazette, June 9, 1959.
214 imported marble: Press-Gazette, September 29, 1930.
214 longtime alderman: Press-Gazette, March 2, 1954.
214 A scratch golfer: Interview with Daniel Gryboski, July 11, 2018.
214 father of eight: Press-Gazette, January 24, 1993.
214 citizens' committee: Press-Gazette, March 9, 1956.
214 since the mid-1940s: Interview with Daniel Gryboski, July 11, 2018.
215 a machinist: Press-Gazette, April 26, 1987.
215 lived next door: Interview with Daniel Gryboski, July 11, 2018.
215 golfed with him: Ibid.
215 no paycheck: Press-Gazette, May 20, 1997.
215 The team's preferred choice: Milwaukee Journal Sentinel, July 15, 2015.
215 He led the Hilltoppers: Milwaukee Journal, December 27, 1964.
216 "cut out some bad roots": Milwaukee Sentinel, November 4, 1958.
216 "A lot of us feel real bad": Press-Gazette, December 15, 1958.
217 Three days later: Press-Gazette, December 17, 1958.
217 an alderman: Press-Gazette, March 30, 1949.
217 mayor of the city: Press-Gazette, March 21, 1976.
217 youngest of nine: 1910 U.S. Census, Brown County, WI, April 23, 1910.
217 grown up on Crooks Street: 1910, 1920, and 1930 U.S. Census, Brown County, WI.
218 hire a general manager: Press-Gazette, December 16, 1958.
218 moved back to town: Press-Gazette, January 26, 1959.
218 "Lambeau Poll": Press-Gazette, January 5, 1959.
223 "like a thoroughbred": Leonard Schecter, "The Toughest Man in Pro Football," Esquire, January 1968.
225 "defeatist attitude": Press-Gazette, April 14, 1959.
225 purchased the contract: Press-Gazette, June 26, 1959.
225 de facto assistant coach: Christl, packers.com, August 17, 2017.
225 over a grocery store: Tim Layden, "Still Golden," Sports Illustrated, July 15, 2002.
225 stenographer and administrative assistant: 1940 U.S. Census, Jefferson County, KY, April 13, 1940.
225 a split T quarterback: Tim Layden, "Still Golden," Sports Illustrated, July 15, 2002.
227 "nothing spectacular": Ed Gruver, "The Lombardi Sweep," The Coffin Corner 19, no. 5 (1997).
227 "If the linebacker tried": Christl, packers.com, May 15, 2018.
229 ran 77 plays: Press-Gazette, December 27, 1960.

14: GREATER GLORY
232 20-plane squadron: Washington Post, October 5, 2008.
232 with his plane inverted: John S. McCain III, "John McCain, Prisoner of War: A First-Person Account," U.S. News & World Report, May 14, 1973.
234 around $100,000: Press-Gazette, July 29, 1961.
235 Such local arrangements: Press-Gazette, July 27, 1961.
235 about $332,000: Press-Gazette, April 27, 1961.
235 judge in Philadelphia: Press-Gazette, July 27, 1961.
235 "Only those fans": Associated Press, August 28, 1961.
235 the Sports Broadcasting Act: Press-Gazette, October 1, 1961.
235 porch lights flickering: Press-Gazette, December 19, 1961.
235 at 8:06 p.m.: Ibid.
235 former fullback Ted Fritsch: Ibid.
235 Chamber of Commerce: Press-Gazette, December 9, 1961.
235 nearly four hours before: Press-Gazette, December 18, 1961.
236 They had then flown: Press-Gazette, December 4, 1961.
236 only 500 people: Press-Gazette, December 19, 1961.
236 Temporary seats: Press-Gazette, December 12, 1961.
236 expanded before the season: Press-Gazette, April 19, 1961.
236 sold 54,000 season tickets: Press-Gazette, December 12, 1961.
236 bedding of straw: Press-Gazette, December 8, 1961.
236 "biggest event ever to hit": Press-Gazette, December 10, 1961.
236 Titletown, USA: Press-Gazette, December 6, 1961.
236 More than 3,500 fans: Press-Gazette, December 24, 1961.
236 50-foot Christmas tree: Ibid.
238 star in the front window: New York Times, January 3, 1962.
238 "The returning prodigals!": Press-Gazette, December 23, 1961.
239 first time in eight weeks: Press-Gazette, December 27, 1961.
239 "Beat the Giants": Ibid.
239 more than 500 fans turned out: Ibid.
239 national sports media: Press-Gazette, December 31, 1961.
239 Game-time temperature: Press-Gazette, January 1, 1962.
241 a red Corvette convertible: Ibid.
241 rising to chief of police: Press-Gazette, December 26, 1961.
241 to fully retire: Press-Gazette, December 6, 1963.
242 "profane cordiality": Press-Gazette, September 11, 1964.
242 shape of a goalpost: Press-Gazette, December 9, 1963.

242 *had met in 1960:* Jennifer Klessig-DuPont, "Door County's Golden Girl Mary Jane van Duyse Sorgel Dated Lambeau," *Peninsula Pulse,* September 9, 2010.

242 *just before 7:30 p.m.:* Press-Gazette, June 2, 1965.

242 *soft rain was falling:* Press-Gazette, June 6, 1965.

242 *included Bears coach George Halas:* Ibid.

242 *flown in the night before:* Press-Gazette, June 3, 1965.

242 *Lombardi had also been:* Ibid.

242 *by Phil Bengtson:* Press-Gazette, June 6, 1965.

242 *Lombardi did not share:* Christl, packers.com, June 1, 2017.

243 *newspaper colleague Jack Yuenger:* Press-Gazette, July 25, 1965.

243 *"What do you mean":* Press-Gazette, January 15, 2007.

243 *City Council voted unanimously:* Press-Gazette, August 4, 1965.

245 *"I think that in the past":* Press-Gazette, July 11, 1967.

246 *"called their own plays":* Interview with Dave Robinson, October 31, 2018.

246 *the result of an accident:* Milwaukee Sentinel, May 12, 1965.

248 *three-point favorites:* Press-Gazette, December 22, 1967.

248 *"might just be the greatest challenge":* Ibid.

248 *20-degree Saturday:* Milwaukee Journal, December 24, 1967.

249 *sacked Gabriel:* Press-Gazette, December 24, 1967.

249 *carried Williams off the field:* Ibid.

249 *junior college record:* Bruce Newman, "The Last Return," *Sports Illustrated,* March 11, 1991.

249 *93-yard runback:* Ibid.

249 *"the biggest touchdown":* Press-Gazette, December 24, 1967.

249 *his home library:* Interview with Chuck Mercein, January 24, 2018.

250 *had initially been cut:* Interview with Bob Ryan, October 9, 2018.

250 *only eight or nine:* Ibid.

251 *"very anticlimactic":* Interview with Chuck Mercein, January 24, 2018.

15: THE LOST GENERATION

258 *rolling down his cheeks:* Press-Gazette, February 2, 1968.

258 *"I am positive":* Ibid.

259 *"Four in a row":* Ibid.

259 *muscle in his throwing arm:* Press-Gazette, October 14, 1968.

259 *a piece of bone:* Montgomery Advertiser, August 14, 1946.

259 *on July 30:* Montgomery Advertiser, July 31, 1946.

260 *broken leg:* Alabama Journal, October 3, 1950.

260 *a 13–0 victory:* Montgomery Advertiser, September 30, 1950.

260 *five more wins and a tie:* Montgomery Advertiser, November 17, 1950.

260 *practice for hours on end:* Press-Gazette, September 7, 2014.

260 *a 9-1 record:* Montgomery Advertiser, November 17, 1951.

260 *On January 17, 1956:* Associated Press, January 18, 1956.

260 *"Bryan Bartlett":* Press-Gazette, January 19, 1956.

261 *"did not want his picture":* Edwin Shrake, "A Fresh Start with Bart," *Sports Illustrated,* August 25, 1975.

262 *never accepting of Devine:* Christl, packers.com, March 22, 2018.

262 *The story goes:* Interview with Chuck Lane, August 28, 2018.

262 *manager of a cigar store:* 1926 City Directory, Eau Claire, WI.

263 *Jerome lost everything:* Interview with Gregory Devine, September 5, 2018.

263 *Dan was the only one:* 1940 U.S. Census, Chippewa County, WI, April 27, 1940.

263 *vanished from the office:* Press-Gazette, November 19, 2011.

263 *openly dismissive:* Press-Gazette, February 3, 1972.

263 *a 12-man formation:* Christl, packers.com, July 12, 2018.

263 *game film:* Press-Gazette, January 8, 1975.

263 *his kind of football player:* Press-Gazette, November 12, 1971.

263 *took the comment as a slight:* Interview with John Brockington, August 28, 2018.

263 *"When I played in college":* Ibid.

263 *Bob Hyland plowed into him:* Press-Gazette, September 20, 1971.

263 *two preseason operations:* Press-Gazette, July 22, 1972.

263 *offensive play caller:* Interview with Scott Hunter, August 28, 2018.

263 *"a lowercase Bart Starr":* Ibid.

264 *"All we had to do was get close":* Interview with John Brockington, August 28, 2018.

264 *took over play-calling:* Interview with Scott Hunter, August 28, 2018.

264 *"It was embarrassing":* Interview with John Brockington, August 28, 2018.

264 *Starr stood by himself:* Ibid.

264 *"vulgar, malicious and ugly":* "Haunted in Green Bay," *Time,* October 7, 1974.

264 *"only four things to do":* Ibid.

266 *told nobody in the organization:* Interview with Chuck Lane, August 28, 2018.

266 *discussed boycotting:* Christl, packers.com, September 18, 2014.

266 *"never seemed to understand":* Press-Gazette, December 17, 1974.

267 *blocked seven kicks:* Press-Gazette, December 11, 1974.

267 *back of the end zone:* Press-Gazette, September 29, 1974.

267 *"I started to negotiate":* Interview with Ted Hendricks, September 10, 2018.

267 *Starr admitted:* Press-Gazette, January 8, 1984.

267 *"I would have stayed":* Interview with Ted Hendricks, September 10, 2018.

267 *stormed out of the draft room:* Press-Gazette, January 8, 1984.

267 *ultimate authority:* Press-Gazette, December 28, 1980.

267 *Lott believed:* Press-Gazette, October 27, 1986.

267 *high on Cal's Rich Campbell:* Press-Gazette, January 8, 1984.

267 *"dashboard injury":* Rick Telander, "He Takes Great Pains with His Passing," *Sports Illustrated,* September 26, 1983.

267 *asked Houston to trade him:* Interview with Lynn Dickey, August 22, 2018.

267 *brakeman on the Missouri Pacific:* Ibid.

268 *Carl Dickey's job:* Ibid.

268 *crippled by polio:* Kansas City Times, October 2, 1969.

268 *"I was all alone":* Interview with Lynn Dickey, August 22, 2018.

268 *industrial engineering major:* Rick Telander, "A Picture-Perfect End," *Sports Illustrated,* December 6, 1982.

268 *qualified for the 1978:* Ibid.

268 *second-longest legal jump:* International Amateur Athletic Federation.

268 *divorced when he was seven:* "Rick Telander, "A Picture-Perfect End," *Sports Illustrated,* December 6, 1982.

268 *brother and two older sisters:* Los Angeles Times, June 21, 1987.

268 *a lieutenant colonel:* Rick Telander, "A Picture-Perfect End," *Sports Illustrated,* December 6, 1982.

268 *"came to camp late":* Interview with Paul Coffman, September 10, 2018.

268 *giving the finger to fans:* Ibid.

268 *Man of the Year:* Los Angeles Times, June 21, 1987.

270 *sung the national anthem:* Ibid.

270 "*did not dink and dunk*": Interview with Lynn Dickey, August 22, 2018.

270 *looked up at the scoreboard:* Ibid.

270 *a rib injury: Press-Gazette,* December 19, 1983.

270 *Shortly before eight:* Ibid.

270 *lost 20 games:* Christl, packers.com, November 16, 2017.

270 "*among this jaundiced crowd*": *Press-Gazette,* December 19, 1983.

271 *24 assistant coaches: Press-Gazette,* January 8, 1984.

271 *three different personnel directors:* Ibid.

271 "*I got 500 letters*": Christl, packers.com, July 13, 2017.

271 "*now in a position*": *Press-Gazette,* December 19, 1983.

271 "*And that's just what happened*": Interview with Paul Coffman, September 10, 2018.

271 *farmer and tavern owner:* 1920, 1930, and 1940 U.S. Census, Brown County, WI.

271 *graduated from Green Bay East: Press-Gazette,* November 11, 1966.

271 *less than two years later: Press-Gazette,* July 2, 1946.

272 *as a special prosecutor: Press-Gazette,* November 11, 1966.

272 *elected to the Packers' board:* Christl, packers.com, July 13, 2017.

272 *His salary as a judge: Press-Gazette,* May 16, 1982.

272 "*essential to the operation*": *Press-Gazette,* May 4, 1982.

272 *lack of football credentials:* Ibid.

273 *in open revolt:* Associated Press, December 14, 1977.

273 "*pathetic mess*": *Press-Gazette,* December 25, 1983.

273 *hiding in a closet:* Paul Zimmerman, "What's New? These Two," *Sports Illustrated,* January 25, 1983.

273 *left him mistrustful:* Christl, packers.com, March 22, 2018.

273 *Thursday Night Club:* Interview with Lynn Dickey, August 22, 2018.

273 "*What was he going to do?*": Ibid.

273 "*to one of the worst*": Ibid.

273 "*win the Super Bowl*": Ibid.

275 *called Green Bay's players: Press-Gazette,* November 26, 1986.

275 *paid her $500: Press-Gazette,* December 19, 1986.

275 *two years in prison: Press-Gazette,* July 28, 1987.

275 *served 15 months:* Associated Press, November 12, 1988.

275 *receivers coach Tom Coughlin:* Frank Deford, "Troubled Times in Titletown," *Sports Illustrated,* May 25, 1987.

275 *glass elevator: Press-Gazette,* April 29, 1985.

275 *arrested and jailed: Press-Gazette,* December 18, 1986.

275 "*embarrassed*": Ibid.

275 "*the Packers could walk to work*": *Leader-Telegram* (Eau Claire, WI), February 9, 1987.

276 *The district attorney said: Press-Gazette,* May 23, 1987.

276 "*didn't have enough evidence*": *Los Angeles Times,* June 21, 1987.

276 *Gregg never suspended him:* Frank Deford, "Troubled Times in Titletown," *Sports Illustrated,* May 25, 1987.

276 *one in 300 people:* Ibid.

276 "*If you're a black man*": Ibid.

277 "*a guy would tell you*": Interview with Dave Robinson, October 31, 2018.

277 *a model franchise:* Jack Olsen, "In the Back of the Bus," *Sports Illustrated,* July 21, 1968.

277 "*We make no issue*": Ibid.

277 "*Vince integrated the city*": Interview with Dave Robinson, October 31, 2018.

277 "*don't have that much to offer*": *Press-Gazette,* January 11, 1981.

277 *mentioned that he might want out: Los Angeles Times,* June 21, 1987.

16: RESURRECTION

280 "*for $60 million or whatever*": Frank Deford, "Troubled Times in Titletown," *Sports Illustrated,* May 25, 1987.

280 "*ridiculous*": *Press-Gazette,* May 22, 1987.

280 "*stairway just going down*": Interview with Bob Harlan, September 23, 2017.

280 *first time since 1951: Press-Gazette,* February 10, 1983.

281 *the botched drafting:* Christl, packers.com, May 24, 2018.

281 *all signing and roster bonuses: Press-Gazette,* June 3, 1986.

281 "*We have found a way*": Ibid.

281 "*The way we were doing business*": Interview with Bob Harlan, September 23, 2017.

281 *one of the last teams: Press-Gazette,* September 19, 1985.

281 *a cost of $5 million: Press-Gazette,* February 15, 1985.

281 *$741,000 of it: Press-Gazette,* June 3, 1986.

281 *$22.8 million in assets: Press-Gazette,* March 8, 1983.

281 *$32.5 million: Press-Gazette,* June 5, 1990.

282 *his personal policy: Press-Gazette,* June 6, 1989.

282 "*consummate football executive*": Ibid.

282 "*always tell people*": Interview with Bob Harlan, September 23, 2017.

283 "*Al did stuff like that*": Ibid.

283 *73 yards in 13 plays: Press-Gazette,* November 6, 1989.

283 *fourth-and-goal:* Ibid.

283 *two-year contract extension: Press-Gazette,* January 17, 1990.

284 *bench-pressed 545 pounds:* Austin Murphy, "The Flip of the Flop," *Sports Illustrated,* July 12, 2004.

284 *his 22-inch biceps:* Rick Telander, "Tony Mandarich Is Very, Very Sorry," *Sports Illustrated,* March 9, 2009.

284 *scout Charley Armey:* Paul Zimmerman, "Don't Cross This Line," *Sports Illustrated,* September 5, 1994.

284 *one and a half sacks: Press-Gazette,* December 17, 1990.

284 "*can't believe how Reggie*": *Wisconsin State Journal,* December 17, 1990.

285 "*simply had to be done*": Interview with Bob Harlan, September 23, 2017.

285 *two-and-a-half-hour meeting: Press-Gazette,* November 21, 1991.

285 *a search committee:* Ibid.

286 *later the same day:* Interview with Ron Wolf, September 24, 2017.

286 "*no clear line of authority*": Ibid.

286 "*take an entrance exam*": *Tampa Tribune,* May 1, 1975.

287 *all 12 NFL teams: Milwaukee Journal Sentinel,* August 7, 2015.

287 "*closed-door society*": Ibid.

287 *moved to Chicago:* Ibid.

287 *returned to Oklahoma:* Ibid.

287 *a history major:* Interview with Ron Wolf, March 2, 2019.

287 *without graduating:* Interview with registrar, University of Oklahoma, September 24, 2018.

287 *roster limit was 33:* Associated Press, August 29, 1963.

287 "*And that's how I learned*": Interview with Ron Wolf, September 24, 2017.

287 "*size and speed*": Doug Farrar, "Ron Wolf Talks Al Davis, Brett Favre and His Hall of Fame Football Life," SI.com, November 13, 2015.

287 *a Cold War spy: San Francisco Examiner,* May 11, 1975.

287 *youngest chief executive: Tampa Tribune,* April 1, 1975.

288 *Wolf resigned: Tampa Tribune,* February 23, 1978.

288 *Culverhouse replaced Wolf:* Ibid.

288 *"I had been through that":* Interview with Ron Wolf, September 24, 2017.

288 *"an impasse": Milwaukee Journal Sentinel,* August 7, 2015.

288 *only four months: Press-Gazette,* August 28, 1994.

288 *Notre Dame and Wisconsin gear:* Interview with Ron Wolf, September 24, 2017.

288 *"Gee whiz":* Ibid.

289 *29,000 no-shows: Press-Gazette,* November 25, 1991, and December 16, 1991.

289 *"We are going to make a change":* Interview with Bob Harlan, September 23, 2017.

290 *"I was really impressed":* Doug Farrar, "Ron Wolf Talks Al Davis, Brett Favre and His Hall of Fame Football Life," SI.com, November 13, 2015.

290 *first official day: Press-Gazette,* December 3, 1991.

290 Who the heck is that?: Interview with Bob Harlan, September 23, 2017.

290 *not let Favre participate:* Interview with Ron Wolf, September 24, 2017.

290 *his chief scout: San Francisco Examiner,* January 27, 1974.

290 *"What it told me was":* Interview with Ron Wolf, September 24, 2017.

290 *and cracked vertebrae:* Leigh Montville, "Leader of the Pack," *Sports Illustrated,* August 23, 1993.

291 *named for Irvin:* Ibid.

291 *seven passes a game: Times* (Shreveport, LA), November 11, 1988.

291 *"Three days before":* Leigh Montville, "Leader of the Pack," *Sports Illustrated,* August 23, 1993.

292 *third on the depth chart:* Ibid.

292 *three years and $1.2 million:* Ibid.

292 *traded down with the Eagles: Press-Gazette,* February 12, 1992.

293 *take a quarterback anyway:* Ibid.

293 *"you think is a great one":* Ibid.

293 *"Some of the worst mail":* Interview with Bob Harlan, September 23, 2017.

293 *"I didn't agree with the switch": Press-Gazette,* September 14, 1992.

293 *a pick 'em: Press-Gazette,* September 20, 1992.

293 *Motor Parts West: Press-Gazette,* September 21, 1992.

294 *mishandled two snaps: Press-Gazette,* September 21, 1992.

294 *some of the oddest formations:* Ibid.

295 *Campen was crying:* Ibid.

295 *"and everything changed":* Interview with Ron Wolf, September 24, 2017.

17: REGGIE AND A RETURN TO GLORY

298 *spent $8.3 million: Green Bay Packers Media Guide,* 2018.

298 *selling out before: Press-Gazette,* February 27, 1990.

298 *In the first season: Press-Gazette,* May 30, 1991.

298 *$42.3 million in revenues:* Ibid.

298 *$128 million to Green Bay:* Associated Press, September 29, 2018.

299 *Two weeks after Plan B:* Associated Press, September 22, 1992.

299 *accept free agency: Philadelphia Inquirer,* January 7, 1993.

300 *only 453 of those residents:* 1990 U.S. Census, Brown County, WI.

300 *Blache and his younger brother:* Interview with Greg Blache, October 14, 2018.

301 *"everybody had Afros":* Ibid.

301 *the hair of inmates:* Ibid.

301 *"If you were a black man":* Ibid.

301 *two-and-a-half-year-old: Philadelphia Inquirer,* September 11, 1988.

301 *baseball and softball:* Interview with Thelma Collier, October 12, 2018.

301 *hosiery mill:* Ibid.

301 *an Army cook:* Ibid.

301 *"best project around": Philadelphia Inquirer,* September 11, 1988.

301 *piles of dirt:* Ibid.

302 *new home in St. Elmo:* Interview with Thelma Collier, October 12, 2018.

302 *Piney Woods Baptist Church:* Ibid.

302 *two Presbyterian ministers: Philadelphia Inquirer,* September 11, 1988.

302 *"Whatsoever thy hand":* Associated Press, December 15, 1983.

302 *five-year, $4 million contract: The Tennessean,* January 19, 1984.

302 *four-year, $1.6 million: Philadelphia Inquirer,* October 31, 1985.

304 *"The good Lord doesn't": Philadelphia Inquirer,* September 11, 1988.

304 *from left end to nose tackle:* Ibid.

304 *"a whole bunch of people":* Paul Zimmerman, "White Heat," *Sports Illustrated,* November 27, 1989.

304 *sent his private jet:* Peter King, "Trip to Bountiful," *Sports Illustrated,* March 15, 1993.

304 *By the end of the first week:* Ibid.

304 *build White a church:* Ibid.

304 *state capitol building: Greenville News,* March 14, 1993.

304 *took him to the Palace: Detroit Free Press,* March 10, 1993.

304 *Clark's by the Bay: Press Democrat* (Santa Rosa, CA), March 31, 1993.

304 *Twenty-four hours later: New York Times,* March 18, 1993.

305 *four inches of snow: Press-Gazette,* March 10, 1993.

305 *"Reggie, this is God": Press-Gazette,* April 1, 1993.

305 *White hit him in the chest: Press-Gazette,* November 16, 1992.

305 *49ers were hamstrung: Daily News* (New York), April 7, 1993.

305 *NFL rules dictated: Press-Gazette,* March 30, 1993.

307 *only $4.4 million in salary: Press-Gazette,* April 7, 1993.

307 *"came down to money":* Interview with Ron Wolf, September 24, 2018.

307 *hit quarterback Jim Harbaugh: Press-Gazette,* November 1, 1993.

307 *"he's near it":* Michael Silver, "Stepping Out," *Sports Illustrated,* May 18, 1997.

308 *"It's crazy that LeRoy Butler":* Ibid.

308 *10-point favorites: Press-Gazette,* January 6, 1996.

308 *15 of his first 17 passes: Press-Gazette,* January 7, 1996.

309 *"It was destiny":* Ibid.

309 *"landscape-changing":* Interview with Ron Wolf, September 24, 2018.

309 *"don't know what they don't know":* Robert Klemko, "How Reggie White Made Green Bay Cool," SI.com, December 6, 2016.

310 *back of Jurkovic's knee:* Peter King, "The Unkindest Cut," *Sports Illustrated,* March 25, 1996.

310 *tearing his MCL: Press-Gazette,* January 15, 1996.

311 *"It was ridiculous":* Ibid.

311 *"will win a championship":* Ibid.

311 *The offense, playing without: Press-Gazette,* November 19, 1996.

311 *also turned down: Tampa Bay Times,* January 8, 1992.

311 *tried to take back his refusal:* Ibid.

311   *Culverhouse rescinded: Tampa Bay Times*, January 19, 1992.

311   *essentially the same terms: Boston Globe*, January 22, 1993.

312   *final year of his contract:* Paul Zimmerman, "AFC East," *Sports Illustrated*, September 2, 1996.

312   *a rift with Patriots owner:* Michael Silver, "Return to Glory," *Sports Illustrated*, February 3, 1997.

312   *midweek press conference:* Ibid.

312   *valuable as a kick returner: Press-Gazette*, July 12, 1996.

312   *"it's almost ridiculous": Press-Gazette*, January 5, 1997.

313   *boasted that they were planning:* Michael Silver, "Return to Glory," *Sports Illustrated*, February 3, 1997.

313   *74 Razor:* Ibid.

313   *maximum-protection blocking scheme:* Ibid.

313   *"touched his leg": Boston Globe*, January 27, 1997.

313   *activated the morning of the game:* Ibid.

314   *"ruined a perfectly good game":* Ibid.

18: INTO THE FUTURE

320   *250 of them: Press-Gazette*, January 28, 1997.

320   *more than three hours:* Ibid.

320   *10-mile route: Press-Gazette*, January 27, 1997.

320   *borders Lambeau Field:* Ward map, Village of Ashwaubenon, WI.

320   *voted to rename: Press-Gazette*, June 25, 1997.

320   *become Lombardi Avenue: Press-Gazette*, August 7, 1968.

321   *chance to go undefeated: Press-Gazette*, August 21, 1997.

321   *11½-point favorites: Press-Gazette*, January 25, 1997.

321   *turned down at least one offer: Press-Gazette*, January 22, 1998.

321   *"I'd rather not deal with": Press-Gazette*, January 24, 1998.

322   *"Certain calls": Milwaukee Journal Sentinel*, December 5, 2009.

323   *lost track of what down:* Ibid.

323   *not run since training camp:* Ibid.

323   *"I think I'll be back":* Ibid.

323   *Nine starters: Press-Gazette*, September 10, 1997.

323   *lost five of them: Press-Gazette*, April 5, 1998.

323   *"crossed the line with me": Press-Gazette*, December 1, 1998.

323   *captured on video:* Ibid.

323   *not only did Seattle: Press-Gazette*, January 9, 1998.

323   *by far the highest-paid coach: Milwaukee Journal Sentinel*, January 9, 1998.

324   *citing concerns over: Philadelphia Inquirer*, December 8, 2002.

324   *agreed to step down:* Associated Press, January 1, 2003.

324   *"things they know I like to do": St. Louis Post Dispatch*, January 5, 2003.

324   *he had been blindsided: Milwaukee Journal Sentinel*, November 12, 2005.

324   *"expected us to be together forever":* Ibid.

324   *announced that it planned: Press-Gazette*, October 10, 1997.

326   *In the first 11 days: Green Bay Packers Media Guide*, 2018.

326   *Residents of Wisconsin:* Ibid.

326   *on Elm Street:* 1930 and 1940 U.S. Census, Brown County, WI.

326   *holes they had dug:* Interview with Tom Konop, October 30, 2018.

326   *Konop was the oldest:* 1940 U.S. Census, Brown County, WI, April 13, 1940.

326   *six children: Press-Gazette*, December 3, 1956.

326   *Nash Motors:* Ibid.

326   *then into the Navy: Press-Gazette*, February 2, 1943.

326   *peanut-vending machines: Press-Gazette*, February 15, 1988.

327   *disposable swimsuits: Press-Gazette*, May 13, 1979.

327   *"My father didn't miss a game":* Interview with Tom Konop, October 31, 2018.

327   *one of the final purchases: Press-Gazette*, March 11, 1998.

327   *wall of his bedroom:* Interview with Tom Konop, October 31, 2018.

327   *in October 1994: Press-Gazette*, October 13, 1994.

327   *concessions, parking: Press-Gazette*, April 2, 1995.

327   *$2.2 million in revenue: Press-Gazette*, May 30, 1996.

327   *ninth out of 30 teams: Press-Gazette*, May 28, 2000.

327   *a steady climb: Press-Gazette*, June 7, 1998.

327   *insisted that he was thrilled: Press-Gazette*, March 17, 1998.

327   *17th in the NFL: Los Angeles Times*, May 13, 2001.

327   *Washington led the league:* Ibid.

327   *heat and water turned off: Press-Gazette*, January 24, 2000.

327   *about $20 million: Press-Gazette*, March 7, 1999.

328   *"Every time a team moved":* Interview with Bob Harlan, September 23, 2017.

328   *From 1995 to 2003:* Albert Breer, "NFL Stadiums Go from Boom to Swoon in Span of a Decade," NFL.com, July 6, 2012.

328   *scrapped his original plan: Press-Gazette*, March 3, 1999.

328   *$295 million renovation: Press-Gazette*, January 23, 2000.

328   *without spoiling: Press-Gazette*, July 8, 1998.

328   *Harlan cited it: Press-Gazette*, February 4, 2000.

328   *modern touches: Press-Gazette*, January 23, 2000.

328   *"I want a red-brick building":* Interview with Bob Harlan, September 23, 2017.

328   *0.1 percent sales tax: Press-Gazette*, February 6, 2000.

328   *rather than being left open:* Jim Palmer, "Miller Park's Forgotten Man," *Milwaukee Magazine*, June 7, 2011.

328   *already rejected a plan: New York Times*, October 7, 1995.

328   *a 52–47 vote: Milwaukee Journal*, September 29, 1995.

328   *vote of 16–15: Press-Gazette*, October 6, 1995.

328   *he turned against it: Milwaukee Journal*, October 8, 1995.

328   *bill was going to fail: Press-Gazette*, October 6, 1995.

328   *removed Petak from office: Milwaukee Journal*, June 5, 1996.

328   *"They were still upset":* Interview with Bob Harlan, September 23, 2017.

329   *Chief among them: Press-Gazette*, February 6, 2000.

329   *a population base: Press-Gazette*, September 13, 2000.

329   *"Why do the Packers": Press-Gazette*, September 4, 2000.

329   *13 cents a day: Press-Gazette*, August 6, 2000.

329   *42 percent of households: Press-Gazette*, September 10, 2000.

329   *by early May it had dropped: Press-Gazette*, May 8, 2000.

329   *support for the tax increased: Press-Gazette*, August 24, 2000.

329   *On the Saturday before:* Interview with Bob Harlan, September 23, 2017.

329   *"I could talk to 20 people":* Ibid.

329   *53 percent to 47 percent: Press-Gazette*, September 13, 2000.

329   *"If the referendum had failed":* Interview with Bob Harlan, September 23, 2017.

329   *on time and on budget: Green Bay Packers Media Guide*, 2018.

329   *jumped up to 10th: Press-Gazette*, June 15, 2003.

329   *One year later: Press-Gazette*, June 20, 2004.

329   *ranks in the top half: Green Bay Packers Media Guide*, 2018.

329   *The sales tax ended:* Ibid.

329   *longest continually occupied:* Ibid.

329   *booked through 2021:* Ibid.

329   *more than 700 events:* Speech by Mark Murphy, St. Norbert College CEO Breakfast and Strategy Series, May 24, 2018.

331 *in effect since 1996: Milwaukee Journal Sentinel,* March 15, 2018.

331 *The earliest it could:* Ibid.

331 *did it all themselves: Green Bay Packers Media Guide,* 2018.

331 *10-year, $100 million: Press-Gazette,* December 30, 2001.

331 *"couldn't envision myself":* Ibid.

332 *"I made a mistake":* Interview with Bob Harlan, September 23, 2017.

332 *"Mike became a different person":* Ibid.

332 *Scouts in the office:* Ibid.

332 *did not talk to reporters: Press-Gazette,* January 12, 2004.

333 *In January of that year: Press-Gazette,* January 16, 2005.

334 *Much of the blame: Press-Gazette,* December 25, 2005.

334 *cut before he was due: Press-Gazette,* February 20, 2005.

334 *purge of expensive veterans: Press-Gazette,* September 25, 2005.

334 *came in April 2006: Press-Gazette,* April 27, 2006.

334 *$39 million deal: Press-Gazette,* July 29, 2006.

334 *Thompson fired Sherman: Press-Gazette,* January 3, 2006.

334 *Thompson's decision:* Interview with Bob Harlan, September 23, 2017.

334 *"they hardly spoke":* Ibid.

335 *hired 49ers offensive coordinator: Press-Gazette,* January 13, 2006.

335 *"I just didn't throw it": Press-Gazette,* January 21, 2008.

335 *"That would have been a steal": Clarion-Ledger* (Jackson, MS), May 14, 2007.

335 *without any input: Press-Gazette,* January 13, 2006.

335 *"There were some games":* Interview with Greg Jennings, December 13, 2017.

336 *"I know I can play": Press-Gazette,* July 12, 2008.

336 *did not want to cut or trade: Press-Gazette,* July 12, 2008.

336 *retire Favre's number 4:* Ibid.

336 *due to make $12 million:* Ibid.

336 *quarterback's unconditional release:* Ibid.

336 *held a rally: Press-Gazette,* July 14, 2008.

336 *to not play football: Press-Gazette,* August 2, 2008.

337 *Favre returned to Green Bay:* Ibid.

337 *"That training camp":* Interview with Mark Tauscher, November 13, 2018.

337 *on the night of August 6: Press-Gazette,* August 7, 2008.

19: THE PEOPLE'S TEAM

340 *"If you vote yes": Press-Gazette,* July 22, 2014.

342 *"people scratch out the P": Press-Gazette,* October 29, 2011.

342 *On July 7, 1944:* War Department memorandum, July 1944.

342 *his 44th mission: Decatur Herald,* September 10, 1944.

342 *son of a refrigerator salesman:* 1940 U.S. Census, Dallas County, TX, April 11, 1940.

342 *had been a copywriter:* Edward W. Rodgers, World War II draft registration card, October 16, 1940.

342 *in the advertising department: American-Statesman* (Austin, TX), September 15, 1940.

342 *During an attack on Vienna: Decatur Herald,* September 10, 1944.

342 *over western Hungary:* War Department memorandum, July 1944.

342 *Rodgers and the 10 men:* Ibid.

342 *First Lieutenant John A. Simmons: Atlanta Constitution,* September 7, 1945.

342 *before he reached the ground:* Missing Air Crew Report, U.S. Army Air Force memorandum, July 9, 1944.

342 *his arms and his jaw:* Interview with Ed Rodgers, December 13, 2018.

342 *Stalag Luft III:* World War II Prisoners of War Data File, National Archives.

343 *POW camp near Nuremberg:* Ibid.

343 *liberated by Russian troops:* Interview with Ed Rodgers, December 13, 2018.

343 *retired in 1963: Santa Maria Times,* October 6, 1982.

343 *last two years on active duty:* Ibid.

343 *three girls and a boy: Santa Maria Times,* October 6, 1982.

343 *offensive line at Lompoc High: Lompoc Record,* November 18, 2004.

343 *California State University, Chico: Reno Gazette,* October 29, 1976.

343 *All–Far Western Conference: Times-Standard,* November 23, 1976.

343 *semipro ball for four years: Lompoc Record,* November 18, 2004.

343 *getting married in 1980: Ukiah Daily Journal,* October 12, 1979.

343 *grew up in Chico: New York Times,* January 30, 2011.

343 *competed against each other: Press-Gazette,* July 24, 2005.

343 *"wanted the ball in my hands":* Ibid.

343 *leading the Vikings:* Tim Layden, "All for One, One for All," *Sports Illustrated,* November 7, 2011.

343 *studying football film:* Ibid.

343 *exceptionally big feet:* Ibid.

343 *A-minus average: New York Times,* January 30, 2011.

343 *scored 1310 on the SAT:* Tim Layden, "Green and Golden," *Sports Illustrated,* February 14, 2011.

343 *no Division I scholarship offers: Washington Post,* December 15, 2015.

343 *a two-year school:* "Tim Layden, "All for One, One for All," *Sports Illustrated,* November 7, 2011.

343 *One day in 2002:* Tim Layden, "Green and Golden," *Sports Illustrated,* February 14, 2011.

344 *"fulfilling a childhood dream":* Associated Press, January 4, 2005.

344 *booed Rodgers: Press-Gazette,* August 4, 2008.

344 *eight of Green Bay's losses: Wisconsin State Journal,* December 21, 2008.

344 *"Not to some people": Press-Gazette,* December 29, 2008.

344 *"just didn't know how to finish":* Interview with Greg Jennings, December 13, 2017.

344 *showered and dressed: Wisconsin State Journal,* December 21, 2008.

344 *Donald Driver used to jump in:* "Tim Layden, "All for One, One for All," *Sports Illustrated,* November 7, 2011.

344 *missed a combined 86 games: Packers Blog, Milwaukee Journal Sentinel,* November 5, 2012.

346 *strong left, trips 27 Tampa:* Tim Layden, "Green and Golden," *Sports Illustrated,* February 14, 2011.

347 *"That one throw":* Ibid.

347 *"We Are the Champions":* Ibid.

347 *"I told Ted back in 2005": Los Angeles Times,* February 7, 2011.

347 *$40 per car: Press-Gazette,* September 7, 2018.

349 *"sought out coaching manuals":* Interview with Aaron Nagler, November 29, 2018.

349 *"best fan blog out there": New York Times,* September 29, 2010.

350 *"my father and two friends":* Ibid.

350 *upwards of 50 people:* Interview with Lori Nickel, October 31, 2018.

350   *most recent stock sale: Green Bay Packers Media Guide,* 2018.

351   *editorial cartoons: Press-Gazette,* November 29, 1981.

351   *Starr threatened to ban Christl: Press-Gazette,* October 31, 1978.

351   *several female reporters: Press-Gazette,* October 7, 1978.

351   *banning all reporters: Press-Gazette,* July 17, 1979.

351   *kept the locker room open: Press-Gazette,* October 4, 1990.

351   *Gregg banned Olson:* Ibid.

351   *an equal-access policy:* Ibid.

351   *no female reporters in the state:* Ibid.

351   *22-year-old reporting intern:* Interview with Lori Nickel, October 31, 2018.

352   *"been pretty good":* Ibid.

352   *reported record revenue: Press-Gazette,* July 17, 2018.

352   *top 10 in the league:* Ibid.

352   *"no small-town feel":* Interview with Lori Nickel, October 31, 2018.

352   *began buying land:* Speech by Mark Murphy, St. Norbert College CEO Breakfast and Strategy Series, May 24, 2018.

352   *knocked down a Kmart: Press-Gazette,* August 21, 2015.

352   *razed a number of houses:* Ibid.

353   *on about 21 acres: Press-Gazette,* August 21, 2015.

353   *was not big enough:* Speech by Mark Murphy, St. Norbert College CEO Breakfast and Strategy Series, May 24, 2018.

353   *by far the smallest market:* Ibid.

353   *for any of its 36 outlets: Press-Gazette,* May 5, 2012.

353   *fourth-best-performing:* Speech by Mark Murphy, St. Norbert College CEO Breakfast and Strategy Series, May 24, 2018.

353   *"the confidence":* Ibid.

353   *former meatpacking plant: Press-Gazette,* August 17, 1960.

353   *more than 27,000 hotels:* AAA Diamond Rating Fact Sheet, January 2018.

353   *has no meeting space:* Speech by Mark Murphy, St. Norbert College CEO Breakfast and Strategy Series, May 24, 2018.

353   *people 65 and over: Press-Gazette,* January 2, 2011.

354   *"That means standing":* Interview with Corey Behnke, January 13, 2019.

354   *25 and over:* U.S. Census Bureau, "American Community Survey and Puerto Rico Community Survey, 5-Year Estimates," July 1, 2017.

354   *best for startup activity:* The Kauffman Index 2018, Ewing Marion Kauffman Foundation.

354   *one of the worst states: Press-Gazette,* July 26, 2017.

354   *46,000-square-foot building: Press-Gazette,* July 21, 2018.

354   *with $5 million each: Press-Gazette,* October 20, 2017.

354   *venture studio:* Ibid.

354   *"Of all the things we've done":* Interview with Mark Murphy, September 7, 2018.

354   *When the plans for Titletown: Press-Gazette,* August 21, 2015.

355   *20 "finalists": Press-Gazette,* July 4, 2008.

355   *winner of the contest was decided:* Ibid.

355   *Green Bay finished third: Press-Gazette,* July 29, 2008.

INDEX

Page numbers in *italics* indicate illustrations.

A

AAFC. *See* All-America Football
Conference
ABC broadcast contracts, 235, 298
Abrams, Frances, 59
Abrams, Isadore, 59
Abrams, Nathan, *12–13, 22–23,* 59, 61
Acme Packing Company, 45–46, 185
Adams, Arnon, 112
Adderley, Herb, *239,* 245, 246, 249
A. E. Staley Manufacturing Company,
36, 45
Afflis, Dick ("Dick the Bruiser"), 202
African American players
AAFC and, 170
breaking color barrier, 170–71
discrimination against, 202–3, 276–77
early 1900s, *34,* 35
NFL history, 73
Packers, 72–74, *74,* 171, 200, 202–4,
225, 276–77, 300–301, 309
Agamiate, Don, 188–89
Agamiate, Sandy, 188–89
Akers, David, 332
Akron Indians, 35
Akron Professionals (APFA team), 37, 38
Algonquin Indians, 2, 3
All-America Football Conference (AAFC),
57, 168–71, 169n, 183–84, 188
Ameche, Don, 170
American Caesar (Manchester), 153
American Football League, 72, 168, 235
American Fur Company, 5
American Professional Football
Association (APFA), 37–39, 45–46,
53–56
American Professional Football
Conference (APFC), 32–33, 35–36
Anderson, Donny, 255, 264
Anderson, Edwin J., 201

Anderson, Heartley "Hunk," 52–53, 52n,
55
Andrews, Leroy, 100
APFA. *See* American Professional Football
Association
APFC. *See* American Professional Football
Conference
Armey, Charley, 284
Army (U.S.), history in Green Bay, *3,* 3–4,
5
Army (West Point team), 17, 50, 153,
222–24
Arness, James, 209
Artoe, Lee, 170
Astor, John Jacob, 5
Astor Hotel, 150, 151
Atkins, Steve, 267
Atkinson, Jerry, 184, 221
Atlanta Falcons
1967 season, 246
1991 season, 289, 290, 292
2002 season, 332
2006 season, 140n
courting Reggie White, 304
Favre drafted by, 292, 316–17
attendance. *See* fan attendance
Atwater, Steve, 322

B

Baldwin, Burr, 172
Baltimore Colts
1947 season, 172
1953 season, 200
1958 season, 216, *219,* 224, 235, 249
1959 season, 261
1967 season, 252
merger into NFL, 207
Barnes, Billy Ray, 229
Barra, Allen, 134
Barrymore, John, 117

baseball
1920s, 32, 51
All-Star Game, 57, 172
The Baseball Encyclopedia, 82
Baseball Hall of Fame, 106
reference books, 82, 84, 85
World Series, 32n, 51, 53
Baseball Cyclopedia (Lanigan), 84
The Baseball Encyclopedia (Neft), 82, 85
Baseball Hall of Fame, 106
bathroom tissue industry, 7, 118
Baugh, Sammy, 76, 162
Baumgartner, Stan, 143n
Bays (football team), 23–24
Beam, Dick, 288
Beban, Gary, 287n
Bedard, Greg, 349
Beebe, Don, 313
Behnke, Corey, 347–50, *351,* 353–54
Belgian immigrants, 14–15
Belichick, Bill, 332n
Bell, de Benneville "Bert," 169, 186, 188,
204, 207, 209, 219–20
Bellevue Park, *48–49, 66–67, 70,* 79–80,
138n
Beloit Fairies, 27–28, 29n, 40, 42
Belonger, Larry, viii
Bengtson, Phil, 225, 242, 251, 258–59,
261–62
Bennigsen, Ray, 207
Bent, Gordon, 120, 122
Bent, Willard, 119, 120–22
Benton, Jim, 172
Berlin Wall, 238
Bero, Henry J. "Tubby," *12–13,* 29, 150,
206, 241
Betsky, Aaron, 192
Biever, Vernon, *254–55*
Birthplace of a Commonwealth (Rudolph),
118
Bishop, Desmond, 346
Blache, Greg, 300–301, 301n, 307–8

PHOTOGRAPHY CREDITS

Associated Press: 136, 259

Athlon Sports/AP: 292

Lee Balterman/SI/ Getty Images: 223

Ernest Bennett/AP: 198

Bettmann/Getty Images: 90, 106, 116, 129, 130, 146, 159, 160, 194–95, 212–13

James V. Biever/Getty Images: 300

Jim Biever/AP: 283, 299, 316

John Biever: ix, 248, 254–55, 256–57, 266, 333

John Biever/SI/Getty Images: 296–97, 315

Vernon Biever/AP: 200–201, 219, 226, 237, 239, 260, 265, 269, 274, 277, 295

David Boss/USA Today Network: ii–iii

Peter Brouillet/Getty Images: 306, 309

The Buffalo Courier: 19

Anthony Camerano/AP: 171

Kevin C. Cox/Getty Images: 338–39

Bruce Dierdorff/Getty Images: 278–79

Mike Ehrmann/Getty Images: 348

James Flores/Getty Images: 233

Focus on Sports/Getty Images: 240

Fordham University/Getty Images: 216

Hannah Foslien/Getty Images: 345

Morry Gash/AP: 318–19, 342

Courtesy of Green Bay East High School: 18

Courtesy of The Green Bay Packers: 51

Courtesy of The Green Bay Press–Gazette: 7, 77, 119, 182, 185

Green Bay Press-Gazette/AP: 156

Green Bay Press-Gazette/USA Today Network: 84, 148–49, 164–65, 188

Jeff Hanisch/USA Today Network: 334

Rod Hanna/USA Today Network: 247

HLK/AP: 172

Walter Iooss Jr./SI/Getty Images: 234

Indian Packing Co.: 25

Courtesy of Bonnie Jerow and Judy Michelson Ambelang: 243

Kidwiler Collection/Getty Images: 220

Kirby Lee/USA Today Network: 193

Lefebvre/Luebke: 142